Asian/Pacific Islander American Women

Asian/Pacific Islander American Women

A Historical Anthology

EDITED BY

Shirley Hune and Gail M. Nomura

New York University Press

NEW YORK AND LONDON

NEW YORK UNIVERSITY PRESS
New York and London

Library of Congress Cataloging-in-Publication Data
Asian / Pacific Islander American women : a historical anthology
/ edited by Shirley Hune and Gail M. Nomura.
p. cm.
Includes bibliographical references and index.
ISBN 0-8147-3632-7 (acid-free paper)
ISBN 0-8147-3633-5 (pbk. : acid-free paper)
1. Asian American women—History. 2. Pacific Islander American
women—History. 3. Asian American women—Social conditions.
4. Pacific Islander American women—Social conditions. 5. United
States—Ethnic relations. I. Hune, Shirley. II. Nomura, Gail M.
E184.O6A855 2003
973'.0495'082—dc21 2003002436

New York University Press books are printed on acid-free paper,
and their binding materials are chosen for strength and durability.

Manufactured in the United States of America
10 9 8 7 6 5 4 3 2 1

For Asian American and Pacific Islander American women

and

In loving memory of my parents,
Don Hune and Jacqueline Gar Yin Hune, and
for the Hune, Chan, and Singham families

S.H.

For my mother, Leatrice Sakayo Nomura,
and my daughter, Emi Fumiyo Nomura Sumida

G.M.N.

Contents

Acknowledgments

This anthology marks an important stage not only in the study of Asian American and Pacific Islander American women's history but also in the development of collaborative efforts among scholars who share this interest. We are grateful to all who expressed interest and support for this anthology. We particularly thank our authors for their valuable research and contribution to this book and to the field of women's history. We thank Jesianne Asagi for contributing her assemblage, *Personal Effects*, for the cover design. We gratefully acknowledge the anonymous reviewers who provided helpful comments and critiques. Thanks are due to our students who have inspired us to compile this anthology and whose questions have shaped our thinking on the subject. We are also grateful for the support of the Graduate Division at the University of California, Los Angeles and the Department of American Ethnic Studies at the University of Washington, our colleagues, and staff. We thank both Ellen Palms and Kenyon S. Chan for their assistance with the many computer program issues that came up and Rosie Baldonado for her general support. Our special thanks go to Jennifer Hammer, editor, New York University Press, for her commitment to this project and for guidance, encouragement, support, and patience in the long process, and to Emily Park of NYU Press for her professionalism and skill. We are also very appreciative of the design and production staff at NYU Press. Finally, we especially thank Kenyon S. Chan, Sparky, Stephen H. Sumida, Emi Nomura Sumida, Maya, and Chibi for their loving support and never-ending patience.

Introduction

Through "Our" Eyes:
Asian/Pacific Islander American Women's History

Shirley Hune

There is a great need for an anthology of recent scholarship on Asian/Pacific Islander American women's history that both centers women and reinterprets their lives through "our" eyes—the viewpoints of the participants themselves and the critical perspectives of scholars of women's history. In this book, we reframe history about Asian/Pacific Islander American women by considering them as historical agents actively engaged in determining their lives and those of their families, communities, and larger entities, albeit within multiple and complex constraints. As such, *Asian/Pacific Islander American Women* recognizes the "simultaneity of oppression and resistance" as a "qualitative difference" in the lives of women of color.[1]

This anthology goes beyond simply contesting male-centered or other privileged analyses of women's lives to present new knowledge and fresh perspectives for both teaching and advancing research. Its purpose is twofold. We are concerned about the absence of curriculum materials on the history of Asian/Pacific Islander American women. Collections of literary writings, criticisms, and contemporary studies are available, but anthologies devoted to historical studies are woefully lacking. Furthermore, much of the new research on Asian/Pacific Islander American women's history remains inaccessible to the classroom, being scattered in monographs, book chapters, journal articles, and unpublished dissertations. This book can serve as a major text in Asian/Pacific Islander American women's courses and as an additional resource in Asian American and Asian/Pacific American Studies,[2] Women's Studies, Ethnic Studies, American Studies, and U.S. history courses.

We also seek to advance research and scholarship by bringing together in one volume some of the best new works in Asian/Pacific Islander American women's history. We have been excited by research that focuses on the women's lives and viewpoints and that gives them voice. Such an approach transforms epistemology—what we know and how we know it—and how we do history. Fresh perspectives, innovative methodologies, and newfound and underutilized sources are contributing original findings and alternative interpretations about Asian/Pacific Islander American women. To better understand how this anthology both is innovative and fills a gap, I briefly assess the current limitations and the common approaches to teaching and scholarly writing on their history to date.

The Difference That Asian/Pacific American Studies and Women's Studies Make and Their Limitations

What do we know about Asian/Pacific Islander American women in history? How do we know what we know about them? And in what ways did our knowledge about their lives, aspirations, choices, and contributions change over the last three decades of the twentieth century? Since the early 1970s, new interdisciplinary fields of study have challenged the omission, invisibility, and misrepresentation of women and of racial and ethnic minority groups in all disciplines, especially history. Asian American Studies, for example, has sought to recover and reclaim Asian Americans, and to a lesser extent Pacific Islander Americans, from the margins of history and to envision a new history of their presence, goals, and activities in the United States and other homelands. Similarly, Women's Studies has sought to transform historical knowledge and practice by centering women's viewpoints and experiences. Both fields have questioned traditional interpretations and methodologies; promoted alternative approaches, such as oral history; identified additional and often undervalued sources, including personal journals and community newspapers; and encouraged new research topics. They also have embedded their analyses in structures of power and linked historical inquiry to social change. In short, epistemological concerns have been and continue to be central issues of Asian/Pacific American Studies and Women's Studies.

The contemporary struggles to make Asian/Pacific Islander American women visible, to give them voice, and to acknowledge their role in community and nation building are an outgrowth of the establishment of Asian/Pacific American Studies and Women's Studies on U.S. campuses after 1969. Nevertheless, numerous scholars have commented on the extent to which women of color are marginalized in history (and other fields). Both Asian American Studies and Women's Studies have illuminated aspects of Asian/Pacific Islander American women's lives, yet these fields are not without their shortcomings. In Asian American Studies, race is the organizing category and the master narrative remains male-centered. Hence the historical significance of women is rendered invisible when their lives, interests, and activities are subsumed within or considered to be the same as those of men. And given the predominance of scholars in the field with Asian American interests, examination of the perspectives, voices, and history of Native Hawaiian and other Pacific Islander American women is rare indeed.

Women's Studies, by contrast, centers women and features gender as the category of difference. But as critiques by feminist scholars of color have demonstrated, Women's Studies has yet to shift from its dominant paradigm of white leisured middle-class women's aspirations, ideologies, and experiences to one that more fully encompasses the complexity and differences that race, class, sexuality, religion, national origin, citizenship status, and other categories bring to women's everyday lives. Here, too, Asian/Pacific Islander American women are marginalized. At best their lived realities with their particular power relationships and intersections are hidden or homogenized within the larger category of women generally or women of color specifically.

Given the current limitations in these two fields, can a focus on Asian/Pacific Islander American women make a difference in teaching and scholarly work about their historical significance and contributions?

The Asian American Women's Survey Course and Scholarly Production

Nancy Kim has documented the evolution of the general survey course on Asian American Women (the most common title) from 1970 to 1998. As Asian/Pacific Islander American women resisted (alongside male counterparts) their exclusion from full participation in U.S. society and demanded curriculum change and access to higher education, they argued for a course of their own. History, contemporary issues, and women's activism are the three major areas of the course.[3]

Asian American women's courses, Kim noted, are generally initiated and housed in Asian American Studies rather than in Women's Studies. The first known women's course was taught at the University of California at Berkeley in 1970. Today, only a few campuses regularly offer more than one course on Asian American women and gender issues related to Asian Americans; more campuses offer a single general women's course, and often only occasionally. Nonetheless, the women's course, Kim concludes, is a case study in *transformative education*. It challenges traditional offerings by legitimating a new curriculum and empowering students and faculty of color. It is also often a site for developing an Asian American feminist pedagogy whereby the traditional hierarchical teacher-centered classroom is converted into a more democratic student-centered one, and knowledge is applied "through collective processes" to serve the community and change social inequities.[4]

Kim found that the women's course gained acceptance in mainstream academia over time. She identifies three phases: experimentation, 1970–1975; institutionalization, 1976–1989; and professionalization, 1990 onward. In phase 1, it was primarily graduate students and staff who taught the course, on a temporary basis. In phase 2, the course was offered on a regular basis, generally taught by full-time faculty, and gained institutional legitimacy with the support and growth of Women's Studies. By phase 3, undergraduate students could take the women's course as part of their general education requirement, and tenure-track faculty recruited specifically for their expertise in Ethnic Studies and Women's Studies were training graduate students in different disciplines on women's topics in Asian American Studies.[5]

The growth in research, scholarship, and curriculum materials on Asian/Pacific Islander American women parallels these phases of the women's course. In the experimental phase, very few written materials were available for the classroom. Women college students produced booklets of reading materials by combining historical research; personal reflections; interviews with mothers, grandmothers, and noted women activists; and editorials about women's conditions in the United States and the Third World.[6] *Roots* and *Counterpoint*, two influential readers adopted in the first Asian

American Studies courses in the 1970s, featured only a few articles on women, and the volumes in no way centered women's experiences and perspectives.[7]

Through the 1980s and institutionalization, the women's course utilized ethnic-specific autobiographies, biographies, and novels to explore historical experiences and social science articles to cover contemporary issues.[8] Kim identifies the publication of *Making Waves* in 1989 as the beginning of the professionalization of Asian American women's studies. It was adopted as a text in most of the women's courses in the 1990s.[9]

From the 1990s on, there has been an outpouring of works about Asian/Pacific Islander American women. Collectively, they are addressing the shortcomings of Asian American Studies and Women's Studies outlined above. The range of genres, including memoirs, life stories, biographies, histories, ethnographies, literary critiques, literary works, and social science and cultural studies, reflects the interdisciplinary training of the authors. Some of the writings, often as monographs, focus on one individual or on an ethnic-specific group. Others are collections of pan-ethnic writings on an array of topics in a disciplinary or multidisciplinary reader, anthology, or special journal issue.[10] In short, the scholarly production of Asian/Pacific Islander American women's writings is vibrant, multifaceted, and multidisciplinary, but historical anthologies are hard to find. This brings us to the second aspect of the purpose of *Asian/Pacific Islander American Women*—to showcase new research that reframes them as active subjects of history.

Historicizing Women

How does this anthology fit into the larger project of reconstructing history generally and Asian/Pacific Islander American women's history specifically? How has the framework of U.S. history changed and been changed by the inclusion of Asian/Pacific Islander American women? In what ways have they been included in history, and how has a particular approach influenced what we know about them?

A number of scholars have noted the limited scholarship on Asian/Pacific Islander American women's history, and some have offered alternative proposals to address women's absence and misrepresentation.[11] It is not within the scope of this introduction to provide a full historiography here. What follows is a brief discussion of common approaches to the study of Asian/Pacific Islander American women—painted with very broad brush strokes—and some of the strengths and weaknesses of these historical frameworks. How are Asian/Pacific Islander American women constructed historically?

Historical Frameworks[12]

Making Women Invisible. In this long-standing historical framework, Asian/Pacific Islander American women are omitted or absented in historical writings in spite of their lived realities. A focus on men's immigration, men's labor, and men's politics that fails to acknowledge women's immigration, women's work, and their activities and organizations, which are concomitant, are a few examples. Hence one learns very little about Asian/Pacific Islander American women in history when they are rendered invisible.

Discovering Women. A few individual women (e.g., Queen Liliʻuokalani) are identified in this framework. Limited categories of women (e.g., picture brides, garment workers) and specific aspects of their lives are also made visible. These women are frequently nameless, however. More important, in uncovering the presence of Asian/Pacific Islander American women, the dominant narrative of a male-centered history prevails. And too often the discovered women are viewed as exceptions, anomalies, or problems—in other words, "deviants" from traditionally defined womanhood.

Marginalizing Women. In this framework, the presence, roles, and contributions of Asian/Pacific Islander American women cannot be dismissed, however, their history is treated as interesting but less important. Thus women are added to the main story but confined to its margins, sometimes figuratively in sidebars and special features of textbooks. At best, their history is considered tangential to the master narrative and its concerns. Consequently, the women enter history primarily in the context of the main narrative and lack significance in their own right. Incomplete and distorted in their representation, Asian/Pacific Islander American women remain the "other."

During the last two decades, many scholars have been engaged in moving marginalized groups to the center of their fields of study. Their efforts have been both welcomed and challenged. Some feminist scholars, for example, have argued that one cannot simply add women into the knowledge mix, stir, and hope to adequately reconstruct history (or other disciplines). They call for new approaches. We too find the conceptual framework of centering women to be complex and ask, *how* are Asian/Pacific Islander American women being centered in history, and through whose eyes? At least three distinct frameworks have been deployed so far.

Centering Women (but within Traditional Parameters). When Asian/Pacific Islander American women's history is moved from the margins to the center, it can still be considered through a dominant lens, such as a male lens or a white feminist lens. These lenses tend to recreate parameters of what is important and valued that continue to misrepresent Asian/Pacific Islander American women's lives in spite of their being centered. For example, the women's experiences as workers and in families cannot be adequately explained within male definitions of work or white middle-class women's dichotomy of public and private domains. Nor are the social networks and activities of Asian/Pacific Islander American women in support of community building fully acknowledged and respected using this construction.

Centering Women as Objects of History. In this framework, Asian/Pacific Islander American women are viewed as historical subjects in their own right but interpreted as objects of history.[13] They may be health care workers, community activists, or military brides, for example, but the women are seen primarily as victims or passive actors caught up in history and societal change. One learns more about their multiple oppressions and the larger social forces and power structures that subordinate women than about what women thought or how they responded. Themes of patriarchy, racism, and class exploitation are common. While a form of women's history, this historical framework can still silence Asian/Pacific Islander American women and ignore their perspectives and resistance. Women may be centered in history, but they remain in the background and diminished.

Centering Women as Active Subjects of History. Asian/Pacific Islander American women are viewed as active participants in history and agents of social change, negotiating complex structures of power. Viewing health care workers, community activists, and military brides as subjects rather than as objects produces a different history when the women's aspirations, voices, activities, and actions are acknowledged. In this framework, women's lives are dynamic, complicated, and multifaceted. Their contributions to family, community, and society; their social and cultural formations and activities; and the simultaneity of their subordination and resistance to multiple forms of oppression, among other aspects, are acknowledged. It can be argued that in this framework the women's lives are conceptualized as Asian/Pacific Islander American women's history. The women are no longer simply in history; they are centered with agency and in the foreground. The chapters in this anthology support and advance this framework.

Engendering Women. Some work is beginning in the area of reconstructing Asian/Pacific Islander American women's history as gendered. For example, attention is given to changing gender roles and ideologies in households when women work outside the home or when men lose their privileged place in society. Such a framework is important in uncovering hidden histories of both women's and men's lives and for analyzing the constructions of femininity and masculinity. A limitation of this framework, however, is the lack of systematic and substantive historical evidence of Asian/Pacific Islander American women's and men's lived realities upon which gender analyses can be made. We view the works in this book and others as providing new evidence for examining the ways in which women's and men's lives and histories are gendered and how gender roles change over time and in specific situations and eras.

These historical frameworks suggest there are many ways in which Asian/Pacific Islander American women can be (mis)represented in history. Some might interpret the frameworks presented here as stages in which one moves from exclusion to fuller inclusion. We are not making that argument here. Instead we introduce these frameworks to enlist readers in considering how specific approaches to the study of history inform Asian/Pacific Islander American women's history. Most important, full inclusion without changing the paradigm of how Asian/Pacific Islander American women are included perpetuates an incomplete and distorted history of their lives.

Spatial frameworks also have entered the historical discourse, and the boundaries of women's history are being extended. The lived realities of Asian/Pacific Islander American women are everywhere—private and public spheres; local, regional, national, and global arenas; and in between. As the goal of reconstructing history is beyond the scope of both this introduction and this book, our intention here is to suggest the challenges rather than to be comprehensive or prescriptive. In such a framework for the future,

U.S. history must be reconceptualized, engendered, and transformed; hence a new synthesis that fully integrates all histories, including Asian/Pacific Islander American women's history. And this new whole would incorporate the perspectives of its many participants in their multiple spaces; especially those whose visions and voices have been heretofore suppressed.

The Contents of This Anthology

This anthology adopts as its framework viewing Asian/Pacific Islander American women as historical subjects with agency and resistance, actively negotiating intricate hierarchies of power including gender, race, class, sexuality, generation, language, religion, community, nation, and the global division of labor in the United States and elsewhere. By incorporating the women's perspectives and voices and those of critical scholars, we uncover a new history of Asian/Pacific Islander American women that is more complex, nuanced, and partakes of more numerous locations—institutionally and spatially—than generally understood.

Asian/Pacific Islander American Women covers a broad terrain geographically and temporally, from Hawai'i in the pre-Western contact period and Asian states prior to large-scale emigration to the Americas, to Guam, the Philippines, and the U.S. continent at the end of the twentieth century. We conceptualize and locate Asian/Pacific Islander American women's history within larger and more dimensions than previously conceived and consider how social forces and changes in their own communities impact on women's lives as well. The spaces that Asian/Pacific Islander American women occupy, negotiate, and seek to transform are various, from the local to the global and from the cultural to the political, and always include the economic sphere. Readers will note the large extent to which many women's lives and activities are transnational and blur private and public domains, from the ordinary and everyday to the state house.

Collectively, the authors present new findings about Asian/Pacific Islander American women, including recent immigrant and refugee groups to the United States and understudied groups. There are chapters on women from the following groups, in alphabetical order: Cambodian, Chamorro, Chinese, Filipino, Hmong, Indian, Japanese, Korean, Native Hawaiian, and Vietnamese Americans. Many works are ethnic-specific; some are pan-ethnic.

This anthology also includes a wide range of women's experiences—as immigrants, military brides, refugees, American-born, lesbians, organizers, low-income workers, professionals, entertainers, beauty contestants, wives, mothers, teenagers, leaders, grassroots activists, and other groupings and situations. Many chapters examine women's lives in historical eras previously neglected in Asian/Pacific American Studies. Other chapters shed new light on topics and periods considered well-covered by scholars. Still others contest existing historical interpretations of Asian/Pacific Islander American women, assess methodological approaches, and provide additional resources about the women. The authors integrate women's experiences within broader topics such as gender, race, historiography, cultural formations, war, colonialism, transnational migration, globalization, social activism, resistance, and others. They also provide fresh analyses of women's everyday lives and give them historical significance.

The chapters are original, that is, previously unpublished, works prepared specifically for this anthology. There were other exciting new studies that could not be included given the limitations of space. Nor does the anthology seek to be comprehensive in the coverage of groups, eras, and topics. Other omissions were due to the unavailability at this time of new studies of women from particular ethnic groups and in specific time periods.

In the second essay of this introductory section, Gail Nomura explains the complexity of (self-)definitions of Asian Americans and Pacific Islander Americans and how these definitions have changed over time. As a general context for the chapters, she also considers how the two groups have come to be linked together, sometimes tenuously, and how we came to choose *Asian/Pacific Islander American Women* for the anthology's title.

The greater part of *Asian/Pacific Islander American Women* consists of eight sections, each organized around a particular topic. Common themes—family, identity, work, community, gender roles, cultural production, and women's struggle for dignity and their resistance against subordination—permeate and link the sections. Parts 1 and 8 are critical overviews of historiography and bibliographic and video documentary materials on Asian/Pacific Islander American women, respectively. Parts 2 through 7 proceed somewhat chronologically. Some works could just as well appear in other sections, given their multiple themes.

Part 1: Re-envisioning Women's History

Part 1 focuses on historiography. Its three chapters challenge long-standing historical and social constructions of Asian/Pacific Islander American women, namely, how the dominant "Western" and male-centered historical literature has interpreted them as "other," whether exotic, Orientalized, or simply invisible. The authors also propose new interpretations of Asian/Pacific Islander American women's lives, roles, and status in their communities and the larger society, based on new research that assesses their lived realities as strong and purposeful women.

Davianna McGregor contests the tourist-based imagery of Native Hawaiian women and constructs a forceful spiritual self-image that invokes female cosmic forces and "chiefly women" as genealogical ancestors to inspire modern Hawaiian women in their leadership roles. Kathleen Uno critiques the impact of Orientalism on Asian family studies, which also distorts images of Asian American women and households. Using revisionist writings, she finds Asian families less patriarchal than previously conceived and women's status far more complex. Within the context of global capitalism and local economies, Sucheta Mazumdar reinterprets why Chinese and Indian women did not emigrate in the nineteenth century, a long-standing and perplexing question—they were needed as laborers in their homelands—and considers the effect of men's absence on women's sexual, social, and economic lives.

Part 2: Revisiting Immigrant Wives and Picture Brides

The dominant historical narrative of Asian American women during the late nineteenth and first part of the twentieth century focuses on their immigration to the United States as picture brides and wives, where they are often seen as adjuncts of men. Only recently have we begun to view this period through the eyes of the women themselves and of feminist scholars. By focusing on women's agency and survival strategies—identified through new archival resources and oral history—the authors in Part 2 uncover a more complex history of immigrant Asian women in this period, albeit within the confines of gender inequity in their households, ethnic communities, and U.S. society.

Three studies, two in this section and the third in Part 3, deal with the Angel Island immigration station, but each offers something unique. Erika Lee demonstrates how the Chinese exclusion laws created additional barriers for her grandmother and other Chinese immigrant women and how women's resiliency and strategies sought to overcome these barriers. Jennifer Gee examines Angel Island as a site of gendered gatekeeping and compares the different treatment of Chinese and Japanese immigrant women at the station according to racial, class, and gender ideologies of U.S. society. In documenting the activities and organizations of early Korean women in Hawai'i, Lili Kim uncovers their role in community and nation building and challenges the male-centered view of community support for the Korean independence movement. Together these three chapters suggest new ways of thinking about gendered immigration patterns, policies, and community organizing. They also document the multiple ways in which women have challenged their unequal treatment and succeeded.

Part 3: Recovering Women's History through Oral History and Journal Writing

Traditional historical methodologies, with their attention to big events and standard practices of documentation, tend to silence "ordinary" people, especially indigenous,[14] rural, immigrant, and minority women. If "official" history is socially constructed and an interpretation, how can "ordinary" women tell their stories and have them heard and legitimated? The two chapters in Part 3 give attention to methodologies—oral history and journal writing—that can empower women by granting them a voice in the writing of Asian / Pacific Islander American women's history. Both methodologies provide new terrain for doing research and can yield rich historical details and first-hand observations whereby women, as historical subjects, become knowledge producers. Like "traditional" approaches to doing history, these approaches are not without challenges, including the skill, encouragement, and sensitivity of mediators and facilitators.

Oral history, an innovative tool of Ethnic Studies, Women's Studies, and contemporary social history, seeks to capture the life story or recollections of an individual through interviews. Judy Yung contrasts the state of the practice of oral history in the mid-1970s and the mid-1980s in revealing the struggles and triumphs of Lee Puey You, who came through Angel Island, and argues for the value of a feminist consciousness and an ethnic sensibility in reclaiming women's lives. Journal writing is another vehicle that allows the subjects themselves to interpret their lives and to specify what is significant for them. Gail Nomura identifies Filipina American journal writing as one such historical resource and outlines the process and techniques developed by Dorothy Laigo Cordova. Using the journal writings of Filipina Americans, she explores their powerful role in recovering personal and community history and examines the tool as an opportunity for ordinary women to document their daily life experiences and contribute to the historical record.

Part 4: Contesting Cultural Formations and Practices, Constructing New "Hybrid" Lives

Part 4 focuses on the first half of the twentieth century, an understudied period in Asian/Pacific American Studies. It also gives attention to American-born Asian and Native Hawaiian women and continues a theme of cultural and social production. The four chapters address the role of girls and women in contesting cultural formations and practices within and outside their ethnic communities to create new ones of their own. By blending ethnic and mainstream ways of being and doing, girls and women are actively engaged in flexing gendered ideologies and practices to expand their opportunities and shape new "hybrid" lives for themselves.

Judy Tzu-Chun Wu analyzes the strategies of Dr. Margaret Chung, as she negotiated the boundaries of mainstream society and the Chinese American community to become a physician and develop her practice. The chapter discusses the complications of gender, race, class, and sexuality in Chung's career development. From an analysis of ethnic newspapers, Valerie Matsumoto uncovers a multitude of highly visible Japanese American girls' clubs in Los Angeles during the 1920s and 1930s and considers how their activities represented a new mix of race, gender, and generational dynamics. Shirley Jennifer Lim explores how Chinese, Japanese, and Filipina American women demonstrated their belonging and cultural citizenship as ethnic Americans by accommodating to and resisting constructions of beauty, such as those in beauty magazines and contests, in the highly politicized early Cold War era. Using conceptual frameworks of foreground and underground, Amy Stillman documents the contributions of Native Hawaiian women in the creation, preservation, and transmission of Hawaiian music and the hula from the nineteenth century to the present, and in some cases, from one generation to another. These chapters open up new areas of exploration about the role of Asian/Pacific Islander American women in creating, resisting, and maintaining cultural and social formations that are gendered.

Part 5: Reshaping Lives and Communities after Militarism and War

A dominant theme in Asian/Pacific American Studies is the role of U.S. involvement—colonialism, military intervention, and wars—in Asia and the Pacific Rim and the implications of militarism and warfare and their ideologies on the lives of Asian/Pacific Islander Americans. In Asian/Pacific American Studies, much attention has been given to the World War II period and Japanese American internment and camp life. Less is known about the eras that framed this period, specifically, about how Asians and Pacific Islanders were affected by U.S. empire building of the nineteenth century and U.S. interventions during the Cold War era. The gendered dimensions of militarism and war during the last half of the twentieth century are the focus of Part 5. The three chapters investigate the impact of U.S. military involvements in Korea and Southeast Asia on different aspects of Asian American women's lives and assess women's initiatives in reshaping their lives and communities.

The everyday lives of Korean military brides in the United States from 1950 to 1996 are considered by Ji-Yeon Yuh, as she examines the sisterhood the women form when they create social organizations to build their own community and resist their marginalization by both U.S. society and the Korean American community. Linda Võ discusses how different groups of first-generation Vietnamese American women survived and adjusted through war, the refugee experience, and resettlement in America, and how they contribute economically to the household and ethnic community, in part, by forming their own economic opportunities and niches. Sucheng Chan considers the countries where Hmong and Cambodian women and girls came from and why they are in the United States. She analyzes the severe traumas they experienced during war and revolution, the years when they were confined in refugee camps, and their resettlement in the United States, as well as their valiant efforts to rebuild themselves, their families, and communities. The bending and extending of women's traditional gender roles and women's resilience in the face of cultural differences and demanding, sometimes life-threatening situations, are commonalities shared by Asian American women in this part.

Part 6: Negotiating Globalization, Work, and Motherhood

The new immigration and demographic diversity of the Asian American population, from the 1960s to the present, marks a turning point in Asian American and U.S. history. Most important, the increased presence of women, their participation in the paid labor force, and the transnational character of many households are among the factors changing traditional institutions and hierarchies of power. How do Asian / Pacific Islander American women deal with the increasing complications of work and family, especially when located beyond national boundaries? The chapters in Part 6 focus on the significance of Asian American women in the post-1960s era as they are integrated into the feminization and racialization of the workforce—the new division of labor—globally and domestically.

To explain the increased emigration of Asian women, especially Filipinas, to the United States and elsewhere, Rhacel Parreñas provides a theoretical discussion of global restructuring from the 1960s to the 1990s and discusses how it has contributed to the transmigration of Asian women as a "cheap" labor source. Xiaolan Bao examines the situation of immigrant Chinese women as garment workers in New York City in the 1970s and 1980s and describes how their dual responsibilities as workers and mothers contribute to their politicization and to demands for daycare centers from their union. Charlene Tung identifies a less-known group of recent transnationals—Filipina live-in elderly caregivers—and considers the new but still gendered ways in which the women maintain family and redefine motherhood and marriage while emigrating alone and working overseas for many years. As these chapters suggest, the challenges that women face in their multiple roles in the twenty-first century continue unabated, as does globalization.

Part 7: Challenging Community and the State:
Contemporary Spaces of Struggle

Asian/Pacific Islander American women's agency and resistance are continuing themes throughout their history and in this anthology. In Asian/Pacific American Studies, some attention has been given to women's organizing efforts as workers or on behalf of workers. This part examines the women's activism during the latter half of the twentieth century and highlights their efforts, in different hierarchical levels and locations, to organize collectively, to make spaces for themselves, and to struggle to be heard and have their issues represented. The four chapters suggest new areas of study pertaining to the ideologies and strategies that bind or divide women's groups and to women's struggles within their own communities and with larger entities (the state and its officials, for example) to determine their objectives. The role of culture in the women's lives as they articulate and advance their rights and concerns and the blurring of the personal and the political remain constant themes.

Trinity Ordona describes collaboration and conflict among Asian lesbians in San Francisco during the 1970s and 1980s, as they sought to create a community for themselves and, in the process, laid the groundwork for the Asian/Pacific queer and transgendered people's movement of today. Catherine Ceniza Choy explores the rise of Filipino nursing organizations in the United States in the 1970s and 1980s, the purpose of which has been to contest the objectification and exploitation of Filipina nurses by both transnational labor recruitment agencies and U.S. nursing organizations. Madhulika Khandelwal outlines the activities of a new generation of South Asian American women in the New York City area, as they exercise leadership through feminist writings and organizations that challenge stereotypes about them and their community's representation as a "model minority." Vivian Loyola Dames analyzes the abortion debates in the early 1990s in Guam through the worldviews of Chamorro women and considers how their worldviews, which are not homogeneous, are intertwined with their notions of being female (womanhood), which in turn is linked to the Chamorro struggle for self-determination.

Part 8: Additional Resources

Part 8 consists of two essays that identify additional resources to support teaching and scholarly work. I provide a bibliographic essay of generally accessible published works on Asian American and Pacific Islander American women as historical subjects, grouped largely by ethnic group. Nancy Kim presents an annotated bibliography of accessible video documentaries organized around topics, each of which places Asian/Pacific Islander American women at the center or is presented from their perspective and hence is seen "in her eyes." The chapter also provides helpful commentary for using the videos in the classroom.

Finally, in answer to those who asked us why we didn't do an anthology about gender instead of women's history: we feel that our approach to women's history in this anthology incorporates gender as a principal category of analysis. Therefore, this book is about gender but grounded in history. We also seek to support historical research that provides the kind of substantive and empirical evidence that is lacking in many areas upon which gender analysis is currently based. The new findings in this book reveal the complexity of women's gendered lives. Most important, there is a need for places to document the details of women's perspectives, voices, actions, and everyday lives, which are part of the larger historical landscape. This anthology is, first and foremost, one of those spaces.

The significance of Asian/Pacific Islander American women's history lies in its power to *transform* knowledge, theory, and practice. Asian/Pacific Islander American women's lives dismantle the notion of a monocultural American experience and a single way of being and doing. Their experiences challenge Eurocentric and male-biased worldviews, as well as universalized white middle-class women's norms, values, and ideologies. They complicate global, national, and ethnic histories by calling attention to women's lives as sites of intersection. Their lived realities suggest new possibilities for understanding history when everyday experiences as well as elite activities and the aspirations and accomplishments of subordinate groups—in this case, Asian American and Pacific Islander American women—are valued and incorporated in community, national, and international formations.[15] We hope that this anthology encourages a dialogue for conceptualizing and doing history. It is but one small step toward envisioning a new, richer, and fuller history of women that is local, global, and in between.

NOTES

I especially thank Gail Nomura for her valuable assistance and comments in preparing this essay. I also thank the authors in this book for their thoughtful suggestions.

1. Rose M. Brewer makes this argument in reference to African American women in "Theorizing Race, Class and Gender: The New Scholarship of Black Feminist Intellectuals and Black Women's Labor," in *Theorizing Black Feminisms*, ed. Stanlie M. James and Abena P. A. Busia (London: Routledge, 1993), 13–30, especially 28.

2. The vast majority of teaching programs use the name Asian American Studies; a few call themselves Asian/Pacific American Studies. I use the terms interchangeably in this introduction.

3. Kim analyzed thirty-eight syllabi and interviewed ten instructors. The courses evaluated were taught at public and private colleges and universities on the U.S. continent, the largest group being in California; a few of those courses included readings on Native Hawaiian women. Nancy I. Kim, "The General Survey Course on Asian American Women: Transformative Education and Asian American Feminist Pedagogy," *Journal of Asian American Studies* 3:1 (February 2000): 37–65.

4. Ibid.

5. Ibid.

6. Early examples include *Asian Women* (Los Angeles: UCLA Asian American Studies Center, 1975), originally published as *Asian Women's Journal* at the University of California, Berkeley (1971); and *Asian American Women* (Stanford: Stanford University Press, 1976).

7. Amy Tachiki, Eddie Wong, Franklin Odo, with Buck Wong, eds., *Roots: An Asian American Reader* (Los Angeles: UCLA Asian American Studies Center, 1971); and Emma Gee, ed., *Counterpoint: Perspectives on Asian America* (Los Angeles: UCLA Asian American Studies Center, 1976).

8. See Kim, "General Survey Course," 48–49, for additional details. It should be noted that a reader of women's topics and testimonies, *Asian and Pacific American Experiences: Women's Perspectives*, ed. Nobuya Tsuchida (Minneapolis: University of Minnesota, Asian/Pacific American Learning Resource Center and General College, 1982), was available but was not identified by Kim's survey as having been adopted in the classroom in the 1980s.

9. Asian Women United of California, ed., *Making Waves: An Anthology of Writings by and about Asian American Women* (Boston: Beacon Press, 1989). See Kim, "General Survey Course," 50.

10. Many of these publications are discussed in chapter 23, "Asian American and Pacific Islander American Women as Historical Subjects: A Bibliographic Essay," in this book.

11. For example, see Alice Yun Chai, "Toward a Holistic Paradigm for Asian American Women's Studies," *Women's Studies International Forum* 8:1 (1985): 59–66; Shirley Hune, "Doing Gender with a Feminist Gaze: Toward a Historical Reconstruction of Asian America," in *Contemporary Asian America*, ed. Min Zhou and James V. Gatewood (New York: New York University Press, 2000), 413–30; Shirley Hune, *Teaching Asian American Women's History* (Washington, D.C.: American Historical Association, 1997); Sucheta Mazumdar, "General Introduction: A Woman-Centered Perspective on Asian American History," in *Making Waves*, 1–22; Gail M. Nomura, "Significant Lives: Asia and Asian Americans in the U.S. West," in *A New Significance: Reenvisioning the History of the American West*, ed. Clyde A. Milner II (New York: Oxford University Press, 1996), 135–57; and Gary Y. Okihiro, *Margins and Mainstreams* (Seattle: University of Washington Press, 1994), chap. 3.

12. This section extends, applies, and builds on frameworks that I have previously explored; for example, see Shirley Hune, *Pacific Migration to the United States: Trends and Themes in Historical and Sociological Literature* (Washington, D.C.: Smithsonian Institution, 1977); "Rethinking Race: Paradigms and Policy Formation," *Amerasia Journal* 21:1, 2 (1995): 29–40; and "Doing Gender." I also draw upon the frameworks of Gilda Lerner, Peggy McIntosh, and other feminist scholars discussed in Marilyn Jacoby Boxer, *When Women Ask the Questions* (Baltimore: Johns Hopkins University Press, 1998), especially 59–68.

13. In a related discussion, Patricia Hills Collins considers how African American women have been treated as objects of sociological knowledge. She argues that it is not until after 1970, as Black women achieve a critical mass as sociologists, that they become subjects and agents of

sociological knowledge. See Patricia Hills Collins, *Fighting Words* (Minneapolis: University of Minnesota Press, 1998), chap. 3.

14. For a deeper discussion of the impact of colonial methodologies on indigenous peoples, see Linda Tuhiwai Smith, *Decolonizing Methodologies: Research and Indigenous Peoples* (London: Zed Books, 1999).

15. For more details on historical significance, see Hune, *Teaching Asian American Women's History*; and Nomura, "Significant Lives."

Introduction
On Our Terms: Definitions and Context

Gail M. Nomura

This anthology explores the experiences, consciousness, and actions of Asian American and Pacific Islander American women from the nineteenth century to the present, examining the intersections of race, gender, class, sexuality, and ethnicity in their lives. Using the voices and perspectives of the women themselves, collectively these works present a new history of Asian American and Pacific Islander American women "on our terms."

Asian American and Pacific Islander American women are diverse groups composed of peoples of many ethnicities, languages, religions, and cultures who have a history with the United States. How did the terms *Asian American* and *Pacific Islander American* come into being? And who decides?

Who Are Asian Americans and Pacific Islander Americans?

The term *Asian American* generally refers to immigrants and those born in the United States of Chinese, Filipino, Japanese, Korean, South Asian (e.g., Indian, Pakistani, Bangladeshi, Sri Lankan, Nepalese), and Southeast Asian (e.g., Vietnamese, Hmong, Lao, Cambodian, Indonesian, Thai, Malaysian, Singaporean) ancestry. Some may expand the term to include peoples of Asian descent in all the Americas and define "Asian" as including peoples from the entire geographical region of Asia.

The term *Pacific Islander American* refers especially to indigenous peoples of Pacific Islands with a history of U.S. colonialism: the state of Hawai'i; the organized, unincorporated territory of Guam; the Commonwealth of the Northern Mariana Islands; the unorganized and unincorporated territory of American Samoa. This term may also include the indigenous citizens of the three sovereign nations that comprise the Freely Associated States (the Federated States of Micronesia, the Republic of the Marshall Islands, and the Republic of Palau [Belau]) who currently migrate to the United States and its territories or possessions under nonimmigrant status. Also, all Pacific Islander immigrants and their descendants born in the United States are included (e.g., Tahitian, Tongan, Maori, Fijian).

It must be recognized that a tension exists between legal categories and self-identity when defining an "American." For example, permanent residents may self-identify as American and, given issues of sovereignty and struggles for self-determination, some Pacific Islander Americans in U.S. colonized territories may not self-identify as "American."

The complexity of "Asian American" and "Pacific Islander American" is illustrated by noting the many ethnicities included in the larger subcategories of "Asian American" (e.g., Southeast Asian American) and the many different indigenous island groups encompassed by "Pacific Islander American." The panethnic terms often obscure distinctions within these synthetic groupings. For example, the term *South Asian American* is often taken to mean Indian American, the most numerous ethnic group under that designation; and even the term *Indian American* masks, for example, regional, religious, and language distinctions. Likewise, many take "Pacific Islander American" to mean the numerically dominant subgroup "Native Hawaiian." Further, if one interrogates a single ethnic category, such as "Chinese American," one finds Taiwanese American and ethnic Chinese of varying national origins and sometimes multiple national journeys. Distinct ethnicities emerge even in what seems to be an unambiguously homogeneous group, as in the case of Okinawan Americans who are usually subsumed under the generic category "Japanese American." Moreover, the boundaries and definitions of categories are contested—as in the case of Filipino Americans, who, some argue, should be included among Pacific Islander Americans since the Philippines is located on the Pacific Rim, in what is called "island" Southeast Asia. Others argue that Filipinos are better situated with Latina/os or Hispanics due to their history of Spanish colonialism. In recent times, some Native Hawaiians have sought to move to the category of Native American and, in fact, are included in pieces of congressional legislation, such as protection of ancestral graves. Adding to the inability neatly to define stable categories of classification are the growing numbers of multiracial, multiethnic peoples who trace their ancestries in part to Asia and/or the Pacific Islands.

Generational differences further complicate relations within and between these groups. For example, some Asian Americans have histories of seven or eight generations in the United States. Particularly since immigration reform in 1965 lifted many discriminatory policies and quotas against Asians, there has been a growing number of immigrants who brought their children with them, the "1.5" generation—a new phenomenon of those who were born in Asia but came as young children to the United States and acculturated rapidly. The Fall of Saigon in 1975 prompted a sudden wave of refugees from Southeast Asia. Thus, the number of Asian-born Americans in the United States more than tripled in the decade of the 1970s and nearly doubled in the decade of the 1980s, rising from 800,000 in 1970 to 5 million in 1990 and 7.2 million in 2000.[1]

With this influx of new immigrants and refugees from Asia, and enhanced by immigration policies that support family reunification, the Asian American population doubled from 1,356,638 in 1970 to 3,726,440 in 1980 and nearly doubled again in the next decade, to 7,273,662 in 1990. It also shifted from a small but predominantly American-born population to one of the fastest growing racial groups in the United States, at present largely comprising immigrants. The 2000 U.S. census counted 11,898,828 Asian Americans; 51 percent (6,119,790) were women.[2]

More than 874,414 Pacific Islander Americans were enumerated in the 2000 U.S. census; slightly less than 50 percent (434,733) were women.[3] Among Pacific Islander Americans one finds generational and regional differences between the indigenous island resident and the off-island Pacific Islander living away or born and raised in the continental United States.

Negotiating Definitions, Self-Definitions

Racial and ethnic categories are dynamic and socially and politically constructed and negotiated. The term *Asian American* arose in the 1960s in the midst of the civil rights, anti-war, anti-imperialism, women's, and yellow power movements. Asian American activists challenged their being designated "Oriental," as imposed on them by the dominant society. "Orient" referred to the compass direction "east" or "the East" and meant, essentially, Asia as opposed to the West (Occident, meaning Europe). And due to a long history of "Orientalism," the terms *Orient* and *Oriental* had an exotic, inscrutable, foreign connotation that reinforced the notion of Asians in America as perpetual foreigners despite their long history in and contribution to U.S. culture and society.[4] Activists contested the Eurocentric view and hegemony that designated Asia as a compass direction east of Europe, denying the region and its peoples their own integrity, and chose instead to self-identify as Asian Americans, reasoning that "Asia" designated a more neutral regional-geographical site. "Asian" was used as an adjective to modify "American." By the late 1970s, a hyphen that often linked the terms was increasingly dropped from use, since "Asian-American" indicated two nouns in a co-equal relationship and thus implied that a person had dual identities or loyalties as Asian and American—a two-headed monster rather than a single, integrated identity.

Asian American activists thus constructed an identity and a political consciousness among peoples with diverse ethnicities, histories, religions, languages, and places of origin. This political construction and self-definition of Asian American panethnic solidarity was based on the discourse of social justice and anti-imperialism that foregrounded the political as opposed to the difficult-to-argue cultural relationships between Asian groups in the United States. By emphasizing the common subjugated positionality of Asian ethnic groups in the United States and linkages to Third World people, Asian American activists built an Asian American panethnic movement for racial justice that countered the potential separatism evoked by the previous tendencies in Asian American communities toward Americanism on the one hand and Asian nationalist politics on the other. This panethnic label was used in the political mobilization of Asian Americans to seek an end to their unequal treatment and to address issues including educational access, political representation, and media stereotyping. The discourse of Asian American panethnicity held the differences among the members in tension rather than in overt contradiction. However, as with any coalition, tensions always threaten to pull apart this alliance.[5] Asian American groups have been able to work in tandem as strategically necessary to promote panethnic alliances as well as to advance ethnic group interests.

The term *Pacific Islander American* has come into use only in recent years. Most Pacific Islander Americans subscribe to distinct island-based indigenous identities, for example, Native Hawaiian, Samoan, Chamoru,[6] Tongan, or Maori, rather than to a panethnic identity. Certainly, they see little in common with Asian Americans, and they see clear sociocultural and political distinctions between different islander groups. But there appears to be a growing movement to forge a pan–Pacific Islander American ethnic identity in the United States. Debbie Hippolite Wright and Paul Spickard point to the formation of formal associations and networks by academics, professionals, and students, such as the Pacific Islander Student Association at the University of Utah, which was known as the Polynesian Club until 1995, and the first National Pacific Islanders in America Conference held in May 2000 at Brigham Young University-Hawaiʻi, whose conference theme was "Who Is a Pacific Islander American?"[7]

Paralleling the efforts of Asian American and Pacific Islander American groups to have their interests addressed, and oftentimes in response to their challenges of being ignored in the allocation of resources, the U.S. government has sought to document more accurately the status of domestic racial and ethnic minorities and to include the Asian American and Pacific Islander population. For example, in 1977 federal agencies were notified of a new statistical policy differentiating populations by racial and ethnic categories. The U.S. Office of Management and Budget (OMB) issued its Statistical Directive 15, which officially fused Asian American and Pacific Islander American into a statistical category by directing all federal agencies to use five racial or ethnic categories for administrative and statistical reporting: American Indian or Alaskan Native, Asian or Pacific Islander, Black, White, and Hispanic.[8] The federal government linked the two umbrella categories "Asian" and "Pacific Islander" under one label in order to make it simpler to allocate funds and categorize people in government analyses. Consequently, OMB Directive 15 institutionalized the representation of Asian Americans and Pacific Islander Americans as an aggregate group. The 1980 and 1990 censuses thus used the category "Asian and Pacific Islanders," though subcategories were counted and disaggregated numbers by ethnic group were reported, in large part because Asian American and Pacific Islander American groups contested and forced changes in classifications and categories. In 1997, in response to discussions with Native Hawaiian and other Pacific Islander American leaders, the OMB decided to disaggregate "Asian and Pacific Islander" into two separate categories: "Asian" and "Native Hawaiian or Other Pacific Islander."[9] The 2000 census used the disaggregated "Asian" (with checkoffs for Asian Indian, Chinese, Filipino, Japanese, Vietnamese, Korean, Other Asian) and "Native Hawaiian or Other Pacific Islander" (with checkoffs for Native Hawaiian, Guamanian or Chamorro, Samoan, Other Pacific Islander) categories.

During and since the 1970s, coalitions of Asian Americans and Pacific Islander Americans formed various political, social services, community, and professional organizations and caucuses with names that included Asian/Pacific American (APA), Asian and Pacific Islander (API), Asian and Pacific Islander American (APIA), and so forth. These umbrella terms pooled the power of increased numbers of people sharing some common issues and collectively brought political clout, representation, and voice to their shared agenda. While efforts at inclusivity were laudable and well intentioned,

Pacific Islander Americans were often marginalized in these expanded panethnic coalitions, and Pacific Islander Americans questioned the commitment to their specific aspirations, issues, and perspectives.[10]

Asian/Pacific Islander American

In constructing a title for this anthology that reflects both groups in its content, we deployed a slash in "Asian/Pacific Islander" to indicate clearly that "Asian" as well as "Pacific Islander" modify American women, lest some readers mistakenly take "Asian" to refer to Asia rather than to the United States. The slash separates yet brings together "Asian" and "Pacific Islander" to modify "American." While many groups use the combination Asian/Pacific American, Asian Pacific American, or Asian and Pacific American, we use Pacific Islander American rather than Pacific American explicitly to designate the indigenous island populations in distinction from nonindigenous people residing in the Pacific who may claim to be Pacific American. Further, the term *islander* is important because some readers may assume "Pacific" to include Pacific Rim countries rather than point to the interior Pacific islands. The term *American* qualifies "Asian/Pacific Islander" to indicate that we are dealing with the U.S. context and not Asia and Pacific Islands outside the U.S. experience.[11]

By using the title *Asian/Pacific Islander American Women*, we are not suggesting that Asian Americans and Pacific Islander Americans are a single homogeneous group. We do not seek to subsume, obliterate, or obscure their distinctiveness but to expand research and interpretative boundaries leading to new ways of understanding a multicultural history of the United States. In this book we address the diverse histories of Asian American and Pacific Islander American women and recognize the heterogeneity within and between these politically constructed, panethnic, umbrella groupings. In short, we seek to explore the many possibilities of alliances and connections through differences as well as commonalities and shared agendas, without perpetuating or reinscribing the same hierarchies and exclusions that have sometimes marred such projects. Effective coalition building constructs a shared agenda that is a work in process, constantly negotiated, debated, and requiring continuous open dialogue to explore boundaries, frontiers, and borderlands of interactions and separations.

Asian/Pacific Islander American Women is a step toward exploring these interactions and separations and enabling readers to begin to examine and push our theoretical constructs and interpretations beyond the analyses of single ethnic groups. The selections in this anthology present new research that explores diverse aspects of Asian American and Pacific Islander American women's history while acknowledging shared experiences as women of color in the United States. Collectively, these works reveal the agency, resistance, and resilience of Asian American and Pacific Islander American women in all their diversity and, in the process, transform our understanding of women's history.

NOTES

I thank Davianna McGregor, Amy Stillman, Rick Bonus, Stephen H. Sumida, John Rosa, Evelyn Flores, Sucheng Chan, and Shirley Hune for their helpful comments and suggestions.

1. See http://www.census.gov/Press-Release/www/2002/cb02-18.html.

2. Numbers include those who reported Asian in combination with one or more other races. Table 5, "Asian Population by Age and Sex for the United States: 2000," in "Race and Hispanic or Latino Origin by Age and Sex for the United States: 2000 (PHC-T-8)," Internet release date: February 25, 2002, http://www.census.gov/population/www/cen2000/phc-t08/tab05.pdf.

3. Numbers include those who reported Native Hawaiian and Other Pacific Islander in combination with one or more other races. Table 6, "Native Hawaiian and Other Pacific Islander Population, by Age and Sex for the United States: 2000," in "Race and Hispanic or Latino Origin by Age and Sex for the United States: 2000 (PHC-T-8)," Internet release date: February 25, 2002, http://www.census.gov/population/www/cen2000/phc-t08/tab06.pdf.

4. See Robert G. Lee, *Orientals: Asian Americans in Popular Culture* (Philadelphia: Temple University Press, 1999).

5. For discussions of Asian American identity and the Asian American movement, see, for example, Yen Le Espiritu, *Asian American Panethnicity: Bridging Institutions and Identities* (Philadelphia: Temple University Press, 1992); William Wei, *The Asian American Movement* (Philadelphia: Temple University Press, 1993); Kenyon S. Chan, "Rethinking the Asian American Studies Project: Bridging the Divide between 'Campus' and 'Community,'" in *Journal of Asian American Studies* 3:1 (February 2000): 17–36; and Daryl J. Maeda, "Forging Asian American Identity: Race, Culture, and the Asian American Movement, 1968–1975" (unpublished diss., University of Michigan, 2001).

6. Although *Chamorro* is the more common spelling, I use the spelling *Chamoru*, which more accurately reflects the phonetic spelling of the original language of the indigenous people of Guam. There are many political nuances and battles that belie what seems at first glance a simple orthographic issue. Who has the power to decide the spelling of a people's language? See also Vivian Dames, chapter 22, especially note 4, in this book.

7. Debbie Hippolite Wright and Paul Spickard, "Pacific Islander Americans and Asian American Identity," in Linda Trinh Võ and Rick Bonus, eds., *Contemporary Asian American Communities, Intersections and Divergences* (Philadelphia: Temple University Press, 2002), 112–15.

8. Yen Le Espiritu and Michael Omi, "'Who Are You Calling Asian?': Shifting Identity Claims, Racial Classification, and the Census," in Paul M. Ong, ed., *The State of Asian Pacific America: Transforming Race Relations, A Public Policy Report* (Los Angeles: LEAP Asian Pacific American Public Policy Institute and UCLA Asian American Studies Center, 2000), 50. See also Juanita Tamayo Lott, *Asian American: From Racial Category to Multiple Identities* (Walnut Creek: AltaMira Press, 1998). Lott points out that OMB Directive 15 was first published in the *Federal Register* in 1978.

9. Espiritu and Omi, "'Who Are You Calling Asian?'" 72.

10. For excellent discussions on inclusions, exclusions, and representations, see, for example, Wright and Spickard, "Pacific Islander Americans and Asian American Identity"; Sharon Lim-Hing, "Introduction," in Sharon Lim-Hing, ed., *The Very Inside: An Anthology of Writing by Asian and Pacific Islander Lesbian and Bisexual Women*, (Toronto: Sister Vision Press, 1994); J. Kehaulani Kauanui and Ju Hui "Judy" Han, "'Asian Pacific Islander': Issues of Representation and Responsibility," in Lim-Hing, ed., *Very Inside*, 377–79; and David L. Eng and Alice Y. Hom, "Introduction, Q & A: Notes on a Queer Asian America," in David L. Eng and Alice Y. Hom, eds., *Q & A: Queer in Asian America* (Philadelphia: Temple University Press, 1998), 1–21.

11. The dialogue over terms and (self-)definitions is also reflected in academe, including professional organizations. In 1979 the Association for Asian/Pacific American Studies (AAPAS) was established and held its first annual conference at the University of Washington on November 6–8, 1980. AAPAS changed its name in 1982 to the Association for Asian American Studies (AAAS) because some Pacific Islander Americans questioned the tokenized treatment of Pacific Islander American studies in the field. This is being reversed. At its annual conference in Salt Lake City in 2002 members at the business meeting passed a resolution sponsored by the Pacific Islander Caucus of the AAAS to discuss renaming the Association to "recognize the increased focus on, participation by, and commitment to Pacific Islanders in the Association." The resolution noted the "increased attention to the issues and concerns of Pacific Islander Americans in research, publishing, and teaching under the rubric 'Asian American Studies' generally. . . ." The Board of the AAAS responded to the resolution by voting to send a ballot to the general membership on a constitutional amendment to change the name of the association. The proposed name change to Association for Asian/Pacific Islander American Studies would recognize a shared academic space in ethnic studies to explore the experiences of Asian Americans and Pacific Islander Americans. See Association for Asian American Studies Newsletter, 19:3 (November 2002), 2–4.

Part 1

Re-envisioning Women's History

Constructed Images of Native Hawaiian Women

Davianna Pōmaikaʻi McGregor

The popular image of Native Hawaiian women as beautiful, graceful, and voluptuous hula maidens has been promoted by the tourist industry to market the romantic allure of the Hawaiian islands. The day-to-day reality of the average Native Hawaiian woman seldom resembles the poster-girl image. In fact, Native Hawaiian women span the broad spectrum of physical features, class, sexual orientation, as well as political involvement and socioeconomic status.

One significant indicator of the actual living conditions of Native Hawaiian women is their health statistics. Historically, Native Hawaiian women have had the shortest life expectancy in comparison to women of other ethnic groups in the islands.[1] Native Hawaiian women have unusually high risk factors for cardiovascular disease and cancer—cigarette smoking, obesity, elevated blood pressure, diabetes, and high blood cholesterol. Due to low income levels, which hinder access to health care, mortality rates for Native Hawaiian women are higher than for women of other ethnic groups in Hawaiʻi for heart disease, cancer, stroke, diabetes, and motor vehicle and other accidents. Between 1988 and 1992, Native Hawaiian women recorded one of the highest cancer-related mortality and incidence rates in the United States, equal with Black women and second to Alaska Native women.[2]

Another relevant indicator of the status of Native Hawaiian women is that the divorce rate of Native Hawaiians is among the highest of the ethnic groups in the islands.[3] This contributes to the high number of Native Hawaiian single-mother households and to the high number of households in which a mother and child live with relatives.[4]

The trials and tribulations of life in modern Hawaiʻi challenge Native Hawaiian women to assume strong physical, social, and spiritual roles in their families and communities. Native Hawaiian women are intelligent, beautiful, powerful, passionate, and enduring, not as constructed by the tourist industry but in a manner that incorporates the images and qualities of their godly and chiefly female ancestors. When Native Hawaiian women construct a self-image as native, the female sacred forces of nature and chiefly ancestors are invoked. This chapter describes the key female cosmic forces and chiefly women who are claimed as genealogical ancestors and why they inspire modern Native Hawaiian women as they assume leadership roles in their families, communities, and nation.

Female Cosmic Forces

In Hawaiian cosmology, female forces of nature play an equal role with male forces in the procreation of the universe. This shared creative energy contributes to the sense of empowerment among Native Hawaiian women today. Native Hawaiians trace their ancestry to earth mother Papahānaumoku, who mated with sky father Wākea to give birth to most of the Hawaiian islands and eventually to the Native Hawaiian people. The daughter, Hoʻohōkūkalani, the maker of stars in the heavens, mated with father Wākea and gave birth to Hāloa Naka, a still-born male fetus. When buried in the earth, Hāloa Naka grew into taro, the primary food plant of the Native Hawaiian people from generations past to present. Their second-born male child, Hāloa, became the progenitor of the Native Hawaiian people.[5] In the tradition of Papahānaumoku and Wākea, it is a woman's powerful creative energy—that of Papahānaumoku and her daughter, Hoʻohōkūkalani—that produced the islands of life, kalo or taro, the staple food plant, and the Native Hawaiian people through mating, as equals, with the male god Wākea. Papahānaumoku is one of the primary female cosmic forces that Native Hawaiian women honor as ancestor.

The goddess Hina, in her many forms—coral reefs, marine reef life, ocean caves, the moon, and tides—is another principal cosmic force. She embodies the female force in the universe, while her husband, Kū, is the male force. Together, their reproductive energies were invoked to produce good crops, good fishing, long life, and family and national prosperity.[6] As mother of the demigod Māui, she guided him in harnessing the energy of the sun, capturing fire from the alae birds, and fishing up the Hawaiian islands from the ocean. In a mating with Wākea when Papahānaumoku had left him in anger, Hina gave birth to the island Molokaʻi-nui-a-Hina.[7]

As the social and political system evolved into a system of ruling chiefs from the thirteenth through early nineteenth centuries, the state religion focused on four principal male gods—Kū, Kāne, Kanaloa, and Lono. Female deities continued to be honored, but as lesser deities in the state temples; in separate temples distinctly established for women; and as ʻaumakua, or family ancestral gods.[8]

Heiau Hale O Papa, or "House of Papa" temples, honored Papahānaumoku and served as special places of birthing, healing, and refuge for women.[9] Hina, wife of the ocean god Kūʻula, is represented and honored with her husband in fishing koʻa, or shrines, throughout the islands. *Moʻowāhine*, dragon lizards who can transform into beautiful women and inhabit fresh water pools in the uplands and along the shoreline, were also honored as family ʻaumakua.[10]

One of the most awesome and magnificent creative forces of nature is acknowledged to be a female nature force and ʻaumakua—Pele, goddess of the volcano. In Native Hawaiian tradition, Pele and her family of deities are the ʻaumakua, or family ancestral gods, of the families who settled and continue to live in the Puna and Kaʻū districts of the island of Hawaiʻi.

Hiʻiaka-i-ka-pouli-o-Pele, youngest sister in the Pele family of deities, embodies powerful forces of healing—the process of evoking life out of the forces of death. This is especially manifest in the new forest growth that eventually heals the lands scorched and covered over by Pele's lava. In the epic myth *Pele and Hi'iaka*, Hi'iaka evolves into a deity who is as powerful as her older sister Pele. She prevails as victor in a series of deadly battles with mythical dragon-like lizard figures, called Mo'o; outwits dishonest human men; and revives the human male lover of her sister Pele from death.

These deities are honored and adopted as female ancestors from whom Native Hawaiian women inherit powerful, passionate, and enduring female qualities and characteristics.

Women in the 'Ohana, Extended Family

As Native Hawaiian society evolved, gender played a major role in defining the lives of the people. The responsibilities of the women revolved around their natural childbearing role and were distinguished from those of the men. The core Native Hawaiian culture established between 600 and 1100 evolved around the productive and reproductive activities that were organized through the 'ohana, or extended family. While responsibilities and roles within the 'ohana were distinguished by both age and gender, only the gender roles were defined under the Hawaiian *kapu*, or sacred rules of behavior. Men were considered *kapu* and sacred, while women, because of their menstruation, were considered *noa*, or not sacred. Men conducted the primary rituals and prayers to the gods while women were restricted in their participation. Men cultivated food plants, did the deep-sea fishing, and prepared all the food. Women's work, although less physically demanding, was nevertheless arduous and tedious and required forethought and planning; it included gathering resources of the forest, streams, and reefs. For example, women gathered and then beat and wove materials used for thatching, clothing, rope, mats, sails, and so forth. Men and women were required to eat separately of food that was also prepared separately, and women were restricted from eating selected foods such as bananas, coconuts, turtle, pork, and red fish.

In the following explanation of the 'aikapu, the restrictive eating rule, University of Hawai'i, Mānoa Hawaiian Studies professor Lilikala Kame'eleihiwa conjectures that the 'aikapu was a means of protecting male *mana*, or power. The reproductive power of women gave them the ability, through the choice of their sexual partners, to reinforce the strength of a genealogical line or to introduce a new and potentially dangerous relationship.

> 'Aikapu is that which prevents the "unclean" nature of women from defiling male sanctity when they offer sacrifice to the male Akua. . . . [T]he foods forbidden to women (pig, coconut, banana, and certain red fish) were not only phallic symbols but also kinolau (one of the many physical forms) of the major male Akua. . . . [F]or women to eat these foods would not only allow their mana to defile the sacrifice to the male Akua, but would also encourage them to devour male sexual prowess. . . . Nor did the haumia [unsacred] nature of women make them inferior to men; rather, it made them dangerous and thus powerful.[11]

Between 1100 and 1400, new influences were introduced through the migration of men and women from Tahiti to Hawaiʻi. The cultures merged both through intermarriage of Tahitian chiefs with women of prominent indigenous genealogical lines and as a result of battles and conquest. Apparently, the lives of the men and women of the ʻohana remained stable and improved with technological innovations in fishing, farming, and irrigation.

Beginning in 1400 and up through European contact in 1778, chiefs emerged as rulers of the Native Hawaiian social system. Women also assumed sacred and chiefly roles in the social hierarchy, whereby they were freed from day-to-day labors and accorded special privileges. However, they were still bound in their activities by the female kapu restrictions, and thus gender rather than class continued to be the principal determinant of the lives of Native Hawaiian women.

Although political rule was patriarchal, highest-ranking women of sacred birth could nevertheless determine which chief's son would inherit rank and privilege through their choice of mates.[12] Often, chiefs of lower rank would attempt to ascend in genealogical status by usurping the sexual power of the sacred "chiefess" before the higher-ranking chiefs. Professor of anthropology Jocelyn Linnekin explains the dynamics of the inheritance of political rank as follows:

> The most critical fact for understanding Hawaiian chiefly politics is that rank was bilaterally determined; although men predominated as political rulers and conquerors, chiefly women were vessels of the highest kapu rank and were critical to the dynastic aspirations of their frequently lower-ranking husband.[13]

The lives of the men and women of the ʻohana remained stable but now involved regular labor service and tribute to the male and female chiefs.

Hawaiian Monarchy

With European and American contact and trade, the development of a capitalist social system in Hawaiʻi engendered the redefining of the roles of chiefs and chiefesses to commoner men and women. In the forty years from the arrival of Captain James Cook in 1778 to Kamehameha's death in 1819, the demand for provisions and sandalwood from ships engaged in the China trade in turn increased demands of the chiefs upon the commoner men and women to provide goods and services. This trade also spread continental epidemic diseases throughout the previously unexposed indigenous population and introduced Western military technology into the wars among the island chiefdoms. In 1804 alone, the Hawaiian historian David Malo recorded, half the population died of maʻi okuʻu, a disease that was either cholera or bubonic plague.[14] Lt. James King had estimated the Native Hawaiian population at 400,000 when he was part of Captain James Cook's expedition in Hawaiʻi in 1778–1779, but in 1823, when the first missionary census was conducted, there were only approximately 135,000 Native Hawaiians.[15] On the military front, High Chief Pāiea Kamehameha took advantage of Western trade and utilized military technology in his battles to conquer and unite the chiefdoms of Hawai'i under his central rule as king.

Reflecting the prowess of their cosmic and godly female ancestors, Native Hawaiian women of chiefly birth also trained as warriors under Kamehameha. According to the Reverend Stephen Desha, in his account *Kamehameha and His Warrior Kekuhaupi'o*, the high-ranking chiefesses accompanied their husbands into the battles. Kamehameha himself had three divisions of chiefly women warriors trained in *lua*, the Native Hawaiian fighting arts.[16] Notably, the warrior chiefesses who accompanied their husbands into Kamehameha's Battle of Nu'uanu on O'ahu were specially trained by the high chief to be adept in the shooting of Western muskets and were the first line of offense against the O'ahu chiefs.[17]

The death of King Kamehameha I in May 1819 signaled a political crisis for his heirs. Rival ritual chiefs who had been defeated in King Kamehameha's rise to power rallied to wrest control over their ancestral chiefdoms back from the Kamehameha chiefs and their allies. Kamehameha's political successors had to devise a means to undermine the ritual authority and rival claims of these traditional chiefs.

High Chiefess Ke'ōpūolani was the highest ranking and most sacred chiefess in the islands and mother of Kamehameha II and Kamehameha III, heirs to the throne. High Chiefess Ka'ahumanu was the most politically influential wife of King Kamehameha, whose brothers and uncles constituted the principal allies of King Kamehameha in his rise to power; upon the death of King Kamehameha, the position of *kuhina nui*, or prime minister, was created so that Ka'ahumanu could jointly rule with King Kamehameha II. The two chiefly women worked with King Kamehameha's Council of Chiefs and his heirs to achieve a successful transition of rule, which excluded the rival chiefs. Key to the transition was the abolition of the system of chiefly *kapu* under which the rival chiefs claimed traditional power, prestige, and rights of succession. Once abolished, the right to rule became secular and based on military power and faithful service to the central government of the king, the *kuhina nui*, and the appointed Council of Chiefs.

Within one month of the death of King Kamehameha, the high chiefesses Ke'ōpūolani and Ka'ahumanu together with King Kamehameha II and the Council of Chiefs carried out the 'Ai Noa, or abolition of the chiefly *kapu*.[18] Notably, the 'Ai Noa also abolished the restrictions upon women and opened the way for the roles of both women and men at all levels of society to be redefined. While the liberation of women, especially those of chiefly rank, was a critical factor in the 'Ai Noa, the primary motivation was to undermine the status of rival ritual chiefs who claimed traditional privilege and rank and threatened to overturn the central government.[19]

High Chief Kekuaokalani, nephew of King Kamehameha I, inherited the guardianship of the war god, Kūkailimoku, and was the leader of the rival ritual chiefs. When King Kamehameha II declared the 'Ai Noa, High Chief Kekuaokalani organized the rival chiefs and led them into battle against the chiefs of the central government. His wife, High Chiefess Manono, as was the custom, went into battle and was killed fighting alongside her husband in defense of the traditional chiefly religion. In contrast to the high chiefesses Ke'ōpūolani and Ka'ahumanu, High Chiefess Manono is honored as one of the leading defenders of Native Hawaiian cultural traditions against foreign influence.[20] The defeat of High Chief Kekuaokalani and the ritual chiefs led to the consolidation of the central government under the authority of the Kamehameha chiefs and chiefesses.

Endurance of 'Ohana, with Women at the Core

With the 'Ai Noa, the division of labor and restrictions on the consumption of resources according to gender ceased. Commoner women assumed a greater role in production for the households of 'ohana, including cultivation and food preparation. Men, freed of the household duties, were increasingly drawn into wage labor outside the household as sailors and stevedores for whaling ships, as teamsters and haulers for merchants, as cowboys on ranches, and as manual laborers on plantations.

The 'ohana of the maka'āinana, or commoner class, bore the burden of social and economic change under the monarchy. The impact of disease on Native Hawaiian families was immeasurable and continued throughout the nineteenth century. For example, Samuel Kamakau, in Ruling Chiefs of Hawai'i, observed:

> In 1826 thousands died, especially in the country districts, of an epidemic of "cough, congested lungs, and sore throat."
> ... In September, 1848, an American warship brought the disease known as measles to Hilo, Hawaii. It spread and carried away about a third of the population.... In 1857 many died of an epidemic of colds, dull headache, sore throat, and deafness.... There is also a large mortality among children and a decline in the birthrate, not because women do not desire offspring. Some Hawaiian women have as many as ten to twenty children, but few grow to maturity.... These country women do not try to do away with their children nor do they frequent houses of prostitution, yet the death rate is large.[21]

Under the traditional social system, land was sacred and could not be owned. The chiefs and later the king provided stewardship over the land, and the entitlement of the 'ohana to live on and cultivate the land for subsistence was recognized and honored, provided they also gave tribute and labor service to the chief. Chiefly control over the land could change with defeat in war or upon the chief's death, but the tenure of the common people on their ancestral lands was continuous and transferred with the land from one chief to the next. The unprecedented establishment of a Western system of private property, beginning in 1848 with the Ka Māhele Act, left the majority of 'ohana landless. When the final land grants were made under the Kuleana Act of 1850, 8,205 maka'ainana received 28,600 acres, or 0.8 percent of all of the lands of Hawai'i. Although all of the 29,221 adult males in Hawai'i in 1850 were eligible to make land claims, only 29 percent received land while 71 percent remained landless.[22]

Some of the women in the burgeoning port towns of the islands were drawn into prostitution. There, Native Hawaiian women also worked as nurses, house servants, washerwomen, and serving women, earning from one to ten dollars a week, about half of men's usual wages.[23] However, in the main it was the women who remained with the families and households of *'ohana* and held them together, day to day. The men periodically had to leave to engage in the market economy in wage labor or trade. Women remained and cultivated the taro and sweet potato fields, and gathered resources upland and in the streams and reefs.

Despite strong economic and social forces pushing to disperse the *'ohana*, Native Hawaiians maintained strong family ties and obligations, with women at the core. In her study of Native Hawaiian women and landholding in Hawai'i after the establishment of a Western property system, Jocelyn Linnekin found that inheritance by women increased in the late nineteenth century because the women remained on ancestral lands while the men moved to the cities to work. She states:

> With the growing proportion of single, mobile Hawaiian men, women were more likely to remain as stable figures on the land, a role presaged by their mythic and symbolic association with land and permanence. As an adjustment motivated by historical vicissitudes, landholding by women served to keep land within the family in the face of historical challenges to the indigenous social order.[24]

Between 1820 and 1845, the role of Native Hawaiian women was equal to that of men. Native Hawaiian women could own property, participate in elections, and freely leave intolerable marriages. Beginning in 1845, however, Western laws were adopted that restricted the rights of women in Hawai'i. From 1845 through 1888, the Hawaiian kingdom adopted a coverture law from Massachusetts under which a married woman surrendered ownership of her property and the right to conduct business to her husband.[25] Upon her death, the husband received one-third interest in the wife's fixed property and the remainder passed on to her heirs. Likewise, upon death of the husband, the widow received a dower of one-third life interest in her husband's fixed property and an absolute one-third ownership of his movable property. In 1850, women were denied the right to vote that they had previously exercised. In 1860, the law required a married woman to adopt her husband's name. The coverture law was repealed in 1888, but the other laws restricting the rights of women remained in place.[26]

Chiefly Women and Queens

The status of Native Hawaiian women, however, varied according to class. While Western laws began to limit the rights of women in Hawai'i, chiefly women, unlike the commoner women, retained significant political power and owned property. The position of *kuhina nui* held by High Chiefess Ka'ahumanu made her equal in power to King Kamehameha II. When he died in London of measles in 1824, his brother became Kamehameha III at the age of nine, and Kuhina Nui Ka'ahumanu served as regent until the king came of age and then continued as co-ruler. Except for the period from 1844 through 1855, the *kuhina nui* were chiefly women from 1819 until the office was abolished in 1864.[27] King Kamehameha V asked Bernice Pauahi Bishop to succeed him as ruler, but she declined. Upon the death of King Lunalilo, Queen Emma, widow of King Kamehameha IV, was a candidate against Chief David Kalākaua to succeed as ruler.

High Chiefess Liliʻuokalani did succeed her brother King Kalākaua as queen and last monarch of the Hawaiian kingdom. Chiefly women also served in the Council of Chiefs and in the House of Nobles. Under the Ka Māhele Act, five of the ten high chiefs to receive lands and ten of the twenty-four lesser chiefs to receive lands were women.[28]

Throughout this period, many daughters of landed Native Hawaiian chiefs maintained their status in the new social system through marriage to American and European merchants and businessmen. Plantations, ranches, and banks were established through the investment of foreign capital on chiefly lands controlled through intermarriage. For example, in 1850, Princess Bernice Pauahi married Charles Reed Bishop, an enterprising young banker from San Francisco, and in 1862, Princess Lydia Kamakaʻeha Liliʻuokalani married John Dominis, son of a New England merchant. Other prominent marriages between landed Native Hawaiian chiefesses and haole entrepreneurs and businessmen included the marriage of Chiefess Rachel Keliikipikaneokoolakala of Kohala to Samuel Parker in 1818; Princess Miriam Likelike to A. S. Cleghorn in 1870; High Chiefess Kinoole to Benjamin Pittman; High Chiefess Kahinu to William Beckley; Chiefess Kamaka to Henry Stillman; High Chiefess Kaumakaokane to Thomas Cummins; and Irene Kahalelauko Iʻi to Charles Brown.[29] The hapa-haole, half-Hawaiian offspring of these marriages formed the core of the Native Hawaiian professionals, politicians, and businessmen in the twentieth century.

Native Hawaiian queens looked after the education, health, and social welfare of their people during their lifetime and upon their passing, in the establishment of perpetual landed estates. One by one, as they passed away in the late nineteenth century, the landed *aliʻi* or lineal chiefs and chiefesses bequeathed their substantial personal landholdings to the common Native Hawaiian people in the form of perpetual charitable trusts. The lands of the Native Hawaiian *aliʻi* were to be used to generate revenues to provide programs for the education, health, and general welfare of the common people.

The private landholdings of the Kamehameha chiefs, totaling 369,699 acres (9 percent of all the land in Hawaiʻi), were consolidated into the Bernice Pauahi Bishop Estate. The revenues generated from the estate were to be used to fund the establishment and maintenance of the Kamehameha Schools for the education of Native Hawaiians. Queen Emma, widow of King Kamehameha IV, willed her private landholdings, totaling 13,064 acres, to a trust that would provide health care to destitute Native Hawaiians through the Queen's Hospital. Queen Kapiʻolani, the widow of King Kalākaua, willed her estate to the maintenance of the Queen Kapiʻolani Maternity Hospital. Queen Liliʻuokalani established the Queen Liliʻuokalani Children's Center with the lands from her estate, totaling 9,793 acres, to provide social services support to orphaned and indigent Native Hawaiian children.[30]

The Overthrow of Queen Liliʻuokalani and the Hawaiian Monarchy

The Hawaiian monarchy, established in 1810, was overthrown on January 17, 1893, by U.S. naval forces, while Queen Liliʻuokalani held the throne.[31] Queen Liliʻuokalani grew to symbolize the sovereignty and national integrity of the Native Hawaiian people. For the generations of Native Hawaiians born in the twentieth century, Native Hawaiian national consciousness and identity were fed, nurtured, and shaped by the bitter knowledge of the loss of sovereignty when the Hawaiian monarchy, in the person of the queen, was overthrown. The image of the queen—regal, beautiful, defiant, proud, enduring—is integral to the identity of Native Hawaiians, especially the Native Hawaiian women. Her motto, *'Onipa'a*, meaning "stand firm in the shifting tides of change," is interpreted as a call to persevere and endure as a people. *'Onipa'a* was a call for future generations of Native Hawaiians to live, practice, and perpetuate the native language, culture, science, spiritual beliefs, and customs and to endure as a distinct people, despite American efforts to extinguish Hawaiian language and culture and to assimilate Native Hawaiians into the American social system.

Queen Lili'uokalani became the focal point of Native Hawaiian protest against American annexation, rule, and assimilation, at the end of the nineteenth century and throughout the twentieth century. Noenoe Silva, professor of political science, documents the role of Native Hawaiian women in organizing the protest to the annexation of Hawai'i in the 1997 issue of *Social Process in Hawai'i*.[32] The Hui Aloha 'Āina, or Hawaiian Patriotic League, was the main organization formed to oppose annexation. According to Silva, by July 1893 the organization claimed a membership of 7,500 native-born Hawaiian qualified voters (out of 13,000 registered voters) and a women's branch of over 11,000 members.[33] In an announcement to women to attend a mass meeting, the women's branch exhorted women to get involved as follows:

> Adolescent women, young adult women, and mature women (mothers) of the Hawaiian Nation are wanted to come to this meeting to discuss patriotic convictions and the caring for (or tending to) the continued independence of this Archipelago.
>
> This is a most excellent thing that Hawaiian women should do out of love for the Land, its Flag, and its permanent independence.[34]

According to Silva, the women's Hui Aloha 'Āina were led by women of *ali'i* or chiefly lineage. Their activities included a letter of protest to Commissioner James Blount, who was sent to Hawai'i by President Grover Cleveland to investigate the role of the U.S. naval forces in the overthrow of the Hawaiian monarchy; a rally of between five thousand and seven thousand people to protest the establishment of the Republic of Hawai'i; letters of protest to the foreign ministers of the United States, Great Britain, France, Japan, Germany, and Portugal; a rally against the annexationist U.S. senator John Morgan when he visited Hawai'i; and a petition against annexation, with the signatures of over twenty-one thousand Native Hawaiians from nearly every district on every island.[35] Silva also contends that one form of native protest to colonialism was the printing of Native Hawaiian legends, songs, chants, and genealogies in independent Native Hawaiian language newspapers. The legends, including accounts of the deities, which I discussed at the beginning of this essay, presented strong female role models, which Silva says were the inspiration for the chiefly women of the anti-annexation struggle. She writes:

It is not surprising that the executive committees of the organized resistance were aliʻi, for these histories and legends, along with chants, songs and genealogies, were part of their education from an early age. In short, knowledge of their powerful mothers and grandmothers was part and parcel of their consciousness of who they were, and surely gave them strength for the fight.[36]

Thus, even as the period of the Hawaiian monarchy drew to a close, the Native Hawaiian female deities were invoked as images and symbols of protest to Native Hawaiian women and men.

Territorial Years

The trend of out-marriage of Native Hawaiian women with Caucasian males continued, but in addition, toward the end of the nineteenth century, Native Hawaiian women of all classes began to intermarry with Chinese men as they left the plantations and entered into trades. Marginal taro-growing lands were leased out to Chinese for the cultivation of rice. Chinese served as middlemen, buying fish and farm produce from Native Hawaiian farmers and trading it in the towns for manufactured goods that, in turn, they peddled among the rural Native Hawaiian farmers. Eventually the Chinese opened stores in rural Native Hawaiian communities. Those who married into Native Hawaiian families helped market fish and products grown on Hawaiian ancestral lands. Some opened poi mills in small rural settlements.[37]

By 1910 the census takers had begun to count "Asiatic-Hawaiian" as a category separate from "Hawaiian" and "Caucasian-Hawaiian." That year there were 3,734 offspring of Chinese-Hawaiian marriages. By 1920, the number had increased to 6,955. In 1930 there were 50,860 Native Hawaiians, of which 22,636 were pure Hawaiian, 15,632 were "Caucasian-Hawaiian," and 12,592 were "Asiatic-Hawaiians."[38]

At the beginning of the twentieth century, after the annexation of Hawaiʻi to the United States, urbanization increased and Native Hawaiian women also entered the workforce. In the tourist industry they worked part time as hula dancers, lei makers, greeters, waitresses, and hotel workers. Native Hawaiian women also worked in the pineapple canneries, as clerical workers, and as telephone operators and entered the professions of teaching and nursing.

In 1920, 1,450, or 10 percent of the Hawaiian and part-Hawaiian women over age ten, worked for wages. These Native Hawaiian women also made up 10 percent of all the women in Hawaiʻi over age ten who worked for a wage.[39] By 1930 the number of Hawaiian and part-Hawaiian women who were wage earners had increased to 2,600, which was 15 percent of the Native Hawaiian women over age ten, and they in turn made up 14 percent of all the working women in Hawaiʻi. By comparison, Japanese women made up 46.9 percent of the women over age ten who worked; Caucasian women comprised 19.2 percent; Portuguese women, 7.2 percent; and Chinese women, 6.8 percent.[40]

In 1930, Native Hawaiian working women made up 21 percent of the territory's teachers, 15 percent of the trained nurses, 17 percent of the clerical workers, and 35 percent of the telephone operators. The proportion of Native Hawaiian women in all these fields had declined from 1920, whereas the proportion of Japanese women in these fields had increased. In agriculture, Native Hawaiian women still represented only a small proportion, 5 percent of the female employees. However, they made up 27 percent of the women operatives in the pineapple canneries.[41] Thus, Native Hawaiian women were represented in all classes of labor, and their condition of life was determined primarily by their class status, rather than according to their gender.

Native Hawaiians and those of part-Hawaiian ancestry were considered to be among the best teachers in the territory. The superintendent of schools Edgar Wood commented in his 1920 biennial report, "The Hawaiian teacher is recognized as among the very best in our schools."[42] In 1921, *The Friend* carried an article on Native Hawaiian teachers that praised their abilities:

> As a class, the Hawaiian group constitutes a particularly desirable element in our teaching corps, because of their familiarity with local conditions, their relatively long tenure of service, sympathetic and kindly qualities, and their Christian-American background.[43]

After suffrage, Native Hawaiians were the first women to become attorneys and to serve in the legislature. Throughout the twentieth century, women also played important roles as the keepers of the culture, as *kumu hula* (hula teachers and chanters) and *kūpuna* (elders). Intermarriage of Native Hawaiians with non-Hawaiians increased throughout the twentieth century.

The book *Notable Women of Hawai'i* (1984), edited by Barbara Bennett Peterson, features 127 women, of whom 39, or 33 percent, were Native Hawaiian women; out of these, seventeen were chiefesses or queens of the nineteenth century. Among the remaining twenty-three women, four had served in the territorial legislature; four were noted *kumu hula*, or master teachers of the hula; three were key figures in large landed family estates and known for their philanthropy; two were Hawaiian cultural experts; two were entertainers; one was an attorney; one was a labor leader; one was an ordained minister; one was an artist; one was in public health nursing; and one was a businesswoman. This collection of biographies gives the reader a sense of the breadth of involvement and talent of Native Hawaiian women as the economy transformed.

Statehood Years and Sovereignty

Hawai'i became a state in 1959. In 1969, after ten years of unprecedented development that transformed the landscape of island shorelines, polluted fishing grounds, drained underground water tables, and displaced Native Hawaiian fishing and farming communities, a Native Hawaiian political movement emerged. Research of Hawai'i's political status and options resulted in documentation that the overthrow of Queen Lili'uokalani by the U.S. military was illegal and that the U.S. government was obligated to provide redress. The queen's book, *Hawai'i's Story by Hawai'i's Queen*, was widely read, and passages were quoted such as "The cause of Hawaiian independence is larger and dearer than the life of any man connected with it. Love of country is deep-seated in the breast of every Hawaiian, whatever his station."[44] Queen Liliʻuokalani became the icon for the restitution of justice and sovereignty for the Native Hawaiian people.

With Queen Liliʻuokalani as the patron of sovereignty, Native Hawaiians seek to improve and uplift the health, education, and standard of living for Native Hawaiian ʻohana. Natural and cultural resources essential for subsistence and persistence of religious and cultural custom, belief, and practice must be protected and sustained. Native Hawaiians seek full redress, including restitution of all of the territory of the Hawaiian nation, compensation for mismanagement and destruction of national lands and resources, and, most important, the re-establishment and recognition of a government to exercise sovereignty and self-determination.

Despite statehood, the consciousness of, pride in, and practice of Native Hawaiian culture and spirituality evolved into a modern renaissance. In rallying to stop U.S. navy bombing of the island of Kahoʻolawe, the traditional concept of aloha ʻāina, that land is sacred and must be nurtured, returned to prominence, and rural Native Hawaiian communities, strongholds of Native Hawaiian subsistence lifeways reliant on and protective of the land, gained significance. Pele practitioners organized the Pele Defense Fund to stop the extraction of geothermal energy out of the Kīlauea volcano as a desecration of the life force of the deity. Traditional navigational arts and skills were revived with trans-Pacific voyages of the Polynesian Voyaging Society on the canoes Hōkūleʻa, Hawaiʻi Loa, and Makaliʻi. Hālau hula, schools of traditional Hawaiian dance and chant, increased and flourished. Lāʻau lapaʻu, traditional herbal and spiritual healing practices, were revived as valid holistic medicine. Hawaiian studies from the elementary to the university level became part of the regular curricula. Hawaiian music evolved into new forms of expression and gained popularity.

In this renaissance, the knowledge and experience of Native Hawaiian kūpuna, or elders, was crucial. Kūpuna shared their knowledge of chants, hula, legends, genealogies, place names, religious rituals, subsistence fishing and planting, astronomy, navigation, and healing practices. Women were prominent among these kūpuna, including kumu hula trained in the Pele traditions, such as Mrs. Edith Kanakaole and Aunty ʻIolani Luahine from the island of Hawaiʻi; those schooled in the traditions of powerful spiritual kahuna and kūpuna from the traditionally spiritual island of Molokaʻi, such as Aunty Mary Lee, Aunty Clara Ku, Aunty Lani Kapuni, and Aunty Harriet Ne; the Native Hawaiian scholar from Kaʻū, Hawaiʻi, who worked as translator, ethnographer, and resource person at the Bishop Museum on Oʻahu, Mary Kawena Pukui; and Oʻahu kumu hula and cultural resource Mrs. Emma De Fries. Through these women, the images of the cosmic gods of nature, powerful spiritual healers, and great rulers—including ancestral female gods and chiefesses—came to be acknowledged, respected, and honored.

For example, Aunty Edith Kanakaole, one of the most influential of these kūpuna, has named in her honor the Hawaiian Studies Building at the University of Hawaiʻi, Hilo, and the stadium where the Annual Merrie Monarch festival is held. She is the principal figure in the perpetuation of Pele beliefs, customs, and practices as kumu hula of Hālau O Kekuhi, a Hawaiian hula school devoted to the perpetuation of the Pele traditions, chants, and hula.

Traditional and contemporary chants performed by the hālau honor and celebrate the beauty and power of Pele by describing the various stages of her eruptive manifestation, from the past to the present. Significantly, new chants reinforce the construction of Pele as a primary ancestress and deity for contemporary Native Hawaiian women. An example of such a chant is "Halulu Ka Hōnua I Ka ʻOlaʻi E," composed by Edith Kanakaole to chronicle the 1977 eruption at Kahaualeʻa, Hawaiʻi. Just before the lava flow, an earthquake struck early in the morning and a gigantic flash of lightning appeared in the sky—manifestations of the goddess Pele. Initially it was thought that the flow would go through Kalapana, and the chant speaks of how the people of the district were concerned. Through the smoke and sulfur manifestations of Pele, which travel down the chain of Hawaiian islands, people of other islands are reminded that Pele still lives and is active on Hawaiʻi. Once the lava began to flow, Pele's eruption headed for the ocean, consuming the forest on the way. The chant honors the primal force of Pele, the woman of the volcanic crater pit.

Halulu Ka Hōnua I Ka ʻOlaʻi E
Halulu ka hōnua i ka ʻolaʻi e
>   The earth quivers with the earthquake
Ilaila o uka o Kalalua
>   There in the uplands of Kalalua
ʻImi aʻela kāhi o Pohakea
>   Searching for a place to break forth
Waʻele ka hōnua, puka aʻela
>   The earth separates, the exit is found
Ua poʻohina la e
>   The blanket of grey appears
Hoʻi ka wahine i ka ʻāina
>   It is the Woman who appears
Pōloli no he ʻai he Iʻa
>   Hungry to consume fish
Hoʻi ihola a pau ke kolu
>   After the third time she returns
Kani hou nā manu
>   The sounds of the birds are again heard
Hoʻolulu ka lehua e
>   The lehua becomes abundant
Nā lehua i hoa me ka maile
>   The lehua and the maile are companions
Kau i puʻu Kauka e
>   At the top of Kauka
Mālamalama he au ua ʻeha
>   An illumination ignited by a piercing energy
ʻEha ka manaʻo he kupa o ka ʻāina e
>   A worrisome sight for the people of the land
E nonome ana a maʻa mau
>   For the creeping flow of lava is evident

Uhi ūhā e manene ai
  Groping, engulfing, fearsome
Ka hana ka wahine o ka lua
  This primal force of the Woman of the pit
He eʻepa ke akua ʻahiʻenaʻena
  The god of intense fiery glow is indeed extraordinary
ʻOwaka ka lani naue ka hōnua
  The heaven is rent, the earth shakes
Poahi ka wahine, pouli e
  The earth is obscure, dark
Paʻapū ka moku o Keawe
  The land of Keawe is concealed in smoke
Ke iho nei ka Pele ʻau i ke kai e.
  Downward marches Pele reaching to the sea.[45]

The continuing composition and performance of these chants construct and reconstruct the existence of Pele in Hawaiʻi to her descendants and followers who believe in her as a deity.

In addition to chants and hula, the potent images of the Pele family forces in nature are constructed and reconstructed in giving their names to children and grandchildren from generation to generation, the presentation of hoʻokupu (offerings) in Native Hawaiian spiritual rituals to them, and family burial rites at the volcano.

One of the most significant ceremonies to commemorate the one-hundred-year anniversary of the overthrow of Queen Liliʻuokalani and to rally support for the restoration of Hawaiian sovereignty was a twenty-four-hour vigil to Pele and her family of deities. Participants gathered around the Halemaʻumaʻu Crater on Hawaiʻi island, identified in chant and legend as the primary residence of the fire deity. Every hour, for twenty-four hours, the participants performed chants honoring the birth of the islands from Papahānaumoku and Wākea, prophesying the unification of the islands into a re-established nation, and calling for focus and vision to sustain the sovereignty movement. This ceremony was expanded to include vigils at sacred sites on every island to welcome in the new millennium in the year 2000.

As Hawaiʻi moves into the twenty-first century, Native Hawaiian women are leaders in the movement for Hawaiian sovereignty and self-determination, and they continue to fulfill a wide variety of meaningful roles across the broad spectrum of a multiethnic society. Native Hawaiian women of every class are empowered by a legacy of powerful, brilliant, and enduring female ancestors who are creative life forces of nature, national leaders, and family matriarchs to take on new challenges and struggles of everyday living.

NOTES

1. Mele Look, Summer Sylva, and Gigliola Baruffi, "The Health of Hawaiian Women," *Pacific Health Dialog* 5:2 (September 1998), 290–96. The life expectancy for women in Hawaiʻi in 1990 was 82.06 years. Chinese women had a life expectancy of 86.11 years.

2. Ibid. The Native Hawaiian Health Care Systems or Papa Ola Lōkahi provides screening for breast cancer and prostate cancer, diabetes, and cardiovascular disease through individual island health care organizations—Nā Pu'uwai for Moloka'i and Lana'i, Ke Ola Mamo for O'ahu, Hui No Ke Ola Pono for Maui, Hui Mālama Ola Nā Ō'iwi for Hawai'i, and Ho'ola Lāhui Hawai'i for Kaua'i and Ni'ihau.

3. Office of Hawaiian Affairs, *1998 Native Hawaiian Data Book* (Honolulu: Office of Hawaiian Affairs, 1998), 62.

4. Ibid., 58. In 1990 the divorce rate for Native Hawaiian women was 9.22 percent and for Native Hawaiian men, 7.55 percent. Statewide, 13.27 percent of the households are headed by single women, and among the Native Hawaiian population 22.5 percent of the households are headed by single women (52–53).

5. David Malo, *Hawaiian Antiquities: Moolelo Hawaii*, Bernice P. Bishop Museum Special Publication 2, 2d ed., translated from the Hawaiian by Dr. Nathaniel Emerson, 1898 (Honolulu: Bishop Museum Press, 1971), 238–44; Samuel Manaiakalani Kamakau, *Tales and Traditions of the People of Old: Na Mo'olelo a ka Po'e Kahiko*, translated from the newspapers *Ka Nūpepa Kū'oko'a* and *Ke Au 'Oko'a* by Mary Kawena Pukui and edited by Dorothy Barrere (Honolulu: Bishop Museum Press, 1991), 125.

6. Martha Beckwith, *Hawaiian Mythology* (Honolulu: University of Hawai'i Press, 1970), 12–14.

7. Ibid., 214–37.

8. Ibid.; Samuel Kamakau, *The Works of the People of Old: Na Hana a ka Po'e Kahiko* (Honolulu: Bishop Museum Press, 1976), 129–45.

9. For example, the Hale O Papa in Hakioawa on the island of Kaho'olawe has several women buried in and around the site. One burial included the bones of a fetus and several other burials included infants, indicating that the *heiau* was connected to prenatal, birthing, and natal care for women.

10. Beckwith, *Hawaiian Mythology*, 122–43.

11. Lilikala Kame'eleihiwa, *Native Land and Foreign Desires: Ko Hawai'i 'Āina a me Nā Koi Pu'umake a ka Po'e Haole, Pehea la e Pono ai? How Shall We Live in Harmony?* (Honolulu: Bishop Museum Press, 1992), 33–35.

12. Ibid.

13. Jocelyn Linnekin, *Sacred Queens and Women of Consequence: Rank, Gender and Colonialism in the Hawaiian Islands* (Ann Arbor: University of Michigan Press, 1990), 16.

14. David Malo, "On the Decrease of Population of the Hawaiian Islands," trans. L. Andres, *Hawaiian Spectator* 2:2 (1839).

15. Robert C. Schmidt, *Historical Statistics of Hawai'i* (Honolulu: University Press of Hawai'i, 1977), Table 1.1.

16. Richard Paglinawan, "Olohe Lua or Master of Hawaiian Fighting Arts" (presentation to Counseling and Treating People of Color Conference, Honolulu, Hawai'i, November 9, 1999).

17. Stephen Desha, *Kamehameha and His Warrior Kekuhaupi'o* (Honolulu: Kamehameha Schools Press, 2000), 35, 44, 151, 400–402, 408–410. The chiefly women warriors had been trained to shoot the muskets by the Kaua'i chief Ka'iana, who had learned the skill during his travels to North America and Europe.

18. Marshall Sahlins, *Historical Metaphors and Mythical Realities: Structure in the Early History of the Sandwich Islands Kingdom* (Ann Arbor: University of Michigan Press, 1981), 55–64.

19. Ibid.; William Davenport, "The Hawaiian 'Cultural Revolution': Some Economic and Political Considerations," *American Anthropologist* 71 (1969): 1–20; A. L. Kroeber, *Anthropology* (New York: Harcourt, Brace, 1948).

20. His Majesty Kalākaua, *The Legends and Myths of Hawaii: The Fables and Folk-Lore of a Strange People* (Tokyo: Tuttle, 1973), 429–46.

21. Samuel Kamakau, *Ruling Chiefs in Hawaii*, rev. ed. (Honolulu: Kamehameha Schools Press, 1992), 236–37.

22. Marion Kelly, cited in Neil Levy, "Native Hawaiian Land Rights," *California Law Review* 63:4 (July 1975): 856.

23. G. W. Bates, *Sandwich Island Notes* (New York: Harper and Bros., 1854), cited in Linnekin, *Sacred Queens*, 1990, 183.

24. Linnekin, *Sacred Queens*, 213.

25. Judith R. Gething, "Christianity and Coverture: Impact on the Legal Status of Women in Hawai'i, 1820–1920," *Hawaiian Journal of History* 11 (1977): 188–220.

26. Ibid.

27. Keoni Ana, the half-Hawaiian son of King Kamehameha's British military adviser John Young and a niece of the king, served as *kuhina nui* from 1844 through 1855.

28. Kame'eleihiwa, *Native Land and Foreign Desires*, 227.

29. *Pacific Commercial Advertiser*, June 12, 1910, sec. 2, p. 1; George Nellist, *The Story of Hawaii and Its Builders* (Honolulu: Star-Bulletin, 1925); A. Grove Day, *A Biographical Dictionary: History Makers of Hawaii* (Honolulu: Mutual Publishing of Honolulu, 1984).

30. Acreage statistics found in Legislative Reference Bureau Report No. 3, 1967, "Public Land Policy in Hawaii: Major Landowners" (Honolulu, 1969), Table 3, 17–18. Note also that when the unmarried King Lunalilo passed away, he willed $25,000 from his estate for the establishment and maintenance of the Lunalilo Home as an infirmary for poor, aged, and infirm people of Hawaiian birth or extraction.

31. Sources on the overthrow of the Hawaiian monarchy include U.S. House of Representatives, 53d Cong., 2d sess., Report No. 243, "Intervention of United States Government in Affairs of Foreign Friendly Governments," December 21, 1893; U.S. Senate, 53d Cong., 2d sess., Report No. 227, "Report from the Committee on Foreign Relations and Appendix in Relation to the Hawaiian Islands," February 26, 1894 (Washington, D.C.: Government Printing Office, 1894); Queen Lili'uokalani, *Hawai'i's Story by Hawai'i's Queen* (Tokyo: Tuttle, 1964); petitions in Archives to Queen Lili'uokalani.

32. Noenoe K. Silva, "Kū'e! Hawaiian Women's Resistance to the Annexation," in Joyce Chinen, Kathleen O. Kane, Ida M. Yoshinaga, eds., *Women in Hawai'i: Sites, Identities, and Voices, Social Process in Hawai'i* 38 (1997).

33. Ibid., 8.

34. Ibid.

35. Nalani Minton and Noenoe Silva, *Kū'e: The Hui Aloha 'Āina Anti-Annexation Petitions, 1897–1898* (Honolulu: Nalani Minton and Noenoe Silva, 1998), 17.

36. Ibid., 7, 13–14.

37. Davianna McGregor, *Kupa'a I Ka 'Āina: Persistence on the Land* (unpublished Ph.D. diss., University of Hawai'i, 1989).

38. U.S. Bureau of the Census, Fifteenth Census of the United States: 1930. Population Second Series, Hawaii: Composition and Characteristics of the Population and Unemployment (Washington, D.C.: U.S. Government Printing Office, 1931), Table 2, p. 6. While the term used was *Asiatic-Hawaiian*, the overwhelming majority of intermarriages were with Chinese rather than with Japanese or Koreans.

39. U.S. Bureau of the Census, Fourteenth Census of the United States Taken in the Year 1920, Hawaii (Washington, D.C.: U.S. Government Printing Office, 1921), Table 7, p. 3.

40. U.S. Bureau of the Census, Fifteenth Census of the United States: 1930, 1931, Table 5, p. 86.

41. Ibid., Table 8, p. 90.

42. Quoted in Benjamin Wist, *A Century of Public Education in Hawaii: October 15, 1840–October 15, 1940* (Honolulu: Honolulu Star Bulletin, 1940), 206.

43. *The Friend* 7 (July 1921): a.

44. Queen Lili'uokalani, *Hawai'i's Story by Hawai'i's Queen* (Honolulu: Mutual Publishing, 1999), 302.

45. Jon K. Matsuoka, Davianna McGregor, and Luciano Minerbi, with Pualani Kanakaole Kanahele, Marion Kelly, and Noenoe Barney-Campbell, "Native Hawaiian Ethnographic Study for the Hawai'i Geothermal Project Environmental Impact Study," for the *Oak Ridge National Laboratories Environmental Impact Study* for the U.S. Department of Energy (1993), 194–96.

2

Unlearning Orientalism
Locating Asian and Asian American Women in Family History

Kathleen Uno

Although experiences of home and family life are part of our everyday world, much work remains to be done to thoroughly understand and analyze Asian and Asian American women in families and households. There is also work to be undone, namely, unlearning Orientalism, which continues to influence the study of Asia and, in turn, permeates the study of Asians in the diaspora. Colonialism has left its mark on how Asian, Asian American, and Pacific Islander societies, including gender, inside and outside families, are analyzed. Those intellectual operations of colonialism have also had an impact on the lives of Asian women who migrate and are born overseas.[1]

"Lotus blossom," "submissive," "less liberated than Western women," "shy," "retiring," "devoted," "subservient," "exotic," and "sexy" are descriptors often applied to Asian women by the media and people in the everyday world, and these labels also stick to American-born and immigrant Asian women. Some Asian American women embrace these stereotypes as a route to personal goals, while others reject them as unwanted barriers. The stereotyping of Asian and Asian American women can be linked to images of Asia, and both sets of images are inscribed by the power of the West to shape knowledge around the globe since the rise of modern imperialism. Edward Said has argued that "the distillation of essential ideas about the Orient—its sensuality, its tendency to despotism, its aberrant mentality, its habits of inaccuracy, its backwardness—into a separate and unchallenged coherence" have characterized images of the Near (or Middle) East, its culture, and its people.[2] Yet the habits of mind formed in the imperialist encounter are not restricted to one geographic area. They have influenced views of societies, cultures, and peoples in other parts of the world, including Asia and the Pacific islands. Nor did those habits of mind vanish with the decline of formal or territorial imperialism in the twentieth century.

Some consequences of Orientalism include a tendency to collapse differences and to obliterate Asian histories, replacing them with a static, timeless present. Moreover, while there are similarities between the broad regions of South,[3] Southeast, and East Asia, there are also social and cultural differences. Differences exist among localities and peoples within the nations that constitute these regions as well, including differences under Western and non-Western (Japanese) colonialism. Rather than offer detailed descriptions of household and family life in major Asian nations that have sent large numbers of migrants to the United States, this chapter focuses on how those interested in finding out more about Asian women may develop fruitful approaches to the history of Asian families and households by examining recent works. For students and researchers alike, (1) recognizing Asian and Asian/Pacific Islander American diversity as well as (2) acts of unlearning, recasting, or demystifying old images through questioning the assumptions of existing research may be as important as learning new facts or doing new research on Asian women in households and families.

As a starting point for understandings of postmigration Asian and Pacific Island culture and social life, this chapter raises questions about the received wisdom of women in Asian households and families since the nineteenth century. Long-standing stereotypes of Asia, Asian women, and Asian family life feed images of women and family life in Asia today and Asian American women in the United States. It is worth casting doubt on these stereotypes that originate in colonial modes of thinking about Asian and Western societies and values, Asian women and men, and household or family values and activities. The historical method calls the questioning of existing assumptions, facts, approaches (or methods), and conclusions "revisionism." At present, much of the path-breaking work in Asian family history and Asian gender history and studies is revisionist. The new scholarship interrogates the received wisdom about women in Asian households, and households in society, in the past and the present. These new findings and revisionist approaches to Asian women's and family history can stimulate fresh perspectives on Asian American women's and family history, especially at a time when studies of recent Asian immigration and of Asians in the diaspora are blossoming.

Some Terms and Concepts

The main argument of this chapter is that Orientalism, or the inscription of power on knowledge under Western imperialism since the late eighteenth century, has marked notions of Asian households, resulting in an exaggeration of both their patriarchal character and the subordination of women. Recent research, much of it by Women's or Gender Studies specialists, including many feminists, is directed toward revising the conventional wisdom about households. The body of the chapter surveys earlier views of women in the household and family in six Asian countries but emphasizes the research that challenges those views. Due to limitations of space, the main geographic focus here is women, households, and families in Asian nations that have sent the largest numbers of immigrants to the United States: China, India, Japan, Korea, the Philippines, and Vietnam.

Present definitions of family as well as persistent, fixed notions of the peoples and cultures of Asia and non-Western regions as inherently different from the peoples and cultures of Western Europe and the United States have deeply influenced notions of Asian families and Asian women. Family ideals in the United States today center on a *nuclear* unit of parent and child that dissolves when the children leave to marry and the parents pass away. Despite ethnic, regional, and individual variations in structure and values, other widely held ideals are companionate spousal bonds, affective bonds with children, equal concern for all children, and the welfare of all family members. Although the family today is generally seen as a co-residential kinship unit comprising mother, father, and children, in the past servants, boarders, and other unrelated persons and cousins, aunts, uncles, and other collateral relatives often lived in households. *Extended* families may be *stem* families—one couple of each generation or *joint* families— all couples of each generation.

Patriarchy is literally rule by the father, but it often indicates male domination in general. Asian patriarchy emphasizes male authority and its opposite, female subordination and submissiveness. *Patrilineality* is continuity of the family line through males, with matrilineality, bilaterality, and other more complex principles constituting alternative descent patterns. Asian patrilineality is often cited as a reason for the marginalization of women in family and society. When women don't belong permanently to a family, what happens to them often may matter less, and when resources are scarce, investing in the care and education of daughters who leave home and village for marriage or work usually is less appealing than investing in the future of a son who stays in the household.

Lingering from the past, Orientalism is so pervasive that not only Westerners but Asians in the "homeland" and in the United States, including women, feminists, and anti-imperialists, cannot completely escape its influence despite their intents and desires. Its major impacts on Asian family studies include (1) the exaggeration of male and female role differentiation, (2) overly negative evaluations of Asian family structures and practices or overemphasis on their divergence from U.S. or Western European practices, and (3) the exaggeration of women's disadvantages in Asian households or family systems. So ghosts from the colonial past haunt our supposedly postcolonial world and can inhabit the minds of Asian Americans and Pacific Islanders today, ordinary people and scholars alike.

In general, Asian patriarchy and patrilineality have figured prominently in descriptions of family and society in China, India, Korea, Japan, and Vietnam, although more strongly for some of these countries than for others. Forms of oppression centered in the home—footbinding in China, bride burning (or dowry murders) in India, and female infanticide in both countries—have come to symbolize or represent the downtrodden status of women in China and India, as in Asia in general, due to the size, population, and cultural importance of these two countries.[4] The multigenerational family is another motif, and it, too, operates to differentiate Asian from contemporary Western families. *Bilateral* descent (tracing lineage through both maternal and paternal relatives) predominates in discussions of the Filipino family, although there are regional variations in the Philippines and nearly all other Asian countries. However, despite the weakness of patrilineality in the Philippines, a theme considered in common with other Asian countries is women under male authority. Contrary to the conventional wisdom, newer research on women and the family points out weaknesses in male authority; greater female agency, authority, or resistance than previously assumed; and active female public participation. Historical research is reclaiming the women's past by showing that patriarchy, patrilineality, and other supposed features of Asian families were weaker or even absent in earlier times.

China

Despite late 1970s sentiments that the Chinese family had been comprehensively studied,[5] subsequent decades saw an explosion of monographs attempting to modify the picture of a starkly oppressive joint family and uniformly miserable women. Typically, the Chinese family is represented as a large, multigenerational unit consisting of a senior male, his wife and concubines, his sons, their wives and concubines, and their children. Subject to the "three obediences," women were said to fall under the authority of their fathers in youth, their husbands in adulthood, and their sons in old age. In addition, due to patrilocal marriage, they had to serve and obey their mothers-in-law and sisters-in-law. A woman kept the surname of her birth family, yet she was generally not recorded in its genealogy because she moved to another home at marriage. In contrast to such evidence of female marginality, sons who carried on the surname were permanent family members and played central roles in the rituals for the ancestors. Footbinding, done by Chinese mothers to their daughters so that they would be desirable marriage partners, was common more in northern regions of the country than in the south. Both outside and inside China, as the twentieth century progressed, footbinding and Confucianism came to symbolize the oppressiveness of gender and family norms.

Questioning the universality of the joint family is a major theme in the new research on Chinese families and women. Lloyd Eastman estimated that no more than 6 to 7 percent of Chinese families lived up to the joint-family ideal.[6] In smaller households, in which a wife's labor at housekeeping or income-earning activities was more necessary, women had a stronger voice in family affairs.

Some studies have challenged the universality of both marriage and its forms in China. Other research has undermined the assumption that young women inevitably went as daughters-in-law to their husbands' families. Arthur P. Wolf and Chieh-shan Huang point out that in some parts of China, more than one-third of marriages involved the marriage of daughters adopted at a young age to their step-brothers (minor marriage), and that *uxorilocal* marriages (husbands living with their wives' families) were frequent, though not predominant in some regions. They also argue that ordinary household values rather than a unique outlook accounted for these practices.[7]

In the early twentieth century, due to strong demand for textile production in some areas of the Canton delta (southeast China), some young women postponed co-residence with their husband and his family and even purchased proxies to serve their in-laws while they resided elsewhere in women's houses. Why did women evading life with their in-laws bother to marry? According to Janice Stockard, their marriages resulted from a belief that, after death, their spirits could never rest unless they had descendants to pay respects to their ancestral tablets.[8]

Recent studies also revise grim images of family life as constant submission and unbroken misery. Instead they emphasize Chinese women's maneuvering to do the best they could for themselves within the family system. Many had responsibilities for managing major aspects of family life. A few elite women excelled in creative activities. Dorothy Ko's research on one region of sixteenth-century China argues against the notion that marriage inevitably equaled women's complete oppression. Thus female agency as well as class or regional differences and historical context can be effectively deployed against what can be called Orientalist notions of Chinese women's unrelieved submission, misery, and passivity.[9] And Neil Diamant argues that, contrary to popular views, rural women in the Communist period were more active than their urban counterparts in seeking divorces.[10]

India

The patriarchal joint family and the fate of women within it have loomed large in popular and scholarly discourse on the Indian family and society. Recent research attuned to class issues and regional variations has questioned the assumption of the joint family as the predominant family form in South Asia.[11] Although elite social groups in some regions could live in multigenerational households composed of fathers and sons plus their wives and children, new data show that the majority, average and poor families, lived in smaller household units.[12] Other scholars found that some regions or localities had family norms other than the patriarchal joint family.[13]

Typically, modernity is portrayed as destroying the traditional joint family, with Indian families becoming more like Western families in their structure and values over time, developing nuclear structure, greater equality between spouses, and a companionate spousal relationship based on western-style romantic love. Against assumptions that modernity brings an inevitable convergence of Western and Indian (or Asian) family life, one stream of recent research argues for the persistence of the joint family as a unit of solidarity and mutual aid but not as a co-resident group. Under modern conditions of geographic and occupational mobility, co-residence of married sons (or brothers) under one roof has become rarer, but joint celebration of rituals, strong affective ties, and mutual aid are still very common.

However, works describing joint family persistence deemphasize patriarchy or co-residence as the joint family's main features. Sometimes this line of argument stages a dual attack on the idea of the joint family as a co-residential unit and the notion of its modern decline. By defining the joint family not in terms of co-residence but in terms of ritual solidarity, emotional bonds, and mutual aid, it is possible to say that the joint family is alive and well despite increasing industrialization, commodification, and urbanization in South Asia. In this way, the joint family can persist despite increased gender equality in family and society, a more companionate relationship between husband and wife, improved status of women in society, and increasing participation of women in the paid labor force.

While most of the existing literature emphasizes disadvantages of the joint family for South Asian women, alternative voices articulate some advantages. Negative aspects include problems in arranged marriages; the subservience of wives to their husband and in-laws, especially the mother-in-law; and restrictions on physical mobility among the upper classes. Also, the killing of brides who bring insufficient dowry to their marriage has emerged as an issue with the rise of a commodified economy, attracting local and international media coverage.

On the positive side for women can be counted the essential role of women in reproducing the family, their active role in maintaining family ties, and the possibility of aid from their natal households, especially from brothers, in times of trouble in a marital household. There can also be advantages to arranged marriages—reliance on more experienced persons in selecting a mate and expectations that affection and love will develop after marriage rather than before. These advantages may be offset by an arranged marriage that is made to enhance family interests rather than to secure the bride's (or even the groom's) happiness. However, marriage ties two families, not just two individuals, together, and it is not acceptable for a man to discard a wife for a younger, richer, more educated, or better-looking woman. Respect for the wife, the mother of one's children, and her family cannot prevent extramarital affairs, physical abuse, or emotional neglect, but it helps protect wives from being left penniless with children to support because a husband's fancy changes.

Korea

Recent studies undermine accounts of the patriarchal Korean family and the powerlessness of women within it. Frequently, Korean families and households in the late Choson (Yi) Dynasty (1392–1910) are described as highly androcentric (male-centered) units. For example, Martina Deuchler states, "The hallmark of Korean society in late Choson was a kinship system that rested on highly structured patrilineal descent groups." It could include thousands of male kinsmen sharing the same surname and ancestral village. The main lines were formed by the firstborn sons of primary wives and lesser branch lines by later-born sons, while sons of secondary wives were not full-fledged lineage members. Lineages and households were perpetuated through *primogeniture* (inheritance by the oldest son), with wives selected from other lineages.[14]

The conventional view of Korean kinship does acknowledge the importance of women to some extent. As bearers of sons, mothers and mothers-in-law enjoyed high status and power in the family. Under the Confucian value of filial piety, mothers as well as fathers were entitled to lifelong respect and obedience. A wife's influence on outside affairs, however, was supposed to be indirect and transmitted through her husband.[15] Thus standard views of Korean family life establish the centrality of small and larger kin groups in Korean society and the marginality of women within those units.

Nonetheless, revisionist writings work against the view of an everlasting, thoroughly patriarchal Korean family. According to Deuchler, extensive lineages were upper-class forms of family organization, limited to the families of government officials. Commoners did not form extensive lineages; their kinship system was "less complex and less ritualized," and they "did not keep genealogies."[16] Other evidence of higher women's status and privileges before the middle of the Choson period includes that women's names were once written into the genealogies and that they had inheritance rights that disappeared in the seventeenth century.[17]

Although late Choson influences linger in attitudes and behavior in the contemporary period, Clark Sorensen's study of actual family practices and ideas in a rural village in the late 1970s both confirms such tenets of male authority as patrilineality, public deference of women to men, and a gender division of labor and uncovers women's agency and power.

Sorenson states that "the actual dimensions of the househead's power over the house mistress [his wife] depend upon the relative contributions of the husband and wife to household economy and on their own personalities. There is no set balance of power . . . but rather a range of possibilities, conditioned by the socioeconomic circumstances of each individual family."[18] For example, in Pujok Paek's poor household in Sorenson's village, husband and wife both work as farm laborers and the wife has a "strong will and sharp temper." . . . [S]he makes most of the household decisions," and when he "lost his wages on the way home . . . he was afraid to come home for two days, much to the disgust and amusement of the other village men." As a wealthy man but a younger son not responsible for ancestor worship, Hanso Kang also seems "less tradition-bound." With much land and only one son to help, his wife participates in "an unusual amount of field labor for a woman in such a wealthy household," while Kang "helps with silk raising, normally a woman's task." Sorenson finds, "Kang and his wife are relatively equal . . . and they consult with each other on major decisions."[19]

New studies such as those of Deuchler and Sorensen are reconfiguring conventional wisdom about Korean kinship by considering the full range of variation in household life. Observing actual household life, Sorensen found families in which men did not possess absolute authority, especially in the households of the poor and of noninheriting sons and of those pursuing nontraditional livelihoods. As a measure of Korean family ideals, the received wisdom is useful. To the extent that households of the poor outnumber prosperous ones and that households of noninheriting sons outnumber those of eldest sons, unqualified descriptions of the Korean family as a patriarchy exaggerate the weakness of adult women and the power of adult men at home and in social life.

Japan

Since the nineteenth century, many writings have called attention to the tenuous position and the oppression of women in Japanese households: "'Women have no home of their own anywhere in the world': when she is born, she is brought up in the house which is her father's; when she is grown and married, she lives in a house which is her husband's; when she is old and being cared for by her son, the house will be her son's. All the . . . property is her husband's property. . . . [W]hen the house is poor, the poverty is her husband's poverty; the wife simply follows her husband in the hardship."[20] But the ideal, eternal family consisted not of a joint household retaining all sons and their wives but a *stem* household of just one couple of each generation, usually the oldest son and his wife, in some regions the youngest son and his spouse or the oldest daughter and her husband. James Ito-Adler has summarized this conventional wisdom as four P's—patrilineality and its associates patriarchy, patrilocality, and primogeniture.[21]

Scholars have questioned conventional views of the Japanese family, offering critiques of Japanese patrilineality similar to those for Korea. Adoption in Korea and

China was basically limited to paternal relatives, while in Japan, maternal relatives or even unrelated persons could be adopted to carry on the household. When a daughter's husband was adopted, the bloodline continued through the daughter, but when an unrelated couple was adopted, only the household, not the bloodline, continued. In Japan, senior household members sometimes disinherited lazy or untalented sons and passed management of the household trade to an able outsider who married a natural or an adopted daughter. Carrying on a bloodline was secondary to business ability and success.[22]

Hence, some researchers question the use of the term Japanese *family* for periods between 1600 and 1945.[23] They argue that *household* or *corporate unit* is a more appropriate term for co-residential units of husband, wife, and other dependents, because of the deemphasis on kinship in adoption practices and the primacy of business aptitude in determining headship and household membership.

Revisionist writings also somewhat weaken the case for Japanese patriarchy. Some studies show that women have been more active in productive labor and in public and family life than conventional notions of the patriarchal extended family would allow. In Japan before 1868, a widow could become the househead following her husband's death, especially if her son was young, and she sometimes stayed on as head of the family and its enterprise even after the son grew up. Also, in ordinary and poor farm and merchant families, the wife's labor was essential. She was regarded as the helpmate and partner of her husband rather than as his property, his servant, or his subordinate.[24] The economic participation of Japanese women in raising rice, making handicrafts, serving customers, and making business decisions benefited the household economy, and savings from thrifty purchases of food, clothing, and other items could be invested in the family enterprise.

Ann Walthall and others found that in some pre-1868 villages, women participated in governance and shrine worship organizations.[25] Controls on sexual behavior among the elite samurai (warrior) class were strict, but in some pre-1868 Japanese villages, premarital sex was the norm, and young people chose their own spouses. Studies of pre-1945 villages also indicate that patriarchal control over married women's sexual conduct was weak.[26] In a rural community on the southern island of Kyushu in the 1930s, women's suggestive talk and dances and pre- and extramarital affairs remained part of village culture.[27]

The Japanese case also reveals the diversity of Asian family values and practices. Although men nominally held more authority in households and in the public world, if we focus too much on male dominance or female powerlessness, we can easily overlook women's authority over sons, daughters, and young people as parents or members of a senior generation. The senior woman, as mother-in-law or mistress, supervised female relatives, daughters-in-law, and servants. By focusing only on male control, we may miss younger males' subordination to older men and women in households. In addition, by fixating on women as "inside persons," we might miss the fact that in farm and merchant households, which were at the same time homes and small businesses, women functioned as field and craft workers, sellers of goods, and even managers. And we might never notice that before modern laws, women could head households and manage businesses in their own right or as part of family business strategy.

But with industrialization and modern schooling, as the private space of the home became isolated from the public spaces of companies and the state, the Japanese government attempted to define the modern Japanese woman's place as the home. Thus modernity involved not only the growth of the army, industry, cities, and educational institutions but also redefinitions of gender and reconfigurations of family life. In modern Japan, middle-class women were kept out of the newly emerging public sphere and relegated to the domestic sphere—to serve the public good by shaping patriotic, industrious citizens for the nation instead of working for wages or participating in politics. But lower-class women remained on the farms and entered the industrial labor force on unequal terms with men.[28] Clearly, the Japanese family and women's place at home and in society were subject to change over time, and women's "modernity" varied by class.

Vietnam

The four P's also dominate descriptions of the Vietnamese family. But compared to patriarchal models in China, India, Korea, and Japan, Vietnamese patriarchy has been asserted in a more qualified way, often countered by statements that suggest historical variability in female strength or its opposite, male dominance. Here, too, there are revisionist findings.

Writing in 1984, Arlene Eisen assumed a "patriarchal family" in its purest form, in which the "Three Obediences" to father in youth, husband after marriage, and son in widowhood "negated all possibility of a woman's self-determination" in twentieth-century Vietnam."[29] The nineteenth-century Gia Long codes took away women's rights to inherit property and provided punishments for "unmarried women caught having sexual relations" and for adulterous wives. They also prevented women from suing for divorce but allowed men to keep concubines and easily divorce their wives. Eisen wrote that the proverb "If you have a son, you can say you have a descendant. But you cannot say thus, even if you have ten daughters" showed the devaluation of women who could not carry on the family line or lead the rituals of ancestor worship.[30]

But even as Eisen asserted male dominance, she described an underlying tension between "patriarchy" and daily female responsibilities and attitudes toward women. In ancient Vietnamese society, fables suggest women's dominant role. "When Tu Tuong proposed marriage to Nu Oa, she challenged him to compete with her in building a mountain . . . and created one far superior to . . . [his]." But under the one thousand years of Chinese rule (to 981 A.D.), the Vietnamese absorbed Confucian ideas of gender from China, including "Respect men, despise women," an axiom resulting in a division of labor that held women responsible for all domestic tasks and much of the agrarian and manual work. Later, in the sixteenth century, a reformist government allowed "women to share inheritance with men and to inherit the entire family fortune if there were no male heirs," but three centuries later, the next dynasty rescinded these rules.

Through labor in the fields and on the docks, and in small-scale trading, women made substantial economic contributions to their households and society but earned little positive recognition. In contrast to Confucian tracts and pronouncements, Vietnamese folk songs and proverbs proclaimed affection and partnership between spouses: "Having pledged eternal love for him, / I will not shun crossing streams and mountains with him . . . / In the way of husband and wife, / depending on each other is essential to guard against the adversities of life."[31]

Pham Van Bich reveals the same contradictions. Bich presents a standard view of Vietnamese family life as characterized by male authority, hierarchy, and mutual solidarity, yet she cannot avoid describing active female roles in family and economy and respect for women at home and in society. Bich points out that because officials were not to work with their hands, upper-class men did not participate in manual labor. Instead, elite wives "had to do everything, including rice production, housework, and trading." Because commerce was inferior and therefore beneath the dignity of men, women "formed the overwhelming majority of all active merchants" and "made up the mass of customers."[32] Even concubines were not strictly for men's pleasure but were often acquired as cheap labor for use in cultivation. And in lower-class families, "[c]ouples had to share the rice cultivation and housework at different levels; nobody had reason to feel superior or inferior, and women were the irreplaceable helpers of their fathers and husbands. . . . [I]f the family had no buffalo . . . women and their children sometimes had to act as draft animals."[33]

Vietnamese women were also essential for the socialization of children. Mothers' companionship, affection, love, and intermediary role countered the emotional distance and harshness of fathers.[34] Thus "wives were often referred to as *noi tuong* [general of the interior]." Referring to married couples, the wife (*vo*) is mentioned first, followed by the husband (*chong*). Peasant men showed high esteem for their wives in the following adages: *Nhat vo, nhi troi* (The wife comes first and the king of heaven second) and *Lenh ong khong bang cong ba* (his kettledrum cannot sound as loud as her gong).[35]

Bich concludes, "In brief, we may say that in spite of the persistence of the Confucian doctrine of 'three obediences,' the Vietnamese women played a significant role in the family, especially among the lower classes and families where the husbands were incompetent or irresponsible."[36] Furthermore, as in the case of Korea and Japan, the privileged position of Vietnamese men has varied historically. Like Korea, Japan, and the Philippines (and perhaps China), Vietnamese women's property and marriage rights were stronger before the early modern and modern eras. Based on detailed analysis of the Le legal codes, Ta Van Thai argues convincingly that, in practice if not in name, in the Nguyen dynasty, as well as sporadically under French colonialism, Vietnamese women were able to inherit and pass on property; daughters were second in line, ahead of adopted sons, to inherit ancestor-worship property; married women retained ownership of the property they had before marriage; widows could inherit property gained during their marriage. Also, divorce by mutual consent existed. Clearly, in the Le dynasty, women had stronger legal rights under its family code than they did in the following Nguyen dynasty.[37] In Vietnam, "patriarchy" varied over time, and Vietnamese women participated in the economy and held higher social status than the general stereotype of "downtrodden Asian woman" allows.

The Philippines

Despite strong evidence of a more egalitarian family heritage, representations of women and family in the Philippines seem to differ little from the conventional wisdom concerning women and family in other Asian regions. However, colonial heritage from Spanish rule and conversion to Catholicism, rather than the native culture, are seen as major wellsprings of an oppressive family and women's subordination to men.

Regional subcultures exist in the Philippines as in nearly all other Asian countries. Nonetheless, overall an image of relative gender equality emerges for precolonial Filipino families and society, an equality that was not completely erased by centuries of colonial domination under Spain and the United States.[38] Bilateral kinship (reckoning descent through the mother's and father's kin or bloodlines) is characteristic of many areas, with children's last names deriving from both the mother's and father's last names. Women participated in economic life, including farming and trade. Under colonialism, women's legal disadvantages increased and their social participation and status decreased. An ideology of female domesticity and dependence prevailed: women should stay at home and stay out of affairs that took them into the public world. The upper classes had the means and greater motivation to conform to Spanish colonial notions of womanhood, but native surname customs remained, perhaps because they fit with Spanish practices. Many ordinary women continued in agriculture and commerce due to family need. Mutual aid as well as godparenting has continued to come from both maternal and paternal relatives.

In the Philippines today, legacies of Spanish and American colonialism combine with the native heritage and the demands of a modernizing economy to produce a complex culture. The tendency to cloister women as a mark of elite status clashes with the benefits of income and newer forms of prestige associated with professional occupations. To help their parents and children and to fulfill personal desires and ambitions, Filipinas are boldly migrating overseas to Asian, American, and European destinations as unskilled and professional workers,[39] yet the image of a quiet, submissive, oppressed Asian female still attaches to them. Yet overemphasizing Filipinas' victimization can lead to neglect of changes in individual and family values, practices, and actions—for example, split families, decisions to migrate and return, negative consequences from the stereotyping of Asian women, and resistance or labor organizing. A focus on what is done to Filipino women by families, employers, and societies can preempt the opportunity to see what Filipinas themselves perceive, choose, and do.

Comparing Women in Asian Families

With the new revisionist writings, the past picture of overwhelming patriarchal dominance and inevitable female denigration and submissiveness in Asia is being challenged by more balanced views that recognize varying degrees of female agency, respect for women in Asian households, female participation in economic affairs, and women's domestic and public leadership.

The term *patriarchy* (or *Asian patriarchy*) has typically, but not invariably, been applied to Chinese, Indian, Korean, Japanese, and Vietnamese households. Such features as patrilocal marriage, arranged marriage, male headship, male inheritance, and limits on the mobility of upper-class women have resulted in neglect of attitudes and behavior that do not fit these practices. With such a focus, it is easy to overlook evidence of women's limited autonomy and agency in households. In addition, tendencies toward multigenerational structure and larger size in a minority of the population, especially the upper classes of Vietnam, China, and Korea, have marked Asian families as different from Western families despite the fact that these tendencies were not characteristic of ordinary and poor families, the majority of the population. And strikingly different practices such as footbinding and widow suicide and bride burning allowed further magnification of differences between Chinese and Indian household organization and families of the West.

Patriarchy or male power and victimization of women or absence of female agency are constant themes in writings about the household and women in China, India, Korea, Japan, Vietnam, and the Philippines, as is patrilineality, or family continuity through the male line. Generalizing from such findings results in standard views of the "patriarchal, oppressive Asian family." If Orientalism operates to preserve the distance between East and West, then Asian families are necessarily constructed as different from those in the West, as are Asian societies and cultures and the women who inhabit them. It is not surprising that Asian families and women are cast as oppressed and the patriarchal nature of Asian households exaggerated despite occasional mention of female authority, economic contributions, and status. But freedom (or greater freedom) from Orientalist blinders can permit both researchers and ordinary people of the West or imperialist nations to see advantages and disadvantages in past and present Asian and Asian American social institutions, including the family, instead of only disadvantages, and to see advantages and disadvantages in Western gender organization, instead of only advantages.

Conclusion

In sum, in no case do we find examples of the Western-written literature exaggerating the advantages of the Chinese, Japanese, Korean, Indian, Vietnamese, and Filipino family systems for women. Rather, in line with what one would expect if Orientalism is an overriding background influence, scholarship highlights the disadvantages or oppressiveness of the Asian family. New research or even rereadings of the existing literature can try to create a more balanced picture. Recognition of women's participation in agriculture, especially of upper-class women in Vietnam and lower-class women in Japan, Vietnam, Korea, the Philippines, and China; their role in trade in Vietnam and the Philippines; recognition of the authority and respect accorded to senior women, including by sons to their widowed mothers, and the partnership between husbands and wives when both must earn income to support the household may begin to correct stereotypes of Asian women as always and forever submissive, powerless, secluded in the home, and excluded from "outside" affairs of economy and government.

In part, distortion by omission in descriptions of Asian households and families may stem from a tendency to imagine a utopia or things desirable in distant times and places. In part it also may derive from the legacy of Orientalism, which portrays non-Western peoples, cultures, and societies as clichés, employing adjectives that range from *backward*, *stagnant*, and *nonprogressive* to (less frequently these days) *inferior*. Lingering Orientalism contributes to representing women of former colonial or semicolonial regions in general terms, rather than as individuals, and as submissive, passive, timid, tradition-bound or ignorant performers of daily tasks. More positive aspects of this imaging can include devotion to husband, children, home, and family. Of course, for those who regard women's place as being solely in the home or domestic domain, the Asian or non-Western woman as the quintessential inside person may be seen as a virtue rather than a detriment. But in either case, Asian women who are active, assertive participants in the world outside the home, who are educated, or who have strong personalities tend to become invisible. And this victimization or invisibility of Asian women contributes to the invisibility of Asian American women.

Due to the influx of recent migration and the conflation of Asian American with Asian women, Asian American and Pacific Islander American women's history faces the task of countering Orientalism. The early works sought to find nearly invisible female faces in the pre–World War II bachelor societies. Later works contradict images of Asian women's passivity and establish female agency. Others find women maneuvering responsibilities or leadership in households, families, and communities. These pursuits parallel the ongoing efforts of revisionist and feminist scholars who are reexamining Asian women in Asian households, families, and societies. In studies of women in Asian and Asian American families, the quest is broadening to take into account factors such as class, religion, immigrant status, and ethnic, regional, and generational differences that generate diversity among Asians and Asian Americans.

In the end, operations of Orientalism may denigrate Asian women and Asian culture and society and prejudice views of Asian migrants and their cultures in their new homelands. Equally important to Orientalism is the valorization of advanced Western cultures, with concepts of egalitarianism and fundamental respect for women cast as the binary opposite of Asian (or other non-Western) cultures. This obscures the gender gap in pay and political representation and ideologies that still proclaim, "Women's place is in the home" (or in between the sheets) in countries such as the United States, Germany, France, and United Kingdom.

It can be argued that by taking colonialist blinders from our eyes as we attempt to learn about or research women in Asian or Asian American families and societies, we have a new freedom to see Asian and Asian American women as individual human beings with a full range of human intellectual, social, spiritual, and psychological possibilities, rather than through Orientalist eyes that limit us to being stereotypes in a generic non-Western culture. But before concluding so optimistically, isn't it necessary to think about why images of patriarchy and the exotic erotic, the submissive Asian, stubbornly persist, why they cannot be erased from books, films, and minds? Reinforcement by mass media on an increasingly global scale is part of the answer. But it also may be that, despite the proliferation of revisionist literature on Asian families and women, we are not living in a postcolonial world. This clearly may be said of Native

Hawaiians and indigenous peoples around the world who are still struggling to attain greater autonomy or to form independent nation-states. And, although most countries in the world have political independence, the practice of neocolonialism (new colonialism—domination of the economy without political control) still relies on operations of difference (race, gender, class, sexual orientation, nationality, and ethnicity) to maintain its rule. If, under colonialism, Orientalism functioned to maintain distance between the dominating and dominated groups, under neocolonialism today the incentive to maintain distance between the dominating and dominated groups remains in our era of multinational corporations and global capitalism. There is still a stake in the maintenance of difference, and that may be a reason why the exaggeration of difference in the Asian family and for Asian women might not fade away, despite the rise of oppositional consciousness and revisionist research.

NOTES

1. Although it is beyond the scope of this chapter, it is important to trace the impact of Orientalism on representations of Pacific Islander women, families, societies, and women. See, for example, Davianna McGregor, chapter 1, in this book.

2. Edward Said, *Orientalism* (New York: Vintage, 1976), 205.

3. From the eighteenth century, much of the Indian subcontinent fell under British rule. Upon independence in 1947, the nations of India, Pakistan, and Sri Lanka were formed, and in 1971, East Pakistan seceded from West Pakistan to form Bangladesh. "India" and "Indian" here refer to the contemporary boundaries of India, while "South Asia" and "South Asian" refer to the subcontinent, a larger geographic unit comprised of several nations. The boundaries of geographic regions change over time and are subject to contestation.

4. For example, Barbara Weightman's geography text *Dragons and Tigers* (New York: John Wiley, 2002) has three inserts on Asian women—on sati (widow suicide), footbinding, and work.

5. Arthur P. Wolf and Chieh-shan Huang, *Marriage and Adoption in China, 1845–1945* (Stanford: Stanford University Press, 1980), v.

6. Lloyd Eastman, *Family, Fields, and Ancestors: Constancy and Change in China's Social and Economic History, 1550–1949* (New York: Oxford University Press, 1989), 16.

7. Wolf and Huang, *Marriage and Adoption*, 26–27.

8. Janice Stockard, *Daughters of the Canton Delta: Marriage Patterns and Economic Strategies in South China, 1860–1930* (Stanford: Stanford University Press, 1989), 49.

9. Dorothy Ko, *Teachers of the Inner Chamber: Women and Culture in Seventeenth-Century China* (Stanford: Stanford University Press, 1994), introduction. Some chapters in Christina Gilmartin, Gail Herschatter, Lisa Rofel, and Tyrene White, eds., *Engendering China: Women, Culture, and the State* (Cambridge: Harvard University Press, 1994), also pursue these issues.

10. Neil J. Diamant, *Revolutionizing the Family: Politics, Love, and Divorce in Urban and Rural China, 1949–1968* (Berkeley: University of California Press, 2000).

11. Leela Mullatti, "Changing Profile of the Indian Family," in UNESCO, Principal Regional Office for Asia and the Pacific, ed., *The Changing Family in Asia: Bangladesh, India, Japan, Philippines, and Thailand* (Bangkok: UNESCO, Principal Regional Office for Asia and the Pacific, 1992), chap. 2, 75–112. There is not one, universal "Indian family" across the diverse religions, classes, castes, and regions of the South Asian subcontinent.

12. Ibid.

13. Ibid.

14. Martina Deuchler, *The Confucian Transformation in Korea: A Study of Society and Ideology* (Cambridge: Council on East Asian Studies/Harvard University Press, 1992), 7.

15. Eui-Young Yu, "Women in Traditional and Modern Korea," in Eui-Young Yu and Earl H. Phillips, eds., *Korean Women in Transition: At Home and Abroad* (Los Angeles: Center for Korean-American and Korean Studies, California State University, Los Angeles, 1987), 16–17.

16. Deuchler, *Confucian Transformation in Korea*, 13.

17. Ibid.; Mark Peterson, "Women without Sons: A Measure of Social Change in Yi Dynasty Korea," in Laurel Kendall and Mark Peterson, eds., *Korean Women: View from the Inner Room* (New Haven, CT: East Rock Press, 1993), 33–39.

18. Clark Sorensen, "Women, Men; Inside, Outside: The Division of Labor in Rural Central Korea," in Kendall and Peterson, eds., *Korean Women*, 71–72.

19. Ibid.

20. Yukichi Fukuzawa, *Fukuzawa Yukichi on Japanese Women*, trans. Eiichi Kiooka (Tokyo: University of Tokyo Press, 1988), 9. This was originally published in June 1885 in his newspaper by Fukuzawa Yukichi, a male Japanese enlightener who dedicated himself to revamping his country's customs, attitudes, and institutions along modern and Western lines; he included the family in his proposed reforms.

21. James Ito-Adler, "Adoption in Japan," specials paper (Cambridge: Harvard University, 1974), 43.

22. Kathleen Uno, "Questioning Patrilineality: On Western Studies of the Japanese *Ie*," *positions: east asia cultures critique* 4:3 (Winter 1996): 569–94.

23. Chie Nakane, *Kinship and Economic Organization in Japan* (London: Athlone Press, 1967).

24. Kathleen Uno, "Women and Changes in the Household Division of Labor," in Gail Lee Bernstein, ed., *Recreating Japanese Women* (Berkeley: University of California Press, 1991), 17–41.

25. Ann Walthall, "Devoted Wives/Unruly Women: Invisible Presence in the History of Japanese Social Protest," *Signs: Journal of Women, Culture, and Society* 20:1 (Autumn 1994): 106–36.

26. Richard Varner, "The Organized Peasant," *Monument Nipponica* 32:4 (Winter 1977): 358–83.

27. Robert J. Smith and Ella Lury Wiswell, *Women of Suye Mura* (Chicago: University of Chicago Press, 1982).

28. Uno, "Women and Changes."

29. Arlene Eisen, *Women and Revolution in Viet Nam* (London: Zed Books, 1984), 7, 15, 14.

30. Ibid., 17.

31. Ibid.

32. Pham Van Bich, *The Vietnamese Family in Change: The Case of the Red River Delta* (Surrey, England: Curzon Press, 1999), 33. See also Ngo Vinh Long, "Background," in Ngo Vinh Long, ed., *Vietnamese Women in Society and Revolution*, vol. 1: *The French Colonial Period* (Cambridge, MA: Vietnam Resource Center, 1974), 3–52.

33. Bich, *Vietnamese Family in Change*, 34–35.

34. Ibid., 39–40.

35. Ibid., 49.

36. Ibid., 40.

37. Ta Van Tai, "The Status of Women in Traditional Vietnam: A Comparison of the Code of

the Le Dynasty (1428–1788) with the Chinese Codes," *Journal of Asian History* 15:2 (1981): 97–145.

38. Stella P. Go, "The Filipino Family in the Eighties," in UNESCO, ed., *Changing Family in Asia*, chap. 4, 239–306; Lilia Quindoza Santiago, "Rebirthing Babaye: The Women's Movement in the Philippines," in Amrita Basu, ed., *The Challenge of Local Feminisms: Women's Movements in Global Perspective* (Boulder, CO: Westview, 1995), chap. 4, 110–28.

39. For example, see Catherine Ceniza Choy (chapter 20), Rhacel Parreñas (chapter 16), and Charlene Tung (chapter 18) in this book.

3

What Happened to the Women?
Chinese and Indian Male Migration to the United States in Global Perspective

Sucheta Mazumdar

Matrilocal societies aside, women form the largest group of migrants in any society, for they move to take up residence where their husbands live.[1] Why was it, then, that in some communities, and at particular times, moving to their husbands' home was the only transfer of residence they made, even when the husband later moved to other countries? The absence of the wives among many of the Asian migrants in the pre–World War II United States, particularly among the Chinese, is the subject of numerous studies. Why did the women not come?

In this essay, I locate two specific examples of Chinese and Indian migration to the United States, and I query standard narratives of migration histories that focus on nation-state boundaries and trace histories of migrants only after they arrive on these shores. The first part of the essay explores how a global and comparative methodology, instead of nationalist paradigms, located within an understanding of how capitalism articulates a new division of labor both locally and globally, allows us to reinterpret dominant narratives of Asian and Asian American migration histories. The second part examines how this process produced a new division of labor within the family/household unit in Asia, recasting women's roles in both family and society even as new forms of labor emerged to attract migrants to the Americas. In considering the ways in which gender relations were restructured, I query the legacies of Orientalism and nationalist mythographies that have constructed these specific histories and distorted the lens of our inquiries.

Studies of Asian migration tend to follow national denominations of diasporas. There is little comparative and connective work that investigates Asian migrations in continent-wide terms. Unlike developments in European migration studies, studies of the Chinese or Indian diaspora are seen as tertiary adjuncts to the "main" narrative of the nation-state, particularly since these national narratives are premised on notions of immobile agrarian populations and all-powerful imperial states opposed to rural mobility. Nineteenth-century Orientalist constructs posited a stagnant "East" versus a dynamic "West," the latter with a mobile European peasantry willing to cross oceans to fulfill their dreams. Notions of Chinese villages with travel-adverse residents have become an uncritically accepted baseline of overseas migration studies.[2] Ample evidence suggests, however, that annual migrations and sojourning anywhere from five to twenty years abroad was a normative pattern for generations of men from particular provinces of China. In the Indian context, reiterations of supposed caste taboos against traveling across the oceans (*kalapani*) similarly ignore the historical evidence of thousands of traders from a variety of communities routinely traveling all over Asia and eastern Africa before and after the nineteenth century.

Orientalist legacies and nationalist narratives are not confined to the other side of the Pacific. Apart from African slave migration to the Americas involving around 10 to 12 million people,[3] massive global migrations across the oceans began only after the 1820s. One of the most significant trajectories was the migration to the United States between 1820 and 1940 of close to 40 million people, mostly from Europe.[4] In historical terms, the nineteenth century migrations are seen as a unique phenomenon embraced under a model of U.S. exceptionalism, rather than one juncture of the global movement of people that has now achieved proportions unimaginable earlier.[5] Additionally, the dominant narrative of nineteenth- and early twentieth-century U.S. history of *im*migration and permanent settlement leaves little space for exploring the frequencies of sojourning that marked the histories of *all* migrant groups to the United States, not only the Chinese. The focus on the Pacific Coast history of Asian migration as the principal model for Asian American history further disconnects this migration from the contemporary and major trajectories of Asian and European migration to other parts of the Americas, including Cuba, Guyana, Suriname, Trinidad, Brazil, and Peru. Asian migration to Latin America and the Caribbean was numerically more significant in the nineteenth and early twentieth centuries than its counterpart to North America, with implications for family formation and community development. I do not intend to obscure the very real context of racism and Asian exclusion that operated in the United States or to argue that local historical specificities do not matter. By drawing attention to the systemic and gendered dimensions of the global economy, I suggest that subsuming U.S. migration patterns under the nationalist ideological narrative of incipient settler families clutching one-way tickets in their hands and the American dream in their hearts is, at best, an inadequate model.[6]

I focus on Chinese migration while integrating dimensions of Punjabi and Sindhi migration as a useful counterpoint. The South Asian cases provide interesting parallels to the better-studied Chinese case. There are striking similarities in how these two agrarian economies and their gender relations were restructured in the nineteenth century in the wake of colonialism, the rapid transformation of their agricultural economies, and social property rights. All these migrations were from extremely localized regions, allowing for a closer investigation of how customary institutions of patriarchy were recast at the local level. The majority of the Chinese migrants to the United States came from eight contiguous counties of Guangdong's Pearl River Delta.[7] Most Indian migrants came from an equally narrow strip of five contiguous districts of Punjab province, while the mercantile group in Honolulu was from the urban enclave of Hyderabad, Sind province.

The Contours of Migration

The relative paucity of women from China and India in the early period is standard commentary in the historiography of U.S. migration. The facts are uncontroversial: in 1900 there were about 4,500 Chinese women compared to almost 90,000 men on the mainland. In Hawaii, 3,471 of the 25,767 Chinese were female.[8] By 1900, only wives of U.S. citizens, merchants, and diplomats were allowed to enter the United States. Wives of Chinese laborers, even if they themselves were not laborers, were barred. Unending interviews and harassment were conducted by U.S. immigration services to determine if entering Chinese women were prostitutes, which deterred the migration of single women.[9] In 1890, of the 104,620 Chinese men in the United States, 24 percent of the married men lived without their wives. By 1940, of the 57,389 Chinese men in the United States, over 38 percent did not have their wives in the country.[10] In the Punjabi case, approximately ten thousand people of Indian origin were living in the United States around 1914, and by 1940, fewer than three thousand, as Indian migration declined rapidly in the early 1920s with legal exclusions and returns to India. The number of Indian women entering the United States never exceeded two hundred.[11] Why did the women not emigrate?

There have been two distinct explanations. Culturalist explanations revolve around reified notions of Confucian filial piety, morality, and taboos about women traveling.[12] A legalist explanation focuses on the role of the U.S. state, the Chinese exclusion laws, and the myriad ways in which Asian migration, but particularly Chinese migration, was restricted and curtailed.[13]

However, while the U.S. laws made it difficult for those who would want to bring their wives, the number of Chinese women migrants never totaled the number of slots open to them.[14] If U.S. restrictions were the sole cause for the low numbers of female migrants, why did so few Chinese women migrate to Malacca, for instance, which had no legal restrictions comparable to the United States and was physically much closer to China? In Malacca, as late as 1911, there were only 204 Chinese women per 1,000 males.[15] The argument that the restrictive laws account for the paucity of Chinese women in the United States is loaded with an ahistorical interpretive burden revolving around three problematic assumptions: (1) that the women would have migrated if given the choice, (2) that male migration from China was atypical and done only under the economic duress of the Opium Wars, and (3) that the decision to migrate was an individual decision instead of a collective household strategy.

I suggest it was unlikely that the married women would have migrated even if the laws had allowed, because the economic system was built around male migration and female domestic labor. By the seventeenth century, cash earnings of young males had become part survival strategy and part strategy for economic mobility in Guangdong and Fujian.[16] By the nineteenth century, male migration was commonplace. Commissioner Lin Zexu, upon his arrival in Guangzhou in 1838 prior to the Opium Wars, noted that "every year at Winter time, when the foreign ships return to their homelands, there are some unemployed paupers who privately recruiting among themselves accept employment abroad. Upon arrival in those countries, they are ordered to excavate mountains and plant trees or do other kinds of heavy work."[17]

Was the migration of Chinese males peculiar in contrast to the European family migration to the United States? A global perspective shows that male migration was the norm for *all* immigrant groups, with a few exceptions. I suggest reconsidering two notions: (1) that marriage was universal and (2) that Chinese male migration was atypical. First, did all Chinese (or other Asian men) marry? Usual birthrate ratios of male and female children precluded universal marriage, for there were not enough women to go around for poorer men when richer men had multiple secondary wives (concubines). Migration and earning money for the bride price overseas may have enabled more Chinese men to marry than would have been otherwise feasible. Second, prior to 1914, predominantly male migration was common for all migrations. Except for the Irish, three-fourths of *all* migrants to the United States were male. Half the migrants to Brazil were male (despite intensive efforts to recruit families).[18] It was not until after 1930 that women outnumber men in overall migration statistics to the United States.[19]

The "sojourner mentality" of the Chinese migrants has received much attention.[20] Such commentary reflects an Orientalist emphasis on the importance of the multigenerational "family" as an immutable fact in China. Chinese migration patterns fit the norm rather than the exception. "Returning home after a season, a year or a few years"[21] was an established pattern also for most Europeans. Between 1857 and 1914, 43.3 percent of the arrivals in Argentina left again. For the United States, we find a high return rate even among well-established communities, with the average rate being between 20 and 30 percent. The return rate for Italians was about 50 percent between the 1880s and 1920 and, between 1908 and 1930, 46 percent for Greeks.[22] Neither Chinese nor Indian male migration patterns were exceptions. The U.S. economy arguably was developed in equal measure through the labors of men who did not "settle" here and those who did. Split households—the spatial separation of the female productive sphere from the male productive sphere—were, and continue to be, a central feature of the restructuring of the family economy that has taken place globally in tandem with the spatial arrangements fostered by capitalism.

Women and Migration

Writing in the mid-1990s, Donna Gabaccia noted that historical studies of international female migration still scarcely exist.[23] Her survey of thirty-five different migrant groups to the United States between 1820 and 1928 reveals that while the percentage of female migrants was very low for the Indian and the Chinese migrations (1 percent and 5 percent, respectively, of all migrants from those countries), the percentage of women migrating from Korea (17 percent) was higher than that of female migrants from Bulgaria or Dalmatia (10 and 12 percent, respectively), and the percentage of Japanese female migrants (33 percent) was higher than that of Greek (23 percent) or Italian female migrants (25 percent).[24] There was a very wide range in the percentage of female migrants to the United States, and predominantly male migration was common to many communities. The normative model of female migration history has come to be dominated by the migration patterns from Northern and Western Europe, specifically Irish and Jewish migration, in which female migrants accounted for 40 percent or more of the migrants. Locating migration not as an individualistic and voluntary process that would focus on the completion of an idealized, nuclear, three-generational Chinese familial unit but as a process integral to the workings of the economy may be more appropriate. What would Chinese women have done if they came?

The majority of Chinese women needed to work. But few employment opportunities were available for most married migrant women. Domestic service was the only female occupation of any significance.[25] Growth in the female labor force in the United States between 1870 and 1920 came through the demand for white-collar workers, but these jobs were seldom open to foreign-born women. The immigrant women's place in the workforce actually dropped from the nineteenth to the twentieth century as more male migrants arrived from all over the globe.[26] Married women of all backgrounds worked at home as domestic workers, were boardinghouse keepers and self-employed shopkeepers, took in laundry, and so on. Outside the home were sweatshops and factories, but these were overwhelmingly located on the East Coast. Apart from prostitution, agricultural work, and domestic work, working from home remained the only option.

For Chinese women, if they were married and had a sliver of space to spare, taking in boarders was a primary occupation. They also worked as seamstresses and at home, raising everything from flowers to bean sprouts in bathtubs for sale.[27] Outside the home, most women found work only as prostitutes. As is well studied, the early migration phase saw some self-employed Chinese prostitutes and independent brothel owners, but the majority were bonded prostitutes; some had been kidnapped. Here again, a comparative perspective is helpful. Chinese women were not the only women who worked as prostitutes in such large numbers. Prostitution was one of the "hidden costs of industrialization." The preindustrial agrarian family structure transformed by the dual processes of industrialization and migration led to enormous increases in prostitution worldwide. William Sanger's survey of women of European origin on the East Coast in 1858 found one prostitute to every fifty-seven men in New York. Destitution and absence of other work were the most frequently cited causes for prostitution.[28] So why the unswerving focus on Chinese prostitutes in the United States?

The overwhelming attention paid by the media, immigration officials, and Christian missions to Chinese prostitution and other practices, such as concubinage and homosexuality—an attention reproduced in much Asian American literature—needs reinterpretation. It is possible to reexamine Chinese prostitution not as a simple narrative of the victimization of Chinese women but rather as a comment, first, on the contemporary attempts by the state and church to establish a normative model of the American and European nuclear family and, second, on how sex workers have become a major commodity on the world market from the nineteenth century onward.

Chinese men and Indian men were coming to the United States at a time when a particular model of the family was becoming established in both the United States and in Europe and when the sexual and reproductive capabilities and services of women were being reorganized. The modernizing states and the church were moving to "standardize" working-class practices everywhere. Given that out-of-wedlock birthrates averaged one in five live births in areas as far apart as southern Germany and northwest Portugal, illegitimacy and working-class immorality had become primary themes for politicians and reformers alike.[29] In the United States, where the emergence of the normative ideal of the nuclear family and "the authority of the father and his capacity for moral supervision were very strong,"[30] transnational Chinese families and Chinese prostitutes were seen as peculiar aberrations. Without the domestic realm to bolster the normative constructs of American masculinity, the Chinese males were effectively feminized in popular imagery. At another level, in the American west, anxieties about Victorian marriage notions of female chastity, companionate marriage, and fidelity to the marriage bed were already coming under stress from Mormon polygamous practices that threatened "the substitution of the Harem for the Home in all our western borders."[31] The salacious focus on Chinese prostitution reflected these anxieties and served primarily to reiterate efforts to define the normative ideal of the "American family."

Chinese prostitutes in the United States supported their families financially in the same manner that male migrants did. The exploitative conditions for the prostitutes were linked to the systems of indenture and bonded labor that existed for men, women and children in China. The economic crisis of nineteenth-century China globalized these systems. Today, the global sex trade continues apace. As a major arena of profit making, it uses Asian women and others as it did during the nineteenth century.

If prostitution became the most visible part of women's labor in the nineteenth-century global economy of migration, the labor of women who did not migrate forms the other, neglected part of the story.

Migration and the Feminization of Agriculture

There are differences in the Chinese and Indian histories of migration to the United States, not the least of which is that migration from Guangdong predated the colonial impact, while Punjabi migration started with colonialism in the mid–nineteenth century.

Migration from Punjab was sponsored first by recruitment into the British Indian army. By the twentieth century, Punjabis made up half the soldiers in the British army; many were sent to work in Hong Kong and Shanghai.[32] In some villages, agricultural work became secondary for the men to working in the army. Migrations also took place through labor recruitment projects: in 1896, out of the nineteen thousand laborers used to build the Ugandan Railway, over half were from the Punjab. As a colonial official described the nineteenth-century *jat* (Punjabi peasant cultivator): "[H]e could be found fattening cows in China, sawing wood in Canada, tinning fruit in California and trading in Australia."[33]

In Sind, a province adjacent to Punjab, international migration networks grew out of Shikarpur and Hyderabad.[34] Mercantile migration from Shikarpur developed during the eighteenth century and extended overland to Russia and China. Hyderabadi mercantile activities emerged in relation to international maritime trading opportunities of the nineteenth century. Many merchants, especially those trading in the Pacific, were Hindus. With trade links in the Philippines, Hong Kong, Shanghai, Tianjin, Yoko-hama, and Kobe and throughout Latin America and the Caribbean, they set up branches in Honolulu prior to World War I. We do not know the size of the Indian com-munity in Hawai'i when the Sindhi Watumull family arrived in 1914, but correspon-dence regarding recruitments from India and sugar-refining companies in Hawai'i sug-gests a few Punjabis probably already were in the islands.[35] Watumull is now a major re-tail trading company with considerable economic and political visibility.[36]

Guangdong, Punjab, and Sind, although having very different origins for trans-Pa-cific migration, all developed into migration-dependent economies by the beginning of the twentieth century. The majority of the migrants to the United States from the Pun-jab, like those from Guangdong, were agricultural smallholders facing changed global economies as the world market pushed domestic commercialization of agriculture si-multaneously with new demands for male migrant labor.

The global division of labor involved both the production of raw materials in the colonies for industrial manufacture and consumption in the metropolitan centers and a total transformation of the agrarian economies, from the introduction of new crops to the expansion of export-oriented food crops and a new sexual division of labor. Home-based manufacturing combined with agriculture had earlier involved both men and women of a household unit; this unit was now separated into discrete sectors. The physical reproduction of labor remained located in the rural sector with the women, children, and the elderly, while the majority of the able-bodied males left to work in the cities or overseas.

The migrants from Guangdong were of varied socioeconomic strata and included merchants, smallholding peasants, as well as coolies, who were among the poorest seg-ments of rural society. Apart from the completely destitute who bonded themselves in return for passage and wages or were abducted and made to work as coolies, the vast majority coming to the United States were members of small- to medium-sized landowning families who paid their own way. They tended to be either middle or younger sons.[37]

Guangdong's Pearl River Delta agrarian economy had an intensive agriculture from the seventeenth century onward in the core counties and included a range of primary commercial crops and secondary activities such as sericulture, pisciculture, and horti-culture. Counties on the delta's peripheries, such as Taishan, cultivated cereals for ex-port to the core counties but did not have labor-intensive sericulture. This pattern of commercial agriculture was intensified in Guangdong in the nineteenth century. World market demands led to regional specializations. Some counties developed mulberry trees for raising silkworms; others grew sugarcane or cultivated palm trees for making fans. Since the seventeenth century, a gender division of labor in the field had emerged as a distinctive feature of the commercialized economy. Notwithstanding bound feet, women always have worked in the fields in Guangdong. Survey data from the 1920s and 1930s show Chinese women performed 38 percent of the farm work and, in some coun-ties, outnumbered male laborers.[38]

Women contributed to the household economy in four distinct sectors. First, they worked with men in the fields, doing weeding and other maintenance work with com-mercial crops, and helped with planting, harvesting, and threshing. The other three sectors depended solely on the labor of women for the survival of the household unit. Women were primarily involved in the cultivation of the subsistence sector and produced food for domestic consumption, such as sweet potatoes, beans, taro, and other vegetables. Except for the wealthy, who could afford rice, most rural families ate sweet potatoes at every meal as the basic staple. Women's work in Guangdong also included the secondary-income-generating sector, such as spinning silk and cotton and raising pigs, geese, and chickens. In the silk-producing counties, women's labor was indispensable for raising the silkworms and spinning the cocoons. By the late nineteenth century, sericulture was the economic basis of so many core counties of the Delta that the family's livelihood depended on women. Last, the routine maintenance of the household was women's work: fetching water, gathering fuel, chopping wood, cleaning, cooking, doing laundry, preserving sweet potatoes, making vegetable pickles—the list goes on.

This gendered dimension of agrarian labor also applied in the Punjab. After the opening of the Suez Canal made it possible to transport Indian wheat to Europe within thirty days, wheat cultivation expanded rapidly in the Punjab. By the turn of the twentieth century, one-third of the land was under wheat. In addition, sugarcane and cotton became major crops. The household's domestic consumption continued to be based on millet and sorghum. Raising cattle was another major source of income. As a British colonial official noted of women's work:

> The women work as hard as the men if not harder. The heavy tasks of bringing in wood and fuel and water fall on them; they have to cook the food and carry it daily to the fields, they have to watch the crops, to them the peeling of sugarcane and picking of the cotton belongs and when there is nothing else to do they much fill up the time with the spinning wheel.[39]

Weeding the fields, feeding and milking the cattle, churning and making butter and buttermilk, cleaning the stalls, collecting dung and making fuel cakes also fell to the women. Women also cleaned, mended, cooked, hauled water and fuel, and took care of children and the elderly. While women from the upper castes did not plow, dig, or drive carts (upper-caste men also did not plow) lower-caste women did these jobs as well.[40] Many local proverbs repeated the importance of women's work: "*ran jatti te hor sab chatti* [a *jat* wife for me—all the rest are a mere waste of money]."[41] Colonial officials found widowers defaulting on loans and unable to keep their farms functioning; such a man was "half-paralyzed" with no one to bring meals to the fields, take care of the home, weed the fields, and pick the cotton.[42]

Given this range of women's work in sustaining the household, the reasons behind the limited married female migration from Guangdong and Punjab seem self-evident: the labor of men could be replaced, that of the women could not. As long as the family farm survived, the role of women in the family economy was indispensable. The labor of sons, especially if they were second and third sons, was dispensable on the farm, while their remittances became indispensable for collective family strategies for land acquisition or for survival in an economy where the cash nexus had been amplified through global economic processes. If the women left, the entire household collapsed.

Renegotiations of Patriarchy

The absence of men and the new access to cash through remittances reshaped migrant families in complex and sometimes unanticipated ways. For most of the women, a husband's absence did not necessarily mean greater "personal" freedom. To imagine a completely individualized entity in the nineteenth century would be anachronistic; the concept of a woman as an individual with vested rights of personhood is still not a universal concept. In the nineteenth century, the "rights" and "freedoms" of men, too, were shaped by the social context of their being, the corporate property-holding unit or lineage, the family unit, and their class.

In South China, the lineage (*zu*, sometimes translated as "clan") determined the right to live in a village, own land, draw water from the village pond, and so on. Belonging to the lineage, retaining one's position in the ancestral temples and burial sites, was essential for both this life and the afterlife. Consequently, many chose to "return" to the homeland after death by having their bones buried in the family plot.[43] In this social context, the decision to migrate was a collective one; the wife and children left behind were part of the collective *jia* (household) and *zu*, and their well-being a collective responsibility. Typically, remittances were not personal, individual property but used by the family for collective consumption needs and controlled by it to buy land, for use in moneylending operations, and so on. The wives could not dispose of landed property even if they were in desperate straits.[44] In Guangdong, the heartland of revolutions and rebellions between 1850 and 1950, villages resembled armed encampments rather than idyllic rural havens, with remittances being used to buy guns.[45] Personal safety for both men and women required a collective domicile.

The proliferation of "Gold Mountain widows," as the Pearl River Delta women whose husbands went off to San Francisco were called, and the increase in the number of young wives without husbands set in motion a more repressive regime of control of female sexuality. Since exogamy was the norm, and the woman lived with and worked for the husband's family, she was surrounded by members of his lineage and agnatic kin, and her physical mobility was controlled through gossip and restrictions on visiting the natal home and on movement outside the village walls. In Taishan county, the villagers kept a close watch on the married women and reported any deviance to each other and to the absent husbands. They ganged up on women who became pregnant through liaisons and drove the lovers from the village. Above all, the families of Taishan sought to promote a cult of chastity. The county gazetteer of Taishan of 1893 printed the names of women who remained chaste after being "widowed" by overseas migration.[46] Somebody must have written to Yee Fon, an irate father from Stockton, California, who wrote back to his son in 1918:

> I heard that your mother often goes to the market, exhibiting more showiness than other people. I ask you whether you are ashamed of yourself to allow that. . . . The clansmen say that since I cannot control my own family, I shouldn't be a man. If you don't feel the disgrace, you should consider my name—whose wife is it that gives such exhibition.[47]

Since the link with the absent son/husband depended on the fidelity of the daughter-in-law/wife, such measures were undoubtedly necessary to ensure the cooperation of all concerned, especially if the financial benefits of the remittances were not enough inducement for chaste behavior.

Even in Taishan, by the 1920s and 1930s, female-headed households in the homeland emerged among nineteenth-century migrants as structures of control by lineage and family eroded. A study of forty first-generation migrant families found that 50 percent had lived in households headed by women. In many cases, the father or the brothers of the male migrant had died, and the economic situation in China did not permit the husband to return. The wife was left running the household, raising the children, and living independently. In such cases the women rented out the land, ran the family farm, and became heads of households.[48] In the areas of Fujian and Chaozhou, which had longer histories of male migration than Taishan, female-headed households were an established pattern. The wife of the migrant who sent the money would emerge as the "acting head of the household" and make decisions that could include "important questions having to do with business, education, marriage, and religious observances."[49] Clearly, women in Taishan were challenging the boundaries. Some had taken to going to the market, as Yee Fon complained from Stockton, California.

While the poetry of women's solitude forms the dominant narrative of Chinese American migration and is repeated in the stories of hardship and loneliness of the migrant men, it is relevant to note that much of this poetry comes from Taishan county. With more men from Taishan living outside the county than in it by the twentieth century, there was no family without migrants.[50] Taishan, however, was not the only type of migrant community, and it had a distinctive economic history. Taishan, along with Enping, Kaiping, and Xinhui were known collectively as the "Sze Yup" or four counties. Predominantly agrarian communities with relatively little manufacturing at the beginning of the twentieth century, these areas were particularly affected by the Taiping Rebellion and had a history of intense lineage warfare. They represent one type of overseas migration community; seven out of ten Chinese in California were from the Sze Yup, and most were from Taishan. The remaining 30 percent of migrants were from counties with significantly different economies—historically greater levels of commercialization of agriculture and manufacturing and higher levels of industrialization by the late nineteenth century.

Shunde county was located in the most prosperous part of the Pearl River Delta and had been a major center of sericulture since the sixteenth century. By the late nineteenth century, when the global demand for silk accelerated, as much as 75 percent of the land was turned over to cultivating mulberry trees, and 75 percent of the population was engaged in raising silkworms and spinning silk.[51] Several silk factories were set up in the area. This intensification of women's work and its wage-earning potential had a major impact on the women's lives and their marriage patterns.

The transfer of the wife to the husband's family is a key ritual in all agrarian societies, and the time that lapses between the ceremony and the actual cohabitation has been mediated throughout history by various types of local customs. Even in the relatively compact Pearl River Delta, there were wide variations in marriage patterns. Unlike Taishan and the other Sze Yup counties, where the transfer took place immediately after marriage, in the counties of Shunde, Panyu, Nanhai, Zhongshan, and Shanshui the dominant cultural form of marriage had been "delayed transfer marriage," where it had been customary for the couple to live together only after three years of marriage.[52] The wife went to visit the husband's family for the major festivals, but pregnancy prior to the three-year limitation was not thought to be "proper." It is possible that the institution reflected the fact that the bride was older than the groom and had to wait for him to reach maturity.[53]

The growth of the silk industry in the nineteenth century and the concomitant avenues for women's employment enabled Shunde women to delay their transfer to the husband's family for as long as ten years with support from their natal families. Did Shunde men take secondary wives (concubines) and migrate for the interim before the primary wife was willing to make the transfer? Some women who refused to live with their husbands bought concubines for the husbands with their earnings at the silk filatures and legally adopted a son born of the concubine for their own old age and afterlife security. These women seem to have controlled a significant portion of their earnings, although given the legal system it is unlikely they would have had rights to patrilineal land.

From the 1880s to the 1910s, at the height of the world market silk boom, there was little out-migration of women from Shunde and the neighboring counties. But later, women from Shunde emigrated to Malaya and Singapore in significant numbers to work as domestics and in the rubber plantations and pineapple-processing factories. When the silk industry in Shunde collapsed during the worldwide depression after 1929, the numbers of women migrants increased dramatically. They became the principal wage earners and providers for their natal families in Shunde and other counties.

Some Shunde women were famous for refusing marriage altogether and sometimes moved from their natal homes into dormitories called spinsters' houses. Such self-organization may have been made possible by institutions such as the independent all-women associations, called Seven Sister Associations, where a major festival and its annual planning were done by pre-marriage-age girls throughout the county. This gave the young women experience in making collective decisions, handling money, and participating in the public sphere, including opportunities to form lifelong friendships.[54] Other practices included sworn sisterhoods of spinsters, women who paid for and participated in a special ceremony that included ritual dressing of their hair, worshiping of the natal family ancestors like a male, and providing a feast for the kin. They continued to wear their hair in a distinctive manner to display their sisterhood status.[55]

Many Shunde and Panyu women also belonged to millennial and messianic religious sects that celebrated chastity and purity, such as the Xian Tian (Former Heaven) sect, which legitimated refusal to cohabit with a man.[56] These practices built on various religious sects in Guangdong, Fujian, and Zhejiang, particularly the powerful cult of Tian Hou (Empress of Heaven)—Ma Tsu in Taiwan—a highly revered deity of seafaring people, whose temples dot the countryside. In her mortal manifestation, Tian Hou was a woman seer who refused to marry, had a special relationship with spinsters, and fasted to death rather than marry an older man chosen by her parents.[57] Could these sects have become more popular with the out-migration of males that made marriage less likely?

The similarities of the beliefs of the Xian Tian sect and the Brahma Kumari sect of Sind, discussed below, would suggest a connection between sect popularity and male out-migration. Practices ranging from local religious belief systems and chastity cults to institutions such as sisterhood associations, spinster dormitories, and delayed transfer marriages suggest that existing patriarchal norms were being transformed and modified in the course of the late nineteenth century. People from outside the Guangdong Delta considered these practices abhorrent, regarding the women as wayward lesbians and too rich for their own good.[58] A young academic from Zhongshan University traveling with the American journalist Agnes Smedley in the 1930s was probably speaking for many when he complained that while the women supported parents, brothers and sisters, and grandparents with their earnings, "They squander their money! I have never gone to a picture theater without seeing groups of them sitting together holding hands."[59]

Many migrants from counties such as Shunde, Zhongshan, Panyu, and Nanhai became merchants in the Chinese American community, while the Sze Yup migrants were often the laborers and domestics. These divergent economies of the home counties and of class backgrounds had different implications for the status of women, the possibilities of female migration, and the ways in which patriarchal relations evolved in a period of rapid economic transition. The erasure of these homeland differences in writings on Chinese America, as if the history of the migrants prior to their arrival mattered not at all, contributes to a flattened model of "Oriental" history where time stood still and the villages and their denizens were indistinguishable from one another.

Across the Himalayas, sexual mores were also transformed in the Punjab during the extensive male migration. Here parallels with Taishan are more apparent than with Shunde, for Punjabi male migration increased patriarchal control of the woman's sexual and reproductive functions.

Punjab, like the rest of India and China, had a strong male-preference culture. The increase in commercial crops by the end of the nineteenth century, the consequent increase in the value of women's labor on the farm, and the increased cash nexus through remittances led to an increase in bride price.[60] The "market price" was also kept high by female infanticide and hypergamy. Bringing in an older bride who could work on the farm as soon as she arrived, and for whom the bride price was lower, became common. As the saying went: "*Badi bahu, bade bhag / chhota bandra ghane suhag* [An older bride, very lucky / a younger groom, luckier still]."[61]

The importance of women's labor also revitalized the institution of the levirate—the marriage of the widowed sister-in-law with her husband's younger brother. Known as *karewa*, widow remarriage was common in many parts of South, Central, and West Asia. By marrying the widow to the dead man's brother, the patrilineal property was kept intact, for under customary law the widow inherited her husband's property.

The increase in male migration brought on an increase in "polyandry," as the British colonial officials termed it. Several brothers of the husband shared the woman, for rather than have fewer children in the family because of long absences of the husband, the reproductive role of the wife was reiterated through agnatic kin control. Only one brother would be formally married but the other brothers had free access to the wife.[62] The children born were technically "fathered" by the man who had had the marriage ceremony, for like the wife, they, too, were part of the *ghar* (the household) and the *biradari* (patrilineal unit).

There is evidence from folklore, women's songs, and women's legal protests that women did not freely choose this system, for it meant, sentiments aside, unending pregnancies to add to their other labors. The colonial state, however, was primarily interested in promoting the consolidation of rural property and supported the levirate system enthusiastically. The state and the husband's agnatic kin found any woman's reluctance to remarry a hindrance. A British judge noted in his memoirs that "if the man (the brother-in-law) seemed a decent man, and the woman could give no better reason than to say 'I don't like him' I said 'stuff and nonsense.' I can't listen to that, the law must be respected."[63]

In Sind, where similar practices of polyandry existed, as in Punjab, the display of an item of clothing belonging to the husband often sufficed to legitimate the birth. However, unlike Punjab, where the women were in the rural sector, the urban centers from which the Sindhi merchants originated probably contributed to many more wives having active financial dealings in their husband's businesses.[64]

More interesting, the political economy of the sex-gender system in Sind, transformed through migration, may have contributed to the rise of a sect called Brahma Kumari. Started in the 1930s by the wives of Sindhi merchants in Hyderabad and a wealthy male benefactor with radical ideas about "harmony between the sexes," the sect's philosophy was built around the "more traditionally feminine qualities of patience, tolerance, sacrifice, kindness, and love as core values," along with vegetarianism and strict celibacy between husband and wife.[65] Prem Chowdhry has suggested that the immense sexual pressures created for the merchants' wives when their husbands returned for the usual six-month stay at home before leaving again for a three-year sojourn abroad may have led to the development of a sect that made conjugal celibacy the cornerstone of its practices, along with cleanliness, purity, and women's spirituality.[66]

The sect generated fierce hostility in Hyderabad and ultimately relocated to Rajasthan in India, where it has grown to an international organization with branches in the United Kingdom and United States. The well-endowed organization still receives support from Sindhi mercantile communities worldwide, including families like the Watumull. Its radical womanist message is striking. It is an organization completely administered by women who see themselves and their followers as the midwives of *satyug*, a millennial vision of an era of Truth and Purity. The descriptions of their "golden age" evoke early twentieth-century feminist utopian novels such as Charlotte Perkins Gilman's *Herland* (1915) and Rokeya Sakhawat Hossain's *Sultana's Dream* (1905). The *satyug* will be a paradise of perpetual spring, with no desires, no cooking, and use of solar power and atomic power for everyday life in an androgynous world where reproduction will transpire through yogic power and not sexual union.[67] Celibacy, withdrawal from society, and asceticism were significant routes to moral and spiritual power in both Buddhist and Hindu traditions. The incorporation of celibacy in popular religious sects, by women who were still very much part of society in various migrant communities from Shunde to Sind, can be seen as an alternative negotiation with dominant patriarchal controls, an effort by women to control their bodies and sexualities.

To sum up, we now know what happened to the Cantonese and Punjabi women: they were busy working in the fields; in the cattle sheds, pigpens, and chicken coops; in the silk filatures and markets; in the kitchen and at the loom. Their labor was too vital for the household unit to let them migrate, especially if the man was going to return within a few years. Why have we known so little about this dimension of the lives of Chinese women? Perhaps it is because many of our images of Chinese women's lives in the nineteenth century come from the writings of Euro-American missionaries. Engaged in constructing the helpless, hapless, heathen Chinese women for their own purposes, the missionaries were typically based in China's urban centers. They had little opportunity to observe the work of women on farms and in fields and consequently wrote little about them.[68] These and similar sources in the United States, including Chinese newspapers such as the *Chung Sai Yat Po*, run by the prominent Presbyterian clergyman Ng Poon Chew, with close links to the Mission Home of Donaldina Cameron—the "white angel to hundreds of Chinese slave girls"[69]—Orientalized Chinese women as passive victims of culture and patriarchy.

Besides work, control of their labor by the husband's family, and immigration restrictions, other reasons explain the absence of Chinese and Indian women in the United States. After all, the women had separate lives that we have yet to study in depth, and the textual sources for such studies may exist only in their personal papers and letters. But as glimpses of their lives indicate, the women had their own ties to kin, natal families, and friends and their own cultural worlds that were important to them. Without some consideration of women's alternative spaces, their agency is obscured, as are the myriad negotiations with patriarchy that they must have undertaken daily in China, India, and the United States (if we assume *a priori* that they wanted to join their husbands in forming a nuclear household and were prevented from doing so only by U.S. racism and restrictions). Anecdotal evidence suggests that the alien world of America was far less attractive to many immigrant women than we would imagine with our nationalist lore. Indeed, records do exist for some Chinese merchants' wives who came to the United States, gave birth, but chose to return home and stayed there for most of their lives, more comfortable with living in China on remittances than in the secluded worlds of Chinatowns.[70]

As we discover that the migration of women along with their men was the exception rather than the rule in the nineteenth and early twentieth centuries, we can ask why the historiography on the subject has focused on the family unit as the normative model of migration. Is it because the increase in migrations of families to the United States in the post–World War II period, and even more so after the 1965 immigration legislation, has made nuclear-family migration seem the norm? It is still far from the norm, possible only for a small number of the migrants, the middle-class professionals who have both the economic means of paying thousands of dollars and the support of U.S. and European states that allows for spousal migration of professionals. Even then, it is not unusual for a family to spend a decade apart before all the children born abroad, the husband, and the wife are united under one roof.[71] As the diverse contemporary trajectories of Sri Lankan, Filipino, and Thai female migrations worldwide show—along with the Keralan and Pakistani male migrations to the Middle East, the Bangladeshi and

Pakistani male migrations to the U.S. northeast, and so on—we are in the process of establishing yet other patterns of social transformations of the gender systems in the Asian homelands. Processes of capitalist economic development and accumulation that constantly produce and reproduce global divisions of labor also produce new gender-divided patterns of migration. The challenge is to move beyond narrow nationalist narratives to recast the contours of Asian migration history as global history.

NOTES

1. Earlier versions of this chapter were presented at the World History Center, Northeastern University, and Association of Asian Studies, 2002. I thank Philip Kuhn, Elizabeth Sinn, Wing-chung Ng, Adam McKeown, Patrick Manning, and Vasant Kaiwar for valuable comments and suggestions, and the audience for sharing important insights.

2. E.g., Wang Gungwu, *Don't Leave Home: Migration and the Chinese* (Singapore: Times Academic Press, 2000).

3. Gérard Challiand and Jan-Pierre Rageau, *Atlas des diasporas* (Paris: Edition Odile Jacob, 1991).

4. Ewa Morawska, "The Sociology and Historiography of Immigration," in Virginia Yans-McLaughlin, ed., *Immigration Reconsidered* (New York: Oxford University Press, 1990), 187.

5. There were over 60 million migrants in Europe alone by 1992. Ewa Morawska and Willfried Spohn, "Moving Europeans in the Globalizing World," in Wang Gungwu, ed., *Global History and Migrations* (Boulder: Westview Press, 1997), 27.

6. The 1965 Immigration and Naturalization Service (INS) regulations on family reunification promoted a new pattern of transnational marriage strategy.

7. The counties of Nanhai, Panyu, Shunde, Xinhui, Toishan, Kaiping, Enping, and Zhongshan (Xiangshan).

8. Judy Yung, *Unbound Feet* (Berkeley: University of California Press, 1995), 243; and Ronald Takaki, "They Also Came: The Migration of Chinese and Japanese Women to Hawaii and the Continental United States," in *Chinese American History and Perspectives* (San Francisco: Chinese Historical Society, 1990), 3.

9. Madeline Hsu, *Dreaming of Gold, Dreaming of Home* (Stanford: Stanford University Press, 2000), 92–99. See also Jennifer Gee (chapter 5), Erika Lee (chapter 4), and Judy Yung (chapter 7) in this book.

10. Hsu, *Dreaming of Gold*, 99.

11. Sucheta Mazumdar, "Punjabi Agricultural Workers in California," in Lucie Cheng and Edna Bonacich, eds., *Labor Immigration under Capitalism* (Berkeley: University of California Press, 1984), 571–72.

12. Culturalist explanations survive as concerns with morality and bonded slave girls in discussions of Chinese prostitution.

13. E.g., Sucheng Chan, "The Exclusion of Chinese Women, 1870–1943," in Sucheng Chan, ed., *Entry Denied: Exclusion and the Chinese Community in America* (Philadelphia: Temple University Press, 1991); Lisa Lowe, *Immigrant Acts: On Asian American Cultural Politics* (Durham: Duke University Press, 1996); and George Peffer, *If They Don't Bring Their Women Here* (Urbana: University of Illinois Press, 1999).

14. Adam McKeown, "Transnational Chinese Families and Chinese Exclusion, 1875–1943," *Journal of American Ethnic History* 18:2 (1999): 73–110.

15. Victor Purcell, *The Chinese in Southeast Asia* (London: Oxford University Press, 1965), 232.

16. Sucheta Mazumdar, *Sugar and Society in China: Peasants, Technology and the World Market* (Cambridge: Harvard University Press, 1998), 206–10.

17. June Mei, "Socioeconomic Origins of Emigration, Guangdong to California," in Cheng and Bonacich, eds., *Labor Immigration*, 234.

18. Walter Nugent, "Demographic Aspects of European Migration Worldwide," in Dirk Hoerder and Leslie Page Moch, eds., *European Migrants: Local and Global Perspectives* (Boston: Northeastern University Press, 1996), 72.

19. Marion F. Houstoun, Roger G. Kramer, and Joan Mackin Barrett, "Female Predominance of Immigration to the United States since 1930: A First Look," *International Migration Review* 18:4 (1984): 908–63.

20. Franklin Ng, "The Sojourner, Return Migration and Immigration History," in *Chinese America: History and Perspectives* (San Francisco: Chinese Historical Society, 1987), 53–71.

21. Walter Nugent, *Crossings: The Great Transatlantic Migrations* (Bloomington: Indiana University Press, 1995), 35.

22. Mark Wyman, *Round Trip to America* (Ithaca: Cornell University Press, 1993), 9–14; Nugent, *Crossings*, 35.

23. Donna Gabaccia, "Women of the Mass Migrations: From Minority to Majority, 1820–1930," in Hoerder and Moch, eds., *European Migrants*, 91.

24. Ibid., 92.

25. Ibid., 95.

26. Ibid., 100.

27. Sucheta Mazumdar, "In the Family: A Tapestry of Oral Histories," in UCLA Asian American Studies Center, ed., *Linking Our Lives: Chinese American Women of Los Angeles* (Los Angeles: Chinese Historical Society of Southern California, 1984), 29–47.

28. Rosalyn Baxandall, Linda Gordon, and Susan Reverby, eds., *America's Working Women* (New York: Vintage Books, 1976), 93.

29. Michael Mitterauer and Reinhard Sieder, *The European Family* (Chicago: University of Chicago Press, 1982), 131.

30. James Casey, *The History of the Family* (Oxford: Basil Blackwell, 1989), 161.

31. Angie Newman, cited in Peggy Pascoe, *Relations of Rescue* (New York: Oxford University Press, 1990), 24.

32. Prem Chowdhry, *The Veiled Woman* (Delhi: Oxford University Press, 1994), 32–33.

33. Malcolm Darling, *The Punjab Peasant in Prosperity and Debt* (London: Oxford University Press, 1928), 38.

34. Claude Markovits, *The Global World of Indian Merchants 1750–1947: Traders of Sind from Bukhara to Panama* (Cambridge: Cambridge University Press, 2000). I draw heavily on Markovits here.

35. Joan Jensen, *Passage from India* (New Haven: Yale University Press, 1988), 121–26.

36. It is now a well-known Indian international philanthropic organization, supporting various educational and health-related activities. See http://www.watumull.com and http://www.indiacurrents.com/199912/indianamericans.htm.

37. Mei, "Socioeconomic Origins," 237.

38. John Lossing Buck, *Land Utilization in China* (Shanghai: Commercial Press, 1937), 290; Chen Hanseng, *Agrarian Problems in Southernmost China* (Guangzhou: Lingnan University Press), 104.

39. *Rohtak District Gazetteer*, Lahore: Civil and Military Gazette, 1910; Chowdhry, *Veiled Woman*, 57–58.

40. Ibid., 60.

41. Darling, *Punjab Peasant*, 36.

42. Ibid., 58.

43. Elizabeth Sinn, "In Between Places: The Key Roles of Localities of Transit in Chinese Migration" (Washington, D.C.: paper presented at Association of Asian Studies, 2002).

44. Hsu, *Dreaming of Gold*, 217, n. 68.

45. Mazumdar, *Sugar and Society*, on rural violence, 220–23, 315–18.

46. Hsu, *Dreaming of Gold*, 104–6.

47. McKeown, "Transnational Chinese Families," 95.

48. Sandra Wong, "For the Sake of Kinship: The Overseas Chinese Family" (Ph.D. diss., Stanford University, 1988), 51.

49. Chen Ta, *Emigrant Communities in South China* (New York: Institute of Pacific Relations, 1940), 123.

50. Hsu, *Dreaming of Gold*, 16.

51. C. W. Howard and K. P Buswell, *A Survey of the Silk Industry of South China* (Hong Kong: Hong Kong Commercial Press, 1925), 15–25.

52. Janice Stockard, *Daughters of the Canton Delta* (Stanford: Stanford University Press, 1989), 9.

53. Marjorie Topley, "Marriage Resistance in Rural Kwangtung," in M. Wolf and R. Witke, eds., *Women in Chinese Society* (Stanford: Stanford University Press, 1975), 82.

54. Ibid., 42–44.

55. Stockard, *Daughters of the Canton Delta*, 70–73.

56. Topley, "Marriage Resistance," 74–76.

57. James Watson, "Standardizing the Gods: The Promotion of T'ien Hou," in David Johnson, Andrew Nathan, and Evelyn Rawski, eds., *Popular Culture in Late Imperial China* (Berkeley: University of California Press, 1985), 297.

58. Agnes Smedley, *Portraits of Chinese Women* (New York: Feminist Press, 1976), 105.

59. Ibid.

60. Darling, *Punjab Peasant*, 53.

61. Chowdhry, *Veiled Woman*, 63. My translation.

62. Ibid., 112; Darling, *Punjab Peasant*, 51.

63. George Campbell, *Memoirs of My Indian Career*, cited in Chowdhry, *Veiled Woman*, 92–93.

64. Markovits, *Global World*, 274–76.

65. See the Brahma Kumari Web site: http://www.bksu.com/about/leaders.html.

66. Prem Chowdhry, "Marriage, Sexuality and the Female 'Ascetic': Understanding a Hindu Sect," *Economic and Political Weekly* 31:34 (1996): 2307–21.

67. Suma Varughese, "Satyug Is as Sure as Death," at http://www.lifepositive.com/Spirit/spirit-centers/brahma-kumari.asp.

68. See various reports of American missionaries: *Chinese Repository* (1832–1851); *China Mission Year Book* (1910–1940), Duke University, Special Collections.

69. Ng married Chun Fa, raised at the Mission Home. See *San Francisco News*, May 4, 1939, report on Donaldina Cameron, "Earthquake Eyewitness Accounts."

70. Great Grandmother Leong Shee in Yung, *Unbound Feet*, 15–16.

71. Children over the age of eighteen are excluded as migrants on their parents' visa. The current waiting period for processing spousal unification visas is two to three years.

Part 2

Revisiting Immigrant Wives and Picture Brides

4

Exclusion Acts
Chinese Women during the Chinese Exclusion Era, 1882–1943

Erika Lee

My grandmother Moy Sau Bik first came to the United States from China in 1931. She immigrated during the Chinese Exclusion era, when U.S. immigration laws excluded all but a few classes of Chinese immigrants. The Chinese Exclusion Act of 1882 changed the course of U.S. immigration history, but little is known about what happened *after* 1882, especially in terms of exclusion's impact on Chinese women and the ways in which they responded. As a child, I was always curious about Paw Paw's (grandmother's) past and her journey to America. But I knew better than to ask too many questions. Like many Chinese Americans, she preferred to keep the years of exclusion buried and refused to talk about the "old days," times that were full of pain and scars that never healed.

The original 1882 Chinese Exclusion Act denied entry to all Chinese laborers.[1] Only Chinese merchants, students, teachers, travelers, and diplomats were considered exempt. Eventually American-born U.S. citizens and the wives and children of merchants and citizens were also allowed to apply for admission.

Immediately after the act's passage, Chinese immigration to the United States dropped dramatically. In 1887, the number of Chinese admitted into the country by immigration officials reached an all-time low of only ten individuals.[2] But despite the Chinese Exclusion Act's intent, it failed to end Chinese immigration altogether. From 1882 to 1943, an estimated 300,955 Chinese successfully gained admission to the United States for the first time or as returning residents and native-born citizens. In fact, the number of Exclusion era Chinese admissions is greater than during the pre–Exclusion era, from 1849 to 1882, when 258,210 Chinese entered the United States.[3] The fact that so many managed to enter the country in spite of the exclusion laws is truly significant. It raises questions about the efficacy of restrictive immigration laws and demonstrates the power of immigrant resistance and agency. The vast majority of these immigrants, however, were men. Of the total number of Exclusion era Chinese immigrants, only ten thousand to forty thousand were women.[4] The exclusion laws and the gendered ways in which they were interpreted and enforced by U.S. immigration officials created additional *exclusion acts* that further restricted Chinese female immigration.

My grandmother's father, grandfather, and great-grandfather were well-established merchants in New York City and Philadelphia.[5] They were fortunate in that their class status allowed them to migrate freely between China and America. Yet their families were not immune to exclusion. Three generations of Moy women stayed behind in China while their husbands and fathers came to the United States. A number of factors likely influenced the family's decision to allow only the men to migrate abroad, but the exclusion laws and the unequal environment that they created made all women, even those from the exempt classes, especially vulnerable to restriction.

In 1919 my great-grandfather Moy Wah Chung decided to move the entire family to the United States. He prepared and filled out all the necessary immigration forms. He claimed that his family consisted of a wife and two sons, but no daughters. While my grandmother's younger brother was included in this family description, my grandmother was never mentioned. According to the official record filed with the immigration service, she did not exist as a member of the Moy family. In her place, using her rightful immigration slot, was her male cousin, Moy Chong Don, who posed as the eldest child in the family. Reflecting the prevailing patriarchal Chinese attitudes that privileged sons over daughters, my great-grandfather apparently believed that his nephew was more worthy of immigration than his own daughter. While the family traveled on to the United States, my grandmother was left behind to live with relatives. She never saw her mother alive again, and my great-grandfather never sent for her to join the rest of the family in America. Ineligible to enter as an independent immigrant herself, and without the sponsorship of her father, my grandmother was effectively excluded from the country. She eventually immigrated only after she married my grandfather, a Chinese merchant in New York.[6] As a member of one of the exempt classes, my grandmother should have been able to immigrate to the United States without restrictions much earlier in her life. But gendered biases within her own family combined with the larger restrictions placed on all Chinese immigration served to exclude her anyway.

Historians have just begun to explore the gendered dimensions of Chinese exclusion through analyses of laws and court cases, demonstrating how exclusion became an "ever-tightening noose" to constrict Chinese female immigration.[7] But laws and court cases tell only one side of the story. A focus on the inequalities created and reinforced through the everyday application of Chinese exclusion reveals the full magnitude of its impact on Chinese women. What soon becomes evident is that Chinese and American conceptions of race, class, and especially gender became enacted, reinforced, and institutionalized in the daily enforcement of the exclusion laws and directly influenced Chinese female immigration.

American fears and stereotypes about Chinese prostitution first caused immigration officials to target all Chinese women for special scrutiny during the Exclusion era. As seen in the interrogation and investigation processes, Chinese women faced additional burdens to prove both their standing as "moral" women and their status as exempt-class Chinese. The exclusion laws also reinforced the gender inequalities in both American and Chinese societies and explicitly positioned most Chinese female immigrants as dependents of their male husbands and fathers. This dependent status affected women's immigration opportunities and even their rights to remain in the United States after they were admitted.[8]

Focusing on the Chinese women's everyday experiences at America's gates also allows us to examine their active agency in confronting exclusion. Their daily acts of negotiation and resistance—what Lisa Lowe has called "immigrant acts"—defy popular stereotypes that portray Chinese women as passive, subordinate victims.[9] Although they often held unequal positions in their own families and communities, as well as in the United States, Chinese women proved to be resilient actors in their own right, finding and using strategies to overcome the barriers erected by the Chinese exclusion laws.

Suspected of Being "Bad Women"

Although the Chinese Exclusion era is often referred to as the sixty-one year period of 1882–1943, American efforts to exclude Chinese immigrants officially began as early as 1875. That year, the U.S. Congress passed the Page Act, specifically targeting Asian contract laborers and women—especially Chinese women—entering for "immoral purposes." The immigration of Chinese prostitutes had first begun in the mid–nineteenth century, when the number of Chinese women in the United States was extremely small. Imported to work as indentured servants in slavelike conditions, Chinese prostitutes came to be viewed as symbols of social decay and "moral and racial pollution" in America. Social reformers and anti-Chinese politicians alike led the campaign to eradicate the business and immigration of Chinese prostitutes.[10] The 1875 Page Act was the first federal law to restrict immigration, illustrating the extent to which Chinese prostitution was considered a threat to the nation.[11] It also paved the way for the eventual passage of the Chinese Exclusion Act seven years later.

The U.S. government's early efforts to stem the immigration of Chinese prostitutes under the Page Law had long-term repercussions. Upon applying for admission into the country, Exclusion era Chinese immigrant women of all classes were routinely suspected of being potential prostitutes by immigration officials. This government scrutiny resulted in further limiting the immigration opportunities open to all Chinese women. Correspondence to and from the immigration bureau in San Francisco in the 1890s, for example, demonstrates that Chinese immigrant men who wanted to bring their wives and children to the United States were explicitly discouraged from doing so. Believing that these applicants and their "alleged wives" were merely dishonest importers and Chinese prostitutes in disguise, immigration officials sought to limit *all* Chinese female immigration. They combined a racialized characterization of Chinese immigrant men as a "cunning," dishonest group, willing to victimize their own women, with another stereotype that linked Chinese women immigrants directly (and only) to prostitution. In 1895, John H. Wise, the collector of customs and chief of the immigration bureau in San Francisco, warned one inquirer that he would

> do as much as I can to discourage Chinese from sending for their alleged wives and children. . . . I am satisfied that . . . many women and young girls [would be] brought for immoral purposes. It is well known that the cunning of Chinese often circumvents the vigilance of the officers.[12]

When pressed to explain what documents Chinese women would need to enter the United States, Wise made it clear that *all* Chinese women would be suspected of being prostitutes until proven otherwise.[13]

The administrative procedures designed to thwart prostitution had profound effects on Chinese women applying for admission throughout the Exclusion era. Routinely suspected of being potential prostitutes, Chinese women were often unfairly detained and/or denied entry. One such case involved Lau Dai Moy, who applied for admission into the country as the wife of a U.S. citizen on June 12, 1917. Her papers were in order, but as part of the regular inspection process at the immigration station on Angel Island in San Francisco, she and her husband, Fong Dai Sing, were brought in for extensive questioning. To immigration officials, Lau Dai Moy's case appeared to be suspicious. She was a wife of a U.S. native—a class suspected of widespread fraud—and she was much younger than her husband. Acting on their suspicion that Lau and Fong were not legally husband and wife (and that Lau was possibly a prostitute), the inspectors grilled the couple about various aspects of their wedding ceremony, their home, and their family. The questions were exacting in their detail, and both Lau and Fong were expected to give specific answers that agreed with one another. Lau's interrogation progressed in part:

Q. What presents or ornaments has your husband given you?
A. The bracelets and rings that I have on now.
Q. When did your husband give you the hair ornament?
A. A few days later [after the wedding].
Q. Did he buy that hair ornament in his home village?
A. No, in the Shek Kee Market place.
Q. Did you really wear the gay head-dress and the bead[ed] veil at your wedding?
A. Yes.
Q. Just when did you wear the head-dress?
A. Soon after I entered the house.
Q. How long did you wear the head-dress?
A. Just for about one hour.
Q. Did you wear it while you served tea?
A. Yes.
Q. Who were the guests that you poured tea for?
A. I don't know all of the gentlemen guests who were there, some of them were friends of my husband.

Such detailed questions reflect not only the gendered procedures of exclusion enforcement—Lau was asked only about strictly feminine activities pertaining to what she was wearing, how she was adorned, and her role as hostess at her wedding—but also the ways in which the government sought to prove or disprove the validity of relationships and marriages. If there were too many discrepancies, immigration officials ruled that the relationship was based on fraud and that the applicant was thus inadmissible. Discrepancies, of course, did not always mean a fraudulent case. In the case of Lau and Fong, the interrogation revolved around minute details of their arranged marriage and wedding ceremony that had taken place a year prior to the interrogation. Other questions involving Fong Dai Sing's native village, house, and their shared life were even more difficult to answer, because the couple had spent only a few months together before Fong returned to the United States. They had not experienced much of a shared life, house, or family, but they were still expected to provide consistent answers or risk a denial. Because of discrepancies between herself and her husband, Lau was detained at the station for six weeks.

The pressure and intensity of the interrogation apparently traumatized Lau. Immigration inspectors had spent several hours asking her details about the wedding. They also asked her how many bracelets her husband had given her as a wedding present. All of these questions were then asked of Fong. During her part of the interrogation, Lau was unsure about the number of bracelets and responded that she had received from her husband only one pair. When her interrogation was completed, she was taken back to the women's barracks. There, she remembered that she had one additional bracelet packed in her luggage. Believing that such a wrong answer would mean certain exclusion, Lau first panicked, then fought to amend her testimony. She rushed up to an interpreter and tried to give an additional statement. "I have two bracelets!" she explained. "The second [one] is in baggage. I do not know why I had been so stupid!" The interpreter took note of Lau Dai Moy's claims and recorded them in her immigration file. In the final analysis of her case, the government's decision was favorable. After six weeks in detention, Lau was finally allowed to land. Though clearly shaken, she had managed to make the system work for her.[14]

Lau Dai Moy's 1917 case reveals how nineteenth-century American presumptions about Chinese women's alleged immorality had lasting consequences. As late as 1940, sociologist Wen-hsien Chen found that "over-suspicion on the part of immigration officers [had] caused great embarrassment to respectable young Chinese women."[15] Chinese women, however, learned to adapt to these biased interpretations and procedures in order to avoid being branded as prostitutes or women of questionable morals. One way was through evidence of "proper character," either through credible testimony, documentation, or clear markers of class. One of the first women to apply for admission through the port of San Francisco after the Chinese Exclusion Act was passed was Leong Cum, a garment maker and U.S. citizen born in Lewiston, Idaho. Applying for readmission in May 1884, Leong distinguished herself as "a woman of excellent reputation and irreproachable character" through affidavits from white acquaintances. One was from Jerome Millian, a Chinese interpreter who likely worked for the immigration service. These affidavits and Millian's endorsement worked in Leong's favor. She was landed two days after her initial arrival.[16]

Chinese women applying for admission as wives of merchants found it necessary to go one step further. At stake was not only their status as respectable women but also their membership in the merchant class. When judging merchant cases, immigration officials looked for a number of factors, including the steamship class by which Chinese traveled to the United States. Merchants and their families were expected to travel in the more expensive and elite upper decks. A first-class steamship ticket was thus considered evidence of class, and for women, proper moral standing as well. At the same time, Chinese women who traveled by third-class passage were suspected of being "bad women."[17]

Based on these presumptions, many Chinese attempted to conform to immigration officials' expectations and notions of class, gender, and respectability. Lee Chi Yet and Wong Lan Fong, a merchant and his wife, delayed their scheduled immigration to the United States in 1926 until they had saved enough money to pay for first-class passage. Such a strategy, they believed, would help them avoid undue scrutiny during the immigrant inspection.[18]

Other Chinese women emphasized physical markers. Because immigration officials expected merchant families to possess fine clothing, a respectable manner, and, especially, bound feet, Chinese women and their attorneys learned to highlight these traits in order to achieve their goal of entering the country.[19] The earliest example of this attention to bound feet involved Jow Ah Yeong and Chun Ah Ngon, a merchant's wife and daughter who arrived in San Francisco in 1885. The application of both mother and daughter emphasized that both applicants had "compressed feet," which the affidavit explained "is a mark of respectability."[20] In 1901, Gee See, a Los Angeles merchant's wife, submitted a full-length portrait of herself dressed in luxurious silk robes, seated in a richly decorated room, and clearly revealing her tiny, bound feet. To provide further proof, she also included an X ray of her bound feet, which was described as showing "conclusively that the feet of this woman are what is known as 'small' or 'bound,' the position of the bones and their abnormally small size distinctly appearing."[21] Chinese immigrant women performed such actions consciously and purposefully. They played to the government's definitions of how a "proper" Chinese woman should look and behave with affidavits, witness testimony, photographs, and even X rays. This smart strategizing facilitated the admission of upper-middle-class women but nevertheless did little to challenge the overarching class and gendered stereotypes held and perpetuated by U.S. immigration officials.

Dependent Immigration Status

At the same time that some Chinese women learned how to mark their class and moral standing in order to facilitate admission into the country, others explicitly challenged their exclusion from the country through the American legal system. Like their male counterparts, they learned to hire the "very best attorneys."[22] Eventually, judicial rulings affirmed the right of American-born Chinese women and merchant wives and children to apply for admission.[23] These court decisions represented important new opportunities for Chinese female immigration, and the numbers of Chinese women immigrating to the United States began to increase steadily.[24] In 1900, women made up only 0.7 percent of the total number of Chinese immigrants entering the country. That figure rose to 9.7 percent in 1910, 20 percent in 1920, and 30 percent by 1930. These statistics do not include American citizens of Chinese descent.[25] Despite this increase, the exclusion laws continued to reinforce old barriers as well as erect new ones for Chinese immigrant women. These restrictions were inextricably linked to the ways in which the exclusion laws privileged and duplicated gendered dynamics of immigration both in their enforcement by government officials and in practice by Chinese immigrants themselves.

During exclusion, women could apply for admission as both independent and dependent immigrants. In practice, however, most women entered as dependents of a male merchant or citizen. This dependent status—both reflecting and reinforcing the gendered face of American immigration law and the power relations between husbands and wives, fathers and daughters—served to limit Chinese women's immigration opportunities and even threaten their rights to remain in the country after they had been admitted.

Chinese women's dependent immigration status was neither automatic nor inclusive of all women's immigration opportunities. The class- and profession-based exempt categories as outlined in the original Exclusion Act (merchants, teachers, diplomats, students, and travelers) did not specify that admissible members of these professions had to be male. Chinese women could—and increasingly did—enter and apply for admission as teachers or students. Nevertheless, few Chinese women were actively engaged in the exempted professions for most of the exclusion period and thus were not eligible to enter independently. To claim that the exclusion laws eventually "opened more doors than it closed," as one scholar has, is to ignore the fact that despite the perceived increase in immigration opportunities, few women were actually eligible to take advantage of those opportunities on their own.[26] Instead, most women applied for admission as dependent immigrants. From 1910 to 1924, 2,107 women (27 percent) entered as independent immigrants or U.S. citizens and 5,702 women (73 percent) entered as dependents.[27]

Dependent immigrant status had clear disadvantages. First and foremost was the fact that most Chinese women derived their right to enter the country only from their male relatives' immigration status. Early Exclusion era court rulings had determined that a woman's right to enter the country was derived from her husband or father.[28] Thus, unless they were exempt from exclusion in their own right, Chinese women were almost completely dependent on their husbands and fathers to sponsor them into the United States. Like my grandmother, many may have been left behind without the freedom to immigrate on their own. While a multiplicity of factors contributed to the lower rates of Chinese female immigration to the United States in general (patriarchal cultural values and patterns of male sojourning already favored the migration of males over females), the restrictions of the exclusion laws and the environment that they created further threatened the remaining immigration opportunities for women.

The exclusion laws turned immigration into a valuable and precious commodity. Families were forced to choose who would immigrate, when, and under which categories. As economic and political conditions in China worsened in the early twentieth century, the desire and need to immigrate to the United States increased among many Chinese in southern China, the native home to the majority of Chinese immigrants prior to 1965. But not all could immigrate, and women were often the ones to be left behind. The disparity in immigration opportunities available to male and female immigrants is seen most clearly in the so-called paper-son practice. Chinese who were not eligible to apply for admission on their own purchased "slots" or false papers belonging to exempt-class Chinese willing to sponsor them into the United States as their own "children." Immigration involving fraudulent papers increasingly became the primary means of Chinese immigration by the early 1900s, but the market in false papers was not evenly distributed between male and female applicants. The majority of paper slots were for male applicants. A 1925 investigation by the San Francisco immigration office revealed that only 49 out of 719 immigration slots recorded that year were for female children.[29] Given such statistics, it is not difficult to speculate that many women, like my grandmother, were deprived of their opportunities to immigrate in favor of their male relatives or other males who purchased their family's immigration papers.

Even Chinese women who were able to immigrate remained hindered by their dependent status under U.S. immigration law. Chinese family members applying as dependents were first held responsible for meeting two sets of requirements, while independent immigrants only had to satisfy one. Wives and children of merchants and citizens had to reconfirm the exempt-class standing of the sponsor himself. They then had to prove that the relationship to their sponsor indeed existed. Dependent immigrants were, in effect, tested twice. Chinese men and boys immigrating as dependents (as sons of merchants and citizens, for example) faced similar scrutiny and burdens of proof. But because there were more opportunities for Chinese men to enter as independent immigrants, Chinese women were more adversely affected by the burdens of dependent immigrant status.[30]

It was not uncommon for problems to arise in the effort to reconfirm the sponsoring immigrant's exempt status or to prove that the marital or parental relationship existed. Even if the exempt-class sponsor was a longtime resident of the United States, the investigations pertaining to immigration status could be lengthy, often causing delays in the cases of exempt-class families. Yong Shee, for example, was detained for two months in 1915 while immigration officials investigated the status of her husband, Lee Kan, a merchant in San Francisco and partner in the Chong, Kee, and Company. Because she was unable to apply for admission independently, Yong Shee's admission was tied to that of her husband. Thus, when immigration officials began to scrutinize the company's holdings in order to determine its qualification as a bona fide mercantile establishment, at stake was not only the status of the business but also Yong Shee's right to enter and reenter the country. The couple hired an attorney, rallied friends and acquaintances to their cause, and were eventually admitted into the country.[31] In another case, Jung Shee was almost denied entry in 1942 because a recent injury had prevented her husband from working and supporting her. Fearful that the absence of a male provider would make Jung Shee "likely to become a public charge," immigration officials released her only with assurances from relatives and social workers that Jung would be able to support herself.[32] Dependent status had severe consequences even for Chinese American women, citizens by virtue of their birth in the United States. Under the 1922 Cable Act, Chinese American women who married "aliens ineligible to citizenship" lost their citizenship and could face problems reentering the country.[33]

The Shadow of Exclusion

For some Chinese immigrants, the nightmare of exclusion ended once they were officially admitted into the country and allowed to land. For many others, the shadow of exclusion haunted and followed them for years afterward. Widespread illegal Chinese immigration and enduring anti-Chinese sentiment motivated U.S. government officials to practice long-term surveillance on suspected Chinese immigrants who had entered or remained in the country in violation of the law. Although they were not the main practitioners of illegal immigration, Chinese women were nevertheless at risk during government crackdowns, because their right to remain in the United States hinged on the legal status and standing of their husbands or fathers. They were also vulnerable to adverse fluctuations in their sponsor's immigration status. For example, immigration laws and regulations established under the 1924 Immigration Act required that Chinese admitted to the United States as students, travelers, or merchants "must maintain the status under which [they were] admitted while remaining in the United States."[34] If such an exempt-class Chinese were to lose or change his or her status, that person could be arrested and sent before a deportation hearing. Because Chinese women could remain in the country only as long their husbands and fathers maintained their exempt status, they were also to be arrested and possibly deported.

Such was the predicament in which Ngoon Shee and Wu Wah, a wife and her merchant husband, found themselves beginning in the fall of 1932. Ngoon Shee was eventually allowed to remain in the country, but only after being hunted by immigration authorities who threatened to deport her over a five-year period. Ngoon Shee arrived in San Francisco in October 1930 and was admitted as the wife of Wu Wah, a resident merchant and member of the firm of Sun Tong Chong Company in Oakland, California. Over the next seven years they had six children together, all born in the United States as citizens. Seven months after his wife's arrival, Wu was forced to sell his interests in Sun Tong Chong, most likely because of the economic depression gripping the entire country. He found work doing odd jobs in restaurants and laundries but was unable to find full-time, gainful employment. With no interest in a mercantile firm, Wu lost his merchant's status and placed at risk both his own and his wife's rights to remain in the United States. On September 17, 1932, immigration officials issued a warrant for the arrest of both Wu and Ngoon. The warrant charged the couple with remaining in the country after failing to maintain the exempt status under which they were admitted and thus violating the Immigration Act of 1924.[35]

The couple took matters into their own hands. Apparently aware of the government's intentions beforehand, they hurriedly left their home in Oakland just a few days before Immigrant Inspector E. C. Benson arrived with an arrest warrant. Benson pursued the couple, attempting to track them down through the U.S. postal system and the California Department of Motor Vehicles. Benson drove northward to Napa and Yountville, California, in an attempt to find them but had no success. Meanwhile, instead of succumbing to the wrath of the Immigration and Naturalization Service (INS), Ngoon and Wu began a fugitive life underground, moving from place to place, keeping their locations secret from all but a few trusted relatives and friends. They never stayed in one location for very long. A frustrated Inspector Benson concluded his March 1933 report with this warning: "Every effort will be made to locate Wu Wah and his wife, Ngoon Shee, and in the event this office should locate this woman, she will be immediately taken into custody."[36] Ngoon remained insistent in her right to remain in the country and stayed one step ahead of immigration officials. One year later, she and her husband were still missing. District director Edward L. Haff responded by sending out a request to all local police departments that they apprehend the suspects. The notice featured the warrant of arrest and photographs of both Ngoon and Wu.[37]

The couple continued to elude arrest for five years. Finally, in July 1937, the persistent Inspector Benson received information leading him to Ngoon and Wu.[38] On July 22, 1937, Benson went to Seventh Street in Oakland to serve Ngoon with the long-awaited arrest warrant. He found his prisoner-to-be in fragile condition, suffering from complications due to childbirth. Her doctor convinced Benson to return another day, and one week later, the inspector successfully served the warrant. A $500 bond was placed on Ngoon until her appearance before the Bureau of Immigration.[39] In September, husband and wife were interrogated concerning their right to remain in the country. They automatically challenged the government's case to deport Ngoon Shee and hired attorney W. H. Wilkinson, a former law officer in the Bureau of Immigration. Wilkinson shrewdly countered the government's claims by pointing to both legal precedent and the service's own regulations which nullified the charges in this case. He first pointed to a 1933 case in which the Northern California Circuit Court of Appeals had ruled against the deportation of a merchant's son following his father's change in status. The court chastised the "absurdities and hardships" of a rule of law that required deportation of the "hapless" and perchance "helpless" family of a merchant who, "because of illness, mishap, economic condition, or other misfortune," has been compelled to change his employment as a merchant and seek other employment.[40] Later in 1933, the Bureau of Immigration eliminated its rule that Chinese must maintain their exempt status in order to remain in the country.[41] These rulings should have provided legal protection to individuals like Ngoon Shee. Nevertheless, she became caught up in a larger government assault on Chinese Americans that ignored not only the immigration service's own regulations, but also a federal court ruling. In October 1937, Ngoon Shee's deportation case was finally closed, five years after it had first been filed.[42] She and Wu Wah had lived through years of hardship imposed by the INS, but they had refused to give up their rights to remain in the country with their American-born children. In the end, they emerged victorious and on the right side of the law.

Conclusion

The Chinese exclusion laws created an unequal environment that affected all Chinese immigrants, but Chinese women were vulnerable to the race, class, and gender biases explicit in the laws in ways that their male counterparts were not. The laws attacked the women along all three lines and created and reinforced unequal immigration patterns. The harsh realities of life under exclusion cast a long shadow over the lives of Ngoon Shee, Lau Dai Moy, my grandmother, and countless others. The U.S. government's efforts to control the immigration of Chinese prostitutes placed all Chinese women under suspicion and had long-term consequences. Chinese women's dependent immigration status, reinforced and institutionalized by exclusion, affected both their opportunities to immigrate and their abilities to remain in the country.

Contrary to popular stereotypes, Chinese women were not passive victims. Instead, they were active agents. Merchant wives used their class status and bound feet as tools to facilitate their admission into the country. Others, like Ngoon Shee, refused to give up even under the most daunting circumstances. Even my grandmother, whose opportunity to come to the United States had been taken away, eventually managed to immigrate and raise a family in America. In her last years, she finally broke her silence. Perhaps believing that she no longer needed protection from the past, she found power and comfort through telling.

NOTES

1. Act of May 6, 1882, 22 Stat. 58.

2. U.S. Bureau of Immigration, *Annual Report of the Commissioner-General of Immigration* (Washington, D.C., 1903), 32 (hereafter cited as U.S. Bureau of Immigration, *Annual Report*).

3. Pre–Exclusion era statistics taken from Judy Yung, *Unbound Feet: A Social History of Chinese Women in San Francisco* (Berkeley: University of California Press, 1995), 22. The figure for the Exclusion era includes immigrants only from 1882 to 1891 and immigrants and returning citizens from 1894 to 1940. Statistics for the years 1892–1893 and 1941–1943 are not available. U.S. Bureau of Immigration, *Annual Reports* (1898–1943); Helen Chen, "Chinese Immigration into the United States: An Analysis of Changes in Immigration Policies" (Ph.D. diss., Brandeis University, 1980), 181; Fu-ju Liu, "A Comparative Demographic Study of Native-born and Foreign-born Chinese Populations in the United States" (Ph.D. diss., University of Michigan, 1953), 223.

4. U.S. government statistics for Chinese immigrant admissions are highly inconsistent. When categorizing by sex, the U.S. Bureau of Immigration recorded 127,012 total Chinese immigrants (9,868 Chinese women) admitted during 1882–1943. When categorizing by immigration status, the Bureau recorded the total number of Chinese admitted for the same period as 422,908. From 1910 to 1924, when the number of Chinese immigrants were broken down by both sex and immigration status, Chinese immigrant women averaged 9.4 percent of the total Chinese immigrant pool. Based on these calculations, the actual number of Chinese immigrant women who entered during the Exclusion era was probably closer to forty thousand. See tables titled "Immigrants Admitted" and "Summary of Chinese Seeking Admission to the U.S." in U.S. Bureau of Immigration, *Annual Reports* (1898–1943); H. Chen, "Chinese Immigration," 201, 181.

5. Moy Dong Kee, File 14/643, and Moy Shai Quong, File 13/322, Chinese Arrival Files, RG 85, Records of the U.S. I.N.S., New York, RG 85, National Archives—Northeast Region, New York; Moy Wah Chung, File 35100/177, Chinese Arrival Files, Records of the U.S. I.N.S., Seattle, RG 85, National Archives—Pacific Alaska Region, Seattle, Washington (hereafter cited as Chinese Arrival Files).

6. Interview with Gladys Huie, Sept. 9, 1993.

7. Sucheng Chan, "The Exclusion of Chinese Women, 1870–1943," in Sucheng Chan, ed., *Entry Denied: Exclusion and the Chinese in America* (Philadelphia: Temple University Press, 1991), 95, 97; Yung, *Unbound Feet*, 18–24. Adam McKeown offers a different perspective in "Transnational Chinese Families," *Journal of American Ethnic History* 18:2 (Winter 1999): 74, 78, 83, and in *Chinese Migrant Networks and Cultural Change: Peru, Chicago, Hawaii, 1900–1936.* (Chicago: University of Chicago Press, 2001), 30–32. On Chinese exclusion's impact on U.S. immigration law in general, see Lucy Salyer, *Laws Harsh as Tigers: Chinese Immigrants and the Making of Modern Immigration Law* (Chapel Hill: University of North Carolina Press, 1995).

8. See also Jennifer Gee (chapter 5) and Judy Yung (chapter 7) in this book.

9. Lisa Lowe, *Immigrant Acts: On Asian American Cultural Politics* (Durham: Duke University Press, 1996), 9. See also Judy Yung, *Unbound Voices: A Documentary History of Chinese Women in San Francisco* (Berkeley: University of California Press, 1999).

10. Robert Lee, *Orientals—Asian Americans in Popular Culture* (Philadelphia: Temple University, 1999), 88–89; George A. Peffer, *If They Don't Bring Their Women Here: Chinese Female Immigration before Exclusion* (Urbana and Chicago: University of Illinois Press, 1999), 28–42; Peggy Pascoe, *Relations of Rescue: The Search for Female Moral Authority in the American West, 1874–1939* (New York: Oxford University Press, 1990), 14.

11. Act of March 3, 1875, 18 Stat. 477.

12. John Wise, Collector of Customs, to W. F. Thompson, Feb. 26, 1895, "General Correspondence from the Office of Collector of Customs," RG 36, Records of the U.S. Bureau of Customs, Port of San Francisco, National Archives—Pacific Region (hereafter "General Correspondence").

13. John Wise, Collector of Customs, to R. R. Swain, Esq., Feb. 14, 1895, in "General Correspondence."

14. Lau Dai Moy, July 17, 1917, File 16327/3-3, Chinese Arrival Files, San Francisco, National Archives—Pacific Region.

15. Wen-hsien Chen, "Chinese Immigration under Both Exclusion and Immigration Laws" (Ph.D. diss., University of Chicago, 1940), 201.

16. Leong Cum, 5-12-84/*SS Oceanic*, Chinese Arrival Files, San Francisco, National Archives—Pacific Region.

17. W. Chen, "Chinese Immigration," 201.

18. Interview with Mary Lee, Feb. 20, 1990.

19. John P. Jackson to the Secretary of the Treasury, March 30, 1899, File 53108/9-B, Subject Correspondence, RG 85, Records of the U.S. I.N.S., National Archives, Washington, D.C.

20. Jow Ah Yeong, File 10-23-85/180, Chinese Arrival Files, National Archives—Pacific Region.

21. File 4098, Oct. 15, 1901, Chinese Segregated Records, Chinese General Correspondence, RG 85, Records of the U.S. I.N.S., National Archives, Washington, D.C.

22. Oscar Greenhalg to Walter S. Chance, March 11, 1899, File 52730/84, Subject Correspondence, RG 85, Records of the U.S. I.N.S., National Archives, Washington, D.C.

23. *Ex parte Chin King; Ex parte Chan San Hee*, 35 Federal Reporter 354 (C.C. D. Ore. 1888); *In re Chung Toy Ho and Wong Choy Sin*, 42 F. 398 (D. Ore. 1890); Chan, "Exclusion of Chinese Women," 114–20.

24. In 1910, 344 Chinese women were admitted. In 1924, 1,284 women were admitted. See U.S. Bureau of Immigration, *Annual Reports* (1910, 1924).

25. Liu, "A Comparative Demographic Study," 233; H. Chen, "Chinese Immigration into the United States," 201.

26. McKeown, "Transnational Chinese Families," 74, 78.

27. U.S. Bureau of Immigration, *Annual Report* (1910–1924).

28. Chan, "Exclusion of Chinese Women," 114.

29. U.S. Bureau of Immigration, *Annual Report* (1925), 23.

30. On the gendered character of U.S. immigration law in general, see Donna Gabaccia, *From the Other Side—Women, Gender, and Immigrant Life in the U.S., 1820–1990* (Bloomington: Indiana University Press, 1994), 26.

31. The case continued in 1916. See Donaldina Cameron to Commission of Immigration, Jan. 26, 1916, File 14894/2-2, Chinese Arrival Files, San Francisco, National Archives—Pacific Region.

32. E. J. Sims to I.N.S. District Director, April 21, 1942, File 38813/7-16, Chinese Arrival Files, San Francisco, National Archives—Pacific Region.

33. Act of Sept. 22, 1922 (42 Stat. 1021); Chan, "Exclusion of Chinese Women," 128–29.

34. Section 15, Immigration Act of 1924, 43 Stat. 153, Rule 18, "Maintenance of Status," U.S. Department of Labor, *Treaty, Laws, and Rules Governing the Admission of Chinese*, Rules of October 1, 1926 (Washington, D.C.: Government Printing Office, 1926), 75; W. Chen, "Chinese Immigration," 236.

35. E. C. Benson, Immigrant Inspector to Commissioner, Oct. 17, 1932, File 12020/21693, Chinese Departure Files, San Francisco, RG 85, Records of the U.S. I.N.S., National Archives—Pacific Region (hereafter Chinese Departure Files).

36. E. C. Benson to Commissioner, March 17, 1933, File 12020/21693, Chinese Departure Files.

37. Edward L. Haff, "Request to Apprehend," April 11, 1934, File 12020/21693, Chinese Departure Files.

38. The record does not indicate how Benson finally tracked down the couple, but it appears the lead was related to news of the birth of their sixth child in 1937. E. C. Benson to District Director, July 29, 1937, File 12020/21693, Chinese Departure Files.

39. Ibid. Interestingly, Benson appears to have taken pity on the couple and recommended that the bond be reduced from its normal $3,000 to a more reasonable $500.

40. *Haff v. Yung Poy*, 68 Federal Reporter (2d series) 203 (9th Cir. 1933), as cited in "Brief for Defendant *In re Ngoon Shee*," Sept. 20, 1937, File 12020/21693, Chinese Departure Files.

41. Order No. 22, Nov. 8, 1933, "Chinese General Orders," File 55853/354, Records of the U.S. I.N.S., I.N.S. History Office, Washington, D.C. My thanks to Marian Smith, I.N.S. historian, for access to this file.

42. W. W. Brown to District Director, Oct. 22, 1927, File 12020/21693, Chinese Departure Files.

5

Housewives, Men's Villages, and Sexual Respectability
Gender and the Interrogation of Asian Women at the Angel Island Immigration Station

Jennifer Gee

When Matsuho Tsune arrived at the Angel Island immigration station in 1910, she confronted a brief but pointed interrogation about her intended role as a married woman in America. Matsuho had worked as a schoolteacher in Japan, but she asserted that she now intended to perform "simply household duties." Deemed a housewife joining a husband who could support her financially, Matsuho gained entry the next day.[1] Chinese immigrant Lee Shee, arriving in 1914, encountered numerous questions designed to ensure that she was the wife of a U.S. resident merchant. Her interrogation, which included minute details about her husband's village in China, proved more difficult than the interrogations typically faced by her male counterparts. At the end of her examination, Lee's identity as a merchant's wife was confirmed by the lack of discrepancies between her testimony and that of her husband as well as by her appearance as a "respectable" woman.[2]

Matsuho and Lee claimed different countries of origin, spoke different languages, and were categorized under distinct U.S. government immigration regulations. At the Angel Island immigration station, however, their experiences merged. Both women's eligibility for entry was influenced profoundly by prevailing standards of women's proper roles and behavior in early twentieth-century American society.

Matsuho and Lee arrived at the Angel Island immigration station during the initial years of its operation. Established in 1910, the station served as a major site of immigrant screening on the West Coast of the United States until its destruction by a fire in 1940. For thirty years, the station functioned as a detention and interrogation center for immigrants of various national origins, including individuals from China, Japan, Korea, and India. Upon docking in San Francisco, arriving immigrants took a ferry to Angel Island. There, each immigrant underwent interrogations by two immigration inspectors. An interpreter translated questions and responses, while a stenographer recorded the exchange. At the end of the interrogations, the inspectors decided whether to admit or deny entry to the applicant.

Studies of the Angel Island immigration station have provided important insights on the establishment of the station and the living conditions faced by detained immigrants. In particular, the discovery in 1970 of Chinese poetry etched on barrack walls has inspired a focus on the experiences of Chinese immigrants at the station. These studies, drawing from barrack poetry translations and oral histories, portray the station as a site of anti-Chinese racial discrimination.[3] This chapter examines transcripts of immigrant interrogations conducted at Angel Island in order to investigate the actual process of immigrant screening. Such an approach sheds light on the specific way in which immigration officials questioned, evaluated, and made the critical decisions to admit or exclude arriving immigrants.

The interrogation transcripts of Asian immigrants of Chinese as well as non-Chinese national origin reveal that race was one of many overlapping concerns and ideologies used to screen new arrivals.[4] Foremost among these was the infusion of gender into the interrogation process. The enforcement of the 1882 Chinese Exclusion Act and the 1907–1908 Gentlemen's Agreement with Japan (discussed below), for example, brought differential treatment to Asian immigrant women and men. Central to immigration officials' decisions to admit or exclude Japanese and Chinese women were concerns about women's labor, domesticity, identities, and sexual morality. The history of the Angel Island immigration station cannot be encapsulated as a gender-neutral "Asian" or "Chinese" experience, for early twentieth-century immigration restriction represented far more than a racial story.[5]

Women Going to Men: Picture Brides, 1910–1920

Inspector Clendenin: Where and to whom are you going?
Nagao Fusako: To my husband, in Salinas, California.
Inspector: Where and how did you marry him?
Nagao: In November, 1911, by photograph.

. . .

Inspector: What do you expect to do in the United States, if admitted?
Nagao: Keep house for my husband.

. . .

Inspector (to husband, Nagao Sakaichi): If this woman is admitted, to be your wife, what do you intend she shall do in the United States?
Nagao: Keep house for me, as my wife.
—Hearing of picture bride Nagao Fusako, Angel Island, 1913[6]

From 1910 to 1920, thousands of Japanese women immigrated to the United States as picture brides.[7] An adaptation of traditional arranged marriage, the picture bride practice arose as one of the ways in which Japanese immigrant men in America married women in Japan. In Japanese arranged marriages, heads of households used intermediaries to choose marriage partners for children or other family members. Pictures were sometimes viewed by negotiating parties during the selection process. In the picture bride system, these photographs were exchanged across the Pacific Ocean. Once both families agreed to the marriage, the wedding ceremony was held in Japan without the presence of the groom. Since Japanese marriages became legal once brides' names were entered into husbands' family registries, Japanese immigrant men did not technically need to be present for the marriage to occur.[8] The Japanese government sanctioned the practice by granting passports to picture brides joining husbands in the United States.

Japanese women who chose to emigrate as picture brides had a variety of motivations for doing so. Some agreed to marriages out of duty to their parents, who had arranged the union. Others sought to aid their families economically by immigrating and sending money back home. Another economic motive was simply escaping poverty. In these cases, traveling overseas to join husbands provided a means for women to secure basic sustenance.[9]

Japanese immigrants' entry was governed by the Gentlemen's Agreement of 1907–1908. The diplomatic agreement between Japan and the United States excluded Japanese laborers but allowed the entry of nonlaborer men and the wives, children, and parents of immigrant men residing in America. These exempted individuals were granted passports by the Japanese government.[10] Although the possession of passports technically sanctioned immigrants' admission, immigration officials imposed their own screening process at Angel Island. If officials found that Japanese immigrants otherwise violated U.S. immigration laws, they could be excluded despite their possession of passports.

In this process of admission and exclusion, gender sharply differentiated picture brides' experiences from those of Japanese immigrant men. Dominant assumptions about women's proper roles in the household were central to their interrogations. Picture brides were frequently asked what type of work they intended to perform if admitted. Like Nagao Fusako, most women responded that they planned to "keep house." Other picture brides stated that they would perform "household duties" or claimed their former occupations in Japan as "housewives" or "helping at home."[11] Husbands who met their wives at Angel Island were also questioned about the roles their new wives would assume in their households. Most gave the same answers as their wives: the husband of Kuranaga Kitsu stated, for example, "She will cook at home for me—housework."[12] Picture brides who claimed that they planned to do housework were readily admitted by immigration officials at Angel Island; they did not face follow-up questions or harassment for their answers, nor were they ever excluded on that basis. Officials accepted housework as the normative function of Japanese immigrant wives, granting entry to picture brides according to their own assumptions about married women's roles in the household.

Immigration officials' approval of housewives' entry supported the class biases of the Gentlemen's Agreement, which targeted laborers for exclusion. When Japanese immigrant women stated that they were housewives, they not only invoked a gendered division of labor but implied a particular class status as well. Housewives, for example, were married to men who could afford to support their wives and families with their incomes alone. Laborers' wives, by contrast, needed to engage in paid labor outside the home and thus could not claim the status of housewife. The ideal of female domesticity had been critical to bourgeois class identity among white Americans since the nineteenth century.[13] That immigration officials so readily admitted picture bride housewives suggests their adoption of these gendered definitions of class; by granting entry to housewives, they attempted to admit members of nonlaboring classes.

While the questioning of picture brides' intended roles reinforced the anti-laborer provision of the Gentlemen's Agreement, immigration officials demonstrated little interest in picture brides' work or class status before their marriage. In fact, many picture brides stated that they had worked as "farm laborers" when asked their occupation in Japan.[14] Their current status as housewives for their new husbands automatically placed them in the nonlaborer category, regardless of their past laborer status. In this way, picture brides' interrogation experiences at Angel Island contrasted with those of Asian immigrant men. Chinese, Japanese, Korean, and South Asian men who claimed that they had worked as laborers in Asia or the United States often faced intense questioning, harassment, and ultimate exclusion as laborers in violation of various immigration laws. That officials disregarded picture brides' past status as laborers made their interrogations more lenient than those faced by their male counterparts.

Picture brides' interrogations were also easier because they were not generally considered eligible for exclusion as "likely to become a public charge," or LPC. Unlike Japanese, Korean, and South Asian men, who frequently faced aggressive questioning and exclusion under the terms of the 1882 class-based law, picture brides did not encounter interrogations focusing on their ability to support themselves financially.[15] Their statements that they intended to perform a nonremunerative occupation as housewives were accepted without comment by immigration officials. Although officials' view of picture brides as housewives in some ways made women's interrogations more lenient than those faced by men, such a gendered view of picture brides also made them vulnerable to exclusion. Since picture brides were considered economically dependent on the men they were joining, their admission was premised almost exclusively on their husbands' status and testimony rather than their own. Picture brides could in fact be excluded as "likely to become a public charge" if their husbands were determined unable to support them financially.[16] Because of this, picture brides lacked control over their entry in that their own status, skills, and testimony had little bearing on the final decision. Women's admission ultimately depended on the testimony of men.

Husbands meeting picture brides at Angel Island faced interrogations that targeted their financial status. Since immigration officials assumed that husbands would be the sole economic providers for their new wives, Japanese men needed to prove that they would not allow themselves and their wives to become public charges. When picture bride Kadota Tsurumi arrived at Angel Island in 1910, for example, her husband was asked his occupation, what evidence he could present to prove his occupation, whether he possessed a bank account, and whether he had brought any money with him. After Kadota's husband presented his municipal and state licenses for his employment agency in San Francisco and showed two hundred dollars in cash, Kadota gained entry. Immigration inspector J. X. Strand's summary of the case demonstrates the significance of Kadota's husband's financial status, while highlighting Kadota's assumed economic dependency. Strand concluded that Kadota was admissible "from the evidence of her husband being a business man and able to support his wife."[17] Kadota's case reveals the way in which Japanese picture brides' categorization as dependent housewives made their entry dependent on their husbands as well.

Picture brides also faced the possibility of exclusion if their husbands could not prove their prior lawful admission. Officials reasoned that if a Japanese immigrant man had entered the country illegally, then he should be deported. This would result in his wife becoming a public charge, since she was a housewife wholly dependent on him for financial support. Again, officials' assumptions about married women's dependency meant that picture brides' entry would be determined by their husbands' status. When Nakamura Kiyoye arrived at Angel Island in 1919, her husband, Nakamura Toragusu, faced a series of questions about his own immigration. Nakamura was asked, for example, whether he underwent an examination when he arrived in San Francisco in 1904. He replied, "Only the sick ones were taken off; all the rest of us were allowed to go." At the end of the interrogation, Nakamura Kiyoye was informed that since her husband did not present documentation proving his legal admission, nor could officials find records of his entry in 1904, she could not enter the United States. Being "totally dependent upon him for support," Nakamura was excluded as "likely to become a public charge."[18]

Immigration officials' efforts to screen picture brides according to white middle-class ideals of domesticity did not result in the entry of Japanese housewives confined to unpaid work inside the home. As immigrant wives in America, picture brides worked at labor camps as cooks and laundresses for large numbers of male laborers; farmed alongside their husbands; ran family-owned laundries, boardinghouses, and restaurants; and worked as domestic laborers for white American families. Women did indeed perform the housework that they told immigration officials they intended to do, but they balanced work in the household and child rearing with labor outside their homes.[19]

The contrast between Japanese picture brides' labor in the United States and their statements at Angel Island that they would be housewives suggests that picture brides and their husbands understood the interrogation process and its requirements for entry. While some women may not have anticipated the type of labor they would perform in America, the frequency of the "housewife" response indicates that picture brides did know that describing themselves as future laborers would not assist their cases. Claiming they were housewives conformed to immigration officials' assumptions about women's domestic roles, while releasing them from the requirement of demonstrating their own financial stability. While this generally made picture brides' interrogations more lenient than those faced by their male counterparts, the accompanying assumption of absolute economic dependency also made them vulnerable to exclusion. Picture brides' roles as workers both inside and outside their homes once they landed demonstrates that their screening had more basis in gender ideology than in the reality of immigrant labor.[20]

Comparative Disadvantage: Chinese Wives, 1910–1940

Inspector Strand: How long did you live in Wong village after marriage?
Jee Shee: Between one and two months.
Inspector: What house did you live in in Wong village?
Jee: 5th row, 7th house.

Inspector: Who lived in the 8th house on that row?

Jee: Chun Mun Ying.

Inspector: Is he married?

Jee: Yes.

Inspector: What kind of feet has his wife?

Jee: Bound feet.[21]

Inspector: How many children has she?

Jee: One boy, no girl.

Inspector: Who lives in the 6th house, your row?

Jee: Gee Wing.

Inspector: What kind of feet has his wife?

Jee: Bound feet.

Inspector: How many children has she?

Jee: Two boys, no girl.

—Hearing of Jee Shee, wife of a Chinese merchant, Angel Island, 1911[22]

Like Japanese picture brides, the majority of Chinese immigrant women arriving at Angel Island were married to U.S. resident husbands. Most joined husbands who had previously immigrated to the United States or came with husbands who had returned to China from America in order to marry. As in the case of Japanese women, Chinese women emigrated for various reasons. Many sought to escape poverty and planned to send money home to help their families survive economically. Such decisions were often reinforced by women's sense of familial duty, as parents sometimes arranged marriages for daughters during times of economic hardship. In addition, some women saw emigration as an opportunity for education.[23]

Chinese immigrant women's entry into the United States was governed by "derivative status." Although the Chinese Exclusion Act of 1882 did not specify women's eligibility for entry, the federal courts ruled that women's immigration status derived from that of their husbands.[24] Thus, because the exclusion act barred the entry of Chinese laborers, wives of laborers were also excluded. Likewise, merchants, as members of an exempted category in the law, were legally entitled to summon wives from China.[25] That Chinese wives of merchants were defined as admissible by immigration law and the federal courts did not necessarily translate into lenient interrogations and easy entry. As in the case of Chinese immigrant men who were merchants, sons of merchants, or returning U.S. citizens, exempted Chinese women often faced grueling interrogations, verbal harassment, and long detentions. But Chinese women's status as women made their experiences at Angel Island distinct from those of Chinese immigrant men. Like Japanese picture brides, Chinese women encountered an immigration process differentiated by gender. Gender, however, played a unique role in the interrogations of Chinese women.

Although most Chinese women arrived at Angel Island as wives of resident men, they were not treated primarily as women going to men. Unlike picture brides, Chinese women did not face interrogations that focused on their roles as housewives dependent on the men they were joining. Rather, the main concern in Chinese women's interrogations, as in those of Chinese men, was proving the veracity of their identity. The focus on Chinese immigrants' identity in Angel Island interrogations stemmed largely from the terms of the Chinese Exclusion Act and its interpretation by the courts. Although nonlaborers such as students and merchants were required to carry Chinese government certificates proving their identities and exempted status, family members of exempted merchants and U.S. citizens carried no official documentation.[26] Immigration officials held responsibility for determining whether arriving wives, daughters, and sons truly were who they claimed to be. By contrast, Japanese wives, children, and parents of U.S. residents arrived with Japanese government passports confirming their identities and eligibility for entry. Because of this, officials did not typically concern themselves with Japanese immigrants' identities, focusing instead on other excludable categories such as LPC.[27]

The enforcement of the Chinese Exclusion Act thus meant the thorough examination of arriving immigrants' identities. As in the case of Chinese men, Chinese women's testimonies about their families, villages, and other details were compared to those of family members, neighbors, and other witnesses. If discrepancies in these testimonies arose, officials could argue that the immigrant had assumed a false identity and thereby deny her admission. Both women and men underwent this rigorous process, but women were placed at a distinct disadvantage due to the gender bias embedded in immigration officials' method of identity testing: the excessively detailed questions encountered by Chinese immigrants emphasized the families and villages of men. Whereas Chinese men faced interrogations on their own families and villages, Chinese women were expected to answer the same questions about the relatives, neighbors, local surroundings, and homes of their husbands. Wives' intimate knowledge of husbands' families and villages was unlikely since marriages usually occurred between women and men of different home villages. Women's acquaintance with their husbands' families and villages was based on the relatively short period of time that they lived with their husbands' families after marriage. Jee Shee, the merchant's wife who arrived in 1911, for example, had resided in her husband's village for less than two months.

Chinese immigrant women did face questions about their own families, but these questions were restricted to their parents, siblings, and children. Similarly, Chinese immigrant men encountered limited inquiries about their wives' siblings and parents.[28] By contrast, women faced numerous questions about their husbands' extended families. In a typical interrogation, Chinese immigrant Gin Shee was asked about her husband's parents, her husband's two brothers, and the brothers' wives and children at her interrogation in 1912. Specifically, officials required her to recite the names of each of the relatives, the ages of her husband's father and nephews, and the precise whereabouts of her husband's brothers.[29]

Questions about husbands' villages involved minute details about the number of houses in the village, the village layout, and village families. While these questions were extremely challenging for Chinese men who were born and raised in the village, they proved even more difficult for women who had moved there only after marriage. Typical interrogations consisted of detailed questions about markets, ancestral halls, schools, water wells, rivers, fish ponds, walls surrounding the village, and the various families residing in the village.[30] Some women faced verbal harassment by immigration officials if they could not recite these details. When Ng Shee failed to provide the names of all the members of a particular village family during her 1917 interrogation, immigration inspector W. Becktell questioned, "How do you happen to know that he lives in that house if you know nothing whatever about his family?" Later in the interrogation, Becktell warned, "You are advised that you must tell all you know about these people otherwise there might be discrepancies sufficiently great to cause us to decide that you are not the wife of Fong Yuen Chang." Ng did not passively accept Becktell's accusations: she asserted, "I am telling you what I know, I can't tell you more than I am telling you."[31] Clearly, officials expected Chinese women to "know" minute details about their husbands' villages, even amid some women's active protests that such expectations were unreasonable.

That women could not easily answer questions about their husbands' villages was due not only to the relatively short period of time they resided there. These questions were also biased against women because they ignored the different roles of women and men in the household. Women's work, for example, was typically more confined than men's to their homes and the immediate vicinity. Women raised children; cared for extended family members; performed domestic labor, such as cleaning and cooking; and engaged in spinning, weaving, and sewing to earn supplementary income for their households. Outside their homes, women fetched water, washed clothing, harvested crops, raised livestock, and gardened.[32] Because of the nature of their work, women may have been less likely to know details of the larger village, such as the village layout or distant neighbors. Ng Shee, for example, explained why she did not know the exact location of a villager's house by stating, "I don't know his house because I don't go out very much in the village."[33] Similarly, a woman named Chun Shee, who arrived in 1913, expressed the difficulty of recalling details about her husband's village. When asked about the size of the village, Chun responded, "I don't know; I stayed in the house most of the time."[34] In this way, the gendered questioning that Chinese women faced extended beyond a focus on the villages of men. Interrogations also emphasized particular aspects of villages that men were more likely to know. Ironically, while immigration officials rigidly defined Japanese picture brides as housewives, they disregarded the way in which Chinese women's assumption of similar roles impeded their ability to pass their interrogations. Officials were clearly more interested in women's future roles in America than in past gendered experiences.

The questioning of Chinese immigrant women was designed to determine whether they were in fact the exempted wives they claimed to be. Their interrogations, as in the evaluation of Japanese picture brides, served the larger class biases of immigration law. Because one of the main exempted categories for wives under the Chinese Exclusion Act was reserved for the wives of merchants, testing wives' identities became a means to ensure that only Chinese merchant families could reunite and reproduce in the United States. At the same time, difficult interrogations administered to Chinese women reinforced racial exclusion by constricting the loophole for exempted wives. Limiting the entry of wives impeded the growth of Chinese American communities through immigration and the birth of a second generation.

Enforcing the Chinese Exclusion Act in the case of Chinese immigrant women had an underlying gendered purpose as well. Verifying that women were wives was also a way of ensuring that they were not prostitutes. White Americans had associated

Chinese immigrant women with prostitution ever since Chinese prostitutes began arriving in California in the mid–nineteenth century. While merchants' wives were at least officially welcomed into the United States because of their class, marital, and supposed accompanying moral status, prostitutes were reviled as lower-class immoral women who were furthermore excluded formally by an immigration law passed in 1875. By interrogating Chinese immigrant wives so closely about their husbands' families and villages, officials sought to ensure that prostitutes were not using the loophole for merchants' wives in the Chinese Exclusion Act. In doing so, they made the interrogation process difficult even for "true" wives, who were expected to know minute details about their husbands' families and villages in order to prove their exempted status.

"Respectable Women": Sexuality in the Immigration Process

Assistant Commissioner Boyce: The applicant has been under your observation since Sept. 15. What has been your impression of her as to her respectability?

Mary E. Greene [Angel Island employee in charge of detained women]: She has been very nice and quiet.

Boyce: Has she behaved in a manner that might lead you to believe she was a respectable family woman?

Greene: Yes. Always.

. . .

Boyce (to Mr. Tang, Chinese interpreter): What is your idea of this woman?

Tang: She is a respectable woman all right.

—Interrogation of Angel Island employees regarding
Chinese woman Ng Shee, 1917[35]

Unlike Asian immigrant men, women encountered assessments of their sexual morality, which profoundly influenced immigration officials' decisions to admit or deport them.[36] The requirement of sexual respectability reflected contemporary racial ideology that defined Asian women as particularly inclined to immorality. Sexuality had been embedded in white Americans' conceptions of Asian women since the mid– to late nineteenth century. During this period, exaggerated stories about Chinese prostitutes in San Francisco appeared in local newspapers and other media. Chinese women, for example, were described as "reared to a life of shame from infancy" and became inextricably linked to prostitution with claims such as "not one virtuous Chinawoman has been brought to this country."[37] By the 1890s, definitions of sexual immorality became attached to Japanese immigrant women as well. One San Francisco newspaper asserted, "The women here are of the lowest class, and, like the Chinese women, are imported only to lead a life of shame."[38]

Attacks on Chinese and Japanese women's sexuality formed the ideological background for the legal exclusion of Asian women in the late nineteenth century. In 1875, the Page Law prohibited the entry of Chinese, Japanese, and "Mongolian" contract laborers, women for the purpose of prostitution, and felons. Although the Page Law did not significantly impact the immigration of men, it was enforced effectively against

Chinese women, all of whom were assumed to be prostitutes.[39] In the case of Japanese women, amendments to legislation in 1891 prohibited particular categories of immigrants, including prostitutes, contract laborers, and paupers. Along with the Japanese government's cooperation in screening potential emigrants who applied for passports, the legislation significantly reduced the immigration of Japanese women during the period.[40]

Angel Island immigration officials had several laws at their disposal that excluded prostitutes and other allegedly immoral persons. In addition to the Page Law, the 1910 White-Slave Traffic Act, aimed at European prostitutes, forbade the transportation "in interstate or foreign commerce" of "any woman or girl for the purpose of prostitution or debauchery, or for any other immoral purpose." Morality-based exclusion was further codified in the Immigration Act of 1917, which barred entry to "prostitutes, or persons coming into the United States for the purpose of prostitution or for any other immoral purpose."[41]

By citing Asian women's sexuality in order to exclude them from the United States, officials tightened further the restrictions of the Chinese Exclusion Act and the Gentlemen's Agreement, thereby reinforcing anti-Asian racial exclusion. When inspectors labeled Asian immigrant women immoral, they constricted the tiny loophole in both regulations that allowed the entry of the wives and daughters of merchants, citizens, and U.S. residents. To gain admission at Angel Island, women were not only expected to prove their identities as exempted wives or housewives of men with financial means; they were also required to pass a stringent and subjective evaluation of their sexuality. Sexuality was, in fact, connected to verifying exempted status as wives, since women's proof of wifely status was integrally tied to disproving they were prostitutes. Screening for sexual immorality also reinforced the class biases of the Chinese Exclusion Act and the Gentlemen's Agreement. Because prostitutes were assumed to belong to nonelite social and economic classes, immorality served as an indicator of lower-class status.

Immigration officials' evaluation of Asian women's sexuality did not always result in their exclusion. Many women who faced scrutiny of their sexuality were deemed respectable.[42] An examination of positive as well as negative assessments of Asian immigrant women's sexuality demonstrates the importance that officials placed on sexual morality as a precondition for women's admission. In the context of prevailing racial and gender ideologies that defined Asian women as particularly prone to immorality, official confirmations of their respectability were critical to justifying their entry.

Immigration officials used a variety of subjective indicators in screening Asian immigrant women according to standards of respectability. For example, they paid particular attention to women's past lifestyle and behavior. Kurita Ine, a Japanese woman interrogated in 1918, faced a series of questions about her behavior en route to Angel Island and as a single woman in Japan. In an effort to determine whether she was a procurer of prostitutes, officials asked Kurita if she "had any women friends on board" when she traveled to Angel Island. They then pursued a series of questions about the names of these women and how she knew them. She was also asked, "Did any women come on this boat in your care?" Kurita subsequently faced numerous questions about her behavior while she lived in Japan that implied sexual immorality: among these were "Did you ever live with any man without being married to him?"; "Were you ever a dancing girl in Japan?"; and "Did you ever work in a tea house?" Even Kurita's husband faced questions about his wife's past behavior: he was asked, for example, "Have you ever had any trouble with your wife, due to her paying attention to other men?"[43] The questions asked of Kurita and her husband demonstrate that officials were concerned with prostitution as well as a broader range of sexual behavior that they considered immoral. Immigration inspectors' concerns with whether Kurita had worked in a "tea house" or as a "dancing girl" mixed implications of sexuality with class status, paralleling conceptions of prostitution: such women were considered simultaneously immoral and of lower-class status because they worked outside the home.

In the case of Chinese immigrant Moy Shee, judgments of her behavior merged with officials' stereotypes about urban and rural environments. Although Moy was ultimately deemed respectable, the manner in which she testified apparently suggested otherwise. Inspector J. H. McCall explained, "The woman appears to me to have been of the respectable class, although she has an open and free manner which, in a Hong Kong woman, would suggest a lengthy examination."[44] Although Moy behaved in a so-called open and free manner during her interrogation, she passed immigration officials' test of respectability because she was *not* a "Hong Kong woman." In Moy's case, her rural origins transcended her allegedly sexually demonstrative "open and free" behavior.

Concerns about whether women lived in cities such as Hong Kong were similarly expressed in the case of Chin Shee, who arrived as a merchant's wife in 1915. Inspector J. B. Warner asked Chin's husband, "Has this woman to your knowledge ever been in Canton or Hongkong until she came to Hongkong to come to the United States?" When he answered, "No," Warner asked, "She is a country girl, is she?" Chin's husband responded affirmatively. In the end, Warner concluded that Chin possessed "the appearance of being a country woman" and was not entering "for an improper purpose."[45] Evidently, immigration officials associated cities such as Canton and Hong Kong with Chinese prostitutes and "country women" from rural areas with respectability. Women of apparently similar class origins faced differential judgments of their sexuality based on an urban-versus-rural divide.

But even status as "country girls" could not exempt women from the label of sexual immorality. Officials also considered linguistic clues during the interrogations. Chinese immigrant Loh Ah Lin encountered judgments of her sexuality based on the dialect she spoke. When she faced her interrogation in 1911, officials believed that she was a prostitute posing as the wife of a U.S. citizen. In reaching this decision, they cited discrepancies in testimony, the unorthodox documentation submitted by her husband, and the dialect Loh spoke. Immigration inspector H. Kennah stated, "The alleged husband speaks See Yup, while the applicant speaks Sam Yup, the dialect spoken by the majority of the Chinese slave girls in the United States."[46]

The subjectivity involved in determining women's sexuality based on dialect was illustrated clearly in immigration officials' assessment of Moy Shee. Officials not only evaluated Moy's behavior and rural status but also considered the dialect she spoke. However, the fact that Moy spoke the Sam Yup dialect brought a very different judgment: immigration inspector J. H. McCall concluded, "[the] applicant speaks the Sam Yup of the Gow Gong subdivision, which, I am informed by Dr. Gardener, is a dialect which suggests respectability."[47] Thus, while Loh Ah Lin faced exclusion because her

Sam Yup dialect apparently proved she was a "Chinese slave girl," Moy Shee received the label of respectability for speaking the same dialect. Immigration officials' focus on language indicates that they considered geography a marker of sexual morality. The subjectivity inherent in labeling an entire language group or geographic region as prone to immorality was compounded by the lack of agreement over which dialect made a woman suspect.[48]

Immigration officials apparently believed that sexual immorality in women was tangible and detectable. Regardless of which subjective methods officials used in evaluating women's sexuality, they displayed a heightened sensitivity to Asian immigrant women's potential status as immoral women. Dominant ideas about women's proper behavior, when combined with racial and gendered definitions of Asian women as distinctly immoral, made sexual respectability a particularly critical requirement for their admission into the United States.

Conclusion

Examining the Angel Island immigration station as a site of gendered gatekeeping highlights the centrality of gender to the overall project of immigrant processing. The history of the Angel Island immigration station was much more complicated than suggested by its common portrayal as a site of anti-Chinese racial exclusion. Immigration officials employed dramatically different standards in determining the admission of Asian women and men. Dominant ideas about women's domestic roles and women's proper behavior shaped the types of questions Asian women were asked as well as the final decisions on their entry. Gender ideology sometimes reinforced and sometimes undercut racial exclusion, resulting in a screening process that negotiated various complementary and competing concerns. Immigrant screening at Angel Island was designed ultimately to distinguish between the "desirable" and the "undesirable"; anti-Chinese sentiment constituted only part of this complex decision-making process.

A focus on the gendered nature of immigrant screening also reconceptualizes the history of Asian exclusion beyond its monolithic definition as a racial phenomenon. If Asian immigrants were judged according to gendered standards at Angel Island, then gender ideology also played a significant role in the exclusion of Asian immigrants from the United States. White middle-class ideas about female domesticity and morality, commonly viewed as unrelated to the history of Asian Americans, became major considerations in the enforcement of anti-Asian immigration regulations in the early twentieth century. Important aspects of the racial ideology underlying Asian exclusion were informed by gender as well. As demonstrated in the enforcement of women's sexual respectability at Angel Island, gendered concerns about women's sexuality intersected with race in the conception of Asian women as particularly, or racially, inclined to immorality.

Requiring that Asian immigrant women conform to prevailing standards of women's roles and behavior was part of a larger process of defining membership in early twentieth-century American society. Screening Asian immigrants according to racial, class, and gender ideologies paralleled contemporary efforts to "reform" immigrants and peoples of color. As an example, Americanization programs during the 1910s and 1920s sought to "uplift" Mexican immigrants in California by imposing domesticity on Mexican immigrant women.[49] Screening Asian women at Angel Island according to these same gendered standards mirrored Americanization programs in the emphasis on women's proper roles as a means of counteracting perceived racial inferiority. At the same time, both processes demanded sexual respectability of women of color who were defined by American society as racially prone to immorality. While "reforming" focused on imposing particular gender roles and behavior on women who already resided in the country, screening ensured that only those who conformed to the same gendered requirements could enter at all. The interrogation of Asian immigrant women at Angel Island according to specific gendered standards was no isolated historical incident. Rather, it represented an integral part of broader efforts to define just who merited membership in American society.

NOTES

I thank Leslie Berlin, Roberta Chavez, Martha Mabie Gardner, Gina Pitti, Judy Wu, and Gail Nomura for their helpful comments on this essay. I also thank Gordon Chang and Estelle Freedman for their critiques of earlier drafts.

1. Hearing of Matsuho Tsune, December 11, 1910, File 10443/6-1, Box 479, Immigration and Naturalization Service Arrival Investigation Case Files, Record Group 85, National Archives—Pacific Sierra Region (hereafter cited as INS AICF, RG 85, NA-PSR). The names of Asian immigrants such as Matsuho Tsune begin with surnames, followed by given names.

2. Letter from Inspector Phillip B. Jones to Commissioner of Immigration, April 23, 1914, File 13376/3-4, Box 790, INS AICF, RG 85, NA-PSR.

3. See Him Mark Lai, "Island of Immortals: Chinese Immigrants and the Angel Island Immigration Station," *California History* 57 (Spring 1978): 88–103; Him Mark Lai, Genny Lim, and Judy Yung, *Island: Poetry and History of Chinese Immigrants on Angel Island, 1910–1940* (San Francisco: HOCDOI Project, 1980; 2d ed., Seattle: University of Washington Press, 1993); Connie Young Yu, "Rediscovered Voices: Chinese Immigrants and Angel Island," *Amerasia Journal* 4 (1977): 123–39; Judy Yung, "'A Bowlful of Tears': Chinese Women Immigrants on Angel Island," *Frontiers* 2 (1977): 52–55; and Judy Yung, *Unbound Feet: A Social History of Chinese Women in San Francisco* (Berkeley: University of California Press, 1995), 63–68. See Judy Yung, chapter 7 in this book for an expanded oral history of a Chinese immigrant woman detained at Angel Island.

4. This study is drawn from a larger analysis of the interrogation transcripts of 411 Chinese, Japanese, Korean, and South Asian immigrants. The following analysis is based primarily on the interrogation transcripts of twenty-four Japanese and sixty-three Chinese women who were examined at the station. See Jennifer Gee, "Sifting the Arrivals: Asian Immigrants and the Angel Island Immigration Station, San Francisco, 1910–1940" (Ph.D. diss., Stanford University, 1999).

5. The gendered processing of Asian women was not necessarily designed to exclude them disproportionately. Rather, it ensured that women entering the United States conformed to specific definitions of gender roles and womanhood. An analysis of 169 Chinese and Japanese immigrant files showed similar admission rates for women and men. See Gee, "Sifting the Arrivals," 204–6.

6. Hearing of Nagao Fusako, February 26, 1913, File 12545/10-8, Box 669, INS AICF, RG 85, NA-PSR.

7. Although official statistics on picture brides are unavailable, some approximations exist: in 1920, Kanzaki Kiichi of the Japanese Association of America reported that between 1912 and 1919, 6,321 Japanese picture brides entered the United States through Seattle and San Francisco. Yuji Ichioka, "Amerika Nadeshiko: Japanese Immigrant Women in the United States, 1900–1924," *Pacific Historical Review* 44 (1980): 343.

8. Ichioka, "Amerika Nadeshiko," 342–43.

9. Ibid., 345–46.

10. The Japanese government imposed its own screening process on potential emigrants. For example, U.S. resident husbands needed to meet minimum employment, income, and savings requirements in order for their wives to secure passports. Laborers were ineligible to summon wives until 1915. Ibid., 344–45.

11. See Hearing of Nagao Fusako; Hearing of Kanemori Uta, January 9, 1911, File 10447.5/1-1, Box 491, INS AICF, RG 85, NA-PSR; Hearing of Nishikawa Nobo, December 4, 1914, File 13955/30-9, Box 866, INS AICF, RG 85, NA-PSR; and Hearing of Shimamura Chie, March 26, 1918, File 17031/4-1, Box 1220, INS AICF, RG 85, NA-PSR.

12. Hearing of Kuranaga Masayaki, April 5, 1919, File 18055/9-13, Box 1354, INS AICF, RG 85, NA-PSR.

13. See Alice Kessler-Harris, *Out to Work: A History of Wage-Earning Women in the United States* (New York: Oxford University Press, 1982), 49–72; Mary P. Ryan, *Cradle of the Middle Class: The Family in Oneida County, New York, 1790–1865* (New York: Cambridge University Press, 1981); and Christine Stansell, *City of Women: Sex and Class in New York, 1789–1860* (Urbana: University of Illinois Press, 1987).

14. See, for example, Hearing of Okamura Masayo, October 30, 1912, File 11316/13-27, Box 644, INS AICF, RG 85, NA-PSR.

15. The LPC law was one of the most frequently cited laws in the exclusion of Japanese, Korean, and South Asian male immigrants at Angel Island. See Gee, "Sifting the Arrivals," 52–53, 106–28.

16. In a sample of twenty-four Japanese women, two were denied entry for this reason. See Gee, "Sifting the Arrivals," 220. Definition as economic dependents, however, made all picture brides vulnerable to exclusion.

17. Hearing of Kadota Tsurumi, December 11, 1910, File 10443/7-3, Box 479, INS AICF, RG 85, NA-PSR. Husbands also presented a certificate from the Japanese consul attesting to their economic status. Those who worked as tenant farmers often brought copies of their leases as financial evidence.

18. Hearing of Nakamura Kiyoye, September 29, 1919, File 18549/9-2, Box 1378, INS AICF, RG 85, NA-PSR.

19. Ichioka, "Amerika Nadeshiko," 348–49. On Japanese immigrant women who worked as domestics, see Evelyn Nakano Glenn, *Issei, Nisei, War Bride: Three Generations of Japanese American Women in Domestic Service* (Philadelphia: Temple University Press, 1986). Valerie Matsumoto discusses the gendered division of labor in Japanese immigrant households in California's San Joaquin Valley; see Valerie J. Matsumoto, *Farming the Home Place: A Japanese American Community in California, 1919–1982* (Ithaca: Cornell University Press, 1993), 67.

20. Picture bride immigration spanned only a decade. Bowing to anti-Japanese sentiment in the United States, the Japanese government stopped issuing passports to picture brides in 1920.

21. Immigration inspectors used bound/unbound feet as an identifying characteristic of Chinese women in the interrogations of Chinese immigrants. Officials sometimes considered

bound feet an indicator of higher class status and accompanying womanly "virtue," both of which tended to influence officials favorably.

22. Hearing of Jee Shee, January 11, 1911, File 10448/2-8, Box 491, INS AICF, RG 85, NA-PSR. "Shee," which meant "from the family of," was common in the names of married Chinese immigrant women. In the case of Jee Shee, for example, Jee was her "maiden" surname, not her married surname.

23. Yung, *Unbound Feet*, 58–63. My paternal grandmother Hom Tiu Gok, who received very little formal education in China, stated that she hoped to go to school in the United States when she immigrated as a merchant's wife in 1935.

24. For a discussion of the court cases that determined how the Chinese Exclusion Act applied to women, see Sucheng Chan, "The Exclusion of Chinese Women, 1870–1943," in *Entry Denied: Exclusion and the Chinese Community in America, 1882–1943*, ed. Sucheng Chan (Philadelphia: Temple University Press, 1991), 94–146; and Lucy Salyer, "'Laws Harsh as Tigers': Enforcement of the Chinese Exclusion Laws, 1891–1924," in Chan, ed., *Entry Denied*, 61.

25. Chinese wives of U.S. citizens were also allowed entry until the passage of the Immigration Act of 1924, which barred the immigration of "aliens ineligible to citizenship." While the Supreme Court ruled in 1925 that wives of merchants would not be affected by the 1924 law because treaties with China allowed the entry of merchants, the court also concluded that wives of U.S. citizens were excludable as "aliens ineligible to citizenship." In 1930, after intense lobbying by Chinese Americans, Congress amended the Immigration Act of 1924 to grant entry to wives of citizens who had married prior to the enactment of the law. See Chan, "Exclusion of Chinese Women," 125–27.

26. The Supreme Court's ruling in 1900 that Chinese wives and children of exempted male immigrants possessed "derivative status" meant that they were not required to carry certificates. See Salyer, "Laws Harsh as Tigers," 61.

27. Officials' focus on Chinese immigrants' identities also stemmed from their awareness of the "paper son" system, in which arriving immigrants claimed false identities as the sons of exempted merchants and U.S. citizens. Contemporary racial stereotypes of Chinese immigrants as "deceptive" and "sneaky" further reinforced officials' suspicions.

28. See, for example, Hearing of Mok Shee, March 14, 1918, File 16995/29-1, Box 1219, INS AICF, RG 85, NA-PSR; and Hearing of Dea Shee, January 29, 1920, File 18814/6-12, Box 1408, INS AICF, RG 85, NA-PSR.

29. Hearing of Gin Shee, October 22, 1912, File 11297/15001, Box 644, INS AICF, RG 85, NA-PSR.

30. See, for example, Hearing of Moy Shee, October 21, 1912, File 11297/9040, Box 644, INS AICF, RG 85, NA-PSR; and Hearing of Wong Shee, September 8, 1920, File 19431/1-5, Box 1450, INS AICF, RG 85, NA-PSR.

31. Hearing of Ng Shee, September 24, 1917, File 16516/3-11, Box 1186, INS AICF, RG 85; NA-PSR.

32. Yung, *Unbound Feet*, 19–20.

33. Hearing of Ng Shee, September 25, 1917, File 16516/3-11, Box 1186, INS AICF, RG 85, NA-PSR.

34. Hearing of Chun Shee, October 14, 1913, File 12973/4-9, Box 735, INS AICF, RG 85, NA-PSR.

35. Hearing of Ng Shee, October 19, 1917, File 16516/3-11, Box 1186; INS AICF, RG 85, NA-PSR.

36. In a sample of 269 interrogation transcripts of Chinese, Japanese, Korean, and South

Asian men, none faced judgements of their sexuality by immigration officials. See Gee, "Sifting the Arrivals," 251–52.

37. Cited in Yung, *Unbound Feet*, 32.

38. *Bulletin*, May 4, 1892, cited in Yuji Ichioka, "Ameyuki-san: Japanese Prostitutes in Nineteenth-Century America," *Amerasia Journal* 4 (1977): 14.

39. George Anthony Peffer, "Forbidden Families: Emigration Experience of Chinese Women under the Page Law, 1875–1882," *Journal of American Ethnic History* 6 (1986): 28–46. See also Chan, "Exclusion of Chinese Women," 105–9.

40. Ichioka, "Ameyuki-san," 16.

41. U.S. Department of Justice, *Immigration and Nationality Laws and Regulations as of March 1, 1944* (Washington, D.C.: U.S. Government Printing Office, 1944), 70, 4.

42. In a sample of eighty-seven women, three were excluded for alleged sexual immorality. See Gee, "Sifting the Arrivals," 251–52.

43. Hearing of Kurita Ine, March 12, 1918, File 16995/7-7, Box 1219, INS AICF, RG 85, NA-PSR; Hearing of Kurita Takejiro, March 13, 1918, File 16995/7-7, Box 1219, INS AICF, RG 85, NA-PSR.

44. Letter from J. H. McCall to Commissioner of Immigration, October 23, 1912, File 11297/9040, Box 644, INS AICF, RG 85, NA-PSR.

45. Hearing of Ngai Ah Sing, February 10, 1915, File 14122/12-7, Box 884, INS AICF, RG 85, NA-PSR; Letter from J. B. Warner to Commissioner of Immigration, February 17, 1915, File 14122/12-7, Box 884, INS AICF, RG 85, NA-PSR.

46. Hearing of Loh Ah Lin, January 15, 1911, File 10448/2-11, Box 491, INS AICF, RG 85, NA-PSR.

47. Letter from J. H. McCall to Commissioner of Immigration, October 23, 1912, File 11297/9040, Box 644, INS AICF, RG 85, NA-PSR.

48. Existing scholarship does not label Chinese prostitutes as predominantly Sam Yup or Sze Yup speakers. Although some studies suggest that prostitutes were more likely from the Sze Yup region because of their class status, women's dialect could hardly have predicted whether they were prostitutes.

49. George J. Sanchez, "'Go After the Women': Americanization and the Mexican Immigrant Woman, 1915–1929," in *Unequal Sisters: A Multicultural Reader in U.S. Women's History*, ed. Vicki L. Ruiz and Ellen Carol DuBois, 2d ed. (New York: Routledge, 1994), 284–97.

6

Redefining the Boundaries of Traditional Gender Roles
Korean Picture Brides, Pioneer Korean Immigrant Women, and Their Benevolent Nationalism in Hawai'i

Lili M. Kim

In 1917 a petite, sixteen-year-old girl left her family in a small village in Kyoung Nam, Korea. With her long black hair neatly braided, she set off for Hawai'i, where she was to marry a Korean man whom she had never met but whose picture she had seen through a "go-between." She had heard that people "can collect money by rake" in America and hoped that her picture marriage would provide the opportunity to pursue wealth in Hawai'i. She survived the grueling fifteen-day journey by sea that nearly left her dead from seasickness and arrived on the shores of Honolulu, to be met by Kim Ja Soon,[1] her husband-to-be, who was all but unrecognizable from the picture he had sent her from his younger days. Nam Soo Young recalled, "When I see him, he was much older, an old man. I was surprised. He cheated his age ten years. He was twenty-five years older than I. 'How can I live with him?' I thought." Trying to buy herself time, she asked to postpone the wedding for one week, but to no avail. With tears running down her cheeks, Nam married her husband and was released from the Immigration Station of Honolulu as the wife of Kim Ja Soon.[2]

Nam was one of an estimated one thousand Korean picture brides who came to Hawai'i and the continental United States between 1910 and 1924.[3] The far-reaching influence of Korean picture brides on the future of the Korean community in Hawai'i is hard to exaggerate. Because sugar planters sought strong, healthy laborers, pioneer Korean immigrants to Hawai'i mostly consisted of single men in their twenties, and a few married men who came with their families. By coming to Hawai'i as prospective wives to Korean bachelor laborers, Korean picture brides solved the problem of the lack of marriageable Korean women in the early years of Korean immigration. Unlike the Chinese, who, due to the Chinese Exclusion Act of 1882, remained largely "single" in the early twentieth century, pioneer Korean immigrants were able to marry picture brides, start families, and create a thriving next generation of Korean Americans.[4]

Furthermore, Korean picture brides significantly shaped and contributed to the Korean independence movement in the United States during the crucial years of overseas Korean nationalism, after Japan's annexation of Korea in 1910. Unlike the small number of pioneer Korean women who came to Hawai'i with their husbands between 1903 and 1905, the picture brides had lived under Japanese colonial rule before coming to

Hawai'i. Their sorrow over losing Korea to Japan and their determination to see Korea liberated made them active community members against the backdrop of the thriving yet bitterly divided Korean independence movement in Hawai'i. Redefining the boundaries of traditional gender roles, Korean picture brides, together with the pioneer Korean immigrant women who came before them, contributed to the Korean independence movement in important and alternative ways. By demonstrating what I call benevolent nationalism—nationalism rendered through valuable social and economic services that focused on the good of the community and future of Korea—Korean picture brides and immigrant women expanded the scope of community activism and altered the contours of the Korean independence movement in Hawai'i. At the same time, their organizational activities to promote Korean patriotism and to preserve Korean culture expedited their Americanization process by challenging and crossing the boundaries of Korean traditional gender roles.

Korean Picture Brides Come to Hawai'i

The picture bride practice began after the United States and Japan reached the Gentlemen's Agreement of 1907, which stipulated that Japan would voluntarily cease issuing passports to all Japanese laborers coming to the United States. This restrictive agreement, however, allowed for the immigration of wives and children who wished to be united with their husbands and fathers in the United States. Unmarried Japanese laborers in Hawai'i also took advantage of this provision by sending for picture brides. With Japan's annexation of Korea in 1910, Koreans were considered Japanese nationals, and Korean laborers in Hawai'i could also bring wives and picture brides from Korea under the Gentlemen's Agreement Act of 1907. The Immigration Act of 1924 prohibited the immigration of anyone ineligible for citizenship and thus stopped virtually all Asian immigration to the United States, including that of Korean picture brides.

Single Korean men sent for picture brides not necessarily because they could not find other women to marry—although that was true in many cases—but mainly because they specifically wanted to marry a Korean woman. Julia Chang Chung spoke of her father's popularity as a prospective husband and son-in-law before marrying her mother, Do Yun Hong, a Korean picture bride:

> Neighborhood people with eligible daughters just wanted to marry their daughters off to my papa. There was this Portuguese man who wanted my papa to marry his nice-looking daughter. There was another Hawaiian family who had to have my papa as a son-in-law. And you couldn't find a better catch than Papa! He invited him for dinner, gave him this and that. He even said, "Marry my daughter, and I will give you a house and a lot." Papa said he wanted the house and the lot, but couldn't think of marrying anyone except a Korean girl.[5]

Like Chung's father, many single Korean men turned to the picture bride practice to find a Korean wife and start a family.

As one can imagine, a marriage agreement based on pictures with short self-descriptions on the back involved a good deal of courage on the part of Korean picture brides. Like Esther Kwon Arinaga's mother, many Korean picture brides were "willing to risk life with a total stranger in a new land, in exchange for the opportunity to further [their] education, escape Japanese domination, and pursue religious freedom."[6] Phyllis Ahn Dunn, who came to Hawai'i as a fourteen-year-old picture bride, recalled, "I begged my mother to let me go to Hawai'i—I was not afraid!"[7] As in the case of Nam Soo Young, inflated ideas about the kind of life available in Hawai'i prompted prospective picture brides to marry men they had never met and to make a new living in a place they had never been to.

For their part, Korean men used the deception that picture marriages allowed to allure prospective wives. Men often sent pictures from their younger days to conceal their actual age. They also tried to give an impression of wealth they did not have by renting a suit or taking a picture next to their boss's automobile. Invariably, then, a Korean picture bride's initial meeting with her husband-to-be was a devastating disappointment. Like Nam's husband, most men looked nothing like the picture. Their workers' clothing and dark tans from working in the sugar plantation fields all day gave away their poor economic standing.[8]

Going back to Korea, however, was not an option for picture brides for two reasons. First, although the prospective husband sent money for the bride's one-way passage to Hawai'i, he would not pay for her to back out of the marriage and go back to Korea; nor could he have afforded to do so. Second, as Nam explained, going back meant a life of unbearable shame in Korea: "I want to go home, but I could not go home too. Because if I go home, I only get big shame. People say that the girl went for marry to Hawai'i, but she come back. She sent back. That would be most shameful abuse for a girl."[9] The only way to stay in Hawai'i legally was to marry their prospective husbands, but some picture brides held out as long as they could:

> I'm so disappointed I cry for eight days and don't come out of my room. I don't eat nothing, but at midnight when everybody sleeps I sneak out to drink water, so I don't die.... But I knew that if I don't get married, I have to go back to Korea on the next ship. So on the ninth day I came out and married him. But I don't talk to him for three months. Later on, it was all right.[10]

Despite a disappointing beginning, many picture brides had happy marriages, with children who became very successful. But in some cases, husbands became abusive out of paranoia. Some husbands, afraid their new wives might run away, had them locked up before going to work each day. Other picture brides eventually divorced their husbands.[11]

Creating a precise profile of the picture brides is difficult, as accurate information on them is hard to come by and existing accounts conflict. Some scholars have maintained that the picture brides who came in the second wave of Korean immigration between 1910 and 1924 were "new women" who benefited from a modernization period during which Korean women received a formal education for the first time. Sharply contrasting with this view, other scholars have insisted that because of prevailing Confucian beliefs, the majority of the picture brides arrived in Hawai'i with very little formal education.[12]

Regardless of their educational level, Korean picture brides changed the traditional gender dynamics in Korean marriages, not only by working outside the home and contributing to the family finances but also by expanding their influence to the public sphere, actively serving in the Korean churches as teachers, Bible study leaders, and committee members. As Margaret Pai recalls in her family memoir, her mother, Hee Kyung Kwon, and other picture brides founded important church organizations, such as the Methodist Ladies Aid Society. Pai writes:

> At her church, she helped form the Methodist Ladies Aid Society, a powerful organization that provided a network of services reaching every Korean family in the community. Although the immigrants were all poor, so dedicated were the Society members that no family went without food or a roof over their heads (immigrant men often lost their jobs); a mother who became ill could depend on other mothers to help her; and a mother with a newborn baby did not have to rise from her bed until she was strong. All these services were rendered despite the fact that every woman was burdened with heavy responsibilities of her own.[13]

Through such community services, Korean women exerted their power outside the home, and their activities helped to form bonds with other women providing and receiving assistance.

Given the powerful role of Christianity in convincing Koreans to emigrate, churches were organized at a furious pace. Korean immigrants founded thirty-one churches and chapels in Hawai'i, and in California many new converts, nearly two-thirds of the Korean population, filled up twelve Korean churches. But more than willing acceptance of Christianity accounts for this rapid growth. Many Koreans saw conversion to Christianity as a way to expedite their Americanization, and the planters, in turn, encouraged them to become Christians in the hope that Christianized Koreans would make more dependable and diligent workers in the fields. To that end, Hawaiian missionaries openly supported Korean efforts to build and establish churches. Although Korean women held important positions in the church, they deferred to male dominance of leadership, unless they organized their own societies. Another public arena where Korean women could exert greater influence through separate, all-female organizations was in the independence movement.

Fractured Community: The Korean Independence Movement in Hawai'i

Away from the watchful eyes of their colonizers, Koreans in Hawai'i and the continental United States launched a full-scale independence movement and rallied for American support after the annexation of Korea by Japan in 1910. The dominant narrative of the Korean independence movement tells the story of bitter factions and rivalries among four prominent male leaders—Syngman Rhee, Kilsoo Haan, Chanho Ahn, and Youngman Pak.[14] Rhee emphasized gradual diplomatic efforts in Washington as the head of the Korean Commission. Pak believed military training was the key to fighting back Japanese aggression. Ahn, who was most active in California, firmly supported education as the most effective way to train and cultivate able Korean leaders. Haan, the leader of the Sino-Korean Peoples' League, to which only about one hundred Korean community members belonged, insisted on more radical tactics, namely, the support of revolutionaries in China who were engaged in a common fight against Japan and the sponsorship of espionage work to provide key military information to the United States.

Rhee was the focal point of the various leadership conflicts, and the most severe rivalry developed between Pak and Rhee. Pak came to Hawai'i in 1912 to become the editor of a local Korean newspaper, the *Korean National Herald*, the official organ of the Hawai'i Korean National Association. Invited by Pak to join him in creating a powerful Korean independence movement, Rhee arrived in Hawai'i at about the same time. Rhee had just completed his doctoral studies at Woodrow Wilson's Princeton University. Because of his education and connections to prominent U.S. officials, Rhee was regarded with deep respect and had a large, loyal following in Hawai'i.[15]

Although Pak and Rhee began as friends, they soon became archrivals. The first of many disagreements between Pak and Rhee began over a Korean language school they both hoped to establish. Pak wanted to build a high school, but Rhee wanted it to be a grade school where students would study not only Korean language and history but also other subjects such as English and science. Rhee won the battle for public approval, and Pak had to turn over the funds he had raised.

Clashing over strategies to restore Korean independence, Rhee and Pak fiercely competed for power and respect in the community and undermined each other's authority. When Pak successfully founded the Kundan, or military academy, in 1914, Rhee quickly maneuvered to curtail Pak's popularity by spreading rumors that Pak was a traitor. Not to be outdone, Pak and his supporters accused Rhee of mishandling the Korean National Association's finances.[16] Soon there were two irreconcilable factions within the Korean National Association in Hawai'i: supporters of Pak and of Rhee. Rhee and his followers formed their own organization, the Tongihoe (Comrade Society), as a separate faction within the Korean National Association. The Tongihoe eventually broke all ties with the Korean National Association in 1930. The split also reflected Korean regionalism: members of the Tongihoe were predominantly immigrants from the southern parts of Korea, and members of the Korean National Association were overwhelmingly northern Koreans.[17] The division between the two factions became even wider after Rhee's dispute with William Fry, the superintendent who oversaw the operation of the Korean Methodist Church. Rhee and his followers started a new place of worship that eventually became the Korean Christian Church. All but one of Rhee's followers left the Korean Methodist Church to join the Korean Christian Church.

The rivalry between the leaders deeply affected their followers and the overall progress of the movement. Reflecting on the tumultuous years of the Korean independence movement, Hazel Park Chung recalled, "When Dr. Rhee came here, he divided the Korean community."[18] This was an understatement, to be sure, for Korean people lost friendships, threw punches at each other, and ultimately hurt the cause of Korean liberation over whether one supported Rhee or not. Julia Chang Chung remembered,

"Whenever there were people from two opposite sides, there were verbal confrontations, and they would start hitting each other. Sometimes they would bring out the knife. When the police came, they would disperse."[19] Demonstrating the severity of the division, Rhee supporters, in extreme cases, would call anti-Rhee Korean members of the community "Japanese." To call a fellow Korean "not Korean" and "Japanese" was indeed one of the most serious insults to a Korean.[20]

Longing for Korea, Braving the New World:
Korean Women's Benevolent Nationalism

The hegemony of the male leaders' role in the current narrative of the Korean independence movement is understandable, for they did occupy the most visible and prominent positions vis-à-vis their interactions with U.S. officials, and effects of their bitter rivalry spared no corner of the deeply divided Korean communities. But as Shirley Hune has pointed out in her critique of current scholarship on Asian American history, male-dominated narratives and representations of Asian American communities view gender as "neutral or separate, at best" and, as a result, render Asian American women "invisible, misrepresented, or subsumed in Asian American history as if their experiences were simply coequal to men's lives, which they are not."[21] A closer examination of women's participation in the Korean independence movement, both at the leadership and grassroots levels, not only reveals Korean American women's accomplishments, but also different, gendered expressions of nationalism that utilized informal networks as well as formal associations. Thus, focusing on Korean American women's participation in and contributions to the Korean independence movement fundamentally alters our understanding of Korean American nationalism and how we historicize it. While by no means completely immune from the factional divisions in the larger community, Korean women in early immigration years contributed immeasurably to the Korean independence movement by providing services to the members of the Korean community in Hawai'i and fellow Koreans in Korea. Further promoting Korean unity and ethnic pride, they bridged the generational gap between the first and second generations.

Responding to unfolding political events in Korea, Korean picture brides and immigrant women mobilized to show their support for Korean independence efforts. Even before Japan took complete control over Korea in 1910, the first Korean women's organization in Hawai'i, the Korean Women's Association (Hankuk Buin Hoe), was formed in 1908 to teach children the Korean language.[22] The March 1 movement of 1919 in Korea directly prompted the formation of the most powerful women's independence organization in Hawai'i.

The March 1 movement, the most important and bloodiest independence effort in Japanese-occupied Korea, began with a peaceful march on March 1, 1919, by thirty-three patriots, who signed the Declaration of Korean Independence as a symbolic rejection of Japanese colonialism. When more than a million people joined the signers of the declaration in the march shouting, *"Teahan Toknip Manse"* (Long live Korean independence), the Japanese law enforcement reacted with ruthless force and brutality. All told, in the following few months of similar, reoccurring protests, over seventy-five hundred Koreans were killed, fifteen thousand injured, and some forty-five thousand people were arrested. During that time, an independent Korean provisional government was erected in Shanghai, later moved to Chungking, and continued to exist in exile.[23]

Inspired by the heroic acts of ordinary Korean men and women who fearlessly put their lives on the line during the peaceful protest that began the March 1 movement, Korean women in Hawai'i recreated a similar peace march in March 1919. Donned in traditional Korean dresses, Korean women marched in downtown Honolulu, singing Korean patriotic songs. After the march, forty-one women representing all the Hawaiian islands gathered in Honolulu, and two weeks later, these women met again to establish the Korean Women's Relief Society.[24] Maria Hwang, leader of the Korean Women's Relief Society, was someone the community people called a "warrior woman" because she immigrated to Hawai'i by herself with her children after leaving her husband, who had a concubine. Although Korean husbands commonly kept concubines in the early 1900s, Hwang did not accept the practice. She allegedly told her husband, "I can no longer live under these circumstances with you. I am taking our children to America and will shame you in the future. These children shall become educated and I shall become a wonderful person. You can remain as you are."[25]

Under Hwang's leadership, the Korean Women's Relief Society demonstrated its benevolent nationalism and at once expanded and redefined the scope of the Korean independence movement. The purposes of the organization, according to its petition, were "to give the needy help in time of their distress, and to promote the mutual human interests, understanding and friendship among the Koreans and Americans, and to encourage the fair and just treatment of all races, familiarizing its members with the Western ideals and equality, and other social activity, promoting the spirit of good fellowship among its members."[26] Emphasizing unity and humanity as its central aim, the Korean Women's Relief Society espoused a greater, universal purpose of peace and harmony beyond the immediate goal of regaining Korean independence.

Members of the Korean Women's Relief society practiced such a philosophy of humanity and compassion primarily through fundraising and charity work. Aside from their annual dues of $2.50, they raised money by going door to door to sell copies of the Declaration of Korean Independence manifesto, signed by thirty-three patriots in Korea during the March 1 movement of 1919. They also cooked and sold homemade Korean food items. Altogether the women of the society raised an impressive total of about $200,000. With the money they collected, they provided financial assistance to families whose members were killed or injured in the March 1 movement and to victims of famine and flood in Korea. They also contributed to the Korean provisional government in China, the Korean Commission in Washington, D.C., and the Korean Independence Army in China and Manchuria.[27]

Such organizational efforts of Korean women were a significant accomplishment. Although the members of the Korean Women's Relief Society took on "traditionally feminine projects," such as the sale of Korean food to raise funds, the extent to which they contributed financially to the independence cause was a tribute to Korean women's ability to redefine and negotiate the boundaries of traditional gender roles. Out of their love for Korea and their ardent hope for its restored independence, women freely gave their time and resources, both financial and emotional.

While giving emotional resources and energy may have been easy, coming up with financial contributions every week or month was much more difficult for Korean women and their families. Considering that on average male Korean plantation laborers worked for a mere sixty-seven cents a day—and Korean women laborers for even less—extra income was virtually nonexistent. Despite this apparent difficulty of financing a political movement with their meager income, Koreans conscientiously gave what they could. One FBI report in Honolulu aptly noted:

> Natural obstacles to their work for independence which were insurmountable received little consideration by the average Korean. For the cause of independence and party politics, the followers unstingily and without consideration of self and kindred, gave much of their hard-earned money for the cause. In connection with local Korean politics, thousands of dollars have been poured into party coffers.[28]

Korean leaders were relentless in asking the community to contribute. An article in the Korean section of the *Korean National Herald–Pacific Weekly* asked:

> Who wants independence of Korea? Every Korean wants independence, and those who are opposed to it are only the Japanese. . . . We, Koreans, the people without government, are trying to regain independence through our dedicated patriotism and resources. . . . Nothing works without money. Money makes army, and army makes victory possible.[29]

The author requested that everyone "with a drop of Korean blood" contribute to the independence cause. Tightening their belts, Korean women made adjustments to their family finances and, together with their husbands, dutifully made contributions to the independence movement.

But aside from organizing independence groups and participating in the Korean independence movement in a traditional sense, Korean women found alternative ways to express their love for Korea. Striving to stay above unproductive divisions caused by factional independence movement politics dominated by men, Korean women focused on the important work of cultural preservation, as well as social and public service both in Korea and Hawai'i. Ha Soo Whang was an important visionary and a leader in helping Korean American women channel their patriotism and love for Korea in ways that were meaningful to Korean American women. Arriving in Hawai'i in 1922 at the age of thirty to accept a position at the International Institute of the Young Women's Christian Association (YWCA), Whang had a remarkable record of achievements to help Korean American women in Hawai'i. She founded a Korean cultural organization called Hyungjay (Sisters) Club. Its primary purpose was to provide a social space where young Korean girls could learn Korean traditional culture and folkways. Her niece Mary Whang Choy, a member of the club, summarized its impact on second-generation Korean girls:

At Hyungjay Club, we learned old folk culture. My aunt Ha Soo recruited Korean men and women who recently immigrated to Hawai'i with expertise in Korean folk music, Korean dancing, and had them teach us Korean folk culture. And from there, productions would be produced. My aunt Ha Soo wrote the play, directed it, and produced it. Young girls would get dressed up and depict old folk tale of Korea. We never lost sight of the fact that we are Koreans. We had a great pride in our heritage. We credit my aunt Ha Soo for her deep feeling for Korea and carrying on old cultural ways, music, and dance to pass them on to the new Korean American generation.[30]

This was a far more effective way to instill ethnic pride in second-generation Korean Americans than forcing factional independence politics on them. Whang opted to express her "deep feeling for Korea" by helping to preserve Korean culture in Hawai'i among second-generation Korean girls.

At the same time, Whang's vision of a strong Korean community embraced the Americanization of Korean women to empower them to become productive members of the Korean community, as well as in the larger Hawaiian community. For elderly Korean women, she created a Mothers' Club, where she taught English and exposed members to American culture. She invited physicians, nurses, and other health experts as guest speakers to discuss health issues pertinent to the elderly.[31] She also catered to the special needs of Korean picture brides in abusive domestic situations by serving as their translator in court. With her sense of public service and commitment to ensuring a productive, thriving Korean community, Whang provided much-needed day-to-day services for women of the Korean Hawaiian community, with immediate as well as future implications for the lives of Korean women.[32]

Her ability to weave in and out of Korean and American culture comfortably made Whang particularly effective in bridging the cultural and language gaps between the first and second generations. The fact that she was born in Korea but educated at an American college (Mills College) before she arrived in Hawai'i made her "acceptable" to both first- and second-generation Koreans. Her special focus of service was "that of adjusting difficulties which arise out of the contacts of the older generation of non-English speaking Koreans with American institutions and with the second generation of Koreans."[33] Whang recognized the importance of uniting different generations and strove for common understanding of the challenges of living in the United States as people of Korean ancestry.

Another benevolent Korean women's club that bridged the political factions was the Young Nam Buin Hoe, or the Southern Women's Society, an organization for Korean women from the southern provinces in Korea. Focusing on social service, the club helped both current members and newcomers. One of the last of the surviving Korean picture brides, Pun Cho Yu, was a member of the Young Nam Buin Hoe. Because of his heart condition, her husband did not work from the time Yu arrived in Hawai'i as a picture bride in 1919. Yu was the primary breadwinner of the family and did not have the time or means to participate in the Korean independence organizations or churches: "I worked day and night. I was too busy working to participate. Other women would curse me for not coming when they saw me. I was too busy working. I had no time." Despite having to work "day and night," she did enthusiastically participate in the Young Nam

Buin Hoe. Its focus on helping people from her hometown region in Korea appealed to Yu more than any political work:

> We helped students from the southern provinces. We collected money to purchase winter coats for new students coming from the southern provinces, because it is cold in the United States. We never fought. We had everyone from Tongihoe and Kuk Min Hur [Korean National Association].[34]

As a member of this organization, Yu found a meaningful connection to Korea and took pride in the services she and other members of the organization provided for fellow Koreans.

Bridging different factions of the community by attracting both Rhee and Pak supporters, the Young Nam Buin Hoe fully supported the Korean liberation cause. After hearing of the plans for the March 1 movement in Korea, the women of the Young Nam Buin Hoe made plans to go back to Korea to participate in the movement. After realizing the daunting logistical task of making this goal a reality, including coming up with funds to pay for their passage to Korea by boat, they elected to pay for one representative, Margaret Pai's mother, Hee Kyung Kwon, to go to Korea. Kwon, with her undeterred patriotism to "do what we can to help," would eventually be captured by the Japanese and jailed in Korea.[35]

More informally, Korean women of all ages in Hawai'i regularly met to socialize and share a Korean meal together. Nam Soo Lee held such events frequently, especially for former Korean picture brides who were widowed. Lee's children have vivid memories of all the Korean women who gathered in their house to socialize and enjoy a special Korean meal that their mother had prepared:

> All the ladies were there. Most of them were very old. Most of the ladies were sick or too old to leave home. They were either widows, or widowed for many years. [Our mother] always provided refreshment. She loved to cook. You can't make a little. You had to make a lot. The old ladies lived by themselves. She felt that the food was the thing to give them.[36]

Whatever the occasion, such meals strengthened their common bonds as Korean women and intensified their nostalgia for Korea. Pai also recalls her mother and her friends hosting meals to welcome a Korean visitor who came to Hawai'i to solicit funds for the independence cause and who served to inform the community members of the deteriorating conditions back in Korea. While such fundraising dinners ended up causing a fight between her mother and her father, who did not share the same degree of independence spirit, the meals that her mother hosted for the Korean visitor reawakened "the old revolutionary spirit" in her mother.[37] Organizing outside the limelight through these informal social gatherings, Korean American women often spearheaded grassroots education and mobilization in the community.

Conclusion

Whether they arrived as wives of plantation laborers with the hope of striking it rich quickly or as picture brides in pursuit of a comfortable home and a husband, discovering the harsh realities of life and conditions in Hawai'i was devastating for Korean women. But nothing demoralized the Korean community in Hawai'i as did the news of the Japanese annexation of Korea in 1910. Doing their part in the Korean independence movement, Korean women effectively carved out their public space and extended their influence outside the home. In a deeply divided community, scarred by factional independence politics, Korean picture brides and pioneer Korean immigrant women in Hawai'i found outlets for their love for Korea through their public service and activism to promote unity, patriotism, and preservation of Korean culture.

While male leaders vied for power and respect in the community, which came at the cost of the overall unity of the Korean independence movement, Korean women's social and economic services and cultural initiatives had a deep, lasting effect on future generations of Korean Americans and their households, and particularly on Korean American women. By organizing purposefully around the goal of promoting Korean nationalism through preserving Korean culture and empowering those who needed assistance carrying on everyday activities, Korean immigrant women and picture brides served as important mediators of the new and old worlds: they helped the younger generation understand the rich cultural and political heritages of the Korean past, and they helped the community members survive and thrive in their new, adopted country. Thus, the dominant historical focus on the activities of a few Korean American male leaders provides a limited view of the Korean independence movement within the community in Hawai'i. Attention to Korean American women, their leadership and activities, illuminates their new roles in the United States and their agency in building their community and participating in political causes.

The legacy of Korean American women's benevolent nationalism in the early years of Hawai'i went far beyond the fundraisers, benefit shows, boycotts of Japanese goods, and other independence activities. Their public service of helping the needy families in both Hawai'i and Korea imparted to the entire community a sense of autonomy and self-sufficiency, even during the bleak moments of Japanese colonialism in Korea. Furthermore, Korean women's benevolent nationalism fundamentally altered the Korean independence movement by shifting its objective of Korean liberation from a political goal to a project of humanity. Driven by both anger at Japanese imperialism and compassion for the suffering of Koreans in occupied Korea, Korean American women focused on providing aid to fellow Koreans on both sides of the Pacific. Through their charity work and social services, Korean American women leaders and participants in the Korean independence movement envisioned and subscribed to nationalism that embraced humanity first and foremost, not politics, without losing sight of the political nature of their work.

Ironically, their very efforts to promote, redefine, and strengthen Korean nationalism facilitated Americanization of Korean immigrant women and picture brides. Politicized by their nationalist activities, Korean American women skillfully challenged and redefined the boundaries of their traditional gender roles in marriage, family, and community. Once confined to their roles as wives and mothers, Korean American women exerted public influence through their collective organizing activities in and outside their homes. While personal factors such as regional ties, direct experiences of Japanese colonialism, and class status varied their ability, intensity, and areas of involvement in the Korean independence movement, Korean American women collectively shaped the ideological basis for and the range of activities of Korean nationalism in significant ways. Focusing on Korean American women's overlooked contribution to Korean nationalism necessarily alters our understanding of the Korean independence movement in Hawai'i during the Japanese occupation of Korea.

NOTES

I am grateful to Shirley Hune for her several critical readings of this essay at different stages that greatly improved the final version. Portions of this chapter were presented at the annual meeting of the Association for Asian American Studies, Toronto, Canada, 28 March–1 April 2001, and at the Berkshire Conference on the History of Women, Storrs, Connecticut, 6–9 June 2002. I benefited tremendously from the encouragement and insightful comments of Alice Yang Murray. Lynn D. Gordon's thoughtful feedback on this essay in its earliest form significantly shaped the central argument. I give special thanks to Michael Macmillan for his assistance with sources, and I gratefully acknowledge the research support of the UCLA Institute of American Cultures Postdoctoral Fellowship in Ethnic Studies during the writing of this essay.

1. I adhere to the Korean naming practice of listing the last name first, followed by the first and middle name, when they appeared so in the original sources.

2. "The Oral Life History of Mrs. Nam Soo Young," conducted by Hwa Ja Kim Park, December 1986, Center for Korean Studies, University of Hawai'i at Mānoa, Honolulu.

3. Warren Y. Kim, *Koreans in America* (Seoul: P. Chin Chai Printing Co., 1971), 22–23. According to his estimate, 951 Korean picture brides came to Hawai'i and 115 more to the continental United States.

4. Some of these seemingly "single" men had wives back in China and therefore were not bachelors. But the point that the Chinese immigrant community, dominated by men, could not reproduce remains valid.

5. Interview with Julia Chang Chung, tape 19, the Roberta W. S. Chang Collection (RWSCC), Center for Korean Studies, University of Hawai'i at Manoa, Honolulu.

6. Esther Kwon Arinaga, "Double Identity: A Korean Experience in Twentieth-Century Hawaii" (unpublished autobiographical paper delivered at the symposium on "Korean Americans in Hawaii: Their Life and Experience," Center for Korean Studies, University of Hawai'i at Manoa, Honolulu, 13–15 January 2000).

7. Interview with Phyllis Ahn Dunn (in Korean), translation by author, tape 21, RWSCC. She was on the last ship from Korea to bring picture brides.

8. Wayne Patterson, *The Ilse: First Generation Korean Immigrants in Hawaii, 1903–1973* (Honolulu: University of Hawai'i Press, 2000), 85–87.

9. "Oral Life History of Mrs. Nam Soo Young."

10. Nancy Foon Young and Judy K. Parrish, eds., *Montage: An Ethnic History of Women in Hawaii* (Honolulu: University of Hawai'i Press, 1977), 75.

11. Interview with Mary Hong Park, tape 3, RWSCC.

12. See Eun Sik Yang, "Korean Women of America: From Subordination to Partnership, 1903–1930," *Amerasia Journal* 11:2 (1984): 1–28; and Patterson, *Ilse*, 84.

13. Margaret K. Pai, *The Dreams of Two Yi-min* (Honolulu: University of Hawai'i Press, 1989), 7.

14. The most comprehensive to date, if overtly anti-Rhee, account of the Korean independence movement, its male leadership, and their differences is Kinsley K. Lyu, "Korean Nationalist Activities in Hawaii and the Continental United States, 1900–1945, Part I: 1900–1919," *Amerasia Journal* 4:1 (1977): 23–90; and Part II: 1919–1945," *Amerasia Journal* 4:2 (1977): 53–100.

15. Robert Oliver, *Syngman Rhee: The Man behind the Myth* (New York: Dodd Mead and Company, 1954), 110.

16. Lyu, "Korean Nationalist Activities, Part II," 68–72.

17. Korean Independence Movement, Report No. 41, 25 April 1942, Research and Analysis Branch, Far Eastern Section, Army Intelligence, Record Group 165, ACS G-2 Intelligence, Korean-American Policies, Box 2496, National Archives II, College Park, MD.

18. Interview with Hazel Park Chung, tape 1, RWSCC.

19. Interview with Julia Chang Chung, tape 19, RWSCC.

20. Frances Sup Sut Lee, "Cooking for Single Men," in Daisy Chun Rhodes, *Passages to Paradise: Early Korean Immigrant Narratives from Hawaii* (Los Angeles: Academia Koreanna, 1998), 108.

21. Shirley Hune, "Doing Gender with a Feminist Gaze: Toward a Historical Reconstruction of Asian America," in Min Zhou and James V. Gatewood, eds., *Contemporary Asian America: A Multidisciplinary Reader* (New York: New York University Press, 2000), 413.

22. Eui-Young Yu, "The Activities of Women in Southern California Korean Community Organizations," in Eui-Young Yu and E. Phillips., eds., *Korean Women in Transition: At Home and Abroad* (Los Angeles: Center for Korean American and Korean Studies, California State University, Los Angeles, 1987), 276.

23. Carter J. Eckert, *Korea Old and New: A History* (Seoul: Ilchokak Publishers for the Korea Institute, Harvard University, 1990), 278–79. Compare these figures to the Japanese official count of only 553 dead and 12,000 arrested during the March 1 movement. Bruce Cumings, *Korea's Place in the Sun: A Modern History* (New York: W. W. Norton, 1997), 155.

24. Yang, "Korean Women of America," 13–15.

25. Sonia Shinn Sunoo, ed., *Korea Kaleidoscope: Oral Histories*, vol. 1: *Early Korean Pioneers in USA: 1903–1905* (Davis, CA: Korean Oral History Project, 1982), 156.

26. "Korean Organization in Territory of Hawaii," Territorial Office of Civilian Defense, 23 December 1941, Romanzo Adams Social Research Laboratory (RASRL) Confidential Research Files, "Koreans—War (World War II)," unprocessed file, Special Collection, University of Hawai'i Archives, Honolulu.

27. Yang, "Korean Women of America," 14.

28. "Federal Bureau of Investigation Survey of Korean Activities in the Honolulu Field Division," 20 March 1943, Record Group 319, Army-Intelligence Decimal File, Box 394, Folder 291.2, "Koreans," 16, National Archives II, College Park, MD.

29. "Who Wants Independence of Korea?" *Korean National Herald–Pacific Weekly* (Korean section), 11 February 1942. Translation by author.

30. Interview with Mary Whang Choy, "They Called Her Komo (Aunt): The Story of Whang Ha Soo," tape 12, RWSCC.

31. Interview with Miss Ha Soo Whang, Korean Secretary of the International Institute of YWCA, 13 October 1927, RASRL Confidential Research Files, "Korean File," Box 12, Folders 18–19, Special Collections, University of Hawai'i Archives, Honolulu.

32. Interview with Mary Whang Choy, tape 12, RWSCC.

33. Interview with Miss Ha Soo Whang.

34. Interview with Pun Cho Yu (in Korean), translation by author, tape 21, RWSCC. Yu, believed to be the last picture bride alive, was one hundred years old when she was interviewed. Rhee founded the Tongihoe after severing ties with the Korean National Association, the Kuk Min Hur.

35. Pai, *Dreams of Two Yi-min*, 8.

36. Interview with Caroline Lee Kanada and Willie Lee, tape 15, RWSCC.

37. Pai, *Dreams of Two Yi-min*, 118–19.

Part 3

Recovering Women's History through Oral History and Journal Writing

7

"A Bowlful of Tears"
Lee Puey You's Immigration Experience at Angel Island

Judy Yung

In 1975, a few years after the discovery of Chinese poems on the walls of the immigration barracks at Angel Island, I embarked on an oral history project with historian Him Mark Lai and poet Genny Lim to document the story of Chinese detention at Angel Island during the exclusion period.[1] After conducting forty-five interviews with ex-detainees and staff and translating 135 of the Chinese poems, we published *Island: Poetry and History of Chinese Immigrants on Angel Island, 1910–1940.*[2] Although none of the poems were written by women, we conducted eight interviews with women, offering us a rare opportunity to hear their versions of the story as well.

One of the women we interviewed was Lee Puey You, who had immigrated to the United States in 1939. She was denied entry by immigration authorities and detained at Angel Island for twenty months before she was deported. She gave us a detailed and moving account of her long stay at Angel Island. Little did I know then how much more complicated and sad her full story was, and how our lack of experience as oral historians had made us overlook the gendered effects of exclusion on women's lives. In hindsight, we should have asked more open-ended as well as follow-up questions; covered more of her entire life history; considered race, class, gender, and memory dynamics in our line of questioning and analysis; and compared her testimony to the transcripts in her immigration file at the National Archives.[3]

The following rewrite and analysis of the interview that we conducted with Lee Puey You in 1975 as part of the *Island* book project is intended to provide a fuller picture of a Chinese woman's experience at Angel Island, told in her own words, as well as a better understanding of how we can best reclaim our past through oral history. The 1975 interview is compared with a second interview with Lee that was conducted ten years later for a film production, *Carved in Silence*, to show what was overlooked in the first interview due to our inexperience as oral historians and the different results that come from working in the medium of film. Excerpts from a third interview conducted by an immigration officer in 1955, when Lee was threatened with deportation for fraudulent entry, are included at the end to reveal the full tragic story of her immigration and life in America that she withheld from us. I did not come across this last interview until after Lee's death in 1996.[4] While I can respect Lee Puey You's sense of privacy and desire to protect her family and us from the painful circumstances of her immigration, I include the full story here with the permission of her daughters as a testimony to the strength of character that Lee displayed in confronting institutional racism and sexual exploitation. Against such odds, she must have cried more than a bowlful of tears in her lifetime.

"A Bowlful of Tears": First Interview for the Book Island

In 1975, we were lucky to find Lee Puey You through a mutual friend of her daughter Daisy Gin. We had heard she was detained on Angel Island for close to two years, probably the longest stay of any Chinese detainee in the history of the Angel Island Immigration Station. And she was willing to be interviewed. So one Saturday afternoon, Him Mark Lai and I, fully equipped with tape recorders and a list of questions, paid Lee Puey You a visit in her North Beach flat in San Francisco. I remember she welcomed our questions and thoughtfully answered them one by one until we ran out of questions after an hour or so.

In many ways hers was both a common and a unique story about detention life at Angel Island. Lee Puey You was born in Chung Tow village in Chungshan (Zhongshan) District, Guangdong Province, in 1916. She was twenty-three years old when she immigrated to the United States in 1939, posing as the daughter of a U.S. citizen.[5] Once admitted, she was to marry a Chinese immigrant in the United States and prepare the way for the rest of her family to come. Unlike most Chinese women immigrating at this time, she was well educated and thus had an easier time memorizing the coaching book for the interrogation.[6] She expected to be detained at Angel Island for a few weeks until she successfully passed the physical examination and interrogation. However, because of discrepancies in her interview and that of her alleged father, she was denied entry.

Slated for deportation, Lee Puey You was told by her "relatives" that they would hire an attorney to appeal her case to higher authorities in Washington, D.C., and that she needed to be patient. The appeal went from the U.S. District Court to the U.S. Circuit Court of Appeals and finally to the U.S. Supreme Court, without success. By this time the war against Japan had escalated in China, and the United States was about to enter World War II on the same side as China. The hope was that Lee would be allowed to land because it would be too dangerous to send her back to China. Instead, after twenty months of confinement at Angel Island, she was deported to Hong Kong. Here, her story took another unique turn. In 1947 she returned to the United States, posing as a war bride, to marry the same man.[7] The immigration station at Angel Island had since closed and been moved to San Francisco, and the Chinese Exclusion Act had been repealed. This time, she was allowed to enter immediately. But the twenty months of prison-like detainment at Angel Island had been forever etched into her mind and heart.

When we interviewed Lee Puey You thirty years after her ordeal at Angel Island, she told us repeatedly how she was made to feel like a criminal and how often she cried in anguish and out of frustration. "Everyone there cried at least once. You know, sitting at Angel Island I must have cried a bowlful of tears, it was so pitiful." We found that because she had been there for such an unusually long time, and because she was an educated woman, Lee observed and understood the detention experience at Angel Island more thoroughly than her peers. She remembered in detail the backgrounds of the women and their emotional state of mind, the poetry on the barrack walls, the interrogation process, and the ways women coped with imprisonment. Mindful of the psychological scars of Angel Island that she still bore, Him Mark Lai and I treaded carefully, perhaps too cautiously, in asking our prepared list of questions. As a result, we saw only a partial picture of the circumstances of her immigration to the United States. Nevertheless, the following is what she told us about what happened to her at Angel Island. The original interview in Chinese has been translated into English and edited to eliminate redundancies and to allow for an organized flow, but the tone and substance of the interview remain hers. Whenever helpful, I have included interview questions and editorial comments in brackets.

I didn't want to come to America but I was forced by circumstances to come. My mother had arranged a marriage for me. I had a passport to come [as a daughter of a U.S. citizen] when I was 16, but I didn't come until I was 23, after the Japanese attacked China.[8] They bombed Shekki[9] and everywhere and there was nowhere to hide so I had to come to America. But my fate was not good. I had never seen my fiancé before, but I knew he was a lot older than me.[10] He said he would give me the choice of marrying him or not after I arrived. My mother wanted me to come so that I could bring the family over later. Because of that, I was afraid to oppose the arranged marriage. I had to be a filial daughter. The situation forced me to sacrifice everything to come to America.

In 1939 I arrived at Angel Island. They told us to put down our luggage [in the storage shed] and then they directed us to the wooden building. We were allowed to bring only a small suitcase of clothes. There must have been over 100 people. The men had their dormitories and the women had theirs. They assigned us to beds [two-tiered bunk beds] and there were *gwai poh* [foreign devil women] to take care of us. We slept there and had three meals a day. Everyday we got up at about 7:00. They yelled, chow, chow! You know those *gwai poh*. They would wake us up and take us to the dining room for breakfast. Usually a plate of vegetables and a plate of meat catering to the Chinese palate. Nothing good. Sometimes scrambled eggs, sometimes vegetables mixed with meat. Their food was pretty bad, not very tasty. But then most people didn't eat their food. Many had relatives in the city who sent Chinese dishes, barbecued duck and pork, packages of food every day. After we ate, they took us back and locked the doors. That's all. Just like in jail. Followed us out and followed us back, then locked the doors. They treated us like criminals. They were always afraid that we would go over to the men's side and talk to them [and thereby corroborate testimonies] or that we might escape or commit suicide. Where would we escape to? I never saw anyone try suicide, but people did cry for death because they were suffering so.

There was nowhere to go. Just a little hallway that was fenced in for us to sun, exercise, or play ball. No longer than my hallway here [about fifteen feet]. The men's exercise area was larger. There was a long table put there for us to use for writing or sewing. From the windows we could see the boats arrive daily at about 9:30 or 10:00 in the morning. At the end of the day we would watch the inspectors and newly released immigrants leave the island on the same boat. That's all. [How did you pass the time?] Sometimes I read or knitted, made some clothes, or slept. When you got up, it was time to eat again. Day in and day out, eat and sleep. Many people cried. Everyone there cried at least once. [The men gambled and had music, how about the women?] No, no mah jongg, no recreation. Once a week they allowed us to walk out to the storage room where our luggage was kept [to retrieve things]. That allowed us to stretch and breathe in some fresh air. We walked around a bit and then returned. [Were you allowed to write letters to your relatives?] Yes, but they examined your letters before mailing them. The same for letters coming in. They opened them to see if there was any coaching information. Any packages or food that were sent to us had to be examined too. Then the *gwai poh* would call our name and deliver the package to you.

[Any other regulations?] Well, when you got sick you were supposed to tell the *gwai poh*. They would send you to the hospital until you got well. They always gave you laxatives, which tasted awful. After a few days, you came back. We couldn't have any visitors, but there was a Miss Moore [Maurer], a Protestant woman who came once or twice a week.[11] She was pretty old. Sometimes she brought me yarn or fabric. She was very nice to me. I still remember her. At Christmas time she gave us gifts. The staff there were pretty nice to me too because I had been there for such a long time. They allowed me in and out of their office. [Did they ever threaten or punish anyone?] Sometimes when they called you to get up to go eat and you didn't feel well enough, they would force you to. They won't let you stay in bed. Or they would make you go to the hospital. But they never hit anyone. They might scold you but they never punished anyone. Sometimes the girls would scold back and they would get into an argument. But some were very nice to us.

[Did you remember seeing any poems on the walls?] Yes, there were some written [not carved] on the walls. It was like songs people would sing. [Did you write any yourself?] Not on the wall, but I did write poetry to console myself. I would write and cry at the same time. You know, sitting at Angel Island I must have cried a bowlful of tears. It was so pitiful.

[Were there other immigrants who were not Chinese there?] There were a few Japanese and Korean women. They lived in a different room next to ours. We had no contact with them. The Japanese were looked up to. They came and went in a day or two. That's probably because we Chinese didn't have the proper papers.[12]

[Was it comfortable living there?] Of course not! We had a bed to sleep in and the bathrooms were adequate, but it was so noisy with so many people—50 or 60 women at one time and a few young children besides. Sometimes the people next to you talked or people would cry in the middle of the night so you couldn't sleep. It was very noisy. Sometimes people didn't get along and argued, but because we were in the same fix, we were generally good friends. We shared food and helped each other out even though I couldn't understand the Sze Yup dialect.[13] Often, those who had been there awhile cried when they saw others leave. So you started to cry. It was very sad.

[The men had their Self-Governing Organization that lodged complaints for them, did the women?] No, we didn't. The women did not dare complain [about the food or the treatment]. If you didn't like the food, the only thing you could do is not eat their food and get your own [from relatives in San Francisco]. Or you could buy things at the small store [in the dining room]. You could buy almost anything there—canned fish, fermented bean cakes, fruit, ice cream, cookies. As a new arrival, you're like a stupid pig, not knowing anything. Whatever they told you to do, you did. There was no recourse for protest.

[What was the interrogation like?] People said that coming to America was like going to heaven, but it was so difficult. You had to memorize all the coaching information—background on your grandparents, your home and neighbors, the distance between places, you know, how many ancestral halls, temples, everything. It was just like in school. You had this vast amount of information to learn. How many brothers and sisters does your father have? What are the names of your uncles? What were their occupations? When did they return to China? Have you ever seen them? When did your grandparents die? Where were they born? Lots of questions and answers going back three generations.

Two or three weeks after my arrival, I was called in for the interrogation. I knew I would be interrogated, but I was still nervous when the time came. There was a typist, an inspector, and an interpreter; three in all. It took three days. We started at 9:30 or 10:00 in the morning. At 11:30 or 12:00 there was a lunch break. Then we went back at 1:00 until 4:00. They asked me about my grandparents, which direction the house faced, which house I lived in, how far from one place to another. It took a long time because they had to interrogate the witnesses too. After they asked me questions, they would ask my father, then my uncles, and then the two witnesses. That's why it took two or three days. [Were the interrogators hard on you?] Sometimes the interpreters were cranky. When I said I wasn't sure or I didn't know, they would tell me to say yes or no. They just treated us like criminals.

After the interrogation, if you failed, they didn't tell you. But when you were allowed to see your father or witnesses, you knew they were going to deport you. You see, if I had passed I won't have had to see the witnesses. I would have been immediately called to land, to gather my things and leave. That's how it usually was. Relatives later told me that they would appeal my case to the higher courts in Washington, D.C. They told me to be patient. My appeal failed the first time and then a second time. They were hoping that when the war finally hit the United States, I would be released. But instead, I was stuck on Angel Island for twenty months. I was there the longest. Most people stayed three weeks or so. Those on appeal left after a few months. But my case was more crooked [complicated] because my paper father had reported twins and it wasn't true.[14] So I wasn't landed.

[Did anything unusual happen while you were there?] Right before I was deported, there was a fire in the middle of the night. We saw flames and inhaled smoke. Everything was burnt in the women's barracks. It was pretty bad so we had to run over to the hospital to live for awhile. Then they moved us to that immigration building on Washington Street [in San Francisco].[15] A few weeks later, I was deported to Hong Kong.

[Upon reflection, how do you feel about what happened at Angel Island now?] Before, that was the system. There was nothing you could do about it. That was the American law then, how can you go against it? But this is how I look at it now. If things checked out at the American consul's in Hong Kong, they should let us come. If not, they shouldn't let us come. That would have spared us suffering twenty days aboard ship, seasickness and all, and then imprisonment at Angel Island.[16] In my case, I had to endure twenty months of prison-like confinement. And then to be deported back to Hong Kong, how sad!

"Carved in Silence": Second Interview for a Film Production

In 1984, when filmmaker Felicia Lowe decided to make *Carved in Silence*, a film about the Chinese immigration experience at Angel Island,[17] I suggested Lee Puey You as a possible subject. Felicia wanted to follow the stories of three immigrants in the format of a docudrama but was having trouble finding ex-detainees who were willing to tell their story on camera and who would come across well on film. Lee agreed to be filmed, and I signed on as a historical consultant to help with the research and interviews. Working with Felicia, I learned that film required a different approach to interviewing. Although the historical background was important, it was the emotional connection that really mattered.

My job was to sit right below the camera and ask open-ended questions that would evoke memories of Angel Island and encourage Lee Puey You to speak expressively but succinctly into the camera. Short answers in a monotonous tone or long answers that skirted the questions would be deadly in this situation. I learned to be both solicitous and persistent in my line of questioning, to rephrase my questions and ask good follow-up questions in order to steer her in the right direction. Felicia was already familiar with Lee Puey You's story from reading the transcript of our earlier interview with her and from interviewing Lee herself a number of times. She knew which stories she wanted Lee to tell on camera. My part was to draw these stories out of Lee as spontaneously as possible, even though we reshot some of the answers a number of times. Although Lee Puey You's voice would be dubbed over in English, Felicia intended to do an exact translation and stay as close as possible to the tone and wording of her responses, which to her credit she did accomplish in the final edit of the film.

The following excerpts from a series of interviews with Lee Puey You in preparation for the filming of *Carved in Silence* show what we learned by pursuing a different line of questioning. In particular, we hear about her life before and after Angel Island, the dire family conditions that forced her to agree to marry a stranger in America, and the poetry she saw in the bathroom of the women's barracks. Since the building that housed the women at Angel Island had been burnt in the 1940 fire, we had given up hope of ever finding any Chinese poetry by women. Yet here was Lee Puey You, reciting one of the poems she had written while at Angel Island, proving that not all Chinese immigrant women were illiterate at the time. Moreover, Felicia prodded her to tell us how she felt having to appear naked before a white male physician, something we had failed to ask in our 1975 interview. She also got Lee to analyze how her upbringing and education in China helped her to endure the twenty long months of confinement at Angel Island.

Then came that unforgettable moment on film when Lee Puey You broke down and began to cry while recalling her return voyage to China. It was totally unexpected and we caught it on film. While it is to Lee's credit as an interviewee that she was willing and able to tell her own story on film as effectively as she did, it still takes a good interviewer and filmmaker to make this possible—to establish the rapport, ask the right questions, and edit the interview so that the significant points are made within a broader historical context. Compared to our cautious approach in interviewing Lee for the book *Island*, Felicia was persistent about exploring Lee's unique background and capturing her emotional response to detention life and deportation on film. The following excerpts from the interview with Lee Puey You have been translated from Chinese into English and edited for an organized flow, but the integrity of her voice has been retained. As before I have also left certain questions in brackets to show what prompted her to answer as she did.

[What were your reasons for coming?] My mother wanted me to come to America so that later on, I could bring my brothers and sisters over to America. At the time, the Japanese were bombing my village. That was another reason why I fled my country. [How was your family doing then?] When I was very young, my father was a wealthy farmer. A flood destroyed all his land and he lost all his money. It was then that our family changed. My brother had to go to work to support me and my mother. I saw how hard he worked, just one job. It was barely enough. Finally I decided to listen to my mother. I would come to America first and then later help my brother and the rest of the family to come over. That was what my mother had always wanted. Here, there was a future. In China we were just too poor and there was nothing we could do.

[What were your preparations before you came to America?] My mother had a girlfriend in our village who wanted to introduce me to her cousin for marriage. She wanted me to come to America to marry him so she bought me a false paper.

[Tell me about your trip to the United States.] From my village, I went to Hong Kong. I stayed with relatives in Hong Kong for six months until I got the papers from America to come. Then I got on a big ship and was on it for nineteen days. I thought it would be very easy for me to land in America. Instead, I had to go to Angel Island.

[Could you describe the physical examination?] When the doctor came, I had to take off all my clothes. It was so embarrassing and shameful. I didn't really want to let him examine me, but I had no choice. Back in China, I never had to take off everything, but it was different here in America. I found it very strange.

[Tell me about the interrogation.] The interrogators frightened me. There were two or three Westerners along with one Chinese at the interrogation. Just looking at them made me scared and nervous. I didn't know what to do or how to act around them. They asked me questions that I could not answer, even how many feet our house was from the house next door. I was bewildered and didn't know how to answer them.

[Were the rest of the women scared like you?] Everyone was feeling low. We all suffered emotionally. No one had any energy. We slept all day. So much mental anguish. You know, we cried more than anything else. It was hard and time went by so slowly. When I was in China, I didn't know it would be so hard in America. Everybody said that coming to America was like going to heaven, but at Angel Island they treated the Chinese as if we were criminals, like we were all thieves and robbers. Because I was there so long, all the new arrivals would ask me questions about Angel Island. They all wanted to learn from my experience. We sympathized and tried to help each other out.

[What else gave you the strength to endure such sadness and hardships?] Sometimes I tried to analyze myself, to understand my inner feelings and emotions. Sometimes I wrote poems to express my feelings. That helped to release some of the tension. [Were there many poems written on the walls of the women's barracks?] The bathroom was filled with poems expressing sadness and bitterness. They were about how hard the stay at Angel Island was, how sad and depressed the women were, not knowing when they would be allowed to leave the island. During one of my more painful moments, I wrote this poem:

> From across the Pacific Ocean to America
> I left my village and all my loved ones.
> Who would have thought I would be imprisoned in this wooden barrack?
> I do not know when I will ever be set free.

In my darkest moment of sadness, I could only turn to God for help.[18] I just prayed everyday. That was the only way I could bear those hardships. I had no choice but to be strong. I had to take care of myself so that I might survive. I had to fulfill my duty as a filial daughter. That was all!

[Tell us how your father influenced your life.] When I was little, my father always told me what to do and how things worked. At fourteen years old, I knew how to lease and how to rent out land. I was considered quite smart. During the poor times, I learned how to dig up plants and roots for cooking. I also knew how to catch fish. I was very capable and helped my mother quite a bit.

[Tell us about your schooling.] I went to school and studied history. We even had a special teacher to teach us the Chinese classics. I have a very good brain so I was able to absorb all the material. This was probably what gave me the extra strength to endure life on Angel Island. It gave me a better understanding of people and of the world. My father always said it was a pity that I was born a girl and not a boy. I had a good business head and was able to help him. I became a housewife after I got married. But I encouraged my husband to buy stocks, a business, and real estate. I had no interest in just staying home and cleaning house. Even today, my goals in life are more like a man's.

[Why were you on the island so long?] My case had to go through two appeals in Washington, D.C.[19] My mother's girlfriend was determined that I stay in America. She did not care how much money or how long it would take. As long as there was a string of light, she wanted me to hang on. I was the only one to stay on Angel Island for such a long time. Twenty months. Anyone else would have just gone back home to China.

[How did you feel when you found out about your deportation?] My heart felt very heavy. I had no face [was ashamed] to see my family back home. My spirit was broken. During my trip back to China on the boat, my heart hurt so much that I finally had to put some rice, some hot rice, against my chest to ease the pain inside (sobs). The anguish that I had suffered is more than anyone can bear. I can't begin to describe it. Then all of a sudden, I had a dream. My appeal was successful! It was like a message from God. Then my heart was at peace. So that's my story from start to finish. It took me fourteen years to come back to America, fourteen long, long years.[20]

[How was your life when you returned to America the second time?] It was a lot easier than life in China. As long as you are willing to work hard, you can make a better living in America. I consider myself lucky that I did not have to work too hard in America. We had a grocery store and since there were enough people working in the store, I was not needed. Later on, after my father-in-law passed away and my brother-in-law left, that left only my husband and me to run the store. I would work every day from 7 a.m. to 9 p.m., fourteen hours a day, seven days a week. But I only did that for five or six years. Now my life is quite settled. I saved enough money to buy a building so that I can live in one apartment and rent the rest of the units out. I should be able to take care of myself for the rest of my life.

[Tell me how you finally sponsored your family over to America.] My mother had wanted me to come to America, hoping that later on I would somehow bring the rest of the family over. Twenty years later, my mother, my brother, his wife and their four children, my sister and her husband and children rode a ship and came to America. It cost me thousands of dollars, but my mother's hopes have finally been fulfilled! Now all of them are doing well. They all have good jobs and their own homes. And all the children have finished college and are making good money. Everyone is happy and my responsibility to them is finally over.

"In the Matter of Yim Tai Muey":[21] *Third Interview with INS*

Sixteen years after the second interview for the film *Carved in Silence*, I came to a different understanding of Lee Puey You's immigration experience and life in America. It had not been as "easy" as she had said. By then, Lee had passed away, and I turned to her daughters, Daisy and Debbie Gin, for help in clarifying some discrepancies in her interviews. Based on the immigration files that Daisy and Debbie found at the National Archives, we learned that in 1955, someone blew the whistle and reported her illegal entry to the Immigration and Naturalization Service (INS). A warrant for her arrest was issued on the grounds that the immigration visa she had used to enter the country in 1947 had been procured by fraud. She was ordered to appear before the INS to show cause as to why she should not be deported. The stakes were just as high as they had been for her at Angel Island in 1939, but this time she had the benefit of an attorney to represent her interest, as well as the support of her second husband, Fred Gin, whom she had married in 1953. She was also apparently prepared to tell the whole story. According to the transcript, part-way through the interrogation and at the prompting of her attorney, she said through the interpreter, "I wish to volunteer the whole facts in the case." Then she proceeded to tell the following story.[22]

I was born in Cr 5-5-3.[23] My name was Lee Puey You at birth. When I was about 13 years old my father died and he did not leave us anything and my family was very poor. It was during the war and my family was having a hard time to make a living. One day a cousin of Woo Tong talked to my mother and told her that he has a cousin in the United States whose wife died recently and that he would like to remarry again and asked my mother whether she was willing to consent to having her daughter marry his cousin in the United States. Later Woo Tong's cousin tell my mother to have a photograph of me to send it to Woo Tong to see whether he liked me or not. Some time later Woo Tong's cousin came and told me that I was to go to the United States under the name of Ngin Ah Oy as a daughter of a son of a native—I was known as Yim Tai Muey at that time—and that after I came to the United States I was to marry Woo Tong as his wife, and I came to the United States in 1939. When I arrived here in San Francisco, I was detained at Angel Island for almost two years. During all of that time I had a very hard time and I was very sad, and every time that someone was released from there I felt sick all over again. I did not know what was happening to my case. I even attempted suicide. Then later I was deported back to Hong Kong. On my way back to Hong Kong I wanted to commit suicide again, but I was thinking about my mother, of the hard times we had together. When I arrived back in Hong Kong, I sold rice on the street in Hong Kong. I was having a very hard time because it was during the war at that time. My mother told me that we have used some of Woo Tong's money and no matter how hard a time I am having I must not get married. She already promised my marriage to Woo Tong. She said that I should wait until after the war, when she could correspond with Woo Tong again and that he will make arrangements for me to go to the United States again. After the war, in about 1947, Woo Tong came to Hong Kong and he came to our house and talked to my mother. Later then, we invited some friends for dinner; then my mother told me it was considered as my marriage ceremony with Woo Tong. Then Woo Tong told me of his plan to bring me to the United States. He said I was to get a marriage certificate with Sai Chan[24] and said I was to come to the United States as Sai Chan's wife and said he would accompany me to the United States. After Sai Chan and I obtained our marriage certificate from the American Consular Office in Hong Kong, he told me that I must go to a husband and wife relationship with him before he could bring me to the United States. I objected to that, but he forced me into that, so I lived with him as man and wife in Hong Kong. Sai Chan and I came to the United States together in 1947. After we arrived in the United States, he took me to Woo Tong's place at 1141 Stockton Street and he left me there. When I get there I learned Woo Tong's wife was still living and that I was not actually to be Woo Tong's wife, but his concubine. I objected to it, but there was nothing I could do because I was now here in the United States. I did not know of anyone to go to for aid, so I stayed with him. During all those times I was living there I was treated very badly by his wife. She treated me as a slave girl. I had to do all kinds of work in the house, take care of her and I also had to take care of one of Woo Tong's buildings. On January 8, 1949 I gave birth to a daughter fathered by Woo Tong. While I was in the Stanford Hospital during my maternity period, Woo Tong made all the arrangements for me. He filled out the birth certificate for my daughter and he filled out the father's name as Sai Chan. Woo Tong died August 18, 1950 in San Francisco. After he died, his wife forced me to continue to work for her. When Woo Tong died, he did not leave money or anything for my daughter and myself. I met Fred Gin in about 1953 and learned his wife had passed away several years before. I found he was a person of good character. I went with him about six months before we got married. I went to Reno and obtained a divorce decree from Sai Chan to clear the record on January 16, 1953. Fred Gin had two sons by his first wife in the United States and after we were married, I bore him a daughter on February 4, 1955.

Then followed a series of humiliating questions regarding her moral character, specifically her sexual relationships with Sai Chan and Woo Tong.

Q During the few days you lived with Woo Tong after that dinner [in Hong Kong], did you have sexual intercourse with him?

Q [After you were admitted to the United States and started living with Woo Tong] did you immediately have sexual intercourse with Woo Tong?

Q When did you last have sexual intercourse with Woo Tong?

Q After you obtained a marriage certificate with Sai Chan, did you voluntarily submit to relationships with him?

Lee Puey You admitted to no wrongdoing and insisted that she was just following her mother's orders, that she had agreed to marry Woo Tong believing he was a widower, and that Sai Chan had forced her to have sex with him after their wedding. In the cross-examination by her attorney, Lee emphasized her newfound happiness at being married to Fred Gin and her desire to remain with her family in the United States.

Q What would happen if you were separated from Fred and the rest of your family?

A I would have a hard time, because I have no one else to go to if I should be separated from my family.

Q Would Fred go with you in the event you should be deported?

A I will not allow him to go with me even if willing, because I don't want him to sacrifice his life for me.

Q Would you take your blood daughters Eva and Daisy[25] if you were separated from Fred?

A No. I will leave them in the United States. Even if they have to beg or starve in the United States, I would leave them because the living conditions here in the United States are better.

When asked by the INS officer if she had anything further to add before the hearing came to a close, she said:

I just wish to say that you give me a chance so that I can remain in the United States to be with my family. I found happiness after I married Fred Gin. Prior to that time the wrongdoing was not due to my fault. I was just obeying my mother, which she make all the arrangements with Woo Tong that I apply for a marriage certificate as the wife of Sai Chan to come to the United States.

The INS officer was evidently not convinced or moved by her testimony and ordered her deported on grounds that her immigration visa had been procured by fraud and that "she [had] lived in an adulterous relationship with Woo Tong" while still married to Sai Chan. Lee Puey You did not give up. She hired another attorney to appeal the decision on her behalf. First, the attorney argued that she was "not innately a bad person of criminal tendencies . . . but a mere pawn—indeed a slave—of men who deserve severe condemnation." Next, he pointed out that because her marriage to Sai Chan, a citizen veteran, was consummated and deemed valid, she had immigrated legitimately as a war bride. Evidently persuaded by the attorney's arguments, the Board of Immigration Appeals sustained Lee Puey You's appeal and terminated the deportation proceedings on March 25, 1956. She became a naturalized U.S. citizen in 1959, which paved the way for her to send for her family from China.

Conclusion

Lee Puey You's full story sheds light not only on the complexities and ordeal of immigration for Chinese women at Angel Island but also on how we can best reclaim that past through oral history. Conceptions of race, class, and gender all played a part in determining who immigrated and their treatment upon arrival. Because of poverty and war conditions at home, and out of filial duty, Lee sacrificed her own happiness in agreeing to marry a man who was thirty years her senior in order to immigrate to the United States. In the process, class and gender inequities placed her in a vulnerable position, to be sexually exploited by men such as Woo Tong and Sai Chan. Then, because of race, class, and gender biases in the exclusionary laws, Lee could come to the United States only by posing as a dependent member of the exempt classes. As such, she was subjected to a double test. In claiming her right to land as the daughter of a U.S. citizen, she had to reconfirm her alleged father's exempt status as well as prove that their relationship actually existed. Later, when she was accused of fraudulent entry as a war bride and threatened with deportation, she had to prove the legitimacy of her marriage to a citizen veteran as well as her moral character by answering humiliating questions about her sexual life. In these ways, race, class, and gender dynamics made the immigration process more difficult for Chinese women like Lee Puey You than for any other group of immigrants during the exclusion period.

In interviewing Lee Puey You, it was important that Him Mark Lai and I were Chinese-speaking, culturally sensitive, and well informed about Chinese American history. For these reasons, we were able to establish rapport with her and encourage her to talk freely about her twenty-month ordeal at Angel Island. But being novice oral historians in 1975 and overly polite at the time, we missed out on the opportunity to learn the full impact of exclusion on her life and how she was able to overcome racial and gender oppression. Working with Felicia Lowe on the film *Carved in Silence* made me realize how important it is to be persistent and analytical in our line of questioning. What influential forces shaped her life and helped her to cope with detention at Angel Island?

Even after knowing this, we did not get the full tragic story. It had not occurred to any of us to question the validity of her story, to read between the lines, to compare the interview with her testimony in the records of the National Archives, or even to ask her daughters what they knew. What made her hide the truth from us? Would she have told us the whole story if we had probed further or showed her the immigration record? Although aware of the pain that full recall might have caused her, I believe that she would have told us more if we had only persisted. In not doing our job well as critical oral historians, we missed the opportunity to better understand her life as well as to vindicate the wrongs committed against her.

Nevertheless, one thing is for certain: Lee Puey You was not a passive victim but an active agent in the making of her own history. She chose to talk to us and then selectively to tell us what she did. That showed good judgment and self-control. After three appeals and deportation to Hong Kong, she ultimately succeeded in her goal of landing in America and sending for her family. That took patience and tenacity. Even though both Sai Chan and Woo Tong betrayed her, she kept her word and went through with the marriages. That showed strength of character. And when threatened with deportation again, she persisted in fighting to the extent of telling and reliving the sordid details of her horrendous past. That required courage and forbearance on her part.[26]

In finally being able to hear her full story, I believe we come to a better understanding of and appreciation for the struggles and triumphs of our foremothers. Lee Puey You's story is an important part of the larger American story, indeed a challenge to the master narrative of the immigration saga, and a reminder that reclaiming our past as women requires a special approach to doing oral history.[27]

NOTES

This chapter is written in memory and in honor of Lee Puey You. My thanks to Daisy and Debbie Gin for sharing their mother's story and immigration file with me; to Michael Frush for his assistance at the National Archives and Records Administration—Pacific Region (San Francisco); to Erika Lee and Jennifer Gee for their insightful analyses of Asian immigrant women's experiences at Angel Island (see chapters 4 and 5 in this book); and to Ruthanne Lum McCunn for her careful reading of an earlier draft of this essay.

1. The exclusion period began with the passage of the Chinese Exclusion Act of 1882, which barred the further immigration of Chinese laborers to the United States, and ended with the repeal of the act in 1943. Between 1910 and 1940, during the time that the Angel Island Immigration Station was in operation, Chinese immigrants were singled out for long detention and subjected to physical examinations and grueling interrogations in order to prove their legal right to enter the country.

2. Him Mark Lai, Genny Lim, and Judy Yung, *Island: Poetry and History of Chinese Immigrants on Angel Island, 1910–1940* (San Francisco: HOC DOI Project, Chinese Culture Foundation of San Francisco, 1980; Seattle: University of Washington Press, 1991).

3. The National Archives and Records Administration—Pacific Region (San Francisco) holds thousands of immigration case files relating to the enforcement of the Chinese Exclusion Act at Angel Island that can be made available to family members and researchers. For details, see Waverly Lowell, "Chinese Immigration and Chinese in the United States: Records in the Regional Archives of the National Archives and Records Administration," National Archives and Records Administration, Reference Information Paper 99 (1996).

4. At my suggestion, Daisy and Debbie Gin looked up their mother's immigration records at the National Archives and Records Administration—Pacific Region in San Bruno, California, and were able to uncover three separate files: documents pertaining to her interrogation at Angel Island in 1939 (Ngim Ah Oy, Folder 39071/12-9, Chinese Departure Case Files, San Francisco District Office, Immigration and Naturalization Service, Record Group 85); the legal briefs of three separate appeals to higher courts not to deport her ("In the Matter of Ngim Ah Oy on Habeas Corpus," Folder 23099R, Admiralty Files, San Francisco District Office, Immigration and Naturalization Service, Record Group 85); and documents pertaining to her deportation hearing in 1955 ("In the Matter of Yim Tai Muey," Folder A6824153, Alien Registration Files, San Francisco District Office, Immigration and Naturalization Service, Record Group 85). The staff at the National Archives could not locate the immigration file of her entry as a war bride in 1947.

5. Chinese wanting to immigrate to the United States during the exclusion period found ways to circumvent the Chinese Exclusion Act by posing as members of the exempt classes—merchants, teachers, students, officials, tourists, and those who claimed derivative U.S. citizenship.

6. Relatives or professionals in the field prepared coaching books for prospective immigrants, giving questions and answers about one's background that immigration officials might ask. For a detailed description of a coaching book, see Judy Yung, *Unbound Voices: A Documentary History of Chinese Women in San Francisco* (Berkeley: University of California Press, 1999), 32–56.

7. The War Brides Act of 1945 was amended in 1947 to allow Chinese American veterans to bring their wives to the United States.

8. In 1937, after Japan's vicious attack on China, war was formally declared between the two countries.

9. Shekki (Shiqi) is the county seat of Chungshan (Zhongshan) District in Guangdong Province.

10. Her fiancé was thirty years her senior.

11. Deaconess Katharine Maurer (1881–1962) was appointed by the Methodist Episcopal Church in 1912 to administer to the needs of immigrants at Angel Island. She was known as the Angel of Angel Island.

12. Because of the diplomatic influence of the Japanese government, and because the Japanese generally had passports and papers to verify their identities, they faced few delays at Angel Island.

13. Most of the women were from the Sze Yup districts of Guangdong Province (Sunwui, Toishan, Hoiping, and Yanping), while Lee Puey You was from Chungshan District, where the Lung Do dialect was spoken.

14. The final report in Lee Puey You's immigration file cited numerous discrepancies in her own testimonies about her birth date and in her alleged father's testimony about his family background and the exact birth dates and different names given to his twin children (Lee Puey You was supposedly the older twin child).

15. Lee Puey You is probably referring to the immigration building at 630 Sansome Street near Washington Street, where she was detained in 1947 on her second attempt to enter the United States. After the fire in 1940, Chinese detainees were temporarily housed at 801 Silver Avenue in San Francisco.

16. Indeed, beginning in the 1950s, decisions on one's eligibility for admission into the United States were made at the port of departure.

17. Felicia Lowe, *Carved in Silence*, San Francisco, Felicia Lowe Productions, distributed by Cross Currents Media, 1987.

18. According to Daisy Gin, her mother never converted to Christianity but was always open to all belief systems.

19. According to Lee Puey You's immigration file, her lawyer actually filed three appeals on her behalf—first to the U.S. District Court, then to the U.S. Circuit Court of Appeals, and finally to the U.S. Supreme Court.

20. It took Lee Puey You fourteen years to come to America, counting from 1932, when she was betrothed and first issued a visa, to 1947, when she was finally admitted into the United States as a war bride.

21. Yim Tai Muey is the name that Lee Puey You used to enter the United States as a war bride in 1947.

22. Lee Puey You gave her testimony in Chinese. Through an interpreter, the transcript was

rendered in English. I have intentionally quoted the transcript as is and not corrected any of the grammatical errors in it.

23. "Cr" refers to the Chinese Republic, which was established in 1912. Lee Puey You was born in the fifth year, fifth month, and third day of the Chinese Republic, or June 3, 1916, according to the Western calendar.

24. Sai Chan (pseudonym I chose to use in compliance with INS regulations) is a U.S. citizen and World War II veteran.

25. At the time of this INS interview, Lee Puey You's youngest daughter, Debbie Gin, had not been born yet.

26. Similarly, according to her daughter Daisy Gin, Lee Puey You led a courageous and a very "in character" struggle with cancer before she died in 1996: "She underwent a mastectomy in 1985 and would insist on taking the bus to her chemotherapy sessions on her own, only to take a taxi afterwards to play mah jong in some Chinatown alley! She then underwent a very major operation for pancreatic cancer in 1990, where most of her digestive system was removed. She was given a prognosis of only six months to a year, even with repeated chemotherapy. She surprised and was marveled by her surgeon and physicians when she passed the five-year mark. She waved off medical advice about diet and diabetes-control measures and said that she knew how to take care of her own body." Email communication to author, September 10, 2000.

27. See Sherna Gluck, "What's So Special about Women? Women's Oral History," *Frontiers: A Journal of Women's Studies* 2:2 (Summer 1977): 3–17; and Judy Yung, "Giving Voice to Chinese American Women," *Frontiers: A Journal of Women's Studies* 19:3 (1998): 130–56.

8

Filipina American Journal Writing
Recovering Women's History

Gail M. Nomura

In 1985, Dorothy Laigo Cordova, founder and executive director of the Filipino American National Historical Society (FANHS), launched the Filipino Women in America: 1860–1985 project, which resulted in a celebrated traveling historical photo exhibit on the history of Filipina Americans. While simultaneously collecting oral histories, documents, and photographs for the project, Cordova started women's journal-writing groups to encourage women to write their own histories and share their stories with their families and community. Through journal writing, Cordova helped the women rediscover and write their personal history.

This chapter offers some preliminary observations on journal writing as a way to access knowledge of women's everyday lives so often left unrecorded in history. When writing women's history, we often are faced with the problem of locating sources to document their daily life experiences. One method to aid in retrieving this record of ordinary women's lives is the use of journal-writing groups. More than mere memories committed to paper, journal writing can be a powerful tool in recovering personal and community history. Cordova's journal-writing project is an example of how this way of collecting history can shed new light on women's history.

"Sharing Our Heritage"

The idea for collecting women's history through journal writing emerged when Cordova attended a conference and heard some older people reading from their journals. At a meeting of a group planning the annual Women's Heritage Month events in Seattle for 1982, Cordova suggested that journal writing might be a good way of collecting history. One of the planning group members was Esther Helfgott, who was writing on Jewish women's history. Having conducted effective journal-writing sessions with Holocaust survivors, she taught the group about a different kind of journal writing that involved a catharsis as people wrote of images and emotions associated with those images. People were not just keeping a private daily journal but were doing group writing exercises led by Helfgott. It was the reading aloud and sharing of their words and emotions that opened people up. Hearing group members read back their journal entries and share emotions enabled people who had been in denial to see that it was okay to speak about even the unspeakable.

Helfgott began training a core group of women planning the Women's Heritage Month activities in her method of leading journal-writing sessions. This led to the "Sharing Our Heritage" project for the March 1982 Women's Heritage Month in Seattle, in which the core members led journal-writing workshops for various community groups, encouraging women to write their own histories. Cordova led a women's journal-writing group on the Filipina American experience. Others led groups focusing on writing Jewish women's history, Nordic women's heritage, and discovering our heritage as lesbian women.[1]

The success of this pioneering effort to blaze a new way of collecting women's history was lauded by the head of Washington Women's Heritage, Susan Starbuck, who called the women "Journal Writers Recovering Women's History." In a letter to the group leaders, Starbuck thanked them "for creating something new." She said that they dared "to redefine not only the content of history, but the form of collection as well—the work the historian has to do on herself included in the process of collecting and writing history." She gave special thanks to Esther Helfgott "for time and sharing of her own process of becoming woman and historian, woman historian, historian of women."[2]

Cordova's Journal Writers Recovering Women's History met on March 21, 1982, at her home in Seattle. Eight of the twelve who met were second-generation Filipina Americans and four were war brides (military brides). The organization of this group became the template for the later 1985 journal-writing groups Cordova conducted. The group first gathered to eat lunch prepared by Cordova and to socialize, then started the journal-writing session. Cordova deployed the process she had learned from the group sessions led by Helfgott to draw out the women's thoughts and emotions from the past into their present consciousness and to commit them to paper.

Two examples from journal writings collected from this first session conducted by Cordova illustrate the usefulness of this technique in providing powerful insights into women's lives. For Teresa Jamero, a second-generation Filipina American who had been born and raised in California, kitchen "represented work." The images she wrote spoke of work: "chop wood, get water, cooking, buy kerosene for coal-oil stove, killing the chicken, killing the rabbits, never sat down to a meal." The emotions associated with these images were:

> Work—My early recollection of my mother working so hard in the kitchen. She not only did the cooking for camp, family, she also worked out in the field. My poor mother worked so hard all her life and I will always remember her working hard. Feelings were of resentment, love and anger at myself for not being more helpful. I didn't cook till I was in later years in H.S. Still didn't know how to cook when I got married.[3]

Teresa Ordona Verfaille, another second-generation Filipina American, wrote about how a young girl's sense of awkwardness about body image affected dating experiences:

Well, in high school I never dated. It was kind of hard for me to date. For one thing, it was an all girl school and I never had a chance to meet any boys. For another thing, I was kind of shy. I was scared to do anything on my own. I had two older sisters that told me what to do and when to do it.

Besides that, in high school I wasn't much to look at. I had glasses that were two inches thick, teeth that were not buck, but they went in.

So my mother and dad never had to worry about me going out with boys. I never had any dates in high school.[4]

A New Way of Collecting History

In 1985, Cordova, as director of the Demonstration Project for Asian Americans (DPAA), received a grant from the Department of Education under the Women's Educational Equity Act (WEEA) to develop a project on the history of Filipina American women. Working under a short, one-year timeline for the grant, Cordova collected materials for this history in multiple ways. She conducted journal-writing workshops for different groups of Filipina Americans throughout the United States in conjunction with traditional archival research, oral history interviews, and use of questionnaires. Recalling the almost superhuman multitasking research she conducted, Cordova exclaims, "When I look back on it I'm thinking I was a crazy lady to do it. I must have been nuts!"[5] Workshop sites included the Bay Area, San Diego, Stockton, Washington, D.C., Seattle, and Portland. Using contacts built on more than twenty-five years of networking, Cordova was able to gather a wide range of women, from older pioneer women in their sixties and seventies to young U.S.-born Filipina Americans in their thirties. Cordova says, "I'm glad I collected when I did," because the older pioneer women were still alive and "sharp" enough to recall and write about their experiences.[6]

Cordova built on her experiences in conducting journal-writing sessions for the 1982 Sharing Our Heritage project. Cordova taught the workshop participants that journal writing is a nonrestrictive form of writing. She explained to them, "There are no mistakes. Keep writing free, flowing thoughts. You are writing 'bits and pieces of you.' Journal writing is a method of 'talking to yourself.' Your journal does not have to be a finished product."[7]

She again used a room in the house, the kitchen, as a trigger word to start the women writing. The kitchen, often a gendered space for women, became the starting point for the women to begin composing their lives. She told them to close their eyes and picture a kitchen, then asked them to write a list of single-word images that came to mind. After writing for five minutes, each person read back to the group what they had listed so that everybody felt a part of the whole process. They then began to see there were similarities and dissimilarities in people's images and perceptions of this commonly shared space, kitchen.

Cordova then made them write phrases for ten minutes about their emotions regarding the single-word images associated with kitchen that they had listed. Again they were asked to share what they had written. By this point in the workshop, the women realized that everyone had written something and that, indeed, everyone can write. Cordova next asked them to write paragraphs for twenty minutes on a single topic, such as growing up brown in America if they were second-generation or their first year in America if they were immigrants. They were told that they should write on anything they felt "compelled" to write about, something in their own lives, something personal that they wanted to share. Again they read back what they had written.

Throughout these exercises, the women were reminded repeatedly that they should not worry about the mechanics of writing, grammar, or spelling. These guided writing exercises gradually gave the women confidence in their ability to write their histories and in the process produced a wealth of information on the lives of the women gathered. They committed to paper stories they shared at dinners and get-togethers with friends and relatives and stories they had never shared before. Some people wrote a lot; some wrote little. All participants were asked to sign release forms and give their writings to the DPAA. Most did contribute their writings to the project, but about a third did not because of the personal nature of what they had written or failure to send their journal writing back to DPAA after having asked to be given time to revise and edit what they had written.[8]

Through these workshops, Dorothy Laigo Cordova uncovered the history of Filipina Americans by asking them about their lives and having them write and share their rediscovered memories with the journal-writing group. It involved risk taking to share their thoughts and experiences, but the women were inspired by Cordova to see the importance of recording and sharing their stories. An analysis of the journal writings produced by two Pacific Northwest women's groups in Seattle and Portland gives a sense of how much can be learned from this method of collecting women's history.

The Seattle Journal-Writing Groups

The Seattle groups met for several sessions at Cordova's house over a month-and-a-half period between July and August 1985. Cordova worked separately with the second-generation women and the immigrant women, but sometimes members of one group would participate in the session of the other group.

At one gathering of second-generation Filipina Americans at Cordova's house on July 30, 1985, the beginning writing exercise on "kitchen" triggered vivid memories for Tina Mamallo:[9]

The Kitchen

The kitchen has always been my favorite area, since I was a child. My fond memories take me back to helping my auntie with the many chores in the kitchen. The wood stove was the biggest chore. Once a month I would help auntie and uncle chop and stack the wood into a woodshed. Always keep the ash trap clean and start a fire 30–45 min before getting the stove at a hot temperature for cooking. It was also the heater before the oil heater was purchased. Heavy irons were heated on the wood stove and were perfect for ironing out wrinkles of heavily stacked clothes. Loads of canning and preserves kept us busy during the summer, which were stored in a walk-in pantry. The week-end trips to pick the vegetables and fruits meant the joy of riding in uncle's car bouncing about in the rumble seat. Uncle was chef at one of the hotels and sometimes would share his good delicious recipes at home. However, auntie did a lot of the cooking and baking. How I enjoyed the batch of cookies which filled a large commercial lard can for the many week-end visitors. How I remembered helping in seeing the bottom before the month ended. Other than the ice box which held a block of ice there was also a winter ice box, which was a wooden crate box nailed to the outside of the kitchen window. Next to that window box was my corner of the kitchen where I would climb on my little footstool, which was "Doing My Thing" (washing dishes after dinner).

Emotions in The Kitchen

It was in the kitchen where auntie taught me the time of day with the big Ben wind-up clock which was frustrating and again at the kitchen table one afternoon she wanted to sing a very special song to me. It was called "The Song My Mother Sang To Me." It was the first time I have heard her sing and the last. However at the time I was so impressed and dry eyed, not knowing that the sentiment in future years would fill my eyes with tears. The most trauma in the kitchen at that time was to help prepare a live chicken for dinner. I couldn't bear what was to take place. If you never felt like a scared chicken, I felt exactly like a scared chicken. A SCARED CHICKEN!!

We learn from the journal writings that Filipino fathers often did the cooking for their families. Marya Castillano, second-generation, born and raised in Seattle, observed that[10]

even though there were always a dozen or more people in our household we had lots of food—always more than one main dish w/ our rice and vegetables. My Dad's livelihood was cooking and he did most of the cooking and it was always good and served artistically. My Uncle Emong (my godfather) lived with us and he was a good cook too— mostly Filipino food.

Ticiang Diangson reported her emotion associated with "kitchen" as "contentment— watching my father prepare big dinners."[11]

Most of the second-generation Filipina Americans wrote about "growing up brown." Marya Castillano related a bittersweet tale of belonging:[12]

When I was about 7 or 8 years old, many of my school friends were "junior" girl scouts or Brownies. It was a very "apple pie" aspiration for a young American girl. I wanted very much to be a Brownie but I never became one. One or more of my older brothers had teased me saying that I didn't need to become a "Brownie" because I already was a "Brownie" (a Filipino). Then they laughed and I cried.

Although Castillano never became a Brownie, she had fond memories of growing up brown in the warmth of the Seattle Filipino American community:

4th of July Community Picnic at Seward Park on "Pinoy Hill"—wonderful, carefree, fun memories! organized games—races; each family had its own picnic table or tables and people visited from table to table. Security in numbers maybe because it was great to be a Filipino on Pinoy Hill on the 4th of July. Filipino dances at Washington Hall or Finnish Hall: Filipino hands playing "Red Sails in the Sunset"—my Uncle Phil Begornea's band I remember most vividly; Filipino sailors doing the jitterbug dancing with young Filipina girls my older sister's age; young kids like me watching from the balconies.

One of the journal writings reveals insights into the experiences of mestiza second-generation Filipina Americans. Born and raised in Chicago, Ticiang Diangson's father was Filipino American and her mother was Polish American. Diangson described "growing up brown":[13]

The first time I figured out I was brown I didn't know I was brown I thought I was yellow. I got chased home from kindergarten for being a "Jap." I was "yellow," I was "slant-eyed," I was "the enemy."

My mother told me that "sticks and stones could break my bones but names could never hurt me." I didn't agree—and the kids were throwing sticks and stones too. I went underground and became as quiet and invisible as possible. I picked as my best friend the only Jewish girl in class. We walked to and from school down the side streets for safety. By the time first grade started, kids were used to us. And there were new kids—with German accents—to make fun of.

My father never said anything about the trouble. But one day one of my girlfriends called me a "Jap" and I spit in her face. My mother made me apologize. She told my father and he turned to me and said "You were right."

When I was eleven years old I was out of school for a couple of months for surgery. When I came back it seemed like almost everyone in class had "grown up"—including me. The boys kept on telling me I had bedroom eyes and looked like a sexy Italian movie star. Everyone used to be envious because I could get a dark tan and they would get sunburn. Whenever anybody asked me what I was I told them I was Eurasian like Jennifer Jones in "The Snows of Kilimanjaro" with Gregory Peck.

The first time I had any consciousness that what I was going thru wasn't just some strange thing that was peculiar to me was when I saw the movie "Pinkie" with Jeanne Crain and Ethel Waters. Jean Crain played a half black/half white woman who could pass in white Southern society. It was then that I figured out that my mother and father were not the only mixed race couple in the world. I can remember when they stopped going to public places together. I had always thought it was because they had had a fight about going bowling. I remember now how people used to stare at my blonde mother and me when we watched my father's bowling team.

Ruth Vega is a second-generation Filipina American woman who was caught in the Philippines during World War II. Born in Seattle, her mother took Vega to the Philippines before the outbreak of war. Vega explained how she was able to return to her father in the United States after the end of the war:[14]

American citizens were liberated from Santo Tomas in April 1945. Shortly after that I heard repatriation back to the U.S. was going on. I decided to finish the month of June as secretary of a refugee home before applying for passage to California where my father was.

Since we lost track of him, the Red Cross got busy and located him in no time at all. I was packed off on the troop ship U.S.S. Gen. Harry Taylor with about 10 or 15 civilians and hoards (seemingly) of soldiers.

Our boat zigzagged its way across the Pacific dodging mines—most of the adult civilians got seasick. I got the job of babysitting and entertaining the kids, distributing crackers and bagoong from the Filipino steward who was not allowed in the women's quarters.

We landed in San Francisco greeted by the Red Cross who showed us where we could buy some warm clothes. Red Cross ladies were very hospitable and accommodating. They drove us around and helped us catch trains to our final destination. She made sure the train conductor knew where I was getting off so I wouldn't get lost. Thermal, Calif. did not have a station and was not a usual stopping place. I was all alone and had butterflies in my stomach all the way.

Maria Batayola, born in the Philippines, immigrated with her family to Seattle as a fourteen-year-old teenager in 1969. She wrote of her impressions of America:[15]

I'm 30 years old. I've gone this far with a promise that if I can just live the same number of years in this country as I have in the Philippines I will be ok—not complete, not whole, just ok. I won't have to choose being one or the other—maybe be more American to continue to grow—but I'm not even allowed that.

I am glad I did not have the intellectual understanding I have now of my instinctive awareness back then of what it is to be oppressed. Otherwise I would have been very depressed, very angry possibly without hope.

I came in 1969, 14 years old with two months notice from my Dad that we could be immigrating. My uncle was ruthlessly murdered leaving my mother without immediate kin, without bonds to the Philippines. Being the second daughter who had chores but did not have to be fully responsible, I was a junior in high school by day and played with dolls by night.

Our whole family (Mom, Dad, older 16 yr. sister Teresita, younger brother 12 yr. old) immigrated. I remember the cold of Seattle coming at Indian summer with Americans wearing shorts while we shivered in our PI made "winter" coats made of satin. I remember my cocky loud cousins giving us a joyride on freeways with frightening speed. I remember speaking with what sounded like a stutter because the cold made my jaw vibrate—speaking in Irish accent to American brown cousins who sounded black. . . .

Coming to my Auntie's house in the heart of black central area—I saw blacks who reminded me of one of my ancestors—negritos. We slept 24 hours exhausted from Uncles and Aunts who are saying "Remember me I knew you when you were this high?" I was so disoriented. I ate cottage cheese and peaches and could not tell of why I was choking back tears of remembering mangoes—that there would be no more mangoes in this cold begotten place. 24–36 hours of sleep was what followed. We were in one bedroom. Mom and Dad in a double bed, Teresita and I in a single bed. I have not slept with my sister so closely since womanhood. I have not slept in a room with my parents much less slept with a man in the room. New things to deal with, I didn't know I was sad—depressed. My mind kept repeating conversations with classmates of "Bring me back some snow" I promised yes in a can, I would imagine similar to the way chorizo cans are packed with white lard. Yes, I'll send you snow—but in my mind, it'll just be water. What I didn't tell them was that I don't want to write them, I don't want to feel sad, I don't want to re-member them.

(skipped to finish)

I could not put up what with I called impoliteness but now call bullshit, arrogance. I know now it is white arrogance. I have been too much of a whole person as a citizen, a woman even in my young years as a pinay. I have been too much of a majority to put up with being a minority.

The immigrant Filipina Americans met at Cordova's house on August 23, 1985. One clear distinction between the experiences and background of the second-generation Filipina Americans and the immigrant women participants is revealed in their writings of kitchen images and emotions associated with kitchen. Unlike the second generation, who wrote about associating work with kitchen, these immigrant women's class back-ground and the economy in the Philippines allowed them to delegate kitchen work to maids. Flori Montante (Gavino), whose father went to the United States, leaving his family behind in the Philippines, explained:[16]

We have housemaids to do all the preparation, dirty work and cleaning, which makes it easy—what you do is just supervise and direct them what to do—when everything is done you just arrange and garnish the food prepared according to your taste or style—you can have as many parties without being burdened of tedious work.

Gloria Adams had similar views about kitchen work. Adams was a school principal in the Philippines before coming to the United States, first in 1966 as an official observer of the U.S. public schools and youth agencies and then in 1968 to work, after marrying an American. She wrote:[17]

The abundance of maids in the Philippines makes it easier to maintain an effective func-tional and tidy kitchen. I hate kitchen work and the kitchen has never been a priority for me and so is the rest of household work.

My hatred for household work tends to limit my social activities at home here while I love to have company at home in the Philippines because I don't have to do anything there.

Obdulia (Dolly) R. Castillo came twice to the United States, the first time as exchange student in 1953 to Arizona, where she met another exchange student. They returned to Philippines and got married and later returned to United States as teachers. Castillo ex-plained the differences between kitchens in the Philippines and the United States:[18]

In the Philippines I seldom went to the kitchen except to snack and check if I smell something burning, or to check if my kitchen needed some groceries. The maids usually cooked and did everything. What we did was just to go and eat when the meals were ready.

In the Philippines we used—especially in the province very "plebian" gadgets—stove made of clay, pots made of clay, ladles made of bamboo and wood carved. Even the "glasses" were made from coconut cups—called "ongot." We used a angoyob to keep the fires burning. The maid cut wood for firewood, food placed in several baskets up in the ceiling. Fish and meat was mostly dried—if we cooked fish and meat we usually ate them with little leftover—or it gets spoiled. We cooked breakfast in salaposop if we have time—corn meal steamed with carrot (not U.S. carrots) and our spices were hanged at the doorway and windows.

In the U.S. all the appliances can be managed by one person, no maids so you do it by yourself—everything is done by one person—from stove, refrigerator, freezer, microwave, garbage disposal and kitchen aide—lots of water and sink and lots of grocery nearby store, lots of food in boxes and ready made—ready to cook. Easy to prepare—all the time-saving devices.

Flori Montante (Gavino) wrote a particularly compelling account of her first impression of the United States. She was a teacher in the Philippines and had saved money to come as a visitor (tourist) to see her father, who had been so long estranged from the family:[19]

IMPRESSION:
When I came to the U.S.—

To see my dad face to face and show myself as his daughter in the Philippines who is not just anybody to be left behind and forgotten—It is petty but it is true—it was sort of to spite him and vengeance in mind.

I succeeded but I regretted—

Later my cousins wanted me to stay and so they got me a teaching job in the Catholic schools and got me my green card and so I became a citizen.

U.S. was disappointing—I thought it better just like—but Seattle was a conservative place.

The Portland Writing Group

The Portland journal-writing group met for a focused one-day workshop at the Filipino American Association community hall. The participants were mainly immigrant women who wrote about the challenges and opportunities of immigrating to the United States.

The Portland Filipina Americans produced vivid descriptions of their first impressions of the United States. Estela B. Feliciano, a nurse who arrived in 1949, wrote:[20]

When I first stepped on U.S. soil I was surprised to see San Francisco surrounded with mountains and beautiful homes built on them. I expected it to be flat like Manila. At home we always think of people up the hills as our poor relations, where as here, only the well-to-do could afford to live there.

It was in the summer month when I arrived, July, yet I found the weather so cold. I think I was the only one walking on the street with a sweater and coat walking hunched over to protect my stomach from the cold winds. The buildings and transportation didn't surprise me as they were the same as those in Manila.

Another thing I found quite different was the taste of the food. They are called the same and looked the same as the ones at home but the taste was just not there. I was quite exhausted when I first landed here because I was sea sick for 19 days out of the 21 days that it took us to get there by ship. I spent my first week in Frisco confined at home and mostly in bed trying to get my bearings but most of all just trying to keep warm. I remember what a funny sight my friend and I must have been sleeping in socks and sweater in our pjs and also a night cap. The Filipinos we stayed with were very kind and understanding.

Concordia G. Hortaleza came to Portland in 1952 as the wife of a naturalized U.S. citizen. She wrote:[21]

When I first arrived here in U.S., I thought everything was beautiful, because it was springtime, but when I first tasted the food like corn on a cob, fish, etc., they tasted different from what we use to eat in P.I. Our food over there is always fresh. Here it was different. I feel cold all the time and I wanted to go home, 'cause you don't have anybody to talk to except your husband. We live in an apartment. The food I enjoyed so much was ice cream. I was so happy when I met several Filipinos. One was my cababayan— Jonny Soy.

As we are starting a new life here, no money, my husband don't make much, I did my washing by hand. I have two sisters who live with me in the P.I. so I depend on them to do all the work as I am always in school. Now I do all the work and I'm very good at it. All the conveniences are here, so I'm so glad about it. Now I love the life here.

Jem C. Winquist, who arrived in Portland in 1972 as the wife of a Peace Corps worker, wrote:[22]

My husband and I arrived July 2, 1972. It was raining and very cold. It was a month of getting to know and getting adjusted to a new country. I watched and observed and got involved in many activities [as] I can. I could not drive so I rode the bus. I learned the town and it's beauty in the different areas. I like the cleanliness, the convenience and the orderliness of everything—from stores, packages meat (as opposed to open market at home), paved streets all over!

I was impressed with the abundance of supply! Light was on in a switch, heat was on in a few minutes, dinner was cooked. Wow! the *instant* magic of time! It seems everything about me moved fast—TIME was of (the) essence! Clocks in buildings, stores, radio, cars, kitchens, living room walls, etc. etc. The telephone was also quite impressive—the instant communicator. Distance was all of a sudden just a dial away! People were also interested in me. They knew I was new—I was asked often how I felt. Buying during my first month was quite trying. Petite sizes were non-existent at the time and I was always sent to the children's department! Well, what do you know, I borrowed a sewing machine and made my *own* designer clothes!!! I was easy to please. I tried everything I could taste. I also noticed people did not walk as much, they drove their cars or rode the bus.

The women's journal writings provide insights into early community building among the Filipino Americans in Portland. Estela B. Feliciano explained the early community formation:[23]

The Filipino American Association of Portland and Vicinity came into existence in 1959 because at that time there were just a handful of Filipinos in Portland and yet we didn't know all of them or have the opportunity to meet and get acquainted. Knowing more townmates helps homesickness. Those of us who were working in the service area and are in contact with so many different nationalities also felt the necessity of being identified as Filipinos—distinct from other Asians who we may resemble in color and looks.

With families—mine included—gathered in a birthday party, the idea of forming an organization was brought up. So I think it was in January of 1959 when we finally met, after calling every Filipino we know within a 30 mile radius, in Mr. and Mrs. Julian Llanis basement. There were 31 incorporated and our first president, Mr. Perlas, was elected. We had 17 officers and that practically took all the membership because not all 31 persons joined the organization then. This handful of people really worked hard to bring the organization to what it is now.

We had a lot of good times when meetings were conducted in private homes. No matter what the number we all felt a closeness that you won't find in a public building. But since we can't stay in stagnant, I suppose some of the good things have to be sacrificed.

The goals of the organization are highly motivated by willingness to help one another in times of need, as in looking for jobs, emergency shelter or food or calamities as death in a family. Also, foster better understanding among each other as well as the country we live in.

Concordia G. Hortaleza further noted that one of the purposes of the Filipino American Association was to do public performances of Filipino culture:[24]

We perform some activities, such as, dancing for other towns and also for the Park Bureau. We exhibit our Filipino dances during (the) Rose Festival of Portland, some schools and join parade of the different organizations, and some towns of Oregon. Even our children form their organization called F.A.Y.A. or Filipino American Youth. I love our Association as it is getting widely known here in America.

Marcelina (Marcing) Pimentel explained why she and her husband joined the association:[25]

Joining the Association was good for the both of us 'cause being from the north end of the Philippines we were able to get acquainted with Filipino people from different parts of the Philippines. I was, as I remember, the youngest member of the association at that time. I felt then, out of place, because they were mostly old people. The way they talk especially when expressing themselves in English, I always thought they were fighting. We had good leaders and we tried to struggle hard to let the American people know we exist. The Association from the beginning of its birth was called to show the cultures of the Philippines in any way. But what was asked for mostly was our folk dances, which we do whenever we can. Portland at this point knew we are around, so every time the city, TV and radio station, churches, schools, clubs and other organizations want Filipino performances we are represented.

Dolores Flores, who came to the United States in 1948 as a bride of a member of the First and Second Filipino Infantry Regiment, explained that her children were one reason she joined the Filipino American Association:[26]

Marcing asked us to join, as she also know I have five children, to get acquainted with other Filipinos in the city, and also my children has to meet their age group while they are growing up. Also they can learn the culture and learn folk dancing that the Filipino American Association offered, especially during our Fiestas.

Also on Christmas time when we have potlucks, you bring your favorite foods—taste everybody's cooking. Meeting new faces in the community. . . . When we have fund raisings—as we have a Filipino-American Hall to pay. We learn how to cooperate and work hard together, no matter what happens.

Milargros F. Castro explained that cultural pride and preservation were one reason she joined the Filipino American Association:[27]

I was born Filipino and I am very proud to be a Filipino. I have a very good respect to all Filipinos and really admire people who are proud of our culture and heritage.

As a Filipino, I joined the organization for Filipino-American Association so I could probably in some ways help them introduce our culture and heritage. I was so involved in Philippine folk dances that I was assigned to be the chairman of the entertainment in our association and director of the dance group. It was my aim to preserve our tradition, beautiful customs of the Filipinos by way of its dances and folk songs. Filipino are very talented in their own capacity and we should be proud of this. Also I am trying my best to be active and helpful in the association for the sake of our younger children.

In my personal opinion, my children were all born here in the United States and I still don't know what my kids will think about Filipinos. So being a Filipino mother, I am trying my best to teach them and introduce to them our beautiful culture so they will have good sight and feelings towards the Filipinos. Being involved in the association together with the children will help them be a real Filipino.

Jem C. Winquist summed up the deeper meaning of community embodied in the act of coming together in the Filipino American Association:[28]

To give myself an extension of "family." There are certain atmosphere, culture, events that come together in a big group. Extending myself in a way to help someone that might be in need. I also have children that are born and are being raised here; I would like them to see, feel and be a part, first hand, what the Filipino heritage is—of which is theirs too, when I continue to expose them to Filipinos in the community.

Festivities and hospitality are the external manifestations of our Filipino organization activities and the underlying caring, gentleness and interest and concern for one another are the main characters that come out when you associate with the organization—That I would also like in my children. Therefore, the organization served as my support group for the ideals I have in preserving the culture. I benefit from the organization and I like the organization to benefit from me.

Conclusion

One of the pioneers in conducting oral history projects, Dorothy Laigo Cordova found that conducting journal-writing workshops was a useful additional method to retrieve history, especially when faced with a highly limited timeframe in which to complete a history project. Oral history involves a long, tedious, and expensive process of transcribing the one- to two-hour taped interviews. Group journal-writing sessions of one and a half to three hours produce a remarkable quantity and quality of writing. Moreover, because the women can write on whatever topics they feel "compelled to write about," the women themselves determine what they write about and how they represent their lives, without the constant mediation of the ever-present interviewer questioning and guiding them according to a standardized interview schedule, as in an oral history project. As Cordova explains, "You know that's [journal writing] a good way because it is in their words."[29]

Over the last twenty years, Cordova has trained many women and men to lead journal-writing groups. She conducts a journal-writing workshop at every FANHS national conference, and in a one-and-a-half-hour session she teaches participants how to do journal writing, making it an engaging and fun exercise. One FANHS group in the Bay Area recently published a collection of their journal writings titled *Seven Card Stud with Seven Manangs Wild*.[30]

Cordova believes that journal writing is a powerful method of collecting information about women's lives and experiences and of accessing women's voices. The personal narratives provide new insight into women's lives and challenge traditional boundaries defining who can write history. Journal writing is a powerful method to retrieve and reconstruct women's history.

Dorothy Laigo Cordova is a woman historian teaching historians of women how women can write our history. She embodies the spirit of the inquisitive historian who just has to know: "I don't know, you know the whole thing about history, there are so many ways of retrieving information if you are curious enough. And me for instance, I'm the type of person if I hear a siren I want to go chasing after it. I've always been like that. I have to know. It is really important for me to know or to at least have some understanding of it." She laughs and exclaims, "And I am always amazed when people don't have that same sense of inquiry!"[31]

NOTES

I thank Dorothy Laigo Cordova for guiding me to these sources and sharing with me her knowledge of journal writing and the invaluable materials she has gathered for the Filipino American National Historical Society Archives. Thank you, too, to Emi Nomura Sumida for her assistance with this project.

1. See draft letter by Ellen Jahoda of the Washington Women's Heritage Project to community groups and draft press release on "Sharing Our Heritage," undated (February? 1982), Seattle/1982 file, Filipino American National Historical Society (FANHS) Archives (hereafter cited as FANHS Archives), Seattle, Washington.

2. Susan Starbuck to Journal Writers Recovering Women's History, March 15, 1982, Seattle/1982 file, FANHS Archives, Seattle, Washington.

3. Journal entry, Teresa Jamero, March 21, 1982, Seattle/1982 file, FANHS Archives, Seattle, Washington.

4. Journal entry, Teresa Ordona Verfaille, Filipino Women Journal Writing Group, Cordova Home/March 21, 1982 file, Seattle/1982 file, FANHS Archives, Seattle, Washington.

5. Interview with Dorothy Laigo Cordova, August 21, 2002, FANHS national office, Seattle, Washington.

6. Interview with Dorothy Laigo Cordova, August 21, 2002.

7. Instructions for Journal Writing Workshops, Demonstration Project for Asian Americans/WEEA Project—Filipino Women in America files, FANHS Archives, Seattle, Washington.

8. Information on the workshop process was derived from instructions for Journal Writing Workshops, and from an interview with Dorothy Laigo Cordova, August 21, 2002.

9. Christina Amado Mamallo, Seattle/July 30, 1985 file, FANHS Archives, Seattle, Washington.

10. Marya Castillano, Seattle/July 30, 1985 file, FANHS Archives, Seattle, Washington.

11. Ticiang Diangson, Seattle/July 30, 1985 file, FANHS Archives, Seattle, Washington.

12. Marya Castillano, Seattle/July 30, 1985 file, FANHS Archives, Seattle, Washington.

13. Ticiang Diangson, Seattle/July 30, 1985 file, FANHS Archives, Seattle, Washington.

14. Ruth Vega, Seattle/July 30, 1985 file, FANHS Archives, Seattle, Washington.

15. Maria Batayola, Seattle/July 30, 1985 file, FANHS Archives, Seattle, Washington.

16. Flori Montante (Gavino), Seattle/August 23, 1985 file, FANHS Archives, Seattle, Washington.

17. Gloria Adams, Seattle/August 23, 1985 file, FANHS Archives, Seattle, Washington.

18. Obdulia (Dolly) R. Castillo, Seattle/August 23, 1985 file, FANHS Archives, Seattle, Washington.

19. Flori Montante (Gavino), Seattle/August 23, 1985 file, FANHS Archives, Seattle, Washington.

20. Estela B. Feliciano, Portland/August 25, 1985 file, FANHS Archives, Seattle, Washington.

21. Concordia G. Hortaleza, Portland/August 25, 1985 file, FANHS Archives, Seattle, Washington.

22. Jem C. Winquist, Portland/August 25, 1985 file, FANHS Archives, Seattle, Washington.

23. Estela B. Feliciano, Portland/August 25, 1985 file, FANHS Archives, Seattle, Washington.

24. Concordia G. Hortaleza, Portland/August 25, 1985 file, FANHS Archives, Seattle, Washington.

25. Marcelina (Marcing) Pimentel, Portland/August 25, 1985 file, FANHS Archives, Seattle, Washington.

26. Dolores Flores, Portland/August 25, 1985 file, FANHS Archives, Seattle, Washington.

27. Milargros F. Castro, Portland/August 25, 1985 file, FANHS Archives, Seattle, Washington.

28. Jem C. Winquist, Portland/August 25, 1985 file, FANHS Archives, Seattle, Washington.

29. Interview with Dorothy Laigo Cordova, August 21, 2002.

30. Helen C. Toribio, ed., *Seven Card Stud with Seven Manangs Wild: An Anthology of Filipino-American Writings* (San Francisco: East Bay Filipino American National Historical Society, 2002).

31. Interview with Dorothy Laigo Cordova, August 21, 2002.

Part 4

Contesting Cultural Formations and Practices, Constructing New "Hybrid" Lives

9

"The Ministering Angel of Chinatown"
Missionary Uplift, Modern Medicine, and Asian American Women's Strategies of Liminality

Judy Tzu-Chun Wu

> Any woman surgeon . . . bucks heavy odds of lay prejudice and professional resentment at usurpation of what many consider to be a man's undisputed field and when that woman is an American of Chinese descent she is granted even fewer mistakes and less leisure.
> —Margaret Chung, *Los Angeles Times*, 25 June 1939

In 1916, Margaret Jessie Chung (1889–1959) graduated from the University of Southern California's College of Physicians and Surgeons, becoming the first known American-born Chinese woman physician. She overcame gender, racial, and economic barriers to attain medical training. As a member of a large, impoverished family, she worked to pay for her own education, barely making enough to pay for tuition and sustenance. In her unpublished autobiography, she recalled, "All the time that I was in Medical College I do not remember having three square meals a day."[1]

Margaret Chung's strategies to establish a career in the predominantly white and male medical profession provide insight into Asian American women's negotiations of gender, sexual, racial, and class boundaries in both mainstream American society and their own ethnic communities during the early twentieth century. Prior to World War II, the overwhelming majority of Asian Americans, immigrants as well as American-born, men as well as women, worked in low-status and labor-intensive occupations. A small but increasing number of Asian Americans succeeded in gaining access to higher education and professional training.[2] However, racial discrimination limited their ability to pursue careers in mainstream society. In addition, female professionals faced obstacles due to gender discrimination. In response, Asian American professionals pursued racial and gender "separatism" as vocational strategies.[3] Like other people of color, they established themselves in segregated communities to offer services to co-ethnics. Women also took advantage of social norms that discouraged gender mixing to provide medical care for other women.

At first glance, Chung's career appears to follow this pattern of professional separatism. She initially wanted to practice medicine in China and eventually founded a clinic in San Francisco's Chinatown. However, Chung's professional efforts there met with mixed results. Seeking to serve other women of Chinese ancestry, she mainly attracted white, male patients. A closer examination of her medical training and early practice provides a more nuanced understanding of changing racial, gender, and sexual dynamics in the mainstream society as well as in the Chinese American community. Her pioneering efforts to enter the medical profession reveal how Asian American women used their liminality, their "in between" gender and racial identities, to negotiate the shifting social boundaries of the early twentieth century.

The "Medical Lady Missionary"

Margaret Chung came of age, both personally and professionally, during a transitional historical period. She was born in late Victorian America, a society founded upon gender inequality and racial hierarchy. Women, viewed as innately incapable of entering the public world of work and politics, were consigned to the private sphere of home and family. Nonwhites, designated as inferior races by prevailing Darwinian theories, experienced an escalation of racial violence and segregation. While Chung was raised in this world, she completed medical training and embarked on a career as the broader society self-consciously entered a modern age that celebrated values of equality and cosmopolitanism. The transformation in social norms at this time occurred unevenly and incompletely. By 1920, women gained the right to vote and increasingly rejected traditional gender constraints. While these changes presaged the merging of gender spheres, both women and men continued to embrace notions of essentialized gender difference. Similarly, the 1920s signaled contradictory notions about race. The 1924 Immigration Act almost completely barred Asians from entry into the United States. At the same time though, middle-class whites "slummed" in working-class and segregated neighborhoods to experience exotic forms of entertainment. Social scientists also entered these communities to further their studies of cultural and racial differences.[4] Chung's motivations for becoming a physician and her strategies for obtaining a professional education reflect the changes as well as the continuities in racial and gender norms during this conflicted era.

Chung's desire to become a physician was inspired by Victorian Christian missionary teachings. Her parents, Ah Yane (1869–1914) and Chung Wong ([1860–1862]–1917), immigrated separately to the United States in the mid-1870s and received religious instruction and support from Presbyterian missionaries in California.[5] The white reformers, who organized themselves as a branch of the *foreign* missionary society, viewed their work with the Chinese in the United States as an extension of their efforts in China, the central site for American proselytizing activities. Influenced by Christian ideals, Chung aspired to become what the religious reformers referred to as a "medical lady missionary," a physician who could bring spiritual as well as physical healing to potential converts, especially to other women.[6] By "ministering to the body," Presbyterian missionaries hoped to "reach the soul" of Chinese women, who in turn could convert their families and communities to Christianity.

This plan of chain conversion relied on traditional conceptions of gender and race separatism to promote educational and professional opportunities for Asian and Asian American women. Missionaries portrayed women's entry into the male realm of medicine not as a departure from but as an extension of traditional female qualities and responsibilities. One publication explained: "Woman with her quick intuitions, her exquisite tact, her tender sympathies, is welcomed as a ministering angel by her suffering sisters in those countries whose customs forbid the presence of a male physician."[7] Female medical missionaries were characterized by their nurturing and moral qualities and not by their rational, scientific minds. Furthermore, women doctors were necessary for societies that uphold social separation of the sexes. In fact, missionaries targeted women for conversion based on traditional expectations of female responsibility over child rearing and moral education.

Similarly, Christian reformers used racial and cultural hierarchy to justify the medical training of Asian women. The missionaries viewed their religion and science as superior to the customs and beliefs of their "native" converts. In their eyes, traditional Chinese medicine demonstrated the culture's "intellectual darkness" and correlated with superstitious beliefs about religion.[8] Despite these derogatory views of Chinese practices, the belief that Chinese people could be transformed and uplifted inspired the reformers to offer a "humane" expression of imperialism abroad and a "benevolent" form of racialism in the United States.

Seeking to train lady medical missionaries from "native" ranks, western proselytizers provided opportunities for the educational and professional training of Asian and Asian American women. During the late nineteenth and early twentieth centuries, they founded female academies, medical schools, and hospitals throughout Asia. In a few cases, Asian Christians were encouraged to travel to the United States to obtain further religious and professional training. In fact, the first Chinese female students to arrive in the United States came to study medicine and eventually returned to their homeland to serve as medical missionaries.[9] Their status as students technically exempted them from the Chinese Exclusion Act of 1882. However, it was their connections with American missionaries that facilitated their entry and created educational opportunities. The combined efforts of creating medical institutions in Asia and sponsoring overseas studies contributed to a sizable population of Asian female physicians. In China alone, women doctors constituted 12 percent of the profession by 1920, more than double the percentage in the United States.[10]

Liminality and the Medical Academy

As an American-born Chinese Christian woman, Chung held similar aspirations of serving her ancestral homeland as a medical missionary. To enter and succeed in the academy, a realm traditionally dominated by white Americans and men, she selectively adapted values instilled by Victorian missionaries to respond to emerging modern social values. Chung crafted her gender and racial identities as flexible assets that demonstrated her ability to assimilate into the professional norm yet also highlighted her embodiment of difference to gain support and recognition. She sought acceptance from the masculine medical profession even as she allied herself with other women and female organizations. She embraced western, scientific culture yet capitalized on her Chinese ancestry to create professional opportunities. Unable to erase her racial and gender difference, she tried to use her "otherness" to her advantage.

Chung's desire to become a medical missionary most likely influenced her decision to pursue preparatory studies and medical training at the University of Southern California (USC). Established by the Methodist Episcopal Church in 1881, USC emphasized its religious affiliation and mission. When Chung began attending the preparatory school in 1907, the university bulletin explained that all students were expected to attend daily chapel exercises and the church regularly.[11] Although the Presbyterian Church also established an academy affiliated with Occidental College, USC may have been more attractive to Chung because the institution housed a College of Medicine that accepted applicants with only high school diplomas.

This criterion for admission was not unusual in the early twentieth century. A variety of schools existed in the United States that provided training in diverse health-care approaches, including herbal medicine, midwifery, homeopathy, and other eclectic forms of treatment. However, "regular" physicians, who allied themselves with "modern" scientific medicine that emphasized laboratory research and hospital-based health care, increasingly sought to regulate the profession by instituting a series of reforms through the American Medical Association and the state. Under pressure to match rising standards for medical training, schools like USC increasingly established more stringent criteria for admission and graduation. Had Chung applied a few years after 1911, she would not have gained entry without college preparation. She also was fortunate to complete her studies in 1916. In 1920, the USC medical college became one of many schools to close due to its financial inability to meet the requirements of a first-rate institution. The contraction of schools, under the banner of promoting "modern" medicine, had a disproportionate impact on women and people of color. "Heterodox" academies tended to have more open admission policies, while "regular" programs at separatist women's and historically black colleges generally lacked the economic resources to improve facilities and training.[12]

Despite her fortune in historical timing, Chung still needed determination and resourcefulness to become a physician. For one thing, the economic instability of her family repeatedly interrupted and delayed her education. Although Chung Wong began his marriage as a merchant, he soon pursued a variety of agricultural occupations—vegetable grower, rancher, and dairy operator—to sustain his family of seven children. The economic precariousness of the Chung family mirrored the experiences of other Chinese Americans in the racially stratified labor market of the American West. As a result of their poverty, the Chungs moved from Santa Barbara, where Margaret was born, to Ventura County in 1899 and then to Los Angeles shortly after the turn of the century. As the eldest child, Margaret contributed to her family's welfare by pitting apricots, caning rattan chairs, mowing hay, and working in a Chinese restaurant. The series of moves as well as the necessity of employment delayed her education.

When Margaret began grade nine at the USC preparatory school, she was nearly eighteen years old.

While Chung's background clearly posed an obstacle to obtaining an education, her gender and racial identity supplied her with assets as well as liabilities in her efforts. Women constituted a small minority during the years that Chung attended medical school (1911–1916). To succeed in this environment, Chung experimented with both integrating into the masculine milieu and seeking support through women's separate organizations.

Chung's choice of clothing and her nickname provide indications of her efforts to assimilate into a male profession. During her second year in medical school, in which she was the only woman out of twenty-three students, the annual photo reveals her practicing partial cross-dressing.[13] While she was publicly known to be a woman, she dressed like a man. Her hair was either short or pulled back, and she wore a dark suit with a tie. Chung apparently enjoyed adopting masculine clothing and a male persona. Her favorite picture during the 1910s through the 1930s featured her in similar attire. She sent autographed versions of the photo to her friends and chose to identify herself as "Mike."

Chung was not alone in her practice of cross-dressing. A number of professional women during the turn of the twentieth century adopted masculine dress and nomenclature to symbolize their entry into traditionally male realms. The practice of cross-dressing both blurred and reinforced gender boundaries. By assuming male dress and identities, women demonstrated their ability to assume masculine occupations and to assert traditionally male privileges. At the same time, the association of men's clothing with independence and professionalization illustrated the gap between gender groups. Chung's status in medical school reflected the unequal incorporation of women into traditionally male realms. P. M. Suski, a Japanese immigrant who entered USC medical school one year after Chung, recalled that she was "a very bright and popular sophomore student" who served as an officer for both her class and the general medical student body that year.[14] In contrast to her preparatory school years, however, in which women had constituted approximately 44 percent of the student population and regularly acted as high-ranking class officers, she occupied the traditionally female office of secretary.

In addition to attempting to assimilate into the male student body, Chung joined gender-segregated organizations. In 1914, she helped found the USC chapter of Nu Sigma Phi, a women's medical sorority. She also participated in the campus Young Women's Christian Association (YWCA). The topic of her speech to the YWCA in October 1913 exemplified the opportunities as well as the tensions in her years in medical school. Speaking on the theme of "friendship," Chung argued for the importance of diversity: "We need the friendship of those whose interests and types of mind differ most from our own. The University offers a great opportunity for such friendship and students cannot afford to be exclusive."[15] Her call for inclusion reflects upon her own achievements of entering a traditionally masculine and predominantly white career world. However, the fact that she spoke this message about diversity to an organization of Christian women suggests that Chung also felt the need for support from those of like minds.

The racial composition of Chung's classes throughout her education at USC mirrored the skewed gender ratio in the medical school. Despite her popularity, Chung, as the only nonwhite student in her medical school class, became a target for discrimination. As she recalled, she "knew the bitterness of racial prejudice."[16]

Similar to her strategies relating to gender, Chung adopted a flexible approach to her cultural and racial identities to relate to the predominantly white student body at USC. Born in the United States and raised by Christian parents, she identified with mainstream culture. She believed in the power of western medicine, especially surgery, and expressed little interest in Chinese herbal medicine. Perhaps as an indication of her educational priorities and/or the result of the moderate numbers of Chinese in the areas where she lived, Chung had limited Chinese language skills. Furthermore, she avoided Chinese dress. While her baby pictures indicate that her parents occasionally outfitted her in Chinese costumes, Chung donned western clothing for her schooling and profession. As one of her medical mentors remarked, "She never wore Chinese clothes, but on all occasions appeared in a thin black tailored suit."[17]

While Chung adopted mainstream cultural beliefs and practices, she also strategically emphasized her interest in China and her Chinese heritage. During her years at USC, the school newspaper revealed a campus-wide interest in the political, cultural, and religious developments in Asia. The overthrow of the Qing dynasty in China and the establishment of a republican form of government there in 1911 sparked debate about the future of democracy and the balance of world power. The university's religious mission also encouraged this attention to Asian people and cultures. School publications explained:

> Here on the Pacific Coast . . . in immediate touch by water with the Great Orient, Californians have a unique position for doing honorable work in the world. . . . Particularly with our own institution . . . where religion has a definite place in the organization and in the curriculum, is there a call to send out representatives . . . west to teaching and missionary posts.[18]

The YWCA particularly was active in sponsoring lecturers and workshops about China and the need for female physicians to serve as missionaries there. The fascination with Asia provided opportunities for Chung to receive economic support for her education and to achieve social recognition. She helped pay for school by giving talks to students, churches, and clubs about China, a country that she never visited. Her advocacy for her ancestral people, particularly for women, gained Chung a reputation as "a leader in her class in the College of Medicine and a strong advocate for the emancipation of Chinese women."[19]

Following Chung's graduation from the USC College of Physicians and Surgeons in 1916, she applied to serve as a medical missionary in China. Her goal of fulfilling a religious calling through the science of healing represented a culmination of her family upbringing and her educational training. Consequently, the denial of her request to serve as a medical missionary both surprised and troubled her. In a 1939 interview, Chung interpreted her rejection as a result of her American birth and Chinese ancestry: "Three times her application came up before administrative boards and three times it was turned down—not because of any lack in her qualifications, but because there was no provision in the rules and regulations governing funds to send American missionaries to China that covered a case of an American of Chinese descent."[20] The refusal of the missionary society to support Chung as a medical missionary reveals the persistence of racial hierarchy, even among those who sought to uplift the Chinese. Of the forty-one missionaries in China sponsored by the Presbyterian Occidental Board from 1875 to 1920, none was of Chinese descent.[21] Chung's credentials would not have disadvantaged her compared with the overwhelming majority of white missionaries, most of whom lacked the language and cultural skills to function in China. However, Chung's Chinese ancestry would have placed her in an awkward social position there. As Jane Hunter argues, Chinese Christians represented marginal figures in the largely segregated white missionary circles.[22] The few Chinese women who received their medical training in the United States were widely respected, but, unlike Chung, they had been born and raised in China and had the ability to develop and put to use connections with political leaders and benefactors there. As an American-born Chinese, Chung was both too American and too Chinese for the purposes of white missionaries.

Chung's failed application to serve as a medical missionary fostered a sense of professional and religious anxiety. One month after graduation, she still had not received an internship. During this time, she also stopped patronizing religious institutions. According to her sister, Margaret "was never known to have gone to church after she graduated from medical school."[23] The rejection of her application left her bereft of a professional as well as religious calling.

A Secular Female Reformer in a "Modernizing" Community

After her completion of medical school, Margaret Chung obtained positions at a variety of medical institutions and developed specializations in surgery and psychiatry. However, her initial postings in the Midwest and southern California proved unsatisfactory. Although she began a private practice that attracted a number of Hollywood entertainers, Chung still persisted in her desire to serve her "own" people.

In 1922, she decided to pursue her original goal of becoming a medical missionary, this time in a secular capacity of promoting "modern" science. She opened a practice in San Francisco Chinatown, the largest community of Chinese in the United States with nearly eight thousand residents. The predominantly but not thoroughly segregated neighborhood was bordered by the downtown financial and tourist districts, the elite society of Nob Hill, and the Italian and bohemian communities of North Beach. As in medical school, Chung sought to use her liminality as an asset to establish a niche in San Francisco Chinatown. Because of her racial and gender background, she could appeal to more traditional notions of community solidarity and female modesty to develop a clientele. With her western scientific training, she could gain a following among more Americanized members of the Chinese American community. Ironically, Chung encountered difficulties attracting patients of her same racial and gender background. The mixed reception she received reveals the internal divisions in presumably uniform racial and gender groups. In particular, her uneasy position in Chinatown exposes the problematic nature of "modern" reform efforts that sought to promote western medicine as well as new gender and sexual norms.

When Chung began her medical practice in San Francisco Chinatown, she became part of a broader movement to transform not only health care in the community but also the identity of Chinese Americans. As Nayan Shah argues in his study on public health in San Francisco Chinatown, civic activism during the twentieth century reshaped the image and social structure of the community.[24] In the nineteenth and early twentieth centuries, "mainstream" Americans largely viewed Chinese as unworthy of cultural and political citizenship. Negative assessments of Chinese religious beliefs, medical practices, and lack of nuclear families among the predominantly male population marked them as outsiders to the American norm. As nationalist modernization movements in China influenced immigrant community leaders and as the second generation came of age during the 1920s and 1930s, Chinese Americans increasingly emphasized their ability to adopt western culture to demonstrate their assimilability. Evidence of acculturation included the promotion of western medicine and the creation of normative families. Chinese American leaders, echoing common conceptions, frequently used the language of modernity versus traditionalism to contrast desirable and undesirable practices. However, not all Chinatown residents embraced western over herbal medicine; nor were they all members of heteronormative families.

In this context of cultural transition and conflict, Chung's attempts to establish a professional niche in the Chinatown community initially met with few productive results. In her autobiography, she recalled that "for a solid month I sat in my offices without a single patient."[25] Her absence of clientele resulted from a combination of factors. First, Chung's view of her role as a medical missionary reinforced her status as a community outsider. To perceive herself as bringing scientific enlightenment to Chinatown entailed a belief in the superior value of her contributions. Her recollections about her first visit to San Francisco reveal this sense of social separation from the Chinese American community. Traveling as a guest of her Hollywood patients, Chung initially toured Chinatown in a chauffeur-driven car. From this position of privilege, she expressed "shock ... [at] the conditions under which many of the Chinese people lived."[26]

While Chung viewed herself as occupying a higher status, she also recognized the disadvantages of being an outsider. When she opened her clinic, she was the second doctor of Chinese descent in the Chinatown community. However, she was the first American-born and the first woman of Chinese ancestry to practice western medicine.[27] As a new female arrival without family or social contacts, Chung had few resources to help her establish her position in the close-knit community. Furthermore, raised in areas with much smaller numbers of Chinese Americans, Chung lacked the language and social skills to function in a large, ethnic neighborhood. As she recalled in her autobiography,

My first few years in San Francisco were rather disheartening. I knew very few people socially, I lived alone in a hotel. I was afraid to go out and visit many Chinese people because of my limited Chinese. They thought me "high-hat" because I didn't accept their invitations where, as a matter of fact, I was embarrassed because I couldn't understand their flowery Chinese.[28]

Chung's early experiences in San Francisco Chinatown reveal class kinship and cultural divisions in the racially segregated community. Her ethnic commonality did not necessarily foster a natural bond with other Chinese Americans.

In addition to the lack of cultural skills and social networks to assist her transition into the Chinatown community, Chung faced resistance to western medicine, especially surgery, as well as competition from white female physicians. She explained: "At the time, Chinatown was divided into two classes—the older generation who still believed in Chinese herbs, and the younger, more modern generation who, if they required medical attention and wanted modern medicine and surgery would go to a white physician."[29] Other Chinese doctors echoed Chung's interpretation.[30] Chinese Americans who valued western practices and culture tended to internalize mainstream racial attitudes that privileged associations with white Americans. Furthermore, white physicians most likely faced less social pressure than Chinese physicians to respond to their patients in culturally appropriate ways.[31] While whiteness did not automatically ensure these physicians greater influence in the Chinese community, the existing racial hierarchy granted more prestige and placed fewer expectations on them than on Chung.

While she faced competition for clients from white female physicians, Chung also encountered distrust from members of the community who preferred Chinese methods of healing. In the 1920s, when there was less than a handful of western-trained physicians of Chinese descent in Chinatown, there were thirty-seven herbal stores that provided medical care for both Chinese and non-Chinese patients.[32] Herbal medicine, diametrically opposed to Chung's preferred specialization of surgery, was essentially a noninvasive treatment that relied on observation, conversation, and pulse detection for diagnosis. Chinese patients, accustomed to this form of health care, held negative opinions of western hospitals. Joseph Lum, who would become the superintendent of the Chinese Hospital in San Francisco, explained, "In those days . . . they [the Chinese American community] did not trust American doctors, and they thought the hospital was a place where you came to die."[33] While critics of these attitudes would argue that the deaths primarily resulted from the reluctance of Chinese patients to enter the hospital "until it is too late," the patients explained the cause of death as a result of "being 'cut-open' . . . and . . . [other] totally unheard of remedies."[34] Although advocates of western health care criticized these fears as evidence of the "backwardness" or "superstitious" nature of traditional Chinese, many Americans actually shared these views of hospitals as unsanitary death traps, which accurately describes these institutions during much of the nineteenth century.

Given the different approaches of western and Chinese medical care, it is not surprising that Chung met with community reluctance to patronize her new practice. After six weeks of inactivity, when she "had almost reached the end of my rope," she suddenly benefited from a historical accident. In her autobiography, she recalled receiving an urgent call from a Chinatown restaurant:

> I walked in and found a young Chinese woman who was seriously ill, practically in shock. Calling an ambulance I rushed her to the hospital. They say that fools rush in where angels fear to tread. . . . I did not realize how my professional reputation and my future livelihood depended upon that case. It hung like a slender thread. . . . God was good to me, for

she was an exceedingly poor risk . . . and if she had died my name would have been "mud" and I might just as well have folded my little tent and gone elsewhere.[35]

Her patient turned out to be a well-respected businesswoman who frequently served as a translator for other Chinese women during their visits to doctors. Chung recalled that "in less than twenty-four hours, the news had gotten around. Business picked up considerably following that successful operation."[36]

As Chung's first case indicates, Chinese American women, who constituted only 22 percent of the Chinatown population, launched her career in the community.[37] Her patient, a wealthy and prominent woman, used her contacts among the female members of the community to promote Chung's practice. The existence of a women's network that shared information about health care reveals the gendered nature of medical care in Chinatown. Both Chung's recollections and oral histories suggest that Chinese American women, particularly mothers, were responsible for the health of their families. The women determined when their children needed medical attention and selected the professionals to provide treatment.[38] Furthermore, Chinese American women apparently preferred female health-care providers, as evidenced by their practice, prior to Chung's arrival, of consulting midwives or white female physicians.

Maternal supervision of health care fulfilled both traditional and emerging expectations of gender behavior. The Chinatown community witnessed a baby boom during the 1920s as the second generation came of age and as the community uncovered loopholes in immigration exclusion laws. In that decade, Chinese American women gave "birth at a rate 90 to nearly 250 percent higher than women in the city overall."[39] A peak of 451 births was reached in 1924, just two years after Chung's arrival in the community. The increase in conjugal families countered negative depictions of Chinatown as a bachelor society that fostered sexual vice. As Nayan Shah argues, the growing emphasis on heteronormative families masked the variety of kinship and social relationships that existed in the community. Nevertheless, maternal authority over health care empowered women who became mothers, as well as women who could provide medical services to facilitate biological reproduction.

The demand for Chung to minister to the medical needs of women and their families is demonstrated by her specialization in Chinatown. In 1925, after years of organizing, fundraising, and lobbying, immigrant and second-generation community leaders finally succeeded in establishing a five-story, fifty-five-bed Chinese Hospital.[40] Following the standards of the California Medical Board, the Chinese Hospital maintained a cultural hierarchy between western and Chinese medicine, but the institution did challenge the existing racial hierarchy. Each department of the hospital was headed by one of the four Chinese American western-trained physicians in the community. They, in turn, presided over the remaining thirty-two white doctors on the hospital's staff. Chung was one of the founding physicians of the Chinese Hospital. Significantly, although she had received training in a variety of surgical procedures, she was not listed under the Chinese Hospital surgical staff. Instead, as the only female physician among the four, Chung led the department of Gynecology, Obstetrics, and Pediatrics.[41]

Although Chung achieved some recognition and acceptance for her ability to facilitate biological reproduction, she also encountered increased ostracism for perceived transgressions of normative gender and sexual roles. By the late 1920s, Chung faced growing competition in the Chinatown market from other Chinese American female physicians. The relatively cool reception that she received is contrasted with the community's warm acceptance of Dr. Rose Goong Wong. A graduate of the Philadelphia Woman's Medical College, the only female institution to survive the modernization reforms in the profession, Wong began her practice in Chinatown in 1927. Despite her later arrival, she played a central role in transforming community attitudes regarding western medicine, hospitals, and childbirth. Like other Americans during the early twentieth century, expectant Chinese parents preferred childbirth at home. Wong, who specialized in obstetrics and gynecology, offered medical treatment to patients in their homes and also coaxed parents to use the services of the Chinese Hospital. According to Shah, with "the popularity of Wong's reassuring bedside manner, the rate of hospital deliveries jumped dramatically, from only 20 percent of all Chinese births in 1929 to 56 percent in 1939."[42] A community history of the Chinese Hospital reveals the disparity in popularity between Chung's and Wong's practices. While Chung is described in positive terms, the author notes that she mainly "had a huge non-Chinese following." In contrast, Wong is characterized as a widely respected community resource, leaving "behind a legacy of twenty-four hour devotion to her patients in which fatigue never dulled her joy."[43]

A variety of factors contributed to the difference in community reception of Chung and Wong. First, Wong's medical expertise and approach to health care proved more suitable for a community focused on biological reproduction yet distrustful of western medicine. While Chung had received training in gynecology and obstetrics, she identified herself as a surgeon, a member of a field dominated by men. In contrast, Wong viewed herself as a specialist in women's illnesses and reproduction. Furthermore, Wong willingly provided free and low-cost medical care to develop her base of Chinatown patients. As a later arrival, Wong may have felt the need to offer these services to establish a clientele.

The contrast in community reaction to Chung and Wong also can be related to distinctions in the women's personal backgrounds. Wong grew up in San Francisco Chinatown and attended the nearby University of California, Berkeley, as an undergraduate. In addition, the differences in the two women doctors' marital status and perceived sexual identity influenced the community's reception. Although both Chung and Wong transcended established gender roles in their choice of professional career and adopted masculine clothing, Wong followed a more traditional path for her personal life. She married and eventually had a family. Chung remained single, a status that became increasingly anomalous in the conjugal family-centered Chinatown community.

As an unmarried woman who cross-dressed, Chung aroused suspicions regarding her sexuality. When Bessie Jeong, another Chinese American female physician who attended the Woman's Medical College in Philadelphia, was asked whether she and Chung shared a sense of camaraderie, she exclaimed defensively: "Oh, no! Margaret and I were as different as [pause] She was a homo, a lesbian."[44] Dr. Jane Lee, whose family operated a pharmacy in Chinatown, recalled that she was fascinated by Chung, one of the few Chinese American female physicians in the community. Interested at an early age in becoming a doctor, Lee tried to learn all she could about Chung. When Lee delivered pharmaceuticals to Chung's office, she prolonged her visits to observe the latter's appearance, mannerisms, and interactions with her patients. However, Lee received numerous warnings from family and community members to stay away from Chung, a reputed lesbian.[45]

The arrival of other Chinese American female physicians and the rumors circulating about Chung's sexuality resulted in the decline of her Chinatown clients, especially female patients. The speculations marked her as a transgressor against the increasing importance of heteronormative families. Just as Chung's racial status did not guarantee acceptance in the Chinese American community, her gender identity did not necessarily create a natural bond with other women.

Medical Tourism: Strategic Uses of Oriental Maternalism

While Chung's blending of cultural and gender identities sparked controversy and created a sense of uneasiness in the Chinatown community, she discovered that this exotic mixture attracted white patients, particularly male ones. Her clientele was not unusual among Chinese American physicians, who faced professional and social pressures similar to those Chung encountered in Chinatown.[46] The phenomenon of white male patients seeking medical care from a Chinese American female doctor appears to invert established gender and racial hierarchies. However, Chung's patients traversed social boundaries not because of their desire to ignore her identity as a Chinese American woman but rather to take advantage of her social difference. Just as middle-class white Americans visited racialized communities during the 1920s for purposes of leisure, Chung's patients engaged in *medical tourism*, that is, they sought health care from an exotic "other," an outsider to their racial and gender group. Whereas the close-knit Chinatown community had more daily interactions with Chung, and consequently more ability to regulate her professional and social interactions, non-Chinese individuals, because of their geographic or cultural distance from her, could view Chung through their preconceptions regarding gender, race, and sexuality.

Chung supplemented her private practice by serving as a house physician at the Hotel Wiltshire, located in the tourist district just on the outskirts of Chinatown. She discovered that among her clientele of hotel guests, which predominantly consisted of white Americans, particularly men, her "otherness" proved an asset. A journalistic account of her life reveals how mainstream Americans perceived her professional persona. In 1924, *Sunset* magazine, a San Francisco–based monthly, featured Chung as an "Interesting Westerner" and dubbed her "the Ministering Angel of Chinatown."[47] As the two phrases suggest, the writer, a white man, attributed Chung's newsworthiness to her gender, cultural, and historical liminality. On the one hand, the designation of Chung as a "westerner" suggested that she exemplified the pioneering spirit, an ethos that celebrated the ability to remake one's identity in the American west. On the other hand, the label of "the Ministering Angel of Chinatown" evoked practices of racial segregation and Victorian ideals of essentialized gender difference. It is precisely this mixture of progress and tradition that the author, and by extension Chung's patients, found so fascinating.

For example, although the writer acknowledged Chung's masculine dress and specialization in surgery, he insisted on portraying her as a traditional, maternal figure: "Professionally mannish are the silk shirtwaist, soft collar and bow tie that Dr. Chung wears, but a woman's tenderness and a mother's love she has showered on a growing family." This desire to assert an fundamentally feminine nature underneath the masculine exterior resonates with Chung's observations regarding her popularity with male patients. She "found that sometimes men prefer to go to a woman to have their surgery done because they think perhaps she might be gentler."[48]

Just as Chung's femaleness allowed male patients to project their desires for maternal nurturance, her Chinese ancestry allowed white patients to fulfill their fantasies about cultural difference. For example, the *Sunset* magazine account describes Chung as "a Chinese woman doctor, thoroughly Americanized . . . [fighting] against the oriental ideal of homebound womanhood, against oriental distrust of everything Western, against the ignorance of sick persons who would die with herbs rather than live with modern medicine."[49] In celebrating Chung's ability to transcend cultural divides, the article also uses the opportunity to assert an essential dichotomy between "oriental" values and "everything Western." While the East is characterized by ignorance and patriarchy, America represents rationality, freedom, and modernity.

Recognizing this dual fascination with border crossing as well as border maintenance, Chung sought to capitalize on her liminal cultural identity. The woman who always dressed in Western clothing decorated her medical office in Chinatown with "furnishings in Oriental artistry."[50] This commingling of the West and the East reflected Chung's cultural identity. Perhaps more importantly, she selected the décor as a conscious commercial and publicity strategy. Chung shared a reception room with a photography studio. Her clinic served as an extension of a staged backdrop to attract patrons curious about the Chinatown milieu. The plan effectively sparked interest. One white visitor remarked that the "very beautiful Chinese furnishings took my fancy."[51] Chinese American writer Pardee Lowe also commented that Chung's "office has become one of the main sights in Chinatown."[52] Dressed in western clothing and practicing western medicine, Chung provided a safe yet culturally distinctive experience for the non-Chinese seeking health care.

Chung's strategy of using her "otherness" to attract white male clients resonated with the efforts of Asian American women and men who sought economic opportunities in mainstream society. Judy Yung notes that few second-generation Chinese American women during the early twentieth century found positions outside Chinatown. The few available jobs used women as "exotic showpieces," requiring them to "wear oriental costumes" to add "atmosphere" for "teahouses, restaurants, stores, and nightclubs."[53] Similarly, Haiming Liu discovered that from the mid–nineteenth through the mid–twentieth centuries Chinese herbalists, who had large clienteles of white Americans, sometimes resorted to dressing in "Chinese robes and round Mandarin hats" to prove the cultural "authenticity" of their medical cures to their non-Chinese patients.[54]

Such self-orientalization, which accentuated Chung's difference from the mainstream, encouraged the patronage of non-Chinese patients who purposely sought medical care providers outside their own community. Just as Chinese herbalists developed a practice among white patients for treating "embarrassing" problems, such as venereal disease and infertility, western-trained physicians of racialized backgrounds received requests to remedy socially disreputable ailments.[55]

Even rumors regarding Chung's sexuality, which did not circulate widely but were discussed privately, may have helped attract patients. For example, Chung became the physician for Elsa Gidlow, a self-identified lesbian, and Gidlow's female lover, Tommy. Gidlow, who suspected that Chung "might be a sister lesbian," was drawn to the physician and felt comfortable revealing that she and her lover resided together.[56] Because of this assumed bond based on their mutual status as outsiders, Gidlow requested Chung's help to obtain an abortion, an illegal procedure at the time, for her unmarried and pregnant sister. Gidlow recalled:

> I had no idea how one went about getting one and was horrified at what I heard about that violent recourse.... Finally, I asked Margaret Chung for advice. She told me what I already knew, that she could not risk such an operation. But she was warmly sympathetic. She had young sisters and would feel as I did. She said, "I'll help you." She wrote a name and an address. "This man is a competent medical doctor and surgeon. He will do a clean, safe job. I'll telephone and tell him he is not to charge you over $50." There are no words to express gratitude for such compassion.[57]

In addition to providing the referral for the abortion, Chung agreed to sterilize another of Gidlow's sisters. Chung apparently provided medical options for other women to control their fertility. In 1950, a letter to the Board of Medical Examiners reported "rather ugly rumors in circulation about the abortion activities of Dr. Cecil A. Saunders [a fellow graduate of USC] and his relationship in business with Dr. Margaret Chung."[58]

It is not clear how much of Chung's practice involved abortion referrals and whether she provided similar services for Chinese American women. Her willingness to assist women in regulating their fertility may have stemmed from recognition of the detrimental impact of multiple pregnancies on her own mother's health.[59] Considering the political and social significance of biological reproduction for the Chinese San Francisco community in the 1920s, Chung's efforts to provide birth control might have contributed to her marginalization in Chinatown. In contrast, she found acceptance among non-Chinese patients because she fulfilled their desires for exotic nurturance and provided discreet remedies for their experiments in social transgression.

Conclusion

Although clearly unique, Margaret Chung's medical career provides insight into the lives of pioneering Asian American female professionals as they sought to negotiate the shifting racial, gender, and sexual boundaries of mainstream society and their own ethnic communities during the early twentieth century. Seeking to transcend traditional social barriers, women like Chung also sought support from those of the similar background. The tensions between assimilation and separatism that these women experienced reflected the broader transformation of social values from the Victorian to the modern era. With the push toward gender and racial equality as well as the persistence of essentialized notions of difference, women like Chung sought to use their in-betweeness, their liminality, to advance their professional as well as personal aspirations.

Ironically, Chung found greater acceptance from white Americans, particularly men, rather than from Chinese American women. Her reception cannot be explained simplistically by viewing white American men as more modern and liberal and Chinese American women as more conservative and backward. Rather, Chung's uneasy position in San Francisco Chinatown reveals the complex ways in which the community awarded social status based on kinship ties, class affinities, professional skills, gender identification, and sexual reputation. In the process of "modernizing" their identities, Chinese Americans accepted some elements of western medicine and female professionalization. At the same time, they also expressed suspicion and rejection for those outside established kinship networks and emerging heteronormative families.

Like members of the Chinese American community, Chung's white American patients navigated shifting social values. Her acceptance by these individuals does not necessarily suggest the prevalence of color-blind or gender-blind attitudes. Rather, mainstream perceptions of her professional identity reveal a society that was fascinated with and sought to capitalize on gender, racial, and sexual difference. Described as "mannish" and "motherly," "Oriental" and "Americanized," Chung symbolizes the desire, prevalent in the early twentieth century, to cross but not to erase gender and racial boundaries.

NOTES

1. Margaret Chung, "Autobiography," Margaret Chung Collection, Box 1, Folder 1, Asian American Studies Collection, Ethnic Studies Library, University of California, Berkeley. The unpublished autobiography is not paginated and not dated.

2. Judy Yung, *Unbound Feet: A Social History of Chinese Women in San Francisco* (Berkeley: University of California Press, 1995), 299.

3. On gender separatism, see Estelle B. Freedman, "Separatism Revisited: Women's Institutions, Social Reform, and the Career of Miriam Van Waters," in Linda Kerber, Alice Kessler-Harris, and Kathryn Kish Sklar, eds., *U.S. History as Women's History: New Feminist Essays* (Chapel Hill: University of North Carolina Press, 1995), 170–88; and Nancy F. Cott, *The Grounding of Modern Feminism* (New Haven: Yale University Press, 1987). On racial separatism, see Gloria Heyung Chun, *Of Orphans and Warriors: Inventing Chinese American Culture and Identity* (New Brunswick, N.J.: Rutgers University Press, 2000).

4. Henry Yu, *Thinking Orientals: Migration, Contact, and Exoticism in Modern America* (New York: Oxford University Press, 2001).

5. Peggy Pascoe, *Relations of Rescue: The Search for Female Moral Authority in the American West, 1874–1939* (New York: Oxford University Press, 1990).

6. Mrs. J. B. Stewart, "Medical Missions," *Occidental Leaves* (San Francisco, 1893), 38.

7. Ibid.

8. Lucy S. Bainbridge, *Woman's Medical Work in Foreign Missions* (New York: Women's Board of Foreign Missions of the Presbyterian Church, 1886), 9 and 14.

9. See Jane Hunter, *The Gospel of Gentility* (New Haven: Yale University Press, 1984); and Weili Ye, "Crossing the Cultures: The Experience of Chinese Students in the U.S.A., 1900–1925" (Ph.D. diss., Yale University, 1989), 263–82.

10. Regina Markell Morantz-Sanchez, *Sympathy and Science: Women Physicians in American Medicine* (New York: Oxford University Press, 1985); and Ellen S. More, *Restoring the Balance: Women Physicians and the Profession of Medicine, 1850–1995* (Cambridge: Harvard University Press, 1999), 99.

11. *University of Southern California Bulletin, College of Liberal Arts Year Book, 1907–1908* (Los Angeles: University of Southern California, 1908), 89 and 188.

12. Darlene Clark Hine, *HineSight: Black Women and the Re-Construction of American History* (Brooklyn: Carlson Publishing, 1994); and Paul Starr, *The Social Transformation of American Medicine: The Rise of a Sovereign Profession and the Making of a Vast Industry* (New York: Basic Books, 1982).

13. See Judy Tzu-Chun Wu, "Was Mom Chung a 'Sister Lesbian'? Asian American Gender Experimentation and Interracial Homoeroticism," *Journal of Women's History* 13:1 (Spring 2001): 58–82.

14. P. M. Suski, *My Fifty Years in America*, English summary (1960; reprint, Hollywood: Hawley Publications, 1990), 21.

15. "Friendship Theme of Y.W. Address," *Daily Southern Californian*, 30 October 1913, 3–4.

16. George F. West, "Battlefields of China Call Dr. Margaret Chung" (clipping found in the private collection of Dorothy Siu), n.d.

17. Bertha Van Hoosen, *Petticoat Surgeon* (Chicago: Pellegrini & Cudahy, 1947), 219.

18. *El Rodeo, 1917* (Los Angeles: University of Southern California, 1916), 18.

19. Manuel P. Servin and Iris Higbie Wilson, *Southern California and Its University: A History of USC, 1880–1964* (Los Angeles: Ward Ritchie Press, 1969), 60.

20. Helen Satterlee, "Two Remarkable Women: The Story of a Persevering Chinese Girl Who Reached the Heights of Surgical Fame," *Los Angeles Times Sunday Magazine*, 25 June 1939, 20.

21. *Forty-Seventh Annual Report of the Occidental Board of the Woman's Foreign Missionary Society of the Presbyterian Church of the Pacific Coast* (San Francisco: A. J. Leary, 1920), 48–54.

22. Hunter, *Gospel of Gentility.*

23. Mariko Tse, "'Made in America,' Research Project for East West Players on Chinese in Southern California" (unpublished paper, June 1979), Judy Yung Private Collection, 10.

24. Nayan Shah, *Contagious Divides: Epidemics and Race in San Francisco's Chinatown* (Berkeley: University of California Press, 2001).

25. Chung, "Autobiography."

26. Pearl P. Puckett, "She's Mom to Two Thousand American Flyers," *Independent Woman* (January 1946), 32.

27. *The Dawning* (San Francisco: Chinese Hospital Medical Staff Archives, 1978).

28. Chung, "Autobiography."

29. Ibid.

30. Philip Choy and Him Mark Lai, "Summary of Interview with Dr. James Hall," 23 August 1970, Belmont, California. Him Mark Lai Private Collection.

31. I thank Lucy Murphy for this insight.

32. Pardee Lowe Papers, "Business Establishments," information quoted from "The Chinese Community of S.F.," Lee and Lee, 1929, Hoover Institution of War, Revolution and Peace, Stanford University, California (hereafter cited as PLP). Also see Haiming Liu, "The Resilience of Ethnic Culture: Chinese Herbalists in the American Medical Profession," *Journal of Asian American Studies* 1:2 (June 1998): 181–82; and Christopher Muench, "Chinese Medicine in America: A Study in Adaptation," *Caduceus* 4 (1988): 5–35.

33. George Kao, *San Francisco Chinatown in 1950* (Hong Kong: Chinese University Press, 1988), 92.

34. Pardee Lowe, "Death a Commonplace in Chinatown," 8–9, Box 326, Folder "Death," PLP.

35. Chung, "Autobiography."

36. Ibid.

37. Yung, *Unbound Feet*, 296.

38. Members of the Square and Circle Club, conversation with author, San Francisco, 17 July 1999; and Dr. Edmund Jung, interview with author, San Francisco, 21 July 1999.

39. Shah, *Contagious Divides*, 207.

40. *The Dawning*; Joan B. Trauner, "The Chinese as Medical Scapegoats in San Francisco, 1870–1905," *California History* 57 (1978): 70–87.

41. "The Opening of the Chinese Hospital," Chinese Historical Society, San Francisco Collection, Box 3, Folder 11, Ethnic Studies Library, University of California, Berkeley.

42. Shah, *Contagious Divides*, 217.

43. *The Dawning*, 7–8.

44. Bessie Jeong, "Oral History," interviewed by Suellen Cheng and Munson Kwok, 17 December 1981 and 17 October 1982, Southern California Chinese American Oral History Project, University of California, Los Angeles, Special Collections.

45. Jane Lee, conversation with author, 13 April 1997, Oakland, California.

46. *The Dawning*.

47. Gerald J. O'Gara, "Interesting Westerners: The Ministering Angel of Chinatown," *Sunset Magazine* (December 1924): 28.

48. Chung, "Autobiography."

49. O'Gara, "Interesting Westerners," 28.

50. Shirley Radke, "We Must Be Active Americans," *Christian Science Monitor*, 3 October 1942.

51. Van Hoosen, *Petticoat Surgeon*, 219.

52. Pardee Lowe, "Chinafication Desired by S.F. People, 1934," PLP.

53. Yung, *Unbound Feet*, 136.

54. Liu, "Resilience of Ethnic Culture," 181–82.

55. I thank Leslie J. Reagan for suggesting this argument.

56. Elsa Gidlow, *Elsa: I Come with My Songs* (San Francisco: Booklegger Press, 1986), 207.

57. Ibid., 255.

58. Percival Dolman, "Letter to Frederick N. Scatena," 29 July 1950, Margaret J. Chung File, Deceased Physicians Files, 1902–1977, Department of Consumer Affairs—State Board of Medical Examiners, California State Archives, Sacramento, California. Chung's method of abortion referral was representative of physicians who engaged in this practice. See Leslie J. Reagan, *When Abortion Was a Crime: Women, Medicine, and Law in the United States, 1867–1973* (Berkeley: University of California Press, 1997).

59. Ah Yane suffered and eventually died from tuberculosis, a disease whose symptoms are aggravated by pregnancy.

10

Japanese American Girls' Clubs in Los Angeles during the 1920s and 1930s

Valerie J. Matsumoto

In 1926, the first letter to the editor of the *Los Angeles Japanese Daily News*'s fledgling English-language section came from a Nisei girl, part of the growing second-generation readership targeted by the ethnic newspaper. Cora Asakura welcomed the Nisei-run section with delight, saying, "I hope we may put our club news in it too."[1] Asakura was one of the many young women who participated in a fast-growing range of Japanese American youth clubs in southern California before World War II.[2] These organizations provided camaraderie and critical resources for second-generation adolescents in an era of segregation and exclusion, exacerbated by economic hardship during the Great Depression. In their clubs, Nisei daughters honed valuable organizational skills, developed strong gender and generational ties, socialized with young men, engaged in social service, and gained high visibility within the Japanese American community. Examining their group activities reveals how girls pushed the boundaries of acceptable gender behavior while maintaining certain gendered practices, such as women's responsibility for food preparation. Club activities also show how the Nisei both challenged and reflected the racial structures of their time. At the intersection of gender and racial dynamics, young women played a vivid symbolic role—which grew increasingly tense with the advent of World War II—as representatives of the ethnic community.[3]

The English-language sections of the Japanese American newspapers in Los Angeles provide a window into the young women's extensive networks. Two newspapers have been particularly useful: the *Rafu Shimpo* (*Los Angeles Japanese Daily News*) and the *Kashu Mainichi* (*Japan-California Daily News*). Preserved in their pages, the cadence and color of Nisei speech bring to life much that was forgotten after World War II. In this chapter I have drawn heavily from the early years of the *Rafu Shimpo*'s English-language section, which offer a treasure trove of "thick description" about club activities. Because of the wartime destruction of so many Japanese American personal records, the ethnic press and oral history recollections remain invaluable sources for examining the prewar community.

Growing Up in Los Angeles

By the second decade of the twentieth century, Los Angeles had become the major population center of Japanese Americans in the United States. The Census Bureau recorded 8,641 living in Los Angeles County in 1910. By 1930 the number had grown to 35,000, of whom half were U.S.-born Nisei. As *Kashu Mainichi* reporter Joe Oyama observed in 1936: "Los Angeles is to the Japanese what Harlem is to the Negro, San Francisco to the Chinese, Stockton to the Filipinos, and Hollywood to the Mid-Western girl."[4]

Japanese American neighborhoods and businesses coalesced in many parts of southern California, particularly as Issei and Nisei farming burgeoned. In Los Angeles County the trade in Japanese American–grown fruit and vegetables fueled a bustling wholesale produce market as well as numerous fruit, grocery, and dairy stores. Some two thousand contract gardeners, many of them living in West Los Angeles, also became a familiar part of the landscape they tended, from the estates of Westwood and Bel Air to Hollywood and Pasadena. A Japanese American fishing and cannery community also developed on Terminal Island across from San Pedro. Because racial discrimination barred Japanese from buying or renting homes in more desirable areas, Japanese enclaves were often located near commercial or industrial sites, and frequently in proximity to African American neighborhoods.[5]

The hub of these diverse southern California communities was "Little Tokyo,"[6] a cluster of stores, restaurants, hotels, and homes in downtown Los Angeles, centering on First Street between Alameda and Los Angeles Streets. Here farm families came on weekends to shop; job seekers headed to employment agencies; and both the Nisei and their immigrant parents, the Issei, spent leisure time with their friends: attending church and club meetings, dancing, gambling, and going to movies, theater performances, and music recitals.

Nisei daughters growing up in this urban setting had more comfortable, less strenuous childhoods than their rural counterparts. They did not, however, lack for responsibility. Whether they lived on a farm or in the city, Japanese American children usually worked in the home and family business. Their labor proved vital to the support of the immigrant family. City girls often helped operate family businesses in the Japanese American enclave, sweeping a tofu store or waiting on restaurant customers. Their chores included housework, from which their brothers were exempt, and supervising younger siblings. However, the city Nisei were more likely to have free time and greater access to leisure activities.

Generally speaking, the Nisei were a very young group. In 1930, the bulk of the second generation in Los Angeles County was under twenty-one years old. In 1934, a journalist reported that the majority of Nisei in the United States were between the ages of fifteen and eighteen. They grew up synthesizing both the Japanese customs of their parents and American mainstream culture. Most of the second generation spoke Japanese with their parents and English with their siblings and friends. When the regular school day ended, their parents sent them to Japanese-language school. Whether Buddhist or Christian, they celebrated a round of Japanese and American holidays, including New Year's Day, Thanksgiving, and Christmas. Nisei girls learned knitting and crocheting as well as *odori* (traditional Japanese dance). Like their non–Japanese American peers, they also practiced the waltz and foxtrot, played basketball, listened to swing bands on the radio, and collected photographs of screen idols such as Deanna Durbin and Clark Gable.

Sheiks and Shebas in Little Tokyo

From the 1920s, urban Nisei girls both challenged and reinforced gender dynamics. Like their brothers, they eagerly embraced many trends of the Jazz Age, including some of the attributes of the "New Woman." They adopted the language and attire of their mainstream peers, called "sheiks" and "shebas" after the romantic characters portrayed by early movie stars such as Rudolph Valentino and Theda Bara. The newspaper advertisements from Japanese-run department stores and beauty salons echoed these styles, suggesting to an ethnic female clientele how they might look with bobbed hair and the latest outfit.

The flapper style and the gender-role shifts with which it was associated caused consternation among conservative critics in the ethnic community and the larger society. An acrimonious exchange of letters to the *Rafu Shimpo* editor in 1926 conveys both the critique advanced by an older Nisei man and the Little Tokyo Nisei women's undaunted enthusiasm for the latest fashions, as well as for their organizations. The irate Akatsuki Sakano wrote to complain about "these slick, knock-'em-dead sheiks and these painted, red-hot shebas that strut about the streets of Little Tokio." The women's outfits and make-up particularly upset him. Sakano criticized them as "short-skirted baby dolls with their artificial rosebud lips and their languishing, mascara'ed eyelashes" who "arrogantly displayed" their "knock-kneed, bowshaped, overgrown limbs." He expressed his dismay that these "sheiks and shebas" were "respectable members of the churches and even Sunday School teachers and leaders of their young people's societies."[7] Sakano's letter, which enraged many of the Nisei in Little Tokyo, conveys a sense of the popularity of flapper-style clothing and cosmetics among the urban second generation, including those considered respectable and active in local youth groups.

Sakano paired his attack on Nisei women's attire with a blistering critique of the proliferation of the Nisei youth clubs; his diatribe revealed the existence of an impressive array. He began with what he called the "little kids" clubs—probably junior high school level—and then moved to the high school girls' clubs throughout southern California, the co-ed social service organizations, women's athletic clubs, church-related youth leagues, and a range of clubs sponsored by the Young Women's Christian Association (YWCA) and the Young Men's Christian Association (YMCA). On the college level he blasted a Nisei sorority and fraternity that had been founded as alternatives to the European American Greek system that did not then admit racial/ethnic members. In 1936, reporter Joe Oyama noted that in Los Angeles there were "some 66 second-generation Japanese organizations, whose members range from 18 years of age and up," and 104 such groups in southern California.[8] Had Oyama included the clubs for younger boys and girls, the figure would likely have been higher. Indeed, the *Rafu Shimpo* estimated in 1940 that there were some four hundred Nisei youth organizations in southern California.[9] Thanks to Akatsuki Sakano's list, it is clear that they were flourishing by the mid-1920s.

Both Christian and Buddhist churches fostered girls' and boys' clubs, but YWCA-sponsored activities were particularly widespread. In 1926, a Nisei male columnist observed, "The work of the Y.W. is well known. Their activities are ever helpful to the women of this community, and the effects of their work are unconsciously felt more or less by every woman of the Japanese community in the Southland."[10] Why did the "Y" have such impact? By the 1910s, YWCA leaders had concluded that "the most different groups—such as industrial girls, Negroes, the foreign-born—would not be reached by the Association without special efforts related to their own life-experiences and cultural backgrounds."[11] Their "special efforts" to reach Japanese American girls seem to have mirrored their practices with regard to African American young women, for whom they established separate branches in ethnic communities, and foreign-born women, out of concern for whom they founded an urban International Institute movement. The establishment of ethnic-branch clubs reflects the delineation of racial boundaries before World War II; as Sucheng Chan has noted, the YMCA and YWCA also set up separate branches for Chinese Americans.[12] The "Japanese YWCA" in Los Angeles was started in 1922,[13] and the YWCA's International Institute in Boyle Heights became a center for young women's club activities, including the Japanese YWCA branch.

Another YWCA development greatly influenced the organization of Nisei girls' clubs: the fast-growing Girl Reserve (GR) movement, begun in 1918, which aimed to enlist seventh- and eighth-grade schoolgirls, junior high school and older high school adolescents, and the younger girls in industry and business.[14] The first Japanese GR club formed in 1918; by 1926 there were five such clubs in Los Angeles.[15] The emphasis of the GR movement on "the developing of [a] program out of the needs and desires of the group rather than as a standardized pattern"[16] may have made it particularly adaptable to the Nisei girls, who flocked to join, picking individual names for their GR clubs and choosing their own activities for the year. The "little kids" groups of which Sakano wrote likely included the junior members of the Girl Reserves.

Stung by his criticism, the Nisei women quickly leaped to the defense of their organizations. Fierce rebuttals appeared in the next issue of the *Rafu Shimpo*. Lily Satow, expressing a group sentiment, decried Sakano's knowledge of the various young people's clubs as being, at most, superficial. She also suggested that "the poor fish must have been disappointed in love, perhaps by one of the very 'painted, short-skirted, bow-legged shebas' whom he so strongly condemns."[17] Another woman wrote, "To my mind, he's a fogey-faced dumb nit-wit wot ain't gotta chance with the so-called shingled Shebas." She asserted that the network of Nisei youth clubs in outlying communities served as "the only means of getting young folks together."[18] This might be a reference to the fact that Japanese Americans and other racial/ethnic youth were excluded in this period from many extracurricular high school and college organizations. She also suggested that group activities might exert social control in checking romantic impulses, contrary to Sakano's assertion that they were just a "rendezvous for amorously inclined males and females."[19] As she put it, "Are not such clubs an aid in keeping young folks from pairing off, as is the tendency where there aren't any clubs?"[20]

The youth organizations had already taken root as community institutions, as subsequent events indicate. It appears that the current of Nisei public opinion ran strongly against Sakano and that this response had a serious effect on him: Three weeks later, his wife wrote a letter to the editor in defense of her husband's character. She announced that, despite his being "a man of great vigor and robust health," "my poor husband is suffering a nervous breakdown because of the terrible criticisms made of him. He is now recuperating in a sanatorium in the north."[21] It is not possible to assess either Sakano's previous emotional stability or the force of the wrath leveled at him, but the backlash that sent him into retreat does convey the growing strength of the Nisei club networks and the loyalty they inspired in their members.

The Multiple Functions of Nisei Youth Clubs

The Nisei youth groups served a variety of functions. According to sociologist Harry Kitano, they were a means of social control and socialization: "During early and late adolescence, Nisei generally were controlled by organizations within the community. These often took the form of leagues and clubs...." Older Nisei peers rather than parents often exercised control of these organizations; as Kitano noted, the groups "were usually guided by the Nisei themselves. The youngsters were left pretty much alone, to make mistakes, to try new things, and to translate their understanding of large community models in ways that could be of use to them."[22] For young Nisei women who, like their Mexican American sisters, "sought to reconcile parental expectations with the excitement of experimentation," youth clubs afforded a heady opportunity.[23]

The resources and opportunities offered by Nisei organizations were especially important in the context of race relations in the 1920s and 1930s and provided a vital alternative for Japanese American children who were often excluded from European American clubs or unable to assume leadership positions in them. "If we hadn't had these ethnic organizations to join," Yoshiko Uchida wrote, "I think few Nisei would have had the opportunity to hold positions of leadership or responsibility. At one time I was president of the campus Japanese Women's Student Club, a post I know I would not have held in a non-Japanese campus organization."[24] The name of the first Japanese American Girl Reserves club in southern California reflected their sense of inclusiveness: the T.M.T.M. Club's name stood for "the more, the merrier."[25] In such organizations, Nisei members received reinforcement of generational and ethnic identification, often finding role models in older Nisei advisers.

Indeed, the Japanese YWCA, under the guidance of dynamic senior Nisei women by the late 1930s, aimed to train young women to become "the leaders of tomorrow." As their pamphlet announced, "The Japanese YWCA is doing its part in the preparing of young people for the responsibilities they will be expected to carry as they grow older."[26] It was this aim of fostering women's organizational skills, Joanne Meyerowitz asserts, that distinguished the YWCA from its brother organization: "Through its sustained efforts to train women for positions of leadership, the YWCA challenged patriarchal prerogatives in ways that the YMCA did not."[27] In this respect, the Japanese YWCA—together with other prewar girls' and co-ed clubs—laid the groundwork for Nisei women's active involvement in a variety of community organizations.

Throughout the prewar period, young women's groups provided socialization in both ethnic and mainstream culture. Some, like the Sumire Kai (Violets Group), a junior women's club, met to learn about the history of Japan and the intricacies of Japanese etiquette. Other groups held classes to teach young women domestic skills. For example, the Japanese YWCA in 1927 offered lessons in "household arts," which included sewing and Japanese cooking.[28]

The Nisei girls' clubs provided a forum in which to explore peer-group and intergenerational issues, as well as to participate in a range of activities common to groups such as the Girl Scouts of America. For example, the Junior Girl Reserves conference in 1932 included in its schedule swimming, hiking, handcrafts, nature study, music, and outdoor sports. The featured topics of discussion reflected the influence of popular culture: "What the Boyfriend Thinks?" "What is 'It'?" and "What We All Think of Dancing?"[29] The leaders also hoped to facilitate intergenerational understanding by offering discussions of mother-daughter relations.

These organizations also introduced the Nisei to American holidays unfamiliar to their immigrant parents. Club Halloween parties became an attraction for children and adolescents across the Southland. In 1926, the Maryknoll Girls' "Halloween merriment" included a costume parade, bobbing for apples in a tub of water, and eating treats such as homemade fudge. The dance performance they enjoyed reflects a mixture of ethnic and mainstream influences: As a reporter noted, one girl "was prevailed upon to render a pretty little Japanese dance. . . . Another wee bundle of nerves, masquerading as a Hollywood sheik, presumably, managed to twist herself into various shapes and designs in her endeavor to present her own conception of the Charleston."[30] Club celebrations of Thanksgiving, Christmas, and Valentine's Day also facilitated the Nisei's participation in American mainstream holidays.

A co-ed Christmas party hosted by the Blue Triangle Girls revealed another ethnic influence: The highlight of the evening was the breaking of a piñata, which was described as "an old Mexican game which is filled with candy, fruits, nuts, and small pickens."[31] Given the proximity of racial/ethnic communities in southern California, it is not surprising that Japanese American youth activities reflected a range of cultural influences and adaptations.

The Nisei organizations enabled the second generation to take part in a wide range of recreational activities, some for girls only and others co-ed. Picnics and beach outings were a staple for southern California clubs. YWCA club members took advantage of their access to the YWCA's Eliza Cottage at Hermosa Beach for weekend and week-long stays. Club outings also introduced Nisei girls to local cultural institutions and to public spaces that few of their parents had leisure to visit. For example, the Emba Girl Reserves made a trip to the Southwest Museum in Pasadena; they found particularly interesting "the latest excavations from Arizona" and the "Oriental room."[32] Another "educational tour" took the S.O.F. (Service, Opportunity, and Friendship) Girl Reserves to the Alfred Ice Cream Plant. As one happy Girl Reserve reported, the guide "showed us how they made Eskimo pies, sundaes, bricks, and last but not least ice cream. . . . When the tour was ended the man presented each of us with two Eskimo pies." She concluded, "We expect to go on more educational tours in the future."[33]

Among the round of Nisei recreations, sports were particularly popular, for girls as well as for boys—numerous baseball and basketball teams for all ages drew enthusiastic crowds. Athletic events fostered a range of friendly interactions among the Nisei. As Brian Niiya has noted, "Formed in part as a reaction to discrimination, the Japanese American women's teams and leagues also served a social function, allowing young Nisei women to meet and socialize with their counterparts in other communities."[34] Reflecting the functions of the teams, the *Rafu Shimpo* anticipated that "[w]hen the Triangle Club girls from Santa Barbara come to Los Angeles to play against the Senior girls of Union Church it will mean the meeting of old friends again."[35] Games also provided opportunities for young men and women to socialize: Kay Moritani Komai recalled that she and her friends in the Blue Circles (a GR club affiliated with the Centenary Church) enjoyed the attention of the Nisei boys' club members who would show up to coach their teams and watch them play.[36]

Sports provided opportunities for interethnic interaction as well. In March 1928, the Blue Triangle Girls played the YWCA "Russian Girls" basketball team, losing to their taller opponents. Afterward, "the two teams had supper together. . . . Vocal solos by members of both clubs enlivened the spirit of the girls during the supper."[37] Next, the Blue Triangles played against the African American "Student Club of the Twelfth Street Center," again losing. The *Rafu Shimpo* reported, "Although the game was a hard fought one, the taller colored girls were at an advantage with their height and they managed to keep the ball most of the time."[38] As this reportage suggests, such club activities may have challenged some boundaries of interracial interaction but also reinforced racial stereotypes.

The groundswell of girls' and young women's interest in sports gave rise to an umbrella organization for Nisei women's athletic competition: In November 1935, twenty girls "met at the Japanese Y.W.C.A. office to mother [a] Japanese girls' basketball league" that quickly grew into the Women's Athletic Union (WAU), a female counterpart to the Japanese Athletic Union organized earlier.[39] In its first year, seventeen teams and 245 members joined the WAU, participating in baseball, basketball, swimming, tennis, ping-pong, and volleyball. The WAU boasted a membership of nearly five hundred by 1939.

Group events reinforced ties among young women's groups and between girls' organizations and boys' groups, which were usually, but not always, brother clubs in the YMCA. Dances and socials were favorite joint projects. As S. Frank Miyamoto observed, the socials, "which the Nisei generally organized totally independent of Issei supervision since the latter had little concept of how such events were fashioned in America, were often settings for the Nisei's first boy-girl relations."[40] Staging benefit programs also frequently required combining club resources. For instance, in 1926 the S.O.F. Girl Reserves worked with the Hi-Y (YMCA) and the Oliver Club to put on a successful Gymnasium Benefit Program. Their show included a novelty dance by the Oliver Junior Girls and a "Minstrel Act" for which members of the male Oliver Club, "painted up like 'darkies,' sang a few songs." The Hi-Y Boys did a musical skit and the S.O.F. Girl Reserves "ably presented" a skit about "a woman who needed a cook . . . describing the character of each applicant."[41] A wide range of such joint club efforts strengthened generational and community ties; this particular collaborative program also mirrors the ironic performance of racial stereotypes and the influence of mainstream middle-class gender-role ideals.

Indeed, co-ed activities sometimes reinforced traditional gender roles, as young women were usually expected to provide "the eats." When the Blue Triangles and the UCLA Bruin Club (mostly male at that time) went on a hike at Mount Baldy in 1928, it was promised that "[t]he girls will furnish all the provisions from sandwiches to 'nigiri-meshi' [Japanese food] and the boys will have enough to eat. . . . There will be no danger of starvation."[42] While this arrangement may reflect the young women's having initiated the hike, it was common for girls to supply the food for co-ed gatherings. When a combined Christian Endeavor group from the Union Church held an outdoor meeting in Eagle Rock, the girls brought the provisions. Whether accurately or with tongue in cheek, a reporter chronicled a sumptuous feast: "The 'light' refreshments which the girls fixed up consisted of ten spring chickens, chipped beef on toast, asparagus with mayonnaise, roasted venison, barbecue, etc." Girls' clubs sometimes were asked to prepare and serve the food for boys' club events, as in the case of the Hi-Y Club's Father-Son Banquet. The *Rafu Shimpo* declared, "The success of the party was due to the splendid way in which the Girl Reserves from M.E. (Methodist Episcopal) and Union Church cooked and served the dinner."[43]

However, the boys' clubs also reciprocated on occasion, treating the girls' organizations to festivities in appreciation of their help. When a *Rafu Shimpo* reporter asked rhetorically, "Did the Girl Reserves and the Hi-Y Boys enjoy the social party that was given by the boys in honor of the Girl Reserves and [their adviser] Mrs. Leech?" the answer was "Hope to kiss the flea they did!" This social, attended by forty Nisei, began "with the game of Domestic Science," and hewing to the gender conventions of the day, the reporter commented that "it is remarkable how many of the kitchen utensils the boys knew." Still, not surprisingly, a girl proved to have greater culinary familiarity: "Celia had the most names and she received a prize which she shared with a boy." After playing various games, "the merrymakers went to another room, and there partook of heavy refreshments." While this reference indicates that the food was more substantial than punch and cookies, it also suggests the gendering of food and the association of "heavy refreshments" with males. The boys appear to have varied in their cooking skill: "Danar Abe and his gang" provided sandwiches and the Hi-Y Club secretary made "Hungarian Goulashes [*sic*] . . . At the end of the social, the secretary was mobbed by the girls who wanted the recipe."[44]

These occasions also provided opportunities for heterosexual flirtation in a controlled environment, under the eye of an adviser: The "last game of the evening was Forfeits. Jimmy Nakamura had to disclose the way he made his living when he was compelled to make love to a girl in order to get back his dime. Tom had a hard time getting out of the double handcuff with Seiko [a girl]."[45] With regard to romantic heterosexual relations, Akatsuki Sakano and his critics were both correct: The Nisei clubs provided ample opportunities for flirtation, socializing, and courtship in the context of monitored events—sometimes regulated by peers—that reinforced group ties and standards of behavior.

The reportage of club events reveals how such organizations established and sometimes gently pushed the boundaries of socially sanctioned activities for Japanese American girls, from charitable endeavors to recreation. The growing popularity of dances throughout the prewar years provides an example of changing cultural mores. In 1936, journalist Bill Hosokawa declared, "Not more than half a decade ago, dancing was looked upon as next to sin by many of the first generation. . . . But times doth change. Any young person now that doesn't dance is practically a social outcast."[46] In this respect, generally speaking, city youth had greater latitude than their rural peers, women as well as men.

Dancing was a favorite pastime for many of the Los Angeles Nisei, such as the Blue Circles, for whom dance practice sessions became a regular activity. Sometimes their club would hold an "exchange" with a Nisei boys' club: The young women would make the refreshments—usually punch and cookies—and the boys' club would bring a record player and records. Because the Centenary Church did not permit dances on the premises, they would meet at the homes of various Blue Circles for these parties; this allowed the girls' parents to meet the young men and thus allayed parental anxiety about the respectability of the gatherings.[47] Club advisers also served as chaperones for formal dances held at rented halls.

Nisei women took the initiative in planning, in regulating, and maybe even in attending dances, as a stern admonition to southern California gate-crashers indicated in 1931: "Men and women who walked in without invites at the last Blue Triangle dance are getting into hot water and the sooner their crusts melt away the better."[48] Leap Year dances planned by the Blue Triangles and Chi Alpha Delta[49] received special notice from the *Kashu Mainichi* in January 1932: "Already two dances are scheduled for February for the benefit of the supposed-to-be stronger sex by the weaker sex."[50] The repeated mention that dances would be "strictly invitational" suggests their success in attracting Nisei youth.[51] Such heterosexual couple dancing would have been unheard of for the Nisei's immigrant parents and still incurred the disapproval of rural Issei parents.

Nisei attitudes about club dances reflect the second generation's sense of appropriate behavior for young women and men; in the ethnic community, as in the larger society, a sexual double standard prevailed. Girls were subject to more surveillance and boys bore the major expense of furnishing transportation and paying for dance admission fees and refreshments afterward. In 1933 a YWCA survey of Nisei male and female club members' opinions regarding dancing showed that the respondents' prescriptions focused mainly on Nisei daughters. Revealing the greater vulnerability of a girl's reputation than a boy's, they said that girls "should by all means notify their parents with whom they are going to the dance. For the boys this is not absolutely necessary." The members also felt it was "better for younger Nisei to go to dances in groups rather than in single couples."[52] Issei parents were more likely to permit attendance if their daughters had the additional check of peer chaperonage; this measure may also have provided girls with some buffering from awkward situations and sexual pressures. Young women's networks were critical to their gaining access to youth social events and also assisted in the maintenance of their respectable standing within the ethnic community.

Many of the Nisei organizations had a social service component; for some, it was a priority. This can be seen in the name of a high school club, the S.O.F. Girl Reserves, whose acronym stood for "Service, Opportunity, and Friendship."[53] Girls in such groups tackled a range of projects in the Japanese American community. For example, *Kashu Mainichi* proudly reported in 1933 that the "Cherry Blossom Girls have purchased the material and are now making 'nighties' for all of the girls in the Japanese Children's Home," a local orphanage.[54]

The young women's clubs often collected food and toys for needy families at holiday time. In 1928 the Blue Triangles, for whom this became an annual activity, gave a large Thanksgiving basket "to the Takenouchi family which consists of a widowed mother and five children."[55] During the difficult years of the Great Depression, the Nisei groups continued to make efforts to ease the plight of families struggling to make ends meet.

Even recreational activities such as dancing provided opportunities for social service. Of five spring dances announced in 1932, three were "benefit dances." Admission to the Savings Association dance required "the presentation of the invitation cards and three large cans of food, preferably Japanese."[56] In May, the Blue Triangles lured the light of foot to their "cabaret-style" benefit dance with the promise of waltz and foxtrot contests and live music to be furnished by Dave Sato's Wanderer Orchestra. Through such measures, the Nisei responded to community needs while enjoying the "excitement of experimentation."

As war approached, the Nisei organizations continued their service activities. For example, the Japanese YWCA Annual Report of 1941 proudly declared, "As the Japanese Branch we give good service to our community. We helped to sell 500 U.S.O. pins, which were 50 cents each. We assisted the local [Japanese American] Citizens League in many ways during its recent 'Nisei Festival' week. Our girls helped to make ticket boxes to put in the votes for the Queen Contest. When they invited [European] American friends to the banquet, our girls ushered and served as hostesses, and when the Interracial group had a tea party at the Exposition Park, our girls served tea in Japanese kimonos."[57]

As the YWCA report and the sports news suggest, the Nisei youth clubs provided some opportunities for interethnic and interracial interaction. Joint activities occasionally brought together young women of various ethnic backgrounds, often under the auspices of church-sponsored events. In 1926 the members of the Japanese High School Girl Reserves Club of the Union Church attended a "rally" at a boarding school for Mexican girls. More than two hundred girls attended, including European Americans. As their part of the rally, the Nisei girls, who were dressed in kimonos, sang songs in Japanese.[58] The Nisei clubs also sent delegates to conferences with which they were affiliated as "ethnic branches." In 1927 six Japanese American girls attended the Southern California Girl Reserves Conference in El Centro. During the conference, they stayed with local Japanese American families. The next year, fifteen delegates from the YWCA's International Institute attended the same conference, this time in Hollywood. This delegation included seven Japanese Girl Reserves and "representatives from the Russian, Mexican, Armenian and the Neighborhood [probably African American] groups."[59] The Nisei girls were asked to present a Japanese dance for the International

Luncheon. The Nisei attendees, it was noted, "would stay at some [European] American home during . . . the conference."[60] The arrangements for these conferences delineate both the openings in and the boundaries of interracial relations in the prewar period.

When they interacted with non–Japanese American youth, the Nisei girls were often expected to serve as representatives of ethnic culture. This meant putting aside their regular clothes and donning Japanese kimonos. They were usually called upon to serve tea, as the YWCA report indicated, or to perform Japanese songs and dances. In 1933, for example, Nisei girls took part in an International Day celebration at the YWCA's International Institute in Boyle Heights. As a reporter noted, the Nisei girls participated in "bringing the color of the Cherry Blossom Isles to the afternoon."[61] On the one hand, such performances can be viewed as an affirmation of immigrant ethnic culture. On the other hand, they also illustrate how the second-generation Japanese Americans were often "typecast" as exotic and foreign, rather than recognized as home-grown Americans.

In fact, Nisei girls clad in "picturesque" kimonos served as highly visible community representatives from the 1920s on, appearing at an array of civic events. In 1926, forty "Cherry Blossom Girls"—dancers from the YWCA, the Higashi Hongwanji Buddhist Temple, and the class of a private teacher—were slated to perform at the "Festival of Nations," a pageant organized to support the work of the Council on International Relations and to "present in a dramatic way scenes that reveal accurately the life of the people in their respective countries."[62] This illustrates how the Nisei, despite their American birth and upbringing, were often identified with Japan. In February 1928, ten Nisei girls danced in the local Roosevelt High School "All-Nations Festival" to raise funds for the Girls' Gymnasium. The *Rafu Shimpo* reported without irony, "Native girls of many nations, wearing their costumes, will give their country's dance at this time."[63] It might be argued that a costume and dance more representative of the urban Nisei girl might have been a drop-waisted dress and the foxtrot. Nevertheless, the prevailing public image of Nisei girls, even in urban settings, may well have been that of the graceful maiden in colorful Japanese robes and ornate sash.

The second-generation women's ethnic-cultural performance adds a gendered twist to the idea of the Nisei's potential role as a bridge of understanding between the United States and Japan. As historian David Yoo states, this metaphor, initiated by the Issei, was tailored by some of the Nisei "to negotiate issues of identity and to balance the demands of Americanization and the expectations of their parents and the ethnic community." However, Yoo points out, "In reality, very few of the second generation could have served as true bridges, since they lacked adequate knowledge of Japanese language, history, and culture."[64] Nevertheless, this notion remained a potent motif in Nisei discourse from the mid-1920s and through much of the 1930s. Part of its appeal lay in the prospect of a significant role that might be played by the Nisei, many of whom struggled with generational and racial issues in addition to economic uncertainty and political vulnerability. With an eye to U.S.-Japan tensions—and the Nisei situation—Miyoko Shimizu declared in a prize-winning 1933 speech, "Even today . . . with the dawn of the Pacific era, the peoples of the different races are not on the terms they should be." This she attributed to white domination of "colored groups." She proposed that the second generation could help to alleviate the international problem by serving as "the medium through which Japan and America will understand each other. . . ."[65] The role of "cultural bridge" was frequently delegated to young Nisei women in the pre-war period.

As war approached, this public role caused increasing discomfort for some Nisei, particularly as it was requested by European American organizations. In an interethnic religious forum, the Reverend Donald Toriumi lamented, "We wish to be treated like the rest of Americans, and yet we are not. . . . Yes, even when we are invited to church gatherings and . . . Americanization meetings, the amazing fact is that, in many instances, we are asked to come dressed in our 'native' costumes, sing Japanese songs and teach the people the secret lores of Oriental culture."[66] This burden weighed heavily on Nisei women, as Toriumi explained: "I have found that most of the girls do not care to wear these Japanese kimonoes [*sic*]. Many of the cute and quaint Japanese songs you have heard were . . . children's songs learned in pre-school days. The secret lores that you have heard were, in many cases, frantically gathered, and thrown into some kind of presentable shape and were given by people who kept their fingers crossed and hoped that no one would ask any embarrassing detailed questions."[67] Toriumi's words conjure images of young Nisei women hastily gleaning bits of information from Issei mothers, and then uneasily relaying them to white audiences that desired to hear Oriental secrets imparted by exotic "Others." This is not to say that all Nisei women did not enjoy or take pride in ethnic-cultural performance but to note that they differed in their level of comfort with it and to acknowledge the tension surrounding this role by 1941.

The image of the Nisei daughter in kimono, though read somewhat differently, was important in the ethnic community as well. As Micaela di Leonardo's research on Italian Americans in California revealed, maintaining and adapting what is considered ethnic culture has been largely delegated to women. Di Leonardo found that both men and women described women's activities as positively defining ethnic behavior,[68] which they located mainly in the home and family. Examining Nisei women's prewar activities suggests that the work of carrying out ethnic-cultural practices also extended into public arenas. Second-generation girls and young women not only introduced American holidays into the ethnic family but also played a vivid symbolic role in ethnic community celebrations. For example, girls in kimonos were often the highlighted dancers at Buddhist commemorations of the Birth of Buddha (*Hana Matsuri*, or the Flower Festival), observed in April. A poem written in honor of the 1927 Flower Festival parade described the delights of bobbing lanterns and floats, ending, "Dancing maidens with picturesque fans / Bring recollections of old Japan."[69] Japanese American community celebrations, however, in contrast to mainstream civic displays, were more likely to showcase Nisei women and men in a range of performances, both Japanese and Western.

Nisei girls in kimonos became part of long-term efforts to attract both Japanese American and mainstream customers to Little Tokyo. As the 1941 Japanese YWCA report observed, female Nisei club members provided support for the Japanese American Citizens League–run Nisei Week festival (still in existence), initiated in 1934 by Issei merchants to entice the second generation to patronize their businesses. Historian Lon Kurashige observes that, under the auspices of the JACL, the festival began as a vehicle utilizing biculturalism to appeal to both Japanese Americans and European Americans: "By joining Japanese dance, music, and cultural and martial arts exhibits with a parade, beauty pageant, and other American traditions, the festival presented a harmonious blending of East and West."[70] Nisei women served as the welcoming face of the ethnic community: wearing kimonos, they greeted and served tea to visitors; competed in the Nisei Week queen contest; walked the runway in fashion shows; and performed as musicians, singers, and dancers. Despite the crucial nature of women's participation, Kurashige notes their exclusion from the male-dominated leadership of the festival, as well as growing tensions over bicultural display with the advent of war. This shift in emphasis can be seen in the cover photo of the *Rafu Shimpo*'s holiday issue for 1940: The Nisei Week queen and princesses beam at the reader, resplendent in tiaras and ball gowns. Above the photo, and beneath a patriotic eagle head and flag-emblazoned shield, is an inscription proclaiming "God bless America / Our Home, Sweet Home!" and identifying the American status of the women.[71] Clearly, the Nisei's role as ethnic representatives, whether within or outside the Japanese American enclave, was a complicated one—a role that still affects the lives of Asian Americans and other children of immigrants today.

The Highly Visible Nisei Club Girl

By the eve of World War II, young women's clubs abounded in southern California. They were so prominent a feature of the Japanese American social landscape that the *Kashu Mainichi* profiled the female club member in its New Year's issue for 1941. The article attributed the large number of girls' clubs in Little Tokyo to the influence of the YWCA, using interchangeably the phrases "typical nisei club girl" and "typical nisei 'Y' girl." Stated the journalist, "Out of the thousands of girls who come into direct contact with the Japanese YWCA, many belong to the 29 affiliated 'Y' clubs in this city or to the WAU [Women's Athletic Union] where they find uninhibited outlet for their social and athletic activities."[72]

The journalist drew a critical but not unsympathetic portrait of the "typical nisei club girl" as a spirited young woman who enjoyed the pastimes of youth culture: "She likes to talk, dance and go to the shows. She reads the newspapers every morning. . . ." This article also shows club activities as a regular feature in the club girl's life: "Gossip she loves, but confines it usually to her monthly club meetings and teas." The effort to keep personal information in the channels of her closest peer networks suggests the young woman's awareness of and sensitivity to the Japanese American community's expectations regarding the behavior of Nisei daughters.[73]

Regardless of how they were perceived by outsiders, the Nisei women clearly saw themselves as Americans. As the journalist concluded, "With her youthful outlook, the typical nisei club girl has striven to do things in the American Way . . . any way which is the opposite of the traditional Japanese Way."[74] Within a year, for all Nisei in the U.S. West, questions of democracy, leadership, and the American way would become concrete, ironic, and engulfing. World War II brought chaos and loss to Japanese Americans, uprooting and scattering them; the social networks they had forged in earlier decades faced severe testing in the crucible of wartime incarceration and resettlement. The Nisei women's organizational skills, strong peer ties, and camaraderie served as valuable resources in the painstaking process of rebuilding lives and communities.

Conclusion

Despite its breezy, flippant tone and limited coverage, the 1941 *Kashu Mainichi* article does convey a sense of the Nisei club girls' high visibility in the ethnic community as well as of the ways in which their activities and ideas reflected the influence of mainstream youth practices. Through planning programs for recreation and fund-raising, they learned to organize effectively, to showcase their talents, and to move with verve in public space. In groups such as the Blue Circles and the Tartanettes, they formed friendship networks that have endured over six decades. Examining the intricate mosaic of their meetings, dances, sports, social service, and performances suggests how these young women both reinforced and challenged gender and racial dynamics in an era of exclusion. Their role as ethnic representatives, both within and outside the Japanese American enclave, reveals the complex chemistry of gender and race. Women's group activities and affiliation reinforced their generational ties and helped create a rich Nisei social world that has shaped postwar Japanese American communities.

NOTES

Thanks to Shirley Hune, Brian Niiya, Gail Nomura, Peggy Pascoe, and Vicki Ruíz for their helpful comments.

1. *Rafu Shimpo*, 28 February 1926.
2. As the ethnic press shows, prewar Nisei youth clubs proliferated, particularly in West Coast urban centers stretching from San Diego to Seattle.
3. See Vicki Ruiz, "The Flapper and the Chaperone: Historical Memory among Mexican-American Women," in *Seeking Common Ground*, ed. Donna Gabaccia (Westport, CT: Greenwood Press, 1992); and Judy Yung, *Unbound Feet* (Berkeley: University of California Press, 1995). They suggest that second-generation Mexican American and Chinese American young women played multiple dynamic roles in the life of the ethnic family and community.
4. *Kashu Mainichi*, 26 April 1936.
5. James P. Allen and Eugene Turner, *The Ethnic Quilt: Population Diversity in Southern California* (Northridge, CA: The Center for Geographical Studies, California State University, Northridge, 1997), 125.
6. A variety of spellings appeared, including "Lil' Tokio" and "Little Tokio." For consistency, I use the spelling "Little Tokyo," which has become standard usage since the postwar period.
7. *Rafu Shimpo*, 28 March 1926.
8. *Kashu Mainichi*, 26 April 1936.
9. *Rafu Shimpo*, 23 December 1940, 16.
10. *Rafu Shimpo*, 8 November 1926.
11. Mary S. Sims, *The Natural History of a Social Institution—The Young Women's Christian Association* (New York: The Womans Press, 1936), 59.

12. Sucheng Chan, "Race, Ethnic Culture, and Gender in the Construction of Ethnic Identities among Second-Generation Chinese Americans, 1880s to 1930s," in *Claiming America*, ed. K. Scott Wong and Sucheng Chan (Philadelphia: Temple University Press, 1998), 143.

13. Japanese Branch Young Women's Christian Association pamphlet ca. 1940, YWCA Collection, Special Collections, California State University, Northridge.

14. Sims, *Natural History*, 64.

15. *Rafu Shimpo*, 8 November 1926.

16. Sims, *Natural History*, 65.

17. *Rafu Shimpo*, 4 April 1926.

18. Ibid.

19. *Rafu Shimpo*, 28 March 1926.

20. *Rafu Shimpo*, 4 April 1926.

21. *Rafu Shimpo*, 25 April 1926.

22. Harry Kitano, *Japanese Americans: The Evolution of a Subculture*, 2d ed. (Englewood Cliffs, NJ: Prentice-Hall, 1976), 50.

23. Ruiz, "Flapper and Chaperone," 151.

24. Yoshiko Uchida, *Desert Exile: The Uprooting of a Japanese-American Family* (Seattle: University of Washington Press, 1982), 44.

25. *Rafu Shimpo*, 8 November 1926.

26. Japanese Branch Young Women's Christian Association pamphlet, ca. 1938, YWCA Collection, Special Collections, California State University, Northridge.

27. Joanne Meyerowitz, preface to *Men and Women Adrift: The YMCA and the YWCA in the City*, ed. Nina Mjagkij and Margaret Spratt (New York: New York University Press, 1997), xii–xiii.

28. *Rafu Shimpo*, 7 March 1927.

29. *Kashu Mainichi*, 15 April and 22 May 1932. The Junior Girl Reserves' discussion of "It" was doubtless a legacy of Clara Bow, the "It Girl," and the promotion of "sex appeal" in the 1920s.

30. *Rafu Shimpo*, 8 November 1926.

31. *Rafu Shimpo*, 20 December 1926.

32. *Rafu Shimpo*, 1 August 1927.

33. *Rafu Shimpo*, 9 August 1926.

34. Brian Niiya, "Introduction," in *More Than a Game: Sport in the Japanese American Community*, ed. Brian Niiya (Los Angeles: Japanese American National Museum, 2000), 39.

35. *Rafu Shimpo*, 7 February 1927.

36. Kay Moritani Komai interview, Temple City, California, 9 August 2000.

37. *Rafu Shimpo*, 12 March 1928.

38. *Rafu Shimpo*, 19 March 1928.

39. *Rafu Shimpo*, 22 December 1939, 23.

40. S. Frank Miyamoto, *Social Solidarity among the Japanese in Seattle* (Seattle: University of Washington Press, 1984), xvii.

41. *Rafu Shimpo*, 20 September 1926.

42. *Rafu Shimpo*, 1 January 1928.

43. *Rafu Shimpo*, 25 July 1926.

44. *Rafu Shimpo*, 20 June 1926.

45. Ibid.

46. *Kashu Mainichi*, 26 April 1936.

47. Kay Moritani Komai interview.

48. *Kashu Mainichi*, 17 November 1931.

49. Chi Alpha Delta was the first Japanese American women's sorority at UCLA, founded in

1929. For more information, see Shirley Jennifer Lim's Ph.D. dissertation, "Girls Just Wanna Have Fun: The Politics of Asian American Women's Public Culture, 1930–1960" (University of California, Los Angeles, 1998).

50. *Kashu Mainichi*, 5 January 1932.

51. *Kashu Mainichi*, 28 November 1931.

52. *Kashu Mainichi*, 28 July 1933.

53. *Rafu Shimpo*, 7 April 1926.

54. *Kashu Mainichi*, 23 November 1933.

55. *Rafu Shimpo*, 17 December 1928.

56. *Kashu Mainichi*, 29 March 1932.

57. "Annual Report of the Japanese Y.W.C.A.," 1941, YWCA Collection, Special Collections, California State University, Northridge.

58. *Rafu Shimpo*, 25 April 1926.

59. *Rafu Shimpo*, 23 January 1928.

60. *Rafu Shimpo*, 30 January 1928. When the Nisei used the term "American," they usually meant European Americans; they often referred to themselves as "Japanese" in the prewar ethnic press.

61. *Kashu Mainichi*, 6 October 1933.

62. *Rafu Shimpo*, 20 September 1926.

63. *Rafu Shimpo*, 20 February 1928.

64. David Yoo, *Growing Up Nisei: Race, Generation, and Culture among Japanese Americans of California, 1924–49* (Chicago: University of Illinois Press, 2000), 31–32.

65. *Kashu Mainichi*, 17 April 1933.

66. *Rafu Shimpo*, 28 December 1941.

67. Ibid.

68. Micaela di Leonardo, *The Varieties of Ethnic Experience: Kinship, Class, and Gender among California Italian-Americans* (Ithaca: Cornell University Press, 1984), 219.

69. *Rafu Shimpo*, 18 April 1927.

70. Lon Kurashige, "The Problem of Biculturalism: Japanese American Identity and Festival before World War II," *Journal of American History* 86:4 (March 2000): 1634.

71. *Rafu Shimpo*, 23 December 1940.

72. *Kashu Mainichi*, 1 January 1941.

73. Ibid.

74. Ibid.

11

Contested Beauty
Asian American Women's Cultural Citizenship during the Early Cold War Era

Shirley Jennifer Lim

Dear Sirs: George Ohashi's article on "Short Cut to Glamor" (SCENE [sic], April) is just what we have been hoping to find in your magazine. Thanks.
—Rosemary Ono, *Scene*, May 1950

Nearly five thousand people enjoyed a July 4th picnic at picturesque Adobe Creek Lodge here under the auspices of the Chinese American Citizens Alliance, and watched the crowning of "Miss Chinatown, 1950." The attendance . . . was the largest single gathering of Chinese in America ever.
—*Chinese Press*, July 1950

CDA [Caballeros de Dimas Alang] Popularity Contest Looms As One of the Biggest Events of Its Kind
Popularity Contest of Manila Post 464 for "Miss Manila" Now in Full Swing
—Los Angeles *Philippine Star Press*, Sept 11, 1950

Introduction

During the early Cold War era (1948–1955), when charges of being "un-American" were tantamount to treason, Asian American women's bodies were at the center of their communities' claims for inclusion in the American polity.[1] The Cold War was not just a political battle between the Soviet Union and the United States but also an ideological and cultural one. Asian American assertions of U.S. citizenship were made through cultural constructions of beauty, as exemplified in queen pageants and magazine articles.[2] The above ethnic press and magazine excerpts show that the issue of women's beauty continually received first-page reportage and magazine covers. Though many feminists suggest that a focus on fashion, makeup, and beauty is of debatable value to women, one of the most striking features of American-ethnic magazines and newspapers of the era is their prominent and repeated portrayal of Asian American women as fashionable and beautiful, which helps explain their appeal to readers. The magazines and newspapers promoted these women's middle-class styles and activities as part of a campaign to demonstrate that Asian Americans knew appropriate modern cultural practices and hence could claim full American citizenship. As researchers of postcolonial nationalisms have documented, in locations that mark race and ethnicity as significant, women have been made bearers of national identity and citizenship.[3] Indeed, during this era, many of the "acceptable" assertions of ethnicity were coded as female.

The Cold War context shaped Asian American and other racial minorities' desires to appear American, democratic, and loyal to the United States, rather than foreign and communist. "Cold War" is the name used to describe the post–World War II conflict between the Soviet-bloc countries and the West (predominantly the United States and Western Europe). This rivalry involved military, political, and ideological competition for adherents to the communist or capitalist systems. Asia was a primary site for these battles; witness the Korean War, Vietnam War, and the "fall" of China to communism. Although past scholars have focused on traditional political histories of the Cold War, new critical attention is being paid to cultural issues. For Asian American communities, beauty culture became a central site for Cold War politics that played out through displays of democratic capitalism and modernity.

Debated and circulated in mediums such as *Life* magazine, hallmarks of normative Cold War American values included heterosexuality, family life in the suburbs, middle-class propriety, and whiteness.[4] In the ensuing hyper-masculine political culture, what is now recognizable as a corresponding super-femininity emerged. Brassieres, *Playboy* magazine, Marilyn Monroe, Jacqueline Kennedy, and Barbie all became icons of American femininity.[5] Ladylike, sexual yet innocent, and determinedly marked as female, this new construction of beauty required inculcation via cultural forms such as magazines and beauty pageants. *Scene* and Asian-ethnic newspapers attempted to create an Americanized Asian-ethnic identity. However, the Asian American version of the American Cold War body portrayed in ethnic presses was strikingly more female than the European American one in mainstream presses or the African American one in African American presses.

For Asian American communities, the very conditions of the Cold War body—American, beautiful, and female—were under debate and negotiation. Given that racial minorities still had not been accepted fully into the American body politic, not only did the terms of the debate have to be forged, but inclusion into the realm of citizen-subject had to be proven. Yet, paradoxically, given the United States' need to prove its superiority to the Soviet Union, the Cold War allowed claims of racial discrimination to be selectively heard. The Soviet Union's assertion of the lack of racial progress in the United States as proof against the fairness of a capitalist democratic political system provided an unprecedented opportunity for Asian Americans (and other racial minorities) to claim a place in the nation. That claiming was imbued with the tension of trying to agitate for equality with whites yet arguing for ethnic particularity and difference.

The twentieth-century racial distinction between immigrant and citizen exacerbated the Cold War political climate. Throughout the nineteenth and twentieth centuries, the legal category of foreigner (as opposed to American citizen) had been built around the bodies of Asian Americans. By seeming more American, one could be recognized as a citizen rather than a perpetual alien. Since it was impossible for most Asian-ethnic Americans to pass as white, they would appear most American if they participated in mainstream cultural activities. Thus the degree to which they wanted to appear American was continually in tension with demonstrating ethnic pride. The Latino Cultural Studies Working Group's definition of cultural citizenship that "names a range of social practices which, taken together, claim and establish a distinct social space for Latinos in this country" also holds true for Asian Americans.[6]

While all Asian-ethnic groups had to prove Americanness, specific Cold War political challenges differed among the groups. For Japanese Americans, healing the distrust exemplified by wartime internment and postwar resettling into communities was a significant issue. For Chinese Americans, the major hurdle was proving they were not communists like the Chinese in the People's Republic of China. For Filipino Americans, Philippine independence challenged them to define themselves not as colonized subjects or nationals but as people with a distinct national origin and identity. Such definitions were compatible with noncommunist American liberal values of egalitarianism, self-making, and progress.

Asian American women both accommodated and resisted placing their bodies at the center of their communities' struggles for acceptance as Americans. To explore these issues, I examined the Japanese American–turned–Asian American pictorial magazine *Scene* and ethnic presses' portrayals of the 1952 Nisei Week, 1950 Miss Chinatown, and 1948 Miss Philippines beauty contests. Since both the presses' beauty-pageant coverage and the magazine primarily focused on Asian American women, they created spaces where Asian American women could see themselves as subjects and agents in mass media and in their own lives.

Women and Beauty

It is from the perspective of mainstream society that national imperatives for claiming beauty, and hence humanity, can be seen. Since the constitution of the racial ethnic minority body as human was a necessary precondition for the enactment of the liberal democratic citizen-subject, beauty as proof of humanity became a contested issue. Asian American forums such as *Scene*, a magazine founded by prominent second-generation Japanese American journalists in 1948, focused on women's bodies in an attempt to circumvent racialized standards of beauty that castigated non–European American women as ugly and subhuman. In the June 1953 edition of *Scene*, the editors featured a letter from a young college fraternity man with Cold War–necessitated military experience in Asia who wanted to prove to his classmates that Asian women were beautiful:

> Dear Sirs: I have returned from 18 months' duty in Korea with the U.S. Air Force, plus another year in Japan. . . . Here at school, I have been telling my friends that the Japanese women are very beautiful, but none of them will believe me. I noticed a few copies of SCENE [*sic*] in the college library, and they interest me very much. I also noticed on your January, 1952 issue, on the cover a picture of Kathleen Asano. . . . I was wondering if it would be possible to obtain an 8x10 glossy copy of the photo to show the boys that I am right. Elwood Schweer, Theta Sigma Tau, Ripon College, Ripon, Wis.[7]

Scene reported that Kathleen Asano's all-American cover generated an unprecedented number of requests for further information and photographs. It is surprising to note that *Scene* was delivered to the library at Ripon College in Wisconsin, presumably a location with few Asian American students at the time. People like Schweer's friends denied the humanity of Asian American women by refusing them the possibility of beauty. Thus it was empowering for Asian American women to be seen and to see themselves as beautiful. However, the ethnic communities' often-used solution of portraying women in beauty-pageant-type clothing, such as bathing suits and evening gowns, and using women who fit Western standards of beauty as a measure of ethnic comeliness further reinscribed the male gaze and patriarchal domination. Other research bears out that African American communities also strove to prove that their women were beautiful.[8] Thus, to advance themselves as assimilated members of U.S. society in a Cold War context, racial/ethnic groups frequently included conformity to Western patriarchy in their cultural activities.

Cultural producers from *Life* magazine to Miss America pageant organizers to the editors of *Scene* magazine insisted that the representative American body was young, female, single, and American born. What, then, was at stake for the young Asian American women who decided to create normative beauty through community contests or *Scene* profiles? Status and power.

First, just as the senior prom queen signaled the most popular girl in high school, winning a community event or being featured in a magazine could "crown" the social power of a particular young lady.[9] Second, pageants acted as "GI Bills" for women in that they provided economic incentives such as cash prizes, scholarships, and gifts, and the beauty industry provided jobs. Third, the grooming process of the pageant and/or the photo shoot taught young women public poise, polish, and the skills to operate in the public sphere. Fourth, the beauty-pageant contestant or model gained status in her family and community. She demonstrated that her parents and extended clan nurtured ideal young ladies through impeccable social reproduction. Fifth, the pageants and magazine profiles functioned as debuts in which young women would be introduced to society as eligible for dating. As a woman was deemed "beautiful," her "dating worth" skyrocketed. Sixth, the excitement and glamour of being at center stage, like a movie star or royalty, at a time when women had very few opportunities to get public attention, was an incentive.

Clearly, not all the prestige elements listed above would be in operation for all people at all times. However, though many young women adamantly refused to participate in public beauty culture because one or more of the prestige elements did not hold true for them, many women did partake.[10] As Filipina poet, activist, and scholar Emily Lawsin has explained, young Filipina American women's families pressured them to enter beauty pageants as a way to show family prominence and to raise money for the community.[11]

Female beauty as a means to gain status and prestige fascinated Asian Americans all over the United States. Los Angeles reader Rosemary Ono reported that the beauty article in *Scene's* April issue was what "we have been hoping to find in your magazine."[12] Ono's use of "we" implies either that she and others, such as friends and relatives, looked at and discussed the magazine together or that she was invoking a readily imagined community of female readers. Women could alleviate their gender anxieties about appropriate public appearances by following the tips in the article. For busy mothers and working women, the short cuts offered in the article saved precious time and energy. They also constructed a raced, classed, and Americanized being. According to both the beauty-pageant officials and the magazine, this being was female, middle-class, and interested in same-sex social activities, fashion, beauty, and fun.[13]

Similarly, young Chinese American women affirmed the *Chinese Press's* coverage of the 1950 San Francisco Miss Chinatown pageant. By June 9, 1950, the organizers had been successful in their attempts to publicize the Chinese American Citizens Alliance (CACA) Miss Chinatown contest and, with the help of the newspaper, had garnered interest and support from all over California. Marion Lowe, the president of the Oakland Chinese Young Women's Society, wrote: "The CACA activities have been always noted with interest, especially your annual Bathing Beauty Contest. Best of luck for a bigger and more successful picnic."[14] Young women, and men, were interested in the models of femininity shown to be successful in the beauty contest. It is significant that Lowe refers to the queen contest as a bathing-beauty contest.

Female newspaper writers celebrated beauty and fashion. For example, the Filipina American newspaper column "Salinas Tid-Bits by Trudy and Glo" enthused over a young woman's fabulous white "New Look" skirt with a tight-fitting belted jacket worn for Easter.[15] Consumer culture and beauty contests provided avenues for displaying beauty. In other columns, Trudy and Glo congratulated queen contest winners and asked Riz Raymundo where she bought the gorgeous black ballerina dress that she wore last night.[16] Thus good taste united with disposable income could give young women the tools with which to achieve beauty.

Women also made direct monetary gains as purveyors of beauty products. On the page after the skin-care profile "Beauty, Basically Speaking," *Scene* ran an advertisement for four beauty-product distributors: Mrs. Mary Suzuki, Mrs. Mae Noro, Mrs. Masai Maeda, and Mrs. Tatsuko Hino. The advertisement showed photographs of the young, attractive women and labeled them "your chicago counselors."[17] The beauty consultants were all married—which was surprising, for one might expect that marriage would end their wage-paid labor. Perhaps the women's success in marriage would lend credibility and respectability to their claims of knowing makeup and beauty. Perhaps the flexible or part-time hours of beauty-product distribution would appeal to married women. Japanese American women were not the only ones to find paid work in the beauty industry; African American women did as well.[18] For the four Japanese American beauty counselors, the race- and gender-segregated labor market ensured that beauty culture would also appeal to them. Given the demand for aestheticians, the typically low equipment start-up costs, and low barriers to entry, working in the beauty trade provided opportunities.

Most important, in opposition to national events, community events provided a forum for nonmainstream standards of femininity to triumph. Women who did not fit certain beauty conventions nonetheless won local pageants and were featured in community-specific publications such as *Scene*. For example, at the "Portrait of Spring" contest, one member of the queen's court wore glasses.[19] The queen herself, though in possession of a lovely smile, did not physically emblemize an Asian American Marilyn Monroe or a tall Kinuko Ito, Miss Japan. Instead she displayed a look and body type to which the majority of Asian American women could aspire. Thus the local and the particular allowed room for counterhegemonic beauty.

Performing the Cold War Body

The importance of beauty pageants was not unique to Asian American communities. During the Cold War era, for working-class and ethnic white American women who had professional and status aspirations, mainstream beauty pageants offered a significant means of advancement. In 1945, Bess Myerson's victory as a Jewish American "Miss America" marked the first time since the pageant began in 1921 that an "ethnic" white woman had won the pageant and the scholarships associated with the event. However, for racial minority women burdened by the double discrimination of race and sex, success at mainstream national beauty pageants was impossible. "Rule Seven" of the Miss America pageant allowed only "whites" to compete. The first African American woman did not advance to the national Miss America pageant until 1970, and none won until Vanessa Williams in 1984.[20] And it was not until well after the end of the Cold War that the first Asian American woman, Angela Perez Baraquio, won the Miss America title in 2001. Historically, however, Asian American attempts to prove Americanness occurred at community or theme pageants, not at the mainstream national pageants.[21]

Civil rights organizations' sponsorship distinguished racial minority beauty pageants from mainstream ones of the period as well as ones founded more recently. Beginning in 1948, a major civil rights group, the Chinese American Citizens Alliance, held patriotic queen contests. Such contests sought to demonstrate the community's identification with and loyalty to the United States. As the focal point for the annual San Francisco meeting, the CACA queen presided over Fourth of July festivities and was given the title "Miss Chinatown." In 1950, the display of all-American culture would provide an antidote to the recent "fall" of China to communism.

Political considerations also prompted the establishment of patriotic Filipina American queen contests. As women were visible symbols of gendered national identity, societal destabilization wrought by Philippine decolonization could be managed through an all-American queen pageant for women. Filipino Americans in Los Angeles, Salinas, and other communities held Independence Day celebrations centered on the crowned queen and her court. The Miss Philippines beauty pageant signified not only the local Los Angeles community but the Filipino American community in California and the United States, as well as nationalism in the Philippines. Beauty-queen competitions were key forums through which Philippine national identity was debated and forged.[22]

Likewise, Japanese American political and community organizations held numerous queen pageants after World War II. As responses to Japanese American internment, these pageants emphasized participation in American culture. One of the oldest continuous and most well known of those contests has been the Los Angeles Japanese American Nisei Week festival.[23] Begun in 1934 as a way for the second generation (Nisei) to make its mark, Nisei Week was also a means for merchants and community leaders to promote Little Tokyo, the business district just east of downtown Los Angeles.

Details of the Nisei Week contest in community newspapers best illustrate how Asian American women adopted the Cold War body politic. The 1952 Nisei Week candidates displayed middle-class American fashion knowledge and manners that were crucial to performing the Cold War era feminine body. As the *Rafu Shimpo* reported on the front page: "[T]he 10 Nisei Week Festival queen candidates . . . chewed on juicy barbequed spare ribs, sipped coffee, and chatted with hostesses, judges, and guests."[24] Although the article reports that the women were at ease, it would have been extraordinarily difficult for them to have been comfortable eating as they talked to the judges. A contestant who spoke with her mouth full of spareribs, who had barbecue sauce on her lipstick, and who fumbled with her coffee cup would probably be marked lower. A smart candidate might have tried to avoid the food, but then she could be rated lower for not being an obliging guest who partook of her host's refreshments. All these balancing skills were vital for post–World War II social-prestige events, such as sorority rushes and debuts, not to mention business functions and in-law meals.[25]

During the early Cold War era, "American" signified middle-class fashion and style. Not only had more Americans achieved that economic status during the postwar boom, but Americans felt compelled to display appropriate identity markers. As opposed to the "drab" socialist or communist proletariat, the middle-class American possessed the gender-specific consumer goods that showed faith in a capitalist society. Conformity to capitalistic values required an emphasis on gender specificity. Although ethnic whites were achieving social mobility, racial minorities were only beginning to make inroads.[26] So for all who were striving to appear middle-class, or for those newly arrived, performing appropriate class status was crucial.

Elimination rounds showed who best fit Cold War feminine middle-class ideals. To find out if they had successfully charmed the judges while eating the messy spareribs, the Nisei Week contenders had to wait by their telephones at an appointed hour. The previous day's competition had whittled down the field to five finalists, who would then participate in the final queen's contest. Being one of the finalists was an honor and obligation, for all five would comprise the queen's court and have official duties.

The language the *Rafu Shimpo* used implied that all the young women—competitors and readers alike—desired to become a queen, and it painted a genteel portrait of family life: "When the resounding bell rang in the quiet of their living rooms where all the girls were 'asked to stay until we give you a buzz' . . ." This was a life without noise, chaos, or family violence, and with enough affluence to afford a house with a separate living room complete with telephone. The paper conjectured that the women who had been eliminated "took the news with maybe a sniffle or a disillusioned sigh."[27] Given that half of the twenty nominated young women had declined to run, a sigh of relief may have also been a response.

Through their reactions, the candidates displayed Asian modesty and graciousness that dovetailed with gendered Cold War American values. As in many beauty pageants, surprise and sisterhood were the major elements reported by the Nisei Week queen contestants in hearing the news that they had been chosen. The *Rafu Shimpo* called each of the finalists immediately after notification so they could report the contestants' emotions to the readers. "'I am very grateful to be within the five, but am still "plumb shocked." I had little hope of getting in,' said Miss Kawasumi who enrolled last week at the General Hospital School of Nursing." Other candidates, such as Miss Abe, expressed sisterhood with the other queen contenders: "She said she was of course thrilled but thought all the others deserved to be in the finals too."[28] Since many of the young women came from similar class and educational backgrounds, they likely developed empathy for one another through the ordeal of the competition.

The five queen finalists not only showed appropriate mannerisms such as poise and modesty but sported the latest all-American styles. All five had "American" first names, whereas three out of five women eliminated had Japanese first names, such as Yoko and Toshe. Although the press photographs of the finalists were in black and white, it was apparent that they conformed to mainstream American ideals of femininity. All five candidates wore almost identical tea-length gowns with similar dark pumps. The contestants appeared to be the same height, with bright white smiles highlighted by lipstick-rimmed mouths. Although some women of Asian descent have naturally curly hair, the majority do not; yet all the finalists exhibited Elizabeth Taylor–esque waves. Indeed, they fit in beautifully with the stylized femininity depicted in *Scene* magazine. Highlighting the reciprocity between the magazine and the pageant, *Scene* devoted space to coverage of local pageants such as Los Angeles' Nisei Week queen pageant in Little Tokyo.[29]

The growth and consolidation of American ethnic beauty pageants during the Cold War era was accompanied by the development of local and regional contests in South America, Asia, and the Caribbean. In the 1930s and 1940s, these contests had grown in popularity as newly decolonizing nations attempted to perform modernity and nationhood. After World War II, these international "local" and national pageants transformed into regional ones, which were then brought together under the auspices of "Miss World" in 1951. The Miss Universe pageant was founded the next year.[30] Thus overseas competitions existed for reasons similar to Asian American ones.

Judging Beauty

Pageant conventions such as who enters, who judges, and what the contestants have to do express the values by which femininity, class, and ethnicity become defined. Local queens acted as liaisons between their ethnic enclaves and the rest of their cities. On the one hand, beauty pageants gave communities forums to debate and celebrate ideas of femininity, which allow them to gain greater cohesiveness. On the other hand, pageants were sites for dissent from community values.[31]

Since the pageant organizers were often connected to small businesses and knew the sponsors, young women who appealed to business owners were most likely to become finalists. For Nisei Week, substantial prizes were donated by Little Tokyo merchants who would act as sponsors for the festival by their contributions, such as an expensive television set for the winner.[32] As a reward for best embodying the Chinese American community, Miss Chinatown 1950 won a grand-prize boat trip from San Francisco to Los Angeles. Indeed, community beauty pageants of all types frequently favor young women who fit small-business owners' definitions of femininity.[33] It can be argued that there was teleology of progress implicit in the idealized notion of femininity articulated by the small-business owners. If women can conform to particular ideals of femininity, then democratic capitalism and modernity can be secured.

As a means of encouraging readers' interest in the 1952 pageant, the *Rafu Shimpo* explained the judging process for the Nisei Week festival queen. Whereas in previous years the queen contestants earned points by selling tickets to the festival, this year it was solely up to the judges to select the final five candidates, according to the criteria of "personality, poise, charm, and character, as well as her looks."[34] Since all the judges were given a criteria chart and a standard numbering system, ostensibly this method would be more "objective" than other ways of evaluating queen candidates.[35] The contest had become even more complex and sophisticated than in the previous years, for there would be four elimination rounds. The organizers incorrectly assumed there would be so many women entering the contest that the best way to choose the winner would be through extra competition rounds. Whereas the first three rounds involved community judges, the fourth and final event would be the actual selection of the queen by outside judges.

By enlisting judges from outside the community, Asian American norms and values could be evaluated against those of mainstream society. In contrast to the prewar Nisei Week pageants, which had secret judging panels, in 1952 the *Rafu Shimpo* named the ten judges, including the Japanese consul general, Kenichiro Yoshida. Most judges were outsiders to the Japanese American community and were European Americans considered to be experts in the world of business or the world of feminine beauty. In this particular case they included a makeup artist, a Northwest Airlines flight attendant executive trainer, the society editor for the *Los Angeles Mirror*, and a United Press Hollywood correspondent.[36] This privileged hegemonic values over ethnic community preferences. Although there was no controversy over the final decision, the opinions of the external judges versus those of the community could potentially cause disagreement over standards of femininity.

One of the European American female judges for the Nisei Week festival queen pageant explained her criteria for judging "winning" Japanese American femininity as a hybrid between Japanese and American, which demonstrated why Japanese American women became such potent symbols of femininity in the postwar era. A supervisor of stewardesses, Carolyn Miller explained: "In personality, the Japanese American girl has developed well her ability for creative thinking, independence, and American know-how. Yet she has not lost the gracefulness, poise, and esthetic love of natural things which has made the beauty of the women of Japan so internationally famous."[37] Miller's categorization renders "masculine" traits such as independence and know-how "American" and "feminine" traits such as poise and grace "Japanese." Thus Japanese American women could be lauded for appearing both feminine and Americanized, whereas Japanese American men would not be valorized for "Japanese" traits such as poise and grace.

Miller's remarks underscore the point that women who are successful in pageants are the ones who have social skills and educational achievements that can be utilized in a variety of public settings. As a judge, Miller observed that the Nisei Week candidates "will more than hold their own in the American business or social world." Having access to the American business world was still very new for women of color, who a mere decade earlier had been largely excluded. This highlights the convergence of gender and race for female narratives of progress in the context of capitalism and its struggles against communism. Thus domestic American narratives of assimilation to mainstream culture were propelled by these Cold War imperatives.

Contested Beauty

People have varying notions of ideal womanhood, and thus the representation of beauty can cause disputes. Since the winner of a beauty pageant signifies her community—composed of many generations and class tastes—to mainstream society, her victory opens up its values to public scrutiny. Magazines such as *Scene* similarly reveal contestations over and formations of community norms. Since racialized Asian American female beauty vacillated between Asian and American traits, judges and audiences debated its ideal.

It is precisely through disputes over issues such as beauty that groups delineate the boundaries of their values and hence themselves. The exchange in *Scene* magazine over Mineko Chado's latest American hairstyle generated controversy in many parts of the United States among both men and women. For example, Buster Shibata of New York City wrote: "My sister says that Mineko Chado's 'new look' hairdo (SCENE [*sic*], April 1950) makes Miss Chado more attractive. I can't see it. . . . The 'before' [pompadour] hairdo makes her look better to me."[38] The letter reveals that Shibata and his sister were interested enough in the magazine and in the hairstyle to discuss it and to write in right away, so that the letter could get published in the subsequent month's edition. Whether or not the latest fashion in hair was suited to Asian American women was considered an important enough issue for Shibata and his sister to argue over it.

From the opposite side of the country, Ruth Iseri of Portland, Oregon, wrote in her opinion: "Dear Sirs: My vote is for the pompadour"—a view that gender-unspecified J. Noda from Philadelphia shared.[39] Through these race-specific mass-media channels, Japanese Americans all over the United States, especially from major metropolitan areas, could debate the symbolic Cold War feminine body.[40] Although these contestations proliferated after World War II, they continued the networking started by 1930s Japanese American newspaper columns.[41]

Queen pageants demonstrated similar contestations over representations of the Asian American body. What this type of pageant shows is the very fluidity of standards of femininity. Although the selection of queen for Nisei Week and Miss Philippines contests showed harmony and accord, the results of the 1950 Miss Chinatown pageant proved to be controversial.[42] Given ambiguity in judging standards, the 1950 Fourth of July Miss Chinatown contest points were very close—the winner had only seven more points than the runner-up and ten more points than the third-place finisher.[43] As could be anticipated by the closeness of the race, not everybody agreed with the official judges' choice. The *Chinese Press* reported: "As Cynthia [Woo] stepped forward unbelievingly, she had all she could do to blink back the tears. The hubbub increased of applause (not unmixed with a few scattered boos), congra[t]ulations, the presentation of many awards, the whirring of the newsreel cameras and the clicking of shutters, and shouts for the crowds to stand back."[44] Clearly, not everybody believed that she best exemplified Chinese American femininity.

As the *Chinese Press* explained, part of what was at stake in the beauty pageant was the ever-changing notion of beauty, which is inextricably linked to politics and culture. The controversy over Cynthia Woo's victory occurred because of the clash between American and Chinese femininity. The paper noted the Americanized version of Chinese beauty displayed at the pageant. "And a note on stature: the height of the eleven young ladies averaged 5 feet 4½ inches, tall for Chinese girls. Long stemmed Chinese-American roses, you might say, with other measurements to match."[45] As befits an organization and event designed to show the Americanness of the community, the women themselves were hybridized emblems of Chinese American femininity.

Yet alongside the Americanized ideals of feminine physical appearance was a Chinese beauty aesthetic that existed in the minds of some community members. The *Chinese Press* columnist commented that the pageant marked a strong difference between American and Chinese beauty aesthetics, the latter epitomized by the T'ang emperor's court favorite Yang Kwei-fei:

> She turned and smiled, there bloom her hundred charms,
> Rendering colorless all the painted girls of the Six Palaces.[46]

Given the vagueness of both beauty standards, and given that it was one of the community's first contests, it is not surprising that the community did not come to consensus over which woman would best represent Chinese Americans. What the pageant does show is the invested interests of community members in beauty, beauty contests, and the cultural construction of citizenship through such events.

Representative Hybridity

Despite the political expediency of showing a mainstream American appearance, community values and customs allowed for partial Asian-ethnic culture to emerge. Such hybridity can signal ruptures in hegemonic power relations. The queen's appearance at public events signaled to the outside world that her community knew appropriate middle-class American signifiers. Yet, in the case of "not quite, not white" queens, ethnicity and race served as markers of difference and imperfect mimicry.[47] As demonstrated in Carolyn Miller's discussion of Japanese American young women, the debates over Cynthia Woo's victory, and Miss Philippines and Nisei Week clothing choices (discussed below), Asian American women performed ethnicity by hybridizing fashion, which showed the extent to which cultural citizenship could accommodate difference.[48]

Despite the imperatives for 100 percent Americanness in clothing, 1952 Nisei Week queen and court showed Japanese dress with Western hairstyles in their public "face," demonstrating hybridity and the possibility of calling attention to hegemonic power relations. Kimono-clad parades and official visits were exceedingly symbolic as the queen represented her community to the City of Los Angeles. Like a movie star or actual royalty, Emily Kato and her court wore kimonos as they rode in a convertible and waved to the public on their way to delivering the official invitation to Nisei Week to the mayor of Los Angeles.[49] As was the case for European-ethnic community queens, the Nisei Week queen was expected to bring favorable attention to her community.[50] Queens attended various public activities that linked multiple communities.[51] Escorted by pageant sponsors, the kimono-clad queen and her court thanked the Little Tokyo merchants.[52]

Given the strong all-American emphasis of the Cold War era, how can we understand the 1952 Nisei Week candidates' decision to wear kimonos? This act indicated the imperfection of translating mainstream criteria into ethnic pageants.[53] For the Nisei Week contenders, the symbolism of public ethnic affiliation proved stronger than blanket acceptance of Western fashion. Since the court was marked by other cues of Western modernity, such as hairstyles and the convertible, partial displays of Japanese fashion were acceptable. Clothing choices for women held contested meanings for the women themselves and the different communities in which they presented themselves.

Women's clothing was linked to Cold War political issues of democracy and modernity. In cultural forums ranging from magazines to movies, the Japanese kimono and mid-twentieth-century Western women's clothing were juxtaposed as "traditional" and "modern" forms of clothing, whose wearers would be judged accordingly. Immediately after World War II, magazine writer Arthur Behrstock reported that the Japanese woman was "refusing to wear the traditional kimono, and, instead, clothing herself in a form-fitting sweater and skirt."[54] Behrstock saw the change in dress as "evidence of Japan's growing attraction for American democracy." Hence, according to this logic, women living in politically democratic countries would wear the latest Western fashions! The Nisei Week court's hybridized fashions showed the limitations of Behrstock's formulation.

Similarly, Filipina American women in the 1948 Miss Philippines contest modeled gowns with Western and Filipino influences. In the publicity photographs, three out of the five candidates wore "modern" Filipino dress. Trinidad Padilla's dress was styled with puffed sleeves and a V-neck, as was Elizabeth Rigor's, which added fur trim. Winner "Cookie" Tenchavez's sleeves and V-neck were far more subdued.[55] Thus Tenchavez's gown best emblemized a hybridized cultural appearance.

Women commemorated the changes that the Filipina dresses had undergone since the advent of American colonialism. For example, in 1951 the Maria Clara Lodge, the female auxiliary of the Caballeros de Dimas Alang, organized a fashion show that high-lighted the "evolution of Filipina Dresses from 1898 to 1950." The "modern style with panuelo" echoed the main features of the 1948 Miss Philippines contest winner's gown.[56]

Although not a requirement in the 1950 Miss Chinatown pageant, in subsequent pageants in the late 1950s the contestants had to wear *cheong-sams*. Given that China had just turned communist, the Chinese Americans in 1950 had the most need to prove American allegiance. Wearing *cheong-sams* in the later Cold War period signaled the community's desire to show both American and acceptable Chinese identities. The body-revealing *cheong-sam* was identified with Madame Chiang Kai-shek and capital-ist Taiwan, versus the body-hiding Mao suit of communist China.

Contesting Beauty

Given all the incentives to be marked as "beautiful," why did women refuse to run in community pageants? Ten out of twenty of the young women nominated for the 1952 Nisei Week festival queen declined to run.[57] Some women refused to subject themselves to continual public scrutiny. Others did not have the time to participate in the ex-hausting competition rounds or in the winners' activities. The competition may also have been too costly for some families.

Chinese American women's reluctance to compete in pageants signaled resistance to acting as the symbol of their communities' body politic.[58] In 1951, the CACA queen contest organizers solicited participation from all over California. Since the CACA was based in San Francisco, the sponsors and community were dismayed that women from San Francisco declined to enter the contest.

The men running the pageant conflicted with women over the sense of what was an appropriate use of their bodies. In the battle over feminine representation of locality and ethnicity, civic boosterism, prizes, and national attention were supposedly reasons why local contestants should discard "false" modesty and enter the contest. The *Chinese Press* exhorted: "Remember, girls, your cooperation adds to the general upsurge of good community spirit. And besides, even without these wonderful prizes, local pride alone should be enough challenge. In short, is or isn't the San Francisco Chinese girl the most beautiful and charming?"[59] The quotation reveals some of the multiple meanings around Chinese Americanness and local chauvinism. Thus, if a San Francisco woman won the contest, it would prove the superiority of San Francisco and its Chinese Amer-ican community.

Although the *Chinese Press* editorial downplayed the impropriety of being judged according to physical criteria, its emphasis clearly indicated that many young women in San Francisco refused to enter the contest because of their concerns over appearing in public in a bathing suit. It is quite probable that the combination of the bathing-suit portion of the competition and the boos that greeted Cynthia Woo's 1950 victory prompted young Chinese American women watching the pageant to eschew future pageants. That year, confirming the sponsors' fears, a non–San Franciscan, Dorothy Lee, won Miss (San Francisco) Chinatown 1951.[60]

Conclusion

Despite the stark gendering of bodies during the early Cold War era, women of color and Asian American women in particular had differing relations to beauty from European American women, because its invocation could signify individual and/or community and/or race uplift. Performing beauty became a strategy for claiming status as citizen-subject. Some women such as Emily Kato accommodated becoming American. Young women from San Francisco, among others, resisted this form of cultural production by refusing to enter the Miss Chinatown pageant. Although such assertions of subjectivity destabilize mainstream values, ethnic communities do not always have complete control over their reception.

Contestations such as those over Mineko Chado's hair and the Miss Chinatown pageant show ways in which local and "marginal" ethnic groups challenged hegemonic, mainstream standards of attractive gendered bodies. In particular, the creation of hybrid Asian and American "beauty" provided an alternative to white mainstream beauty standards. Hybridity was one way to resolve the tensions between racial and gendered discourses of sameness and difference surrounding the civil rights and women's rights movements: the legal impetus for equality with European Americans and men, respectively, versus the racial power movements. These contestations over beauty—for example, "Black is Beautiful"—influenced the direction of civil rights movements.

In the post–Cold War era, beauty is still central to ethnic communities. *Scene* no longer exists, but *FACE* and *A* attest to the popularity of Asian American magazine culture. The Nisei Week, Miss Chinatown, and Miss Philippines contests all continue today. They have been joined by numerous other pageants—the winner of the Nisei Week pageant goes on to attend the Miss Nikkei contest in Brazil; Los Angeles has its own Miss Chinatown pageant. Other Asian-ethnic groups have developed pageants, such as the Vietnamese Hoa Hau Ao Dai contest and the Miss India Georgia pageant.

The dawning of the new millennium may signal a shift in the cultural importance of racialized gendered bodies. On October 14, 2000, a Filipina American, Miss Hawaii Angela Perez Baraquio, was crowned Miss America for 2001. A few years earlier another Miss Hawaii, a mixed-race part–Asian American woman named Brook Antoinette Mahealani Lee, won not only the Miss U.S.A. competition but the title of 1997 Miss Universe. Such victories do not necessarily mean full acceptance for Asian Americans into the American body politic. However, they do signal a breakdown in the hegemony of European American standards of beauty. This may mean that America's acceptance of racialized bodies comes in particularly gendered ways, such as male sports heroes and female beauty queens. It may be capitalism's attempt to manage race through the promotion of culturally racialized bodies at the expense of the political. Given the global commercial popularity achieved by racialized but not overtly politicized figures such as Lucy Liu, Jennifer Lopez, and L'il Kim, I anticipate that such trends will continue. However, even if global consumer capitalism frames the meanings of racialized gendered bodies, we as the consumers have the power to disrupt, question, and reformulate their significance.

NOTES

I thank Valerie Matsumoto, Gail Nomura, Shirley Hune, Amanda Frisken, Cynthia Tolentino, and Matthew Christensen for commenting on this chapter. I salute Brian Niiya who first alerted me to the existence of *Scene* magazine.

1. Elaine Tyler May, *Homeward Bound: American Families in the Cold War Era* (New York: Basic Books, 1988); Lary May, ed., *Recasting America: Culture and Politics in the Age of Cold War* (Chicago: University of Chicago Press, 1989); Joanne Meyerowitz, "Beyond the Feminine Mystique: A Reassessment of Postwar Mass Culture, 1946–1958," *Journal of American History* 79:4 (March 1993): 1455–82. I am defining the early Cold War era as 1948 to 1955.

2. Lisa Lowe argues it is through culture that the subject marks itself as American; in her *Immigrant Acts: On Asian American Cultural Politics* (Durham: Duke University Press, 1997).

3. R. Radhakrishnan, "Nationalism, Gender, and the Narrative of Identity," in Andrew Parker, Mary Russo, Doris Sommer, and Patricia Yeager, eds., *Nationalisms and Sexualities* (New York: Routledge, 1992), 77–95.

4. May, *Homeward Bound*.

5. Barbara Ehrenreich, *The Hearts of Men: American Dreams and the Flight from Commitment* (New York: Anchor Books, 1983).

6. William Flores, with Rina Benmayor, "Constructing Cultural Citizenship," in *Latino Cultural Citizenship: Claiming Identity, Space, and Rights* (Boston: Beacon Press, 1997), 1.

7. *Scene* denied Schweer's request, stating that they did not send photographs to readers. *Scene*, June 1953, 3.

8. Meyerowitz, "Beyond the Feminine Mystique," 244.

9. Vicki Ruiz has found that for Chicana women, popular culture offered a legitimate alternative to parental expectations and church authority. See her *From Out of the Shadows: Mexican Women in Twentieth-Century America* (New York: Oxford University Press, 1998), 67.

10. Sarah Banet-Weiser, *The Most Beautiful Girl in the World: Beauty Pageants and National Identity* (Berkeley and Los Angeles: University of California Press, 1999); Robert Lavenda, "'It's Not a Beauty Pageant': Hybrid Ideology in Minnesota Community Queen Pageants," in Colleen Ballerino Cohen, Richard Wilk, and Beverly Stoeltje, eds., *Beauty Queens: On the Global Stage* (New York: Routledge, 1996), 31–46; Dorinne Kondo, *About Face: Performing Race in Fashion and Theater* (New York: Routledge, 1997), 13.

11. Emily Lawsin, private e-mail, May 2000. Although Lawsin's family pressured her to participate in the Seattle queen pageant, she adamantly refused.

12. *Scene*, May 1950, 8.

13. Margaret Beetham, *A Magazine of Her Own? Domesticity and Desire in the Woman's Magazine, 1800–1914* (London: Routledge, 1996), 2.

14. *Chinese Press*, June 9, 1950, 1.

15. *Philippines Star Press*, April 9, 1948, 5.

16. *Philippines Star Press*, March 8, 1948, 5.

17. *Scene*, May 1950, 60.

18. Kathy Peiss, "Making Faces: The Cosmetic Industry and the Cultural Construction of Gender, 1890–1930," in Vicki L. Ruiz and Ellen Carol DuBois, eds., *Unequal Sisters*, 2d ed. (New York: Routledge, 1994), 383.

19. *Scene*, June 1952, 8.

20. Banet-Weiser, *Most Beautiful Girl in the World*, 127.

21. Shirley Jennifer Lim, "Girls Just Wanna Have Fun: The Politics of Asian American

Women's Public Culture, 1930–1960" (Ph.D. diss., University of California, Los Angeles, 1998).

22. Arleen G. de Vera, forthcoming Ph.D. dissertation, Department of History, University of California, Los Angeles.

23. Lon Kurashige, "Made in Little Tokyo: Politics of Ethnic Identity and Festival in Southern California, 1934–1994" (Ph.D. diss., University of Wisconsin, 1994).

24. *Rafu Shimpo*, August 4, 1952, 1.

25. Lim, "Girls Just Wanna Have Fun," chaps. 1 and 3.

26. George Lipsitz, *The Possessive Investment in Whiteness: How White People Benefit from Identity Politics* (Philadelphia: Temple University Press, 1998); Karen Brodkin Sacks, *How Jews Became White Folks, and What That Says about Race in America* (New Brunswick: Rutgers University Press, 1998); and Matthew Jacobson, *Whiteness of a Different Color: European Immigrants and the Alchemy of Race* (Cambridge, MA: Harvard University Press, 1998).

27. *Rafu Shimpo*, August 11, 1952, 1.

28. Ibid.

29. *Scene*, September 1951, 40.

30. Banet-Weiser, *Most Beautiful Girl in the World*, chap. 5.

31. Lim, "Girls Just Wanna Have Fun," chap. 5.

32. *Rafu Shimpo*, August 4, 1952, 1.

33. Anthropologist Robert Lavenda has observed that Czech American women who entered a Minnesota community queen contest tended to appeal to members of the small-business community; see "'It's Not a Beauty Pageant,'" 33.

34. Since tickets were frequently a measure of community clout or family wealth, judging by people outside of the community instead of selling tickets could lead to discrepancies with community values. *Rafu Shimpo*, July 28, 1952, 1.

35. The editors obligingly printed clip-out entry forms.

36. *Rafu Shimpo*, August 11, 1952, 1.

37. *Rafu Shimpo*, August 20, 1952, 5.

38. *Scene*, May 1950, 8.

39. Ibid.

40. Benedict Anderson, *Imagined Communities: Reflections on the Origin and Spread of Nationalism* (London: Verso, 1983).

41. For more on the Japanese American press, see David Yoo, *Growing Up Nisei: Race, Generation, and Culture among Japanese Americans of California, 1924–49* (Urbana: University of Illinois Press, 2000).

42. Lim, "Girls Just Wanna Have Fun," chap. 5.

43. The judges were supposed to derive 80 percent of the points from a contestant's face and figure.

44. *Chinese Press*, July 7, 1950, 7.

45. Ibid.

46. Ibid.

47. Homi Bhabha, "Of Mimicry and Man: The Ambivalence of Colonial Discourse," in *The Location of Culture* (New York and London: Routledge, 1994), 85–92.

48. Lowe, *Immigrant Acts*, 66.

49. *Rafu Shimpo*, August 19, 1952, 1.

50. Lavenda, "'It's Not a Beauty Pageant,'" 37.

51. *Rafu Shimpo*, August 19, 1952, 1; Judy Yung, *Unbound Feet: A Social History of Chinese Women in San Francisco*, (Berkeley: University of California Press, 1995), 97.

52. *Rafu Shimpo*, August 19, 1952, 1.

53. No matter how effective the mimicry, unavoidably the subaltern peoples are "not quite, not white" a fact that implicitly threatens the colonizers' hegemony. See Bhabha, "Of Mimicry and Man," 85–92.

54. Arthur Behrstock, "Japan Goes American," *American Magazine*, May 1947, 16. Cited in Caroline Sue Simpson, "American Orientalisms: The Gender and Cultural Politics of America's Postwar Relationship with Japan" (Ph.D. diss., University of Texas at Austin, 1994). 184.

55. *Philippines Star Press*, May 7, 1948, 1.

56. *Philippines Star Press*, January 22, 1951, 1.

57. *Rafu Shimpo*, August 4, 1952, 1.

58. Judy Wu, "'Loveliest Daughter of our Ancient Cathay!' Representations of Ethnic and Gender Identity in the Miss Chinatown U.S.A. Beauty Pageant," *Journal of Social History* 31:1 (Fall 1997): 5–31.

59. *Chinese Press*, August 10, 1951, 4.

60. *Chinese Press*, September 28, 1951, 2. See Wu, "'Loveliest Daughter.'"

12

Passed into the Present
Women in Hawaiian Entertainment

Amy Kuʻuleialoha Stillman

Since the late nineteenth century, Hawaiian music and dance have been enjoyed by residents and visitors to Hawaiʻi and have served as a promotional tool for performers who toured and played nightspots outside Hawaiʻi. Women were an integral part of Hawaiian entertainment. Yet, on close examination, women's contributions cluster into two principal areas: featured soloists and caretakers of knowledge. In this chapter, my purpose is to provide a historical overview of women in Hawaiian entertainment, particularly in the twentieth century, in order to show how women's contributions have been absolutely essential to the perpetuation of Hawaiian music and dance.

Hawaiian entertainment is inscribed in the historical record of Hawaiʻi's peoples. Indigenous legends attribute the hula tradition to Hiʻiaka, favored younger sister of the volcano goddess Pele. The opening scene in the epic tale of Pele and Hiʻiaka takes place on the beach at Puna, where Hiʻiaka's friend Hōpoe and her companion Hāʻena are engaged in a dance. Upon Pele's request for a dance from her sisters, Hiʻiaka responds, dancing to a song that, according to the legend, marks the invention of the hula.[1]

> Ke haʻa la Puna i ka makani
> Haʻa ka ulu hala i Keaʻau
> Haʻa Hāʻena me Hōpoe
> Haʻa ka wahine
> ʻAmi i kai o Nānāhuki la
> Hula leʻa wale i kai o Nānāhuki e!
>
> Puna dances in the breeze
> The pandanus groves at Keaʻau dance
> Haena and Hōpoe dance
> The woman dances
> Hip-swaying in the waters of Nānāhuki
> Dancing with enjoyment in the waters of Nānāhuki![2]

The saga of Pele and Hiʻiaka details how the sisters confront love, betrayal, loyalty, and vengeance, as Hiʻiaka is sent on a journey to fetch Pele's lover from Kauaʻi island.

Throughout her journey, Hiʻiaka's adventures are memorialized in both narrative prose and poetry. The epic is a foundational text for hula students, both in its relating of the genesis of hula and in its encasing of numerous pieces of hula repertoire, many of which have passed into the present.

Out of this episode emerged the hula tradition, the performance of which combines dance movement, poetic composition, vocal recitation, and percussive instrumental accompaniment. Other legends relate the arrival of the sharkskin-covered temple drum with the chief Laʻa-mai-Kahiki at around the twelfth century. The religious system associated with these settlers and the sacred drum required the observation of elaborate ritual practices, among them the safeguarding of sacred and esoteric knowledge. The hula's mythic origins were encompassed by restrictions surrounding the training of performers and the transmission of sacred repertoire.

While specific details of how the elaborate state religious system intersected with gender in Hawaiian society are beyond the scope of this essay, what is important here is that women were involved in hula performance from its beginnings. After the arrival of Europeans in 1778 and the subsequent success of American Calvinist missionaries in converting Hawaiians to Christianity by the mid-1820s, Hawaiian society underwent radical social transformation throughout the nineteenth century. Hawaiian performance was transformed as Hawaiians embraced Anglo-American Christian hymns, and missionaries promoted musical literacy in the use of musical staff notation; yet, despite missionary-inspired prohibitions of the hula, adherents quietly took it underground until later in the nineteenth century, when its performance was once again encouraged. The visual record throughout is rich with images of women performers, in drawings, photographs, and postcards. By the late nineteenth century, women composers were enriching the historical record with songs, and the advent of sound recording added the dimension of women's voices by the start of the twentieth century.

The contrast of foreground and underground provides a convenient conceptual frame for considering two areas of women's contributions to Hawaiian entertainment that I wish to focus on here. As featured soloists, whether as singers or dancers, women are foregrounded by virtue of being onstage. Likewise, in photographic sources, women are foregrounded in a purely statistical manner, outnumbering men performers on postcards by a landslide, for reasons that are elaborated below.

Although the notion of foreground is usually contrasted with background, I suggest that "underground" offers greater nuance. Over the course of the twentieth century, the primary lens through which Hawaiian music and hula have been openly accessible, especially outside Hawaiʻi, has been that of tourist entertainment. There is no one moment that can be designated as the advent of tourism to the islands, for the archipelago became an intended destination from the moment the British sea captain James Cook charted the islands' location in 1778 (and he himself was the first return visitor later that year).

Throughout the nineteenth century, published travel accounts enjoyed a broad public readership in the United States and Europe. Many readers aspired to visit the islands eventually. Scheduled visits became possible with the establishment of regular transportation routes, in place by the 1880s; this was followed immediately by government-sponsored promotional efforts that continue in the present, as tourism has become Hawai'i's top economic sector. In this context, activities not directly related to onstage performance become part and parcel of workings intended to be transparent to the gaze of tourists, not essential to their appreciation of performance activity. The notion of underground is taken here in reference to tourism. What are underground, then, are activities that are community based, church based, and research based—activities critical to the perpetuation of the performance tradition but virtually invisible outside their own arenas.

Women's contributions to Hawaiian entertainment have been absolutely crucial to its perpetuation. Women have been involved in a broad spectrum of roles, not only as singers and dancers but as composers, instrumentalists, teachers, educators, scholars, and policymakers. Importantly, in numerous cases, women's impact begins within their own families, and the descendants of prominent matriarchs embody the fruits of their teaching and practice. While the lens of foreground offers an opportunity to view the valorizing of women singers and dancers as a focal point, the lens of underground reveals the more crucial contribution of women in keeping the Hawaiian performance tradition truly alive. Moreover, this case underscores the importance of looking past that which is foregrounded, in plain view, to identify women's contributions in domains not in plain view yet crucial to that which is foregrounded.

Featured Soloists

In Hawaiian entertainment, featured performers take front and center stage. Arguably, women featured as soloists are appreciated not only for vocal skill but for visual appearance as well. Photographs of women soloists with male instrumental ensembles emphasize the contrast in dress and adornment: women singers attired in floor-length dresses, often either white or bright colored floral fabrics, stand out against men in suits, and the women's abundance of floral adornment in lei and hairpieces is countered by minimal floral adornment on men—with the exception of men who are featured soloists and thus stand out from men whose roles are accompaniment. One variant that has highlighted women performers is their attire in hula costumes—raffia skirts—in contrast to male musicians wearing western-style suits or dress shirts, trousers, and shoes.

Pitch is another dimension in which women soloists stand out. Women's voice ranges rise above men's and even above many instruments, giving women a sonic foregrounding in the musical texture. In the Hawaiian music tradition, there are two distinct subtraditions of women soloists who sing in the high ranges.

The first subtradition can be termed "art songs," the performance of which originally aspired to concert-style presentation by singers whose voices demonstrated training and cultivation. This trained-voice style of performance was particularly associated with the genre of songs called *mele Hawai'i*, which prevailed in the late nineteenth century; many songs of that period remain widely known. *Mele Hawai'i* were songs that were modeled on the alternating verse-chorus song form of the gospel hymns initially introduced by Protestant missionaries, starting in the 1820s.

By the 1860s, Hawaiian composers were composing songs with secular (i.e., non-Christian) lyrics. Moreover, many of the composers were musically literate in western musical notation, which they used to notate their songs. In the late nineteenth century, new songs were premiered in concert recitals that were announced in the newspapers. These events usually included selections of western classical music, and the *mele Hawaiʻi* songs were performed with piano accompaniment—in the manner of German *lieder* and French *chanson*.

Mele Hawaiʻi songs have been a prominent part of the repertoire of the Royal Hawaiian Band, an institution in the history of Hawaiian music, formed under royal patronage in the late nineteenth century and continued in the present under municipal auspices. Initially an all-male ensemble, women were accepted as instrumentalists only after the mid–twentieth century. However, the band apparently has always featured a woman vocalist. Included in this cadre are such singers as Nani Alapai, Julia Chilton, Annie Lei Hall, Jennie K. Akeo, Lena Machado, Lizzie Alohikea, Yvonne Perry, and Nalani Olds Napoleon. To this day, women vocalists featured in the band's weekly concerts stand in front of a group of instrumentalists who remain overwhelmingly male, and no woman has yet been appointed as bandmaster. Yet the sonic presence of women is unmistakable, with soprano voices soaring above the majority of the instruments.

The second subtradition is associated with the repertoire and performance of *hula kuʻi* songs. In contrast to the literate composition of *mele Hawaiʻi* songs that circulated as published sheet music, *hula kuʻi* songs circulated mostly orally, and their performance incorporates vocal techniques that emanate from the older, indigenous system of chant. *Hula kuʻi* songs were staples in party and nightclub entertainment, removed from the rarified realm of concert and recital halls, where *mele Hawaiʻi* songs reigned. The headlining women singers who emerged after World War II projected a self-confident panache manifested as earthy vocal flamboyance. The flair corresponded to the penchant in *hula kuʻi* songs for double meanings in the lyrics, which singers would emphasize vocally through the use of chant-derived articulatory techniques.

The recordings of Genoa Keawe exemplify the vocal earthiness applied to *hula kuʻi* songs. Her nearly six-decade recording career began in the late 1940s with the Honolulu-based 49th State Record Company, and her clear, bell-like voice, crisp enunciation, and widely admired use of yodeling, referred to as *haʻi*, have constituted a standard against which other singers are often compared.[3] Other singers who have enjoyed headliner status in the *hula kuʻi* subtradition of Hawaiian music include Nora Keahi Santos, Pauline Kekahuna, Linda Dela Cruz, Myra English, Myrtle K. Hilo, Leinaala Haili, Kealoha Kalama, Leilani Sharpe Mendez, Karen Keawehawaiʻi, Darlene Ahuna, and Amy Hanaialiʻi Gilliom.

There are some notable qualifications to the dichotomy drawn above. First, despite the contrasting performance practices commonly associated with *mele Hawaiʻi* and *hula kuʻi* songs, the repertoire is not mutually exclusive with respect to singers' abilities. Singers select their repertoire on the basis of the subject matter of the lyrics and the musical materials (melody, harmonizations, tempo, etc.). Yet certain singers tend to gravitate toward a certain repertoire, depending on what their vocal techniques allow them to exploit—be it the rarified elegance of *mele Hawaiʻi* songs or the rambunctious *joie de vivre* of *hula kuʻi* songs.

In this respect, the singer Lena Machado stands out as exceptional, in excelling in both repertoires. A featured soloist with the Royal Hawaiian Band in the 1930s, she was also an admired singer of *hula kuʻi* songs to whom many would correctly point as the model for subsequent vocalists. Even more extraordinary, Lena Macado was also an accomplished song composer, and her *hula kuʻi* songs—which constitute the bulk of her recordings currently circulating as reissues—were particularly suited to showcasing her skill in the *haʻi* yodeling technique.[4]

Moreover, while a majority of featured women singers are noted for singing in the high soprano range, the contralto Haunani Kahalewai enjoyed three decades of prominence as one of the featured singers on live weekly broadcasts of the *Hawaii Calls* radio show, which ran from 1935 into the early 1970s. Her low, sultry voice was featured on dozens of commercial recordings; successors could conceivably include Marlene Sai, Melveen Leed, and Kuʻuipo Kumukahi.

In hula, women dancers have been foregrounded since the late 1800s. It is not difficult to understand why. As objects of desire, native Hawaiian women engaged the fascination of visiting European and American men. These men were among the earliest visitors to the islands in the late 1700s and the early 1800s; even as women travelers and settlers to the islands increased, especially after the arrival of the first party of American missionaries in 1820, men exerted a definite edge in publishing accounts of their travels and in taking photographs, contributing to a greater overall interest in images of women subjects than in men. And because entertainment provided a break from the activities of everyday subsistence, hula enjoyed the preference of artists and photographers over more pedestrian activities such as cooking or fishing.[5]

Hence in historical photographs and postcards since the 1860s is traceable a gradual disappearance of men as dancers. Photographs from the 1880s include men dancing alongside women or men dancers posing in studio portraits alongside women dancers. By the turn of the century, poses of hula troupes were dominated by women; when men were included in photographs, it was most often as accompanists.

The most widely circulated images of women dancers are those associated with the Kodak Hula Show. This show, which ran from 1932 to 2002, was intended to provide an opportunity for tourists to take their own souvenir photographs of hula performances, during daylight hours and in an outdoor setting; this was to compensate for the fact that the lighting in nightclub shows was too low for amateur photographers. Over the decades, numerous commercial hula-related products have been issued, ranging from photographs and postcards to slides, viewcards, 8 mm film, and VHS videotape. The commercial photos capture the three kinds of hula costumes used in the show: (1) the knee-length hula skirt made of ti leaves, worn with a shoulderless fabric blouson; (2) the floor-length figure-hugging *holokū* gown with train; and (3) the loose long gown with a kerchief tied around the hips, used by comediennes.

Also emerging in the 1930s was the figure of the featured, solo hula dancer, who stood out from the typical chorus line of the troupe. Performers who achieved soloist stature were not only graceful dancers; they embodied a particular exotic beauty that tourism marketing was quick to harness graphically on travel posters and advertisements. The ideal was a slender long-limbed mixed-race woman of medium color, not too fair yet not dark.[6] In shows, soloists often perform dances set in a slow tempo that emphasize grace and control; they are attired in glamorous gowns and an abundance of floral ornamentation in neck lei and hairpieces. It is interesting to note that the connections between hula and celebrated ideals of feminine beauty are most clearly seen in beauty pageants, where so many contestants elect to perform hula as their talent—not only at the Miss Hawaiʻi state pageant level but also in the Miss America pageant.[7]

The role of the featured hula soloist had its counterpart in Hollywood movies, where non-Hawaiian starlets were showcased in hula production numbers. Despite coaching in many instances by authoritative consultants, many starlets ended up shimmying fairly meaninglessly in numbers that showcased them visually but still cause trained hula dancers to cringe at their lack of technique. In one notable exception, tap dancer Eleanor Powell, in the 1940 film *Honolulu*, starts out the finale production number in a pseudo-hula that very quickly dissolves into a tap-dancing display only costumed to look like hula.

In the wake of the cultural revival of the 1970s and the establishment of hula competitions as premier venues for hula troupes, contestants for the title of Miss Aloha Hula in the oldest and most prestigious event, the Merrie Monarch Hula Competition, have altered the rules of the game. Contestants are judged not only on technique but also on Hawaiian language competence, demonstrated in chanting, and the extent to which their dancing conveys an understanding of what they are dancing about.

In the cultural world of hula competitions, in different spotlights from those of tourist entertainment venues, soloist contestants are not eye candy but rather knowledgeable exponents of hula technique. Headshot portraits of soloist contestants are included in the program book; those portraits often show poses associated with glamour photography, and subjects are dressed in elaborate attire and coiffure. Since talent and technique are valued above appearance, however, there is a wider range of body size and appearance among the contestants—all of whom represent competing troupes—and the winners. In a venue decidedly antithetical to tourist commodification, hula competitions have helped restore a broader visual spectrum more representative of contemporary Hawaiian women. But the ideal of featuring a woman dancer as soloist is still upheld: contests for male soloists are fewer, far less prominent (the Merrie Monarch competition, for example, does not include a solo men's category), and virtually ignored in the media.

Matriarchs of Tradition

Watching a formal performance of Hawaiian music or hula involves viewing a finished product. The performers must possess a minimum level of skill in singing, playing instruments, and dance; those skills are focused on specific songs that are taught and rehearsed. The formal performance adds two additional elements: costuming and staging. Performers must be attired in costumes that complement the program of songs that will be presented, particularly in the choice of floral materials for the neck, wrist, and ankle wreaths that adorn dancers. Staging involves how performers are spatially arranged on stage and how they enter and exit.

What is presented onstage constitutes the foreground of Hawaiian music and hula performance. For the vast majority of tourists, this is all that is visible. Among audiences of Hawai'i residents, some will see only the finished performance, while others may have opportunities to observe parts of the teaching and preparation (especially parents of children enrolled in hula classes). In this sense, what happens backstage is analogous to what happens underground, out of sight. And this is precisely where women have reigned supreme. Throughout the twentieth century, it is possible to trace not only the staging of Hawaiian entertainment but also the continuity of the performance tradition in the hands of women.

To focus on women is not to deny or denigrate the contributions of men in the teaching and perpetuation of Hawaiian music and hula. A handful of men commanded respect as teachers of hula, such as Pua Ha'aheo, Antone Ka'o'o, Bill Lincoln, Tom Hiona, Henry Pa, Samuel Naeole, George Na'ope, and Darrell Lupenui. Men also clearly dominated as instructors as well as performers on instruments such as guitar and 'ukulele. Men dominated music publishing as well: Henry Berger, Charles Hopkins, A. R. "Sonny" Cunha, Charles E. King, Ernest Kaai, and Johnny Noble all published major collections of song compositions and individual sheet music.[8] From the perspective of historical distance, however, one thing becomes apparent: despite the prominence of men as performers and publishers, it has been largely the work of women that has borne fruit into succeeding generations.

Consider some statistics. In 1970, the University of Hawai'i Committee for the Preservation of Hawaiian Language, Art and Culture identified five masters as *Loea Hula* (literally, skilled hula expert) for their deep knowledge of rarely taught aspects of the hula tradition. All five were women: Lokalia Montgomery, Mary Kawena Pukui, Iolani Luahine, Eleanor Hiram, and Kau'i Zuttermeister. In 1984, the Kalihi-Palama Culture and Arts Society published a volume, *Nānā i Nā Loea Hula,* that documented profiles of prominent hula teachers; women were the focus of sixty of the book's seventy-eight profiles. The follow-up volume with the same title, published in 1997, reflects a nurturing of men hula teachers: twenty-one of the book's fifty-seven profiles are of men.

The dominance of charismatic women teachers brings into view the concept of hula lineages, of tracing one's knowledge through prior generations of teachers. In the twentieth century, another aspect of lineage comes to the foreground, and that is the matriarchal nurturing of one's blood descendants among the students to whom the traditions and knowledge are passed.

Lineages of prominence in the history of Hawaiian music and dance are too numerous to enumerate fully here. Through four case studies, we can see many of the ways in which the teachings of matriarchal figures continue in the present. The two figures whose impact on Hawaiian music is detailed below are Vicki I'i Rodrigues and Imrgard Farden Aluli. Both women were heirs to family legacies in Hawaiian music and hula. Both women have achieved renown as composers whose work has been widely recorded and performed. Both women gave birth to children who grew up to carry on their traditions. And both women have nurtured generations of students who also carry on their traditions.

Vicki Iʻi Rodrigues was a highly regarded musician and a respected authority on Hawaiian music. Like many musicians and enthusiasts, "Auntie Vicki" (as she was affectionately known) maintained a personal book of songs. Some were compositions by her grandmother, Katie Stevens Ii; others were compositions by her grandfather, Thomas Sylvester Kalama. To this legacy she has added her own compositions, which have, in turn, passed on to her children and students. Her five children have all worked as entertainers; three in particular—Nina Kealiʻiwahamana, Boyce Kaʻihiʻihikapu, and Lani Custino—were long-standing performers with the *Hawaii Calls* radio show and have appeared on the numerous commercial recordings issued under the show's auspices.

In the late 1950s, Auntie Vicki and her five children collaborated on an LP titled *Na Mele Ohana*,[9] which called attention to the multigenerational contributions of her family in Hawaiian music. Auntie Vicki's legacy as a teacher extends to many students, among whom two in particular stand out. Contemporary *kumu hula* (hula master) Leimomi Ho credits Auntie Vicki as her only hula teacher and evolved her own styling of hula movement and choreography that for many years stood out as distinct from the stylings of *kumu hula* from other lineages. The accomplished falsetto singer Tony Conjugacion has served as a musical repository of Auntie Vicki's vast repertoire, which he has been recording in his own prodigious output; his 1996 recording *O Ka Wā I Hala* (Of the Time Past)[10] consisted mostly of Auntie Vicki's own compositions.

Irmgard Farden Aluli was one of thirteen siblings who were born into a musical household, grew up to be accomplished musicians, and are the subjects of a book-length biography.[11] Throughout her life, Auntie Irmgard composed hundreds of songs. One in particular has become standard for all musicians and dancers: the song "Puamana" praises her family's home of that name in Lahaina, Maui.

Puamana, kuʻu home i Lahaina	Puamana is my home at Lahaina
Me nā pua ʻala onaona,	With fragrant flowers,
kuu home i aloha ʻia	my home is beloved.
Kuʻu home i ka ulu o ka niu,	My home in the coconut tree groves
ʻO ka niu kū kilakila,	The coconut trees stand upright
e napenape mālie.	and wave gently.
Home nani, home i ka ʻae kai la	Beautiful home on the beach
Ke kōnane a ka mahina	The reflection of the moon
Ke kai hāwanawana	Shines on the whispering sea.
Haʻina ʻia mai ka puana	The story is told
Kuʻu home i Lahaina	My home in Lahaina
I piha me ka hauʻoli	Is filled with happiness.[12]

The song is well suited for beginning hula dancers, as it is filled with basic images to depict using hand and arm gestures: a home is depicted by showing the angled roof pitch with both hands; the coconut trees standing tall are depicted by holding one forearm across the chest, supporting the other arm held straight upright; the beach and ocean are depicted by hand gestures placed below the waist that sketch gentle waves washing onto the shore; and happiness is a playful shrug of the shoulders.[13]

Professionally active in entertainment throughout her life, Auntie Irmgard founded a quartet in the 1960s, which she named Puamana after her family home and the song about it. After years of inactivity, Puamana was resurrected in the 1980s with an all-family membership: daughters Mihana Aluli Souza and ʻAʻima McManus and niece Luana McKenney. The group maintained an active performance schedule in the community and issued one CD, *From Irmgard with Love*,[14] consisting of Auntie Irmgard's songs. After Auntie Irmgard's passing in 2001, Mihana Souza issued a solo CD,[15] and her daughter Mahina Souza formed a duo, Kahala Moon, with cousin Kahala Mossman; they issued their debut CD, *Collage*,[16] in 2002. Mahina Souza represents yet another musical generation to come out of a family lineage of musical households.

In hula circles, women have had an even greater impact on the survival of traditional styles of performance that contrasted with the westernized styles in which Auntie Vicki Iʻi Rodrigues and Auntie Irmgard Aluli excelled. Hula in the performance tradition that supposedly predates westernization has always been more closely guarded by knowledgeable exponents. Attributes of sacredness permeate much of the material necessary for continuing ritual aspects of hula, particularly in the process of transmission and in the preparation for performances. By the mid- to late 1800s, many Christianized Hawaiians felt that Hawaiian ritual beliefs and practices were best left to pass. Some exponents took it on themselves to continue to teach these things clandestinely, especially to students who demonstrated a commitment to respect these traditions and to exercise appropriate caution in passing them further.

When, in the late 1960s and 1970s, Hawaiians began to reclaim those aspects of culture that had almost been suppressed out of existence, it was through the efforts of a handful of women teachers that this knowledge could be accessed and the practices brought back out into view. Two teachers in particular, Lokalia Montgomery and Edith Kanakaʻole, exemplify the perpetuation of traditional hula practices not generally staged for tourist consumption and entertainment. These teachers are important not only because they transmitted their knowledge but because their students have also been extremely active in bringing about widespread participation in these traditions, in a pyramid kind of effect.

Lokalia Montgomery conducted classes in the living room of her Kapahulu home for years. In her classes, Lokalia focused on pre-twentieth-century repertoire not generally presented in tourist entertainment venues. At a time in the twentieth century when Hawaiians were raised as native speakers of English, Lokalia emphasized understanding of the poetic texts, many of which contained esoteric cultural knowledge. And at a time when westernized Hawaiian music provided the public soundscape, Lokalia's teachings kept alive the older, pre–*hula kuʻi* chanted styles.

Among the legions of students who passed through her door, one in particular, Maiki Aiu Lake, was notable for training students who would continue to expand on Lokalia's teachings. Auntie Maiki clearly stands out as having exerted a major significance on hula generally: around 1970, she took the unprecedented step of opening a class specifically to train students who would go on to become teachers themselves. The first class graduated in 1972; over the next eleven years, she graduated forty-two students as teachers.[17]

The new cadre of teachers emerged precisely at the time when interest in studying hula had suddenly multiplied exponentially, and the respect for hula traditions that she instilled in her students became a cornerstone in their teaching of hula: in the orbits of Auntie Maiki's students, hula was not merely casual recreation but a serious endeavor to gain understanding of culturally rich traditions. Furthermore, her students included men who went on to establish schools that brought a vigorously masculine look to dancing and that were significant in drawing increasing numbers of men back to hula.

Most important, Auntie Maiki understood that living traditions are changing traditions. To this end, she instilled in her students a deep respect for what was handed down from the past; she drilled mastery of basic technique, and then she stood back and encouraged her graduates to innovate, confident that they would do so on a firm foundation. It was a potent combination of training, talent, and daring that Auntie Maiki had unleashed on the hula world, but one that has ultimately contributed to the flourishing of a truly vibrant range of idiosyncratic hula stylings.

A number of Auntie Maiki's students have, over the course of the years, directed award-winning hula troupes and made successful recordings that include notable amounts of traditional, as opposed to westernized, material. Although Auntie Maiki had also recorded her chanting, the recordings were only released posthumously in 1992 and clearly encapsulate a conservative approach to performing hula repertoire when placed next to the innovations of her students.[18]

Another example of a prominent hula lineage—and one that clearly dismantles any suggestion of an Oʻahu-island dominance in Hawaiian entertainment—is the Kanakaʻole family in Hilo, Hawaiʻi. Auntie Edith Kanakaʻole brought her family's tradition into the late twentieth century, having inherited it from her mother and grandmother and having trained her own daughters, especially Nalani Kanakaʻole and Pualani Kanakaʻole Kanahele, who assumed directorship of the school after Auntie Edith's passing in 1979. Auntie Edith's chanting and traditional repertoire were released on a 1977 recording, *Haʻakuʻi Pele i Hawaiʻi*;[19] this was followed by a recording of Auntie Edith's singing of her own compositions, *Hiʻipoi i ka ʻĀina Aloha*.[20]

The Kanakaʻole family's tradition is of particular significance for hula, because it is through the hula practice in this family that the repertorie associated with Pele, goddess of the volcano, has been transmitted continuously into the present (including the text cited at the beginning of this chapter, "Ke haʻa la Puna"). The family's proximity to Kilauea volcano accounts for a continuity of ritual practices surrounding the hula. The volcano, whose destructive eruptions gives birth to new land, is also clearly understood as the energizing source for the school's deep-bent-knee, bombastic hula style, low to the ground. In the wake of the vigorous cultural revival of the 1970s, the Kanakaʻoles' style has been widely emulated in hula schools throughout the islands and even in hula troupes in the continental United States.

In 1993, the National Endowment for the Arts honored the two sisters as National Heritage Fellows. Throughout the 1990s, they have turned their creative energies toward theatrical innovations in the presentation of the hula legacy that they guard. To date, two full-length shows have been staged, *Holo Mai Pele* and *Paiʻea*. The latter production toured California in 1998. The earlier production debuted in 1995, and in the fall of 2001 a one-hour film version was broadcast on PBS's *Great Performances* series, underscoring hula as a serious cultural tradition in a national venue.[21]

As the two direct heirs of Auntie Edith Kanaka'ole's traditions advance in age, the next two generations of the family have blossomed onto the hula scene. Kekuhi Kanahele, daughter of Auntie Pua, trained in the family hula traditions since childhood and designated as a co-successor (along with cousin Huihui Mossman) to her mother in directing the school, has come into her own as a singer, recording artist, and composer, having released three compact discs since 1996.[22] Kekuhi's son Lopaka Santiago, of college age at this writing, was also trained in the family hula traditions since childhood and has emerged as an award-winning vocalist in the falsetto tradition. He is preparing his first recording.

There are numerous other families who have been prominent in perpetuating Hawaiian music and dance, and whose eminence can be traced to the efforts of women who safeguarded the knowledge they received. Names such as Beamer, Puku'i, and Zuttermeister come to mind immediately. While space limitations do not allow a full consideration of those families' contributions, suffice it to note that in all cases, knowledge was passed into the present through the hands and voices of women.

In the context of hula competitions—venues of prestige that have emerged since the early 1970s[23]—there has emerged yet another way in which family dynasties are visibly manifested. At the start of the 1970s, an overwhelming majority of hula teachers actively teaching were women. Among women teachers, many of their daughters have since grown up around hula and have started to succeed their mothers in teaching hula and running the hula schools. For mother-daughter teams, competitions for solo titles have become a goal toward which to aspire. In the Merrie Monarch Hula Competition, the contest for the title Miss Aloha Hula has become a venue in which the daughters of prominent hula teachers do very well.

The most well known example is Aloha Dalire, *kumu hula* of Keolalaulani Halau 'Olapa o Laka. She was the very first winner of the soloist contest in 1971, when her mother was teaching hula; in the 1990s, all three of Aloha's daughters who have entered the contest have also won the title—Kapualokeokalaniakea in 1991, Kau'imaiokalaniakea in 1992, and Keolalaulani in 1999.[24] Other daughters of *kumu hula* who have won the title include Twyla Ululani Mendez (1984), daughter of Leilani Sharpe Mendez; Natalie Noelani Ai Kamau'u (1990), daughter of Olana Ai; Pi'ilani Smith (1989), daughter of Alicia Smith; Maelia Loebenstein (1993), granddaughter and successor of Mae Loebenstein; and Ku'ukamalani Ho (1996), daughter of Leimomi Ho. The prevalence of daughters of *kumu hula* being strong contenders drew much media commentary in 2002, when three contestants vying for the title were daughters of well-regarded *kumu hula*.

The prominence of women guardians of the hula tradition is not limited to Hawai'i. Indeed, the relocation of Hawaiians to the continent has spurred the growth of hula schools, especially in California and Washington State. Again, women have dominated in the organization of schools and community events since the 1960s, and daughters are moving into positions of responsibility. In Hayward, California, *kumu hula* 'Ehulani Lum founded a hula school in the 1970s and launched the annual Iā 'Oe E Ka Lā Hula

Competition in 1981; her work is continued by her daughter Gordean Lum Villiados. Across the San Francisco Bay in San Mateo, longtime teacher Esther Correa has handed the reins of her school, Hula Halau ʻo Kuʻuleinani, to her daughter, Renee Kuʻuleinani Price. In Los Angeles, *kumu hula* Sissy Kaʻio was featured with her sons and daughters in the 1992 production titled *California Generations*, which toured the state; this program highlighted how cultural traditions are being perpetuated through multiple family generations. In San Diego, longtime teacher Auntie Barbara Finneran has been co-teaching for years with her daughter, Karen Kealoha Finneran, as has the mother-daughter team of Kauʻi Brown and Donna Merghart.

Tracking Women's History in Hawaiian Music and Hula

Space limitations required focusing on a handful of case studies rather than systematically surveying the richness of women's contributions in Hawaiian music and dance. In general, however, it is possible to sketch two broad contours. Onstage, women are featured soloists, as much for their visual appearance as for their technical skill in singing or dancing. Behind the scenes, out of casual sight lines, and despite challenges that have threatened the continuity of hula (for example, conversion to Christianity in the early 1800s, when hula was deemed pagan and targeted for suppression), deep knowledge of esoteric traditions has been passed into the present by women. Not only did women safeguard knowledge of older ways when those ways were out of fashion; women exerted matriarchal authority in ensuring that students they trained would be respectful and responsible caretakers of knowledge they received. In the case of Auntie Maiki Aiu Lake, students were grounded in traditions so that they would be appropriately cautious as well as informed about how they chose to innovate.

The history of Hawaiian music and dance is replete with strong women who exerted significant influence on the careers of many entertainers. Moreover, it is clear that a history of native Hawaiian women must be viewed in terms of both what is publicly visible "onstage" and what is carefully guarded underground. Many aspects of Hawaiian culture have survived because one or more women held them close until they decided to pass on whatever they were protecting. The case of Hawaiian music and dance is particularly suggestive, because so much performance has been publicly visible. It is always difficult to know whether what is plainly visible is all that there is, or whether there is a bigger backdrop framing it. How much one can see then becomes a matter of where one is standing—inside, among the accepted acolytes, or outside, among the neophytes.

Hawaiian music and hula offer yet another dimension for further consideration. Hawaiʻi's multiethnic population, along with liberal incidents of interethnic marriages, suggests that Hawaiian performance traditions may be of interest to historians of Asian American women. Not only is it the case that Hawaiʻi residents include people of various ethnic heritage; the historical trend of interethnic marriages and the customary Hawaiian practice of adoption have blurred many lines between ethnicities and cultural practices. The very names of various hula teachers, such as Beverly Muraoka, Victoria Holt Takamine, and Denise Ramento, inscribe a multitude of complex histories of interaction. What is visible is perhaps not all that there is to know about how women in Hawaiian music and hula have passed tradition into the present.

NOTES

1. Nathaniel B. Emerson, *Pele and Hiiaka: A Myth from Hawaii* (Honolulu: Advertiser, 1915), xv–xvii, 1–2. Emerson's published version has been the basis for contemporary knowledge of this saga and of the poetic repertoire associated with hula. Recent research by S. Kuʻualoha Hoʻomanawanui has identified multiple versions of the Pele and Hiʻiaka legends, which are already revising our reception of Emerson's published version.

2. The Hawaiian text is based on Emerson with some revision of punctuation; the translation is mine.

3. Genoa Keawe's discography includes hundreds of songs on 78 rpm, 45 rpm, LP, cassette, and CD. Two highly recommended recordings are *Party Hulas* (Hula Records H-507, 1965) and *Luau Hulas* (Hula Records H-514, 1967); both have been reissued on compact disc (http://www.hawaiian-music.com/). Individual songs recorded on the 49th State label have been reissued on various compact discs in the series "Vintage Hawaiian Treasures," produced by Cord International (http://www.cordinternational.com/).

4. Lena Machado's recordings of her song compositions, dating from 1935 to 1962, have been reissued on *Hawaiian Song Bird* (Hana Ola HOCD29000, 1997; http://www.cordinternational .com/wahine.htm).

5. Several rich collections of photographs of hula since the mid-1800s have been published in recent years: see especially Mark Blackburn, *Hula Girls and Surfer Boys 1870–1940* (Atglen, PA: Schiffer Publishing, 2000) and *Hula Heaven: The Queen's Album* (Atglen, PA: Schiffer Publishing, 2001). Popular culture iconography of hula girl figurines and representations appears in Chris Pfouts, *Hula Dancers and Tiki Gods* (Atglen, PA: Schiffer Publishing, 2001). To place postcards depicting hula dancers in the context of postcards of Hawaiʻi generally, see Keith Steiner, *Hawaiʻi's Early Territorial Days 1900–1915 Viewed from Vintage Postcards by Island Curio* (Honolulu: Mutual Publishing, 2001).

6. Jane Desmond has painstakingly traced these visual formations in relation to racialization and the marketing of Hawaiian entertainment. See her *Staging Tourism: Bodies on Display from Waikiki to Sea World* (Chicago: University of Chicago Press, 1999), 34–121.

7. Interestingly, the first Miss Hawaiʻi to win the Miss America title, in 1991, was not a hula dancer. When pageant producers decided to institute a salute to the home state of the outgoing Miss America in 1992, Carolyn Sapp was cast as a central focus in an elaborate hula production number with the Brothers Cazimero and dancers associated with their show, then at the Royal Hawaiian Hotel.

8. For a bibliographic survey of Hawaiian songbooks and a historical contextualization of these particular compilations, see Amy K. Stillman, "Published Hawaiian Songbooks," *Notes* 44:1 (December 1987), 221–39.

9. Hula Records H-501.

10. Mountain Apple Company MACD 2031.

11. Mary C. Richards, *Sweet Voices of Lahaina: The Life Story of Maui's Fabulous Fardens* (Aiea: Island Heritage, 1990).

12. Chikao Toriyama, *Musical Images of Hawaiʻi* (Honolulu: Chikao Toriyama, 1996), 77. Translation is mine.

13. The song "Puamana" was also the structuring device used in the documentary film of the

same name about Auntie Irmgard, produced by Les Blank, Meleanna Aluli Meyer, and Chris Simon. See *Puamana* (El Cerrito, CA: Flower Films, 1991).

14. Mountain Apple Company MACD 2049, 1998.

15. I. Mihana, *Rust on the Moon* (IM Records 777, 2001).

16. Kahala Moon, *Collage* (Keala Records 1218, 2002).

17. Rita Ariyoshi, *Hula Is Life: The Story of Hālau Hula o Maiki* (Honolulu: Maiki Aiu Building Corporation, 1998), 66–67.

18. Maiki Aiu Lake and the Kahauanu Lake Trio and Singers, *Maiki: Chants and Mele of Hawaii* (Hula CDHS-588, 1992). Chant recordings by her students include three by Keli‘i Tau‘a—*The Pele Legends* (Pumehana PS-4903, 1977), *Kamehameha Chants* (Pumehana PS-4918, 1979), and *Pule Mua* (Mountain Apple Company MACD 2032, 1996)—and two by John R. Kaha‘i Topolinski—*Nā Mele Kupuna* (Pumehana PS-4906, 1978) and *Nou E Kawena* (Pumehana PS-4926, 1986). Robert Cazimero can be heard on over twenty recordings issued by the popular Brothers Cazimero duo, but his creative work with traditional hula is not yet represented on commercial sound recordings. The work of Auntie Maiki's students can be seen in commercial videotapes of televised broadcasts of hula competitions, in particular the prestigious Merrie Monarch Hula Competition.

19. Hula Records HS-560, 1977.

20. Hula Records HS-568, 1979.

21. The companion book by Pualani Kanaka‘ole Kanahele, *Holo Mai Pele* (Honolulu: Pacific Islanders in Communication and Hilo: Edith Kanaka‘ole Foundation, 2001), contains song texts, translations, and explanations of the Hawaiian-language repertoire seen on film. The school also issued a compact disc, *Uwōlani* (Liko Records LRCD-2003, 1998), which includes more traditional material in the troupe's repertoire.

22. *Hahani Mai* (Punahele PPCD004, 1996), *Kekuhi* (Mountain Apple Company MACD 2054, 1998), and *Honey Boy* (Mountain Apple Company MACD 2089).

23. For an overview of hula competition events, see Amy Stillman, "Hawaiian Hula Competitions: Event, Repertoire, Performance, Tradition," *Journal of American Folklore* 100 (1996): 357–80.

24. For newspaper coverage, see Cynthia Oi, "Dancing across the Generations," *Honolulu Star Bulletin*, April 9, 1999; online at http://starbulletin.com/1999/04/09/news/story2.html.

Part 5

Reshaping Lives and Communities after Militarism and War

13

Imagined Community
Sisterhood and Resistance among Korean Military Brides in America, 1950–1996

Ji-Yeon Yuh

The lives of Korean military brides, women who immigrated to the United States as wives of American soldiers, can be described as a complex struggle for survival, one characterized by what I call "everyday resistance." By this I mean resistance that is woven into the fabric of daily life, often covert, usually subtle, and rarely identified as resistance. It is part of a struggle for survival that goes beyond physical survival to include emotional and cultural survival as well, the survival of the whole self, intact with dignity, history, and self-respect. It is a struggle fought on many fronts, for the women are isolated from both Korean and American societies and from their own relatives and within their own families as well. They also face various kinds of disapproval, discrimination, and humiliations from all these sources, as well as various pressures to change and conform to American ways and minimize, even erase, their Korean identities.

Resistance is characterized by an outward deference to the authority of husbands, in-laws, and American culture and society, accompanied by an insistent, backstage privileging of the women's own desires and opinions and of Korean culture and identity. It is expressed in conversations among the women when they criticize their husbands and children or make jokes about American ways, in opinions they do not change even though they may change behavior to suit external demands, and most of all in their creation of an imagined community of sisters.[1]

This creation was something I gradually discovered as I conducted field research and oral history interviews from 1993 through 1996 in the Philadelphia–New Jersey–New York area. I first made contact with military brides through personal referrals and by beginning fieldwork at a Korean church whose congregants were primarily military brides and their families. Through these initial contacts, I was introduced to the three regional military-bride organizations. The majority of the women I met were from the working class or lower middle class, had one or more children, and worked outside the home. Some juggled two or three jobs. Some were in the middle of second or third marriages, and few had experienced stable married lives. Some were divorced and living alone. Only 2 of the more than 150 women I met could be described as solidly middle-class or higher, and only 1 had graduated from college. Among them, the earliest to arrive immigrated in 1951 and the latest in 1995.

The contours of military-bride community were gradually revealed during innumerable meetings. As the women themselves recounted it, it started from the simplest impulse, the desire to meet other Koreans like themselves, and gradually evolved into a network of organizations and personal contacts stretching across oceans and continents. This creation of community reveals a salient characteristic of their resistance. These women are not simply struggling *against*; they are struggling *for*. Their resistance is marked by creation of community and affirmation of self. Both are then used for subtle renegotiations of power dynamics in their own families that can provide them with increased freedoms, recognition from family members, and an explicit means of expressing their particular identities as Korean women.

This chapter focuses on the kinds of isolation and domination these women encounter and their varied responses, as well as the networks—both formal and informal—that facilitate their imagined community. It discusses the emergence of formal organizations that reinforced the women's efforts to maintain both their identity as Korean women and their personal dignity as individuals.

Chasing the American Dream

For the overwhelming majority of the women, coming to America represented the fulfillment of a dream. In Korea, the women had faced dominations and deprivations stemming from poverty, patriarchy, and Korea's subordinate status vis-à-vis Japan and the United States. In this context, marriage to an American soldier was itself a form of resistance. For women like Mrs. N, who was 1 of 11 Korean wives of American citizens who arrived in 1951, it was resistance to Korean patriarchy and to Korean backwardness. She saw escape from an impoverished, patriarchal Korea dominated by foreign powers as the only hope for obtaining some of the freedoms and privileges being enjoyed first by the Japanese colonizers and then by the American occupiers. It was wonderful luck, she said, to meet and fall in love with a nice young man who could take her to America. For women like Mrs. L, who arrived in 1972, it was resistance to a past, and a looming future, as a debt-ridden, impoverished camptown prostitute serving American soldiers stationed in South Korea. Despite his alcoholism and his womanizing, she married an American soldier in the hopes that they could build a life together in America. For a woman like Mrs. Q, who arrived in 1991, it was resistance to a bland future as a penny-pinching, middle-class housewife indistinguishable from other middle-class housewives. For all of them, it was a leap into a fairy-tale future, into the gilded America Dream.

Some ninety thousand Korean women took that leap between 1950 and 1989, entering the United States as wives of American soldiers. This migration of Korean women represents about 13 percent of the nearly seven hundred thousand Koreans admitted as permanent residents between 1950 and 1990. Unlike war brides from Europe or from

Asian countries such as Japan, the number of Korean military brides steadily increased until it reached a peak of forty thousand in each decade of the 1970s and 1980s.[2] Anecdotal evidence indicates Korean women are continuing to migrate to America as military brides as the twenty-first century unfolds.

The best available explanation for this phenomenon lies in the continued U.S. military presence in South Korea and the effects of this presence on Korean society, particularly on Korean women.[3] America fought a war in Korea from 1950 to 1953, ostensibly to ward off the communist threat in Asia. The war ended in a ceasefire and left Korea divided between north and south. It also provided the rationale for maintaining U.S. troops in South Korea—as a defense against communist North Korea—and, despite troop reductions over the years, some thirty-seven thousand troops remain stationed there. This military presence not only embodies the economic, political, and military influence that the United States wields over South Korea; it also has served as the primary gateway for American culture to enter Korea. The "American fever," a desire to emigrate to America and the belief that things American are vastly superior to things Korean, ran rampant throughout South Korea, reaching its peak in the 1970s and 1980s.[4] At the same time, the U.S. military presence created camptowns and militarized prostitution and offered on-base employment to Korean women as cashiers, clerks, secretaries, and waitresses, thus facilitating encounters—and eventual marriages—between American soldiers and Korean women.[5] In a social context where America was viewed with awe and American men were figured as knights in shining armor in contrast to Korean men, who were cast as sexist pigs, marriage to an American soldier could become the ideal expression of a Korean woman's desire for a different and better life.

This was particularly true for women from lower-class backgrounds and for women who wished to escape from bad marriages and stigmas such as divorce, rape, or experience in the camptowns. Except for a few women, most of whom married their American soldier husbands in the 1990s, the overwhelming majority of the more than 150 military brides I met during the course of my research came from lower-class backgrounds, were impoverished, or had a past that they wished to put behind them. They met their husbands while working as secretaries, cashiers, or waitresses on U.S. military bases, through the introduction of friends, at neighborhood cafés, and sometimes in or near camptowns.

Isolated on All Sides

Although the camptown is only one of many locales where Korean women can meet American men, most Koreans, whether in Korea or in America, associate military brides with camptowns and prostitutes. Bluntly put, most Koreans believe that military wives are former prostitutes. This has been a major factor in the ostracism and discrimination, even outright contempt, that military brides have faced from Koreans. They are not allowed full access into mainstream Korean society or the U.S. Korean immigrant community, and derogatory names familiar to every Korean-speaking Korean dog them constantly. If a military bride falls on difficult times, becomes divorced, has family troubles or business troubles, or if her children misbehave, Koreans nod knowingly and say, "Well, what can you expect from that kind of woman."

Even family members who have accepted the help of their military-bride relatives often shun them for fear of being tainted by association. Numerous women described sponsoring siblings and other relatives for immigration, helping them adjust to American society, finding them housing and jobs, smoothing their children's entry into schools, translating bureaucratic letters, and performing other, sundry tasks that require a working knowledge of English and American society. But once their usefulness was over, many of the women found that they were no longer welcome in the homes of their relatives. As a result, military brides have found themselves isolated not only from fellow Koreans but also from kin.

This isolation extends to American society and their own families. Although their husbands may provide some access to American society, being the wife of an American has provided neither acceptance as Americans nor the fulfillment of the American Dream of prosperity. As immigrant Asian women, they found themselves faced with patriarchy and poverty American-style, racism, and cultural isolation. As nonnative speakers of English, as interculturally and interracially married women, and as workers in the lower tiers of the economy, they were consistently forced to contend with a wide variety of demands, indignities, and humiliations inflicted by both society at large and the people closest to them.

The domination they experienced was based primarily on gender, race, language, and cultural difference. It is not so much a case of separate, multiple dominations—of racism on the one hand and sexism on the other—but of a domination woven out of all the strands. It is most often expressed in demands that the women tailor their lives to suit the needs of others. For example, they are expected selectively to retain traits of docility, deference, and domesticity that their husbands—in an expression of Orientalist prejudice—assume they possess as Asian women. These are traits that the husbands often view as "better" than those of "modern" American women because they more closely match the characteristics of traditional, old-fashioned women. Since the 1970s, the women have also been increasingly asked to serve as a window to another culture and thereby to provide nonthreatening multicultural experiences for Americans and to contribute to the multicultural milieu of American society, one that conveniently glosses over persisting racial and cultural inequalities.[6]

The demand that they Americanize is perhaps the primary expression of domination. Made by husbands, in-laws, and society at large, the pressure to Americanize has manifested itself most clearly in the demand that the women use their domestic, cultural, and reproductive labor to keep an American household and raise American children, not bicultural Korean American children. For many women, raising American children has meant raising children who will view their mothers as different, perhaps inferior, and thus being forced to deal with a profound sense of cultural distance between themselves and their own offspring. This is usually the isolation that military brides find most difficult to bear, and the one that they most often seek to rationalize and minimize.

Finding Each Other

Korean military brides' responses to the demands and isolation of their lives in America collectively bear the marks of strategies for survival, a complex mix of compliance and resistance, such that resistance is often fashioned out of seeming compliance. This is resistance that takes place on the small stage of everyday life, in the private spaces of home; in personal encounters and relationships with husbands, children, in-laws, supervisors, neighbors, the children's teachers, and the cashier at the local grocery store. It is rarely overt, hostile, or accompanied by an articulated critique of the domination under which they live. Like the Malaysian factory women studied by Aihwa Ong, Korean military brides in the United States display few, if any, signs of Western-style oppositional consciousness. Ong argued that this apparent "lack" did not mean that the Malaysian factory women did not critique and resist this domination. They protested the imposition of capitalist discipline through the inventive use of their own cultural practices, such as spirit possession, to stop production on the work floor.[7] Resistance slips in, in disguise, in forms not immediately recognizable to those in power. For people in subordinate positions without the power to push blatant resistance to successful conclusions, disguised resistance is often the only viable option.

This is the situation for most military brides, who find that much of the domination they face comes from close family members on whom they are dependent or whom they love. They usually do not hold sufficient power—economic, cultural, social, personal—to engage in blatant struggle without incurring heavy penalties. Furthermore, they may not wish to treat husbands and other family members as if they were enemies and aggravate strife within their households. Thus military brides use strategies that can be characterized as "infrapolitics," what James C. Scott describes as "a wide variety of low-profile forms of resistance that dare not speak in their own name" and "practices that aim at an unobtrusive renegotiation of power relations."[8] Their strategies are similar to those described by Robin D. G. Kelley in his studies of African Americans: small acts committed in the routine of daily life by individuals, which together amount to a collective resistance and consciousness with the potential to blaze into outright rebellion.[9]

Among these small acts is finding and connecting with each other. Because most of the women followed their military husbands from base to base, they met and made friends in numerous geographical locations. These friends would also move from place to place. As a result, many women had a web of friends and acquaintances spread across the United States. Nearly everyone I met, for example, spoke of friends in other states, adding explanatory remarks such as "We met in Germany." They often exchanged information about the areas where they lived and about the situation of Korean military brides. Women who were plugged into these networks had access to a wide variety of information, ranging from how to make imitation red pepper paste to how to find a job. These networks sometimes coalesced into formal organizations, sometimes remained informal groupings of friends, and sometimes were based in churches. Membership in these networks often overlapped, so that churches, organizations, and informal groupings were linked through personal ties and mutual members.

In forming these networks, Korean military brides were adapting familiar social forms to their unfamiliar situations as intermarried Korean immigrant women. Networks of female friends and women-only organizations have played significant roles in Korean women's lives throughout the twentieth century. Usually formed among women attending the same schools or living in the same neighborhoods, these friendship networks have provided women with companionship, information, and a peer group against which to measure themselves and their lives. Indeed, a few military brides maintain contact with their friendship networks in Korea. Women in South Korea have also organized themselves to address various issues in their lives.[10] Factory women have played a major role in the labor movement, and middle-class housewives have organized consumer associations, parent associations, and neighborhood associations. Although these housewife organizations ostensibly focus on traditional female domestic concerns such as children's education and the proper way to keep house, they have also used the rhetoric of domesticity to expand the boundaries of acceptable activities for respectable women. In addition, these seemingly conservative organizations—often derided as groups where "idle housewives" meet to socialize—can become forums for women critically to question their condition and the forces shaping their lives, and thus become a site for subversive action.[11]

Most military brides are not directly acquainted with these organizations. But, in a similar fashion, their efforts to find familiar companionship in a strange new world have created spaces where the women can define themselves and their world, provide critical assistance to one another, and affirm themselves as they affirm one another. Through their socializing, then, they have created community and sisterhood out of their common status as Korean military brides. Their informal networks began to coalesce into formal organizations, and they began to use Korean immigrant churches—primarily those located near military bases, whose mission was to minister to military brides—for their own purposes. By the 1970s and 1980s, military brides newly arrived in the United States or just moving to a new area were able to tap into these organizations and find assistance as they settled in, companionship, and the opportunity to belong to a community of their own. Unlike those women who arrived in the 1950s and 1960s, they were not dependent on sympathetic in-laws or husbands to meet one another, and they were not "alone in a sea of foreign faces."

In the area of my research, there are three regional Korean military-bride organizations with a combined membership of several hundred. The women themselves founded these organizations with little or no prodding from others, such as husbands, social workers, or ministers. In all three cases, the women themselves felt the need for a group and set about organizing one. The two military bases in the region also have their own Korean military-bride organizations, as do many U.S. military bases around the nation and the world. Although the on-base associations are loosely sponsored by the military as one of numerous military dependent organizations, such as other military wives' associations that are expected to provide volunteer service, the regional associations are independent of any external sponsorship. The base associations are often an arena where women compete on the basis of the husband's rank and promotions, so that a social hierarchy emerges among the women that mimics the military hierarchy of their husbands. Service in such on-base associations can sometimes influence a husband's promotion, and association presidents are invariably the wives of officers. The regional associations, however, offer a more relaxed atmosphere of fellowship. This is largely because most members of the regional association are a step or two removed from the military, their husbands now living civilian lives. Women who had participated in both on-base and regional associations saw the on-base associations as just an "activity" but viewed the regional associations as tightly knit communities. These regional associations offer not only companionship but also the chance to be part of a community and feel a sense of belonging, a chance that many military brides are denied by both mainstream American and Korean immigrant communities. Some organizations also offer opportunities to work for causes that military brides feel are close to their interests, such as assisting Amerasians in Korea or sister military brides who have come upon hard times.

The community and sisterhood created by Korean military brides should not be exaggerated. There is no national organization that formally links the numerous regional organizations. Links between organizations are often tenuous and dependent on personal connections. The women have not yet been able to create institutions of their own that fully meet their common needs. Most organizations are social clubs rather than associations devoted to community service for military brides. Dependent on volunteers, organizations are often limited in the scope of activities they can engage in. Although the women as congregants can exert a great deal of control over their churches, the churches are nevertheless under the formal control of denominational organizations. Ministers are Korean men who often have little knowledge or understanding of military brides before they are assigned to a military bride church.[12] The nomadic life of military families results in an ever-changing congregation for most of these churches, and this serves to weaken the women's influence over these particular institutions. It is impossible for these organizations and networks to reach all Korean military brides. I met numerous women who were isolated from these organizations and lived rather solitary lives. Nevertheless, Korean military brides as a whole have built a network of ties—personal and organizational—that connect them to one another and often provide valuable, practical assistance. Perhaps more important, they have imagined themselves into a coherent community with common interests, a community in which they can express and receive affirmations of self and of sisterhood.

A Group of Our Own

The growing isolation that military brides felt as they were shunned by both Korean immigrants and mainstream Americans led them to develop their own community, explained Mrs. C, a founding member of a regional Korean military-bride organization:

> It's hard to associate with Americans, they call us *Oriental, Oriental girl* and this and that, but if we try to get involved in Korean communities, then they label us as internationally married women and say this and that about us, so there's no place for us to go. So that's why this *group* started.[13]

The organization, which I call the ABC Korean American Wives Association, held its first meeting in 1979 and drew its members from a wide area that included an army base, an air force base, and a major metropolitan area with a sizable Korean immigrant population. Co-founders and initial members included not only women who had married American soldiers but also Korean women who had married other foreigners, such as the daughter of Korean novelist Yi Kwang Soo, who had married a South Asian and taught at an American university, and Chon S. Edwards, who had married an American civilian in the early 1950s and became an exemplary example of the internationally married woman as civilian ambassador.

According to Mrs. K, another founding member, several women had talked among themselves for three or four years about the need for an organization for internationally married Korean women. Finally, they decided to form one. After contacting several other women, they held an organizational meeting in 1979. About eight women attended that first meeting. Once the organization was founded, she said, so many women became members that people wondered where they all had come from. The organization grew to several dozen members. Several dozen more women, although not members, were acquainted with the organization.

They organized fundraisers for Korean orphans and Amerasians, held social gatherings for military brides, and spoke out in the local Korean media about the successful lives of military brides in an effort to combat negative stereotypes. They also organized to help those military brides who suffered from domestic violence, whose husbands abandoned them, or who needed jobs. As the organization grew, it spun off a second organization, which I call the XYZ Korean American Wives Association. The two organizations divided their geographical territory, so that the original ABC Association drew its members from outlying suburban and semi-rural areas, while the splinter organization drew its members from the major metropolitan area. Both organizations remain active, sometimes sponsoring joint activities. Several women note that only the dedication and unity of the women has kept the two organizations running these many years.

Early in its history, the original group nearly dissolved over relations between women married to U.S. soldiers and women married to Americans who were not in the military. The military brides felt that the other women did not show them respect. Often denied respect by other Koreans as well as Americans, the women demand respect from one another and show little tolerance of sister internationally married women who are unable to respect them. Having joined an organization where they expected to enjoy companionship and mutual respect with other women like themselves, they were dismayed to find members who failed properly to respect everyone and displayed biases similar to those readily encountered among mainstream Korean immigrants. Such biases had no place in the community that the women had envisioned for themselves.

The episode also reveals that while other Koreans categorize all Korean women who marry non-Korean men as "internationally married women," the women themselves make finer distinctions. A fundamental distinction is that between women married to soldiers—the military brides—and women married to civilian foreigners. Women in the latter category often strive to set themselves apart from military brides and the camptown shadow that falls on them by using the label "internationally married women." Perceiving themselves to be superior, some women simply avoid the company of military brides, while others try to assume leadership roles over women they view as uneducated and in need of uplift. This is partly a class division based on the husbands' status, for the civilian husbands are often well-educated professionals, such as scholars in Asian Studies and related disciplines, diplomats, or businessmen engaged in international trade, while the military husbands are generally enlisted men. In part, it was this division between military brides and other internationally married women that threatened to destroy the organization. Rather than being resolved through a coming together across differences, however, the divisions were side-stepped as the military brides took control of the organization and the other internationally married women stepped down into peripheral roles or dropped out altogether. The solidarity that emerged is more a solidarity of military brides than a solidarity of internationally married women generally.

A Cause of Our Own

Around the same time that the ABC Association was founded, Mrs. S and another group of military brides were also forming a regional organization. Although the women had numerous friends and contacts who were military brides, they were often too busy to stay in touch. The early years of working, raising children, and adjusting to American life had left them with little time for developing friendships or organizing formal activities. When one of the women passed away, her death became the impetus for forming an organization. Their grief was suffused with a deep regret that they had not been able to make the time to develop intimate ties with the deceased woman. A formal organization, the women felt, would provide an excuse for regular fellowship and a forum where bonds could be forged. Said Mrs. S:

> It was so sad. We had not been able to see each other that much, we just worked all the time. We came to America and just worked and then we had to part like that, so we said, let's form a group. . . . That was in 1978, we said let's form a group. Only Korean women married to Americans, it had to be that way. *We are same, so we talk everything.* There's nothing to be ashamed of.

Mrs. S and other founding members felt that the organization needed a concrete purpose, so that the women could work together for a common goal rather than simply socializing. They settled on orphans in Korea, particularly Amerasian children, as their cause. The organization's major event is the annual December dinner, which raises funds for Korean orphanages or organizations that provide services to Amerasians in Korea. The dinner features Korean food cooked by the women, a raffle for prizes such as round-trip tickets to Korea, and music and other entertainment. Some years it raises as much as $3,000.

Other annual events include a yearly vacation for women only and a holiday party for the women and their families. Embedded in these activities is the women's sense of community and affiliation with others. The vacation is just for them, the party includes family and friends, while the fundraiser is a chance to promote a positive image of military brides to outsiders and acquaintances, both Koreans and Americans, and to obtain support for their cause. The activities place the women at the center of widening circles of family, friends, acquaintances; in short, at the center of a world of their own.

The communities formed by military brides serve other practical functions as well. They exchange information about jobs, often referring each other to job openings. They babysit each other's children and cook food for one another. They take in newcomers and teach them how to survive in America.

When a young woman arrived in 1995 with her air force husband straight from a U.S. Air Force base in Korea, the women at the church organized to get her settled in. They showed her how to get her driver's license, where to buy Korean foods and other items unavailable at the post exchange (PX) and commissary, gave her advice on various on-base facilities that might come in useful, and quickly drew her into the weekly round of church activities. A similar welcome was shown to those who moved from other areas of the United States, but it was clear that this woman was receiving special care, for she was not only a newcomer to the area but also a newcomer to the country.

She was the beneficiary of a community that had been created where there had been none. Women who arrived in the 1950s and 1960s noted that they had not seen themselves as part of a community; they could not, for one did not exist. In contrast, women who arrived in later decades, especially in the 1980s and 1990s, spoke a great deal about military-bride community. For them, the community was something that already existed and to which they gained entrée through their marriage to Americans.

Some women plugged into these community networks before they even arrived in the United States. Mrs. Q, for example, participated in an on-base association of Korean military brides after she married in Korea. There she became acquainted with the world of Korean military brides, hearing stories about life at other U.S. military bases such as those in Germany and Japan and getting tips for adjusting to life in the military and in America.

Once she arrived in the United States in 1991, Mrs. Q used these networks each time she followed her husband to a new posting in a different state. Her minister, whose church in most cases was near the base and whose congregants were primarily Korean military brides, would usually refer her to a Korean church in the area she was moving to. Military brides with whom she became friends would sometimes also be able to put her in touch with their friends in the area. In this way, Mrs. Q moved to each new location equipped with personal introductions to a new set of contacts.

Initially brought together by shared ethnicity, gender, and status as military brides, the women consciously developed those ties as they constructed community among themselves. The women's choice of activities reflects their efforts to define themselves and their community. Aware that many military brides had difficult lives in the United States, they sought to help their less fortunate sisters. As mothers of biracial children, they took on the cause of Amerasians in Korea. They chose this cause even though they risked strengthening the camptown shadow that loomed over their lives.

In choosing activities that they linked to their own lives as military brides, the women acknowledged their difference from both mainstream Korean immigrants and Americans, while simultaneously asserting that that difference does not equal inferiority. They were also proposing and reinforcing a vision of community that binds people together not on the basis of personal acquaintance but on the basis of their shared position as wives of Americans. They were creating what Benedict Anderson has called, in the context of nations and nationalisms, "imagined communities." These communities, however, were sustained not by printed material but by word of mouth. They came to feel that even if they did not directly know one another, they were somehow connected. The ability of military brides during the 1980s and 1990s to tap into Korean military-bride networks, as Mrs. Q did, and smoothly to move from one regional community to another is a tangible manifestation of this overarching imagined community.

Although Anderson argued that the printed word played the crucial role in constructing the imagined communities of nationalism, I argue that face-to-face encounters linking people together in everyday life also play a critical role.[14] Military brides' sense of community was created and sustained by these direct encounters. Their imagined community was created through a web of personal relationships that served as conduits for information about one another's lives and situations. Learning about each other from each other, their sense of community then transcended direct, personal contact to include people they had never met and were unlikely ever to meet. Their face-to-face encounters facilitated the development of their belief in shared community, based on a shared status as Korean military brides.

"We Are Korean Women Together"

The imagined community that military brides have constructed is distinctly, even deliberately, Korean. This is a response largely to the forced Americanization and consequent cultural deprivations that many women undergo, but it is also a response to other Koreans who see them as impure and "not really Korean." By emphasizing their ties to Korean culture, the women are claiming the Korean identity that both Koreans and Americans would deny them. The women express their ties through food, language, and the affirmation of what they see as Korean patterns of thought. It is no accident that these are also the areas in which many women have been forced to adopt American ways.

The annual vacation is perhaps the most overt expression of military-bride sisterhood and resistance to husbandly authority. The women take off for a weekend or even a week, leaving husbands behind to fend for themselves. The first vacation included husbands, but consequently it was no fun for the women. Explained Mrs. S:

> You have to worry about food, you have to go around with them all the time. We women just want to have fun together talking and enjoying, but if the husbands come along, it's no fun. . . . You have to look after everything for them. What are you doing? What do you want to eat? What shall we eat? If we go by ourselves then we can just cook Korean food for ourselves, but if we take the men along then we have to prepare American food for them and it's just a nuisance.

She also noted that when the women are among themselves they can talk in Korean, but that if the husbands come along, then they have to use English. It just isn't the same, she said, explaining that the whole atmosphere, the entire feel, of the vacation is altered. The vacation is meant to be a break from daily life, but if husbands come along, the burdens of daily life intrude. Mrs. S's comments indicate that those burdens are cultural ones as well: the burden of adapting oneself to American culture in order to perform one's role as the wife of an American. The vacation allows the women temporarily to forget these burdens, and it is so important that some women continue to participate despite the objections of their husbands.

Mrs. S's description of one vacation indicates that it is also a vehicle of resistance against stereotypes held by mainstream Americans about Asian women. She laughs with delight as she describes the reactions of Americans to the sight of a hotel lobby or nightclub full of Korean women dancing, laughing, talking, and having a boisterous good time:

> This is what is so *fun* about it. We go into a hotel. *They are really wondering.* How come so many Asian women are coming here alone? There are more than one or two things that are surprising. And then of course these people think that Korean women are just sooooo quiet. But we like to *enjoy* and we are very lively, so these people just don't know what to do. We like to dance, too, so when the music comes on we all go out to dance and it's just filled with Asians, with women, dancing. Because all of us women dance together, wherever we go people are surprised, they are really startled. Some Americans ask us why we are only women. They think we came from a foreign country, they don't realize that we live in America. When we say that we left our husbands at home, they ask us how we can do that. They are so surprised, Americans, because they don't do that. They always travel together. So they are so startled. They ask us how come the husbands don't say anything. A lot of things surprise them.

Although such "women-only" trips may be unfamiliar, even strange, to most Americans, they are contemporary extensions of intimate female friendships common in Korean society. Some middle-class women in Korea, for example, go on trips with their women friends during college and again after their children are grown and married. Americans unfamiliar with these customs, however, tend to view Asian women as quiet, docile, and subservient to husbandly authority. Mrs. S's comment that American couples always travel together can be read as a subtle gesture to assert the freedom of Korean military brides in comparison to supposedly liberated American women. It is a way of saying that Americans think that Korean women are bound to their husbands, but in actuality it's the American women who do not have freedom.

A Positive Image

The gaze of outsiders—both other Koreans and Americans—has been a continuous force in the lives of the women, for one of their goals has been to show the world what military brides can do and thereby to combat the prejudice that they have felt so keenly. Awareness of this gaze, for example, motivated Mrs. K to take a leadership role at a crucial moment in the ABC Association's history. One of the organization's early goals was to let the Korean community know that military brides were intelligent, well-educated women living interesting and productive lives. Said Mrs. K:

> We showed them the reality of military brides, in a grand way; we showed them that there were these fine women. *They think, but* . . . they think that we are all Korean women who did, you know, and then married foreigners, that we are all uneducated. But we showed them that we military brides are really something.

Similarly, Mrs. S displayed newspaper articles in both Korean and American newspapers reporting on the activities of her organization. The organization's work, she said, helps break stereotypes about military brides.

Military brides also often assume a civilian ambassador role, presenting Korean culture for the consumption of mainstream American society. Although certain events sponsored by Korean immigrant associations—street festivals, Korea Day parades, and the like—play this function as well, the role of military brides may be far greater. While Korean immigrant associations usually operate in metropolitan, multiracial, multiethnic contexts such as New York, Los Angeles, and Chicago, military brides are often operating in primarily white American communities. As schools and community associations across the country began to hold multicultural festivals, those in rural areas, small towns, and outlying suburbs often turned to military brides to represent Korea, for many women spoke of participating in these events.

Since 1990, for example, the local school has called on the women at the church I attended to participate in its annual multicultural festival. Wearing traditional Korean clothes, the women prepare and sell Korean foods such as stuffed dumplings, barbecued beef, glass noodles with meat and vegetables, and rice-and-seaweed rolls. They also display their prized valuables to show Americans Korean cultural goods, lacquered jewelry boxes, embroidered screens, ceramic vases, and jade jewelry. Eager to show Americans that Korean culture—and thus, by extension, Korean people—is worthy of appreciation, they are often oblivious to the ways in which multicultural discourse can set them apart as aliens even as it advances "culture" for the appreciation of Americans.[15]

For the military brides, multicultural festivals are an opportunity, however limited, to show Americans the beauty of Korean culture, and thus an opportunity to receive positive validation from Americans (rather than solely from sister military brides) as they affirm their Korean identity. For those women living in families where children dismiss their maternal reprimands with an offhand "This is America, Mom" and husbands refuse to eat Korean food, it is a rare opportunity to feel accepted among Americans as a Korean woman. These can be moments that nurture confidence and self-esteem. Said one woman:

> They are so interested. They ask all kinds of questions, about my clothes, about the food. One man told me that before, he only thought of war when he thought of Korea. Now, he said, he can think of beautiful silk dresses and fine art work.

This made her feel, she said, that she was spreading a positive image not only about military brides but also about Korea itself. One woman who arrived in the mid-1970s noted that her husband often made derogatory comments that painted Korea as a god-forsaken, backward country that depended on Americans for its national defense. Like other women whose husbands made disparaging comments about Korea, she felt such comments were intended to put her down; they often surfaced when he was angry with her. When her husband accompanied her to one of these multicultural festivals, he was surprised to see that the Korean display was popular. It affected his behavior, albeit only temporarily, as he commented favorably on the display several times over the next few weeks and uttered fewer insults about Korea. Seeing this, she said, made her realize that while she could not change his attitudes, the positive reactions of other Americans to Korean culture could.

Embedded in the stories of these two women is the possibility for resistance to the hegemonizing discourse of multiculturalism and for the reappropriation of that discourse by those meant to be subordinated to it. Although the festivals are aimed at affirming an ethnic American identity stripped of substantive difference, the women themselves used those festivals to affirm identities rooted in that very difference. The woman whose husband disparaged Korea, for example, stated that she wished Americans could see that the beauty of Korean culture is connected to the suffering of the Korean people. Clearly, she senses that multicultural festivals, through their display, are displacing cultures, delinking them from history and community. She herself relinks them, placing Korean culture within her understanding of Korean history as suffering. Thus she articulates two critical observations that directly attack the underpinnings of multiculturalism.

Military brides' insistence on expressing their culture and seeking ways to form spaces in which to do so subverts multiculturalism's insistence that cultural identity be superficial. For Korean military brides, cultural identity is critically important. Women who attended monthly meetings of regional associations sometimes came over the opposition of husbands. Mrs. D, who accommodated her husband's wishes in most cases, "giving up" many expressions of her culture for the sake of family harmony, also insisted that husbands have no right to forbid their wives to attend these meetings, even if they run past midnight.

Communities of Resistance

The dominant Korean self-identity is based on notions of racial and cultural homogeneity, which fail to recognize the diversity in Korean American society. According to Kyeyoung Park, for example, 1.5-generation Korean Americans have their own distinct sense of identity, one that incorporates and transforms elements of their Korean and American upbringings.[16] Korean adoptees and many second-generation Korean Americans may not seem recognizably "Korean" to South Koreans or to the immigrant generation, but they too claim membership in Korean and Korean American societies. Mixed-race people who are part Korean are increasingly claiming their Korean heritage and insisting that "full-blooded" Koreans recognize their claims to inclusion. This diversity—marginalized, suppressed, and ignored—belies the dominant Korean discourse of homogeneity.

At the same time, the insistence of these "deviant" Korean Americans on claiming and expressing racial and cultural difference in the face of efforts at erasure, suppression, and appropriation can also be read as a challenge to the homogenizing discourse of American multiculturalism. As one adult Korean adoptee wrote: "[W]e're being told that our cultural displacement had a purpose—multiculturalism. By growing up in white families, we can be examples, Luuk. We can show others that racial harmony is possible. We just can't show our burdened backs."[17]

The imagined community of military brides is likewise a challenge to both Korean and American definitions of self. Military-bride community is primarily based on an acknowledged sense of sisterhood that flows from shared identities as Korean women with intimate ties to America, as "internationally married women" and, more specifically, as Korean women who married American soldiers. Although mainstream Koreans and Korean Americans often see them as "less Korean" due to their links with American society, the military brides themselves do not. They reject the notion that they are no longer "really" Korean due to their outmarriage and immigration to the United States and have created their own forms of Korean identity. This identity—gender-specific and particular to their situation—challenges the validity of a monolithic Korean identity and opens up spaces for difference in Korean communities.

At the same time, their insistence on substantive difference—language, modes of thought, history—challenges the valorization of "ethnic" in American multiculturalism, for they are in effect refusing to become ethnicized. Their communities stand as eloquent rebuttals to mainstream Americans who would like to see them assimilated in American families, as refutations of the multiculturalism that would render their culture a mere accessory to the ongoing creation of American exceptionalism, and as refusals to relinquish their Korean identity even when the demand might come from their husbands. But even as they maintain and construct their Korean identity, they are also insisting on their right to do so in America. The women have no plans to leave America, and many consider this country to now be their home.

Through their community, military brides are struggling to move beyond resistance—against both American and Korean prejudices—toward transformation. Whether consciously or not, they are pressing for a transformation of both Korean and American identities, away from the narrow and exclusive and toward the broad and inclusive. To both Americans and Koreans, they are posing the same question that bell hooks asked in another context: "Why do we have to wipe out the Otherness in order to experience a notion of *Oneness*?"[18]

NOTES

This essay is drawn from my book *Beyond the Shadow of Camptown: Korean Military Brides in America* (New York: New York University Press, 2002).

1. I borrow this term from Benedict Anderson's work on nationalism, *Imagined Communities*, rev. ed. (New York: Verso, 1991), and use it to indicate that group identity is constructed via the imagination by investing certain connections with special meanings.

2. See Daniel B. Lee, "Korean Women Married to Servicemen," in *Korean American Women*

Living in Two Cultures, ed. Young In Song and Ailee Moon (Los Angeles: Academia Koreana, Keimyung-Baylo University Press, 1997), 96–97. Statistics on the actual number of Korean women who entered the United States as wives of U.S. military personnel are not kept by any agency but must be teased out of records kept by the U.S. Immigration and Naturalization Service, Seoul City Hall's records of marriages between Korean citizens and citizens of foreign countries, and records kept by the South Korean Emigration Office. Using these sources and others, Lee has compiled the most complete figures available on this subject.

3. An extended discussion can be found in chapter 1 of Ji-Yeon Yuh, *Beyond the Shadow of Camptown: Korean Military Brides in America* (New York: New York University Press, 2002).

4. See Nancy Abelmann and John Lie, *Blue Dreams* (Cambridge, MA: Harvard University Press, 1995), especially chap. 3.

5. For a discussion of the camptowns, see Saundra Pollock Sturdevant and Brenda Stoltzfus, *Let the Good Times Roll: Prostitution and the U.S. Military in Asia* (New York: New Press, 1992).

6. For critiques of multiculturalism, see Lisa Lowe, "Imagining Los Angeles in the Production of Multiculturalism," in *Immigrant Acts: On Asian American Cultural Politics* (Durham and London: Duke University Press, 1996), 84–96; and E. San Juan Jr., "The Cult of Ethnicity and the Fetish of Pluralism," in *Racial Formations/Critical Transformations* (Atlantic Highlands, NJ, and London: Humanities Press, 1992), 31–41.

7. Aihwa Ong, *Spirits of Resistance and Capitalist Discipline: Factory Women in Malaysia* (Albany: State University of New York Press, 1987).

8. James C. Scott, *Domination and the Arts of Resistance* (New Haven: Yale University Press, 1990), 19 and 190. See also his *Weapons of the Weak: Everyday Forms of Peasant Resistance* (New Haven: Yale University Press, 1985).

9. Robin D. G. Kelley, *Race Rebels* (New York: Free Press, 1996) and *Hammer and Hoe* (Chapel Hill: University of North Carolina Press, 1990).

10. Women in North Korea may well have done the same, but as I am not aware of any studies that discuss this in any depth, beyond mentioning the activities of women's organizations sponsored by the government, I limit my discussion of women's organizations in post-1945 Korea to the south.

11. Yi Soong Sun et al., "Housewife Movement," in *Jubu: Geu Makhim-gwa Teuim* (Housewife: That closing and opening), ed. Ddo Hana-eu Munhwa (Seoul: Ddo Hana-eu Munhwa Press, 1990), 308–20.

12. A group of Korean ministers have begun holding annual conferences to discuss how best to minister to military brides. Their second annual conference was held in Las Vegas in 1997.

13. All interviews, unless otherwise indicated, were conducted in Korean and translated by the author. Interviewees often sprinkled English words throughout their speech. These words were not translated and are rendered here and in subsequent quotes in italics.

14. Taking their cue from Anderson, other scholars have analyzed the role of broadcast media in the construction of imagined community. For example, Purnima Mankekar, "Television Tales and a Woman's Rage: A Nationalist Recasting of Draupadi's 'Disrobing,'" *Public Culture* 5:3 (1993): 469–92.

15. Lowe, "Imagining Los Angeles." See also San Juan, "Cult of Ethnicity," 31–41.

16. Kyeyoung Park, "I Really Do Feel I'm 1.5!" *Amerasia Journal* 15:1 (1999): 139–63.

17. Kari Ruth, "Dear Luuk," in *Seeds from a Silent Tree: An Anthology by Korean Adoptees*, ed. Tonya Bishoff and Jo Rankin (Glendale, CA: Pandal Press, 1998), 144.

18. bell hooks, *Outlaw Culture: Resisting Representations* (New York: Routledge, 1994), 234.

14

Managing Survival
Economic Realities for Vietnamese American Women

Linda Trinh Võ

Since we moved to the United States in 1979, my mother has worked in an assembly line at a factory, operated a mom-and-pop Oriental food market, transported garment pieces between the factories and seamstresses who sewed from their homes, served Chinese fast food at the mall, and become a beautician, an occupation she still maintains. In Vietnam, she worked as a waitress at a restaurant and as a maid in a hotel, both of which catered to foreigners in Vietnam. As a war bride, she does not represent the "typical" Vietnamese American story; however, the jobs she has held are typical of women of her ethnicity. I have seen her overcome her linguistic and educational limitations, work tireless hours, and struggle against exploitation. I begin with the story of my mother's experience to bring into focus the economic realities of Vietnamese refugee and immigrant women who survived the turmoil of war, dislocation, and resettlement. Far from the perception of them as fragile and passive victims of war, they are resilient and strong survivors who have sought to control the often bewildering and uncertain socioeconomic transformations that have confronted them.[1]

Unlike other Asian immigrant groups, Vietnamese Americans were not brought to America to fulfill labor needs, although they have in fact fulfilled the demands of U.S. capitalism, particularly in the service sector and production work. Like other Asian American women, Vietnamese American women who are sole providers for their families and who contribute to a family income engage in a variety of income-generating activities for economic survival and self-sufficiency.[2] Ironically, as a result of racism and sexism, they have been provided economic niches where they find themselves in segregated occupations defined by their status as women, minorities, and immigrant/refugees. In some cases, employers' preferences for Asian immigrant women in the paid labor force has given Vietnamese American women more employment options than their male counterparts.

The general American public likes to believe that Vietnamese Americans are the quintessential embodiment of the "model minority," who basically arrived with nothing and, as a result of hard work, have achieved the American Dream.[3] However, a closer examination reveals that this myth masks the multiplicity of their economic experiences and overlooks how gender and racial factors impact their lives. In this chapter, I analyze Vietnamese American women's socioeconomic diversity and the various resources and strategies they have used to cope with their economic circumstances. Structural conditions growing out of decades (even centuries) of resistance to colonial powers, along with civil war and their diaspora, are powerful forces that have altered women's economic experiences, in both oppressive and liberating ways.

The economic history of Vietnamese women in this country is shaped by a legacy of economic, political, social, and cultural interventions by foreign powers in Vietnam. The Vietnamese experienced one thousand years of Chinese domination, over three hundred years of French colonial influence, Japanese occupation during World War II, and attempted recolonization by the French that was followed by approximately ten years of occupation by U.S. military forces in the Vietnam (American) War. The North Vietnamese Communists declared victory on April 30, 1975, when they captured the southern capital of Saigon, ending the longest war in modern history. This war contributed to the massive displacement of approximately one-third of the South Vietnamese population. It is estimated that over 4 million Vietnamese soldiers and civilians on both sides were killed, representing more than 10 percent of the total population, and countless others were wounded. The war also created over 879,000 orphans and over 1 million widows.

In the 1960s, there were approximately three thousand Vietnamese in the United States, and most were university students from elite families; some were diplomats or military employees. The majority of the Vietnamese women were wives of U.S. military personnel or U.S. civilians. Since 1975, some Vietnamese women have arrived as refugees, while others came through provisions set aside for immigrants and Amerasian children and their families. In the early 1970s, there were about fifteen thousand Vietnamese in the United States. By 2000, there were over 1 million, concentrated in California and Texas but living in all regions of the country. Each immigrant's occupational experience is affected by the life of her family in Vietnam, her method of arrival, and the resources available to her.

The Pre-1975 Groups: International Students, War Brides, and International Brides

Prior to 1975, in addition to male military personnel and diplomats, elite groups of Vietnamese exchange students, some of them women, were dispersed in colleges across the United States. They were expected to return to prominent political and economic positions in Vietnam and to institute pro-capitalist and pro-democracy policies. Many of those in America after 1975 declared their status as political refugees and have since remained in this country. Others who returned to Vietnam eventually found ways to come back to the United States, albeit under different circumstances. Overall, their educational and class backgrounds and their linguistic and cultural skills have given them privileges in the United States when compared to other Vietnamese Americans who later joined them.

An inadvertent outcome of U.S. military intervention in Vietnam has been transnational, interracial marriages between American men and Vietnamese women. The women were called war brides, implying that the women were married to U.S. servicemen during a period of war. This does not accurately capture the experiences of women married to men working in the private sector or those who were missionaries, diplomats, or students (although one might argue that their presence was connected to U.S. militarization of the region); hence, *international brides* is the term more widely used to incorporate the experiences of these women.

That these women were from different social classes is revealed in the limited documented information available and in anecdotal evidence. One might contrast, for example, the personal histories depicted in the autobiographies of Le Ly Hayslip, who came from a poor farming family, and Duong Van Mai Elliott, who was part of the Vietnamese urban elite.[4] The former was working as a cocktail waitress in Vietnam when she met her American husband-to-be; the latter met her American husband-to-be while they were both college students in the United States during the early 1960s. Hayslip depicts her struggle for economic and political survival during the war years and as a widow and, later, as an abused wife to another European American husband. In contrast, Elliott has been in a long-term, supportive relationship with an academic. Little is known about the Vietnamese women who married U.S. men or were living as common-law wives in Vietnam but were divorced, separated, or abandoned, so that they never lived with their husbands in the United States as a couple. A number of these women would eventually make their way to the United States.

As a result of the contact between Vietnamese women and American men, sexual or romantic relationships developed. With rural economies ravaged by the war, many young Vietnamese women were forced to relocate to urban areas to help support their families. U.S. men had personal contact with women who worked as maids, nurses, housekeepers, secretaries, sales clerks, translators, cooks, librarians, launderers, and other service-sector workers near or on U.S. military bases. Other Vietnamese women met their American husbands while they worked as hostesses or prostitutes in bars around U.S. military stations. Although prostitution was illegal in Vietnam, "militarized prostitution" mobilized for the war was informally sanctioned by both the Vietnamese and U.S. governments.[5] For young girls and women, prostitution provided gainful employment when options were limited, and they could earn $100 a month, four times what male Vietnamese government officials earned at the time.[6] The all-time high for the number of women working as prostitutes during the war is estimated at five hundred thousand.[7]

Suzan Ruth Travis-Robyns captures the travails of Xuan Ngoc Nguyen, an ethnic Chinese Buddhist from the Cholon district in Saigon.[8] The author argues Nguyen is a "veteran" of the war, whose life was altered and scarred by wartime events and who continues to struggle with post-traumatic stress disorder (PTSD).[9] After her family became refugees when Americans bombed their house, she became a prostitute for American GIs at age fourteen. The money she earned paid for her brothers' educations, was used to bribe the government not to conscript a brother, and helped feed her family. She states:

> I fought my war every night in bed with men. Who talks about my war. Who asks me if I'm hurt or wounded? Nobody asks. Not even the closest person to me, my mother, knows or asks. No one knows, it's just a silent war that I have inside of me. . . . I know a lot of women

in this country who are ex-prostitutes, they have the same feeling, but we are still in the closet, we are ashamed, embarrassed. We aren't just criticized by American society but the Vietnamese society too. . . . Even my own people, the Vietnamese community here in the United States, they look down on me because I did something that brought shame to our ancestors.[10]

Xuan moved to Oregon with her second son to marry his father, a U.S. Air Force pilot whom she met in Vietnam, and was a battered wife. In the postwar years, these invisible victims of the war who worked in the sex industry found that they were ostracized and condemned by their families and communities.

Ironically, the assumption also exists that these women are privileged because they married American men who would provide them with a better life in the wealthiest country in the world. These transnational, interracial marriages were often difficult for couples who confronted linguistic, cultural, social, and religious differences. While some Vietnamese women found themselves in economically secure relationships, others found themselves working in occupations similar to those of other refugee women in order to support themselves and their families. Although rarely noted by the community, Vietnamese brides have played a crucial role in the chain migration process by helping to sponsor and resettle Vietnamese relatives[11] and by sending remittances to support family members still in Vietnam in the post-1975 period.

The 1975 and Post-1975 Exodus: Refugees and Immigrants

Although Vietnamese refugees and immigrants who arrived in the United States are often viewed as a homogeneous group, they comprise a diverse population. I have divided them according to the way in which they left Vietnam and were admitted into the United States: (1) refugees, many of whom were elites; (2) boat people of ethnic Vietnamese and ethnic Chinese Vietnamese descent, of mixed class background; and (3) other groups who were state-sponsored immigrants who came through the Orderly Departure Program, the Humanitarian Operation Program, and the Amerasian Program. The economic adaptation of these refugees and immigrants depends on when and how they left their homelands, how much assistance they received upon arrival, and the amount of human capital (education and skills) they possessed.

1975 Refugees and Operation Frequent Wind

The refugees, referred to as involuntary immigrants, were escaping political and economic persecution by the Communist government. The majority of the first-wave refugees were elites who were officers of the South Vietnamese government and military. Others were employees of U.S. agencies and private companies and their families, who escaped in the last days of April 1975 as North Vietnamese forces overtook Saigon. Fearing persecution and retribution from the new government, 129,000 Vietnamese left by air in "Operation Frequent Wind." They were evacuated by sea to U.S. bases in Guam, Thailand, and the Philippines; and were flown to temporary sites on military bases in Camp Pendleton, California; Eglin Air Force Base, Florida; Fort Indian Town Gap, Pennsylvania; and Fort Chaffee, Arkansas.[12]

The U.S. government accepted the refugees out of humanitarian sympathies for their former allies and as a political statement against the new Vietnamese regime. However, the public reception to this first wave was indifferent or hostile, given America's negative feelings about the war and racial stereotypes about the Vietnamese. The economic recession contributed to these sentiments, with a 1975 Gallup poll reporting that 54 percent of the American public felt the Vietnamese would place a burden on public assistance funds and be competitors for their jobs.[13] Government funds, along with contributions from private individuals, nonprofit agencies, and religious organizations, provided the refugees with cash assistance, medical care, social services, English-language instruction, educational programs, and vocational training. A considerable number of the first wave were well-educated, urban professionals who benefited from the financial assistance provided and used their human capital to adjust. After six months, most of the refugees were dispersed across the country through the government's efforts to assimilate them quickly and to avoid financially burdening any one community. Nevertheless, through a process of secondary migration, the refugees counteracted this policy by establishing ethnic settlements or enclaves, where they could be close to co-ethnics and find viable employment.[14]

Boat People and Land Refugees

In the late 1970s, a second wave of refugees with more varied class backgrounds followed. They also lived under the Communist regime and left under extremely dangerous conditions. The new Communist regime imprisoned an estimated 1 million South Vietnamese, sending them to "re-education" camps where they did hard labor and many became sick or died.[15] When released, these men and women, along with their families, often faced exclusion and persecution. Deteriorating economic conditions as a result of the U.S. embargo and poor harvest seasons in 1978 and 1979 made the situation desperate for many. Some escapees referred to as "land refugees" paid guides to walk them through Laos and Cambodia, a dangerous and difficult journey, to the camps in Thailand. Most were "boat people," the estimated five hundred thousand men, women, and children who fled by boat. They used their savings to pay for passage, sometimes losing their money repeatedly to dishonest transporters or when caught by Vietnamese patrols who imprisoned escapees.

It is estimated that approximately 10 to 15 percent of those fleeing died on the treacherous high seas in makeshift, often overcrowded boats with insufficient water and food.[16] In addition, pirates, mainly from Thailand, took advantage of their vulnerability on the open seas and attacked the escapees. The pirates robbed them of their few possessions and food supplies. Girls and women were assaulted, raped, abducted, and tortured, and some were murdered and tossed overboard by sea pirates in the Gulf of Thailand.[17] Statistics from the United Nations High Commission for Refugees (UNHCR) indicate that those crossing the Gulf of Thailand heading to Thailand and Malaysia were the most vulnerable to piracy, with reports that half of the boats were attacked.[18] Those who survived made their way to temporary refugee camps in countries of first asylum—Malaysia, the Philippines, Hong Kong, Indonesia, Singapore, and Thailand—before being permanently settled.

Often overlooked is the exodus from Vietnam of ethnic Chinese who were forcibly expelled by the new regime. In the 1970s, it is estimated, over 1.5 million ethnic Chinese were in Vietnam. Some Chinese Vietnamese came from families who had been in Vietnam for generations but spoke mainly a Chinese dialect and followed Chinese customs, while others had adopted Vietnamese traditions and intermarried with the Vietnamese. When the Chinese-Vietnam border wars of 1978 escalated, Vietnamese Communists, suspicious of the ethnic Chinese's loyalties and wanting to "indigenize" their economy, confiscated their property and threatened their lives, thus forcing the ethnic Chinese to leave Vietnam. Of the approximately 1 million refugees who would leave Vietnam between 1978 and 1989, 60 to 70 percent were Chinese,[19] with an estimated two hundred fifty thousand escaping north to mainland China. A number of them had limited education, with men and women working mainly in the fishing industry or as laborers.[20] Although they were "refugees" like other Vietnamese, the conditions that forced them to leave have left bitter resentments toward ethnic Vietnamese, leading some Chinese Vietnamese refugees to identify principally with the overseas Chinese community.

The refugees who came after 1978 had survived the harsh conditions of the Communist government, faced traumatic escapes, and lived in temporary refugee camps awaiting resettlement, some for years. Many lacked the human capital of the first wave. Unfortunately for those who came in the mid-1980s, U.S. government assistance was cut from three years to eight months. After one year they could apply for permanent residency status, and after four more years they could petition for citizenship and qualify for regular assistance provided to other Americans. While some have established middle-class lives, others struggle in dire poverty and have a difficult time adjusting.

Orderly Departure Program

The Orderly Departure Program, established in 1979 and coordinated by the UNHCR, provided a legal alternative to dangerous boat escapes. Countries of first asylum could not cope with the large-scale arrival of refugees, so the world community pressured the Vietnamese government to devise a solution. This controlled immigration policy allowed Vietnamese who had obtained official exit permits from the Vietnamese government and approval from the receiving country to emigrate. It gave preference to those with close relatives already in the United States and to others with ties to Americans, such as those who had worked alongside or for the U.S. military. By the early 1990s, three hundred thousand Vietnamese, many entering through the family reunification provision, arrived in America.

Humanitarian Operation Program

The Humanitarian Operation Program of 1989 allowed approximately seventy thousand former political detainees of Communist "re-education" camps, who had served at least three years, and their families to immigrate to the United States. Not only had they been imprisoned, some for over a decade, but once released they and their family members were denied educational and employment opportunities. These former religious leaders, South Vietnamese government officials and military personnel, and others who had worked for the U.S. government found it especially difficult to survive. The majority were men; however, women such as Hong Nga and Thanh Thuy Nguyen immigrated through this program.[21] Nga, a former captain in the South Vietnamese army who anchored the official evening news, was imprisoned for four years. Nguyen, once a major general in the South Vietnamese army in the women's secret police unit, was incarcerated for thirteen years. Although often neglected in Vietnamese and Vietnamese American historical accounts of the war, women were involved in the anti-colonial, anti-imperialist movements and also fought on the front line. Vietnamese women's experiences as warriors and militiawomen have been overshadowed by male veteran stories, so the narratives of women veterans, official and unofficial, who would later become refugees and immigrants have been largely undocumented.[22]

Amerasian Program

Amerasians, who came under special immigration provisions, constitute part of the third wave of refugees. Vietnamese Amerasians, the children of Vietnamese mothers and American fathers who were U.S. servicemen and civilians, have existed in Vietnam since the 1950s, the beginning of U.S. military presence there.[23] They have been the "side effects" of the colonial, imperialist, military, and political-economic domination of U.S. involvement in Asia.[24] Some children were the product of brief sexual encounters; others were the children of couples involved in long-term relationships, which sometimes became official marriages. In many cases, the men abandoned the women when their duties were over or couples lost contact with each other during the chaos of war.[25]

Approximately twelve thousand to fifteen thousand Amerasians, degradingly referred to as *bui doi* (dust of life), *con lai* (people of mixed blood), or *my lai* (American half-breed), were left in Vietnam in 1975.[26] Some mothers of Amerasian children suffered from racial discrimination and were disowned by their families for having mixed-race offspring of the "enemy."[27] As outcasts from society in Vietnam, they and their children suffered severe hardship finding employment or housing in the postwar years, while some spent years with their children in the New Economic Zones, which were forced-labor sites in rural areas. Excluded from Vietnamese educational, economic, and social opportunities because of the stigma of their mixed racial backgrounds, their mothers' sexual relationships with enemy men, and their fatherless status,[28] some children were sent to live with relatives, abandoned at orphanages, or left to fend for themselves on the streets.

In the 1970s, the U.S. government was principally interested in severing diplomatic ties with the Vietnamese government and did not acknowledge the existence of these "American" children. The government could have resettled them as young children; instead officials and politicians waited until political and public pressure forced them to accept their responsibility for the children left behind.[29] By the time the U.S. Congress passed the Amerasian Act in 1982 and the Amerasian Homecoming Act in 1987, the thousands who arrived were in their late teens or early adulthood, the average age being

18.5 years, making their adjustment more difficult. Some left as unaccompanied minors or orphans, but most left with family members or nonkin families who conveniently adopted them, sometimes misusing them as a "golden passport" to the United States.[30] Between 1988 and 1994, approximately seventy thousand Vietnamese Amerasians and their accompanying relatives arrived in the United States.[31]

The mothers of Amerasian children have confronted the same dilemmas of other refugees and in addition cannot rely on co-ethnic support, since the Vietnamese community in America marginalizes them. As Nga Tran, who lives with her children in the Washington, D.C., area, states: "My children and I suffered so much under the Communists, I hoped that in this free country everyone would love each other. . . . I am Vietnamese, too, but I feel prejudice against people like me with Amerasian children, whether black or white."[32] Although classified as "immigrants" under the Homecoming Act, the Amerasians were given the same type of public assistance offered to those with refugee status. Most Amerasians have limited English-language skills, minimal education, and few marketable job skills. Some were emotionally traumatized, especially unaccompanied minors; not surprisingly, many have had a difficult time adjusting. Their mothers confront similar occupational choices available to other Vietnamese women, along with being challenged by conditions of chronic poverty.

In the 1970s and 1980s, opportunities for resettlement were available to Vietnamese refugees, but by the 1990s, "compassion fatigue" set in as countries feeling overburdened by refugee populations began refusing to accept them. In 1989, the United States along with fifty-one nations agreed to a Comprehensive Plan of Action that established a cutoff date for denying refugee status. Also, camp countries tired of refugees draining their resources sent the refugees back to Vietnam, an action condemned by overseas Vietnamese. With the forced repatriation of Vietnamese who were considered "economic migrants" and the end of programs for Amerasians and former political prisoners, arrivals now are immigrants sponsored by co-ethnics.

Occupational Constraints and Opportunities

Although Vietnamese women have been defined as controlled by Confucian ideals of patriarchy, historically the status of Vietnamese women has also been influenced by matriarchal practices. For example, Vietnamese women had the right of inheritance; were allowed to receive some education; worked as farmers, fishers, and peddlers; participated in or owned small businesses; and managed the financial affairs of the household.[33] This is not to deny that they were subordinate to men in public and private affairs; however, it points to their historical role in the economy of the family.

Women had to become resilient in order to survive the dislocations and disruptions brought on by the war and the poverty caused by wartime inflation. Women headed about 30 percent of the households when male family members were at war, had disappeared, were injured, were held in detention camps, or were killed.[34] The depiction of Vietnamese women as fragile and homebound, with lives determined by rigid sex-role divisions, is contrary to their actual experiences, since women were mobilized into the war industry, whether they worked as secretaries, soldiers, street peddlers, or prostitutes.

In the postwar years, dire poverty in the country made women's labor a necessity. In the early 1990s, women headed 20 percent of the households; constituted 52 percent of the workforce, with 70 percent of working-age women employed; and made up 65 percent of the agricultural workforce.[35] N. Yen Tran worked as a secretary before the war and, to support herself and her child, in the postwar years worked on an animal farm; sold fruit, juice, and vegetables; made tires; and raised chickens to sell their eggs, while her husband was in a re-education camp or could not find work.[36] After she came to America in 1993 through the Humanitarian Operation Program, she continued to work to support the family.

Overall, the occupation of Vietnamese women varies according to their human capital and the availability of services provided when they arrived, such as English-language classes, vocational training, and cultural orientation programs. Even when programs were available, they reinforced inappropriate gender roles, as in one resettlement camp in Fort Indian Town Gap, Pennsylvania.[37] Through English-language lessons taught in the classes, sex-role education socialized men for employment. In contrast, it confined women's roles to housework and child rearing, contradictory to the economic roles they had had in Vietnam and impractical since many women would have to work once they left the camps. Additionally, contrary to the belief that Vietnamese American women accept their subordinate role, one survey found that 90 percent of the Vietnamese American women believed men and women should have equal rights in the family, and 65 percent did not agree that women should be submissive to keep the family happy.[38]

Many Vietnamese American women work at low-wage jobs that are segregated by gender and ethnicity, with no opportunities for advancement, and that lack medical insurance coverage. Others choose to remain on public assistance to receive Aid to Families with Dependent Children (AFDC), which was replaced by Temporary Assistance to Needy Families (TANF) in 1996, and also medical care for themselves and their children through Medicaid. In New York City, the workfare program, part of the Personal Responsibility and Work Opportunity Reconciliation Act of 1996, forces the disabled, elderly, and women with young children to work, often in unsafe environments with inadequate child care. Such work pays below minimum wage and lacks substantial job training or mobility.[39]

Many Vietnamese American women have found jobs that require little education, training, or English-language skill. Some have found ways to supplement their modest welfare checks by participating in the informal sector, or underground economy, in which they are paid in cash or in kind. Those who live in ethnic enclaves, such as the "Little Saigons" across the country, can find jobs in co-ethnic businesses, many of which struggle to survive and do not always pay minimum wage. Others have found low-level service-sector jobs as custodians in commercial centers, housekeepers in hotels, and servers in the restaurant industries. In many cases these workers, who are employed seasonally or temporarily, do not receive health insurance or unemployment or other work benefits and have problems paying for adequate childcare services.

The manufacturing industry has employed many Vietnamese American women as blue-collar workers and, in fact, prefers immigrant women workers. In the southern regions, notably in the Texas Gulf Coast, they work in the seafood packing industries. In the Silicon Valley of northern California and other high-tech industrial regions, they have found jobs in computer and electronic assembly or manufacturing industries. Being "small, foreign, and female," they are, according to employers, preferred workers, especially for their small fingers for delicate work, and are perceived to be easier to control and less likely to complain and to unionize.[40] In the Midwest, Vietnamese women work in the meatpacking and poultry industries, which have been recruiting a labor force comprising refugees and immigrants. The companies expect that by hiring female family members they will add stability to the labor force, and packinghouse managers consider female workers more docile than male workers.[41]

Many Vietnamese American women are employed in the garment industry, part of a global reindustrialization process, often on a seasonal basis. While some work on site in factories, others do piecework in their homes for small contractors or subcontractors, often owned by other Asian immigrants. Piecework involves assembling clothes using their own sewing machines, tools, and electricity for low wages. While allowing them to work while caring for their children and soliciting the help of family members, it is no different from the oppressive industrial conditions that European immigrant women faced a century ago. For example, a Vietnamese immigrant woman, whose home I visited, showed me her assembled pieces for the garment industry in downtown Los Angeles, over an hour away from her apartment; her husband rebuilt old cars and sold them to other refugees. In their small ground-level apartment, greasy automotive parts were strewn in the living room next to piles of garment pieces, her sewing machine occupied the dining area, and in a small corner was a television for their four young children. Ironically, these women labor under exploitative circumstances similar to those that women and girls employed by Asian, European, and U.S.-based companies in the global garment industries face in Asia, including Vietnam.[42]

Vietnamese American women entrepreneurs have seized available economic opportunities and established economic niches. Some were shopkeepers or vendors in Vietnam, part of the bazaar economy during the war, and have used their entrepreneurial experiences to establish businesses in this country.[43] In ethnic enclaves, their labor may be crucial to the survival of the family business, or they may be the sole proprietors of ethnic restaurants, groceries, retail stores, or other businesses that cater exclusively to immigrant needs. From their homes, they operate catering businesses and childcare facilities. With limited occupational options open to them, immigrant and refugee women will continue to seek new entrepreneurial opportunities.

Thanh Thuy Nguyen, owner of a food-to-go business, who served thirteen years in the re-education camps in Vietnam and came through the Humanitarian Operation Program, explains her ability to overcome hardships:

> It was agonizing torture of the body and mind through which I trained myself to adapt to any difficult living conditions. Actually there was consistent starvation and forced labor, in addition to scarcity of food and clothing, not to mention the tormenting cell keepers and the absence of family. I was compelled to farm all day long, came back to my overcrowded

unit, had bland grains for dinner without bath. We didn't even have water to drink. Sanitary was a big problem. I willed myself to become enduring and tolerant. Because of that, working in the United States comes as less burdensome for me comparing to others. The more you work, the more you earn; whereas in Communist prison, you toiled to death without even getting the minimum amount of food for your stomach. Unlike what people imagine, a prisoner in Communist bondage works all day long and also at night on building dams, transferring construction materials. . . . It was heavy work day after day without weekend break. At night, I had to grow vegetables and fetch water. In the United States women are proud to contribute to the family financial well-being, and for me, that is the most exciting thing.[44]

Throughout the country, Vietnamese American women work as pedicurists, hairstylists, manicurists; some own beauty salons, particularly nail salons. This profession requires only limited education in cosmetology schools, minimal English-language skills, easy licensing, and modest start-up funds. A 1996 study found that 30 percent of the twenty-two thousand nail salons across the United States were owned by Vietnamese Americans. In Los Angeles County in the late 1980s, 80 percent of the over fifteen thousand licensed manicurists were Vietnamese Americans, and Vietnamese Americans, mainly women, owned 80 percent of the nail salons. Start-up funds were about $6,000, and incomes ranged from about $20,000 to $24,000. By bringing down the cost of acrylic, artificial fingernails, to $25 or less from $60, they transformed this beauty industry by making services once available only to elite women more accessible to middle-class women. The majority of the businesses nationwide are established in non-Vietnamese neighborhoods, and their clientele, depending on the location, includes African American, European American, and Latino women.[45] The drawbacks are the competitive nature of the business, the women's constant exposure to toxic chemicals that are suspected of causing health hazards,[46] and their dislike of the service nature of their jobs.

Although some owners can make large profits, most employees' incomes are relatively modest; however, this provides women with better options than employment in the mainstream sector and in the ethnic economy, where wages are lower.[47] For business owners, it provides a sense of independence and allows them to bring their young children to work, cutting down the expense of childcare. For example, Cam Van, who has worked as a manicurist since 1981, states, "I was going through a bitter divorce from my husband, who said to me that I could not make it on my own if I left him. He thought I would be a welfare mother with three small children. I wanted to prove myself and to show him that I could make my own business without help from anybody."[48]

This first generation faced many challenges to establish themselves as professionals. Those who were well educated and once professionals in Vietnam found it difficult to reestablish their careers, since their credentials and work experience were not recognized. Those who are fluent in English have found clerical or office work as secretaries, while others are employed as social service workers and as interpreters. Suzie Xuyen Dong-Matsuda, a clinical social worker in Orange County, California, has worked with Vietnamese American women and men in group therapy. At age sixteen, she left Vietnam as a boat person; lived in the refugee camps, where she escaped being assaulted several times; and resettled in America without the support of family members or proficiency in English. She eventually managed to earn a master's degree in social work.[49] Her knowledge of social work practices along with her personal experiences and bilingual and bicultural skills have enabled her to advocate for better services for the community.

In larger ethnic concentrations, Vietnamese Americans have found work or established their own professional businesses in real estate, medical care, legal services, and financial assistance catering to co-ethnics. One study finds that Vietnamese American women working as professionals and large-business owners were able to adapt well to a new culture and reported high job satisfaction, similar to their male counterparts.[50] Younger generations of educated, acculturated women are finding more career opportunities, particularly in the areas of teaching, nursing, and pharmacology in the mainstream society, unattainable for the earlier generation.

The reported income levels for Vietnamese Americans must be interpreted with caution. Women's employment, even temporary, allows the family to accumulate capital to start family businesses, to pay for a family member's vocational training, to send their children to college, and to make large purchases. The data on incomes do not necessarily correlate with their standard of living, since income, reported and unreported, is often sent to Vietnam to support family members or used to make return visits to Vietnam. Many work not just to support their families in the United States but also to send "packages" of medicines and other goods, which are then resold on the black market by their natal families and other relatives in Vietnam or in other parts of the world where their families have resettled. Additionally, the over $1 billion of remittances in the form of cash and investments that overseas Vietnamese, referred to as Viet Kieu, send back plays a major role in helping to support the Vietnamese national economy.

One of the unintended consequences of the relocation disruptions is that they have made Vietnamese American women more independent and resourceful, since they were not constrained by traditionally structured male-dominated households. For example, Xuan Pham, who had been a farmer, came to the United States with her husband, a soldier in the South Vietnamese army, and their three young sons through the Humanitarian Operation Program in 1990. She discusses her first job experience after they were settled by a Christian organization in Tennessee:

> After one month, I started to work. My job was to clean up a house and do the garden for a white American doctor. It was funny because that was the very first time in my life I had ever seen a lawn mower. I tried to cut grass without a covered bag on the lawn mower. Thus, when the machine moved, the grass was all over my hair and my clothes. They told me to clean the swimming pool and I mistakenly used the chemical for cleaning the kitchen to clean the pool. However, the family was very nice, they paid me $45 for the horrible job that I had done.[51]

Xuan Pham moved to southern California after four months to be near relatives and since then has averaged ten hours a day working as a seamstress in a Vietnamese-owned factory. She explains how she feels about her job and the impact it has had on her relationship with her husband:

I am satisfied with my life here. I know that I have been working very hard, but I have no choice. I have to support my family here and my relatives back in Vietnam. Besides, working hard makes me feel happy because at least it proves that I am still useful. . . . My husband is old now so he has to stay home and take care of my children. He has been so nice to me since the day we got here. Before, in Vietnam, he used to yell at me, and even hit me when he got mad. But not anymore, now he usually helps me to do the housework when I am so busy with my job. Our relationship has become very nice. Maybe changing the living environment makes us understand each other more and love each other more.[52]

As women have contributed to the household income, and in some cases played a crucial role in helping the family regain its former economic status, essentially disrupting the typical expectations of men as the primary breadwinners, they have gained more bargaining power in domestic relations.[53] However, although gender roles may be more flexible, like other women, Vietnamese American wage-earning women who work full time still often bear the burden of household chores and childcare responsibilities. According to the 1990 U.S. Census, in contrast to half of American households with children under age eighteen, over two-thirds of Vietnamese households have dependent children.[54] Overall, while some Vietnamese American women have regained their social status, and others have found opportunities to become socially mobile, many have experienced a decline in their comparative incomes.

Conclusion

Dire political and economic conditions forced Vietnamese American women to determine ways to support themselves and their families in Vietnam and in the United States. They have endured economic hardships, but these conditions have also created unexpected options and benefits. They have managed to survive the ravages of war, resettlement, and adjustment, and they contribute economically to support their families and ethnic communities. While many are now living comfortable lives, others struggle with meager earnings or are largely dependent on social services. And childcare remains largely a woman's responsibility. Clearly, they are not a homogeneous "model minority" but are internally diverse in their economic experiences. In the last decade of the twentieth century this first generation, along with a new generation of Vietnamese American women, were moving from the "survival" mode to finding new economic opportunities and niches.

NOTES

I truly appreciate Gail Nomura's, Shirley Hune's, and Sucheng Chan's close reading of my essay and helpful suggestions for revisions. My thanks to Anne Frank, librarian of the Southeast Asian Archive at the University of California, Irvine, and Trangdai Tranguyen, researcher at the Center for Oral and Public History at CSU Fullerton, for helping me find invaluable resources. The wonderful students in my Vietnamese American Women and Southeast Asian American Experience courses at UC Irvine deserve credit for helping me shape this project. I acknowledge my mother, Thuy Hanlon, who continues to inspire me to write "her" story, and my daughter, Aisha, who defines my work. Over the years, I have been fortunate to meet and know incredible Vietnamese American women who have taught me what it means to build community, to be compassionate, and to be courageous—this is for you.

1. My data is based on secondary sources along with primary research in nonprofit organizations involving Vietnamese Americans, ethnographic observations of Vietnamese American communities, and discussions with Vietnamese American women.

2. Keiko Yamanaka and Kent McClelland, "Earning the Model-Minority Image: Diverse Strategies of Economic Adaptation by Asian-American Women," *Ethnic and Racial Studies* 17:1 (January 1994): 79–114.

3. Hien Duc Do, *The Vietnamese Americans* (Westport, CT: Greenwood Press, 1999); and Linda Trinh Võ, "The Politics of Social Services for a 'Model Minority': The Union of Pan Asian Communities," in *Asian and Latino Immigrants in a Restructuring Economy: The Metamorphosis of Southern California*, ed. Marta López-Garza and David R. Diaz (Stanford, CA: Stanford University Press, 2001), 241–72.

4. Le Ly Hayslip, with Jay Wurts, *When Heaven and Earth Changed Places: A Vietnamese Woman's Journey from War to Peace* (New York: Plume, 1989); Le Ly Hayslip, with James Hayslip, *Child of War, Woman of Peace* (New York: Doubleday, 1993); *Heaven and Earth*, directed by Oliver Stone (Warner Brothers, 1993); Duong Van Mai Elliott, *The Sacred Willow: Four Generations in the Life of a Vietnamese Family* (New York: Oxford University Press, 1999). See also Mai Thi Tuyet Nguyen, *The Rubber Tree: Memoir of a Vietnamese Woman Who Was an Anti-French Guerrilla, a Publisher and a Peace Activist*, ed. Monique Senderowicz (Jefferson, NC: McFarland & Company, 1994).

5. Cynthia Enloe, *Bananas, Beaches, and Bases: Making Feminist Sense of International Politics* (Berkeley: University of California Press, 1990).

6. Suzan Ruth Travis-Robyns, "What Is Winning Anyway? Redefining Veteran: A Vietnamese American Woman's Experiences in War and Peace," *Frontiers* 18:1 (1997): 145–67.

7. Kathleen Barry, "Industrialization and Economic Development: The Costs to Women," in *Vietnam's Women in Transition*, ed. Kathleen Barry (New York: St. Martin's Press, 1996): 144–58.

8. Travis-Robyns, "What Is Winning Anyway?"

9. See also *Regret to Inform* (1998), a documentary directed by Barbara Sonneborn, Sun Fountain Productions, for personal interview footage of Xuan.

10. Cited in Travis-Robyns, "What Is Winning Anyway?" 153.

11. Curtiss Takada Rooks, "Alaska's Multiracial Asian American Families: Not Just at the Margins," in *The Sum of Our Parts: Mixed Heritage Asian Americans*, ed. Teresa Williams-León and Cynthia Nakashima (Philadelphia: Temple University Press, 2002), 71–79.

12. Gail Paradise Kelly, *From Vietnam to America: A Chronicle of the Vietnamese Immigration to the United States* (Boulder, CO: Westview Press, 1977).

13. D. Kneeland, "Wide Hostility Found to Vietnamese Influx," *New York Times*, May 2, 1975, 1.

14. Linda Trinh Võ, "The Vietnamese American Experience: From Dispersion to the Development of Post-Refugee Communities," in *Asian American Studies: A Reader*, ed. Jean Yu-Wen Shen Wu and Min Song (New Brunswick, NJ: Rutgers University Press, 2000), 290–305.

15. Anh Do and Hieu Tran Phan, "Millions of Lives Changed Forever with Saigon's Fall," special report on the Survivors of Camp Z30-D, 1075–2001, *Orange County Register*, Sunday, April 29, 2001.

16. Bruce Grant, *The Boat People: An 'Age' Investigation* (London: Penguin Books, 1979); and

Barry Wain, *The Refused: The Agony of the Indochinese Refugees* (New York: Simon & Schuster, 1981).

17. N. D. Phuc Tien and V. T. Thuy, *Pirates on the Gulf of Siam* (San Diego: Boat People SOS Committee, 1981).

18. U.S. Committee for Refugees, "Vietnamese Boat People: Pirates' Vulnerable Prey," American Council for Nationalities Service, February 1984.

19. Lynn Pan, gen. ed., "Vietnam," in *The Encyclopedia of Chinese Overseas* (Cambridge, MA: Harvard University Press, 1999), 228–33.

20. Nhi Quynh Luong, "A Handbook on the Background of Ethnic Chinese from North Vietnam" (M.A. thesis, California State University, Sacramento, 1988).

21. Do and Phan, "Millions of Lives."

22. On women who fought for the North Vietnamese Communists, see Sandra C. Taylor, *Vietnamese Women at War: Fighting for Ho Chi Minh and the Revolution* (Lawrence: University Press of Kansas, 1999); and Karen Gottschang Turner, with Phan Thanh Hao, *Even the Women Must Fight: Memories of War from North Vietnam* (New York: John Wiley & Sons, 1998). See also *The Long-Haired Warriors* (videorecording), Under-Arm Productions (Berkeley: University of California Extension Center for Media and Independent Learning, 1998).

23. Thomas Bass, *Vietamerica: The War Comes Home* (New York: Soho, 1996).

24. Philip James Mabry, "'We're Bringing Them Home': Resettling Vietnamese Amerasians in the United States" (Ph.D. diss., University of Pittsburgh, 1996), 289.

25. Marilyn Lacey, *In Our Fathers' Land: Vietnamese Amerasians in the United States* (Washington, DC: United States Catholic Conference, Migration and Refugee Services, 1985).

26. Chung Hoang Chuong and Van Le, *The Amerasians from Vietnam: A California Study* (Folsom, CA: Southeast Asia Community Research Center, 1994).

27. Pamela Constable, "For Area's Amerasians, More Struggle; Many Children of GI's Find It Hard to Adjust," *Washington Post*, April 13, 1998, B-1.

28. Kieu-Linh Caroline Valverde, "From Dust to Gold: The Vietnamese Amerasian Experience," in *Racially Mixed People in America*, ed. Maria P. P. Root (Newbury Park, CA: Sage Publications, 1992), 144–61.

29. In contrast, when the French were defeated by the Vietnamese in 1954, they immediately evacuated the Franco-Vietnamese children to France, guaranteeing them citizenship and an education.

30. *Between Worlds* (videorecording), filmed, edited, written, produced, and directed by Shawn Hainsworth (Berkeley: University of California Extension Center for Media and Independent Learning, 1998).

31. Robert S. McKelvey, *The Dust of Life: America's Children Abandoned in Vietnam* (Seattle: University of Washington Press, 1999).

32. Cited in Constable, "For Area's Amerasians, More Struggle," B-1.

33. Mariam Darce Frenier and Kimberly Mancini, "Vietnamese Women in a Confucian Setting: The Causes of the Initial Decline in the Status of East Asian Women," in Barry, ed., *Vietnam's Women in Transition*, 21–37; and Nazli Kibria, *Family Tightrope: The Changing Lives of Vietnamese Americans* (Princeton, NJ: Princeton University Press, 1993).

34. Enloe, *Bananas, Beaches, and Bases.*

35. UNICEF, *Vietnam Children and Women: A Situation Analysis* (United Nations Children's Fund, 1994).

36. Beatrice Nied Hackett, ed., *Pray God and Keep Walking: Stories of Women Refugees* (Jefferson, NC: McFarland & Company, 1996), 104–7.

37. Gail Paradise Kelly, "To Become an American Woman: Education and Sex Role Socialization

of the Vietnamese Immigrant Woman," in *Unequal Sisters: A Multicultural Reader in U.S. Women's History*, ed. Vicki L. Ruiz and Ellen Carol DuBois (New York: Routledge, 2000), 554–64.

38. Hoan N. Bui and Merry Morash, "Domestic Violence in the Vietnamese Immigrant Community: An Exploratory Study," *Violence against Women* 5:7 (July 1999): 769–95.

39. Eric Tang, "State Violence, Asian Immigrants, and the 'Underclass,'" in *States of Confinement: Policing, Detention and Policy*, ed. Joy James (New York: St. Martin's Press, 2000), 230–44. See also *Eating Welfare* (videorecording), produced by the Youth Leadership Project of CAAAV (The Bronx, NY: Youth Leadership Project, 2001).

40. Karen Hossfeld, "Hiring Immigrant Women: Silicon Valley's 'Simple Formula,'" in *Women of Color in U.S. Society*, ed. Maxine Baca Zinn and Bonnie Thornton Dill (Philadelphia: Temple University Press, 1994), 65–93.

41. Janet Benson, "The Effects of Packinghouse Work on Southeast Asian Refugee Families," in *Newcomers in the Workplace: Immigrants and the Restructuring of the U.S. Economy*, ed. Louise Lamphere, Alex Stepick, and Guillermo Grenier (Philadelphia: Temple University Press, 1994), 99–126.

42. Angie Ngoc Tran, "Global Subcontracting and Women Workers in Comparative Perspective," in *Globalization and Third World Socialism: Cuba and Vietnam*, ed. Claes Brundenius and John Weeks (New York: Palgrave, 2001), 217–36.

43. Nazli Kibria, "Patterns of Vietnamese Refugee Women's Wagework in the U.S.," *Ethnic Groups* 7 (1989): 297–323.

44. Thanh Thuy Nguyen, interviewed by Trangdai Tranguyen, Oral History Interview, Center for Oral and Public History, Fountain Valley, CA, December 6, 1999.

45. Craig Trinh-Phat Huynh, "Vietnamese-Owned Manicure Businesses in Los Angeles," in *Reframing the Immigration Debate: A Public Policy Report*, ed. Bill Ong Hing and Ronald Lee (Los Angeles: LEAP Asian Pacific American Public Policy Institute and UCLA Asian American Studies Center, 1996), 195–204.

46. A chemical called methyl methacrylate, a bonding liquid that is used to adhere the acrylic tips used by discount nail shops, has been blamed for a host of possible problems, such as nail infections; eye, skin, and lung irritations; and other internal organ dysfunctions. See Booth Moore, "Pointing a Finger at Discount Nail Salons," *Los Angeles Times*, January 28, 2002, A-1.

47. According to various sources and my discussions with women who work in the business, salaries for nail technicians start at $400 a week, including tips, at a busy shop; however, they usually pay $100–$200 or more a month to rent a chair at a salon.

48. Huynh, "Vietnamese-Owned Manicure Businesses," 198.

49. Discussion with Susie Xuyen Dong-Matsuda, clinical social worker, Orange County Health Care Agency, California, February 8, 2001.

50. Cindy Thuy Phan, "Comparing the Success in Cultural Adaptation of Vietnamese Refugee Women and Men" (Ph.D. diss., Leadership and Human Behavior, United States International University, 1994).

51. Aaron Tea and Van T. Phan, "Experience of the First Generation American Women That Came through the Humanitarian Operation Program" (unpublished research paper for Vietnamese American Women course, Department of Asian American Studies, University of California, Irvine, Winter 2002). A pseudonym has been used to protect the privacy of the interviewee.

52. Ibid.

53. Kibria, *Family Tightrope*, 125.

54. Rubén G. Rumbaut, "Vietnamese, Laotian, and Cambodian Americans," in *Asian Americans: Contemporary Trends and Issues*, ed. Pyong Gap Min (Thousand Oaks, CA: Sage, 1995), 232–69.

15

Scarred, yet Undefeated
Hmong and Cambodian Women and Girls in the United States

Sucheng Chan

Many of the Hmong and Cambodian women and girls now living in the United States suffered severe traumas before they ever set foot on American soil. Some have never recovered from the unspeakable horrors they experienced; others not only have survived but have valiantly rebuilt their lives. They are actively reconstituting families or starting new ones and are working hard to make the communities they now live in into viable social entities. This chapter discusses where they came from and why they are here.

The Hmong originated in China, where more than 5 million of them still live. In the early nineteenth century some Hmong migrated to Thailand, Laos, and Vietnam to escape Chinese persecution. The descendants of these migrants now live in the hills of mainland Southeast Asia and practice slash-and-burn agriculture. The Hmong in the United States all came from Laos, where they are but one of sixty ethnic groups and, being a minority, are dominated by the lowland Lao.

The Hmong social structure is based on clans, which number about twenty. The kinship system, like that of the Chinese, is patrilineal, patrilocal, and patriarchal. Although Hmong women have inferior status vis-à-vis men, in their homeland they do some of the most strenuous work in their communities. They cultivate and harvest crops (usually without the aid of draft animals), husk grain, carry heavy containers of water from mountain streams, gather firewood and lug it home along steep and slippery paths, spin yarn, weave cloth, sew by hand all their families' clothing, and take care of their families, domestic animals, and vegetable gardens. Hmong men are responsible for hunting, clearing jungle plots for cultivation, making decisions, and controlling their families and clans.

In contrast to the Hmong kinship system, that of the Khmer—the major ethnic group in Cambodia—is neither patrilineal nor patrilocal. Rather, it is cognate or bilateral, counting descent through both the male and female lines. After a young couple marries, they can live with or near the husband's family or the wife's family or somewhere else by themselves. Although Khmer women are still subject to male control, Khmer gender roles are complementary rather than hierarchical: women clean house, cook, raise children, and obey and serve the men folk in their families, but they also participate in decision making by advising their husbands and managing family finances.

Khmer culture places great emphasis on female comportment: women must look beautiful, dress and carry themselves modestly, and speak softly and soothingly. Whatever status they enjoy is based on their virtuousness, especially as others perceive it. The reputation of Khmer men, meanwhile, depends mainly on their ability to grow enough food or to earn sufficient wages to support their families.

Neither Hmong nor Khmer women would have come to the United States in sizable numbers had Americans not fought a war in Vietnam and had that war not also involved neighboring Laos and Cambodia.[1] To understand what they went through before they arrived in the United States, it is important to know something about what happened to them during the conflicts that engulfed their countries, because those wartime experiences continue to haunt many of them.

Surviving War and Revolution

The 1954 Geneva Accords that ended the First Indochina War (1946–1954) set aside two provinces in northeastern Laos for the Pathet Lao (Laotian Communists) to regroup their troops. American policy makers feared that the Pathet Lao might take over neighboring provinces, so they looked for ways to prevent such a possibility. The United States had to act clandestinely because both the 1954 and 1962 Geneva agreements stipulated that Laos remain neutral during the Cold War. Thus, the U.S. Central Intelligence Agency (CIA), which can operate secretly, became a key player in Laos. CIA agents had heard that the Hmong were fierce fighters, so they began, in 1959, to recruit Hmong young men into a mercenary army, which U.S. Special Forces, commonly called the Green Berets, trained and equipped.

The secret war in Laos devastated the lives of Hmong men, women, and children. During the peak of the fighting, out of a Hmong population in Laos of about three hundred thousand, some forty thousand men at a time were at war, suffering the highest casualty rate among all the groups involved in the wars in Vietnam, Laos, and Cambodia. Hmong families were moved from their homes in the mountains to the highlands surrounding the Plain of Jars so that the CIA, using its private airline, Air America, could airdrop rice, ammunition, and other supplies to them, as the Hmong could no longer practice slash-and-burn agriculture with war raging on land and in the air.

By disrupting the Hmong pattern of subsistence, Americans unwittingly deprived Hmong men and women of their traditional responsibilities in the gendered division of labor. Since everyone living around the Plain of Jars now depended on the CIA for their daily necessities, women lost much of the status they had enjoyed as their families' providers. Those women who remained in the mountains had to survive as best they could. Blia Lee, who now lives in Montana, describes how she got through those years of hardship:

> My husband went to fight . . . and the Communists killed him, leaving me with four children. Americans dropped lots of bombs on the Communists and burned the fields so the Hmong had no place to farm. We moved from location to location and later hid in the jungle for two years. . . . In the jungle we ate leaves, jungle fruit, and *yaj thawj* (a potato-like

tuber). Some ate the wrong kind of plants and were poisoned and died, and many children died who were given opium to quiet them. Some people died from the landmines and some died from bombs. I feel very lucky to be alive.[2]

Many women became widows as a result of the heavy casualty rate among soldiers. Hmong tradition mandated that widows marry the brothers of their deceased husbands even when the latter already had wives. Becoming secondary wives lowered the women's status, but they had no other choice because women were not supposed to live without male heads of households. Thus, in addition to skewing the sex ratio by killing off so many men, the war increased the rate of polygamy in Hmong communities. But since polygamy was a part of the Hmong cultural tradition, most women learned to view it with equanimity. Says Chue Vue, now a resident of California, who is her husband's third wife:

I realized I shouldn't feel terrible because I was not the only person in the whole world to become a third wife. It was really common at the time. So, overall, I didn't feel anything bad about it. It was part of the Hmong culture.... I learned to live with it. To me, after so many years I see a beauty in all of this. Second Wife's children are my children, and my children are her children. They all call me mother, just like they call her mother.... But I would not like to see my daughters in my position—especially not in America because I know they have choices that I didn't have.[3]

While Hmong women lost social standing and suffered uncommon hardships, wartime conditions nevertheless emboldened a few to claim a measure of freedom for themselves during their husbands' prolonged absence at the front. Vue Vang, who now lives in Minnesota, moved in with her husband's parents when he went off to war in the early 1960s, but "[l]iving with my husband's family was desperately hard," she recalls. After her first child was stillborn,

I refused to continue to live with my husband's family. They made me work too hard, constantly lifting heavy loads on to the horses and carrying equally heavy loads myself, with no one to help me. Many a time, I had to lead three or four horses, each with a heavy load on its back, up and down the mountain . . . many times I got trampled by the horses. If I was behind them, I had to run after them, grabbing their tails in order to keep up with their pace. I felt such hard work had caused the complications that led to my son's death.[4]

So she moved out—an act that defied tradition and took great determination and courage.

In early 1975, the Pathet Lao began to take measures to gain full control over the country, so CIA operatives decided in May of that year to evacuate the Hmong leader, General Vang Pao, his large extended family, and other important persons, lest the Pathet Lao kill them all after taking over the country. In mid-May, approximately ten thousand people jammed the runway at Long Cheng, the headquarters of the Hmong army, but only about twenty-five hundred were flown out. The evacuation was chaotic.

Sao Mee Vang, the wife of one of General Vang Pao's close associates, had an extraordinary experience. Since she was nine months pregnant, Vang Pao authorized his personal pilot to fly her out in his small, twin-engine Cessna airplane. She tells what happened:

> When we get onto the airplane I know the baby is coming soon. I am already having pain, but it is not yet contractions. . . . When we take off, I sit in the chair. Not long after that, I feel the baby is coming, so I put a piece of plastic and a cloth down on the floor, and I sit on that.
>
> My husband is in front with the pilot, and nobody is there to help me. The water comes out, and the baby is born. I deliver the baby by myself. That is the first time I do by myself, but I am prepared! I carry scissors and string. I cut the cord and tie it with the string by myself. . . . When we land in Nam Phong, I walk off the plane with the new baby. People are surprised when they hear the story.[5]

Such recollections illustrate the courage of many Hmong women and their ability to remain calm under trying circumstances.

What happened in Cambodia was even more tragic than the secret war in Laos. Cambodia's ruler, Prince Norodom Sihanouk, an ardent nationalist, tried his best to keep his country neutral during the Cold War. But the United States, troubled by the fact that Vietnamese Communist forces repeatedly crossed over the Vietnamese-Cambodian border to escape American bombs and South Vietnamese ground attacks, began a secret bombing campaign over eastern Cambodia in 1969 to destroy the Ho Chi Minh trail (which North Vietnam used to send men and supplies to the south) and the Vietnamese Communist sanctuaries on Cambodian soil.[6] In March 1970, Sihanouk was ousted by Lon Nol, his pro-American prime minister, and Prince Sirik Matak, one of Sihanouk's cousins. Soon thereafter, American military and economic aid to Cambodia increased dramatically.

No sooner had Lon Nol established the Khmer Republic than a civil war broke out between his forces and a coalition formed by Sihanouk and the Khmer Rouge (Cambodian Communists). The civil war lasted from 1970 to 1975, during which American bombs not only destroyed military targets but also killed a significant number of civilians. Ironically, these bombing raids enabled the Khmer Rouge to win over large numbers of peasants, who developed a hatred for Americans as bombs destroyed their homes, crops, domestic and draft animals, and family members. Peasants also resented the overthrow of Sihanouk and joined the Khmer Rouge "in order to help the prince come back."[7]

The Khmer Rouge emerged victorious. On April 17, 1975, they marched into Phnom Penh, the capital, and established a regime called Democratic Kampuchea that turned out to be one of the most brutal the world has ever known. Within days, they forced the city's 2 million–plus inhabitants, as well as the people who lived in smaller cities and towns, to march into the countryside carrying only a week's rations. The apparent goal of the evacuation was to prevent people from forming groups to resist the new government and to make the entire country subservient to the Khmer Rouge. Tens of thousands of people perished from starvation, exhaustion, illness, and exposure to the elements, while military and political leaders, as well as some common soldiers who had served in Lon Nol's army, were executed.

Two Cambodian women have written about the social and psychological effects of the coerced evacuation. Var Hong Ashe, who now lives in Great Britain, explains how forcing people to leave their homes facilitated the disintegration of existing social relations:

> [A] loudspeaker truck moved slowly down the street, ordering everyone to leave the city . . . the Khmer Rouge were clearing out one section of the city at a time . . . we occasionally passed bodies of government soldiers which had been left lying on the side of the road where they had been shot. . . . The heat, the dust, the crying children, the lack of food and water, and the terror combined together to begin a breakdown of social and family structures and ties.[8]

Teeda Butt Mam, now a California resident, reveals how severely the forced march disoriented and demoralized its victims:

> They kept moving us around, from the fields into the woods. They purposely did this to disorient us so they could have complete control. . . . We were timid and lost. We had to be silent. We not only lost our identities, but we lost our pride, our sense, our religion, our loved ones, our souls, ourselves.[9]

In December 1975, the Khmer Rouge ordered a second evacuation, forcing an already weakened population to crisscross the country once again, thereby causing additional deaths.

The Khmer Rouge leaders made Cambodia into one giant forced-labor camp. People had to plant crops, dig irrigation ditches, build dams and canals, and engage in other heavy labor with their bare hands. To transform every aspect of society, the Khmer Rouge abolished private property, money, and markets; defrocked monks and desecrated Buddhist temples; and closed schools. Food was severely rationed. Malnutrition and illness, as well as sleep deprivation, took their toll. During the three years and eight months that the regime lasted, approximately 1.7 million people, out of a 1975 population of about 7.8 million, perished.

The Khmer Rouge also tried to destroy the family—one of the two foundations of Cambodia's social structure (the other being Theravada Buddhism). They forced some young people to marry mates chosen for them by Khmer Rouge cadres, thus robbing parents and traditional matchmakers of their roles. To deprive families of the bonding that occurred during meals, they made people eat in mess halls. Worse, they used children to spy on their parents and to expose and denounce the latter. They separated men and women, parents and children, and sent the different family members to work in different locations. Children above the age of seven were organized into children's brigades, working miles away from their parents and living in their own camps supervised by teenaged Khmer Rouge soldiers or cadres. Children who lacked the care of parents, an adequate diet, and medicine when they became ill died in large numbers. Not only that, but the birthrate also declined: many women, worked to the limits of their endurance and on the verge of starvation, stopped menstruating. Since few conceptions occurred, few babies were born in those years.

The Khmer Rouge severely punished even the smallest infractions, often by death, but the number of people killed does not tell the full story. The real horror was in the brutal and sadistic manner in which they were killed. To save ammunition, the Khmer Rouge usually did not shoot their victims; instead, they clubbed them to death, or buried them alive in holes the condemned persons were forced to dig, or suffocated them in plastic bags. Some particularly sadistic Khmer Rouge soldiers swung small children around by their limbs and smashed their bodies against tree trunks, causing their brains and innards to splatter. They forced women to watch their husbands and children being murdered and killed the women if they dared to gasp, cry, scream, close their eyes, or shed any tears. People survived by pretending to be dumb, deaf, and blind. Since a far larger number of men than women were killed, more female than male survivors have had to live with memories of the gruesome events they witnessed.

By 1977, the murderous revolution began to devour its own leaders and cadres. Pol Pot, Democratic Kampuchea's leader, became so paranoid that he began purging the leaders of other Khmer Rouge factions who opposed his policies. Those who were not killed formed a resistance movement. In December 1978, dissidents who had escaped to Vietnam returned to Cambodia, supported by 120,000 Vietnamese troops, to drive the Khmer Rouge out of power. On January 7, 1979, they established a new regime headed by two former Khmer Rouge mid-level officers, Heng Samrin and Hun Sen.

Tragically, the end of war and revolution did not bring peace to the people of Vietnam, Laos, and Cambodia. Since April 1975, approximately 3 million people have escaped from these countries; an unknown but significant number of these died during their flight. About half of those who survived now live in the United States, which took in a million Vietnamese refugees and immigrants (the latter through the Orderly Departure Program) and more than 150,000 each of the lowland Lao, Hmong, and Cambodians. (These figures include ethnic Chinese from the three countries.) The rest went to Canada, Australia, France, and other countries, while those whom no country would accept were eventually repatriated to their homelands.

Becoming Refugees

The first wave of refugees out of Southeast Asia included approximately 130,000 people, of whom more than 125,000 were Vietnamese. Although five thousand slots were set aside for Cambodians, only eight hundred actually left before Phnom Penh fell. The other forty-six hundred Cambodians who formed the first wave were individuals who happened to be outside Cambodia when the Khmer Rouge triumphed. No slots were set aside for the lowland Lao and Hmong because Vientiane, the capital of Laos, did not "fall" overnight as did Phnom Penh and Saigon. Only twenty-five hundred Hmong were evacuated along with General Vang Pao in May 1975. A year and a half after the United States completed the resettlement of the first wave of refugees, new groups began to pour out of Vietnam and Laos. They consisted of "boat people" from Vietnam, who escaped in overcrowded, often unseaworthy boats, and "land people" from Laos and Cambodia who crossed the Mekong River into Thailand. The second-wave exodus lasted two decades, numbered in the millions, and sorely tested the humanitarian and problem-solving capacities of dozens of nations.

Since the Hmong had been allies of the United States, the new Pathet Lao government singled them out for extermination. Even after General Vang Pao left, many Hmong refused to lay down their arms; instead, they went deep into the mountains to continue waging guerrilla warfare against the new regime. In retaliation, the Pathet Lao dropped bombs and chemicals over these hideouts to quell the resistance. Meanwhile, women, children, and old people dispersed to their old villages or into the jungle, keeping as low a profile as possible. As life in the villages and jungle became ever more difficult, tens of thousands of Hmong made their way to Thailand. Mai Hang, a Hmong woman now living in Minnesota, recalls:

> The communist soldiers saw that all the young men were nowhere to be seen. Only the elderly people, women, and children were left in the village. They got very angry at everyone. They were especially furious at parents and wives. They took many of the fathers to bunkers to punish and keep as prisoners. They demanded to know where the young men were. Most fathers and wives didn't tell them. And they killed a couple of the fathers . . . Not too long after, . . . they started bombing our homes, valleys, and our mountains. . . . We could not live in the village anymore. It was decided that everyone must go to the jungle to hide.[10]

After holding out for more than two years, the Hmong were dying in such numbers that they decided they had no alternative except to flee to Thailand. During the escape, many Hmong mothers suffered a special agony. When they could not quiet their crying babies, some mothers abandoned the children, lest the babies' cries betray the presence of the entire group. To lull the infants to sleep, they gave them small wads of opium. In some instances, the amount was too large and the children overdosed and died.

The story of a girl named Ia Vang, both of whose parents had died, illustrates in yet another way how strong and tenacious Hmong females can be. During her escape, she hung on to the family heirloom against the wishes of her older brother:

> My grandmother raised us. . . . In 1977, we had to leave the village and go into the jungle, so we separated. . . . Grandmother divided my mother's embroideries between us and told me, "No matter what happens, you must carry these with you . . . as a remembrance of your mother." For two years we hid in the jungle. My oldest brother died during that time when I was only twelve years old, so I took care of his little daughter. I carried my bundle of embroideries around my waist and my niece on top of the bundle. Together with my little sister and my third oldest brother, we decided to escape to Thailand even if it meant we might die trying. When we got to the bank of the Mekong [River], my brother told me to throw away my bundle and just carry my niece. I said, "No, I have to carry it because I want to do what my grandmother told me." My brother was really upset. People with money could pay Thai boatmen to carry them across, but we didn't have any money. We blew up our plastic tubes and tied them together. My brother called to the spirits of my

mother and father when we were about to swim, to help carry us across the Mekong river. It took three hours to cross. I think [the spirits of] my mother and father helped us, because if they hadn't, I would have died when my tube popped and the water came up over my neck.[11]

Compared to the refugees from Vietnam and Laos, it was well nigh impossible for Cambodians to flee their homeland before 1979 because the Khmer Rouge mined the borders and killed anyone caught trying to escape. Only about thirty-four thousand Cambodians successfully reached Thailand between 1975 and early 1979, but more than two hundred thousand people—mostly ethnic Chinese and ethnic Vietnamese then living in Cambodia—managed to make their way eastward into Vietnam. After the Khmer Rouge were overthrown, people were so busy searching for lost relatives that they neglected to harvest that year's rice crop or to plant a new one in the spring. As the scepter of famine loomed, hundreds of thousands of emaciated Cambodians streamed to the Thai-Cambodian border. Attempts by international relief agencies to deliver food to them got mired in the most incredible political tangles.[12]

In spite of the fact that the Cambodians were in even worse shape than the Vietnamese, lowland Lao, and Hmong escapees, Thai officials treated the Cambodians with greater wariness, terrified by the possibility that 5.5 million still-alive-but-starving Cambodians might flood into their country. They also feared that the potential depopulation of Cambodia would undermine its traditional role as a buffer state between Thailand and Vietnam. Thai leaders did not relish the thought that hundreds of thousands of Vietnamese troops and civilians might amass along Thailand's eastern border should Cambodia cease to exist as a viable country. Therefore, to stem the flow, Thailand closed the Thai-Cambodian border, classified Cambodians as "illegal immigrants," and did not allow the United Nations High Commissioner for Refugees (UNHCR) and private relief agencies to care for them. The only Cambodians who could be interviewed for potential resettlement abroad as refugees (as that word is defined by the United Nations) were those who had reached UNHCR holding centers before February 1980. In the next decade and a half, only 250,000 Cambodians were resettled in France, the United States, Canada, Australia, and other countries. The United Nations set up a temporary agency called the Border Relief Operation (UNBRO) to provide food, shelter, and medical care to the less fortunate people who were placed in so-called border camps and denied the possibility of resettlement abroad. United Nations peacekeeping forces escorted approximately 350,000 of these "border Cambodians" back home between October 1991 and May 1993.

Life in both the UNHCR holding centers and the UNBRO border camps was full of hardships and danger. The residents did not always have enough to eat or enough clean water to drink. Robbers from the outside, as well as inside the camps, stole the few possessions the camp residents still had. Young women suffered additional degradation: Thai camp guards, who were supposed to protect them, raped them at will. Samkhann Khoeun, now a resident of Massachusetts, explains how the camp guards in Khao I Dang—the main UNHCR camp holding Cambodians—identified which families to molest: "In the daytime, [the Thai guards] ... went from place to place, so at night, after the UNHCR staff went back to their residences ... the guards knew who had daughters and possessions. They took the girls at night and robbed the refugees."[13] Under such conditions, many people felt helpless and despondent.

Life for the Hmong in the Thai refugee camps was likewise characterized by boredom, uncertainty, anxiety, and violence. Khou Her, who now lives in California, gives us a glimpse of what camp life was like for her, as well as for everyone else:

> The camp where we were kept was surrounded by barbed wire. No one was allowed to go outside without permission. . . . If you tried to leave the camp without permission, the Thai would kick at you or kill you. . . . A lot of kids . . . were so sick that their eyes turned grey. There was nothing to eat almost. The food that was sent into the camp by trucks was only given twice a month. . . . It was almost impossible to survive on what we got. . . . In the camp we were in jail, like the chickens and pigs in Laos. We were that helpless and trapped.[14]

Even being resettled abroad in Western countries did not end their suffering, for still more difficulties lay ahead.

Life in the United States

While Southeast Asian refugee women share many experiences with other Asian immigrant women, there *are* significant differences. I discuss two major differences and one important similarity. The most obvious difference is the multiple, often violent ruptures that Southeast Asian refugees have endured and the continuing impact of such dislocations on their present lives. While immigrants and refugees alike experience acculturative stress, refugees tend to be more sorrowful and psychologically burdened, as they have lost their loved ones, homes, livelihood, social status, countries, cultures, and meaning in life. Moreover, the pain caused by some of these losses is exacerbated by culturally enforced silence. For example, although many of the refugee women were raped, often more than once, during their flight and in the refugee camps, they usually feel too ashamed to reveal the violations that have seared them so indelibly that their sufferings are ineffable. Most damaging of all, the devastations of the Khmer Rouge era caused many Cambodians to lose all trust in other human beings.

The multiple traumas have affected some Cambodian women in a peculiar way. Dozens have developed a condition that has puzzled doctors, who, for a lack of scientific explanation, have called it "psychosomatic blindness." These patients claim they cannot see, even though tests show no physiological causes for their loss of sight.[15] Journalist Alec Wilkinson, who wrote a long magazine article about two such women, Long Eang and Im Cheann, reports:

> It strikes Eang as strange that, no matter how many things she forgets and how much difficulty she has remembering, she never forgets the things that happened to her in Cambodia. The images that arrive in her mind without invitation are so clear that they seem almost as if they are happening again. . . . [D]espite having met and become fond of many people who have helped her since she came to America, she never sees the faces of those

people when she closes her eyes but sees only the faces of the Khmer Rouge soldiers. . . . What happened to Im Cheann and Long Eang in the war . . . was too horrific, and it went on too long ever to reside peacefully within them. . . . They are pursued by their memories; their memories harass them, and they cannot get rid of them. . . . A part of them came to a standstill in the war, and they are drawn back to it with a frequency that is punishing.[16]

It seems that having witnessed more brutal behavior than any human being can be expected to endure, these women have gone blind in order to shut out a world that, in their experience, has been truly grotesque. It may be particularly difficult for Cambodian Theravada Buddhists, who believe in *karma* and who assume responsibility for the adversities they experience, to be healed. For them, post-traumatic stress syndrome and perhaps psychosomatic blindness are not just physical and mental illnesses but moral ones as well.

Compared to Cambodian women refugees, Hmong women refugees seem to be relatively better off. Those who have told their life stories seem generally satisfied with their present lives. Pang Yang of California talks about how much easier a housewife's life is in the United States than in Laos:

I am thankful that the American people let us stay in their country. They are very nice, and I am honored to have them as my neighbors. My neighbors bring my children cake and candy, and I cook many Hmong snacks and offer them to my neighbors in return. . . . Cooking food here is very fast and efficient. We do not have to gather wood, we do not have to stoke the fire, we only need to turn on a switch and the stove is on! . . . I have grown to like the American stove so much that I cook a lot.[17]

While certain Hmong families seem to be adapting relatively well to life in American society, most Cambodians continue to harbor an inconsolable sense of loss. Consequently, they feel an even stronger obligation to retain their cultures than do most immigrants because they cannot forget how the Khmer Rouge tried to eradicate all aspects of Khmer culture. Since the family is the bedrock of Cambodian society, and since Khmer women are expected to be modest, chaste, and deferential to men, the heaviest pressure in Cambodian ethnic communities to preserve the culture of origin falls on young women, who are not allowed to date or stay out late, even with girlfriends. And of course, premarital sex is absolutely forbidden.

Given the heavy emphasis that Khmer culture places on female virtue, parents and other adults pay an extraordinary amount of attention to how their daughters dress and carry themselves. As a teenage Cambodian American girl in California puts it:

They [the old people] don't like it if you leave the house wearing a tank top or something. They think you're a hooker already. They think everything is wrong. They never trust you. They don't understand . . . how American kids dress. . . . They never give us a chance to do what we want . . . they won't give us a chance to be ourselves, fit in. Some girls do act bad because they are always accused of being bad.[18]

There are even a few reported instances of fathers becoming so angry with their daughters for dating secretly or for walking down the street alongside young men that they have beaten their daughters until the young women passed out.[19]

Young Hmong American women are likewise experiencing conflicts with regard to the differential behavior expected of men and women. Says Yer Her of Wisconsin:

> Many Hmong girls don't like the way Hmong men think about girls. They know it can be different in [the] U.S. for girls. Not so hard like in Laos. . . . Boys want it like before. Then girls have to do what they say. They only want to marry young girls, not old ones like me. They don't like [it if a] girl is smart. They say she [is] too much trouble. . . . Marriage [is] good for the man, not for the girl. Too much work for her to take care of everything at home. It's always like that—women work, men sit and talk. Women [are] in the kitchen to make food, men sit at [the] table and eat everything good. When women get to eat after the men, nothing good is left.[20]

Another Hmong woman, Elizabeth Mee Vang of California, resents the sexual double standard that Hmong young men and women in the United States are still expected to abide by:

> I have had culture conflicts over being a Hmong woman in the U.S. constantly, every day, every minute of my life. When I was young I had to decide, "Should I date? Should I have sex before marriage? Should I just kind of be assertive?" . . . It was so difficult. I was always, always into a culture clash. . . . I believe there are certain things in the Hmong culture that should be kept and remembered and practiced, like respecting the elders is good. But there are certain things that you must let go of, like marrying a second wife or having a mistress all the time. We should never, never, never practice that again. If my husband marries another wife . . . I should be allowed to divorce, and I should be allowed to marry another man. . . . Those women back in Laos could accept such things, but not me. . . . I never got the chance to ask men how they would feel if I was sleeping with two men. I'm sure they would be as mad as we women are when we see them sleep with two women. . . . We Hmong women are human, too.[21]

Given the difficulty that parents in the United States have in trying to control every aspect of their children's behavior or to keep their daughters locked up, some refugee parents have resorted to marrying their girls off at even younger ages than they did in their countries of origin, to ensure that the girls will be virgin brides. Teenage brides abound in Hmong and Khmer refugee communities in America.[22] Such measures are considerably more extreme than those taken by families in other Asian ethnic groups.

The second critical difference between refugee women and immigrant women is that government policies and programs affect the two groups differently. Immigrants are not closely monitored by the state after they arrive. They are free to settle wherever they wish, but neither do they receive any special assistance. Refugees, in contrast, are "processed" by layers of bureaucracy, each there simultaneously to aid and control them. Since a vast majority of the refugees depended on sponsors to ease their incorporation into American society, their settlement pattern was strongly influenced by the interaction of three factors: the federal policy of dispersal, the location and practices of voluntary agencies that helped resettle the refugees, and the desires of the refugees to maximize their own well-being.

The U.S. government tried to spread the population out in order to minimize the fiscal and social impact of the refugee influx on any single locality. This dispersal policy was reinforced by the voluntary agencies, many of which are affiliated with churches, which sent the refugees either to cities and towns where they had branch offices or to congregations, parishes, and families that were willing and able to serve as sponsors. Since the sponsors were scattered across the face of America, clusters of refugees from Vietnam, Laos, and Cambodia were placed in many small towns in which few, if any, other Asians had ever lived up to that point. Despite the federal government's and the voluntary agencies' best efforts, the dispersal policy did not work: as soon as the refugees acquired some familiarity with American life, many moved to places with warmer climates, better employment opportunities, higher public assistance payments, or where their relatives and friends were.

While bureaucracies have partly helped to determine refugee settlement patterns, their impact in this regard has been gender-neutral. Other forms of government assistance, however, have had a significant influence on gender relations in the Southeast Asian refugee communities. When the refugees first arrived, they were eligible for various kinds of assistance, including Refugee Cash Assistance, Refugee Medical Assistance, English-as-a-Second-Language classes, and vocational training. When their eligibility period expired, those who had not yet found work could apply for public assistance, or "welfare." The major federal welfare program for needy families in existence during the years of the peak refugee influx, in the 1980s and the first half of the 1990s, was AFDC—Aid to Families with Dependent Children. (AFDC has been replaced by Temporary Aid to Needy Families, or TANF, since "welfare reform" took effect in 1996.) AFDC was a woman-centered program. The fact that it was women who received the government's monthly checks tipped the balance of familial power toward them. When women become breadwinners (whether by employment or through welfare), their status is usually enhanced. That enables the more assertive among them to claim more decision-making power in various aspects of family and personal life.

The American legal and law enforcement systems have also affected gender relations in refugee and immigrant families. The relative ease with which divorces can be obtained in the United States has encouraged some Asian immigrant and refugee wives to leave their husbands. In the United States, women can find jobs more easily, however poorly such jobs may pay or however low their status may be; there are fewer negative sanctions against divorcees; and in many cities there are shelters and counselors for battered women, even though few Asian-ancestry women use them. Some women (and children) have learned to dial 911 for help when men in their families physically abuse them.

Anthropologist Nancy Donnelly tells the story of Mai Yang, a Hmong woman in Seattle, who dared to deviate from the gendered teachings of her culture. Vang decided to divorce her husband, who had several girlfriends and who beat her up when she complained about that fact. When he also hit their young son, she called the police.

With Donnelly's help, she obtained an injunction against him and eventually had the marriage dissolved by a court. However, other Hmong women criticized her actions because "instead of accepting her husband's behavior as an ideal wife should, she was striving to end the marriage by turning to the American legal system."[23]

The main way in which the lives of Asian immigrant and refugee women are similar is that the consequences of female paid labor are the same for both groups. In Laos and Cambodia, very few girls received an education. At most, they attended school for only two or three years. But here in the United States, all children are required to go to school, and public schools are tuition free. Many Hmong and Khmer girls who are not married off in their mid-teens are doing well in school, often better than boys are doing. More and more of them are going to college or even to graduate school. College graduates, especially if they are bilingual, are able to get fairly well paid professional jobs, often in occupations that serve their fellow refugees. But even those women who have not been able to use education as a channel for upward social mobility have entered the labor market in significant numbers and are now wage earners.

As more and more Hmong and Cambodian women earn money, some husbands resent their wives' increased financial power, while others adapt quite well to the new situation. Sirathra Som, a middle-class woman from Cambodia who never had to work in her natal country, is now a successful businesswoman in California. She possesses an important trait that has enabled many refugees to survive—a flexible attitude. When she first arrived, she took a job that, in Cambodia, would have been totally beneath her station. She recalls:

> We arrived in California with nothing, nothing. . . . My first job was at the Sheraton Hotel in San Francisco as a domestic. . . . One of the first things you learn in America is that you need money. . . . [W]e needed two incomes and I went to work. I know my husband did not like it, but it could not be helped. . . . I could work easier than he could and I began to do well and I supported the family. I became the breadwinner. He had bad feelings about this. . . . Eventually, we were divorced.[24]

In comparison, a Cambodian woman named Ramsey, living in upstate New York, is more fortunate—at least from a feminist perspective. Her husband is very cooperative and helpful as she earns a living to support their family:

> When I come home from work . . . I open the door and I hear the kids crying. I say, "Oh, my goodness!" . . . And I tell my husband, "Can you take the kids and let them play over there?" And my husband says to the kids, "Your Mommy is so tired. Let her sleep a little while. Can you come with me, please?" He's so busy with the kids. He helps me a lot when he's home. When he's home, I just sit down.[25]

Changes in the balance of power between men and women, and between parents and their children, are not new phenomena. They are current versions of an old story that has replayed itself many times within immigrant families in America. However, the experiences of Hmong and Cambodian refugee women and girls are far more complex and more heart-wrenching than those of most immigrants. Although beaten down by war, a misguided revolution, flight, confinement in prison-like refugee camps, and the challenges of adapting to a completely different environment as they move from peasant societies to the world's most technologically advanced country, these women are survivors in every sense of the word. They have survived because they are strong, courageous, tenacious, and adaptable. Their stories show how some women may be scarred yet remain undefeated.

NOTES

For additional pertinent references, readers may consult three bibliographies I have published: "A Selected Bibliography and List of Films on the Vietnamese, Cambodian, and Laotian Experience in Southeast Asia and the United States," in *New Visions in Asian American Studies: Diversity, Community, Power*, ed. Franklin Ng, Judy Yung, Stephen S. Fugita, and Elaine H. Kim (Pullman, Wash.: Washington State University Press, 1994), 63–110; "Selected Bibliography," in *Hmong Means Free: Life in Laos and America* (Philadelphia: Temple University Press, 1994), 247–64; and "Selected Bibliography," in *Not Just Victims: Conversations with Cambodian Community Leaders in the United States* (Urbana: University of Illinois Press, 2003), 275–85.

1. On the Hmong role in the war in Laos, see Kenneth Conboy, with James Morrison, *Shadow War: The CIA's Secret War in Laos* (Boulder, Colo.: Paladin Press, 1995); Jane Hamilton-Merritt, *Tragic Mountains: The Hmong, the Americans, and the Secret War in Laos, 1942–1992* (Bloomington: Indiana University Press, 1993); Tim Pfaff, *Hmong in America: Journey from a Secret War* (Eau Claire, Wis.: Chippewa Valley Museum Press, 1995); Roger Warner, *Shooting at the Moon: The Story of America's Clandestine War in Laos* (South Royalty, Vt.: Steerforth Press, 1996); and the introduction in Sucheng Chan, *Hmong Means Free: Life in Laos and America* (Philadelphia: Temple University Press, 1994). On Cambodia, see David P. Chandler, *The Tragedy of Cambodian History: Politics, War, and Revolution since 1945* (New Haven: Yale University Press, 1991); Craig Etcheson, *The Rise and Demise of Democratic Kampuchea* (Boulder, Colo.: Westview Press, 1984); Ben Kiernan, *The Pol Pot Regime: Race, Power, and Genocide in Cambodia under the Khmer Rouge* (New Haven: Yale University Press, 1996); and Sucheng Chan, *Survivors: Cambodian Refugees in the United States* (forthcoming).

2. Susan Lindbergh Miller, Bounthavy Kiatoukaysy, and Tou Yang, eds., *Hmong Voices in Montana* (Missoula, Mont.: Missoula Museum of the Arts, 1992), 25.

3. Lillian Faderman, with Ghia Xiong, *I Begin My Life All Over: The Hmong and the American Immigration Experience* (Boston: Beacon Press, 1998), 138–39.

4. Chan, *Hmong Means Free*, 190–210.

5. Gayle L. Morrison, *Sky Is Falling: An Oral History of the CIA's Evacuation of the Hmong from Laos* (Jefferson, N.C.: McFarland, 1999), 116–17.

6. How the Nixon administration managed to keep this bombing campaign secret is told in William Shawcross, *Sideshow: Kissinger, Nixon and the Destruction of Cambodia* (New York: Simon & Schuster, 1979; rev. ed., 1987).

7. Kate Grace Frieson, "The Impact of Revolution on Cambodian Peasants, 1970–1975" (Ph.D. diss., Monash University, Australia, 1992), 83.

8. Var Hong Ashe, *From Phnom Penh to Paradise: Escape from Cambodia* (London: Hodder and Stoughton, 1988), 25, 29–34.

9. Teeda Butt Mam, "Worms from Our Skin," in *Children of Cambodia's Killing Fields: Memoirs by Survivors*, comp. Dith Pran (New Haven: Yale University Press, 1997), 14–15.

10. Betty Chang, "An Interview with Mai Hang," in *A Free People: Our Stories, Our Voices, Our Dreams* (Minneapolis: Hmong Youth Cultural Awareness Project, 1994), 83–84.

11. Miller, Kiatoukaysy, and Yang, eds., *Hmong Voices*, 24.

12. The story of that tragedy within a tragedy is told in Linda Mason and Roger Brown, *Rice, Rivalry, and Politics: Managing Cambodian Relief* (Cleveland: Notre Dame University Press, 1983); and William Shawcross, *The Quality of Mercy: Cambodia, Holocaust and Modern Conscience* (New York: Simon and Schuster, 1984).

13. Interview with Samkhann Khoeun, Lowell, Massachusetts, August 23, 1995.

14. Faderman and Xiong, *I Begin My Life*, 71.

15. Gretchen B. Van Boemel and Patricia D. Rozee, "Treatment for Psychosomatic Blindness among Cambodian Refugee Women," *Women and Therapy* 13:3 (1992): 139–66.

16. Alec Wilkinson, "A Changed Vision of God," *New Yorker*, January 24, 1994, 68.

17. Chan, *Hmong Means Free*, 221–22.

18. Susan Lee Holgate, "Early Marriages of Khmer High School Students: Influences and Consequences of Culture, Education, and Intergenerational Conflict" (M.A. thesis, California State University, Stanislaus, 1994), 101.

19. Sharon Sloan Fiffer, *Imagining America: Paul Thai's Journey from the Killing Fields of Cambodia to Freedom in the U.S.A.* (New York: Paragon House, 1991), 40; and Nancy J. Smith-Hefner, *Khmer American: Identity and Moral Education in a Diasporic Community* (Berkeley and Los Angeles: University of California Press, 1999), 117.

20. Beth Leah Goldstein, "Schooling for Cultural Transition: Hmong Girls and Boys in American High Schools" (Ph.D. diss., University of Wisconsin, Madison, 1985), 108 and 86.

21. Faderman and Xiong, *I Begin My Life*, 143–44.

22. Mark Arax, "The Child Brides of California," *Los Angeles Times*, May 4, 1993, A-1; Holgate, "Early Marriages"; Ray Hutchison and Miles McNall, "Early Marriage in a Hmong Cohort," *Journal of Marriage and the Family* 56 (1994): 579–90; Sharon Rolnick, "Reducing Teenage Childbearing in the Hmong Community: First Year Results," *Vietnam Generation* 2:3 (1990): 53–61; and Smith-Hefner, *Khmer American*, 181.

23. Nancy D. Donnelly, *Changing Lives of Refugee Hmong Women* (Seattle: University of Washington Press, 1994), 173–81.

24. Siratha Som, "The Doughnut Queen," in John Tenhula, *Voices from Southeast Asia: The Refugee Experience in the United States* (New York: Holmes & Meier, 1991), 180.

25. Florence Sue Mitchell, "From Refugee to Rebuilder: Cambodian Women in America" (Ph.D. diss., Syracuse University, 1987), 81.

Part 6

Negotiating Globalization, Work, and Motherhood

16

Asian Immigrant Women and Global Restructuring, 1970s–1990s

Rhacel Salazar Parreñas

Genny O' Connor, a Filipina domestic worker in Los Angeles, left her office job in the Philippines in hopes of seeking a much higher paying job in the United States. In the Philippines, her salary could barely cover her day-to-day expenses and, needless to say, did not leave her with many resources to provide her family with the financial support expected of her as a single daughter. Having attained a bachelor's degree in the Philippines, Genny had not anticipated that without documents in the United States she would find a job only in the low-wage informal sector. Even after years in domestic work, she is still trying to adjust to her experience of underemployment. She states:

> I was crying all the time. (Laughs.) When my employer gave me the bucket for cleaning, I did not know where I had to start. Of course we are not so rich in the Philippines, but we had maids. I did not know how to start cleaning and my feelings were of self-pity. I kept on thinking that I just came to the U.S. to be a maid. So that was that. I would just cry and I wanted to go home. I did not imagine that this was the kind of work that I would end up doing.[1]

Like many other immigrant women, Genny O' Connor faces severe underemployment. Her participation in the U.S. labor market entails a sharp decline in occupational and social status.

Ever since she was a young girl in the Philippines, Beth Orozo had dreamed of working as a nurse in the United States. Growing up in a not-so-well-to-do family, Beth aspired to leave the Philippines in order to provide financial support to her parents. Since arriving in 1992, Beth has worked as a registered nurse in a convalescent hospital, which is the easiest avenue available for Philippine nursing graduates to enter the United States. Now earning much more than the average nurse, Beth works as a supervisor at a skilled nursing facility. On average, she works one hundred hours every two weeks, logging in overtime hours to increase her pay. Overall, she likes her life in the United States and feels proud that she can provide for her parents in the Philippines. However, her path to the United States was not an easy one. For one thing, it was made difficult by various examinations, the first being the Commission on Graduates of Foreign

Nursing Schools, which she had to take two times, and the second being the State Nursing Board Examination of California. Having overcome these obstacles, Beth has been able to put to use the education she earned in the Philippines and describes her migratory experience as one of "success."[2]

The stories of Genny O' Connor and Beth Orozo are but two of the many different experiences of Asian immigrant women in the U.S. labor market. Post-1965 Asian women migrants to the United States include professionals who correct the labor shortage in certain skilled professions, immigrant entrepreneurs who fill abandoned labor markets in declining urban economies, and workers who provide low-wage labor in service and decentralized manufacturing employment in global cities.

The recent labor migration of Asian Pacific American women takes place in the context of global economic restructuring.[3] This macrostructural process refers to the integration of national economies into a single global labor market. From advanced capitalist nations such as the United States to developing nations such as the Philippines, countries trade goods and services, export products to achieve a viable economy, and depend on multinational corporations and foreign direct investments to increase domestic production.[4] This chapter situates the labor market experiences of recent Asian immigrant women in the globalization of the market economy.

It examines three categories of workers—unskilled laborers, entrepreneurs, and professionals. In this chapter, I show that, each in their own way, these three groups of workers provide "cheap labor" to the U.S. economy—meaning, the costs of their labor are cheap acquisitions for U.S. society and/or the conditions of their employment are below prevailing labor standards. The shared experience of providing cheap labor should be underscored because it is a platform for coalition among diverse classes of immigrant Asian women.

Global Restructuring

As the development of a single global market economy contributes to the formation of a decentered global labor market—that is, multiple consumer markets in different regions of the world—it also results in the relocation of production. Under globalization, manufacturing activities have moved from advanced capitalist countries such as the United States to developing countries such as the Philippines and newly industrialized nations such as Korea; for as an intratrade industry develops in globalization (i.e., countries trade similar goods), domestic producers must compete with foreign producers and businesses more than ever to find low-cost resources (e.g., labor and materials) to reduce production costs and maximize profits. Consequently, 25 percent of U.S. manufacturing is done outside the country's national borders.[5]

A new global division of labor is forming from the relocation of manufacturing production. As manufacturing has declined significantly in advanced capitalist nations, export-oriented economies have emerged across the globe. There is a difference between the growth potential of nations that export primary goods and those that export more highly demanded manufactured goods. As shown by the economic boom of the newly industrialized countries in East Asia, the latter are more likely to achieve rapid economic growth.

Globalization does not bode as well for export-based nations without highly demanded goods. Nations such as Sri Lanka and the Philippines not only seek investments of transnational corporations and export products or goods manufactured in free-trade zones; they also export the bodies of their citizens to introduce foreign currency into their economies. The Philippines is doing so to a growing extent, as the number of emigrants (who send remittances) has increased steadily since the 1970s. Numbering fewer than 50,000 in the early to mid-1970s, the number of overseas contract workers annually deployed jumped to 266,243 in 1981 and to more than 700,000 workers in 1994. Of these workers, roughly 60 percent are women.[6]

Globalization induces labor migration from export-oriented developing countries to both newly industrialized nations such as Singapore and Malaysia and advanced capitalist nations in North America and Europe. In the case of newly industrialized nations, the traditional proletariat female workforce, who would otherwise perform low-wage service jobs, now seek higher-paying manufacturing positions. This shift in labor market concentration generates a need for the lower wage labor of women, prompting emigration from neighboring countries such as the Philippines.

In advanced capitalist countries, secondary tiers of manufacturing and service industries have expanded under globalization. To compete with low production costs in developing countries, corporations now increasingly rely on post-Fordist modes of production, decentralized and deregulated forms of manufacturing such as those reflected in assembly lines and sweatshops. Low-wage service jobs have also increased because of the emergence of global cities, where multinational corporations with production facilities across the globe maintain their central operations. Specialized professional services (e.g., legal, financial, accounting, and consulting services) in these new economic centers (e.g., New York and Los Angeles) generate a need for low-wage services to maintain the lifestyles of professionals.[7] The vulnerability of Asian immigrant women, who face social, political, and cultural barriers (e.g., language), makes them a target group to fill various low-wage positions.

Globalization also spurs the migration of skilled workers. Both newly industrialized nations and advanced capitalist nations fill labor shortages by recruiting professionals from developing countries. In a stratified global economy, such workers are attracted by the higher wages offered in more developed nations. Moreover, they seek the knowledge brought about by the greater technological advances in these nations. However, sending nations usually lose, as skills are transferred out of their country. Migration consequently results in the shortage of certain skilled labor in export-oriented nations. In contrast, receiving nations benefit from the skills of immigrant professionals without having to invest in the costs of the education and training needed to reproduce their skilled workforce.

Not surprisingly, the Immigration Act of 1990 put into effect legislation that responded to the economic need for the U.S. workforce to have a supply of highly skilled professionals and technicians. At the same time, this law acknowledged the existing need for the U.S. economy to maintain a supply of low-wage workers. Under this act, the United States raised the number of occupational preference visas from 534,000 to 738,000 by 1995.[8] Preference was given to migrants with "extraordinary ability," for example, those with advanced degrees, or professionals. Eligibility was also given to ten thousand "other workers," including the unskilled.

An Overview of the Labor Market Activities of Asian Immigrant Women

Since the 1930s, women have for the most part outnumbered male migrants in the United States.[9] The shift from a male- to a female-dominated flow of immigrants took place with the prioritization of family reunification as an immigration criterion, beginning most critically with the War Brides Act of 1945.[10] This trend continued with the Hart-Cellar Act, or 1965 Immigration Act, which ended four decades of Asian immigration restrictions and increased the immigration quota to twenty thousand for each country. This law radically changed the composition of the Asian population by gender and level of educational attainment with the direct recruitment of skilled workers. Taking advantage of the priority given to family-based migration, these workers, in turn, have sponsored the migration of their relatives. In fact, most Asian immigrants, including the Chinese, Asian Indians, and Filipinos, enter the United States via family-preference categories.[11]

Due to the large inflow of migrants, the Asian American population grew exponentially, from 1.5 million in 1970 to 3.7 million in 1980 and to 7.3 million in 1990. The majority of Asians (65.6 percent) in the United States in 1990 were foreign-born.[12] This flow is also women dominated. Between 1975 and 1980, working-age women immigrants from China, the Philippines, Taiwan, Korea, Burma, Indonesia, Japan, and Thailand outnumbered men.[13] The notable exception has been India, where men constitute a greater number of working-age migrants, likely due to the high demand for their skills in science and technology.

Most Asian women migrate as part of a family unit. Approximately 75 percent of professional Asian immigrants who entered the United States between 1988 and 1990 migrated with their families. Moreover, Southeast Asian refugees usually enter the United States with their families.[14] While many Asian women enter the United States as "secondary migrants," to create or reunite a family, they also enter as primary migrants who sponsor the migration of families. This is especially true of Filipinos. The heavy recruitment of nurses spurred the primary migration of women in this community.

Regardless of their mode of entry into the United States, Asian immigrant women actively participate in the labor market. They contribute to the family income and maintain dual-wage-earning households so as to make up for their husband's earnings, which are generally lower than those of native-born men. Income pooling is the primary reason for the high median family income of Asian Americans.[15] Of the general female population age sixteen years and over, 56.8 percent are in the paid labor force.[16] As Table 1 indicates, the percentage of labor market participation of Asian immigrant women compared to immigrant men varies by ethnic group.

Notably, the rate of labor force participation among Filipina immigrant women far exceeds that of the general population and of other Asian groups and is much higher than in the Philippines, where women's labor force participation was 33.7 percent in 1992.[17] Their higher labor force participation has various reasons, including their better command of the English language and concentration in wage labor. Filipinos have the lowest rate of self-employment in the United States, at thirty-two per thousand. In contrast, the rate of self-employment for the general U.S. population stands at 69.74 per 1,000 and is even higher for other Asian ethnic groups: 180.46 per 1,000 for the Koreans and 72.77 per 1,000 for the Chinese.[18] Thus, it is likely that the rate of labor market participation for other Asian immigrant women is undercounted because the assistance they offer as wives in family businesses is not officially recognized as paid labor activity.

For Asian immigrant women, their generally high levels but also diverse range of educational attainment within and across ethnic groups have implications for their employment. In 1990, 20.3 percent of the U.S. general population had completed four years of college.[19] In contrast, the level of educational attainment of foreign-born Asian women in the five largest ethnic groups is significantly higher (Table 2). Only Southeast Asian refugees have a much lower percentage than the general population.

Filipina and Chinese women occupy a wide variety of jobs in the labor market, while other Asian ethnic groups are more highly concentrated in particular occupational categories, for instance, Koreans in self-employment and Vietnamese in low-wage employment. In some ethnic groups, the labor market incorporation of women is bifurcated.

TABLE 1

Labor Market Participation of Asian American and Asian Immigrant Women (by percentage), 1990

	All	Foreign-born
Japanese	47.5	40.8
Chinese	65.4	57.8
Filipina	77.7	73.1
Korean	61.0	55.5
Indian	56.9	59.6
Vietnamese	56.9	55.8

Source: U.S. Census, *1990 Census of the Population, Asians and Pacific Islanders in the United States.* Washington, D.C.: U.S. Government Printing Office, 1993.

TABLE 2

Educational Attainment of Bachelor's Degree or Higher of Asian American and Asian Immigrant Women, 1990

	All	Foreign-born
Chinese	35.0	32.4
Filipina	41.6	44.5
Japanese	28.2	22.2
Asian Indian	48.7	49.0
Korean	25.9	25.5
Vietnamese	12.2	12.7
Cambodian	3.2	3.1
Hmong	3.0	3.0
Laotian	3.5	3.4
Thai	24.9	24.9

Source: U.S. Census, 1990 *Census of the Population, Asians and Pacific Islanders in the United States.* Washington, D.C.: U.S. Government Printing Office, 1993.

For example, 24.6 percent of employed Chinese female migrants are in managerial and professional occupations and 29.7 percent are in service and manufacturing production employment.[20] This contradicts the common description of immigrant women as mostly disadvantaged low-paid workers in dead-end jobs, with limited financial security and upward mobility.[21]

Although the generally high level of educational attainment among Asian immigrant women has allowed them to seek a wider range of occupations than their Latina and Caribbean counterparts, the educational capital of Asian immigrant women does not necessarily mirror the characteristics of their labor market incorporation. Skilled Asian immigrant women have turned to lower-skilled occupations because of restrictive measures against foreign-trained professionals as well as language barriers.[22] For instance, in 1990, 23.7 percent of Asian Indian women migrants held professional and managerial occupations, even though 49 percent of them had completed four or more years of college.[23]

Underemployment is a quintessential way that Asian immigrant women provide "cheap labor" for the skills that they bring into the U.S. labor market. An example is the case of migrant Filipina domestic workers. In my study of Filipina domestic workers in Los Angeles, I found that seventeen of twenty-six interviewees have achieved some years of college.[24] Ten had education degrees and worked as teachers prior to migration. As domestic workers, they enhance the low-cost services that they provide employers by offering free tutoring and other educational services to their wards.

To summarize, Asian immigrant women have a high rate of labor market participation and a diverse range of levels of educational attainment. Unlike other immigrant women, they hold a wide variety of occupations in the U.S. labor market and actively participate in the labor force in myriad ways.

Asian Immigrant Women and Global Restructuring

How are the labor market activities of contemporary Asian immigrant women situated in global restructuring and linked together? Addressing a similar question, Lisa Lowe illustrates the material links that tie the activities of low-wage manufacturing Asian women migrant workers to those in Asia by situating them in global restructuring. As she describes:

> Women migrate from countries of origin formerly colonized by the United States, or currently neocolonized by U.S. corporate capital and come to labor here as racialized women of color. In this sense, despite the obstacles of national, cultural, and linguistic differences, there are material continuities between the conditions of Chicanas and Latinas working in the United States and the women working in maquiladoras and low-cost manufacturing zones in Latin America, on the one hand, and Asian women working both within the United States and in Asian zones of assembly and manufacturing, on the other.[25]

The material continuities that Lowe draws between low-wage women workers across advanced capitalist and developing nations should be extended to include other groups of Asian migrant workers, as they are also part of the singular socioeconomic process of globalization and in various ways provide low-cost labor for the benefit of the U.S. economy.

Low-Wage Workers

Asian immigrant women fill the labor market need for low-wage manufacturing and service workers in urban centers of the United States. They are in decentralized industries, particularly in the garment industry, performing low-wage assembly jobs, and they provide services, including affordable manicures, to middle- and upper-class professionals.

With the offshore relocation of manufacturing, the production that does remain in the United States (e.g., garment, electronics, and furniture production) is decentralized and informal. For instance, the garment industry is structured like a pyramid. Manufacturers cut the costs of production by subcontracting to garment shops and awarding contracts to the lowest bidders. Consequently, they do not leave contractors with much capital to pay seamstresses wages that meet prevailing labor standards. As a result, native women usually shun this work. Without the same opportunities and human capital (e.g., language proficiency) as their native counterparts, immigrant women, including Asian women, fill this existing demand in the labor market.

Garment shops tend to be located in ethnic enclaves such as Chinatown, where the access of potential immigrant entrepreneurs to a pool of co-ethnics as a cheap labor force makes them more attractive and lucrative. Immigrant entrepreneurs are also attracted to sewing shops because they require fewer investment and lower overhead costs than other businesses. For instance, in Oakland, newspaper ads indicated that "$25,000 is sufficient to start a ten to fifteen person shop."[26]

By using immigrant labor, small-business operators facilitate the process of global restructuring. In the garment industry, they give manufacturers direct access to the low human capital of immigrant women. In this way, manufacturers can remain flexible to the constant turnover in fashion trends and at the same time remain competitive against production in the Third World. Overworked and underpaid, immigrant seamstresses are usually paid by piece rate and often lack overtime pay, as well as health insurance and other work compensations.[27]

In the global cities of New York, San Francisco, and Los Angeles, sewing jobs have pulled a large number of Chinese female immigrants into the bottom rungs of the garment industry and made them "the garment workers par excellence." In New York City, over half of Chinese immigrant women workers are in the garment industry, with most of them working as sewing-machine operators.[28] In the San Francisco Bay Area, 90 percent of garment workers are women, with over 80 percent of them Chinese-speaking.[29] In Los Angeles, approximately 10 percent of the estimated 120,000 garment workers are Asians.[30]

Streamlining production is another way that U.S. manufacturers reduce overhead costs. For the most part, low-level manufacturing employment has been divided into simpler and simpler tasks and is therefore low-paying. These jobs are often unsafe (e.g., they expose workers to hazardous materials), are monotonous, and require few skills.[31]

In the Midwest, meatpacking plants increasingly rely on the low-wage labor provided by Southeast Asian refugees. For Vietnamese and Laotian women, packing plants are often their best option for employment, as the work requires few skills (e.g., jobs are set up as mechanized assembly work), provides better pay than other available low-skill employment, and is now shunned by the Anglo American men who traditionally dominated the industry.[32] In Silicon Valley, one study indicates that in the late 1980s women made up approximately 80 percent of production workers, with most being members of minority groups and with Filipina women as the largest group of recent migrants entering assembly-line manufacturing.[33]

Low-wage service work is another way that Asian immigrant women provide cheap labor to the U.S. economy. Many of the available low-wage service jobs are considered women's work, as they have been relegated to women historically in a sex-segmented labor market. These personal and industrial services are provided in different economic sectors, including the informal sector (e.g., domestic workers), the formal industry sector (e.g., hotel housekeepers, restaurant workers, and certified nurse's aides), and ethnic economies (e.g., manicurists and restaurant workers).[34]

Providing low-wage service is difficult work. Domestic work such as elder care may require twenty-four hours of labor.[35] Trinidad Borromeo, a sixty-eight-year-old woman whom I interviewed in Rome, describes a daily work routine that generally reflects those of her counterparts in Los Angeles.[36]

> I begin at seven in the morning. I change her, feed her, give her all of her injections and medication. Then I clean the apartment. When you take care of an elder, the first thing you have to have is patience. If you don't have it, you won't last. For example, when you feed her, it can take up to an hour. It gets hard when they don't want to open their mouth or swallow the food. But taking care of an elder like this one is better than a mobile one. Those ones are demanding. You wipe them already then they want you to wipe them again. They have no shame. These types are better . . . you just move them around from the bed to the chair. You have to just clean her bed everyday because it will smell like pee around the house if you don't. . . . I wake up at four in the morning just to check that the woman is still alive. Then if there is no problem, I sleep until a little bit before seven and I am done with her by nine. I just serve her coffee and biscuits. I sleep around midnight or one in the morning.

Despite their nonstop labor, elder caregivers seldom take a day off because of the tremendous emotional dependence of their elderly patients.[37]

Along with their Caribbean and Latina counterparts, contemporary Asian immigrant women respond to the demand for low-wage service labor in various global cities in the United States, but they do so to a much lesser degree. Yet they are more heavily concentrated in this labor market sector in certain cities. For example, according to the Pilipino Worker's Center, immigrant Filipina workers dominate elder caregiving in Los Angeles, in both personal (e.g., private home) and industrial (e.g., nursing home) services.[38] In the Filipino immigrant community, recent women migrants frequently turn to domestic work because of their limited options in the labor market.[39] In a study of undocumented women in the San Francisco Bay Area, Chris Hogeland and Karen

Rosen found that 41 percent of fifty-seven survey participants from the Philippines are elder care or childcare workers and an additional 23 percent are employed as house-keepers.[40]

Other groups of Asian immigrant women provide low-paid services through ethnic economies. For instance, ethnic entrepreneurs have taken up running nail salons to take advantage of the concentration of service professionals in global cities.[41] In this way, Asian immigrant women provide cheap labor by making this luxury affordable to a wider range of consumers. Any visitor to New York or Los Angeles will notice the abundance of nail salons operated by Korean and Vietnamese women who provide low-cost services to compete with each other. One study found that Koreans operate up to 80 percent of nail salons in New York City.[42]

Small-Business Entrepreneurs

Contemporary Asian immigrant workers contribute to the economic development of global cities in another crucial way. They spur economic growth with the operation of small businesses. For example, they provide convenient services such as dry cleaning to the growing professional class and run contracting shops that are part of the informal manufacturing economy.

Immigrant Koreans have entered the deteriorating urban centers of the United States in full force; more than 50 percent of them operate small businesses.[43] Many of these businesses are not enclosed in ethnic enclave economies (e.g., Koreatown) but instead cater to a larger urban clientele. These types of urban businesses include greengrocers, dry cleaners, liquor stores, and retail shops of Asian manufactured goods (e.g., wigs, clothing). Opening a business in an urban area is more affordable for prospective entrepreneurs than in, for example, the safer area of the suburbs. High levels of crime and poverty have made urban neighborhoods—ghettos and barrios—what Jennifer Lee calls "vacant niches," as local economies have been abandoned by large corporations such as gasoline companies and supermarkets.[44] Taking advantage of these abandoned neighborhoods, Koreans have franchised gasoline stations and opened groceries and liquor stores in these "high-risk" markets. In doing so, they give big businesses access to these once-deserted markets but at the same time absorb the risks that the big businesses choose to avoid.

Immigrants are often disadvantaged to compete against the native-born in the primary labor market because they are unable to put to use their educational and occupational capital, face language difficulties and discrimination, and are unfamiliar with American cultural practices.[45] To avoid low-wage jobs like those performed by Chinese garment workers or Filipino hotel housekeepers in San Francisco, immigrants with class and ethnic resources may choose to operate small businesses to better negotiate the segmented U.S. labor market. In doing so, they take advantage of the business know-how brought by their human capital (e.g., high levels of educational attainment) and the ethnic resources (e.g., rotating credit associations) that make available financial capital required to open a business.[46]

Although they have more resources and advantages than contemporary Asian immigrant women in low-wage manufacturing and service employment, small-business entrepreneurs provide cheap labor as well.[47] First, the maintenance of such businesses requires long hours. As Kyeyoung Park describes, "Korean men and women involved in small business often work more than twelve hours daily and six or seven days a week. According to an August 1987 survey by the Korean American Small Business Service Center of New York, 85 percent of Korean proprietors kept their stores open more than ten hours per day. Some 70 percent used family labor."[48] Second, businesses also rely on the unpaid labor of wives and children. How do long hours and family work translate to cheap labor? Edna Bonacich explains, "If one adds up the hours of work put into many immigrant enterprises and divides that number by the money taken out of business to live on, the result is not infrequently a very low rate of earnings."[49]

In general, small ethnic businesses could not possibly survive without family labor, most importantly the often unrecognized labor of women. While unrecognized, the work of women in small businesses also suffers from a gendered hierarchy that relegates the "less skilled" and thus more monotonous work to them. For instance, men often take over the managerial tasks (e.g., accounting) that are required in the daily operation of small Korean businesses. Similarly, in Chinese take-away shops in England, Miri Song observed that mothers often performed the more labor-intensive and unskilled labor in the kitchen.[50] By relegating the less-skilled and seemingly less important work to women, men are able to justify their own lower contributions to housework. As a result, the "double day" plagues women in small businesses as well as in low-wage work. Women are not only expected to keep long hours in small businesses but are also relied upon to perform the bulk of domestic chores in the household.[51]

Professional Women

The global labor market also needs to attract the highly skilled professionals to their global cities. In this way, advanced capitalist countries such as the United States economically benefit from immigrants' know-how while amending the shortages in certain skilled professions that have been created by cutbacks in social spending.

The growth of capitalism in the United States has led to the greater reduction of social, health, and education benefits to society.[52] As such, the labor shortage of professionals in the United States, which is an acute problem in the fields of science, engineering, and health, is an institutionalized structural problem that has been mended in part by the recruitment of Asian professionals. These workers provide cheap labor in that their educational training did not cost the United States any money. By facilitating their entry, the U.S. government can avoid the consequences of its failure to invest in the reproductive costs of the country's labor force. The highly skilled labor of Asian immigrants, particularly women, is also arguably cheaper than that provided by their native-born counterparts. One study found that Asian women who are employed in core industries earn $2,179.06 less than white female scientists and engineers.[53]

Recent Asian immigrants have helped fill the professional labor force shortage. From 1988 to 1990, more than half of the 150,000 highly skilled migrants who entered the United States originated in Asia.[54] That they have done so more than any other group is a legacy of U.S. colonialism.[55] In particular, the modeling of the educational infrastructure in Asia after that in the United States has homogenized educational standards and objectives to create an expanded international labor pool of professionals who constitute an available resource for the U.S. labor market.[56]

Due to the direct recruitment of Asian professionals into the United States, the percentage of Asian American scientists and engineers increased from 2 percent in 1970 to 7 percent in 1990. Moreover, the numbers of scientists and engineers increased by 603 percent, escalating from just 21,000 to 150,000 in two decades.[57] While the majority of professional immigrants are men, 42 percent of the highly skilled Asian migrants who entered the United States from 1988 to 1990 were women.[58]

A high percentage (68 percent) of highly skilled women from the Philippines entered the United States during this time. As the Philippines is the largest source of foreign-trained health professionals in the United States, many entered as nurses, for which the labor shortage is estimated at 370,000.[59] The reluctance of the United States to invest in the reproductive costs of its labor force is much to blame for this shortage. As Paul Ong, Edna Bonacich, and Lucie Cheng describe:

> The United States has been reluctant to spend money on the training of health personnel, such as nurses, in a general effort at cost containment for health care. The ultimate goal is to reduce health care costs for capitalist employers by lowering the costs of their benefits packages. This policy creates a shortage of nurses in the United States and a demand for immigrant nurses.[60]

Yet the process of labor migration is neither easy nor convenient. In most cases, Filipina nurses first enter as temporary workers. During this time, they are ineligible to sponsor the migration of their families, whom they are forced to leave behind in the Philippines. Foreign-trained nurses also relieve the sponsoring medical facility of the costs of their recruitment and bear most of the costs of their labor placement. On average, migration to the United States costs Filipino nurses $7,000, which is usually deducted from their pay.[61] This debt binds them and consequently leaves them vulnerable to the sponsoring facility. Once in the United States, they also find themselves with the most demanding and stressful jobs. In the mid-1980s, one survey found that 82 percent of Filipino nurses work in hospitals, versus 53 percent of non-Filipinos.[62] Often these hospitals are concentrated in inner cities and are more congested and busier than other health facilities.

At the same time that the "cheapening of labor" in the United States has forced employers to turn to the recruitment of professional Asian workers, it has also deepened the cheap labor pool and limited the opportunities of underprivileged members of society. As Ong, Bonacich, and Cheng describe:

> In general, the cheap labor approach to restructuring has the impact of curbing the development of local professionals by limiting the opportunities of the local working class. People who work for minimum wage can hardly afford to send their children to college. Attacks on the working class thus have the consequence of undermining the strategy of reorganization and innovation by limiting the growth of the class that can implement it. This contradiction sets the stage for the immigration of professionals and managers.[63]

Thus, while the entrance of professionals into receiving nations such as the United States helps deepen the cheap labor pool, global restructuring also generates the need for their recruitment.

Conclusion

The labor market activities of recent Asian immigrant women indicate that their economic adaptation is unlike that of other groups of immigrant women. They can be found in a wide variety of occupations in the U.S. labor market, both cross-ethnically and within ethnic groups. As such, it is difficult categorically to address their labor market incorporation in a singular framework that is inclusive of the diverse range of their labor market activities. The high rate of labor market participation of Asian immigrant women as well as the diversity of their labor market activities attest to the feminization of the wage labor force under globalization. However, the conditions of their labor market incorporation and their low standards of employment suggest that women still hold a fairly low status in the labor market.

By surveying the labor market activities of recent Asian immigrant women and by viewing these activities as processes embedded in global restructuring, I argued that they provide cheap labor in the U.S. economy in myriad ways. The concept of cheap labor is one that I loosely describe to mean that in some way the costs of their labor are "cheap" acquisitions for U.S. society and/or the conditions of their employment are below prevailing labor standards. This definition applies to unskilled workers, ethnic entrepreneurs, and professionals. For instance, it is applicable to the experiences of migrant Filipina nurses whose training did not come with any financial costs to the United States, to the Korean women who operate small businesses for long hours, and to the Chinese immigrant women who dominate the needletrade in various global cities in the United States.

The women workers in the three categories I have surveyed have unequal levels of mobility. They face different opportunities and constraints. While they may share the opportunity to earn more than they would in their countries of origin, a nurse such as Beth Orozo and a domestic worker such as Genny O'Connor cannot be considered equally displaced by the capitalist system in the United States. For one, Beth has been able to transfer her educational capital, while Genny clearly has not. Thus, our understanding of their labor market activities should not disregard their differences.

So as not to ignore the diversity of the labor market participation of Asian immigrant women, my analysis emphasizes the specificities in the location of three groups of workers in the larger schema of global restructuring. My analytical approach accounts for the specific contexts of each of these groups' labor market incorporation. Employing such an approach shows that the material realities of their labor are quite different. At the same time, it shows that from their specific location in global restructuring, Asian immigrant women contribute some form of "cheap labor" to the United States.

NOTES

1. Rhacel Salazar Parreñas, *Servants of Globalization: Woman, Migration, and Domestic Work* (Stanford, CA: Stanford University Press, 2001), 150.

2. Personal interview with author, Iloilo City, Philippines, May 2001.

3. By recent immigrants, I refer to those who entered after 1965, which is when the United States eliminated discriminatory racial barriers and established an open-door policy based on the criteria of occupational skills and family reunification.

4. David Held, David Goldblatt McGrew, and Jonathan Perraton, *Global Transformations: Politics, Economics, and Culture* (Stanford, CA: Stanford University Press, 1999), chaps. 3–5.

5. Harold Perkin, *The Third Revolution: Professional Elites in the Modern World* (London and New York: Routledge, 1996), 19.

6. Parreñas, *Servants of Globalization*, chap. 2.

7. Saskia Sassen-Koob, "Notes on the Incorporation of Third World Women into Wage Labor through Immigration and Offshore Production," *International Migration Review* 18:4 (1984): 1144–67.

8. Kitty Calavita, "Gaps and Contradictions in U.S. Immigration Policy: An Analysis of Recent Reform Effects," in David Jacobson, ed., *The Immigration Reader: America in a Multidisciplinary Perspective* (Malden, MA: Blackwell, 1998), 105.

9. Marion F. Houstoun, Roger G. Kramer, and Joan Mackin Barrett, "Female Predominance of Immigration to the United States since 1930: A First Look," *International Migration Review* 28:4 (1984): 908–63.

10. This law facilitated the entrance of more than two hundred thousand Asian war brides, fiancées, and children into the United States. See Judy Yung, "Appendix: A Chronology of Asian American History," in Asian Women United of California, eds., *Making Waves: An Anthology of Writings by and about Asian American Women* (Boston: Beacon Press, 1989), 423–31.

11. See Bill Ong Hing, "Asian Immigrants: Social Forces Unleashed after 1965," in Jacobson, ed., *The Immigration Reader*, 144–82; and Pyong Gap Min, "An Overview of Asian Americans," in Pyong Gap Min, ed., *Asian Americans: Contemporary Trends and Issues* (Thousand Oaks, CA: Sage Publications, 1995), 10–37.

12. U.S. Census, *1990 Census of the Population, Asians and Pacific Islanders in the United States* (Washington, D.C.: U.S. Government Printing Office, 1993).

13. Yen Le Espiritu, *Asian American Women and Men* (Thousand Oaks, CA: Sage Publications, 1997), 63.

14. Ibid., 62.

15. Alejandro Portes and Rubén Rumbaut, *Immigrant America*, 2d ed. (Berkeley: University of California Press, 1998).

16. U.S. Census, *Census of Population and Housing, 1990 PUMS* (Washington, D.C.: U.S. Government Printing Office, 1993).

17. Sylvia Chant, *Women-headed Households: Diversity and Dynamics in the Developing World* (New York: St. Martin's Press, 1997).

18. Portes and Rumbaut, *Immigrant America*, 72.

19. U.S. Census, *Census of Population and Housing, 1990 PUMS.*

20. U.S. Census, *1990 Census of the Population, Asians and Pacific Islanders in the United States.*

21. According to Linda Miller Matthei, half of immigrant women enter low-wage employment in operations and services, because they lack educational credentials and have few employment skills. See "Gender and International Labor Migration: A Networks Approach," in

Susanne Jonas and Suzie Dod Thomas, eds., *Immigration: A Civil Rights Issue for the Americas* (Wilmington, DE: Scholarly Resources Inc, 1999), 77.

22. Examples are provided by Esther Chow, "Asian American Women at Work," in Maxine Baca Zinn and Bonnie Thornton Dill, eds., *Women of Color in U.S. Society* (Philadelphia: Temple University Press, 1994), 203–27.

23. Keiko Yamanaka and Kent McClelland, "Earning the Model Minority Image: Diverse Strategies of Economic Adaptation by Asian American Women," *Ethnic and Racial Studies* 17:1 (January 1994): 79–114.

24. Parreñas, *Servants of Globalization*, introduction.

25. Lisa Lowe, *Immigrant Acts: On Asian American Cultural Politics* (Durham, NC and London: Duke University Press, 1996), 165.

26. Miriam Ching Louie, "Immigrant Asian Women in Bay Area Garment Shops: 'After Sewing, Laundry, Cleaning and Cooking, I Have No Breath Left to Sing,'" *Amerasia Journal* 18:1 (1992): 1–26.

27. See also Xiaolin Bao, chapter 17, in this book.

28. Nancy Foner, "Benefits and Burdens: Immigrant Women and Work in New York City," *Gender Issues* 16:4 (1998): 8.

29. Louie, "Immigrant Asian Women," 2.

30. Richard Kim, Kane K. Nakamura, and Giselle Fong, with Ron Cabarloc, Barbara Jung, and Sung Lee, "Asian Immigrant Women Garment Workers in Los Angeles," *Amerasia Journal* 18:1 (1992): 69.

31. Karen Hossfeld, "Hiring Immigrant Women: Silicon Valley's 'Simple Formula,'" in Zinn and Dill, eds., *Women of Color*, 765–93.

32. Janet E. Benson, "The Effects of Packinghouse Work on Southeast Asian Refugee Families," in L. Lamphere, A. Stepick, and G. Grenier, eds., *Newcomers in the Workplace: Immigrants and the Restructuring of the U.S. Economy* (Philadelphia: Temple University Press, 1994), 109.

33. Rebecca Villones, "Women in the Silicon Valley," in Asian Women United of California, eds., *Making Waves*, 172.

34. See Ivan Light, Georges Sabagh, Mehdi Bozorgmehr, and Claudia Der-Martirosian, "Beyond the Ethnic Enclave Economy," *Social Problems* 41:1 (1994): 65–79. By definition, *ethnic economy* refers to the self-employed with co-ethnic employees.

35. Charlene Tung, "The Cost of Caring: The Social Reproductive Labor of Filipina Live-in Home Health Caregivers," *Frontiers* 21:1/2 (2000): 72.

36. Parreñas, *Servants of Globalization*, 159.

37. Tung, "The Cost of Caring," 76.

38. Informational brochure provided by Pilipino Worker's Center, 1996.

39. This is caused by a combination of their undocumented status, their inability to put to use their training and work experience from the Philippines, and the ethnic niche in caregiving that has developed in the Filipino migrant community from the large flow of nurses into the United States.

40. Chris Hogeland and Karen Rosen, *Dreams Lost, Dreams Found: Undocumented Women in the Land of Opportunity* (San Francisco: San Francisco Coalition for Immigrant Rights and Services, 1990).

41. Millian Kang, "Manicuring Race, Gender, and Class: Service Interactions in New York City Korean-owned Nail Salons," *Race, Gender, and Class* 4:3 (1997): 143–64.

42. Kyeyoung Park, *The Korean American Dream* (Ithaca, NY: Cornell University Press, 1997), 117.

43. Pyong Gap Min, "Korean Americans," in Min, ed., *Asian Americans*, 199–231.

44. Jennifer Lee, "Striving for the American Dream: Struggle, Success, and Intergroup Conflict among Korean Immigrant Entrepreneurs," in Min Zhou and James Gatewood, eds., *Contemporary Asian America: A Multidisciplinary Reader* (New York: New York University Press, 1999), 284.

45. Ibid., 280.

46. Ivan Light and Edna Bonacich, *Immigrant Entrepreneurs: Koreans in Los Angeles, 1965–1982* (Berkeley: University of California Press, 1988).

47. Edna Bonacich, "The Social Costs of Immigrant Entrepreneurship," *Amerasia Journal* 14:1 (1988): 119–28.

48. Kyeyoung Park, "Impact of New Productive Activities on the Organization of Domestic Life: A Case Study of the Korean American Community," in Gail M. Nomura, Russell Endo, Stephen H. Sumida, and Russell C. Leong, eds., *Frontiers of Asian American Studies* (Pullman: Washington State University Press, 1989), 147.

49. Bonacich, "Secret Costs," 120.

50. Miri Song, *Helping Out: Children's Labor in Ethnic Businesses* (Philadelphia: Temple University Press, 1999), 55.

51. Park, "Impact of New Productive Activities," 140–50.

52. Paul Ong, Edna Bonacich, and Lucie Cheng, "The Political Economy of Capitalist Restructuring and the New Asian Immigration," in P. Ong, E. Bonacich, and L. Cheng, eds., *The New Asian Immigration in Los Angeles and Global Restructuring* (Philadelphia: Temple University Press, 1994), 3–35.

53. Shang-Luan Yan, "The Status of Asian American Women Scientists and Engineers in the Labor Force," *Race, Gender, and Class* 6:3 (1999): 119.

54. William Kanjanapan, "The Immigration of Asian Professionals to the United States: 1988–1990," *International Migration Review* 291 (1995): 15.

55. John Liu and Lucie Cheng, "Duality of Post-1965 Asian Immigration," in Ong, Bonacich, and Cheng, eds., *New Asian Immigration*, 80.

56. Ong, Bonacich, and Cheng, "Political Economy of Capitalist Restructuring," 3–35.

57. Paul Ong and Evelyn Blumenberg, "Scientists and Engineers," in Darrell Y. Hamamoto and Rodolfo D. Torres, eds., *New American Destinies: A Reader in Contemporary Asian and Latino Immigration* (New York: Routledge, 1997), 166.

58. Kanjanapan, "Immigration of Asian Professionals," 20.

59. See Paul Ong and Tania Azores, "The Migration and Incorporation of Filipino Nurses" in Ong, Bonacich, and Cheng, eds., *New Asian Immigration*, 164–95.

60. Ong, Bonacich, and Cheng, "Political Economy of Capitalist Restructuring," 25.

61. Information obtained from informal interviews I conducted with recruitment agencies and prospective migrants in the Philippines between January and July 2000.

62. Ong and Azores, "Migration and Incorporation," 164. See also Catherine Ceniza Choy, chapter 20 in this book.

63. Ong, Bonacich, and Cheng, "Political Economy of Capitalist Restructuring," 25–26.

17

Politicizing Motherhood
Chinese Garment Workers' Campaign for Daycare Centers in New York City, 1977–1982

Xiaolan Bao

What impact does women's labor force participation have on transforming their positions in the family and their perceptions of life?[1] This has been an issue of major concern to scholars of women and labor in the last two decades. Various conclusions, often bifurcated and sometimes conflicting, have been reached in the studies of different groups of working women, focusing on different aspects of their lives, and written from different perspectives. Varied as the conclusions are, these studies have effectively challenged any simplistic attempt to dichotomize family and work by revealing the complex ways in which they intersect to shape the lives of working women.[2]

Unlike many studies that try to understand working women by studying the various forces that shape their lives, this chapter places women workers at the center of its analysis. Through an in-depth examination of a campaign for daycare centers initiated and organized by Chinese women garment workers in New York City, it reveals women immigrant workers' agency in reshaping their destinies in their new homeland and addresses some of the issues raised in the scholarship on women and labor.

The questions to be asked include: What are the major factors that have contributed to the rise of labor activism among the Chinese women workers? What strategies did they use, and how did these strategies contribute to their final success? What political implications did this campaign have for the workers, their community, and the labor movement in the United States? In what ways can this campaign complicate our understanding of women immigrant workers in the United States?

The analysis in this chapter is primarily based on information in the Chinese community newspapers and the author's interviews with individuals in the community from 1989 to 1998 for a larger project.[3] Some of these individuals have actively participated in the daycare campaign. This study begins with a brief discussion of the history of the Chinese community in New York City, the impact of the Chinese garment industry on the city and the community, and women's changing roles in the Chinese immigrant working-class families. It then proceeds to analyze the causes of the campaign and to examine its development, and it explores the campaign's political impact on the women workers, their families, and their community, as well as its implications for the study of women and labor.

Women, Family, and the Garment Industry in New York's Chinatown:
A Brief History

Unlike the situation in the major Chinese communities on the West Coast, the garment industry was not a part of the landscape of New York's Chinatown until the late 1960s. A principal reason for its absence was the scarcity of women in the community. Although the gender ratio was unequal in almost all Chinese communities in the United States before the end of the Second World War, it was even more so in New York City. By 1940, when the Chinese male-to-female ratio had dropped to about three to one nationally and two to one in California, it remained at more than six to one in New York City, and at more than nine to one among those fifteen years of age and older.[4] Given the garment industry's long-standing tradition of relying on low-paid female immigrant labor, it is not accidental that New York's Chinatown had not been a center for the city's garment production.

The Chinese gender ratio began to change during and after the Second World War, following a series of changes in U.S. immigration laws.[5] Women formed an overwhelming majority of the Chinese immigrants in the immediate postwar era. Between 1947 and 1952, 90 percent of the Chinese immigrants who entered the United States were women.[6] Since many of these new immigrant women settled in New York City, the city's Chinese gender ratio dipped from more than 6 men to 1 woman in 1940 to 1.7 to 1 in 1960.[7]

Women's immigration in the post–World War II era has revitalized the economy of the community. For decades, restaurants and laundries remained the city's two major Chinese businesses and employed primarily men. After the war, with married women entering the community in significant numbers, many of the Chinese restaurants and laundries were transformed into family businesses and grew significantly. Women's economic contributions were largely ignored, however, because they worked primarily at home. Particularly in the Chinese family laundry businesses, women, sometimes with their children, worked in the living quarters behind or above the store, while fulfilling their household responsibilities, and their husbands took care of the family businesses at the storefront, dealing with their customers. Since most of the businesses registered under the names of their male family heads, and since women's labor at home was largely ignored by the society, it should come as no surprise that as late as 1950, U.S. Census data show that less than one-quarter of the adult Chinese females in New York State were in the labor force.[8] The percentage was even lower among those who were foreign-born.[9] This societal refusal to acknowledge women's domestic contribution, coupled with the peculiar setting of their family businesses, reinforced the concept of traditional gender roles in Chinese working-class families.

Things changed significantly after 1965, when Congress passed an amendment to the McCarran-Walter Act. The family reunification preferences and the abolition of the discriminatory national quota system in this amendment triggered "chain immigration" from Asian countries. By the mid-1970s, Asian immigrants who arrived as family members of U.S. citizens or permanent residents constituted four-fifths of the total number of quota immigrants from Asia, and nearly one-fifth of those who arrived between 1965 and 1990 were Chinese.[10]

New York City, as the "port of immigrants," received the largest number of Chinese immigrants of any city in the nation. More than one-fifth of the Chinese immigrants who arrived between 1966 and 1976 registered New York City as their place of intended residence. With a fourfold increase in their numbers—growing from 32,831 to 124,764—Chinese began to account for 1.8 percent of the city's population. Women continued to form more than one-half of the Chinese immigrants coming into the city. As a result, the city's Chinese gender ratio reached a balance in 1980.[11]

Many of the Chinese immigrants who arrived in the city during this period lacked skills marketable in the United States. The 1979 unpublished data of the U.S. Immigration and Naturalization Service (INS) show that 70 percent of the Chinese immigrants who came to the city and reported their previous occupations had been blue-collar workers. This lack of skills was even more pronounced among immigrant women: only 28 percent of them reported having any previous employment experience, and of those who had been employed, 30 percent had worked in a factory and only 8.2 percent had experience in white-collar positions.[12] However, for the survival of their families they took whatever jobs that were available to them in their new homeland, since many of their husbands worked in restaurants or other low-paid labor sectors. Hence, new Chinese women immigrants became a much-desired labor reservoir for the city's garment industry.[13]

Chinese-owned garment shops first appeared in New York's Chinatown in the late 1940s, but their numbers remained small: about three in 1952 and eight in 1960. Many factors contributed to the growth of the Chinese garment industry in the late 1960s.[14] The most important one was the emergence of ample, inexpensive Chinese female immigrant labor at a time when the city's garment industry was severely crippled by a labor shortage. As Chinese women entered the industry in large numbers, the number of jobs in the Chinatown garment production center grew from eight thousand to sixteen thousand between 1965 and 1980, while those in the midtown garment center fell from forty thousand to twenty-five thousand. By 1981, Chinatown had become the largest garment production center in New York City, contributing at least $125 million annually to the city's economy in the form of wages and profits.[15]

The growth of the Chinatown garment industry was vital to the city's industry. As early as the 1920s, capital from the garment industry began to flow out of New York City. Although the absolute numbers of employees in the city's garment industry continued to grow, its share in the national industry declined rapidly. The growth of the Chinatown garment industry was not able to curb the continual decline of the city's garment industry, but it did help moderate it.[16] By the early 1980s, producing two-thirds of the sportswear for the manufacturers affiliated with the International Ladies' Garment Workers' Union (ILGWU) Local 23–25—work that otherwise would have been shipped out of the city—the Chinatown manufacturing center had effectively anchored the garment industry to New York City.[17]

The growth of the Chinatown garment industry also revitalized the economy of the Chinese community in the city. Beginning in the 1940s, and particularly in the 1950s and 1960s, the traditional Chinese laundry businesses were gradually edged out by the introduction of washing machines and dryers into the home and by the rise of laundromats in the city.[18] It was at this historical juncture, when the Chinese working-class families were hard hit by the decline of this traditional trade, that the Chinese garment industry began to take off. As early as the 1970s, it replaced the laundry business as one of the major sources of income for these families. By the early 1980s, four out of ten Chinese households in the city and six out of ten in Chinatown had members working in the garment industry. Annually contributing at least $32 million to the economic activities in Chinatown and $14 million to those in other Chinese neighborhoods in the city, the garment industry was central to the economy of the Chinese community in New York City.[19]

The impact of the garment industry on the community was not merely economic but also cultural. With plenty of employment opportunities provided by the Chinatown garment industry, the number of the Chinese women in the labor force grew rapidly. As early as 1970, almost half of adult Chinese women were gainfully employed. The percentage continued to rise in the following decade.[20] Like their European predecessors in the city's garment industry, the Chinese immigrant women workers were hard-working and determined to build a better life in their new homeland. However, unlike their predecessors, more than 86 percent of Chinese immigrant women in 1980 were married, and many had young children.[21] In a community where more than half the households were working-class and had members working in the ethnic economic sector, this high rate of married women's labor participation in the garment industry had a strong impact on transforming its working-class family culture. This cultural transformation has to be understood in terms of the economic structure of the community as well as women's increasingly important role in their families.

Since most of the working-class Chinese men worked in the low-paying labor sector, and their jobs offered no employment benefits, women's employment in the garment industry became crucial for the well-being of their families. Both their economic contribution, which was indispensable to their families, and the benefits, particularly the family health insurance that came with their employment in the unionized garment industry, which their families would not otherwise have been able to obtain, were essential. The prolonged absence of the husbands due to long hours of work also led many women garment workers to play dual roles as major "rice winners" and care providers in the family. A new type of mother-centered culture thus began to emerge in many Chinese working-class families.

What was the impact of this change on women? It was mixed. Like working mothers almost all over the world, Chinese women garment workers had to shoulder double and even triple burdens in their lives. As family tensions were aggravated by the reversed gender roles, some women had to endure additional stress in their lives from strained relationships with their husbands and other family members.[22] However, in many families, women's increased responsibilities also won them growing respect from their family members, particularly their children. Many sons and daughters of garment workers, some of whom are now playing important roles in the community, have singled out their mothers as the driving force in their lives.[23] In some families, the increasingly interdependent relationship between the women workers and their husbands also had the potential to create a more equal relationship between them.

How did women workers themselves react to these changes? Many whom I interviewed took pride in the increased respect they enjoyed in their families and defined the goal of their lives as to fight for a better future for their families. This reaction should not be interpreted simply as the influence of an ethnic culture that valued traditional gender roles. Rather, it must also be understood in the context of their lives after their immigration to the United States. In a new social environment that offered them few alternatives, many women have developed their own visions of a better life. Influenced by a culture that considers education a major channel of upward mobility and that holds children responsible for the lives of their aging parents, the prospect that their wage-earning labor could help them provide their children with a better education led women to see the positive aspect of their labor in the garment shops, however hard it was. The dynamics generated by this interaction of the influence of their ethnic culture and their realities encouraged them to struggle against any conditions at their work-places that they perceived to be in conflict with their goals. Only in this context can we understand why, from the outset of the Chinatown garment industry, many Chinese women immigrant workers who appeared to be so culturally bound would have en-gaged in various forms of resistance to mistreatment imposed on them in the shops.

Like their counterparts in the earlier history of the city's garment industry, most Chinatown shops were contract shops. To make a profit out of the margin between pay-ments offered by the manufacturers and the piece rates they offered their workers, many Chinese employers stretched the limits of labor laws. They argued that the flexi-ble work hours in the garment shops had offered women workers an opportunity to balance their work and family responsibilities. However, the degree of flexibility that the workers presumably enjoyed was more myth than reality. Since work in the garment industry was seasonal and operated at piece rates, the working environment on the shop floor was highly competitive.

Nevertheless, for all the disadvantages of their workplaces, working in the garment shops provided the Chinese immigrant women with an important window to the world beyond their own ethnic setting. Unlike other ethnic enterprises in Chinatown, most of the Chinatown garment shops were unionized. The International Ladies' Garment Workers' Union began to organize the Chinese workers in the 1950s. With Chinese workers joining the union in increasingly large numbers, as early as 1971, Local 23–25 had become the largest ILGWU local and had the largest Chinese membership of any U.S. trade union. Being part of the city's garment industry and the only industry in Chi-natown that was unionized by a major national labor organization, the Chinatown gar-ment industry was structurally bound to the city's and the nation's economy. It could serve as an important link between the Chinese community and the larger society.

There were, however, problems embedded in the unionization of the Chinatown garment industry. A major one was the union's indifference to the particular interests of its Chinese members. This was reflected in its attitude toward the workers' childcare problems. Nevertheless, unionization also exposed the women workers to conditions outside their own ethnic community. The union benefits they enjoyed allowed them to envision a better life in their new homeland. Learning to pressure leaders of their union and other institutions to improve their lives thereby became an important component as well as an index of their acculturation in the United States. This was demonstrated fully in their campaign for daycare centers from 1977 to 1982.

Politicizing Motherhood:
The Campaign for Daycare Centers and Its Impact

To a person outside the community, the initiative of the campaign may appear to be accidental. However, it was by no means accidental to members of the community. The lack of childcare facilities was a problem faced by working women in almost all ethnic groups in New York City, but it was even more salient among Chinese women workers. This had a lot to do with their particular childbearing patterns, caused by the economic conditions of their families.

The 1983 *Chinatown Garment Industry Study* reports that the birthrate of New York's Chinese community dropped from 22.4 per 1,000 people in the 1970s to 13.1 in 1980, despite the fact that Chinese women of childbearing ages immigrated into the city in large numbers during this period. The study suggests that the drop was largely caused by the economic condition of many new immigrant families and the high cost of living in the city.[24] My interviews with Chinese garment workers further reveal that not only did they choose to have fewer children, but they also preferred shorter intervals between the births of their children. The women workers reasoned that raising more than one child at a time would add only a little more work than raising one, but longer intervals between children would shorten their work years. Since most of their husbands worked in low-paid jobs, their families could not afford to have the women stay out of the wage-earning labor force for any long period.

This particular childbearing pattern accentuated Chinese women workers' need for childcare facilities. Unfortunately, such facilities were few in Chinatown. In 1981, for example, when union members in Chinatown shops had an estimated one thousand preschool children and approximately ten thousand children needed childcare services, there were only about twelve daycare centers in the Chinatown neighborhood, with a capacity for serving fewer than twenty-five hundred children.[25] The waiting list was so long that even if their parents put them on a list from the day they were born, the majority of children were not admitted to a daycare center before they were ready for kindergarten. There were also few daycare centers in the city; most were expensive and difficult to find. Many workers noted that even if they managed to find such a facility, the fees usually amounted to 50 or 60 percent of their income from working in a Chinatown shop.

Many therefore took their children to work. Older children worked side by side with their mothers after school, contributing to the family income. Those too young to work played on the floor, and babies were placed in cardboard boxes next to their sewing mothers. Taking children to the shops was both illegal and dangerous. The shops not only contained dust, which was harmful to the children's health, but also had potentially fatal hazards. On February 22, 1979, for example, in an old building with a broken elevator, a twelve-year-old girl fell to her death as she left her mother's workplace.[26] Frightened by the dreadful shop conditions, many workers left their children at home, without adult supervision. This was equally risky. In 1982, on the eve of Mother's Day, when a mother was working in a Chinatown garment shop, her ten-year-old daughter at home, in the care of her teenage sister, fell to her death while trying to reach an air conditioner placed on an unstable windowsill.[27]

Left with no better options, some women simply sewed at home, doing piecework. This was by no means a better solution. Women had to accept whatever work, and at whatever rates, offered by their employers. Although most of them were fully aware of the exploitative nature of their work, working at home remained the only possibility for them to resolve the conflict between their family responsibilities and economic need. Regrettably, for years, leaders of their union and major institutions in their own community ignored the workers' need for childcare facilities. It was therefore not surprising that the workers decided to take matters into their own hands.

In September 1977, when a public school building in Chinatown was available for other uses, a group of workers who were also union members issued their first call for a daycare center. They published an open letter to the union in the Chinese community newspapers, which begins as follows:

> We are members of Local 23–25 and workers who are busy with their work. It is difficult for us to choose between our work and our children. If we bring them to work, it is very dangerous; the union will not allow that, and it is also illegal; if we leave them at home, it is also extremely dangerous. Among members of our parents' association, some leave their children at home, others bring them to work. We do not know what to do, especially on public holidays when we have to work. . . . It is indeed very hard on us working mothers who are torn between their financial need and their children. Children become victims under such circumstances. We are forced to leave them at home without any care.
>
> In truth, a generation gap already emerged in many of our families due to parental negligence or insufficient care. This problem is aggravated by the fact that most parents do not know English and cannot help their children when they have difficulty with their homework. This lack of a loving mother's attention will lead to misunderstanding and problems in the future. With all this adding to our already very stressful life, our work is made even harder and our children find us even more disappointing. We are indeed torn between our work and our children.

The women workers then reported in great detail the childcare problems they faced. Shrewdly, they emphasized that they did not realize how important it was for a child to go to a daycare center until they saw how much their children had benefited from an after-school center run by a group of volunteer students at the City University of New York. These students, as they put it, "understood the difficulties in our lives and had kindly helped us to solve the problems." The women said they were saddened to see that the center was closing down because the building was reclaimed by the city but "saw a gleam of hope" when they found out that the building in Chinatown that had housed the former P.S. 23 was available. They decided to appeal to the union for help.

In the letter, they emphasized the importance of their cause and made concrete suggestions to the union about how it could help them pursue their cause. In the end, they reiterated their concern: "We, therefore, sincerely hope that the union will take our request seriously, extend us a hand in this matter, and will not let us give up halfway and end up being disappointed."²⁸ This carefully written letter did not receive any response from the union, however.

The call for a daycare center was reissued in October 1981, after a lapse of four years. About fifteen women workers decided to petition the union when they sat down to talk about their lives and the difficulty of finding childcare facilities surfaced again. This time, they were determined to fight to the end. To demonstrate workers' need for day-care centers, they spent their precious lunch hours climbing up and down the narrow stairs of the tenement and industrial buildings in Chinatown to gather signatures of support. The response was immediate. As Katie Quan, a longtime labor activist in the Chinese community who herself was a garment worker and a daycare activist at that time, recalled, "We went up and down the factories using the bosses' P.A. systems to say what we were there for, and about 99 percent of the people in every shop signed."²⁹

Fearful that the union would not take them seriously, the women workers decided to garner support in their own community. On October 9, 1981, with crying babies in their arms, the women workers met with community newspaper reporters at the Chinese Staff and Workers' Association (CSWA) office.³⁰ At this press conference, rather than emphasizing the contradictions they faced in their lives as both mothers and workers, they gave the press a detailed report of the difficulties working-class families faced due to the lack of childcare facilities in the community.

As they argued, working-class families in the community would face severe financial problems if women simply stayed home taking care of their children, because the income earned by their husbands could be easily exhausted. However, if women sewed at home, not only would it make the situation difficult for the union to regulate piece rates, but it would also be harmful to the health of the children. Furthermore, they argued that women who sewed at home could not concentrate on their work, nor could they provide their children with adequate attention. As a result, cases in which children were injured due to accidental falling or fighting with each other while their mothers were sewing were not uncommon in these workers' families. To divert their children's attention from one another, some workers who sewed at home simply turned on their televisions round the clock, which led to a peculiar phenomenon in their families: two-year-old children were shortsighted and had to wear glasses. Discouraged by the problems those who worked at home faced, some workers placed their children in the care of other women while they were working in the shops. However, they were distressed to find that their wages were half gone after they paid the caregivers. Some elements in the women's report might be disputed, such as watching television being the sole cause of children's poor eyesight. However, their appeal for support touched the right chords in the community, since the shortage of childcare facilities was an acute and widespread problem in Chinatown.

The daycare activists continued to work closely with the community press after their first press conference. They informed the newspaper reporters of every move they would take or had taken. A major event was their meeting with union leaders, after they had successfully amassed more than twenty-five hundred signatures from workers in Chinatown. To ensure support from the community, they held another press conference prior to the meeting. The women explained to the press that they were not being unreasonable with the union. They were only expecting the union to take the lead in fundraising and to partially finance the future daycare center. Fully aware of the intense political divisions within the community, they made it clear that they were not affiliated with any political organization, nor had they contacted any leaders of such organizations for support. They initiated the campaign simply because of their own experience as working mothers.[31] By publicizing their purpose for meeting with the union leaders, the women workers drew the community's attention to the event, which exerted a significant degree of pressure on the union before the meeting.

On the day of the meeting, November 11, 1981, the ways in which the women dealt with their own childcare problems were themselves a powerful demonstration of the seriousness of the problem. Four daycare activists, either carrying babies on their backs or holding them in their arms, went to the union headquarters in midtown Manhattan. However, the two sides gave very different reports on the meeting thereafter. Jay Mazur, the secretary-manager of the ILGWU Local 23–25 at that time, described it to the press as "friendly, congenial and open and above board," but the workers did not think so. According to them, the union's attitude was indecisive and evasive. The meeting lasted for almost two hours, with Mazur doing most of the talking, leaving them with little time to present their case. Even though the union leader said he was "100 percent" sympathetic with the workers and that they had his full support, Mazur also insisted that providing daycare was unprecedented in the history of the local and that the local did not have sufficient resources for this purpose. When the women tried to argue for their case, he became so impatient that he slapped the table, startling a child from her sleep and making her cry. No wonder that one of the workers called him a master of "shadow-boxing" (game of evasion). The meeting did not lead to any immediate result.[32]

However, the daycare activists refused to give up. They did not wait for the union's decision to move on. Rather, they took the initiative to explore potential resources to pursue their cause. In January 1982, for example, when the board of the Confucian Plaza, a high-rise residential building for middle-income families in the Chinatown area, announced its decision to turn its basement into a rental for a daycare center, the women activists wasted no time in jumping at the opportunity and approached the building management. Although their efforts did not lead to a fruitful ending, many community members were moved by their sincerity in fighting for their cause.

In the meantime, the activists also learned to mobilize their fellow workers to support their cause. This effort, as Quan later recalled, proved very challenging. While the activists themselves were inexperienced in organizing, the women workers whom they tried to mobilize were overwhelmed by their work and household responsibilities. It was extremely difficult to find a meeting time to accommodate the schedules of all the workers. It was equally difficult to maintain order when the meetings were finally held. Those who did come talked about daycare centers, their kids, and their families while changing their younger children's diapers and yelling at their older ones, almost all at once.[33] Nevertheless, the activist workers persisted.

Their dedication won the support of the community. From the outset, responses to their appeal, particularly from the progressive press, were strong and immediate. The *China Daily News* not only publicized every move they took and its outcome but also conducted its own investigation and published a series of reports in early 1982, detailing the childcare problem in the community.[34] Sui Fu, a reporter who wrote six out of the seven pieces published in this newspaper, estimated that three-fourths of the young children in the community were left without care when their mothers were working in the garment shops and thus concluded that the need for daycare centers was urgent. Firmly siding with the women workers, he portrayed them as women who had "a very strong sense of family obligations" and who regarded bringing up their offspring "as a duty bestowed from heaven."[35] Emphasizing the hardships of Chinese working-class families and the acute shortage of daycare centers in Chinatown and elsewhere in the city, he spoke highly of the daycare activists and their cause: "For half a year, the Chinatown workers of Local 23–25 have been soliciting help from every possible source. . . . They used their free time to work on the issue. . . . Their enthusiasm to fight for the interest of their sister workers is indeed *ke ge ke qi* [moving one to sing and cry for them]."[36] The newspaper coverage effectively rallied community support for the campaign. With this strong support behind them, the daycare activists were even more determined.

On March 17, 1982, shortly before the beginning of negotiations for a new union contract, the ILGWU Local 23–25 held a meeting to gather support from its members. More than one thousand members attended the meeting, and one-third of them were Chinese. At the meeting, the Chinese daycare activists courageously raised the issue of childcare. They detailed the problems women workers faced and proposed a daycare benefit be included in the new contract. Union leader Jay Mazur again dodged the issue by emphasizing the need to investigate the situation and the union's lack of financial resources for that purpose. Persistently, the Chinese daycare activists asked how he could be so sure the costs would supercede the amount that the union could afford even before investigating the actual situation and exploring other potential funding sources. The same question was in the mind of almost every Chinatown worker.[37]

Negotiations for a new union contract began shortly after the meeting. However, the talks were deadlocked when Chinese employers refused to sign the contract, which had been signed by other employers in the city. The Chinese employers claimed that they were underrepresented in the negotiation process and that both the union and the contractors' association, being dominated by other ethnic groups, ignored their demands. Concerned about the unfavorable outcome of this deadlock, the daycare activists, along with other Chinatown workers, pressured the union to call a strike. When the union finally decided to do so, they again played an important role in mobilizing Chinatown workers, volunteering their time to serve at information centers and phone banks organized by the union. Thanks to their efforts, more than twenty thousand Chinese garment workers took to the streets to attend the two union rallies on June 24 and July 15. A strike began after the end of the second rally. Although it lasted for only a couple of hours, as the Chinese contractors rushed to sign the contract, it is to date the largest labor strike in the history of New York City's Chinatown. Chinese women garment workers stood firm in defending their right to a union contract in this final showdown with their employers. In doing so, they demonstrated their capacity for militant activism.

Impressed by its Chinese members' determination and collective strength, the union leadership formed a committee to champion a daycare center in Chinatown, almost immediately after the strike. Susan Cowell, then Jay Mazur's assistant, was assigned to lead the committee. As she explored funding sources in the city, the Chinese activists endeavored to locate potential sites in Chinatown for a daycare center. With financial contributions from the union, the employers, and the city, this joint effort between union officials and its Chinese rank-and-file members finally led to the opening of a Chinatown daycare center for the children of women garment workers in late 1983. The formal dedication of this center took place in January 1984, seven years after the Chinese women workers issued their first call.[38]

This daycare center gained publicity in almost all major city and community newspapers. Although its capacity was limited, offering care for only seventy preschool children per year, it brought the needs of Chinese women workers to the attention of the community and the union. As early as 1983, when a major building was proposed to be built in Chinatown and the discussions about the use of its space ensued, for the first time in the history of New York's Chinatown saving space for a daycare center was placed on the agenda of its decision-making committee, made up of community leaders and union representatives. Shui Mak Ka, a former garment worker and a major organizer of the 1982 strike, who began working in the union's research department after the strike, served on the committee. In 1993, with the union and other institutions contributing to fundraising efforts, the second union-involved daycare center was established in the newly constructed Chung Pak Building at the center of Chinatown. Although the two daycare centers are insufficient in meeting the tremendous needs of working mothers in the community, they are evidence that childcare as an issue could no longer be easily brushed aside by the two major institutions in the lives of Chinese women workers: their community and the union.

Women, Work, and Family: Some Reflections

The Chinese women workers' campaign for daycare centers allows us to revisit some issues raised in the scholarship on women and labor. Although participation in wage-earning labor does not necessarily transform women's position in the family and their perception of life, it did for many women garment workers in New York's Chinatown. This has to be understood in the changing context of their community and their lives after immigration.

As the economic structure of their community changed, so did the gender roles in many Chinese immigrant working-class families. While changing gender roles might aggravate tensions in many families and add additional burdens on women workers, family life in many cases provided women with emotional support and instilled in them hope and self-esteem in their new homeland. When this increased optimism and confidence contradicted the reality at their workplace, characterized by its low return for workers' hard labor and the union's failure to deliver its promise, it generated an enormous dynamic of labor activism among the workers. Not only the workers' daily resistance on the shop floor but also their determination and courage in initiating and organizing the daycare campaign, which culminated in the historic 1982 strike, demonstrate this labor activism. The Chinese women workers' experiences challenge scholars to enlarge the scope of their investigations to encompass not only workplaces and families but also all major intersections of working women's lives. Without understanding fully the contradictions they encounter at various sites of their lives and how these contradictions intersect to shape their perceptions, one cannot fully understand these working women.

The language and strategy employed by the Chinese daycare activists can also enhance our understanding of the contested meanings of women workers' traditional gender roles. Under different circumstances, the Chinese daycare activists shifted the emphasis in their presentation. However, motherhood remained at the center of their rhetoric. This strategy contributed significantly to the successful outcome of their campaign. To understand why this strategy worked, we need to consider its political implications in different contexts.

While dealing with leaders of their union, the activist workers emphasized the difficulty of their lives as mothers and workers, as well as the union's responsibility to its members. This approach was effective because it left the union leaders with no legitimacy to publicly deny their request, since the union had long been advocating a pro-family policy and had taken pride in its history of fighting for the interests of its members and their families. However, facing their own community, most of whom still held onto traditional gender roles, no matter how invalid these were in reality, the workers changed the focus of their presentation. Rather than detailing the difficulties in their lives, they emphasized the retarding impact of the lack of childcare facilities on the lives of working-class families and presented themselves as working mothers and wives fighting for their families' interest. By projecting an apolitical image of themselves as concerned and responsible mothers and wives, an image reinforced by the community newspaper coverage, they managed to galvanize the broadest possible support in a relatively conservative community split by political factions.

In both cases, motherhood and the family were politicized. They enabled the daycare activists to gain additional credibility to challenge the authority of their community and the union. In challenging these two largely male-dominated institutions, the workers' role as mothers allowed them to subvert the patriarchal structure under which they operated. The campaign for daycare centers also empowered them in other ways. Through participating in the campaign as working mothers defending their children's interest, they learned about the U.S. political system and labor laws. They also gained experience in delivering public speeches, dealing with establishments such as labor institutions, and organizing workers. All this prepared them to become a new driving force of the U.S. labor movement in the years to come.

It should therefore come as no surprise that many of the daycare activists played an important role in the historic 1982 strike and continued to reform the union from within afterward. In 1984, together with other labor activists, they formed the Chinese Committee of the Coalition of Labor Union Women (CLUW). Since the committee's founding, the members have actively participated in various union activities, particularly those aimed at linking their community with the outside world. Some of these workers attended the UN Conference on Women in Nairobi in 1986; others attended the Beijing conference in 1995. By so doing, they have become part of the larger labor and women's movements in the United States and the world. In the course of their struggle, a number of women have risen to leading positions in the union. The most prominent is Katie Quan, who was elected the first Chinese vice president of UNITE in 1997, the union that emerged after the former ILGWU merged with the Amalgamated Clothing Workers of America in 1995.[39]

The women workers' campaign for daycare centers might not appear as significant as the historic 1982 strike. However, in fostering labor activism among the Chinese women workers and preparing them for future militant action, it can be considered a prelude to the 1982 strike. Unlike the 1982 strike, in which the union claimed a leading role, the daycare campaign was initiated and carried out by the women workers themselves. It challenges scholars to broaden their scope of study and to question their preconception of immigrant women workers. The Chinese women workers' strategy in this campaign has forcefully put to the test any simplistic proclivity to treat their rhetoric as a transparent representation of their lives and their minds. A closer examination of how the women modified their language and self-representation for different situations and the political implications of these variations reveals the workers' agency in shaping their circumstances to achieve their goals. Such an analysis of the meanings embedded in their rhetoric and representation contests stereotypical notions of Chinese immigrant women as passive and bound by traditional ethnic culture. It enables us to better understand their complex lives as working-class women and their potential to become a dynamic force in the U.S. labor movement.

NOTES

1. This essay is revised and expanded from the discussion of the campaign in my book *Holding Up More than Half the Sky: Chinese Women Garment Workers in New York City, 1948–1992* (Urbana: University of Illinois Press, 2001), 185–87. A large part of the discussion about the history of the Chinese garment industry in New York City also appears in the same book, chap. 3.

2. For essays that explore the interrelationships between various aspects of working women's lives and challenge the dichotomizing of women's private and public lives, see Carol Groneman and Mary Beth Norton, eds., *"To Toil the Livelong Day": America's Women at Work, 1780–1980* (Ithaca, N.Y.: Cornell University Press, 1987); and Dorothy O. Helly and Susan M. Reverby, *Gendered Domains: Rethinking Public and Private in Women's History* (Ithaca, N.Y.: Cornell University Press, 1992). For scholarly reflections on the issues raised by Louise Tilly and Joan Scott more than two decades ago in *Women, Work, and Family* (New York: Holt, Rinehart and Winston, 1978), see *Journal of Women's History* 11:3 (Autumn 1999): 9–30.

3. For the larger project, see Bao, *More than Half the Sky.*

4. *U.S. Census of Population,* 1940.

5. They included the repeal of all the Chinese Exclusion Acts in 1943, the amendment of the War Bride Act in 1946, and the passing of a series of Displaced Persons and Refugee Relief Acts in the late 1940s and 1950s. On changes in U.S. immigration laws between the 1940s and 1960s, see David Reimers, *Still the Golden Door: The Third World Comes to America* (New York: Columbia University Press, 1982), 21–29; Roger Daniels and Harry H. L. Kitano, *Asian Americans: Emerging Minorities,* 2d ed. (Englewood Cliffs, N.J.: Prentice-Hall, 1995), 16–18; and Sucheng Chan, *Asian Americans: An Interpretive History* (Boston: Twayne Publishers, 1991), 121, 140–41.

6. See U.S. Immigration and Naturalization Service (hereafter INS), *Annual Report*, for 1948–1953.

7. *U.S. Census of Population*, 1940 and 1960.

8. *U.S. Census of Population*, 1950.

9. No statistics are available for this category in 1950. However, U.S. Census publications report that only 16 percent of the foreign-born were gainfully employed in 1940, as compared to about a quarter of all adult Chinese women in the city that year. See *U.S. Census of Population*, 1940.

10. *U.S. Census of Population*, 1980.

11. Abeles, Schwartz, Haeckel, and Silverblatt, Inc., *The Chinatown Garment Industry Study* (New York: ILGWU Local 23–25 and the New York Skirt and Sportswear Association, 1983), 97–98 (hereafter *Study*).

12. *Study*, 98–99, Table 20. However, my interviews show that the majority of the new immigrant women who registered themselves as "housewives," with an implication of no previous employment experience, had worked on the farm in China or engaged in wage-earning labor at home in Hong Kong. On homeworkers in Hong Kong in the 1960s and 1970s, see Janet W. Salaff, *Working Daughters of Hong Kong: Filial Piety or Power in the Family?* (Cambridge: Cambridge University Press, 1983; New York: Columbia University Press, 1995), 259.

13. See Bao, *More than Half the Sky*, chap. 1.

14. Ibid., 66–68.

15. *Study*, 5.

16. The city's garment industry declined by only 3.6 percent between 1975 and 1996, as compared to 23.6 percent from 1958 to 1974. See Roger Waldinger, *Through the Eye of the Needle: Immigrants and Enterprise in New York's Garment Trades* (New York: New York University Press, 1986), 54; and Mark Levitan, "Opportunity at Work, The New York City Garment Industry" (New York: Community Service Society of New York, 1998), 24.

17. *Study*, 5.

18. While the laundry business employed 42 percent of all gainfully employed Chinese male workers in New York State in 1930, the percentage had dropped to 19.5 percent by 1950 and was less than 16 percent in 1970. See *U.S. Census of Population*, 1930, 1950, and 1960.

19. *Study*, 5.

20. *U.S. Census of Population*, 1970 and 1990.

21. For the percentage of married women among the Chinese women garment workers in 1980, see Min Zhou, *Chinatown: The Socioeconomic Potential of an Urban Enclave* (Philadelphia: Temple University Press, 1992), Tables 4-2 and 8-3.

22. This also includes their relationship with their mothers-in-law and other members traditionally in an authoritative position in the family. For more details, see Bao, *More than Half the Sky*, chap. 5.

23. For example, both Fay Chew, the former director of the New York Chinese American Historical Museum, and Doris Ling-Cohan, an attorney dedicated to serving the community, are daughters of women garment workers. They both considered their mothers their role models when they looked back on their early lives. For an interview with Cohan, see *Justice* 125:3 (April 1993): 11.

24. *Study*, 93–94.

25. See *China Daily News* (hereafter *CDN*), February 26 and March 3, 1982. The statistics there are different from those given by Katie Quan. Quan noted only three daycare centers, with a capacity of serving five or six hundred children, when ten thousand openings were needed. See Ruth Milkman, "Organizing Immigrant Women in New York's Chinatown: An Interview with

Katie Quan," in *Women and Unions: Forging a Partnership*, ed. Dorothy Sue Cobble (Ithaca, N.Y.: ILR Press, 1993), 288; and Katie Quan, "Chinese Garment Workers in New York City," *Migration World* 14½ (1986): 49.

26. *CDN*, February 22, 1979.

27. *CDN*, May 12, 1982.

28. *CDN*, September 21, 1977.

29. Milkman, "Organizing Immigrant Women," 290.

30. *CDN*, November 13, 1982; and Milkman, "Organizing Immigrant Women," 290.

31. *CDN*, November 13, 1981.

32. *CDN*, November 16, 1981.

33. Interviews by the author with Katie Quan, New York, April 27 and 29, 1989, in a mixed language of English and Cantonese. Also see Milkman, "Organizing Immigrant Women," 289.

34. See *CDN*, February 26 and 27; March 3, 8, 15, 17, and 18, 1982.

35. *CDN*, February 27, 1982.

36. *CDN*, March 15, 1982.

37. The above discussion is based on *CDN*, March 20, 1982. Jay Mazur later denied having said this. Katie Quan's account in the interview by Ruth Milkman in 1990 was somewhat different. According to Quan, after they collected all the signatures, the union said it was for daycare and they did not have to go through all this. See Milkman, "Organizing Immigrant Women," 290.

38. For a brief discussion of this collaborative effort between the union officials and the workers, see Milkman, "Organizing Immigrant Women," 290–91.

39. Quan soon resigned and accepted a new position at the Institute of Industrial Relations of the University of California, Berkeley.

18

Caring across Borders
Motherhood, Marriage, and
Filipina Domestic Workers in California

Charlene Tung

Lita stands in line waiting to enter the U.S. Embassy Consular Offices in Manila on April 30, 1990. She stifles a groan as she observes the queue snaking around the building and toward the front doors. She waits, knowing this is her opportunity to find work in the United States as a live-in caregiver to the elderly, just like her hometown neighbor Sally, and to earn almost four times the amount she is now making through her beauty shop. This is her chance to start over far away from her husband and alone to provide for her children's education. She silently rehearses what she will say to obtain a tourist visa to enter the United States.

"I'd like to visit friends, see Disneyland, and visit Hollywood," she explains to the officer behind the window. "This is my dream. I have never been to the U.S." The officer looks at her skeptically. Undeterred, Lita continues, "Of course I won't stay very long. I have my business as well as my four children here. But still, I am looking forward to a vacation with my friends." The officer nods briefly and gives her a date to return for the decision.

Returning a week later, Lita learns that the officer, ostensibly convinced that she will return to the Philippines to care for her children and run her business, has granted her a six-month tourist visa. Lita walks out breathing a sigh of relief, mentally running through a "to-do" list before she leaves for the United States. Back inside, the consular officer watches Lita walk away, sighs, and remarks to no one in particular, "See you in five years."

This opening scene of Lita's first steps on her journey to the United States is a fictionalized account based on twenty oral histories and in-depth interviews of Filipina transmigrant workers employed as live-in elderly caregivers (home healthcare workers) in Southern California.[1] Live-in caregivers are "domestic workers" who care for the terminally ill and the elderly while living in their patients' homes, assuming the companionate and light medical care of elderly persons but also the household care, cooking, and grocery shopping. For many reasons, including a growing demand for eldercare in the United States as well as U.S.-Philippine neocolonial relations, which have laid the groundwork for chain migration, in the last two decades of the twentieth century,

Philippine women have been emigrating in increasing numbers to fill this specific economic niche. Upon their arrival, they find themselves negotiating the demands of providing care for both the elderly in the United States and children left behind in the Philippines.

The case of Filipina transmigrant domestic workers illustrates the enduring centrality of social reproductive labor in women's lives despite migration. While social reproductive labor refers to the "array of activities and relationships involved in maintaining people both on a daily basis and intergenerationally,"[2] it becomes "transnational" as the women engage in this as they cross national borders. It is this labor, paid and unpaid as well as underpaid, that Filipina live-in caregivers provide on a daily basis in their work lives in the United States and for family remaining in the Philippines.

Yet, historically, migration studies have overlooked women. Evelyn Nakano Glenn writes, "When women are looked at in relation to labor migration, they are usually treated as a marginal category: as dependents of male migrants or as part of the debris left behind in the home country when the males depart."[3] However, as contemporary Filipina women illustrate, far from being left behind, women are migrating alone to provide for families as men did in earlier decades. The migration literature's myopia also renders near invisible the unique experience of women migrants who experience labor stratification shaped not only by race/ethnicity but also by gender.[4] Further, women's migration experiences are largely absent from recent scholarly work on globalization.[5] Yet the imposition of destructive structural adjustment policies that plunge developing countries further into debt disproportionately and negatively impacts on rural and working-class women of nations such as the Philippines. Rural-to-urban migration, as well as overseas migration in search of work, has been one of the inevitable results.[6]

This chapter examines how on one level, despite globalization and independent (im)migration, women from the Philippines are unable to leave "the home" and the social reproductive labor that characterizes that space, even as they migrate across oceans as the primary financial providers for their families. Yet, on another level, two institutions in which social reproductive labor is central—mothering and marriage—are nevertheless redefined through the transmigration experience.

(Trans)National Benefits

Filipina women provide the emotional and physical labor upon which the Philippine state, the U.S. home healthcare system, and both Philippine and U.S. families rely in various ways. For instance, Filipina women employed as overseas caregivers are part of the global Philippine diaspora, whose labors benefit the Philippine state. In fact, women make up an estimated 60 percent[7] of the more than 6 million overseas Filipina/o transmigrant workers. Their remittances help decrease the estimated $45 billion national debt by at least $5 billion per year.[8] Philippine government officials have thus dubbed these women "the heroines" of the Philippines—this, while opening the Philippines to foreign investment and exploitation (of both its workers and the environment) by encouraging multinational investments and export-based industries. Dependence on global financial institutions such as the International Monetary Fund continues, further disabling local economies as the government directs its resources toward debt repayment rather than toward agricultural reforms or social services for its people.[9] Under such conditions, Philippine state-sponsored overseas migration emerges.

Filipina transmigrant workers benefit the United States as they contribute toward filling the demand for in-home care. Demographic projections indicate the number of elderly requiring in-home care in the United States will increase from 2.5 million in 1984 to 6.5 million by 2025.[10] While no absolute statistics exist, interviews with caregivers, social service agencies, home healthcare agencies, and hospitals indicate that Filipina women are predominantly filling this economic niche in California, in locales such as San Diego, Los Angeles, and the San Francisco Bay Area. Although Filipina/o registered nurses (RNs) are visible in urban hospitals, researchers and policy makers alike have overlooked the burgeoning numbers of Filipina non-RNs who provide in-home care.[11] The service these women provide to the U.S. elderly remains invisible because the work takes place in the confines of private homes, often as part of the informal economy. Further, Filipina live-in caregivers are involved in what is stereotypically considered women's work, or that which emerges from women's supposed "natural" inclination toward caring and relational thinking.[12] And although feminist scholars have worked to redefine this *as* work, and specifically as social reproductive labor, the work remains undervalued, as do the workers.[13]

Filipina Live-in Caregivers in the United States

It's expensive to come [to the United States]. And a lot of those who come here ... belong to the middle income or maybe above [in the Philippines]. And many of those who come here are college graduates, educated ones who can speak English—so we can communicate [with our patients].   —Filipina live-in caregiver[14]

The typical live-in elderly caregiver in this study had at least two years of college education from the Philippines. Almost all had assets in the form of inherited family land or a house. Slightly less than half of the women hailed from the Metro Manila area.[15] The women earned, on average, $75 per day (for twenty-four hours on call). All the women were mothers.[16] With an average age of fifty-two, half the caregivers had three or more children; one woman was mother to eight children. Eighty percent of the women had children under the age of eighteen when they left the Philippines—either for the United States directly or first to other countries—to work as domestic workers.[17]

In the Philippines, most of the women had been small-business owners (e.g., operating a fish farm or neighborhood beauty shop) or were professionals/white-collar workers (e.g., teachers or clerical assistants). Notably, none possessed any kind of formal training in nursing prior to coming to the United States. While most eventually obtained certification as certified nursing assistants (CNAs) once in the United States the CNA certification was a prerequisite in only a few cases.[18]

Once in the United States, Filipina women usually obtained jobs through a network of other Filipina caregivers. Word of mouth and home healthcare placement agencies were the two primary methods among the women studied here that were used to gain live-in work. Generally, the patient procured home healthcare agency services, and workers signed up with an agency in hopes of obtaining work. Once the agency matched a caregiver with a patient, patients were charged a monthly placement fee, in addition to the caregiver's salary. It was that additional monthly (sometimes daily) fee that both patients and caregivers often objected to. As a result, caregivers often dropped the agencies after placement. In this way, caregivers could be paid directly by patients (or patients' families) and earn approximately $20 to $30 per day—the money previously paid to the agency—more than they had earned as agency workers.

Whether jobs were found through an agency or through friends, the caregiver's work situation was largely informal and unregulated.[19] The worker herself had to verbally negotiate all working conditions, including such things as required tasks, time off, working hours, phone privileges, cooking privileges, and the condition and extent of living quarters. These negotiations were complicated by the fact that as a live-in, the caregiver was always, in a sense, on her employers' turf.

While live-in elderly caregivers experienced challenges similar to live-in childcare workers and maids (e.g., tremendous isolation, difficulty in job negotiations, and lack of time off), unlike other domestics these caregivers *preferred* live-in work over day work. Alternative work opportunities such as clerical or nursing home work had distinct disadvantages. For example, while live-in work offered one-on-one patient-worker ratios, board and care facilities and nursing homes required three to eight patients per worker. Office work translated into costs for professional clothing and transportation to and from the workplace. Further, in addition to free room and board, as well as an invisibility afforded to those undocumented women who had overstayed their visitor visas, a primary advantage of live-in work was the ability to work "six, seven days a week if you want to" and thus earn more money to send home. However, despite the choice of live-in work over live-out alternative work, one largely unforeseen challenge was the emotional cost inherent in live-in eldercare work.

"You Have to Have Compassion": Emotional Labor in Eldercare

In caring work such as paid eldercare, workers are required to perform both physical and emotional labor. Emotional labor can be defined as the "the conscious or unconscious induction and suppression of feelings in order to fulfill the psychological, physical, or monetary needs of both workers and employers."[20] For Filipina caregivers this took the form of dealing with their patients' constant demands, moods, and needs, twenty-four hours a day, nearly seven days a week.[21]

The women provided far more than physical duties such as administering medicines, preparing meals, assisting in physical movements, personal care (e.g. brushing teeth, bathing, taking to the bathroom), or cleaning homes and doing laundry. They were also the sole daily confidantes and companions for elderly persons who often suffered from depression and dementia. Daily activities included playing cards, watching television, and, for those with mobile patients, trips outside the home to the doctor, for shopping, or to senior centers. For those with bedridden and or mentally deteriorated patients suffering from Alzheimer's disease, their days were considerably slower-paced and often more physically and emotionally taxing.

One caregiver, Lillian, emphatically stated, "In this kind of job you have to have compassion. You have to have a big heart. If you don't have that, better not work like this."[22] She explained the specific strategies she used to deal with her patient's tendency to lash out verbally and physically in frustration at her caregivers. For example, it was common for her patient to throw physical tantrums while refusing to eat. Instead of fighting her, Lillian waited until her patient tired out. She then asked, "Can I help you? I love to help you." She explains, "I learned from her to ask . . . I say, 'Can I wipe your beautiful nose?' . . . Otherwise it's like conquering her privacy [or] insulting her." She concluded, "We have to understand [this]." Lillian, like most of the women encountered, insisted on the provision of "love," or what Emily Abel and Margaret Nelson have called "caring about" while "caring for."[23] As another caregiver carefully explained, "I have been taking care of her really, like she were my mom you know?"

As the solitary daily companions to their patients over many years, the caregivers often grew quite emotionally attached. Caregivers found their patients welcome company, given their own isolation from family. And depending on the physical and mental condition of their patients, this relationship could be reciprocal. Caregivers especially expended emotional labor in those cases where they saw their patients through physical and mental deterioration and death.

Beyond the intensive emotional and physical labor inherent in caring for the elderly, Filipina women must contend too with the emotional costs of mothering from afar. For these Filipina caregivers, their roles as mothers and wives remained highly relevant to their lives once in the United States.

Crossing the Borders of Marriage and Motherhood

The Filipina women's marital situations deeply influenced their decision to migrate abroad. Similar to Filipina domestics worldwide (e.g., Singapore, Italy, Hong Kong, Saudi Arabia), troubled marriages combined with poor economic conditions were typical motivations for leaving the Philippines.[24] This breakdown of marital relations, highlighted by women's migration, is markedly distinct from the ideology of marriage in the Philippines. The ideology of Filipina women's dutiful place as wives and mothers finds much support not only in this study but also in Philippine state and religious institutions.[25] Motherhood, regardless of class and education, is viewed as an assumed condition following from marriage, and self-sacrifice, a natural response to husbands and children.[26]

This ideology of motherhood combines with an ideology of the wife to enforce women's figurative place in the home both socially and legally:

In [Philippine] society where a man's infidelities were tolerated, where the role of the mistress was accepted, one could argue quite convincingly that the absence of a divorce law (divorce is not legal in the Philippines) was oppressive to women. . . . It encouraged complacency among men, who knew for certain that despite their transgressions (women's infidelities were frowned upon), the wife had no choice [but to stay].[27]

This lack of choice is reflected clearly in the legal codes governing separation (in the absence of state-sanctioned divorce).[28] Although legal separation is allowed, it is bureaucratically and financially difficult to secure, and neither person is legally allowed to remarry. Further, a sexual double standard is reflected in the nation's written penal code on separation, which holds men and women to differing standards of fidelity.[29] While a man may have grounds for a legal separation based on the mere fact that his wife slept with another man, a woman must prove that her husband slept with another woman in certain places and under "scandalous" circumstances. Such state-imposed (and Catholic Church–supported) policies make obtaining separations even more difficult for women.[30] Under such conditions, migration abroad is inviting.

Further, prohibitions against birth control in much of the Catholic Philippines contribute to the high birthrate among the women. In this study as in others, in cases of separation, responsibility for the numerous children generally fell upon the women. Given such constructions of motherhood and marriage, as well as the Philippines' debt, women have found informal separation through migration to be the answer to singly supporting often large families. Overseas jobs are simply more lucrative than what is available in the Philippines. The women in this study chose to migrate in order maritally to separate but also to enable themselves singly to provide for their children's financial needs.

The discourse and ideology of woman as wife and mother endures despite their crossing of national borders and oceans. The strength of the ideology, as illustrated above, contributes to the challenges the women face. However, through becoming transnational mothers, daughters, and to some degree spouses, these Filipina women necessarily reorder the place and space of women in the Philippine family. For those who have maritally separated from husbands, they maintain a space of "in-betweenness" as they work to recreate their roles as mothers and wives. Such women sustain ties to their children, and sometimes their husbands, despite the length of time and the distance that separate them, but by no means do they fit traditional Western-based middle-class notions of motherhood and marriage.

Like migrant women workers from the Caribbean and Mexico, Filipinas have experienced the challenge of mothering from afar.[31] This leave-taking of one's own children goes against popular notions in the United States of what it means to be a "good mother."[32] Accordingly, leaving one's children for years in order to work in a foreign country caring for another's elderly parent (or young children) is unimaginable.

Yet, in shifting the perspective to the workers themselves, it becomes clear that they understood themselves to be better mothers for being able to better provide for their family's needs financially.[33] Expanding on the notion of "sacrifice," the women themselves prominently expressed the connection between motherhood and self-sacrifice. As one Filipina woman, whose two children were ages four and ten when she left (and are now being cared for by her parents), explained, "It's worth it you know, because I can give [them] whatever [they] like. Not really everything, because I'm not there, but I can send them to good schools. I can buy them what they like. . . . I miss their growing up. But what can I do? I sacrifice." For these Filipina women, securing a future for their children by being able to provide for them financially far outweighed any belief that quality mothering was necessarily achieved only by living with their young children.

Transnational Mothering

I have been gone seven long years now. When I return, I will have to build up relationships
all over again with my children.   —Filipina live-in caregiver

The above woman astutely pinpoints how Filipina elderly caregivers in the United
States redefine traditional notions of motherhood. "Transnational mothering" refers to
overseas mothers' efforts to mother from afar. This phenomenon impacts not only on
themselves and their children but also on their sisters and mothers through the imposition of "extended mothering" (or the use of extended kin networks to take on the immediate daily responsibility of children).[34]

Maintaining mothering across distance and time involves constant challenges. Clare
left for overseas work in 1991 while her two children, aged four and ten, remained in
the Philippines with her mother. She explained:

My first few months, I really got to the point of going back. I cried a lot. Like every night
when I watched TV and I would see kids there . . . I could just feel the tears coming
down my cheeks. I would miss my kids. But then ultimately I got used to it. Especially
because I also kept talking to them [by phone] on the weekends. I got used to it and it's
ok now.

Other women shared similar emotions. One caregiver explained, "I never spent a long
time being with them. You see what I'm saying? As a mother . . ." Here, she alludes to her
own internalized belief that true "mothers" ought to be with their children. Echoing
this, another mother of five, whose youngest was nine when she left, said, "You always
have that guilty feeling. You know you're supposed to be there, beside them." Touching
upon the impact of the dislocation, one woman related, "I don't know actually, the life
of my kids. That's the problem of Filipinas living here." In spite of this, the women do
manage to "mother," but not without monetary and emotional costs.

Monetary costs were inevitable. The women's phone bills ranged from an average of
$150 to $400 per month. Most of the women in this study had weekly phone contact
with their children or families and often even more frequent than that. Letter writing
did not hold the same immediacy or intimacy, as one caregiver explained: "If you sit
down and write [to] them, it takes so long [to get there]. I'd rather hear their voices. It's
like they're just at your side." While expensive phone calls may appear counter to the
women's goal of saving money, they considered it necessary toward maintaining familial connections.

The technicalities of the phone calls underscore the concerted efforts required of the
women. For example, one caregiver arranged to call her children every weekend. She
and her four children would set a date and time, and those away at college in the cities
would travel back "home" to the provinces to await the call. Gathering at a single phone
decreased total costs to their mother.

Aside from phone calls, mothering from afar is also reflected through remittances.
As the Philippine government has expected and hoped, these overseas workers sent
home, on average, over 50 percent of their monthly salaries. This was possible due to

their frugality and low cost of living (room and board are covered for live-ins). Remittances ranged from $500 to $1,500 a month, depending on the number of children to support, their ages, and on how "invested" the mothers were in activities in the United States. For example, if the women were part of Philippine hometown associations in the United States or had met new husbands, their expenses for socializing and food were higher than for those who remained isolated in their patients' homes.

The contents of packages (*balikbayan* boxes) sent home reveal how mothering from afar occurs. For example, one woman's export declaration and packing list from LBC Mabuhay USA Corporation read "white socks, men's briefs, magazines, chocolates, vitamins, flashlight, watercolor, disposable razors, t-shirts, marshmallows, cookies." As an alternative to the postal service (both the U.S. and Philippine), such packages were sent through shipping companies that were often owned and operated by Filipina/o Americans. In other cases, women bypassed postal and shipping companies, preferring to have money and smaller gifts hand-carried by Filipina/o friends from the States who were returning to the Philippines for visits.

Furthermore, mothering from afar requires the help of extended family. That these Filipina caregivers could leave their children was in large measure dependent on the availability of sisters, mothers, and even elder daughters remaining in the Philippines.[35] The caregivers in this study usually sent money for food, clothing, schooling, and household finances to immediate family members. But while the children's grandmothers or aunts could provide oversight and authority, elder siblings (daughters) took on a good deal of the day-to-day household responsibility and care of younger siblings.

For example, Terry turned over household finances to her eighteen-year-old daughter (the middle child of her five children). She felt that this daughter would be best able to coordinate paying tuition, household bills, food allowances, and other expenses. When this daughter moved away from home in her mid-twenties, the responsibilities shifted to the youngest daughter, then sixteen years old, who took care of finances for herself and her thirteen-year-old brother.

Conflicting Demands of Mothering and Marriage

As transnational mothers, the Filipina women inevitably found themselves juggling the conflicting demands of eldercare work, providing for their children in the Philippines, and relations with ex- and even new husbands. Although these women generally expected to return to the Philippines within a few years, they instead ended up remaining in the United States for eight to ten years on average, enduring continuous separation from their young children. The long separations are not necessarily by choice.[36] The social stigma attached to divorce in the Philippines was central to the women's dilemma as mothers and wives. This stigma influenced their choice to remain married for an average of *eighteen* years before separating from their husbands (through migration). Terry, who was married for twenty-four years before she separated, shares her experience:

> In my family, when you get married, it's expected you're going to be together for the rest of your life! Divorce is not legal there. I just couldn't accept it . . . that I would be the very

first in my family to have a broken home. For me, it meant failure. The biggest failure in my life.

Her sentiments were shared by all the separated women in this study. Kinship ties were extremely important to the caregivers, particularly the notion of *hiya* ("shame," "disgrace"—also "not losing face") for the sake of the extended family. Marital troubles were minimized or kept secret not only by the couple involved but also by their parents, uncles, and aunts. All these factors combined to further complicate and limit Filipina women's options.

Moreover, the same stigma that makes it difficult for women to leave their husbands makes it difficult for them to return to the Philippines after separating. While a Filipino man who enters a new relationship after a failed marriage suffers little to no stigma, a Filipina woman is considered to be living "in sin" and faces stronger social sanctions.[37]

So, for the women in this study, remarriage to either a non-Filipino or a Filipino American created obstacles in returning to the Philippines permanently or even temporarily to visit their children. Terry, the mother of five children, explained the predicament should she desire to remarry: "We [could not] get married. It's not allowed. The marriage would not be legal. We can live together [in the Philippines], but without benefit of, you know, being really accepted by people over there." Another woman, recently remarried to an American citizen, echoes this social censure: "It's not good, not good in the Philippines to look like I'm there going home with a new husband, and my [first] husband has no wife. It's bad in the eyes of Filipinos." In her case, she had been in the United States almost nine years and consequently had missed out on her oldest daughter's marriage and birth of three grandchildren. And while she very much would like to visit the Philippines, the combination of her new marriage and the fact that her ex-husband still lives in her family home makes it an impossibility thus far. One woman noted that her children, aged seven and fourteen, wanted her home as "one family." However, now remarried to a Mexican American man, she finds herself pulled between a new husband in the United States and her children in the Philippines. In these ways, the women's decisions to migrate overseas in some cases condemned them to a life without (in varying degrees) their children, their homeland, or close companionship.

Further, some women had to contend with the additional trauma of having been abused by their husbands. These women juggled their desire to see their children with the pain involved in encountering their abusive husbands once again. In all cases, the first or ex-husbands remained living in the same hometown or nearby. As a result, these women felt they could not avoid their husbands, or their husbands' attempts to reconcile, should they visit the Philippines.

Finally, the women's *new* marriages in the United States were also caught between their responsibilities and commitments to their children in the Philippines and to their elderly patients. Because of those children's financial needs, women continued their work as live-ins after remarriage; thus the caregivers did not live with their new husbands.[38] Rather, they saw their husbands once or twice a month, usually over a "weekend," generally defined as Saturday morning until Sunday evening. Maria, who takes three consecutive days off once a month to visit her husband, explains her situation by first citing her children: "Because I really need money for them [my children]." She continues, next citing her concern for her patient: "He [her new husband] understands that I have to sacrifice [living together] because my patient really needs me." Similarly, Sally explained, "Instead of leaving [my patient], I can't because . . . I am attached to her. I am getting used to her, see?" Here Maria and Sally reveal that the demands on them as both mothers *and* caregivers conflict with the demands of their new marriages.

The caregivers' current marriages were by and large characterized by physical distance and financial independence from new husbands. Moreover, primary responsibilities still directed them toward providing for children back in the Philippines. And while it is not certain how long-term such arrangements are likely to be, it is clear that these women's second (or third) marriages were a distinct departure from traditional marriages both in the United States and the Philippines.

Redefining Motherhood and Marriage

This last section brings us back to the transnational migrant woman worker and social reproductive labor broadly. Filipina women's engagement in social reproductive labor as live-in elderly caregivers in the United States, and as mothers and wives, remains central to their lives—though fraught with contradiction and conflict.

On one level, woman's place in "the home" perseveres despite globalization. Yet, on another level, the women can be understood to be restructuring motherhood and marriage. Changes in Philippine governmental, International Monetary Fund, and World Bank policies would certainly help restore Philippine domestic economic development and enhance women's economic and social power. But in lieu of such macro-level changes, individual women are making choices to ensure the material well-being of their households that inevitably change the structures of families.

Personal Triumphs: Marriage and Motherhood

> Some [women in the Philippines] asked me, "How can you leave [your husband]? How can you leave the Philippines? You can't take care of yourself over there!" . . . Well, five months later, heeeere I am! And one year later? I'm driving. I showed them.
>
> —Filipina live-in caregiver

Women's economic independence is definitively forged through their migration. Without downplaying the limited freedom and dangers that overseas women workers face, Elizabeth Uy Eviota writes that in migration, "women are able to seek a way out of situations they find subordinating or oppressive and to exercise options for themselves. By means of remittances women have also begun to play a central role in the maintenance of their families."[39] And this, despite the continued definition of their lives through caring, emotional labor and social reproductive labor, accurately describes what occurred for live-in home healthcare workers in this study.

The Filipina women expressed great satisfaction in terms of personal growth as independent women singly providing for their children, far from family and community support. All the newly single women, particularly those who left unsatisfying or abusive relationships, heralded their newfound "independence," proclaiming their confidence in being able to provide for themselves "anywhere":

> Being alone . . . I'm peaceful at least. Over here [in the United States], you love me as I am, take me as I am. . . . I dress how I like. It's my own decision. This is my face. This is my body, just simple, just me.

The self-confidence exuded by the women reveals the positive aspects of their migration experiences. Some even found that migration allowed them the space and time to look upon Philippine society and openly to critique the norms regarding women's roles—ranging from the silence surrounding domestic violence to the Catholic Church's official position on family planning. Several of the women made connections between the lack of public discussion on birth control and their consequent responsibility for large families when marriages failed.

For the single, remarried, or separated women in this study, this was the first time that their incomes were entirely at their disposal to use toward the sustenance of their immediate households (their children). In many cases, when these women lived in the Philippines, they, not their husbands, ran the household finances. But, echoing the on-going scholarly debate on whether women have "power" through running households, these women did *not* control any surplus.[40] Whether or not women in the Philippines have legitimate power through running household finances generally, as migrant women they are in control of both earning and spending the household finances *in the absence of men*. Hence, they are significantly more empowered than prior to separation.

Further, several of the women with grown children, in combination with the independence gained from living alone, found they were looking forward to this new phase in their lives. As one woman shared: "[My children] are grown up. They're young adults. They have a mind of their own. So now I'm free! I don't have to worry about them anymore." The women who had adult children were, without exception, proud of having brought their children up with little support from male partners. In particular, they emphasized markers such as high school and college graduations, steady jobs, and marriages. Those women who experienced difficulties with their children back in the Philippines (e.g., early marriage, drug use, drinking) steadfastly felt that their ability to support their children financially made the difficulties worthwhile.

Continuity and Change

For all the instances of personal empowerment and success in their children's educational attainments, the women continue to experience structural gender inequalities maintained through political, social, and economic conditions. While Filipinas employed as live-in caregivers in the United States do indeed gain economic independence in the absence of male control, they also remain principally responsible for the children left behind. They also must still engage in underpaid work within the larger international sexual division of labor. And, underscoring that gender inequality in the Philippine household remains in place, there is no escaping in these cases that mothers, sisters, and daughters remaining in the Philippines are taking on the bulk of the responsibility of daily childcare for the overseas workers' children. Further, the women, as separated, divorced, or remarried (arguably sources of their empowerment), must carry the social stigma of that marital "failure" with them. As mothers, they must then endure the daily separation from their children. And it remains to be seen in future studies what effect transnational mothering has had on the children themselves.

Despite the appearance of having "left the home" to work overseas to provide for their families, these Filipina women's lives are defined through "women's work." Filipina elderly caregivers expend much physical and emotional labor in being social reproductive laborers, not only for their husbands, children, and parents but also for their patients in the United States. As one caregiver bluntly commented, "[T]aking care of young children or sick people is basically the same." And while certainly she may be exaggerating to make her point, she has astutely focused on the continuity of social reproductive labor in her own life as well as in the lives of so many other women.

Facing these societal constraints, Filipina women are a living testimony to the possibility of change. Through their very migration, they inevitably redefine the institutions of Philippine motherhood and marriage and thereby their roles as social reproductive laborers. They do not, however, escape these roles. Motherhood and marriage have historically been and continue to be major sites of Filipina women's strength and struggle.

Finally, I emphasize that there is nothing particularly "natural" about the centrality of emotional labor and caring in Philippine (or any) women's lives. The caring work and sacrifice invested by the women in this study are neither happenstance nor arising from some mistakenly assumed innate ability of Filipina women. Women's social reproductive labor is kept in place and reproduced through systematic global political and economic conditions and institutions, enforced by the Philippines and the United States.

It is not by chance that the issues of marriage and motherhood, or family formation, arise most commonly in the discourse on migrant women. Women are the so-called bearers of culture, maintaining the social reproduction of families (children, parents, and husbands) precisely because their choices have, in large part, been limited to these spheres through a sexual division of labor in both the Philippines and the United States. This is not to say that women themselves do not choose to take such responsibilities on and do not gain satisfaction and fulfillment from them. However, it is a mistake to remain blind to institutional (political, economic, and social) and structural limitations on women's lives worldwide.

NOTES

My sincerest appreciation to Shirley Hune for her comments on earlier drafts and to both her and Gail Nomura for their encouragement and enthusiasm for this work. Thank you to Evelyn Nakano Glenn, Barrie Thorne, Arlie Hochschild, and UC Berkeley's Center for Working Families Fall 2001 workshop participants for their support and feedback. Thank you also to Dorothy Fujita Rony, Kitty Calavita, and the women who shared their stories.

1. Parts of this essay appear in different form in "The Cost of Caring: The Social Reproductive Labor of Live-in Home Healthcare Workers, *Frontiers* 21:12 (2000): 61–83. I use the terms

elderly caregivers (used by the women) and *home healthcare worker* (used by social services/home healthcare industry) interchangeably. This essay draws from my dissertation, "The Social Reproductive Labor of Filipina Transmigrant Workers in Southern California: Caring for Those Who Provide Care" (University of California, Irvine, 1999), conducted in two Southern California counties over a two-year period, 1996–1998.

2. Evelyn Nakano Glenn, "From Servitude to Service Work: Historical Continuities in the Racial Division of Paid Reproductive Labor," *Signs* 18 (1992): 1.

3. Evelyn Nakano Glenn, *Issei, Nisei, War Bride: Three Generations of Japanese American Women in Domestic Service.* (Philadelphia: Temple University Press, 1986), 14.

4. Since the mid-1970s and throughout the 1980s, married Philippine men migrated to the Middle East to work construction jobs and/or to teach. However, the implications for women's family roles remain largely unexplored.

5. "Globalization" here refers to movements of goods, services, institutions, and people. It involves the encroachment of multinational corporations into developing nations, structural adjustment policies (e.g., import substitution imposed by the International Monetary Fund and World Bank), and subsequent international development strategies involving export processing zones (see, e.g., William Tabb "Progressive Globalism: Challenging the Audacity of Capital," *Monthly Review* 50:9 [1999]), 1. Globalization also involves a distinct change in the composition and volume of transnational migrants (and communities) from so-called Third World or developing nations to destinations throughout the world. For more discussion of global restructuring, see Rhacel Parreñas, chapter 16 in this book.

6. The outflux of Filipina women employed as domestics worldwide has been increasingly documented. See Rhacel Parreñas, *Servants of Globalization: Women, Migration, and Domestic Work* (Stanford: Stanford University Press, 2001), a comparative analysis of domestic-worker communities in Los Angeles and Rome. Also see Nicole Constable, *Maid to Order in Hong Kong* (New York: Cornell University Press, 1997).

7. Jose Brillantes, "Addressing the Problems of Filipino Migrant Workers," in *OCWs in Crisis: Protecting Filipino Migrant Workers,* ed. Ateneo Human Rights Center (Makati: Ateneo Human Rights Center, 1995), 15–20.

8. 1997 Philippine Central Bank figures in Kim Scipes, "Global Economic Crisis, Neoliberal Solutions, and the Philippines," *Monthly Review* 51 (1999): 5.

9. See Sylvia Chant and Cathy McIlwaine, *Women of a Lesser Cost* (Manila: Ateneo de Manila Press, 1995); and Rosalinda Pineda-Ofreneo, *The Philippines: Debt and Poverty* (Oxford: Oxfam, 1991).

10. Grace Kovar, Gerry Hendershot, and Evelyn Mathis, "Older People in the United States Who Receive Help with Basic Activities of Daily Living," *American Journal of Public Health* 79 (1989): 778–79.

11. Filipina/o registered nurses are beneficiaries of "foreign nurses" training and recruitment programs initiated between the United States, Canada, and the Philippines. See Catherine Ceniza Choy, "Asian American History: Reflections on Imperialism, Immigration, and 'The Body,'" *Amerasia Journal* 26:1 (2000): 119–41.

12. The quotes around "natural" signal that this is a disputed understanding.

13. A review of the racially and gender segregated history of paid domestic work in the United States reveals that Filipina migrant women of today are merely a continuation of a long line of mostly women of color (African American, Latina, and Asian) employed as domestic workers. Bonnie Thornton Dill, "Our Mother's Grief: Racial Ethnic Women and the Maintenance of Families," *Journal of Family History* 13 (1988): 415–31; Mary Romero, *Maid in the USA* (New York: Routledge, 1992); and Glenn, *Issei, Nisei, War Bride.*

14. All quotes from live-in caregivers were obtained through personal interviews conducted 1996–98. While self-identification for class status usually results in a "middle-class" designation, these designations were supported by information regarding the Filipina caregivers' parents' and their own lifestyles, including ownership of land, property, and/or businesses and educational attainments.

15. Metro Manila refers to the metropolitan hub surrounding the capital city and the financial center, where one-third of the entire urban population of the Philippines resides. Chant and McIlwaine, *Women of a Lesser Cost,* 67.

16. There were two exceptions to biological motherhood. One woman officially adopted a niece and nephew. The other woman took in a friend's children when that friend left for the United States to be a caregiver.

17. Filipina live-in elderly caregivers in the United States were generally older than Filipina workers in Hong Kong, for example, who average between twenty-five and thirty-five years old. Constable, *Maid to Order in Hong Kong,* 69.

18. Home health placement agencies sometimes require that caregivers be CNAs. For patients, hiring a noncredentialed caregiver was far cheaper ($3.33/hour) than hiring a licensed vocational nurse (LVN), licensed professional nurse (LPN), or registered nurse (RN) ($31.00/hour). In most cases, a caregiver eventually took on many of the duties of more highly trained persons through on-site training from visiting nurses or doctors. See Tung, "Cost of Caring," 61–83.

19. In no case in this study did a caregiver's agency provide healthcare or negotiate required duties or basic necessities.

20. Tung, "Cost of Caring," 69.

21. In some cases, a patient's medical condition (e.g., requiring the checking of trachea tubes) necessitated that caregivers awake every couple of hours. In other cases, patients constantly called the caregiver (e.g., for water, food, comfort)—making sleeping through the night impossible.

22. Pseudonyms are used throughout.

23. Emily Abel and Margaret Nelson, *Circles of Care* (New York: SUNY Press, 1990), 4.

24. Stella Go, *The Filipina Family in the Eighties* (Manila: Manila Social Development Research Center, 1993), 13; and Keith B. Richburg, "Filipino Diaspora Led by Its Maids," *Washington Post,* Nov. 3, 1995, sec. A.

25. Belen Medina, *The Filipino Family: A Text with Selected Readings* (Quezon City: University of the Philippines Press, 1991), 133, 193.

26. Delia Aguilar, *Toward a Nationalist Feminism* (Quezon City: Giraffe Books, 1998), 116, 127.

27. Mina Roces, *Women, Power, and Kinship Politics: Female Power in Post-War Philippines* (Westport, CT: Praeger, 1998), 100.

28. Exceptions include (1) if the marriage is annulled; (2) if one originally married a foreigner and divorce was obtained abroad; and (3) if one person converts to Islam, in which divorce is recognized by Philippine law. Go, *Filipina Family,* 42, 54.

29. Chant and McIlwaine, *Women of a Lesser Cost,* 14.

30. Although the 1990 Philippine census records showed only 1.3 percent of Filipinas as separated or divorced, the percentage is likely much higher in reality. Since the Philippines government does not allow absolute divorce, it is unclear how divorced women would choose to report. Further, underestimation of female-headed households is probably widespread because most separations are informal arrangements (i.e., not legally binding). Single mothers are often subsumed under the census count of their sisters' or parents' homes. See Chant and McIlwaine,

Women of a Lesser Cost, 14, 18; and Sylvia Chant and Cathy McIlwaine, "The Social Construction of Sexuality," in *Sex and Gender in Philippine Society*, ed. Elizabeth Uy Eviota (Manila: National Commission on the Role of Filipino Women, 1994), 53–82.

31. See Parreñas, *Servants of Globalization*, 116–49; Pierrette Hondagneu-Sotelo and Ernestine Avila, "'I'm Here, but I'm There': The Meanings of Latina Transnational Motherhood," *Gender and Society* 11 (1997): 548–70; and Shellee Colen, "'Just a Little Respect': West Indian Domestic Workers in New York City," in *Muchachas No More: Household Workers in Latin America and the Caribbean*, ed. Elsa Chaney and Mary Garcia Castro (Philadelphia: Temple University Press, 1988), 171–96.

32. Essays in Evelyn Nakano Glenn, Grace Chang, and Linda Renney Forcey, eds., *Mothering: Ideology, Experience, and Agency* (New York: Routledge, 1994), illustrate the contradiction surrounding the ideology and experience of mothering. For example, mothers are romanticized as self-sacrificing and selfless bearers of life and at the same time demonized as overbearing, destructive, and smothering—seen as all-powerful in raising future "leaders," yet powerless.

33. Colen, "'Just a Little Respect,'" 172–73; and Romero, *Maid in the USA*, 17–45.

34. For more on extended mothering, see Pierrette Hondagneu-Sotelo, *Domestica: Immigrant Workers Cleaning and Caring in the Shadows of Affluence* (Berkeley: University of California Press, 2001), 22–27.

35. Virginia Miralao, "The Impact of Female Employment on Household Management," in *Women in the Urban and Industrial Workforce: Southeast and East Asia* (Canberra: Development Studies Centre Monograph, 1984), 379.

36. The women are also constrained by the 1996 Illegal Immigration and Immigrant Responsibility Act, which includes provisions barring entry for a period of three to ten years to those who overstay their U.S. visitor visas, depending on length of overstay. Further, both the INS and the Labor Department fail to acknowledge the demand for these workers (unlike for professional nurses). Post–September 11th INS regulations further constrain these workers' choices as visa overstayers.

37. Jurgette Honculada, "The Family Household," in Eviota, ed., *Sex and Gender*, 14.

38. More than half the women were remarried. Over the course of the two years of the study, all the remarried women continued to live separately from their new husbands.

39. Elizabeth Eviota, *The Political Economy of Gender: Women and the Sexual Division of Labour in the Philippines* (London: Zed Books, 1992), 143.

40. See Rae Blumberg, ed., *Gender, Family and Economy: The Triple Overlap* (Newbury Park, CA: Sage, 1991); and Chant and McIlwaine, *Women of a Lesser Cost*, 256–303.

Part 7

Challenging Community and the State
Contemporary Spaces of Struggle

19

Asian[1] Lesbians in San Francisco
Struggles to Create a Safe Space, 1970s–1980s

Trinity A. Ordona

Introduction

On October 12–15, 1979, more than six hundred Black, Latino, American Indian, Asian, and white people attended the First National Third World Gay and Lesbian Conference in Washington, D.C. That same weekend, the First National March for Gay and Lesbian Rights gathered more than one hundred thousand people in the nation's capital to dramatize their stand against a fierce anti-gay assault led by a coalition of New Right religious fundamentalists and Republican Party neoconservative politicians. Two hundred conferees, including a dozen Asians, marched as a Third World Contingent.[2] Later, Michiyo Cornell spoke for the newly formed Lesbian and Gay Asian Collective and told them:

> We are called the model minority, the quiet, passive, exotic erotics with the slanted cunt to match our "slanted" eye or the small dick to match our small size. But we are not. . . . We share the same problems that other Third World lesbian and gay men share. Because of fear of deportation, because of Asian American dependence on our families and Asian American communities for support, it is very difficult for us to be out of the closet. But we need to come out of the closet. For not to do so, we would be living a lie, and the great lie, which is America, can use that weakness not only to destroy Asian American lesbians and gay men, but also our Third World lesbian and gay sisters and brothers.[3]

Exhorting an anti-racist politics and a liberationist vision, Michiyo then challenged the race and class privilege of the assembled white gays and lesbians:

> You share oppression from homophobia with us, but unless you begin to address your white skin privilege and actively support Asian American lesbian and gay men, you will not have our support and you will lose out on a chance to build the kind of world we all need, to live decently and lead full productive lives.[4]

Together, the 1979 Third World Conference and National Gay Rights March gave birth to a seminal Asian gay and lesbian movement. Soon afterward, Asian lesbians and gay men renewed their organizing efforts in New York and San Francisco, while new gay men's groups formed in Boston, Philadelphia, and Toronto.

Homosexuality, bisexuality, and transgenderism do not discriminate. They are found across time in every gender, race, ethnicity, nationality, class, and social group of the world. In the United States, where gender and sexual minorities are stigmatized, the gay, lesbian, bisexual, transgender, and queer (GLBTQ)[5] movements launched in the 1970s pushed American social, cultural, and political boundaries and gained some degree of acceptance and civil rights protection. But Asian and Pacific Islander[6] sexual and gender minorities—and all queer people of color, for that matter—are not recipients of the full bounty of those advances. While fighting stigma from the broader American society, queer people of color also face marginalization within the GLBTQ movement as well as from their ethnic families and communities. The 1979 Washington, D.C., events described above marked a turning point for all queer people of color. Today, an overlapping local, regional, national, and international network of hundreds of GLBTQ Black/African American, Latino, American Indian, Asian, Pacific Islander, and South West Asian/North African individuals, groups, and organizations strives to confront racism, sexism, and homo/bi/transphobia on multiple fronts.

This is a brief history of Asian lesbians in San Francisco in the 1970s and early 1980s and their struggles to build a community. During this same period, Asian and Pacific Islander gay, lesbian, and bisexual people in Honolulu, Los Angeles, and New York City launched similar organizing efforts.[7] While the San Francisco women's experience is not unique, their story typifies the cultural barriers, political inexperience, and lack of resources that challenged everyone in the beginning. Collectively, the efforts of this generation laid the foundation for the Asian/Pacific Islander and broader people of color GLBTQ community and movement of today. This is just one small part of that story.

Unchallenged Homophobia in 1960s Movements

How did queer people of color find themselves on the outskirts of entire movements that purported to fight racism or homophobia but failed to include their queer or colored members? This conjunction can be traced back to the race, gender, and sexuality contradictions in the civil rights, women's, and anti-war/anti-imperialist movements that exploded with the emergence of "Black Power" in 1966.

Black Power articulated the desire from Black people for militant all-Black organizations to lead the Black struggle. This idea took powerful hold in the youth wing of the civil rights movement, the Student Nonviolent Coordinating Committee (SNCC). SNCC began the 1960s with idealism, dedication, and a deep-seated belief in direct-action nonviolent politics as they organized voter registration drives throughout the South. However, after a decade of unchecked violence from racist state police and vigilante forces and a profound disillusionment with liberalism, many in SNCC questioned the reforms won by the newly passed Civil Rights and Voting Rights legislation. Intent on uprooting institutionalized racism, they looked instead to the self-determinationist politics of the newly decolonized African states and the armed revolutionary movements in Asia and Latin America. In 1966, SNCC changed direction under the

Black cultural nationalist leadership of Stokely Carmichael (a.k.a. Kwame Ture). He supported the call for SNCC to become "black staffed, black controlled and black financed" and to "cut [themselves] off from white people."[8] Straining under convoluted race, class, gender, and sexual internal dynamics that had already polarized Black versus white and men versus women in SNCC, the white people in the organization were eventually asked to leave.

This decision marked a deep split that not only separated Black people from white people in SNCC but prompted all social movements to follow suit. The political empowerment organizing tendencies that rose with Black Power quickly transformed into various forms of cultural nationalism in the Black, Latino, American Indian, Asian, and Pacific Islander communities, led by organizations such as the Black Panther Party, La Raza Unida, the Young Lords Party, the American Indian Movement, and the Red Guards. Under their influence, people of color community organizing moved rapidly forward on a separatist trajectory in parallel with, yet distinctly apart from, the white anti–Vietnam War, women's, and homophile[9] movements.

Although a disconcerting period for white activists who had previously looked to the Black movement for leadership, this was an effusive period of individual and collective discovery and challenge for young Black, Latino, American Indian, Asian, and Pacific Islander activists. For Asian and Pacific Islander people on the West Coast and in Hawai'i, collective empowerment gathered hundreds who reclaimed a common past and worked toward a common future. In the 1970s, the pan-Asian/Pacific movement came alive with the energy and ideals of young activists who crisscrossed daily in various community and campus struggles.

But in all the cultural nationalist movements, sexism, misogyny, and homophobia were unchallenged. Machismo, violence, and death were idealized as acts of manhood;[10] femininity was defined as submissiveness;[11] and homosexuality was proclaimed "a sickness, just as baby rape."[12] Despite support of the gay struggle from Black Panther Party chair Huey Newton,[13] the gay movement was viewed as illegitimate at best, and at worst a corruption of politics because civil rights were advocated for a group that should be criminally policed, punished, and eradicated. Additionally, for Asian American activists who looked especially to China for inspiration, Maoism declared "homosexuals cannot be communists."[14] But it was Cuba's anti-gay position that slammed the door on *out* Black, Latino, and Asian gays and lesbians in their own communities.

Cuba, the first socialist country in the Western Hemisphere, came to power in 1959 and was blockaded immediately by the United States. In 1969, however, the anti-war organization Students for a Democratic Society (SDS) organized the first "Venceremos Brigade," a group of North American volunteers who helped with the sugarcane harvest in Cuba.[15] In the first years of the Brigade, some openly gay Brigadistas tried to hold workshops and distribute Gay Liberation Front materials in Cuba. After an initial period of ambiguity, however, the Cuban Communist Party stated in 1971 that "all manifestations of homosexual deviations are to be firmly rejected and prevented from spreading" and that offenders would suffer severe penalties.[16] The Venceremos Brigade then criticized those members who had appeared in drag or acted in an overtly sexual manner at parties as "imposing North American gay culture on the Cubans."[17] Thereafter, North American gays were excluded from Cuban solidarity work until a policy change in 1984. In the intervening years, Brigadistas returned home and played leading roles in the Asian, Latino, and Black communities, and for the most part, Cuba's anti-gay politics went with them and took root.

"I Could Not Tell Anybody"

Sylvia Savellano, a Filipino American from Oakland, met her first Brigadistas at Grove Street College. Syl was impressed with the Brigadistas' community work and viewed communism as "communities working together."[18] Syl was twenty years old when she went on the Third Venceremos Brigade to Cuba in 1970 and was joined by two hundred other politically radical young men and women of all races from across the United States. The six-week experience of working in the sugarcane fields, living in bunkhouses, meeting young Cubans, and visiting institutions was a turning point for her and her companions.

Before Syl went to Cuba, however, she was seeing a Honduran woman. She thought about coming out during the Brigade selection process but decided against it. Since Cuba viewed homosexuality as a "crime against the people,"[19] upon her return Syl knew that it was impossible to be a gay person in the movement. So she buried her feelings, volunteered at the San Francisco International Hotel, and was one of the first (among very few) women activists in the Kearny Street Asian American Movement.

Syl led a double life, an assumed *straight sister* in the Asian American movement during the day and a *pervert* at night in gay dance clubs. Recalled Syl, "It was isolating. It was a quiet thing. I could not tell anybody. Any inclinations, I had to can it. . . . I came out to my family because of the I-Hotel. But to my Movement friends I lived with . . . they did not know what was going on."[20] Then it all came to a head when one of Syl's fellow Brigadistas called a meeting to start a chapter of the Third World Women's Alliance (TWWA) in the Bay Area in 1971. Syl, along with her girlfriend and several other lesbians of color, piled into a car and enthusiastically went to the first meeting called for women of color:

> We thought we could express our sexual identity. Wrong. . . . We were isolated. We felt bad. We all picked up that we were not welcome, at least to not talk about our lesbianism. So we pulled out. We got the cold shaft. . . . In the Asian and Third World movement, we could have been treated better. It felt like our own people [were] stabbing us. [Name withheld] said, "We are not going to have any of 'that' here; we have too many bigger issues." So we boycotted [the TWWA]. We did not want to go. It was only for straight women. It was not the place to go."[21]

Syl never spoke about this incident to her other Brigade friends. Afterward, she left her Brigade house collective and moved to her brother's place.

Fortunately, Syl was Filipina and found a place in the Filipino radical group KDP (*Katipunan ng mga Demokratikong Pilipino*, Union of Democratic Filipinos). Homosexuals were allowed in KDP because one of its founding national leaders, Melinda Paras, was a lesbian. Melinda, born and raised in Madison, Wisconsin, was a young teenage Asian American anti-war activist and Venceremos Brigadista when she went to the Philippines and joined the revolutionary nationalist movement. She joined one of the revolutionary nationalist groups, *Kabataan Makabayan* (Patriotic Youth), and eventually worked with the American GI movement on the U.S. bases to develop support for the Philippine cause. On September 23, 1972, immediately after the declaration of martial law in the Philippines by President Ferdinand Marcos, Melinda was arrested and deported back to the United States. Returning to the Midwest, Melinda immediately linked up with other anti-Marcos nationalist Filipinos and Filipino Americans to organize the overseas community to stop U.S. aid to the Philippines.

A year later, the radical members of the Philippine support network formed KDP. Melinda was elected to its three-person national executive leadership committee, along with Cynthia Maglaya and Bruce Occena. In October 1973, Melinda left Madison, moved into the KDP's national headquarters in Oakland, and soon began a relationship with another female KDP member (this author) who also lived at the headquarters. Melinda immediately informed her leadership group of her personal situation. There was no problem with her lesbianism, as Cynthia's older sister was a lesbian and Bruce was supportive. Melinda's stellar political credentials as a revolutionary movement activist and deportee also deflected any question that homosexuality had suddenly transformed her into a "social parasite." Melinda's standing as one of the KDP national leaders, however, was paramount to protect. Fearful that KDP's detractors would use Melinda's homosexuality to discredit the organization, the couple did not disclose their relationship. But it was a well-guarded *known secret* in the organization, and eventually there were a dozen gay and lesbian KDP members. As a result, Filipino lesbians and gays in KDP gained political skills not available to other queer people of color, equipping them to contribute substantially in later years to a wide range of movement-organizing efforts.[22]

"If You Don't Want Me, I Don't Need to Be Here"

In the meantime, lesbians and gays were pushed out of the Asian American movement of the 1970s. Born in Hong Kong and raised there until she was five, Kitty Tsui moved to England and then to the United States as a young adult, with her parents and grandmother. At age twenty-three, Kitty entered San Francisco State University in 1970, at the tail end of the Third World Strike for Ethnic Studies. Immediately thrust into the midst of radical race, gender, and anti-imperialist politics, Kitty became part of a small circle of Asian American writers, poets, and theater artists (now the "who's who" in Asian American literature). A rising talent, Kitty was busy giving poetry readings and working with the Asian American Theater in a few years. Then, in 1975, she fell in love with a Chinese woman. Elated with her newfound happiness, Kitty simply told everyone and came out publicly as a lesbian in a poetry reading that same year. Kitty's maternal grandmother, who raised her in Hong Kong, readily accepted her granddaughter's homosexuality; Kitty's mother reacted with tears and self-blame.[23] They have never talked about it since. Kitty, however, was most disappointed by her circle of ostensibly progressive Asian American men and women:

All of sudden, I realized I began to feel coldness and hostility. I told everybody. I was not hidden about it. I think for myself that I retreated from the Chinese American and Asian American community and tried to find a community with the gay and lesbian community. "If you don't want me, I don't need to be here." From 1975–78 I was very involved with my two lovers. That was my way of retreating. I did not go looking for support in the white community. I just isolated myself with my lovers, Chinese women.[24]

Like the Black Power Movement, the Asian American movement was sexist, heterosexist, and homophobic. One Japanese American lesbian and media activist recalled that the women's role was "to protect the manhood of the men" and "consider ourselves more as Asians than as women."[25] Kitty also noted that the first significant collection of writings by Asian American writers, *Aiiieeeee!* published in 1974, had no women on the editorial team. (Furthermore, the 1990 edition begins with Frank Chin's notorious harangue against the work of Maxine Hong Kingston, Amy Tan, and David Henry Hwang for their portrayal of emasculated and sexually repellent—read homosexual—Chinese men.)[26]

Asian Lesbians Find a Home among Gay People of Color

The liberationist politics that took off in 1969 with the Stonewall Rebellion did not deliver on its promise of rainbow inclusion. Within a few short years, the radical call for *gay power* was replaced with *gay pride* and mainstream inclusion of its white middle-class majority. With the dominance of single-issue (read gay-only) politics in the gay movement by 1973, few white brothers and sisters in the gay and lesbian movement were exposed to anything other than "gay" issues and soon became oblivious to the problems faced by gay people of color. The 1970s was the heyday of Gay and Lesbian Pride, as people came out of the closet in droves. Gay parades, discos, and rainbow flags sprouted up everywhere, while popular music, movies, novels, television shows, and politics reflected this changing reality across the country.

While many Black, Latino, American Indian, Asian, and Pacific Islander people found relative acceptance in the white gay community on an individual basis, the relegation of the struggle against racism to the sidelines left them with little alternative but to organize themselves for the struggle on multiple fronts of racism, sexism, and homophobia. Cross-racial coalitions and race-specific organizations formed across the country, mirroring the separatist practices of their brothers and sisters in the straight movements. By 1975 in San Francisco, the Gay American Indians and Gay Latino/a Alliance had formed, while Black gay men and women formed several networks. In 1977, the same year as the New Right's first assault, Asian lesbians in San Francisco began to organize.

Doreena Wong, a second-generation Chinese American, was a shy, studious young woman from a middle-class family in Millbrae, California, when she entered the University of California, Santa Cruz in 1969. The campus, however, was in turmoil over racism in the anti-war movement. Asian American activists had observed that the movement was concerned only for the loss of American (read white), not Vietnamese (read Asian), lives. Asian American activists soon formed their own group and began a long, bitter fight with the anti-war movement to take a stand against racism.[27]

Doreena joined other Asian Americans and attended the anti-war rallies and helped out at the International Hotel. But soon after graduation, Doreena fell in love with her roommate. It was very traumatic: "I was really scared. I really did not want to be a lesbian, to be outside the norm and not getting married. . . . I knew my family would disapprove. They were rigid. They knew what they wanted. . . . The further away I went from their expectations, the further away I might be from the family. So I first had to find out, for sure, if I was gay or not."[28]

In 1975–76, Doreena moved back home to live with her parents, but she visited San Francisco often, scouring the women's community for lesbian support groups. The consciousness-raising (CR) groups she found were all white, and she did not feel comfortable enough to talk in them. Doreena, who had previous political experience with groups, vacillated between passivity and frustration. She felt misunderstood and invisible. "I couldn't just say, 'My family was the first to move into an all-white neighborhood,' and be understood. The women did not have the personal experience to know what that felt like. I always had to explain myself. . . . I actually went to several different groups. . . . But I was usually the only lesbian of color in the groups."[29] After six months of these discouraging experiences, Doreena formed a support group for women of color. This group had monthly potluck meetings in Berkeley and was a welcome improvement. Still, Doreena was the only Asian woman in that group, too.

Canyon Sam, a second-generation Chinese American lesbian writer and performance artist from San Francisco, came out in the lesbian feminist community at nineteen years of age. Recalled Canyon, "I came out in 1975. . . . What was really exciting for me was the political atmosphere, especially around feminism—radical feminism, radical lesbian feminism. Consequently a lot of women at that time, including myself, came out with this two-prong coming out—personal and political."[30] It was an exciting time of meeting interesting women, holding long discussions about feminism and separatism, reading women's magazines, listening to women's music, and attending women's events. Like Doreena, Canyon was usually the only Asian woman. Worse yet, she was underage and constantly thrown out of the lesbian bars. Eventually she moved to Oregon, where she found a lesbian feminist community. There she lived on the land, worked with tools, and built homes. Affirmed by these experiences, Canyon told her parents of her sexual orientation, and they responded well. But the cultural isolation she experienced as the only woman of color was a constant problem. Then, fortunately, she met Doreena, who had just visited to make connections with lesbians of color on the land. Shortly afterward, in 1977, Canyon returned to San Francisco and looked up Doreena. They quickly became friends and began to organize.

Canyon and Doreena called an ad hoc support-group meeting that later became known as Asian American Feminists (AAF). They posted notices in the local feminist newspapers and bookstores and sent cards out to people they knew. Besides Doreena and Canyon, Kitty Tsui, Barbara Noda, Allison Chop, and Zee Wong came to the first meeting. They were all feminists *and* lesbians. Doreena recalled:

We were all ecstatic and talked about being together. It was only six of us, but at that time, that was a lot—with always being the only one all the time! . . . [T]hen we kept meeting for two years. Sharing your story with a group of people is a very intimate, personal thing to do and I guess the process of doing it drew us all together. I had never experienced that kind of closeness before. . . . Some of the stories were very sad. There were some very hard struggles that people went through; their hurts, their pains. Of course, as Asian women, the sexism in our culture was something we all shared in our struggles, too, so our stories had familiarity. It took a lot of trust to tell your story and it built trust in the process of doing it.[31]

Over the next two years, they were joined by more than a dozen other Asian women.[32] Eventually some of the lesbians began dating each other and forming couples. Inevitably, "old" couples broke up to form "new" couples—an emotional process that caused some women to leave the group for a while. After everyone had shared their stories, AAF meetings ended in 1979. That time was a precious incubation period when everyone needed and appreciated each other. These friendships were soon tested by difficult political and ideological differences.

A Community Grows, Falters, and Moves On

In the 1980s, this circle of friends and lovers evolved into a small community that grew steadily. In 1979, AAF member Zee Wong co-founded *Gente* (People), the first lesbian of color group in the Bay Area; soon Zee held the first of many annual Women's Get-Togethers where Asian, Black, Latino, and white lesbian friends gathered. Gisele Pohan, a Japanese-Indonesian lesbian, went to the 1979 March on Washington and later worked at the Artemis Cafe, a woman-only restaurant and cabaret that served the women's community. Canyon and Crystal Jang, a Chinese American lesbian teacher, joined the public-speaking campaign against the Briggs Initiative, which threatened to prohibit homosexual teachers in public schools.

The late 1970s and early 1980s were also a period of path-breaking cultural work by women of color, and Asian lesbian writers were active participants. Pat Parker, a San Francisco poet and outspoken Black lesbian activist, was performing in many local venues. The year 1981 saw the publication of *This Bridge Called My Back*, edited by Chicana lesbians Cherrie Moraga and Gloria Anzaldúa. This landmark radical women of color anthology, which later received the prestigious Columbus Book Award, included works by Asian feminists Nellie Wong, Barbara Noda, and Merle Woo.

In June 1981 the Asian American Theater Company presented Barbara Noda's one-act existential play *Aw Shucks (Shikata Ga Nai)*, about three stereotypical women devoted to pleasure, money, and spirituality. Jill Togawa, from Hawaii and then New York, where she trained on scholarship with the Martha Graham Dance School, moved to San Francisco and eventually formed her own all–women of color dance company, the Purple Moon Dance Project. Willyce Kim joined the new genre of lesbian fiction novelists with *Dancer Dawkins and the California Kid* (1985) and *Dead Heat* (1988). Merle, Barbara, Willyce, Kitty, and Canyon performed singly or together in numerous groups, productions, and poetry readings throughout the 1970s–1980s. Asian lesbians and gay men were even acknowledged in *Bridge*, the premier Asian American movement magazine.[33]

The most significant cultural contribution by Asian lesbians in this period was the formation of Unbound Feet (UF) in 1979. The first feminist Chinese American women's performance group, UF was composed of Canyon Sam, Kitty Tsui, Nellie Wong, Nancy Hom, Genny Lim, and Merle Woo. Using the metaphorical image of *bound and unbound feet*, from a poem by Genny and a four-line chorus written by Nellie, the group challenged the stereotypes of passivity and servitude that *bound* Chinese women in their mind. The signature piece that opened each program described the crippling process in which a young girl's toes were bent back to her heel and held in place by bandages. With feet thus bound—made small to fashionably emulate a lotus bud—Chinese girls were painfully initiated into womanhood. Closing with a choral refrain, however, the poets declared themselves unbound women—writers, workers and free. Through individual and group performance, they creatively addressed sexism, immigration, and family issues and developed a huge following of straight Asian Americans and lesbians. The women themselves—six very talented, strong, and powerful women—were the key to the group's popularity. Kitty, Canyon, and Merle, who were lesbian (stated in the program notes) and openly challenged homophobia by their public disclosure, were greatly admired, especially by other lesbians. In fact, Zee Wong's UF after-parties were popular gathering places for new Asian lesbians coming into the community.

A calendar of scheduled performances, a book contract, and a possible engagement in Hong Kong were all in the works when an irreparable split in the group brought everything to an abrupt halt.[34] Unable to reconcile their differences, Unbound Feet broke up. When Merle, Nellie, and Kitty wanted to continue to perform under the name Unbound Feet–Three, the remaining three (Canyon, Nancy, and Genny) vigorously disagreed. Their dispute was carried out in public through lengthy letters to the editor in a women's community newspaper for the next five months.[35] The divide deepened as statements, counterstatements, and a picket line forced sides to be taken. After a year without the group meeting again or a concession from either side, the struggle for the control of UF's legacy ended, and with it an otherwise effective public education forum on Asian women's issues.

The end of UF was a setback for the Asian American movement and could have also ended the fragile community among Asian lesbians. But it did not. Merle, Canyon, and Kitty had performed together before Unbound Feet. After UF was over, they never spoke to each other about it but continued to participate in the Asian lesbian community. According to Kitty, no one was excluded from the community "unless you took yourself out, unless you said that you were no longer a lesbian."[36] Earlier too, during the days of the Asian American Feminists, when personal relationships led to love triangles and messy breakups, a lesbian was not excluded from the community. The women would keep their distance and friends would comfort each other. Some would leave, but they could always come back when they wanted.

Personal Contacts Build a Community Network

Despite the Unbound Feet debacle, the small community of mostly American-born local Chinese and Japanese women grew, and the women renewed their efforts to organize a group. One of the driving forces behind this move was Lisa Chun. Lisa had moved from the Midwest to San Francisco in the early 1970s to find her roots. In 1979, she was engaged to a young Chinese man, but a month before her wedding she discovered her lesbianism. Lisa called everything off and immediately told her family, who after the initial shock were accepting. She then explored gay life, but she met only white lesbians who were insensitive to the racial and cultural issues Lisa faced. Eventually, Lisa met some Asian lesbians who took her to her first potluck party. The potluck parties were a "safe space" for Asian lesbians to meet, socialize, make friends, fall in love, build relationships, and develop their lesbian lives away from the prying eyes of family, friends, and co-workers.

Together with Zee Wong, Lisa compiled what would become the Asian Women's Group's mailing list. In 1977 there were only 6 women, but by 1983 there were 112 people. Initially, however, the mailing list was controversial. At the time, most of the women were from San Francisco Bay Area; many were in their twenties and still lived at home; fewer than a dozen were out to their families. The mailing list was available to anyone on the list itself, with this condition stated at the top: "Word of caution: These names, addresses and phone numbers are confidential. For personal use only. Do not add them to another organization's mailing list, unless you have each woman's consent. Discretion is advised when using phone numbers, since many women live with relatives."[37] The strict confidential use of the mailing list and abstention from using the "L" (lesbian) word were matters of survival.

Usually, a young Asian woman faced her family's expectation that she would marry and have children. This pressure would not end until she was thirty-five or forty years old—ten to fifteen years ahead for the women on the Asian Women's Group list. Resisting marriage was an effort, but hiding one's homosexuality was a struggle. Asian cultural traditions value filial piety and obligation of children to the family unit. Like most of society, Asian parents also viewed homosexuality with disdain and horror. Homosexuality was a volatile combination of stricture and stigma. These women knew that their nonnormative sexual orientation could result in being disowned by their families. To guard themselves and their parents from the possible pain, most bound themselves to silence. Explained Canyon:

> The white culture is not as family based. In . . . the Asian culture, your family is sticking to you, even if you move away; whereas white women, [they] just split. I know white women who have not seen their parents in eight–ten years, had not spoken to them. They don't have that emphasis on the family unit. [For us] it was always an issue if you came out to your parents. What would it do? Would it give them a heart attack? . . . [So] to meet in a group with lesbians in an organized way who were Asian and lesbian—that was a big deal! That was like being out in a certain way.[38]

Inspired by the example of Black, American Indian, and Latino gay and lesbian organizations, Lisa Chun, Janet Tom, and a few others created Asian Women's Group (AWG). (Notably, the word *lesbian* was not in their name, for the reasons described above.) AWG's goals were to build a "sense of self-identity, pride ... [and] community" among Asian lesbians.[39] AWG wrote a survey and held the first publicly advertised Asian lesbian event, an "Asian Women's Potluck: A Gathering for Asian Lesbians," on June 19, 1983, at the Swedish American Hall in San Francisco. Later that month, the June 1983 Gay Parade Program featured a full-page story on Asian lesbians and gay men in San Francisco.[40]

Asian lesbian political identity was growing too. On October 20, 1983, Lisa and a friend dropped by Ollie's, a lesbian bar in Oakland. To their horror, they found it was "Oriental Night," where the bartender and employees wore "Oriental" costumes. Lisa Chun wrote to the owner of Ollie's:

> Thinking perhaps the bartender was unaware of the racist concept of the term, "Oriental," I explained to her that "Oriental" is no longer an acceptable term. That it in fact perpetuates the stereotype of the meek and passive Asians. . . . I was [then] told that there was a "Western Night" and "Army Night," and now this was "Oriental Night." Although a "Western and Army Night" theme may be both novel and fashionable, we find that having an "Oriental Night" in the same context is demeaning and condescending.[41]

While many agreed with Lisa's initiative, a few others thought it improper to be "so out there." Divergent opinions had already surfaced on earlier issues, such as being out, putting "lesbian" in the name, and holding Asian-only functions. What should AWG do? Before the community really had an opportunity to discuss and settle these important questions, AWG's organizing momentum derailed after a contentious community meeting.[42] Unlike earlier conflicts over personal relationships and the disappointing breakup of Unbound Feet, *inexperience and errors in handling political disagreements within the community* led to this heartbreaking episode of discord and disunity. Everyone resigned from the AWG core group, including Lisa.

Six months later, in an effort to keep some community spirit alive, a group of women started a newsletter, eventually named *Phoenix Rising*. The first issue was published in May 1984. (In Egyptian mythology, the phoenix is a bird that consumed itself by fire, but after five hundred years it rose again, renewed from its ashes.) *Phoenix Rising* did not bring the community together organizationally, but it was a way to communicate again. With articles on movie reviews and recipes produced on a manual typewriter and put together at paste-up parties, the newsletter was a welcome community staple. In 1985, a few women organized the first of many annual Chinese New Year banquets, held at a local San Francisco Chinese restaurant.

Sports also brought Asian women together again. San Francisco's Women's Basketball, Softball and Volleyball League games provided an accessible and popular meeting place. Many Asian lesbians "found" each other at ball games. They even arranged challenge games with their Asian lesbian sisters in Los Angeles. In 1984 an all-Asian softball team formed. Two years later, under the tutelage of their new coach, Miki Adachi, the team took the first of three league championship titles. Renamed the Tom Girls in 1987, after their sponsor, Diane Tom, the team played until 1992, when injuries and age forced many to retire from the game. With time, friendships prevailed and the fledgling community survived. But the issues that divided them—being "out" or not, being a political group or a social group—would take center stage in the late 1980s as a new generation of "out, loud, and proud" Asian lesbians stepped forward.

Conclusion

In the 1970s, when the Black, Latino, American Indian, Asian, and Pacific Islander communities took separate paths to political empowerment, their queer members were shunned and pushed aside. Misogyny and narrow cultural nationalism powerfully combined to justify outright homophobia and heterosexism in communities of color. The gay and lesbian movement, which followed the path of "Black Power" to proclaim "Gay Power" in 1969, soon fell back to an accommodationist goal of mainstreaming for white middle-class gay men, while a separatist vision led lesbians to build women-only cultural spaces and social institutions. "Rainbow inclusion" of GLBTQ people of color proved illusory.

As a marginalized people in a marginal community, GLBTQ people of color organized together and separately and eventually established a political and cultural identity that integrated their queer, colored, and gendered selves. The first stage of that process was the creation of a "safe space," a community of like-minded people with whom to socialize, develop relationships, and build a life that would enable them all to struggle against the daily assaults of racism, sexism, and homophobia from society, their families and ethnic communities, and the gay and lesbian movement itself.

The First National Conference of Third World Gays and Lesbians, organized in 1979 at the initiative of the National Coalition of Black Gays (later, National Coalition of Black Gays and Lesbians), provided the first national opportunity for Asian gay men and lesbians to meet, organize, and address their specific issues. In San Francisco, a budding Third World gay movement organized conferences, campaigns, groups, and cultural productions that provided a nourishing environment in which Asian lesbians could meet, gather, and organize. In this environment, Asian lesbians created a community hidden from family, friends, and co-workers. It was a conservative strategy, but one that served them well in the beginning. Almost ten years later, in 1986, the First San Francisco Lesbians of Color Conference (June) and the Fourth International Gay and Lesbian People of Color Conference (November) provided a platform for a new stage and strategy to emerge. Through discussion and networking made possible by these conferences, a new activist core launched the "out, loud, and proud" phase of the movement, setting into motion the forces that became the national Asian/Pacific gay, lesbian, bisexual, transgender, and queer people's movement of today.

Stimulated by the 1986 gatherings, the next generation of Asian lesbians in San Francisco held the first Asian/Pacific Islander–only retreat in May 1987, which inspired a new effort to organize a visible and vocal presence in the lesbian and gay community *and* Asian and Pacific Islander communities. Linking up the following year with key

Asian and Pacific Islander lesbian and bisexual women leaders in Honolulu, Seattle, Los Angeles, Chicago, Boston, Philadelphia, New York, and Washington, D.C., the Asian/Pacific Lesbian Network (APLN) was formed in 1988. (APLN later became APLBTN to reflect the later inclusion of bisexual women and transgendered people.) Over the next fifteen years, this loose national network of individuals and organizations organized a succession of Asian/Pacific Islander–only local, regional, and national retreats and conferences focused on internal political issues of community building, identity, and inclusion. The most recent national conference was held in Los Angeles in 1998 and attended by three hundred Asian/Pacific Islander queer women and transgendered people from across the country. The 1990s will be remembered as the time when Asian and Pacific Islander queer women and transgendered people came into their own.

The space limitations of this chapter do not permit me to relate the trials, tribulations, and triumphs of the national community building process in this later period. But the efforts of this generation of out Asian and Pacific Islander GLBTQ activists were built on ground settled in earlier years by people, like these women who created a place for themselves and, in so doing, assured a place for future generations.

NOTES

1. The women in this essay used *Asian* and *Asian American* interchangeably to identify themselves through the 1970s and early 1980s, but by the late 1980s *Asian* had become the preferred term.

2. See *Gay Community News*, 27 October 1979; and *The Gay Insurgent: A Gay Left Journal* (Summer 1980): 6.

3. Michiyo [Margaret Nishiko] Cornell, "Living in Asian America: An Asian American Lesbian's Address before the Washington Monument (1970)," in Russell Leong, ed., *Asian American Sexualities: Dimensions of the Gay and Lesbian Experience* (New York: Routledge, 1996), 83–84.

4. Cornell, "Living in Asian America." Sadly, Cornell committed suicide a few years after the 1979 Washington march.

5. I use the term *GLBTQ*, and otherwise *queer*, to characterize what has become today's community and movement of sexual (gay, lesbian, bisexual) and gender (transgender) and inclusive/undefined/nonspecific (queer) minorities.

6. Pacific Islander lesbian and bisexual women were not part of the San Francisco Asian lesbian community in the 1970s and 1980s described in this chapter. Therefore, "Asian/Pacific" lesbian is not used in the title or text of this specific account. Though few in number, Pacific Islanders have organized with their Asian sisters and contributed significantly to the overall Asian and Pacific Islander lesbian and bisexual movement since the 1980s. This is reflected in the term *Asian/Pacific*, used in the names of the communities and organizations of the late 1980s, such as Asian/Pacific Lesbian Network and Asian/Pacific Sisters. Of particular historical note are the contributions of such notable Native Hawaiian leaders as Katherine Ekau Amoy Hall (co-founder of the Asian Lesbians of the East Coast, New York, 1983); Lani Kaʻahumanu (co-founder of several bisexual organizations in San Francisco and national leader of the U.S. Bisexual Movement); and Kuʻumeaaloha Gomes (co-founder of Asian/Pacific Lesbian Network [APLN], 1988, and Na Mamo o Hawaiʻi, Honolulu, 1994). For a more complete discussion of their contributions, see Trinity A. Ordona, "Coming Out Together: An Ethnohistory of the Asian and Pacific

Islander Queer Women's and Transgendered People's Movement of San Francisco" (Ph.D. diss., University of California, Santa Cruz, 2000), 219 (Hall), 256–74 (Gomes), 292–97 (Ka'ahumanu).

7. Asian and Pacific Islander gay and bisexual men and transgender people underwent a parallel process of community and movement building at local and national levels. Their story is beyond the scope of this paper. For one account, see Eric C. Wat, *The Making of a Gay Asian Community: An Oral History of Pre-AIDS Los Angeles* (Lanham, MD: Rowman & Littlefield, 2002).

8. Position paper of the SNCC Atlanta Project cited in Clayborne Carson, *In Struggle: SNCC and the Black Awakening of the 1960s* (Cambridge: Harvard University Press, 1981), 198.

9. Before the 1969 Stonewall Rebellion, the movement for gay and lesbian rights called itself the homophile movement. See John D'Emilio, *Sexual Politics, Sexual Communities: The Making of a Homosexual Minority in the U.S., 1940–1970* (Chicago: University of Chicago Press, 1983).

10. For example, Stokely Carmichael, upon the assassination of Dr. Martin Luther King Jr., predicted a violent struggle in which Black people would "stand on our own feet and die like men. If that's our only act of manhood, then Goddammit, we're going to die." A dozen cities burned that night. See Carson, *In Struggle*, 288.

11. Angela Davis recalled when she worked with a group of cultural nationalists in Los Angeles that women were told not to play a leadership role and that to do so was "aiding and abetting the enemy, who wanted to see Black men weak and unable to hold their own." See *Angela Davis: An Autobiography* (New York: Bantam Books, 1974), 180.

12. James Baldwin (1924–1987), African American essayist, novelist, and playwright, wrote passionately and eloquently about racism and was the country's most prominent black writer during the 1960s. While in jail, Eldridge Cleaver wrote of his initial admiration, then later dismissal of Baldwin for his homosexuality, which he viewed as a love for whiteness and white men. Eldridge Cleaver, "Notes on a Native Son," in *Soul on Ice* (New York: Dell Publishing, 1968), 110.

13. Huey P. Newton, "A Letter from Huey to the Revolutionary Brothers and Sisters about the Women's Liberation and Gay Liberation Movement," originally published in the *Black Panther*, August 21, 1970. Reprinted in Mark Blasius and Shane Phelan, eds., *We Are Everywhere: A Historical Sourcebook of Gay and Lesbian Politics* (New York: Routledge, 1997), 404–6.

14. Los Angeles Research Group, "Toward a Scientific Analysis of the Gay Question," in Pam Mitchell, ed., *Pink Triangles: Radical Perspectives on Gay Liberation* (Boston: Alyson Publications, 1980), 117–35. Many radical gay liberationists participated in the civil rights, anti-war, and women's movements; see Karla Jay and Allen Young, eds., *Out of the Closets: Voices of Gay Liberation* (New York: Douglas Books, 1972). A decade earlier, in the 1960s, Bayard Rustin, a well-known Black civil rights activist, was publicly attacked as a communist, draft dodger, and homosexual by arch-conservative and segregationist U.S. Senator Strom Thurmond in an attempt to discredit the 1963 March on Washington for Civil Rights. Despite internal and external pressure to disavow Rustin, key civil rights leaders defended him. Rustin remained the lead organizer of this now historic event. See Jervis Anderson, *Bayard Rustin: The Troubles I've Seen* (New York: HarperCollins, 1997), 247–51.

15. Allen Young, "The Cuban Revolution and Gay Liberation," in Jay and Young, eds., *Out of the Closets*, 206–28.

16. "Declaration, Cuban First National Congress on Education and Culture," *GRANMA: Daily Organ of the Communist Party of Cuba* (May 1971), reprinted in Blasius and Phelan, eds., *We Are Everywhere*, 408–9.

17. Venceremos Brigade, "Policy on Gay Recruitment (January 1972)," reprinted in Blasius and Phelan, eds., *We Are Everywhere*, 411–12.

18. Sylvia Savellano, interview with the author, December 13, 1998.

19. Ibid.

20. Ibid.

21. Ibid.

22. In addition to this author, former KDP members and notable Filipino lesbian and gay activists are Jaime Geaga (Filipino Task Force on AIDS, San Francisco); Gil Mangaoang (Asian Pacific AIDS Intervention Team, Los Angeles); Melinda Paras (National Gay and Lesbian Task Force, Washington, D.C.); Syl Savellano; Jeanette Lazam (International Hotel Tenants Association, San Francisco); and Douglas Yaranon (Gay Asian/Pacific Alliance Community HIV Project, San Francisco).

23. Kitty Tsui, "A Chinese Banquet," in *The Words of a Woman Who Breathes Fire: Poetry and Prose* (San Francisco: Spinsters Ink, 1983).

24. Kitty Tsui, interview with the author, April 5, 1994.

25. Liz Tanaka [pseud.], interview with the author, December 12, 1998.

26. For an excellent critical analysis of this controversial aspect of Chin's work, see Daniel Y. Kim, "The Strange Love of Frank Chin," in David L. Eng and Alice Y. Hom, eds., *Q&A: Queer in Asian America* (Philadelphia: Temple University Press, 1998), 270–303.

27. William Wei, *The Asian American Movement* (Philadelphia: Temple University Press, 1993).

28. Doreena Wong, interviews with the author, January 17 and May 3, 1996.

29. Ibid.

30. Canyon Sam, interview with the author, January 13, 1994.

31. Wong interviews.

32. Two heterosexual women attended Asian American Feminists meetings, though the majority was lesbian.

33. For early articles, interviews, and poetry of Asian gay men and lesbians, see *Bridge: An Asian American Perspective* 3:4 (February 1975); 7:1 (Spring 1979); 8:3 (Summer 1983).

34. Unbound Feet member Merle Woo had also been a lecturer in Ethnic Studies/Asian American Studies for four years at UC Berkeley when she was dismissed in 1978, after the term limit changed from eight years to four years. Woo claimed her dismissal was the "result of her activism, her strong support of student and workers rights on campus, and her insistence on including the issues of race, sex, class, and sexuality in her teaching." Merle wanted Unbound Feet, as a group, to support her, but they were divided on the issue and subsequently broke up. In 1984, Merle won the lawsuit against the university. See Stephen Stewart, *Positive Image: A Portrait of Gay America* (New York: William Morrow, 1985), 114–15; and Wei, *Asian American Movement*, 88.

35. "Letters to the Editor," *Coming Up!* (San Francisco), September 1981, 6; November 1981, 8; December 1981, 5; January 1982, 4–5.

36. Tsui interview.

37. Asian Women's Group, mailing list, 1977, Trinity A. Ordona Private Collection.

38. Sam interview.

39. Asian Women's Group, "Statement of Purpose," 1982, Trinity A. Ordona Private Collection.

40. "Asian Awakening," 1983 Lesbian and Gay Freedom Day Program, Trinity A. Ordona Private Collection.

41. Lisa Chun, letter to the owner of Ollie's bar, October 27, 1983, Trinity A. Ordona Private Collection.

42. On October 23, 1983, the Asian Women's Group sponsored "A Sunday Bash" dance at Clementina's Bay Brick Inn in San Francisco, attended by over 125 Asian women. Canyon Sam, however, had some rude interactions at the dance with a customer who snickered about it with

the bartender. Canyon wrote a letter of complaint and called on others to withdraw their patronage from Clementina's. A dozen women signed Canyon's letter, but the AWG core group did not. Canyon reported the bar incident to the community at the November 18 meeting, but many people had no idea what had happened, who to support, or what to do. The confusion turned into disagreement that escalated to shouting and yelling at Canyon. While the conflict that erupted remains unresolved today, Canyon said that some people made unsolicited apologies for their rude behavior toward her, including one person who apologized two years after the meeting.

20

Relocating Struggle
Filipino Nurses Organize in the United States

Catherine Ceniza Choy

In U.S. hospitals today, nursing is no longer exclusively practiced by white women in white uniforms. Between 1965 and 1988, more than seventy thousand foreign nurses entered the United States, with the majority coming from Asia. Although Korea, India, and Taiwan are among the top Asian sending countries, the Philippines is the biggest supplier of nurses to the United States.[1]

Complex factors have historically shaped this phenomenon. In the early twentieth century, U.S. colonial education programs, which introduced Americanized professional nursing training and English-language study, prepared Filipino nurses to work in the United States. After World War II, U.S. nursing shortages created new migration opportunities that encouraged and facilitated the mass immigration of foreign-trained nurses to the United States. In the Philippines, high unemployment and escalating international debt shaped an export-oriented economy that promoted labor export and further pushed Filipino nurses to work abroad.[2]

While these transnational contexts are significant, the story of Filipina nurse Elvie Santos (a pseudonym) reminds us that embedded in these migration patterns are individual stories of hope and disappointment. In 1974, Elvie faced deportation by the U.S. Immigration and Naturalization Service (INS). She lamented:

> I first came to the United States on Jan. 14, 1974 with the understanding that I would work as a nurse and make money—much more [than] what I was receiving as a nurse in the Philippines. I am so disappointed at the outcome or turn of events and now I am wondering if my coming here is worth my leaving my family behind.[3]

Originally, a U.S. agency had recruited Elvie to work as a nurse in the United States by paying $100 to a Philippine agency. However, upon her arrival in Washington State, the U.S. agency assigned her work as a nurse's aide in a nursing home. Elvie performed the duties of a registered nurse (RN) but received half of an RN's salary. She then faced deportation proceedings in 1974 because she had worked in the United States as a nurse's aide under a temporary work visa (called an H-1 visa) and had not passed the U.S. nursing licensure examination. Foreign-trained nurses were eligible for H-1 visa status only if they were employed, and thus licensed, as RNs in the United States.

In the mid-1970s, Filipino nurses entered the United States through new visa categories and encountered new licensing requirements. Transnational recruitment agencies took advantage of new migration opportunities by exploiting Filipino nurse migrants with misleading advertisements, low wages, and poor working conditions. By the late 1970s, exploitative recruitment practices, controversial nursing licensing examinations, and a growing awareness of their complex and unique situation in the United States compelled Filipino nurses to "relocate" their struggles and focus on the pressing problems they faced in America.

While many Filipino nurses in the United States were critical of these practices and examinations, their critiques differed considerably. These differences led to the formation of three U.S. national organizations: the National Federation of Philippine Nurses Associations in the United States (later renamed the National Organization of Philippine Nurses Associations in the United States, and then the Philippine Nurses Association of America); the National Alliance for Fair Licensure of Foreign Nurse Graduates (NAFL-FNG); and the Foreign Nurse Defense Fund.

This chapter explores understudied but pivotal moments in the history of Filipino nurses in the United States by analyzing these Filipino nurse organizations in the context of complex developments on both sides of the ocean during the 1970s. During this decade, new migration opportunities helped transform Filipino nurses from national traitors into the Philippines' "new national heroes." At the same time, however, new licensing requirements in the United States transformed Filipino nurses from welcome exchange visitors and immigrants into an alleged threat to the U.S. health care system.

The rhetoric of Philippine government officials and American nurses often rendered Filipino nurses as objects: objects of affection, objects of domestic production, and objects of international consumption. This chapter re-presents Filipino nurses as historical subjects who have struggled to ameliorate their situations as health professionals and Filipino Americans. The main objective is to present a transnational perspective that takes seriously historical developments in both the Philippines and the United States but that also places human faces on Filipino nurses, whose struggles are often subsumed in scholarly literature by statistics. By doing so, this history documents a rich diversity of Filipino nurse activism in the United States; challenges the prevailing view of "docile" and "submissive" Filipino women and nurses; and cautions against sweeping generalizations about their political agendas.

Nursing Changes on Both Sides of the Ocean

The origins of Filipino nurse mass migration to the United States lie in the U.S. Exchange Visitor Program of the 1950s and 1960s. During these decades, more than eleven thousand Filipino nurses entered the United States as exchange visitors who worked and studied abroad for two years, after which they were supposed to return to the Philippines.[4] However, many Filipino exchange nurses employed numerous strategies to remain abroad: migrating to Canada, petitioning U.S. hospitals to extend their stays, marrying U.S. citizens. In 1965 the new occupational immigrant visas created by the passage of the U.S. Immigration Act favored the immigration of professionals with needed skills, such as nurses, and facilitated this phenomenon of Filipino nurses working and residing in the United States on a more permanent basis.

At first, Philippine health officials harshly criticized these nurses for betraying the Philippine national cause, emphasizing the increasing maldistribution of health personnel in the country. However, by the early 1970s this harsh criticism gave way to praise for Filipino nurses who chose to work abroad and remain there. In his 1973 address to visiting Filipina nurses from abroad, Philippine Secretary of Health Clemente S. Gatmaitan proclaimed:

> As head of the Health Department, I consider you as "Long-Lost Daughters"—prodigal children so to speak, who have returned temporarily to the fold. Personally, I wish you for good. But on second thought, we in the Health Department are happy that you have elected to stay and work abroad. . . . We receive glowing reports from abroad. . . . Another benefit that accrues from your work is the precious dollar you earn and send back to your folks at home. In this manner, you help indirectly in the improvement of our economic condition.[5]

In the early 1970s, Philippine president Ferdinand Marcos committed the Philippine government and economy to a new model of development based on export-oriented industrialization, which included the export of people as well as goods. Through these new measures, the Marcos government attempted simultaneously to alleviate unemployment in the Philippines and to accumulate much-needed foreign currency. Ferdinand Marcos's address at the 1973 Philippine Nurses Association convention directly connected the new economic policy with the change in attitude toward migrant nurses: "And so, in short, what is the policy of nursing? . . . It is our policy to promote the migration of nurses."[6]

Marcos's address also revealed the commodification of Filipino nurses vis-à-vis their mass production for an international market:

> I repeat, we will now encourage the training of all nurses because as I repeat, *this is a market* that we should take advantage of. Instead of stopping the nurses from going abroad *why don't we produce more nurses? If they want one thousand nurses we produce a thousand more.* (Emphasis mine.)[7]

These changes in Philippine government officials' attitudes toward the mass migration of Filipino workers abroad led to the implementation of an official overseas labor policy. In 1974, the government created the Overseas Employment Development Board, which publicized the availability of Filipino labor in overseas labor markets, evaluated overseas employment contracts, and recruited Filipino laborers for work abroad. However, while the Philippine government vigorously promoted the migration of Filipino nurses to the United States, escalating tensions between Filipino and American nurses over U.S. nursing licensing examinations complicated the "glowing reports" about Filipino nurses in America.

The controversy over U.S. nursing licensing examinations was linked to the creation of a new category of foreign nurse-migrant, the H-1 visa nurse. In the late 1960s and early 1970s, as the use of the Exchange Visitor Program decreased, occupational immigrant visas became the major avenue of entry for Filipino nurses wishing to work in the United States. However, as foreign professionals took advantage of available occupational immigrant visas, backlogs for these visas increased.[8] In 1970, an immigration amendment dramatically increased employment opportunities for temporary foreign workers with H-1 visas by allowing them to fill permanent positions.[9]

Nurses from the Philippines dominated the number of H-1 visa nurses entering the United States. Between 1972 and 1978, 15,291 H-1 visa nurses entered the United States, and of this group, nurses from the Philippines constituted approximately 60 percent (9,158) of the total.[10]

Changes in the U.S. licensure of foreign-trained nurses placed H-1 visa nurses at the center of a U.S. nursing controversy. In the United States, licensure for nurses is regulated by separate laws in each of the states. Reciprocity was often granted to Filipino nurses who had licenses to practice as RNs in the Philippines.[11] For example, in the 1950s and 1960s in New York State, foreign-trained nurses individually petitioned the State Board of Regents for endorsement of their license, and the state board then evaluated each applicant. However, in 1971, New York State amended this approach. Foreign nurses were required to pass the State Board Test Pool Examination (SBTPE), an examination to test knowledge of U.S. nursing practice.[12] Five test areas—medical, surgical, psychiatric, and obstetric nursing and the nursing of children—made up the SBTPE. According to a 1975 report on foreign nurse graduates in the United States, the increasing cultural diversity, as well as numbers, of foreign nurses in the United States made individual evaluations more burdensome and problematic.[13] By 1977, all state boards abandoned licensure by endorsement and required foreign-trained nurses to take the SBTPE.

Furthermore, some states implemented policies that shortened the amount of time H-1 visa nurses could prepare for the examinations. For example, in Michigan, H-1 visa nurses were initially issued a renewable temporary work permit. However, a new 1974 policy eliminated the possibility of renewal and compelled H-1 visa nurses to pass the SBTPE within six months of their arrival to the United States.

According to a 1976 national report, 77 percent of foreign-trained nurses who took the SBTPE failed the examination.[14] In individual states, the failure rates were even higher. In California, affirmative action officer Delfi Mandragon Shakra observed that Filipino nurses specifically suffered from high failure rates on these licensing examinations: 80 to 90 percent failed the examination in the 1970s.[15] These failure rates of foreign-trained nurses were particularly alarming when contrasted with those of U.S.-trained nurses. The vast majority of U.S.-trained nurses, 85 to 90 percent, passed the SBTPE.[16]

Rosario DeGracia, a professor of nursing at Seattle University and president of the local Filipino Nurses Association, hypothesized about the causes of these high failure rates based on her work and personal observations. One cause was Filipino nurses' lack of training in psychiatric nursing, in particular its clinical aspect, and hence their difficulty with passing that area of the SBTPE. Some Filipino nurses also claimed that the multiple-choice type of questions in the examination was confusing. In addition to these factors, DeGracia pointed out that "taking an examination can be a literally 'frightening' and anxiety-filled experience to those who have been away from school for many years."[17]

Failure of the examination had a detrimental effect on the status of H-1 visa nurses. Their temporary work visa status was revoked because, on failing the licensing examination, they were unable to practice as registered nurses. Like Elvie Santos, they then faced the threat of deportation. These deportations could profoundly affect specific hospitals and communities. In Texas, one of the six states that employs the most foreign-trained nurses, the potential loss of this critical labor pool led to a battle between nursing and hospital professional associations over professionalism, authority, and standards.

In the early 1970s, the Board of Nurse Examiners in Texas granted temporary work permits to H-1 visa nurses until they passed the SBTPE. As these temporary permits became available, the number of foreign-trained nurses working in Texas increased exponentially, from 60 in 1970 to 1,752 in 1973. However, their high failure rates on the SBTPE became a cause for alarm. Only one of every four or five foreign-trained nurses passed the examination. In 1973, the Board of Nurse Examiners refused to grant any temporary permits. As a result, the INS stopped issuing H-1 visas for Texas-bound foreign-trained nurses and informed H-1 visa nurses already in the state that their visas would be revoked if they did not pass the SBTPE. The Texas Hospital Association protested the decision, claiming that the removal of H-1 visa nurses would be "a catastrophic experience for Texas hospitals."[18] It argued that anyone could practice nursing in a Texas hospital under the direction of a physician, and it successfully persuaded the INS to reverse its previous decision.

The experiences of H-1 visa nurses were subsumed by debates on hospital management and professional autonomy. One report about the Texas controversy characterized H-1 visa nurses as a commodity, a "million-dollar investment" by Texas hospital administrators who had organized costly recruitment programs in the Philippines and other parts of the world.[19] Ruth Board, executive director of the Texas Nurses Association, linked this issue to the protection of American public safety: "The law is intended to protect the public, not the nurse. There is no measure in Texas other than the State Board Test Pool exams to assure the public that a nurse has the minimum competency necessary to provide safe nursing care."[20] In 1974, the American Nurses Association (ANA) also became involved in the controversy over foreign-trained nurses, licensure, and practice, illustrating that the struggle had become national in scope.

Professional Resolutions and Pre-Screening Examinations

In June 1974, the ANA Commission on Nursing Services presented a resolution at the ANA biennial convention. Its objectives were twofold: (1) to remove the preferential status of foreign nurses in U.S. immigration regulations and (2) to support the authority of state nurses associations to evaluate the practice of foreign-trained nurses. However, whereas the Texas controversy focused on Texas hospitals' use of H-1 visa nurses who had high failure rates on the SBTPE, the ANA Commission's resolution lumped all foreign-trained nurses together. Of the resolution's twelve points justifying its objectives, three focused on the professional incompetence of foreign-trained nurses in general. The ANA Commission claimed that "many foreign graduates are *not prepared to work* in roles expected of them"; "some employers place foreign nurse graduates in roles for which they are *unprepared*"; and "United States professional schools of nursing cannot provide sufficient educational programs to foreign nurses with *academic deficiencies*"[21] (emphases mine).

Filipino nurse Clarita Miraflor characterized the resolution as a form of nativism and racism: "The implicit racism and know-nothing attitude that permeates this resolution has no place in our profession, which prides itself upon its dedication to the service of mankind."[22] Miraflor and several other nurses formed an ad hoc committee and worked on an alternative resolution, which highlighted the role that U.S. hospital recruiters played in the problems of foreign-trained nurses in the United States. The resolution called for the ANA to collaborate with the International Labor Organization and World Health Organization and to participate in the elimination of misleading U.S. recruitment practices.[23]

The ad hoc committee also proposed the creation of a prescreening examination for foreign-trained nurses, claiming that "many problems could be eliminated if nurses had the opportunity to be tested for communication skills and professional preparation in their country of origin before migration."[24] The ANA hearing committee and house of delegates passed the alternative resolution with minimal opposition.

In 1977, the ANA and the National League of Nursing co-sponsored the creation of a new nonprofit U.S. nursing organization, the Commission on Graduates of Foreign Nursing Schools (CGFNS), which would oversee the implementation and administration of the prescreening examination, known as the CGFNS examination. The examination involved two parts: a nursing competency section, which included nursing areas covered by the SBTPE, and an English-language competency section.

The commission's leadership attempted to cover the multiple concerns about foreign-trained nurses by emphasizing both American patients' safety and foreign-trained nurses' welfare. Executive Director Adele Herwitz acknowledged the "great disappointment" of foreign-trained nurses who failed their state board examinations: "They have often felt discriminated against and disenchanted with the United States. . . . [Others] have been hired as nurses' aides and then pushed into taking registered nurse responsibilities on unpopular night shifts and/or in out-of-the-way communities. This has not contributed to safe patient care."[25]

However, the commission, the INS, and the U.S. Department of Labor used the CGFNS examination in ways that angered Filipino nurses and inspired them to organize three U.S.-based organizations: the National Federation of Philippine Nurses Associations in the United States, the National Alliance for Fair Licensure of Foreign Nurse Graduates (NAFL-FNG), and the Foreign Nurse Defense Fund. These organizations had distinct agendas and interpretations of the 1970s controversy regarding licensure and foreign-trained nurses. National Federation leadership endorsed licensure requirements as they struggled for mainstream recognition of the professional contributions of Filipino nurses in the United States. NAFL-FNG leadership demanded an end to what they claimed to be a culturally biased nursing licensure examination. The

Foreign Nurse Defense Fund used civil rights legislation to oppose what they considered to be a racist nursing licensure examination.

From Overseas Chapters to National Federation

In 1979, members of local Philippine Nurses Association (PNA) chapters throughout the United States formed a new U.S. national nursing organization, the National Federation of Philippine Nurses Associations in the United States. H-1 visa nurses' problems and the CGFNS controversy were the immediate concerns that compelled these nurses to form a national organization. However, the formation of the National Federation was also linked to the transnational origins of these local chapters and the changing relationship between them and the Philippine Nurses Association in the Philippines.

In the 1960s and 1970s, Filipino exchange-visitor and immigrant nurses in New York, California, Illinois, and Hawaii established PNA organizations and then actively pursued affiliation with the Philippine Nurses Association in the Philippines as overseas chapters. For example, after receiving official recognition as an overseas chapter, PNA-Chicago leaders told the Philippine Nurses Association in the Philippines that the "success of the organization lies in your hands. We are therefore hoping for your guidance and inspiration in all the things we do."[26] By the mid-1970s, overseas PNA chapters had also formed in Michigan, Pennsylvania, New Jersey, and Texas.

However, bureaucratic inefficiency contributed to alienation from the Philippine Nurses Association. The PNA seemingly ignored even the most devoted chapters abroad, such as PNA-Michigan. The PNA-Michigan president communicated to the Philippine organization:

> I have been anxiously waiting receipt of our membership cards for 1974 and it seemed Col. Luzon never got my letter and your response proved that it did reach the Manila office.... [T]hough we *never received the membership cards* ... we would like to *receive copies of the Phil. Journal of Nursing regularly* ... (I have not received a single copy!). (Emphasis hers.)[27]

Furthermore, even when the Philippine Nurses Association sought to alleviate the hardships of Filipino nurses abroad, it had little power to affect exploitative recruitment practices and the high failure rate on American licensing exams. In 1975, PNA president Fe Valdez attempted to help Filipino nurses abroad by writing to ANA president Rosamund Gabrielson and proposing that Filipino nurses be given three chances to take the licensing exam before their right to practice nursing was fully revoked. In her response, Gabrielson implicitly rejected the proposal by pointing out that licensure for nurses in the United States was regulated by separate laws in each of the states.[28]

At first, PNA chapters in the United States attempted to alleviate these problems on an individual chapter basis. For example, PNAs in Chicago, Washington, D.C., Southern California, Michigan, New Jersey, and New York offered review courses and tutorials to Filipino nurses at minimal or no cost. However, by 1979, PNA leaders in the

United States recognized that the problems were similar in many states across the country. According to the minutes of the national organizational meeting:

> [A]fter much deliberation and discussion, a decision was reached that we formally organize because of the pressing problem on [H-1] visa confronting the Filipino nurse and only through concerted effort of all PNAs we may be able to alleviate the problems affecting the Filipino nurses in the United States.[29]

PNA leaders in the United States also opposed the ways in which American nursing organizations implemented the CGFNS examination. First, they opposed the mandatory use of CGFNS testing in the United States. The Commission on Graduates had conducted research on foreign-trained nurses who had entered the United States as dependents of U.S. citizens and had concluded that this group of foreign-trained nurses needed to pass the CGFNS examination before taking the SBTPE. According to the CGFNS study, 0.7 percent of forty-five hundred women entering the United States as dependents were nurses. Despite this miniscule percentage, a commission member concluded that "the Commission will have to consider how to handle this group, who will require pre-screen testing in this country."[30] As a result, the commission offered the CGFNS examination in cities in the United States, such as Los Angeles, Chicago, and New York, claiming that "in this way, these nurses will not have to return to their country to take the CGFNS exam."[31] The PNA-New York met with the New York State Nursing Association's Human Rights Committee to protest CGFNS testing in the United States. They claimed that such a rule appeared to contradict the commission's purpose of screening foreign nurses "while they are still in their own countries." They questioned, "Why is the CGFNS examination imposed on these nurses that are already in the U.S. when the State Board examination alone is final in meeting the same purposes?"[32]

Second, PNA leaders in the United States criticized the use of the CGFNS examination as a visa requirement. In 1977, the Commission on Graduates convened a meeting with divisions of the INS, U.S. Department of State, and U.S. Department of Labor and successfully lobbied for the use of the CGFNS certificate in the visa applications of foreign nurse graduates.[33] Clarita Miraflor, who became the first president of the National Federation, claimed, "The concept of a visa qualifying exam is highly discriminatory." Objecting to its use on "humanitarian" grounds, Miraflor pointed to those Filipino nurses who had waited up to ten years for their H-1 visas and would have been denied visas if they failed the CGFNS exam.[34]

Third, Filipino nurses criticized what they considered to be an exorbitant $70 examination fee, which, during the late 1970s, was equivalent to approximately one and a half months of the average Filipino nurse's salary.[35] PNA-Chicago president Maria Couper characterized the commission, along with Philippine recruitment agencies and U.S. employers, as an exploiter of Filipino nurses.[36] She urged other PNAs in the United States to adopt PNA-Chicago's critical position about the CGFNS examination. The need for a national organization became more apparent.

The National Federation acknowledged the uniqueness of its constituency through its ANA-influenced constitution and active communication with both U.S. and Philippine national nursing organizations. According to the chairperson of the by-laws committee, Filipinas Lowery, they had patterned the National Federation's by-laws after U.S. professional nursing organizations "because the people that we're serving are here."[37]

Yet the National Federation continued to maintain dialogue with the Philippine Nurses Association. For example, in June 1981, members of the National Federation (who officially renamed the organization the National Organization of Philippine Nurses Associations in the United States, or NOPNAUS, that year) met with the president of the Philippine Nurses Association to discuss the problems regarding Filipino nurses' recruitment, licensure, and practice in the United States. NOPNAUS attempted to unify Filipino nurses in the United States by voicing the concerns of this group to both U.S. and Philippine national nursing organizations. However, their appeals to unity were challenged by the rise of other organizations.

Fair Licensure: A Cause for the Filipino Community

During a two-day conference in 1977, more than one hundred Filipino nurses and community activists formed the National Alliance for Fair Licensure of Foreign Nurse Graduates (NAFL-FNG). Whereas the National Federation had attempted to unite Filipino nurses specifically, the NAFL-FNG included nonnurses as well as nurses. Its national co-coordinators included community activist Aimee Cruz and a registered nurse, Christina Hing. Organized by the Katipunan ng mga Demokratikong Pilipino (KDP), an anti-imperialist and anti-racist organization, the NAFL-FNG attempted to unify all Filipinos in the United States on the basis of their "minority" status.[38] It argued that the licensure of foreign-trained nurses was a problem for the entire Filipino community because "the nature of the problem clearly challenges our commitment and ability as a minority group to unite and fight discrimination in any area—whether in employment, housing, education, and others."[39]

The NAFL-FNG called for the simplification of English in the CGFNS examination, an investigation into potential biases of the SBTPE, a minimum eighteen-month temporary license for foreign-trained nurses in the United States, and the establishment of licensure examination review programs in educational institutions throughout the United States. They advocated for "deferred voluntary departure" status, which would enable former H-1 visa nurses who lost their immigration status after they failed the SBTPE to obtain another opportunity for legal employment.

At the 1977 conference, Aimee Cruz urged participants to "depart from our traditional notion of conferences as 'talk festivals' where nice sounding resolutions are passed on paper and remain on paper."[40] NAFL-FNG members responded to this call through petition campaigns and pickets. In 1977, the NAFL-FNG launched a petition campaign addressed to INS Commissioner Leonel Castillo, demanding "deferred voluntary departure" status for H-1 visa nurses who had failed the SBTPE. In 1978, it organized another petition campaign addressed to Secretary Joseph Califano Jr. of the Department of Health, Education, and Welfare to demand low-cost and specialized review centers for foreign-trained nurses. In October 1979, the NAFL-FNG organized pickets in Los Angeles, Chicago, and New York to protest the use of CGFNS examinations in the United States.

The NAFL-FNG differed from the National Federation in its views on the U.S. nursing licensure examination. According to NAFL-FNG member Trinity Ordona, the test did not take into account language or cultural differences.[41] However, some National Federation leaders disagreed. According to Filipinas Lowery:

> For some reason there was this radical group of non-nurses going around saying that the licensing exam was discriminatory. And what we said was . . . being that we're nurses, we recognize that there's one exam to be taken by everybody. Whether you're American-educated or foreign-educated, you've got to meet one standard.[42]

However, a 1980 Adverse Impact Assessment report by the California Department of Consumer Affairs supported NAFL-FNG claims of cultural bias and further concluded that the SBTPE was racially biased. According to the report, 45 percent of Asians, 62 percent of Blacks, 55 percent of Filipinos, 40 percent of Latinos, and 40 percent of Native Americans failed the SBTPE, in contrast to the 12 percent failure rate of white test takers.[43] As a result, the NAFL-FNG participated in a coalition with other organizations, including the Service Employee International Union Locals 400 and 723, Asian Law Caucus, Mexican American Legal Defense and Education Fund, National Association for the Advancement of Colored People, Chinese for Affirmative Action, and National Organization for Women, Bay Area. This coalition supported a proposal to extend the temporary work permits of foreign-trained nurses to twenty-four months.[44]

The NAFL-FNG also collaborated with immigrant advocacy organizations such as the National Filipino Immigrant Rights Organization (NFIRO). Together they organized an emergency campaign demanding that the INS stop the deportations of H-1 visa nurses until a "bias-free licensure exam" could be developed.[45]

Defending Foreign Nurses: "Coolies of the Medical World"

In the late 1970s, Filipino nurses organized yet another group, the Foreign Nurse Defense Fund, which defended the rights of foreign nurses in the United States through the use of civil rights legislation. Filipina nurse Norma Ruspian Watson was the executive secretary of the organization. Personal experiences of discrimination in the United States informed her activism. Watson arrived in the United States in 1973 with an occupational immigrant visa and passed the licensure examination in 1974. She and seven other Filipino nurses applied for employment at the Letterman Army Medical Center (LAMC) in California. According to Watson, "[W]e were all denied employment applications, and I was told to my face that LAMC does not hire brown skinned Fillippinas [sic]."[46] She later applied for work in a private hospital, Mary's Help Hospital in Daly City, California. In 1979, Watson filed a complaint with the Equal Employment Opportunity Commission after discovering that she was not being compensated for her seven years of professional nursing experience in the Philippines and was being paid as a new nursing graduate.[47] In her critiques of the U.S. treatment of Filipino nurses, Watson referred to racial and neocolonial hierarchies:

> Do we bring our nursing skills to the USA as professionals, and to fill a needed medical health care crisis as such, or are we brought to the USA as their little brown-skinned sisters to empty bedpans and work in nursing homes?[48]

Watson conducted research into the problems of other Filipino nurses in the United States. In her letter to President Ronald Reagan on behalf of the Foreign Nurse Defense Fund, Watson accused the National League of Nursing of violating state and federal civil rights laws through its development of a "racist and discriminatory" licensing examination. After securing documents through the Freedom of Information Act, she also accused government officials from the Department of Health, Education, and Welfare and the INS of "criminal conspiracy" through their use of the SBTPE as a basis for deportation of foreign nurses in the United States.[49] An outspoken activist, Watson argued:

> Foreign nurses, particularly *Fillippinas* [sic] *are the,* "COOLIES OF THE MEDICAL WORLD," *we have educated ourselves in our countries of origin at no cost to the american [sic] taxpayer, and all you have to do today, is look in any hospital in America and you will see our brown faces everywhere you look. We are sick and tired of being subservient and culturally non-aggressive, and now are taking pages out of the black Civil Rights Movement in this country, and will do what Martin Luther King had done. I would like to see all foreign nurses walk out of the hospitals in this country, and see what happens.* (Emphasis hers.)[50]

Watson's vision of a foreign nurses' walkout never materialized. My research findings suggest that the NAFL-FNG and Foreign Nurse Defense Fund dissolved in the early 1980s. Political gains contributed to their demise. In 1981 in California, the coalition of organizations successfully persuaded the state's Board of Registered Nursing to break away from the national nursing establishment by developing its own nondiscriminatory and job-related licensure examination. The state board also decided to extend the temporary visas of thousands of foreign nurses who faced possible deportation after failing the controversial SBTPE. In July 1982, the National Council of State Boards of Nursing replaced the SBTPE with a new NCLEX-RN (National Council Licensure Examination for Registered Nurses) examination. The NCLEX-RN examination was designed in a way that permitted nurses to take the examination an unlimited number of times without compromising testing accuracy, nurse competency, and safe patient care.

New political, labor, and personal conflicts also hastened the end of these organizations. Different revolutionary movements had divided KDP members (who had organized the NAFL-FNG) and led to the dissolution of the KDP in July 1986.[51] By the mid-1980s, Norma Watson had become embroiled in a hospital controversy about the use of protective clothing when taking care of AIDS patients.[52] Only the National Organization of Philippine Nurses Associations in the United States remained active throughout the 1980s, a period marked by the political domination of President Ronald Reagan and the Republican Party and rollbacks in race-, gender-, and class-based organizing. NOPNAUS's focus on mainstream recognition and integrationist tactics complemented this conservative political environment and reflected what Rick Bonus has found to be a pattern in Filipino American styles of politicking. According to Bonus, common concerns of Filipino American organizations include "their emphasis on recognition and group action. 'Doing politics' for them is always an effort, first, to calculate and respond to the effects, in the past and present, of having no representation in mainstream politics and no access to it, and second, to facilitate the establishment of self-reliant networks of support and mutuality—appropriated from the homeland—as alternative spaces of collective action."[53]

From Racism to Recognition

When I asked Phoebe Andes, who became the second president of NOPNAUS from 1982 to 1984, if the ANA influenced its activities, she responded, "I don't think so. We wanted probably to be *recognized by the ANA* and that's why when there was a convention in Louisiana, we participated by offering a program in their workshop"[54] (emphasis mine). Andes characterized the National Organization's presentation of that program, "The Asian Nurse in the Health Care Delivery System: Issues and Trends in the 80s," at the ANA's 1984 convention as one of the major achievements of her presidency. She related:

> I thought that was giving us a positive image. It made us probably think we are a large, cohesive, and powerful group *in the eyes of the Americans*, being printed in the whole program.... [T]o get into the program was an accomplishment. (Emphasis mine.)[55]

During Maria Couper's presidency from 1984 to 1986, she further pursued ANA recognition by successfully negotiating with the ANA to include NOPNAUS in the procession of dignitaries during ANA conventions' opening ceremonies.

At these specific moments, NOPNAUS leadership attempted to present an image of their organization as "large," "cohesive," and "powerful." However, the organizational histories of the NAFL-FNG and the Foreign Nurse Defense Fund problematize these images of unity and cohesion. Problems regarding foreign-trained nurses, licensure, and practice had divided Filipino nurses in the United States. As they protested exploitation, their conflicting agendas revealed the professional and political diversity among them and ultimately limited their ability to effect changes in U.S. nursing licensure and transnational recruitment practices. Exploitative recruitment practices continued in the 1990s, as did the controversial use of the CGFNS examination in most states.

In the 1970s, Filipino nurses in the United States organized several organizations that protested what they considered to be exploitative transnational recruiting practices, discriminatory immigration requirements, and biased nursing licensing examinations. Although the rhetoric of Philippine government officials and U.S. nursing leaders reduced Filipino nurses in the United States to the inferior status of commodities, daughters, and unprepared workers, this chapter has suggested that the rise of different Filipino nursing organizations contested (albeit in distinct ways) this objectification and subordination.

NOTES

1. Paul Ong and Tania Azores, "The Migration and Incorporation of Filipino Nurses," in *The New Asian Immigration in Los Angeles and Global Restructuring*, ed. Paul Ong, Edna Bonacich, and Lucie Cheng (Philadelphia: Temple University Press, 1994), 164.

2. See Catherine Ceniza Choy, "Exported to Care: A Transnational History of Filipino Nurse Migration to the United States," in *Immigration Research for a New Century: Multidisciplinary Perspectives*, ed. Nancy Foner, Rubén Rumbaut, and Steven J. Gold (New York: Russell Sage Foundation, 2000).

3. Case profile of Elvie Santos [pseudonym], August 13, 1974, Demonstration Project for Asian Americans, Seattle, Washington.

4. Purita Falgui Asperilla, "The Mobility of Filipino Nurses" (Ph.D. diss., Columbia University, 1971), 52.

5. Clemente S. Gatmaitan, "Closing Address for Visiting Filipino Nurses," *Philippine Journal of Nursing (PJN)* 42:2 (April–June 1973): 90.

6. Ferdinand E. Marcos, "Address of His Excellency, President Ferdinand E. Marcos," *PJN* 43:1 (January–March 1974): 21–22.

7. Ibid., 22.

8. By 1970, the waiting period for a third-preference visa from the Eastern Hemisphere was approximately thirteen months. U.S. House of Representatives, "Excluding Executive Officers and Managerial Personnel of Western Hemisphere Businesses from the Numerical Limitation of Western Hemisphere Immigration," 91st Cong., 2d sess., *Congressional Record*, 3 March 1970, vol. 116, pt. 5, 5730.

9. Ong and Azores, "Migration and Incorporation of Filipino Nurses," 175.

10. I have calculated these totals using Tomoji Ishi's table on temporary worker nurses admitted to the United States. See Tomoji Ishi, "Class Conflict, the State, and Linkage: The International Migration of Nurses from the Philippines," *Berkeley Journal of Sociology* 32 (1987): 290.

11. In 1966, Minnesota, Missouri, New Jersey, Ohio, Washington, Washington, D.C., Tennessee, and Hawaii granted reciprocity to Filipino registered nurses. See Soledad A. Buenafe, "On Reciprocity," *PJN* 35:3 (May–June 1966): 191.

12. Nalini M. Quraeshi, Zahir A. Quraeshi, and Inayat U. Mangla, *Foreign Nursing Professionals in the United States* (New Delhi: International Labour Organisation, 1992), 85.

13. "Report of the Conference, Immigration of Graduates of Foreign Nursing Schools, Bethseda, Maryland, June 23–24, 1975," Health Manpower References, DHEW Publication No. (HRA) 76–84, p. 1, CGFNS Collection, N119, Box 1, Folder 4, Boston University Special Collections.

14. Ishi, "Class Conflict, the State, and Linkage," 300.

15. Joan McKinney, "Filipino Nurses Fight for Licenses," *Oakland Tribune*, August 12, 1979, California Nurses Association 23.3, Carton 7, University of California, San Francisco Special Collections.

16. In California, Shakra observed that 90 percent of U.S.-trained nurses passed the state examination (ibid.). A national report indicated that in 1978, 19 percent of foreign-trained nurses passed the examination, in contrast to 85 percent of U.S.-trained nurses. See "Fourth Screening Exam for Foreign Nurses to Be Given April 2, 1980; Proposed New U.S. Immigration Rule to

Require Passing Exam for Preference Visa," 5 October 1979, 3, CGFNS Collection, N119, Box 1, Folder 4, Boston University Special Collections.

17. Rosario T. DeGracia to Dorothy L. Cordova, 27 February 1974, Letters/Communiques File, Filipino American National Historical Society (FANHS) Archives, Seattle, Washington.

18. Rhea Felknor, "Trouble in Texas: Institutional Licensure for R.N.s?" *RN* (April 1974): 79.

19. Ibid., 29.

20. Ibid., 80.

21. American Nurses Association (ANA), "Proposed Resolutions," 10, as cited by Purita Falgui Asperilla, "Problems of Foreign Educated Nurses and Job Satisfactions of Filipino Nurses," ANPHI (Academy of Nursing of the Philippines) Papers (July–September 1976), 7.

22. Janet Henning, "How One Foreign Nurse Organization Fights Back," *Modern Healthcare* (May 1975): 24.

23. "Battle at ANA Convention, Resolution Discriminatory to Foreign Nurses Defeated," *Chicago-Philippine News*, June 13–19, 1974, 1 as cited by Purita Falgui Asperilla, "Problems of Foreign Educated Nurses," 7–8.

24. Ibid.

25. "Guidebook Issued on Qualifying Examination for Foreign Nurses Wishing to Immigrate to U.S.; Interested Nurses Urged to Submit Application Promptly," February 13, 1978, 3, CGFNS Collection, N119, Box 1, Folder 2, Boston University Special Collections.

26. Carmelita C. Matias to Rosario S. Diamante, 2 August 1966, "In Our Mail," *PJN* 35:4 (July–August 1966): 194.

27. Georgiana Rose C. Tutay to Fe M. Valdez, n.d., "Letters from Nurses Abroad," *PJN* 44:3 (July–September 1975): 144–45.

28. Fe M. Valdez to Rosamond C. Gabrielson, 2 May 1975, and C. Gabrielson to Fe M. Valdez, 12 August 1975, "In Our Mail," *PJN* 44:4 (October–December 1975): 203.

29. Minutes of Organizing Meeting, April 21, 1979, National Federation of Philippine Nurses Association [sic] in the United States, 2, Phoebe Andes personal collection.

30. Core Group on the Commission on Graduates of Foreign Nursing Schools, "Foreign Nurses Coming to U.S. as Dependents," January 5, 1977, 5, CGFNS Collection, N119, Box 1, Folder 9, Boston University Special Collections.

31. "Fourth Screening Exam for Foreign Nurses," 2.

32. "PNA-NY Meets with NYSNA Human Rights Committee," *Philippine-American Nurse* 2:1 (Spring 1984): 4–5.

33. "Technical Proposal," 1977, 10, CGFNS Collection, N119, Box 1, Folder 14, Boston University Special Collections.

34. "New Test Requirement Upsets Foreign Nurses," *Health Planning and Manpower Report*, 12 September 1979, 4.

35. Ibid., 3.

36. Maria Redona Couper, letter to the author, 13 August 1995.

37. Author interview with Filipinas Lowery, 27 April 1995, New York City.

38. For an informative history of the KDP, see Helen C. Toribio, "We Are Revolution: A Reflective History of the Union of Democratic Filipinos (KDP)," *Amerasia Journal* 24:2 (1998): 155–77.

39. "Support the H-1 Nurses, Sign Up for Justice," petition campaign launched and coordinated by the National Alliance for Fair Licensure of Foreign Nurse Graduates, n.d., Norma Watson file, FANHS Archives, Seattle, Washington.

40. "Nurses Target Cultural Bias in Licensure Exams," *Ang Katipunan*, May 1–15, 1977, 6.

41. McKinney, "Filipino Nurses Fight for Licenses."

42. Filipinas Lowery interview.

43. Ibid.

44. "Extend Interim Permits for Nurses; Oppose Racist Licensure," n.d., flyer, Sue Englander personal collection.

45. "Foreign Nurses and the U.S. Nursing Crisis," National Filipino Immigrant Rights Organization (NFIRO) and National Alliance for Fair Licensure for Foreign Nurse Graduates (NAFL), n.d., Sue Englander personal collection.

46. Norma Ruspian Watson to U.S. Commission on Civil Rights, 1 May 1979, Norma Watson file, FANHS Archives, Seattle, Washington.

47. "Nurse from Philippines Files a Job-Rights Complaint on West Coast," *New York Times*, 8 April 1979, 41.

48. Ed Diokno, "Medical World's 'Coolie': Federal Agencies Look into FNG's Complaints," *Philippine News*, 3 March 1979, 15.

49. Norma Watson to President Ronald Reagan, n.d., Sue Englander personal collection.

50. Norma Ruspian Watson to U.S. Commission on Civil Rights, 1 May 1979, Norma Watson file, FANHS Archives, Seattle, Washington.

51. Toribio, "We Are Revolution," 176.

52. See Mark A. Stein, "Nurses, S.F. Hospital Clash over AIDS Danger," *Los Angeles Times*, 23 August 1985, Home Edition, 3.

53. Rick Bonus, *Locating Filipino Americans: Ethnicity and the Cultural Politics of Space* (Philadelphia: Temple University Press, 2000), 94.

54. Author interview with Phoebe Cabotaje-Andes, 16 February 1995, South Plainfield, New Jersey.

55. Ibid.

21

Opening Spaces
South Asian American Women Leaders in the Late Twentieth Century

Madhulika S. Khandelwal

In 1995, participation in the annual India Day Parade in Manhattan, New York City, became a contested issue. The Federation of Indian Associations (FIA) of New York, an established community organization of Asian Indians who sponsored the parade, denied permission to march to several progressive South Asian American organizations. In the years immediately preceding 1995, Sakhi (meaning a woman's female friend), a pioneer women's organization for South Asian women in the United States, had approached established organizations such as the Association of Indians in America (AIA) and the FIA for permission to represent their programs and perspectives at their respective public events. Although denied permission at other events, when Sakhi received FIA's permission to march at an India Day Parade, Sakhi members invited some barred organizations, such as the South Asian Lesbian and Gay Association (SALGA), to march with them.

The 1995 India Day Parade was symbolic of Sakhi's informal alliance with emerging progressive organizations; it also pointed to the pivotal role that South Asian American women's organizations such as Sakhi played in providing new community leadership. In the 1990s, the new leadership was characterized by distinct perspectives on the ethnic community, generational issues, and a progressive political agenda—one that sought social justice for disadvantaged members of the community and the larger society—and its women leaders ensured that women's rights and feminist perspectives had a key place in defining these initiatives.[1]

This chapter examines how South Asian American women exercised leadership in defining and organizing their own communities in the last decades of the twentieth century. By forming women's organizations and forging ahead in a variety of public fields, they challenged stereotypes of Asian women and proposed new paradigms of community service and advocacy. The discussion focuses on the New York area, where several women's organizations emerged in the 1980s and the 1990s, but these developments took place in the context of new women's leadership all around the country.[2] This analysis intentionally focuses on documenting women's agency in shaping their own and their community's history during the 1980s and 1990s.

Search for New Paradigms

For a long time, Asian American women have been depicted like other American immigrant and minority women, as having linear stories of empowerment after arriving in the United States. According to this perspective, women in Asia are uniformly subservient and powerless persons who learn to struggle for women's rights because of their being in a Western society. Such an approach not only treats gender in Asia in an ahistorical fashion, decontextualizing it from the socioeconomic and political changes over several millennia,[3] but also ignores the complex realities of immigration, racism, sexism, class, and cultural issues faced by minorities in the United States.

In the 1980s and the 1990s, as the post-1965 immigrant populations established themselves in the United States, a number of South Asian American women emerged in various arenas of American public and professional life. Most of them had high education levels and professional skills and worked for income. However, few among them subscribed to mainstream American feminism or any parts thereof, and most rejected the dichotomized notions of "tradition" and "modernity," especially the manner in which they were used to represent Asian and Western societies, respectively. Both in theory and by their own examples of leadership, they challenged mainstream feminisms, as well as established leadership in their own community. Although women spearheaded these new directions, they were by no means "women-only" initiatives; men often participated with them in common struggles, and alliances were forged with organizations pursuing other progressive issues. Altogether, women opened up new ways of leading their own communities and defining community issues, and they linked gender inextricably with other social factors.

South Asian American women's leadership may be distinguished by their efforts to look for new paradigms for defining "community" and its agenda. To discuss the various ways in which this effort was carried out, three aspects of their leadership have been selected here. First, there was a sincere attempt to bridge theory and practice by starting organizations where women's rights and perspectives could be implemented. Second, though the women leaders espoused protection of women's rights, they consciously aimed at and demanded basic change in related areas, such as labor issues, immigration matters, cultural practices, and community representation. Third, South Asian American women leaders took the challenge of crossing established boundaries in several areas—stretching beyond the confines of narrow identities within their own community, reaching out to others beyond their own ethnic group, and attempting linkages between local and global feminisms.

A noteworthy aspect of the women's leadership under discussion was their boldness in bringing out their perspectives. In the 1990s, many South Asian American women, well versed in feminist theories and struggle representing minority women's perspectives, did not hesitate to make their views public. Some started women's organizations that would provide both service and advocacy to women's issues, and others wrote from and about gendered perspectives. Still others assumed leadership roles in causes such as organizing cab drivers, youth organizations, and civil rights struggles.[4] Most leaders were articulate in presenting their views and used literature, art, and scholarship as their medium of expression, enhancing the visibility of their issues among a wider audience, beyond the South Asian American population. Thus, on the one hand, some South Asian American issues, such as domestic violence, came to be better known by the wider American society; on the other, these leaders provided grounds for outreach and coalition among groups across ethnic and racial lines. Considering such new paradigms required stepping out of established modes of thinking, challenging stereotypes of Asian women, and building new leadership. These efforts faced many challenges and cannot be viewed as unqualified successes, but the women were able to open spaces for different kinds of community leadership. This also created new ways for Asian American women and their contributions to be understood in the United States.

South Asian American Communities in the Late Twentieth Century

The context for South Asian American women's leadership is provided by post-1965 immigration, which witnessed rapid growth in the number of people of South Asian descent coming to the United States. This ongoing immigration for over three decades was accompanied by efforts to build new communities amid new conditions. The period is also distinct as the post–Civil Rights era, when, after winning the struggles for minority rights—both for women and for ethnic and racial minorities—minority groups continued to face the challenge of implementing and consolidating the victories of the 1960s and 1970s. At the same time, accelerated globalization and transnational activities emphasized, among other processes, frequent exchanges between local and international feminisms and the need for new paradigms for Asian American feminism, not framed solely by national boundaries.[5]

The post-1965 South Asian population in the United States comprised immigrants from South Asian countries such as Bangladesh, India, Nepal, Pakistan, and Sri Lanka, although significant numbers also arrived from far-flung diasporic communities such as in Guyana, Britain, Canada, Hong Kong, Fiji, East Africa, South Africa, Mauritius, and Trinidad and Tobago.[6] Immigrants from India dominated this composite group, both numerically and in image, and often other South Asian groups were perceived as minorities in comparison to the dominant majority of Indians.[7]

While the term *South Asian* is used throughout the present discussion, it is important to note that it was not much in usage until well into the 1990s, when a growing number of progressives, including many women activists, began to use it as a category more inclusive than nation-specific labels.[8] While the nation-based identities are supreme in this predominantly immigrant population, many interactions and networks transcending such divisions were often witnessed in celebrations of common religious or cultural traditions as well as in friendships or business links.

I also adopt the usage of "South Asian American" here, which I use interchangeably with "South Asian" but especially in situations to distinguish distinctly U.S.-based and -focused individuals and organizations. This, too, is a terminology that is coming into being only with the increased numbers of second-generation Americans of South Asian descent and the recognition among the immigrant generation that their primary interests and communities are in the United States.

Through the 1980s, most South Asian American community-based organizations fell into one of two categories. First were nation- or culture-based organizations whose main goal was to maintain home-country traditions in the United States and to represent them to "Americans." Thus, in the 1970s and 1980s, many Indian leaders in this country perceived themselves as informal ambassadors of India and formed multiple organizations based on their national identity. A host of other organizations based on regional or religious identities celebrated India's diverse traditions and observed religious practices but were meant to serve members of that particular subgroup; apart from occasional welcomes, they did not attempt collaboration with other Indians or non-Indians.[9]

Second, South Asian Americans also created a number of professional organizations that represented occupation-based interests of immigrants. Given the domination of middle-class and professional immigrants, such organizations generally represented professional or business interests; political and labor organizing or service organizations were conspicuous by their absence. This bipartite organizational picture well captures the goals and mindset of this immigrant population: they were in the United States to avail themselves of economic and career opportunities and would like simultaneously, though separately, to continue social and cultural traditions without substantial changes.

In the 1980s, a set of changing demographics impacted on South Asian communities in the United States and created the prospects for new leadership. Immigration patterns, economic changes at national and local levels, and family reunification resulted in a population with a wider socioeconomic profile. The change was felt most strongly in metropolitan areas, which showed growing numbers of lower-middle-class and poorer immigrants with clear economic needs.[10]

A spate of racist violence against Indians in New Jersey in the second half of the 1980s made the community realize that it was not immune to American racism. As a backlash to the growing presence of the Indian population in the state, a number of racist attacks were made on Indians, the most well known incident being the Navroze Mody case, in which a bank professional by that name was beaten up by a group of teenagers and died a few days later. One hate group called Dot-busters—referring to the colored dot most Indian women wear on their foreheads—came to be widely known.[11] While the struggle against such incidents brought out the community's opposition to such violence, it also revealed serious internal divisions among Indian organizations. These experiences would be recalled in subsequent years as examples of racial violence against South Asians in the United States that necessitated new organizing efforts and coalitions.[12]

An early sign of new leadership was an Indian women's organization called Asian Indian Women in America (AIWA), founded in 1980 by a group of well-educated and professionally employed immigrant Indian women.[13] These women had been members of pan-Indian organizations such as the Federation of Indians in America of New York but felt the need for a separate group to address women's issues, and particularly those of Indian immigrant women struggling to adapt to American society. AIWA held job fairs for immigrant women and represented Indian women at various Indian and multiethnic forums in the city. Through these activities, AIWA was able to create a name for itself and established some networks with Indian women beyond the New York area. However, despite being a women's organization, its leaders shared the upper-middle-class agenda of the pan-Indian organization leadership. Indeed, through the 1980s, AIWA continued to be a member of FIA. It intervened effectively in some cases where Indian women professionals faced racial discrimination, but its links to immigrant women from lower educational and economic backgrounds were limited. At the same time, when women's cries for help against domestic violence started reaching AIWA, it did not develop an effective response.

In the 1980s, women's organizations, social services, and political initiatives were too few or not strong enough to create a new leadership. The South Asian American community was led by middle-class professionals or entrepreneurs, most of whom were immigrant men who represented their class interests and their national identities. In pursuing this agenda, they woefully neglected the pressing socioeconomic needs of a growing South Asian American population who, because of being either female or from lower social strata or both, were rendered "invisible" in the celebratory nature of their organizations.

In the 1990s, a number of progressive South Asian American scholars critiqued this leadership for subscribing to "a model minority" image for their community, assigning it a distinguished and an ideal place free of problems and needs, especially in comparison to other minorities. This challenge to established community leadership was contemporaneous with, and strengthened by, the emergence of a younger generation of South Asian Americans, whose identities and interests contrasted with that of the immigrant generation. The term *model minority* itself became widely used in struggles between divergent ways of defining and leading the community.[14]

Theory and Practice

South Asian American women consciously tried to bridge theory and practice by forming new organizations that reflected their ideology and agenda. In 1985, several women came together to form an organization in New Jersey called Manavi. One of its cofounders, Shamita Das Dasgupta, describes its formation thus:

> In the 1970s, I was part of a mainstream feminist organization where we joined sit-ins and rallies. I was constantly asked to bring Indian women to join these activities arranged for freedom of women. I tried to include issues of colonialism and community traditions in this organization's debates on feminism, but was not successful in getting even attention, not to say anything about serious consideration. What was worse is that I was made to feel constantly sorry for my culture, for my people, and to almost be apologetic about their remaining in arranged marriages and families. After several years of trying to find common grounds, I gave up and walked out of this organization.
>
> Discarding the security of the mainstream feminist movement was not easy. Neither was my conscious decision to wed my feminist agenda with my ethnic identity. Until then my relationship with my Indian community had been based only on my birth; now my relationship became an act of choice. As a symbol, I gave up wearing all western clothing.

However, this was not enough. I had to develop a feminist agenda in the context of the South Asian community. I realized that I was not alone in my efforts. Serendipitously, I came together with five other Indian women, all runaways from mainstream feminism.[15]

Some AIWA members claimed Manavi as a chapter, but Manavi perceived itself as an independent organization that simultaneously addressed service needs and offered new approaches to feminist practices. It considered itself to be the first organization to cater to all South Asian American women, and not only Indian women. The early activities of Manavi included compiling its *Resource Directory for Asian Indian Women in America* and a self-help guide to assist women facing domestic violence; seeking temporary emergency shelter; dealing with rape or other sexual assaults; combating workplace sexual harassment and discrimination on the basis of sex, race, or national origin; and seeking a lawyer. Manavi members worked on cases of domestic violence and child custody disputes and also sought to advance debate on feminist theory and international feminist issues. While rooted in the needs of immigrant women, Manavi also was connected to women's issues in India. Its tenth anniversary newsletter in 1995 reported on Manavi's local activities as well as "Indian Women and National Identity" and "Beijing '95: A Global Referendum on the Human Rights of Women."

In the late 1980s, another group of women—all graduate students or young professionals from India—met in New York City to start a women's organization. After looking at the existing organizations and assessing the service and advocacy needs of South Asian American women, they founded Sakhi in 1989 as a hotline for battered South Asian women in the United States. Within a short period, the number of calls to the hotline seeking help from Sakhi friends grew rapidly. Sakhi's staff and volunteers connected their increasing caseload to appropriate local service agencies specializing in domestic violence intervention.

Sakhi also mounted awareness-raising drives and demonstrations, including one in front of a male batterer's home in Jamaica, Queens, where placards read "Is It Your Business if Your Neighbor Beats His Wife? You Bet Her Life It Is" and "Domestic Violence Destroys Our Communities." As Sakhi's newsletter of the summer of 1996 later reported, "We circled around the family house to the sounds of chants such as 'Wake up fathers, Wake up brothers. If you abuse, you will lose!' We also delivered a poster-letter to the family warning them to stop their terrorization of Ms. [the victim] . . . and SAKHI remain determined to bring Mr. [the perpetrator] to justice and warn families like his that they cannot get away with sheltering those who terrorize women." Sakhi's public outcries against domestic violence shocked the Indian community, particularly its established elite leaders, but at the same time, Sakhi was being recognized by progressives as one of the foremost new feminist organizations in New York City.

In selecting domestic violence as their leading agenda item for organizing, the new women leaders were well aware that, besides being a service issue, it was also a strategic choice for community leadership: addressing domestic violence in one's own community—and thereby acknowledging its presence—meant opening debate on a host of community and feminist issues. Several women practitioners utilized domestic violence work as a basis for their political analyses of their community. For example, Purvi Shah, a staff member of Sakhi, wrote:

Such dichotomies as politics/culture and public/private make it nearly impossible to show how family structures and institutions such as marriage can perpetuate or promote violence against women. The idea that home is private, its affairs governed by culture, makes it possible to justify male superiority and domestic violence—they are simply the result of "tradition," "heritage," and culture. The separation of politics from culture is similarly used to silence activist messages, by barring progressive groups from participating in community events and constructing a sanitized version of culture that suits elite interests and power.[16]

In yet another example of a practitioner-advocate, Anannya Bhattacharjee critiqued the individualist assumptions that underlay many existing domestic violence organizations in the United States, particularly in comparison to a more suitable strategy of collective support for the battered women and against the batterer:

> Domestic violence organizations in the United States balk at such [collective] methods because, above all, they believe in the bourgeois notion of good citizenship, which means abiding by the law even when written by the oppressor. . . . Thus, the concept of women guarding one another, vilifying batterers so that they cannot dare to harm the woman, and other similar tactics are not even contemplated.[17]

In the following years, South Asian American women's organizations encountered a host of other issues that indicated their simultaneous engagement with theory and practice. They debated if men should be part of their active membership, how advocacy work should be balanced with case workload, and if they should open their own shelters.

An example of differences among women's organizations in their approach toward theory and practice is seen in an analysis made by Jyotsana Vaid, herself one of the South Asian American women leaders. From an extensive survey and analysis of South Asian American women's organizations nationwide, Vaid concludes:

> There gradually emerged two models of organizing around the issue of marital violence— one institutionalizes intervention, viewing the problem solely in terms of individuals in need of specific services, the other seeks to raise public awareness of underlying causes of the phenomenon, including awareness about the patriarchal assumptions that implicitly condone violence, while responding to individual cases as needed. Manavi, Sakhi, Saheli, Maitreyi, Narika, and Sawera appear to fit within the awareness model while Apna Ghar, Raksha, Sahara, Aasra, Hamdard Center and MFAIS (and perhaps Daya) appear to fit into the social service model.[18]

In an article discussing organizing to combat violence against women, Bhattacharjee highlighted class issues in Sakhi's work and went on to explain why Sakhi staff members working in its Domestic Workers Committee had to break from the parent organization and form a new organization called Workers' Awaaz (Workers' Voice) in 1997.[19] Sakhi's leaders, in contrast, maintained that organizing household workers was a cause separate from working with survivors of domestic violence, Sakhi's original mission. The acrimonious nature of this split and the ensuing debate surprised many South Asian community advocates, particularly as the debate became public.[20] Besides indicating the deep ideological differences between the two organizations, the split also highlighted the tenuous relationship between theory and practice in community organizations.

A significant characteristic of South Asian American women's leadership has been the close relationship between scholars and practitioners; in many instances it is difficult to distinguish one from the other. As evident from our discussion, a number of practitioners were articulate in expressing their ideologies in a scholarly manner. The emergence of progressive South Asian American women's organizations is coterminous—and deeply connected—with a number of writings on women issues. A few examples of this trend can be seen in anthologies and collected works edited by South Asian women or contributions by South Asian women to volumes on Asian American or to other women-centered publications.[21] Such efforts resulted in the creation of a number of scholar-advocates among South Asian Americans, many of them women leaders. This feature has had considerable impact on the nature and development of community organizations, as many written analyses of feminist struggles became publicly available in a relatively short time. Margaret Abraham advanced this relationship to a considerable degree by conducting an in-depth scholarly study of what she calls marital violence in South Asian communities in America and outlined the challenge of combining academic research with access to women served by domestic violence organizations.[22]

Contextualizing Women Struggles

A hallmark of South Asian American women leaders has been that while they are deeply committed to women's struggles for empowerment, they do not view their work as limited to women only. As evident from their words and actions, their goal has not been to find their voices or to locate a space merely for themselves. They perceive women's issues as community issues and gender as inextricably linked to other societal aspects. Although some women's organizations aimed at facilitating immigrant women's lives in the United States, many others pursued an aggressive agenda of raising questions about established community practices and leadership. In the article titled "Beyond a Space of Our Own," Jyotsana Vaid categorized South Asian women's organizations in the United States by their agenda and emphasized that in order to engage in a struggle for social change, "it is critical that the spaces claimed go beyond the assertion or celebration of identity."[23]

Many South Asian American women advocates had long felt that women's issues, particularly those of minority women, should be addressed in the context of their sociocultural background. There has been a general sense of a lack of cultural sensitivity on the part of mainstream women's organizations and services. It was widely recognized that deep-rooted social barriers prevented South Asian women in the United States who were confronting domestic violence from seeking help outside their family. However, when some did overcome these barriers to seek mainstream social service agencies or shelters, they frequently faced cultural barriers, ranging from language issues to stereotyped and negative images of South Asian marriage and family relationships. In a number of cases, service providers were unaware of dietary, language, and religious features in diverse South Asian cultures and did not understand the background of South Asian gender roles that underlay the case. South Asian American women leaders emphasized the sociocultural context of women's issues and argued that cultural awareness was inextricably linked with women's struggles.[24]

In championing women's rights, South Asian American women joined progressive voices beyond the South Asian American community. Sakhi coordinator Prema Vora, for example, opposed welfare reform provisions in the mid-1990s by stressing their implications for South Asian immigrant women. As she stated in *Newsday* on June 26, 1995, "The decision to leave an abusive husband or a partner is always a difficult one. . . . The decision to leave is perhaps even more difficult for an immigrant woman who speaks little English, is unfamiliar with her surroundings and, most [of all] depends on her abuser for her immigration status."

Meanwhile, Sakhi broadened its agenda and sponsored film festivals, cultural performances, and fund-raising programs presenting women artists and activists. In one Sakhi "Speak Out" night, several South Asian women told personal stories of love, anger, happiness, and bitterness, and several of Sakhi's film festivals screened acclaimed films made by and about South Asian women.

In the late 1990s, New York City became a hub for South Asian American cultural activities, with a busy year-round public calendar of music and dance performances and artistic and literary presentations. While such activities had been going on among South Asian immigrants for some years, this time they had a distinctive progressive and younger-generation flavor. Women's organizations cannot be entirely credited for this cultural efflorescence, but their membership often overlapped with that of new progressive ethnic networks.

Building a Community

Through their work on women's issues, South Asian American women leaders aimed to build new communities based on new paradigms in which women's rights—together with other progressive agendas—could be secured. This goal of a new community was noticeable in two respects: (1) the building of feminist communities among and beyond South Asians in the United States, with both local and international dimensions; and (2) an ethnic community based on progressive issues that transcended national and religious identities.

The search for new paradigms was apparent in locating the genealogies of their feminisms. South Asian American women's leadership had a clear purpose of charting their own feminist directions. Their organizations, together with other South Asian American women writers and scholars, offered critiques of both the traditional patriarchal system of South Asian society and mainstream American feminism.

Anannya Bhattacharjee, a co-founder of Sakhi, voiced widely shared criticisms of mainstream American feminism:

Western feminists have established that for the collective condition of women to change, women must project their experiences of oppression in their private lives into the public. "Public," in this analysis, has been generalized as outside-the-family-home. . . . Implicit is the assumption of the existence of available public spaces, to intervene in and transform. . . . The absence of analysis of the nation-state in the U.S. mainstream feminism leads to the uncritical and automatic assumption of a public whose subject then, is a U.S. citizen. . . . Immigration laws have *privatized* the nation; it is now a bounded space into which only some of the people can walk some of the time.[25]

This effort to build their own feminist agenda included cross-referencing gender with colonialism, social and economic hierarchies, as well as other forces of conservative politics. They also aligned themselves theoretically with Third World women movements and with women of color in the United States.[26] The confluence of South Asian feminism and progressive South Asian communities in the United States was not a coincidence; these organizations consciously placed their work in the immigrant nature of their community, drawing attention to gender in transition between the two cultures and two societies.

South Asian American feminists traced their lineage to contemporary and earlier generations of feminists in South Asia and maintained strong links with them.[27] These networks extended to women's groups in diasporic South Asian communities as well as international feminist circles. As scholar-activist Jyotsana Vaid describes a progressive South Asian effort of the 1980s, "COSAW sought to focus its efforts on creating awareness about the growing women's movement in the subcontinent, starting in the mid-1970s, and South Asian women's concerns in Britain, issues about which there was little coverage in either mainstream or immigrant media."[28]

Such transnational links were present in many other organizations, as well as in literature and arts. South Asian women's writing was shared across national boundaries, and frequent travels supported these links.[29] In fact, discourses about home, language, and culture became part of South Asian intellectual life, and women played prominent roles in sustaining them. South Asian American women were in the forefront of linking the issues of South Asian women in the United States to those of Third World women and placed gender within debates on colonialism, patriarchy, globalization, and war.[30]

At the same time, the women's organizations remained committed to their work in local communities. While linking the local and global feminisms made for an attractive theoretical debate, it remained an enigma for the practitioner who had to operate in conditions directly rooted in the local and national realities. Work in immigrant communities necessitated interfacing with U.S. immigration policies or encountering the state or city educational systems. Although the women leaders were not successful in resolving all the problems of bridging the local and global dimensions of feminist practices, they remained aware of the challenge. This awareness itself marked a qualitative change in the leadership of the South Asian community in America.

Another challenge faced by women leaders involved their relationship with the established community leaders in the United States. While the women questioned the existing definitions of community along the narrower identities of nation or religion, they strove to establish new relationships with the more open sections of the community. In discussing Manavi's work, Shamita Das Dasgupta wrote about this approach to the community:

> Reclaiming our community was an intricate task. We had to dig through its surface crust of conservatism, absolutism, and androcentrism. In turn, the community had to receive us in our many-faceted roles: mothers, activists, professionals, students, wives, feminists, single women. For a while it was touch and go. Through this turmoil, Manavi was born. . . . My work with Manavi has taught me to be an activist and a feminist not by dismissing the immigrant community but working within it. I suppose the community has also learned that we will not go away.[31]

Another woman leader, a co-founder of Sakhi, wrote about the origins of that organization:

> Some of us [the founding members] had been politically active in other communities in the United States and hungered to work with our own. We identified ourselves as South Asian, as we recognized historical commonalities shared by peoples from this region and were drawn to the notion of transcending nationalistic divisions. We also identified ourselves as women of color, with roots elsewhere because of our immigration status and our heritages in the "Third World." We imagined building a community on this gendered and ethnic identity.[32]

Thus, transcending the boundaries of narrower identities such as nation and religion, which were pervasive in the immigrant population, and promoting a broader and more composite ethnic identity of South Asians in the United States were key features of the women's leadership. Until the 1980s, the term *South Asian* was rarely in use, among both other Americans and South Asian Americans themselves. Manavi and Sakhi may be considered pioneers for consciously addressing issues of and serving *all* South Asian American women, and not only the dominant population of Asian Indians. Manavi presented itself as the first organization for South Asian women, and Sakhi adopted its original full name "Sakhi for South Asian Women." These conscious name-related decisions impacted on policy decisions in pan–South Asianism and greatly contributed to the formation of a pan–South Asian ethnic identity in the United States. These women's initiatives were contemporaneous with the emergence of a U.S.-reared younger generation of South Asians who could not identify with the national, religious, or regional identities integral to their parents' generation. Fortified with a progressive agenda, the pan–South Asian appeal of women leaders pioneered a new brand of South Asian American activism.[33]

This newly formed pan–South Asian community in the United States was supported by coalition building with activists from other groups. Women leaders were once again, though not exclusively, at the forefront of such transethnic and transracial networks. In the process of reaching out to other progressive issue-based organizations and to progressives in other ethnic communities, South Asian American women leaders both defined their own cultural community and contributed to multicultural alliances on issue-based struggles. In its early years, Sakhi looked for support from pan-Asian organizations such as the New York Asian Women's Center and Committee against Anti-Asian Violence. In the following years, Asian American and other civil rights organizations became more than familiar with South Asian American women's organizations.

In the 1990s, a significant number of South Asian American activists turned to women's organizations for their orientation to progressive ethnic organizing. At the same time, a spate of progressive organizations with "South Asian" in their names were founded in New York City: for example, South Asians for Action (SAFA), South Asian Lesbian and Gay Association (SALGA), and South Asian AIDS Action (SAAA). These organizations were small in size but distinctive in their progressive agendas. Despite having separate organizational entities, they were united in their members' deviation from immigrant leadership. Sakhi was commonly perceived as a leader of such South Asian American organizations.

The contest between these two groups of leaders—the established and the new—over the definition and agenda of an ethnic community became public at the India Day Parade of 1995. Although the issue of inclusion of "South Asian" organizations in a national-pride parade celebrating India's independence from the British was not resolved for years to come, the approach of the two kinds of leadership was emblematic of their difference. While FIA continued to organize the India Day Parade without much basic change, the progressive organizations rallied local governmental and media agencies to their cause. The latter organizations were supported by a wave of expressions and critiques, through literature, journalism, art, and other media that informed and engaged a wide audience about why "South Asian" was preferable to national identities such as Indian or Pakistani. Despite outstanding issues about the internal workings of diversity under the label "South Asians," it would become an established term in academic and progressive circles.[34]

In the aftermath of the September 11 attacks—both the American war in Afghanistan and the U.S. engagement with the Indian-Pakistani tensions—the term *South Asian* took off in the American mainstream media. While the American public and political interest in the South Asian region was unprecedented, many activists became concerned about the civil liberties of South Asians in the domestic arena (overlapping with those of Arab/Muslim Americans). Once again, women leaders would stand in solidarity with other South Asian American activists and argue how gender issues were intricately linked with those of larger community, immigration, and minority rights.

Conclusion

By 2000, the South Asian American community had an alternative leadership significantly different from that of the established immigrant leaders. Women took a lead in redefining and organizing South Asian communities in the United States and combined gender with other progressive issues such as poverty, sexuality, organizing working-class interests, social service needs, and political representation. In addition, they contextualized gender with racism, colonialism, patriarchy, and social class and other hierarchies and attempted a coming together of local and global feminisms. Most of all, they effectively challenged the established images of passive and docile Asian women and imparted agency not only to their gender but also to their communities.

NOTES

1. On the politics of New York City's India Day Parade, see Madhulika S. Khandelwal, *Becoming American, Being Indian: An Immigrant Community in New York City* (Ithaca, NY: Cornell University Press, 2002), chap. 8; and Purvi Shah, "Redefining the Home: How Community Elite Silence Feminist Activism," in *Dragon Ladies: Asian American Feminists Breathe Fire*, ed. Sonia Shah (Boston: South End Press, 1997), 46–56.

2. The geographic focus of my own ethnographic research has been New York City. See Khandelwal, *Becoming American*.

3. Chandra Talpade Mohanty, Ann Russo, and Lourdes Torres, eds., *Third World Women and the Politics of Feminism* (Bloomington: Indiana University Press, 1991). See also Kathleen Uno, chapter 2, and Sucheta Mazumdar, chapter 3, in this book.

4. As a few leading examples of this phenomenon, Urvashi Vaid led the issues of lesbian and gay communities; Sayu Bhojwani founded and directed the first community-based youth organization, South Asian Youth Action!; and Bhairavi Desai led New York City cab drivers in their strike against unfair city regulations.

5. Shirley Hune, "Doing Gender with a Feminist Gaze: Toward a Historical Reconstruction of Asian America," in *Contemporary Asian America: A Multidisciplinary Reader*, ed. Min Zhou and James V. Gatewood (New York: New York University Press, 2000), 413–30.

6. See Parminder Bhachu, *Twice Migrants: East African Sikh Settlers in Britain* (London: Tavistock, 1985); Tilokie Depoo, ed., *The East Indian Diaspora: 150 Years of Survival, Contributions, and Achievements* (Flushing, NY: Asian/American Center, Queens College, City University of New York, 1993); Madhavi Kale, "Projecting Identities: Empire and Indentured Labor Migration in Trinidad and British Guiana," in Peter van der Veer, ed., *Nation and Migration: The Politics of Space in the South Asian Diaspora* (Philadelphia: University of Pennsylvania Press, 1995), 73–92; and Khandelwal, *Becoming American*.

7. In the 1980 U.S. Census, the first time the new subcategory "Asian Indian" was placed under the "racial" category of "Asian and Pacific Islanders," Indians numbered approximately 365,000; they numbered 865,000 in 1990 and 1,670,000 in 2000.

8. Among the few exceptions were organizations such as South Asian Forum, based in New York, and the Committee of South Asian Women (COSAW), operating from Texas, whose outreach to broader immigrant communities were limited.

9. Khandelwal, *Becoming American*.

10. Ibid.

11. Hindus wear a colored dot as a symbol of respect for themselves. While men wear it only in religious places or on select occasions, this practice is widespread among women, for whom it is integral to their spiritual, cultural, and fashion identities.

12. Deborah N. Misir, "The Murder of Navroze Mody: Race, Violence, and the Search for Order," *Amerasia Journal* 22:2 (1996): 55–76.

13. This New York–based AIWA is to be distinguished from the pan-Asian women's organization Asian Immigrant Women's Alliance, also using the acronym AIWA.

14. Margaret Abraham, *Speaking the Unspeakable: Marital Violence among South Asian Immigrants in the United States* (New Brunswick, NJ: Rutgers University Press, 2000); and Kamala

Visweswaran, "Diaspora by Design: Flexible Citizenship and South Asians in U.S. Racial Formations," *Diaspora* 6:1 (1997): 5–29.

15. Shamita Das Dasgupta and Sayantani Dasgupta, "Journeys: Reclaiming South Asian Feminism," in *Our Feet Walk the Sky: Women of the South Asian Diaspora*, ed. The Women of South Asian Descent Collective (San Francisco: Aunt Lute Books, 1993), 123–30.

16. Shah, "Redefining the Home," 46. For an in-depth discussion of domestic violence and its relationship to community organizing, see Abraham, *Speaking the Unspeakable*; and Satya P. Krishnan, Malahat Baig-Amin, Louisa Gilbert, Nabila El-Bassel, and Ann Waters, "Lifting the Veil of Secrecy: Domestic Violence against South Asian Women in the United States," in *A Patchwork Shawl: Chronicles of South Asian Women in America*, ed. Shamita Das Dasgupta (New Brunswick, NJ: Rutgers University Press, 1998), 145–59.

17. Anannya Bhattacharjee, "A Slippery Path: Organizing Resistance to Violence against Women," in Shah, ed., *Dragon Ladies*, 36.

18. Jyotsana Vaid, "Beyond a Space of Our Own," *Amerasia Journal* 25:3 (1999/2000): 119–20.

19. Bhattacharjee, "Slippery Path," 29–45.

20. See Abraham, *Speaking the Unspeakable*; Shahbano Ailani, Shahensham Begum, Rokeya Mollah, Sushila Patil, and Biju Mathew, "Loud and Clear: A Conversation with Workers' Awaaz," *Amerasia Journal* 25:3 (1999/2000): 183–93; and Athima Chansanchai, "Maid in the U.S.A.," *Village Voice*, Oct. 7, 1997.

21. For example, see Women of South Asian Descent Collective, ed., *Our Feet Walk the Sky*; Sunaina Maira and Rajini Srikanth, eds., *Contours of the Heart: South Asians Map North America* (New York: Asian American Writers' Workshop, 1996); Sonia Shah, ed., *Dragon Ladies*; Mohanty, Russo, and Torres, eds., *Third World Women*; and M. Jacqui Alexander and Chandra Tolpade Mohanty, eds., *Feminist Genealogies, Colonial Legacies, Democratic Futures* (New York: Routledge, 1997).

22. Abraham, *Speaking the Unspeakable*, 199–204.

23. Vaid, "Beyond a Space of Our Own," 124.

24. Das Dasgupta and Dasgupta, "Journeys."

25. Anannya Bhattacharjee, "The Public/Private Mirage: Mapping Homes and Undomesticating Violence Work in the South Asian Immigrant Community," in Alexander and Mohanty, eds., *Feminist Genealogies*, 308, 316–17.

26. Mohanty, Russo, and Torres, eds., *Third World Women*.

27. Das Dasgupta and Dasgupta, "Journeys"; Radha Kumar, *The History of Doing: An Illustrated Account of Movements for Women's Rights and Feminism in India, 1800–1990* (New York: Verso, 1993); and Kumkum Sangari and Sudesh Vaid, eds., *Recasting Women: Essays in Colonial History* (New Delhi: Kali for Women, 1989).

28. Vaid, "Beyond a Space of Our Own," 116.

29. For examples of the transnational appeal of English literature by South Asian women writers, see works by Meena Alexander, including *The Shock of Arrival: Reflections on Postcolonial Experience* (Boston: South End, 1996) and *Manhattan Music* (San Francisco: Mercury House, 1997); Kali for Women, eds., *Truth Tales: Contemporary Stories by Women Writers of India* (New York: Feminist Press of the City University of New York, 1986); and Jhumpa Lahiri, *Interpreter of Maladies* (Boston: Houghton Mifflin, 1999).

30. Inderpal Grewal, "The Postcolonial, Ethnic Studies, and the Diaspora: The Contexts of Ethnic Immigrant/Migrant Cultural Studies in the US," in *The Traveling Nation: India and Its Diaspora*, ed. Amarpal K. Dhaliwal, special issue of *Socialist Review* 24:4 (1994): 45–74; and Mohanty, Russo, and Torres, eds., *Third World Women*.

31. Das Dasgupta and Dasgupta, "Journeys," 126–27.

32. Bhattacharjee, "Slippery Path," 29.

33. In the late 1990s, *South Asian* became a commonly used term for scholars of South Asian descent from different states in the subcontinent. For example, see the works in Maira and Srikanth, *Contours of the Heart*; and Biju Mathew and Vijay Prashad, eds., "Satyagraha in America: The Political Culture of South Asians in the U.S.," *Amerasia Journal* 25:3 (1991/2000). "South Asian American" is also coming into use; see, for example, the title of *Emerging Voices: South Asian American Women Redefine Self, Family and Community*, ed. Sangeeta R. Gupta (Thousand Oaks, CA: Sage Publications, 1999).

34. However, the issue of internal diversity among South Asians in the United States remains alive among immigrants and university students. To reflect on the formation of an ethnic identity, from 1998 to 2002, I taught a course titled "Becoming South Asian" in the Asian American Studies Program of the University of Massachusetts, Boston. See also Naheed Islam, "In the Belly of the Multicultural Beast I Am Named South Asian," in Women of the South Asian Descent Collective, eds., *Our Feet Walk the Sky*, 242–45.

22

Chamorro Women, Self-Determination, and the Politics of Abortion in Guam

Vivian Loyola Dames

I am taking a stand as a woman, as a Chamorro and as an American.　　　　　—Jacqueline Quitugua-Bettis[1]

A classic point of departure between many Western feminists and most Chamorro women relates to fundamental differences in their attitudes about motherhood. Feminists generally view the child-bearing role as the source of female subordination. In contrast, the centrality of mothers in Chamorro culture and the power and authority linked with the maternal role make it difficult for Chamorro women . . . to view motherhood as a source of oppression. Rather, it has been a traditional source of power and prestige for them.

　　　　　—Laura Marie Torres Souder[2]

If you do not know anything about Chamorros and about our struggles, you will miss the point about our decision to protect life. . . . We are proposing a simple idea. We choose to exercise self-determination in the moral imperative even as we pursue self-determination in the political arena.

　　　　　—Archbishop Anthony Sablan Apuron[3]

In 1990, Guam became embroiled in one of the most divisive social policy debates in its forty-year history as a U.S. territory when a Chamorro[4] woman senator introduced a bill virtually banning abortion.[5] This legislation was passed unanimously by a twenty-one-member legislature with seven women senators.[6] The local activism this controversial bill catalyzed, its enactment, and the immediate challenge to its constitutionality catapulted Guam into the U.S. national media as a frontrunner in the race to overturn *Roe v. Wade*, the 1973 U.S. Supreme Court ruling that established a woman's decision to have an abortion as a constitutionally protected right.[7]

At the time there was a complex interaction over abortion among activists, interest groups, legislatures, governors, and courts being played out in several states. This was sparked by the July 1989 Supreme Court ruling in *Webster v. Reproductive Health Services*, which opened the door for states to test the limits of how far they could go in restricting access to abortion.[8] Guam's law, characterized by an American Civil Liberties Union (ACLU) attorney as a "Pearl Harbor for women,"[9] was a remarkable legislative success. However, the lower courts ruled the law unconstitutional, and the decision to invalidate the law was left standing when, on appeal, the U.S. Supreme Court denied review. Because the challenge to its constitutionality failed to overturn *Roe*, many observers view this episode as an unequivocal victory for the pro-choice movement in the United States. However, a more complex story emerges when analyzing Chamorro women activists on both sides of the conflict as agents of resistance and transformation in the context of Guam's history of colonization and the unsuccessful attempt of the people of Guam to attain decolonization through its "Quest for Commonwealth."[10]

While this law, like others in the race to overturn *Roe*, was a local response to national policy development, it was embedded in growing local frustration over the impasse with the U.S. Congress to act on Guam's proposal to change its political status. The signing of this bill and the appeal of the lower court's decision all the way to the Supreme Court provided a high-profile opportunity for Guam's governor to link his personal moral justification for the ban on abortion with a broader political cause. Just as a pregnant woman, especially in the case of first conception, is "betwixt and between fixed points of classification,"[11] so Guam exists politically in a "liminal space, betwixt and between, somehow outside the normal order of sovereignty or integration."[12] I have suggested elsewhere that in Guam, the pregnant woman and the associated issue of individual self-determination (the right of the woman versus the right of the "unborn") became a potent analogue to Guam's political limbo and the issue of the right of the Chamorros, as an indigenous people, to political self-determination. This claim and its implications for Chamorro identity lie at the heart of the political-status question. Once the governor resolved to defend Guam's ban on abortion against a common foe of Chamorro self-determination, namely, the U.S. Constitution, then the politics of abortion and the commonwealth quest became irrevocably entangled.[13]

That a challenge to *Roe* would come from a territory was unexpected. This was not the first time, however, that a Pacific island was at the vanguard of American abortion politics. In 1970, Hawai'i captured national attention by becoming the first state to repeal its restrictive abortion law.[14] In striking contrast to the reform movement in

Hawaiʻi, in Guam it was indigenous women who played central roles. Furthermore, two main protagonists in the Guam story—Elizabeth (Belle) Arriola, the senator who introduced the anti-abortion bill, and Anita Arriola, the attorney who represented the plaintiffs in the legal challenge—are mother and daughter. What does this conflict reveal about the multiple, sometimes conflicting identities of Chamorro women, about the significance of motherhood as both a source of strength and a site of resistance, and about the role of indigenous women at the intersection of church and state?

The abstractions of the contemporary abortion debate and national policy take on shape and meaning in particular places, framed by local interpretations.[15] Of the localized studies of people who do the concrete, sustained work in the opposing movements, two studies, both conducted in the pre-*Webster* period, explore how the contemporary debate over abortion is part of a long history of change in both its cultural meaning and social practice, and hence help illuminate the complex layers of the Guam conflict from a more women-centered perspective.

Kristin Luker, a sociologist, analyzed the relationship between the social values fostered by these movements and the beliefs of individual activists in California where, as in Hawaiʻi, abortion was legal before the *Roe* decision.[16] Her study revealed that the abortion debate has been transformed because it has "gone public" and called into question individuals' most sacrosanct beliefs. Centering on "women's contrasting obligations to themselves and others, the abortion debate has become a *referendum on the place and meaning of motherhood*" (italics in original).[17] She found that these two groups of activists clash in their worldviews, life expectations, and life choices. Of particular relevance here is that while almost 80 percent of the women active in the pro-life movement in Luker's sample were Catholic, no pro-choice activist claimed to be a Catholic at the time of the interview.[18] In Guam, where Roman Catholicism is the dominant religion and central to Chamorro identity and culture, activists who identify as Catholic were on both sides of the abortion conflict.

Faye D. Ginsberg conducted a more localized ethnographic study in Fargo, North Dakota, and found that pro-choice and pro-life activists do not divide neatly along ethnic, occupational, or even religious lines.[19] At the local level, where activity is strongest, grass-roots activists on both sides of the abortion issue tend to be primarily white, middle-class women.[20] This challenges essentialist notions of women and provides support for the view that women, even with similar race, class, and cultural backgrounds, rarely experience themselves or act as a homogeneous social group with a universal set of interests. In abortion debates, not only is motherhood up for grabs, as Luker argues, but so is the very definition of what it means to be female.[21]

In this chapter I analyze the abortion conflict in Guam through the worldviews and discursive strategies of Chamorro women activists.[22] This analysis permits a view of indigenous women as engaged citizens and social actors who are actively reworking ideologies about the place of women in society from a politically and geographically marginalized site in the American landscape. In a situated contest such as this, one can see more generally how abortion comes to signify not only conflicting personal and social ideologies but also national and political identifications capable of mobilizing and polarizing people. In a small island community where indigenous women are connected through a web of relations, these polarizations are deeply felt. I argue that this conflict

over abortion arises from competing views of gender and its transactions with nationality and religion. What is at stake is not only what it means to be a woman but
also what it means to be Chamorro, Catholic, and American in an unincorporated U.S.
territory.

I begin with a historical perspective on the status and roles of Chamorro women
and the cultural basis for resistance to Western feminism as perceived in this context.
I then describe the worldviews of pro-life activists, highlighting the narrative of Senator Arriola and her catalytic role in the mobilization of local pro-life forces. I contrast
this with the worldviews of pro-choice activists and the narrative of Lou Leon Guerrero, a nurse, who assumed the leadership role in the island's first pro-choice organization. I conclude by reflecting on what happened to the key women and organizations described here and what this conflict and its aftermath reveal about contemporary Chamorro womanhood and the meaning of self-determination in the Guam
context.

Chamorro Culture and the Role of Women

The history of the Chamorro people is replete with historical constructions and recon-
structions of Chamorro identities in dynamic interaction with foreign ideas and practices.[23] One of the few sources on the role of women in Chamorro culture is a conspec-
tus by Laura Marie Torres Souder, a self-described feminist and Chamorro rights activist who describes the *hagan-haga'*, or blood daughters of Chamorro ancestors like
herself, as the "embodiment of many contradictions" in their simultaneous roles of culture bearer, cultural preservationist, and agent of change. Souder contends that
Chamorro women organizers manifest "the dialectic between the colonizers and the
colonized, between tradition and modernity,"[24] that can be traced back through Guam's
extended colonial history. It is against this backdrop that I situate the 1990 conflict over
abortion.

Gender identity for Chamorro women is rooted in an origin myth that reflects a belief in a female spirit as a life-giving force, and in an ancient caste society where lineage
and descent were reckoned through the female line, which conferred considerable prestige on women and power over family life, property, and inheritance.[25] A turning point
occurred with the introduction of Roman Catholicism in the 1670s and ensuing colonization by Spain through 1898. Once militarily defeated by the Spanish, the ancient
gynocentric worldview was replaced by a view of creation by a paternal, Judeo-Christ-
ian God. With Catholicism the Chamorros also embraced a reverence of Mary, the
mother of Jesus, and Marianisma, which defined three possible roles for women—as
virgin, wife, and mother.[26]

Souder argues that prior to Western contact, Chamorro culture was also matrifocal,
or mother-centered. While the position of Chamorro women in relation to their husbands changed as a result of changes in sexual practices and the institution of marriage, the centrality of motherhood has not. Motherhood provides a context through
which Chamorro women exercise power and control, in both the family and other
spheres of society.[27] Through this dialectical exchange, a hybrid traditional culture

evolved that persisted up through the early twentieth century, at which time a second disruption occurred.[28]

The United States wrested possession of Guam from Spain in 1898. Under U.S rule, matrilineage was outlawed and patriarchical marriage laws were imposed. The transformation of the subsistence economy into a cash-based market economy also created new arrangements in the division of labor, which separated home from the workplace. Men became wage earners, and the domestic sphere became identified as the woman's place. Gradually, the Chamorro-Spanish culture "amalgamated with American ways to form a pool of syncretic cultural traits which present day Chamorros call *custumbren Chamoru*, or traditional Chamorro culture."[29] Women, especially mothers, are looked upon as having particular responsibilities as bearers of *custumbren Chamoru*.

In 1950, Guam became an unincorporated territory of the United States, and the people became American citizens. With this came a new political consciousness of being legal persons with individual rights. The prevailing assumption during the following decade was that becoming American necessitated a break with the past. This created a problem for Chamorros. In the process of becoming citizens, political identity was confused with cultural identity.[30] Until the 1970s, with the emergence of the indigenous rights movement, there was no conceptual framework for asserting a Chamorro national identity. The prevailing view was that Chamorros, as a people, no longer existed. Only second-class American citizens, an "ethnic" minority—not a separate and distinct nationality—remained.[31]

While Americanization contributed to the decline of certain aspects of traditional power, advances in reproductive technology provided women a new source for personal autonomy and self-determination. Many Chamorro women began to use artificial contraceptive methods to plan their families. At the time of the *Roe* decision in 1973, abortion in Guam was a crime. While illegal and taboo, it was not unknown.[32] Several interviewees gave accounts of individuals known (or suspected) of performing illegal abortions or of women they know personally who had aborted themselves. All informants emphasized the secrecy and *mamahlao*, or shame, surrounding abortion, regardless of the circumstances.[33]

Five years passed before a local statute mirroring *Roe* was enacted in Guam. Concepcion Barrett, a Chamorro and the only woman senator in the Thirteenth Guam Legislature, quietly took the initiative to amend the new Penal Code to include a section permitting abortion by a physician upon demand. There was no local activism advocating reform or any public opposition to the enactment of this law. I attribute this to the absence of any feminist-identified organizations, a general reticence to challenge publicly the formidable power of the local Catholic Church, and Senator Barrett's low-profile legislative strategy. Also, many who were politically aware and engaged were embroiled in the contentious issues of political status, the movement for a nuclear-free Pacific, and a referendum to legalize casino gambling.

By the late 1970s, New Right leaders in the United States sought to create an unprecedented alliance between Catholics, right-wing politicians, and Protestant fundamentalists, in order to recast the right-to-life position in its most conservative interpretation, linking it to their vision of the proper role of government, family, and sexuality.[34] This occurred at the same time that local resistance to Americanization was festering, an indigenous cultural renaissance was taking root, Chamorro identity was becoming politicized, and the clamor for a change in Guam's political status was intensifying. These dynamics provided a unique angle of reflection and refraction in the worldviews of Chamorro women.

Pro-Life Activists and Mobilization

According to Luker, "[T]hose areas covered by a 'world view' are those parts of life we take for granted, never imagine questioning, and cannot envision decent, moral people not sharing."[35] Women for and against abortion divide most clearly in their view of the causes for and solutions to the unequal effects of sexual activity.[36] Pro-life activists believe that men and women are intrinsically different, and this is both a cause and a product of the fact that they have different roles in life: men are best suited to the "public" world, women to the "private" world of the home. Ginsberg found that while both pro-life and pro-choice activists express a concern for the preservation of nurturance, their interpretation of what this means differs. For pro-life activists, nurturance is linked more directly to biological reproduction than to nurturance as a source of cultural value and female authority, as understood by most pro-choice activists.[37]

Within this pro-life worldview, reform efforts are directed toward creating and promoting a social and political context that will protect pregnancy and motherhood. Dawn Leon Guerrero, a Chamorro mother of five and spokesperson for the pro-life coalition, put it this way: "If I, as a woman, have this natural ability to have a child, I think this is a God-given grace in me and I think I have no right to destroy that child."[38] Abortion represents a devaluation of motherhood and hence a threat to Chamorro women's reproductive role and position as bearers of the culture.

When the Supreme Court in 1989 invited renewed battles in state legislatures over tougher abortion laws, leaders of national organizations on both sides began to mobilize. The call rallying pro-life Americans to action resonated immediately with Belle Arriola, a mother of eight, devout Catholic, senior Democrat in her fourth term in the Guam legislature, and chair of the Committee on Youth, Senior Citizens and Cultural Affairs. The personal experiences that Belle brought to her public role as "guardian of the family"[39] help explain why banning abortion was a primary goal of her political career.

Born in 1928, Belle was the eldest in a family of six boys and three girls. From the age of six months to almost twelve years, she lived with her grandmother and aunt; her father died when she was eleven. Belle had a strict Catholic upbringing, graduated as salutatorian from a Catholic girls' high school, and attended a Catholic college in Pennsylvania. She left the island as a stateless ward of the U.S. Navy; she returned in 1952 as a proud American citizen. The view that U.S. citizenship provided, rather than displaced, a preexisting "national" identify is supported by Belle's statement that until 1950 she was a "woman without a country."[40] For Belle, being Chamorro is a cultural, not a political, identity.

The Organic Act of 1950 not only conferred a new political identity, "American," to the people of Guam but also ushered in new arenas for social action. At age twenty-five,

Belle married a Chamorro attorney and soon became the first president of the Women's Democratic Club of Guam. Two life transitions, her children growing up and separation from her husband, preceded her becoming a politician. She coped by extending the value she placed on nurturance as a mother to assuming leadership in organizations concerned with what she viewed as threats to the family.

Belle's assumption of an activist role came through the personal invitation of Bishop Felixberto Camacho Flores, who asked her to co-chair the anti-casino-gambling campaign. Reflecting on this first campaign, Belle said: "I think that's what makes it a winner, because the Church is there."[41] With her confidence in the political efficacy of using the influence of the church to codify public moral standards, Belle was elected senator in her second bid for office in 1982.

Even prior to becoming a legislator, Belle had been following the abortion issue closely. Emboldened by the pro-life movement in the States, Senator Arriola saw in the *Webster* decision a way to create greater awareness of the violence being committed against those that she saw as the most vulnerable and defenseless, the "unborn." Moved also by a concern for the decreasing "native" population in Guam, Senator Arriola instructed her legal counsel to draft a bill.

Belle moved quickly. On July 10, 1989, one week after the *Webster* decision, the senator introduced Bill 848. Concerned that Belle's proposal was too restrictive, three fellow Democrats introduced an alternative, Bill 842, permitting abortion in cases of pregnancy due to rape, incest, or when the fetus is believed to be grossly deformed, as well as requiring advance notification of parents of minors. Belle was optimistic because her party controlled the legislature and all but one of the senators was Catholic. With ready access to the leadership and resources of the local Catholic Church, an ecumenical Pro-Life Coalition was quickly organized to support passage of the bill.

While abortion had been legal in Guam for twelve years, it was still a taboo subject. The introduction of Bill 848 made it known that abortion was legal. For some this was a shocking realization.

The Christian Mothers, whom Arriola had effectively mobilized to defeat the legalization of casino gambling, showed up in full force for the public hearing, held five weeks after Bill 848 was introduced. Most of the thirty-three individuals who presented testimony represented church groups and religious organizations. There were no feminist or civil rights organizations in Guam. Given this political vacuum of organized opposition, the dominant discourse in support of the measures concerned the personhood of the "unborn" and the immorality of abortion based on religious beliefs.

Only four women presented testimony in opposition. The only Chamorro to oppose the bill publicly was Lou Leon Guerrero, who testified as president of the Guam Nurses Association. She argued that Bill 848 "totally ignores individual human rights, decreases access to health care, and increases the potential for adversity in the human condition."[42]

It took five months for the attorney general, Elizabeth Barrett-Anderson, Guam's first woman attorney general and daughter of Senator Barrett, who had authored the 1978 local statute making abortion legal, to provide a legal opinion. The attorney general argued against both bills as violating a woman's constitutional right of privacy, as enunciated in *Roe*. Once this statement was released, many thought the anti-abortion campaign had been thwarted and the bill was dead. However, one week later, both bills were placed on the legislative docket for action.

An anti-colonial agenda surfaced during the legislative session on March 8, 1990, when Senator Arriola introduced a compromise bill worked out in party caucus. It contained three additions. The first was a preamble similar to that contained in the *Webster* decision, in which the fetus drops out of sight and, except during the technical discussion of viability, becomes "the unborn child."[43] While drawing from this judicial language, the spokesperson for the Pro-Life Coalition emphasized, "This was a piece of legislation that we drafted locally. We didn't have it mailed to us from Americans United for Life or any other right-to-life organization. . . . *Culturally, it is ours*" (italics added).[44] Whereas in the United States "Saving the Fetus" and "Saving America" became part of a larger conservative agenda of the New Right, in Guam the anti-abortion campaign became linked with an anti-colonial agenda: "Saving the Fetus" became an analogue to "Liberating Guam" and "Saving the Chamorro People."

The second and third additions addressed the question "Who decides?" Two exceptions were added to the definition of abortion.[45] Section 7, the third addition, mandated an island-wide referendum to repeal the law, if enacted.

On the floor, Senator Arriola stated her intent as wanting to "close the door on abortion on demand in Guam" and to establish the legal personhood of the unborn:

> Let me tell you at the rate that Guam Memorial Hospital is aborting children, between 400–600 a year, and most of them are not even reported. Where are the lives that we are going to protect and preserve? Here we go talking about indigenous rights and self-determination. What good is all that if we don't have our followers to follow and enjoy the fruits of our labor, of this generation's labor, of your labor and my labor to fix this island and have autonomous rights to govern our people.[46]

Bill 848 as modified was unanimously approved. Senator Arriola attributed its passage "to each senator's own personal belief and principle, culture, family ties, tradition, etc."[47] She also spoke of the importance of getting prior commitments from the senators and of the formidable presence of Archbishop Apuron and the Christian Mothers in the legislative hall when the vote was taken. While pro-life supporters were jubilant about the bill's passage, pro-choice advocates were shocked that the vote was unanimous, as certain women senators, perceived as having feminist views, were expected to oppose a complete ban.

Although the governor asserted when he signed the bill (P.L. 20–134) that this was a local concern, the presence of U.S. national organizations and media in Guam at the time and their subsequent interventions underscored the broader significance of this law.

The media attention given to the Guam case had a snowball effect, creating other opportunities to showcase the local movement nationally. For example, in April 1990 a group of approximately fifty people from Guam made a pilgrimage to the nation's capital to join the annual Rally for Life. Pat Perry, a Chamorro spokeswoman for Guamanians United for Life, delivered a four-minute speech, televised live by CNN, in which she described "the evils of the world, such as the near-genocide at the hands of the

(Japanese military) conquerors" and the invasion of Guam during World War II "that nearly destroyed the people and the family." While national media emphasized the Guamanian threat to American free speech and liberal principles resulting from the Guam law, Perry described the *Roe* decision as "another [federal] imposition enforced on us [without our consent]." She likened the Supreme Court and organizations such as Planned Parenthood to World War II and the Japanese occupation, which "created another form of bloodshed among our people." She gave tribute to Senator Arriola, a "popular and courageous woman," for introducing the law that "corrects a great injustice in our island territory." While pro-choice advocates on their separate pilgrimage to Washington, D.C., emphasized Guam's membership in the American family and the universality of the category "woman," Perry emphasized Guam's difference, pointing out that, unlike the United States, the island is "matriarchal . . . [and] it is the women who decides what happens in our society." While the pro-choice group sought national support for the legal challenge to Guam's ban on abortion, Perry called for pressure to be put on the federal court judges and politicians to reshape their values and do what Guam leaders had courageously done, to "uphold life from the first moment of conception until natural death."[48]

The mutually reinforcing connection between local and national pro-life activity was dramatized through a symbolic "Chain of Life." On October 8, 1990, thousands of supporters in Guam joined people across the United States to form a "Life Chain." The local chain wound along a five-mile distance of Marine Drive, the island's main highway, from one site honoring Chief Quipuha, immortalized for challenging Spanish colonization, to another site honoring President John F. Kennedy.

The actual ban on abortion in Guam was short-lived, lasting just four days. On March 23, 1990, Maria Doe, representing herself and all other women who needed abortions or counseling and information, and others as a class challenged P.L. 20-134 as violating the U.S. Constitution and the Guam Organic Act.[49] They obtained a temporary restraining order and a preliminary injunction enjoining and suspending the operation, enforcement, and execution of the law until May 8, when the case was scheduled for trial.

The defense of Guam's anti-abortion law was presented in large measure as a protection of Guam's special identity and heritage. Social and religious leaders of Guam presented the cultural arguments in very explicit terms, by insisting that the Chamorro language lacks a term for abortion and that abortion was nonexistent in indigenous Chamorro culture.[50]

Subsequent to this injunction, Maria Doe was dismissed as a party to the suit, and the lead plaintiffs became the Guam Society of Obstetricians and Gynecologists and the Guam Nurses Association. With the loss of Maria Doe, the personal story of this anonymous Chamorro woman receded, and physicians and nurses took the lead for the legal challenge. But the restrictiveness of the law left little legal room to maneuver, and the available evidence was inadequate to support a defensible cultural argument.

Although the cultural argument was set aside as the case made its way through the appellate process, it was further articulated by Archbishop Anthony Sablan Apuron in a presentation made at a national pro-life conference. He boldly presented Guam's pro-life stance not as an outcome of an ecumenical pro-life movement but as the outcome of "a Catholic people, called Chamorros," with a distinct culture, language, and religious beliefs, who for centuries have been "obscured, ignored, or trampled on." In the final analysis, he asserted, "our struggle to protect the sanctity of life is tantamount to the preservation of our cultural heritage."[51] The very existence of a matrilineal tradition in Guam, the archbishop argued, underscores the particular importance of motherhood as the source of female power. Implicit in this statement is the assumption that it should be the responsibility of all women in Guam, irrespective of identity or allegiance, to assure the continuity of the Chamorro people and culture. This was a burden of representation that neither the U.S. judicial system nor some people in Guam could support.

Pro-Choice Activists and Mobilization

The worldview of pro-choice supporters centers on a belief in reason rather than faith alone to understand and alter the environment. This leads to a worldview where life consists of a social and a biological dimension. The embryo, for example, is only a potential person, in large part because it has not yet begun to have a social dimension to its life, only a physical one. A pregnant woman's rights, being both social and physical, transcend those of the embryo. For this group, quality of life evokes a vista of human intellect directed to resolving the complicated problems of life—such as ill health, poverty, and inequality.[52] Inequality between the sexes is viewed as rooted in social, legal, and cultural forms of gender discrimination. From this viewpoint, safe and legal abortion is an essential safeguard against the differential effects of pregnancy on men and women.[53]

What distinguishes Chamorro pro-choice women I have interviewed is the high value assigned to women's moral agency and individual self-determination. These women value the importance of motherhood to their gender identity and to society. But they hold to a conviction that freedom for women must necessarily encompass the power to make a free and informed choice as to whether, when, and with whom they will have children. Being pro-choice does not reflect a rejection of their Catholic faith but rather the adoption of a stance as a "critical Catholic," one who does not accept uncritically the teachings of the church—or any authority. Whereas *hagan-haga'* of the prewar generation define being Catholic as devotion to the sacraments and religious practices such as attending Mass and saying the rosary and novenas, the postwar generation, especially those with the benefit of higher education and travel, place priority on living their faith through engaging in the transformation of their environment toward what they view as a more just society.

Ginsberg identified two themes that emerged consistently in the narratives of pro-choice activists: first, a recounting of the woman's birth or childhood that emphasized her difference and independence from others in her family; second, an encounter with the protest movements of the late 1960s and early 1970s, especially the feminist movement, as being transformative. Both Anita Arriola and Lou Leon Guerrero came of age during this era. Also, both graduated from the Academy of Our Lady, where Belle taught, and attended U.S. mainland universities. What stands out about the local pro-choice strategy is how the women made use of both local and transnational professional networks in their campaigns. For Anita this meant teaming up with a mainland ACLU attorney to defend the civil rights of women, while Lou, who was elected president of People for Choice, drew from the resources of the American Nurses Association to advocate for legal and safe abortion as a fundamental right of all women and as a health concern.

Anita Arriola, daughter of Senator Arriola and a single thirty-four-year-old graduate of Smith College and Georgetown University Law Center, had worked for several years as a partner in a nonprofit law firm in San Francisco prior to returning to Guam to take up private practice. As soon as the anti-abortion bill was passed by the legislature, Anita was in contact with a friend and professional colleague, Janet Benshoof, director of the ACLU Reproductive Freedom Project based in New York City, which was monitoring attempts by states to limit access to abortion. Benshoof immediately flew to Guam to assist Guam's pro-choice activists and was instrumental in making the Guam case a *cause célèbre*.

Lou Leon Guerrero describes an upbringing that set her apart from how girls were traditionally raised. Her family was very "vocal about things . . . very politically involved." As the only daughter, sandwiched between two brothers, she says, "I always had to be fighting for my place, for equality in the family structure." After graduating from high school, Lou left to attend an all-women Catholic school in Wisconsin but found it "stifling" and transferred to California State College, Los Angeles, where she completed her bachelor's degree in nursing, then a master's in public health. It was through participation in a women's consciousness-raising group that she became pro-choice. Lou also attributes her becoming pro-choice to her Catholic education, which, she says, helped women like Anita and her to become strong, unafraid to speak out about their beliefs.[54]

Nonetheless, the decision to become a pro-choice activist in this conflict was extremely difficult for these women, for respect toward one's elders and harmony within the family are highly valued.[55] A paramount concern for Lou was how her activism would affect her prominent family. Her father is the founder of Guam's first locally owned bank; both parents were active in the Catholic Church; and she has an aunt who is a nun. Two things were important in her decision to accept this leadership role. First was her role as a mother:

> The bottom line that made me decide to do it, was this: . . . If this bill becomes law . . . that means that if my child was raped . . . and she went to have an abortion and found that she could not, she's going to come to me and say, "Mom, what did you do to fight for my right as a woman to decide on my own?" . . . And that's when I said, "If I don't join this, even if it loses, the consoling thing for me is that I tried my best." And that's all I can say to my daughter.[56]

Second, Lou understood this was not just a local issue. The law, if upheld, had profound implications for women across the country.

For Anita, taking a stand meant opposing her mother publicly. She met in advance with her mother and seven siblings and said that "everybody agreed that if my mother

and I don't attack each other personally, we could each express our views politically."
While the elder Arriola admitted that Anita's actions "hurt me personally,"[57] each respected the other for acting on her convictions. On the first day of the preliminary hearing, while an estimated fifteen hundred pro-life supporters gathered to hear the governor and other speakers, a smaller group of about three hundred pro-choice supporters
gathered several hours later to "mourn the loss of freedom of choice." When Anita Arriola took the microphone, she addressed head on her personal dilemma by emphasizing the importance of individual moral choice over filial respect:

> Tonight, I'm the proudest and happiest person in the whole wide world, to see women here
> on Guam fighting for freedom of choice. There are many people who have asked me how
> can I go against my mother, how can I go up against the Catholic Church, and my response
> to them is this: How can I go against my conscience?[58]

To defend freedom of choice in this context was not without disturbing consequences.
Subsequent to this rally, Anita received death threats requiring periodic security checks
at her residence and office.[59] Another woman related how her parish priest asked her
identical twin sister, who is pro-life, to stop serving as a liturgical minister at Mass for a
while. When Lou later ran for political office, opponents used her activism to wage a negative campaign against her. The pro-choice advocates drew strength from the encouragement received behind the scenes from other women, including nuns, who could not
express their support publicly, and from family and friends who supported their activism
even though they did not understand their position or share the same views.

The links with national organizations were important in reducing a sense of marginalization for these activists and in reinforcing an identification with being American.
In addition to the legal support provided by the ACLU, People for Choice was assisted
by the National Abortion Rights Action League (NARAL). NARAL provided financial
support for local organizing, which made it possible for one member, Sylvia DeLong,
to attend a conference for organizers in June 1990. Four members, all professional
women, were assisted to travel to Washington, D.C., to urge Congress and national
abortion rights leaders to keep the pressure on Guam. What was more important than
monetary support, they say, was that NARAL provided a sense of solidarity and connection with the broader struggle for women's rights in the United States. This helped
them to see how "this anti-abortion law is (just) another example of how repression
works in Guam."[60] At the same time, these linkages with the American Nursing Association (ANA), ACLU, and NARAL reinforced a quintessentially American rights-laden
discourse that pitted Chamorro women against each other. This worked against their
being able to engage an alternative discourse such as matrifocal power or a shared
Catholic faith to establish common ground and work through the conflict.

Chamorro Womanhood and Self-Determination

What became of the key actors and organizations that came head to head in this conflict? And what does this reveal about contemporary Chamorro womanhood and the

meaning of self-determination in Guam? While the opposing organizations no longer exist, their activist experience left an indelible imprint in the political consciousness of these women.

The Pro-Life Coalition was disbanded soon after the Ninth Circuit Court decision became public. Several women organizers whom I interviewed remain active in Guamanians United for Life and a subcommittee, the Catholic Pro-Life Committee. While the women say their church group cannot be "involved politically," their participation in the politics of abortion raised their awareness of the impact of national policy and the limited autonomy Guam has to establish its own laws as a moral and political community. For this reason, several reported becoming politically "radicalized" and more ambivalent about what they see as the social and moral cost of being American.

Dawn Leon Guerrero, once a statehood advocate, expressed support for either independence or free association with the United States as desirable political-status options, "simply because it would allow us to create our own legislation and constitution . . . and empower us to decide on the pro-life issue."[61] They remain intent on the ultimate goal of a complete ban on abortion, which would reaffirm in one fell swoop the importance of biological reproduction to Chamorro womanhood, Catholic doctrine on the sanctity of life, and the legal personhood and citizenship of the "unborn." This "moral imperative" and "self-determination in the political arena" advocated by Archbishop Apuron and pro-life supporters, represents a threat to the individual self-determination of all women in Guam.

Senator Arriola was reelected along with almost all incumbent senators who ran in 1992; so was Governor Ada. This led many to conclude that the archbishop's statement was accurate: "To be pro-life and against abortion is to represent the aspirations of the Chamorro people."[62] Senator Arriola vowed to "continue her crusade to outlaw abortions" but was unsuccessful in a subsequent attempt to introduce another anti-abortion bill.[63] She continued to appear at pro-life events until she suffered a fatal stroke in June 2002.

People for Choice became inactive after the Supreme Court denied review and was officially dissolved in 1997. Like the pro-life activists, pro-choice women described how their activism helped them become more aware of how laws and economic and social realities shape women's lives. They recognize the importance not only of advocating for the individual right of a woman to choose but, more important, of creating the contexts needed to make choice real for all women. As Lou Leon Guerrero explained, in the oppositional discourse of the woman's right to choose versus the fetus's right to life, "We forgot the woman. We forgot the mother—and the importance of her quality of life."[64]

These pro-choice activists continue to act on their commitment to improve the status of women through elected office, civic organizations, and their workplaces. Lou Leon Guerrero was elected senator in 1994 and reelected in 1996. In 1998 she ran unsuccessfully as a candidate for lieutenant governor, but she returned to the legislature in 2000 and was reelected for a fourth term in 2002. Unlike her first race, opponents in subsequent elections did not use her pro-choice stance to wage an overt negative campaign.[65] For Lou and other pro-choice activists, success was not in defeating the law but, more important, in claiming a voice in the political vacuum that made it possible for the Catholic and evangelical churches to wield combined influence virtually unchallenged. They feel confident they could mobilize again when needed to. As one woman put it: "We're not going to be sideswiped by the Church again."[66]

There are several indicators that an anti-abortion campaign could be easily mobilized again, next time by a younger generation of leaders influenced by a growing evangelical movement and increased political conservatism. In 1997 the Guam Youth Congress introduced a bill that was more extreme than the 1990 law.[67] In 1999 a bill was introduced to ban late-term or "partial-birth" abortions. It was never scheduled for a public hearing, I was told, because its intent was only to restrict abortion. The current speaker of the Guam legislature, a father of twelve who lost his bid for governor in the 2002 Republican primary, predicts that it is "very likely" that once there is an opportunity for the people of Guam to write their own constitution to replace the Organic Act of 1950, it will include a provision that would define legal personhood as beginning at conception.[68]

Conclusion

Although this chapter focuses on the activism of Chamorro women in the "new" politics of abortion, this study is part of a broader concern, both intellectual and personal, with the meaning of American citizenship, national identity, and belonging from the perspective of indigenous peoples. Political self-determination is an issue of Chamorros not as individuals but as a collectivity whose common needs, position, and consciousness are organized around the colonial nature of federal-territorial relations and the task of decolonization. In both struggles for self-determination, analyses of the structures of domination and oppression are occluded by the construction of citizenship as meaning only individual membership of a state.

The framing of the abortion issue, especially in the adversarial U.S. legal system, as a clash of individual rights made it impossible for indigenous women with different views on abortion to find an alternative discourse and common ground for affirming indigenous values and the social power of Chamorro women as a collectivity. Instead, women were forced to position themselves as adversaries and, according to the terms of the debate, as either pro-choice or pro-life.

How can indigenous women in liberal democracies resolve conflicts that arise from their multiple positioning and belonging to different national communities? What potential is there in the concept and practice of matriarchal power as a discourse and as a defining aspect of Chamorro culture for creating a transformative feminist politics that is not based on the exaltation of women's biological capacity to mother but applies to society as a whole the values attached to that role: care, nurturance, and morality?[69]

Souder suggests that cultural survival has been the "cornerstone" of the Chamorro woman's position in society and could form the "bedrock of an organized movement of Chamorro women."[70] The goal of political self-determination provides a challenge and opportunity for Chamorros to coalesce and organize to create a socioeconomic environment conducive to the values and beliefs that are meaningful to the local people. But neither national identity nor gender identity is a monolithic construct; both are themselves contested within Chamorro culture. This episode illustrates how political coalescence for Chamorros across gender, class, generation, and religious divides may be difficult to achieve, even for indigenous women as a collectivity.

The opposition of women's identities and of the value of individual and collective self-determination, publicly represented by daughter and mother, reveals both the importance and the limitations of the rhetoric of rights. The language of rights not only filters out other discourses; it simultaneously infiltrates them.[71] In this case, an alternative local synthesis could not be achieved because of the American tendency, which Guam has adopted in its political culture and legal institutions, to frame social issues in terms of a clash of rights instead of drawing on an indigenous language of relationship and responsibility.[72] I suggest what Mary Ann Glendon critically describes as the "impoverishment" of American political discourse[73] not only impedes compromise, mutual understanding, and the discovery by Chamorro women of common ground on the issue of abortion; it similarly impedes progress toward resolving Guam's political status.

NOTES

1. Statement made at a pro-choice rally, March 23, 1990, by Jacqueline Quitugua-Bettis, lobbying coordinator for People for Choice.

2. Laura Marie Torres Souder, *Daughters of the Island: Contemporary Chamorro Women Organizers on Guam* (Mangilao, Guam: Micronesian Area Research Center, University of Guam, 1987; reprint, Lanham, Md.: University Press of America, 1992), 235.

3. Archbishop Anthony Sablan Apuron, PFM Cap., D.D., "Guam's Culture Offers a Unique Approach to the Pro-Life Stance"/*UnikuNa Pasahi Ginen I Kotturan Guahan Put i Para-Lina'la'Na Pusisison*" (paper presented at the Unity '90 Conference, Chicago, Illinois, June 30, 1990).

4. *Chamorro*, or *Chamoru*, is the term for the indigenous people and language of Guam and the northern islands of the Marianas archipelago in the western Pacific. In 1994 the Chamoru Language Commission announced a change in the spelling from "Chamorro" to "Chamoru." However, this spelling has not been officially adopted, and "Chamorro" is still commonly used.

5. Bill 848, enacted as Public Law 20–134. The law also criminalized the person performing the abortion as well as the woman seeking it.

6. This is the largest percentage of women in the history of the Guam legislature.

7. See, for example, Dan Balz, "Guam Surprises Abortion Activists," *Washington Post*, March 24, 1990.

8. *Webster v. Reproductive Health Services*, 109 S. Ct. 3040 (1989).

9. Jane Gross, "Stiffest Restriction on Abortion in U.S. Voted in Guam," *New York Times*, March 16, 1999, 1A.

10. Guam is one of five insular areas under the United States, the others being the territories of American Samoa and the Virgin Islands and the commonwealths of Puerto Rico and the Northern Mariana Islands. Guam also has international legal status as a Non-Self-Governing Territory. For more than two decades, Guam pursued what became known as the "Quest for Commonwealth," a policy in which U.S. authority could be exercised only with mutual consent of the Commonwealth of Guam government. This began in 1982 with two political-status plebiscites through which Guam voters overwhelmingly chose "Commonwealth" over five other political-status options. In 1988, one year before the *Webster* decision, the Guam Draft

Commonwealth Act was introduced in Congress. It was reintroduced in every subsequent Congress until finally heard in Washington, D.C., in 1997 and rejected by federal officials. See Vivian Dames, "Rethinking the Circle of Belonging: American Citizenship and the Chamorros of Guam" (unpublished Ph.D. diss., University of Michigan, 2000), esp. chap. 1.

11. Faye D. Ginsberg, *Contested Lives: The Abortion Debate in an American Community* (Berkeley and Los Angeles: University of California Press, 1984), 232, citing Victor Turner, in *Dramas, Fields and Metaphors* (Ithaca, N.Y.: Cornell University Press, 1974).

12. Ronald Stade, *Pacific Passages: World Cultures and Local Politics in Guam* (Stockholm: Gotag, 1998), 47.

13. Dames, "Rethinking the Circle," 403–6; also, *Ada v. Guam Society of Obstetricians and Gynecologists*, 113 S. Ct. 663 (1992).

14. Patricia G. Steinhoff and Milton Diamond, *Abortion Politics: The Hawaii Experience* (Honolulu: University Press of Hawaii, 1977).

15. Ginsberg, *Contested Lives*, 218.

16. Kristin Luker, *Abortion and the Politics of Motherhood* (Berkeley: University of California Press, 1984).

17. Ibid., 193.

18. Ibid., 196.

19. Ginsberg, *Contested Lives*, 6.

20. Ibid.; also, Daniel Granberg, "The Abortion Activists," *Family Planning Perspectives* 13:4 (1981): 158–611.

21. Ginsberg, *Contested Lives*, 6.

22. This chapter is based on semi-structured interviews I conducted in 1997 with Chamorro women leaders and separate peer-group interviews with Chamorro women activists on both sides of the conflict, selected through a snowball sampling method. I also examined archival material of the local pro-life and pro-choice organizations, media accounts, editorials, and legislative records.

23. Vicente M. Diaz, "Repositioning the Missionary: The Beatification of Blessed Diego Luis de San Vitores and Chamorro Cultural and Political History on Guam" (unpublished Ph.D. diss., University of California, Santa Cruz, 1992), 34.

24. Souder, *Daughters of the Island*, 38.

25. Ibid., 204.

26. Anita Agueda Johnston, "The Ethnic Identity Experience of Chamorro Women" (unpublished Ph.D. diss., California School of Professional Psychology, July 1980), 6.

27. Souder, *Daughters of the Island*, 51, 53.

28. Ibid., 8.

29. Ibid.

30. Katherine B. Aguon, "The Guam Dilemma: The Need for Pacific Island Education Perspective," in *Hale'ta-Hinasso': Tinige Put Chamorro (Insights: The Chamorro Identity)*, vol. 1 (Agana, Guam: Political Status Education Coordinating Committee, 1993), 96.

31. Dames, "Rethinking the Circle," esp. 227–36.

32. Ann M. Workman, Randall L. Workman, and Linda Cruz-Ortiz, "Abortion on Guam: Demographic Trends and Fertility Data," in *ISLA: A Journal of Micronesian Studies* (Dry Season 1992), 188.

33. Dames, "Rethinking the Circle," 37.

34. Ginsberg, *Contested Lives*, 46–47.

35. Luker, *Abortion*, 158.

36. Ginsberg, *Contested Lives*, 6.

37. Ibid., 172.

38. Dawn Leon Guerrero, transcription of author's interview with members of the Pro-Life Coalition, May 29, 1997, lines 32–35.

39. Dubbed such by Diaz, "Repositioning the Missionary," 54. Unless otherwise indicated, statements attributed to Senator Arriola are taken from the transcription of my interview with her, March 3, 1997, and from Souder, *Daughters of the Island*, 181–90.

40. Elizabeth Arriola, transcription of author's interview, Tumon, Guam, March 3, 1997, lines 124–25.

41. Quoted in Souder, *Daughters of the Island*, 188; also cited by Stade, *Pacific Passages*.

42. Testimony of Lou Leon Guerrero on Bill 848 submitted to Guam Legislature, September 16, 1989.

43. Rosalind Pollack Petcheskey, *Abortion and Woman's Choice: The State, Sexuality and Reproductive Freedom* (Boston: Northeastern University Press, 1990), 317.

44. Dawn Leon Guerrero, transcription of author's interview with members of the Pro-Life Coalition, May 29, 1997, lines 1217–18, 1225.

45. These exceptions were "an ectopic pregnancy" or "at any time after the commencement of the pregnancy if two (2) physicians reasonably determine substantial risk to the mother."

46. *Legislative Daily Journal*, March 8, 1990, 5.

47. Elizabeth Arriola, personal communication to the author, August 20, 1991.

48. Ken Miller, "Pro-Life Leader Addresses Rally," *Pacific Daily News*, April 30, 1990, 1, 4.

49. *Maria Doe v. Joseph Ada*, 113 S. Ct 663 (1992), Plaintiff's Complaint, 3.

50. Donald H. Rubinstein, "Culture in Court: Notes and Reflections on Abortion in Guam," *Journal de la Société des Océanistes* 94, 1 (1992): 35–44, 35.

51. Apuron, "Guam's Culture."

52. Luker, *Abortion*, 189–90.

53. Ginsberg, *Contested Lives*, 7.

54. Unless otherwise indicated, excerpts cited here are from a transcription of an interview, October 19, 1998.

55. Lou Leon Guerrero, transcription of author's interview, October 16, 1998, lines 546–51.

56. Ibid., lines 842–53.

57. Gross, "Stiffest Restriction on Abortion."

58. Graziella Conte and Jacqueline Chandler, "Rallies Draw Out Sides in Abortion Issue," *Triton's Call*, April 24, 1990.

59. Tambra Maddock, "Threatened Attorney Watched by GPD," *Pacific Daily News*, March 30, 1990.

60. Ken Miller, quoting Lou Leon Guerrero, "Pro-Choicers Rally Mainland Support," *Pacific Daily News*, June 23, 1990.

61. Dawn Leon Guerrero, transcription of author's interview, lines 1554–56.

62. Apuron, "Guam's Culture," 9.

63. Liz Avanar, "Arriola Plans 2nd Anti-Abortion Bill," *Pacific Daily News*, August 25, 1990.

64. Lou Leon Guerrero, transcription of author's interview with members of People for Choice, April 30, 1997, lines 1293–96.

65. Ibid., lines 1316–26.

66. Ibid., lines 1204–5.

67. See bill (number not assigned) concerning "An Act . . . Relative to Regulating the Practice of Circumstantial Abortion," Twenty-first Guam Youth Congress, 1997. This mock bill makes but one exception for abortion, ectopic pregnancy, and establishes a minimum sentence of twenty years to life, with no possibility of parole, for the felony of abortion.

68. Antonio Unpingco, speaker, Twenty-fourth Guam Legislature, personal communication with the author, April 1997.

69. Seth Koven and Sonya Michel, eds., *Mothers of a New World: Materialist Politics and the Origin of the Welfare State* (New York: Routledge, 1993), 4.

70. Souder, *Daughters of the Island*, 239–40.

71. Mary Ann Glendon, *Rights Talk: The Impoverishment of Political Discourse* (New York: Free Press, 1991), 177.

72. I use the term *indigenous* here to refer to Chamorro language and culture. Mary Ann Glendon marshals evidence to make the case that Americans possess several "indigenous languages of relationship and responsibility that could help refine our language of rights." See Glendon, *Rights Talk*, esp. chap. 7.

73. Ibid.

Part 8

Additional Resources

Asian American and Pacific Islander American Women as Historical Subjects
A Bibliographic Essay

Shirley Hune

Asian/Pacific Islander American women's history is being rewritten, stimulated by new and underutilized sources, by methodologies that better incorporate women's perspectives and voices, and by a critical mass of historians with an interest in women's lives, gender, and feminist perspectives. The chapters in *Asian/Pacific Islander American Women* underscore this intellectual endeavor. To enhance teaching and research, I identify here additional published works that both are generally accessible and view Asian American and Pacific Islander American women as subjects with agency centered in history, as reflected in this anthology's framework. I define historical writings broadly here and include works by social scientists, especially life histories and ethnographies. The social sciences also provide analyses of post-1965 history, a critical period for many Asian/Pacific Islander American groups. I have omitted the chapters in this anthology for obvious reasons. I also exclude literary works and fictionalized histories or biographical novels. Given the constraints of space, I have limited my selection to primarily U.S.-based works. This list is only part of the burgeoning new scholarship in this area. I am mindful that a bibliographic essay[1] is a moving target and is easily outdated.

The existing literature on Asian/Pacific Islander American women's history, their individual groups, specific eras, and topics covered, is uneven. Such shortcomings are due, in part, to less attention by scholars and, for some groups, their relatively shorter time in the United States. I begin with general historical resources and works that view Asian/Pacific Islander American women as pan-ethnic groups. Biographical and related studies are treated separately as a genre. The vast majority of the publications are ethnic-specific and are clustered here by ethnic group. Not all Asian/Pacific Islander American groups are included. For a broader listing than history, see Alice Y. Hom, comp., "Asian American Women," in Vicki L. Ruiz and Ellen Carol DuBois, eds., *Unequal Sisters*, 3d ed. (New York: Routledge, 2000), 643–46; Brian Niiya, comp., "Asian American Women," in Ruiz and DuBois, eds., *Unequal Sisters*, 2d ed. (1994), 590–93; and Linda Trinh Võ and Marian Sciachitano, "Introduction: Moving beyond 'Exotics, Whores, and Nimble Fingers,'" *Frontiers* 21:1/2 (2000): 1–19.

General Works

Two general Asian American history texts include women's history. Sucheng Chan, *Asian Americans* (Boston: Twayne Publishers, 1991), has a chapter on "Women, Families, and the 'Second-Generation Dilemma'" that covers the neglected period between World Wars I and II. In *Strangers from a Different Shore*, updated and revised (Boston: Little, Brown and Company, 1998), Ronald Takaki chronicles Asian immigration to the United States by ethnic group and uses women's and men's voices to document their struggles against injustice.

For general readers on Asian American women, see *Making Waves*, ed. Asian Women United of California (Boston: Beacon Press, 1989), and *Asian American Women and Gender*, ed. Franklin Ng (New York: Garland Publishers, 1998). Ruiz and DuBois, eds., *Unequal Sisters*, 2d ed. (1994) and 3d ed. (2000), have several essays on Asian American women reprinted from other sources. Specific articles in these readers are cited elsewhere in this essay. Some contemporary aspects of Asian American women can be found in *Making More Waves*, ed. Elaine H. Kim, Lilia V. Villaneuva, and Asian Women United of California (Boston: Beacon Press, 1997).

On the historiography of Asian American women, a few scholars ask what Asian American history would look like if women were placed at the center and viewed as agents of history. See "Beyond Bound Feet: Relocating Asian American Women," *Magazine of History* 10:4 (Summer 1996): 23–27, and "General Introduction: A Woman-Centered Perspective on Asian American History," in *Making Waves* (1989), 1–22, both by Sucheta Mazumdar; and Gary Y. Okihiro, *Margins and Mainstreams* (Seattle: University of Washington Press, 1994), chap. 3. See Connie Young Yu, "The World of Our Grandmothers," in *Making Waves* (1989), 33–42, on the importance of oral history in claiming and uncovering women's experiences. Alice Yang Murray discusses the challenges and rewards of doing oral history in "Oral History Research, Theory, and Asian American Studies," *Amerasia Journal* 26:1 (2000): 105–18.

The place and role of women are being restored in U.S. immigration history. Sydney Stahl Weinberg, "The Treatment of Women in Immigration History: A Call for Change," in *Seeking Common Ground*, ed. Donna Gabaccia (Westport, Conn.: Greenwood Publishing Group, 1992), 1–22, considers how the incorporation of women, including Asian American women, contributes to alternative views of immigrant culture and institutions.

Asian/Pacific Islander American Women

Two works on Hawai'i incorporate both Asian American and Native Hawaiian women. Joyce C. Lebra, *Shaping Hawai'i: The Voices of Women*, 2d ed. (Honolulu: Goodale Publishing, 1999), features oral histories of octogenarians from Asian and European ethnic groups and Native Hawaiians, as they reflect on their challenges and accomplishments as pioneers. Joyce N. Chinen, Kathleen O. Kane, and Ida M. Yoshinaga, *Women in Hawai'i: Sites, Identities, and Voices*, special issue of *Social Process in Hawai'i* 38 (Hon-

olulu: University of Hawai'i Press, 1997), is a collection of articles focusing on historical and contemporary issues and experiences of multiethnic women of Hawai'i.

Many works treat Asian American and Pacific Islander American women of distinct
ethnic backgrounds as a collective pan-ethnic group and focus on a specific topic. For
example, on wives/brides, Alice Yun Chai describes the survival strategies of Asian picture brides in "Picture Brides: Feminist Analysis of Life Histories of Hawai'i's Early Immigrant Women from Japan, Okinawa, and Korea," in Gabaccia, ed., *Seeking Common
Ground,* (1992), 123–38. Bok-Lim C. Kim assesses the circumstances and needs of
American war brides from different Asian countries since World War II in "Asian Wives
of U.S. Servicemen: Women in Shadows," *Amerasia Journal* 4:1 (1977): 91–115. Venny
Villapando discusses contemporary mail-order brides from Asia in "The Business of
Selling Mail-Order Brides," in *Making Waves* (1989), 318–26.

For an overview of Asian American women's labor history in the United States from
the mid–nineteenth century to the 1990s, see "Climbing Gold Mountain: Asian American Women," in Teresa L. Amott and Julie A. Matthaei, *Race, Gender, and Work,* rev. ed.
(Boston: South End Press, 1996), 193–256. Esther Ngan-Ling Chow considers the
workplace obstacles and conditions women face in "Asian American Women at Work,"
in *Women of Color in U.S. Society,* ed. Maxine Baca Zinn and Bonnie Thornton Dill
(Philadelphia: Temple University Press, 1994), 203–27. Contemporary work experiences in the garment industry are documented in Joyce Chinen, "Sewing Resistance
into the Grain: Hawai'i's Garment Workers at Work and at Home," *Race, Gender and
Class* 4:3 (1997): 165–79; Miriam Ching Louie, "Immigrant Asian Women in Bay Area
Garment Sweatshops: 'After Sewing, Laundry, Cleaning, and Cooking, I Have No Breath
Left to Sing,'" *Amerasia Journal* 18:1 (1992): 1–26; and Richard Kim, Kane K. Nakamura, and Gisele Fong, with Ron Cabarloc, Barbara Jung, and Sung Lee, "Asian Immigrant Women Garment Workers in Los Angeles: A Preliminary Investigation," *Amerasia Journal* 18:1 (1992): 69–82. Karen J. Hossfeld describes the racial and gender exploitation of Asian immigrant women in the electronics industry in "Hiring Immigrant
Women: Silicon Valley's 'Simple Formula,'" in Zinn and Dill, eds., *Women of Color*
(1994), 65–93. Women's occupational segregation is explored by Deborah Woo in "The
Gap between Striving and Achieving: The Case of Asian American Women," in *Making
Waves* (1989), 185–94.

Studies on lesbians and bisexual women, their struggles, and their growing empow-
erment include Pamela H., "Asian American Lesbians: An Emerging Voice in the Asian
American Community," in *Making Waves* (1989), 282–90; Alice Hom, "Stories from the
Homefront: Perspectives of Asian American Parents with Lesbian Daughters and Gay
Sons," *Amerasia Journal* 20:1 (1994): 19–31; chapters in *Asian American Sexualities,* ed.
Russell Leong (New York: Routledge, 1996); and Sharon Lim-Hing, ed., *The Very Inside:
An Anthology of Writing by Asian and Pacific Islander Lesbian and Bisexual Women*
(Toronto: Sister Vision Press, 1994).

Studies on women's organizing activities in contemporary social movements, such
as feminism, unions, American politics, and ethnic struggles, include Esther Chow,
"The Feminist Movement: Where Are All the Asian American Women?" in *Making
Waves* (1989), 362–77; Judy Chu, "Asian Pacific American Women in Mainstream Politics," in *Making Waves* (1989), 405–21; Pei-te Lien, *The Making of Asian America through*

Political Participation (Philadelphia: Temple University Press, 2001), chap. 6; Susie Ling, "The Mountain Movers: Asian American Women's Movement in Los Angeles," *Amerasia Journal* 15:1 (1989): 51–67; Sonia Shah, ed., *Dragon Ladies: Asian American Feminists Breathe Fire* (Boston: South End Press, 1997), which covers a wide range of Asian American women's groups and issues from health care to domestic violence; Yoichi Shimatsu and Patricia Lee, "Dust and Dishes: Organizing Workers," in *Making Waves* (1989), 386–95; and William Wei, *The Asian American Movement* (Philadelphia: Temple University Press, 1993), chap. 3. In "Liberation of Asian American Women: An Uncertain Quest," *International Journal of Sociology of the Family* 24 (Spring): 1–22, Proshanta K. Nandi and Marilyn Fernandez uncover contradictions in women's attitudes toward their struggle for equality in the workplace and in the home.

For analyses of how a gender lens reinterprets Asian American women's and men's lives, see Yen Le Espiritu, *Asian American Women and Men: Labor, Laws, and Love* (Thousand Oaks, Calif.: Sage Publications, 1997), and Shirley Hune, "Doing Gender with a Feminist Gaze: Toward a Historical Reconstruction of Asian America," in *Contemporary Asian America*, ed. Min Zhou and James V. Gatewood (New York: New York University Press, 2000), 413–30.

For the perspectives and voices of contemporary teenage girls on growing up Asian American as they explore identity and cultural dynamics, see *Yell-Oh Girls!* ed. Vickie Nam (New York: Quill, 2001). Asian American and Pacific Islander students, faculty, and administrators provide insights on gender and race barriers in academe in Shirley Hune, *Asian Pacific American Women in Higher Education: Claiming Visibility and Voice* (Washington, D.C.: Association of American Colleges and Universities, 1998).

Autobiographies, Biographies, Life Histories, and Memoirs

Autobiographies, biographies, life histories, and memoirs of individual Asian American and Pacific Islander American women and/or their families provide observations and sensibilities of women's lives and shed light on their aspirations, activities, and challenges. They range from individual or family life stories to larger histories that seek to integrate individual and/or family lives with far-ranging national and global events and social transitions. Many are personal reflections of a time and events rather than historical studies. In some cases, these works are among the few that are available for a specific ethnic group, topic, or time period. Collectively, this genre reveals commonalities among women's experiences as well as differences.

For example, in *Through Harsh Winters* (Novato, Calif.: Chandler & Sharp Publishers, 1981), Akemi Kikumura describes her mother's life in Japan and her initiatives and hardships as an immigrant in the United States over much of the twentieth century. *Sweet Bamboo* (1989; reprint Berkeley: University of California Press, 2001), by Louise Leung Larson, is a daughter's memoir of economic and gender roles in a prosperous Chinese American household in Los Angeles in the first half of the twentieth century and its subsequent impoverishment and survival strategies. Mary Paik Lee, a pioneer Korean woman, recounts her hard-working life in Hawai'i in the early 1900s and in California's agricultural and mining communities in *Quiet Odyssey* (Seattle: University of

Washington Press, 1990). In *The Dreams of Two Yi-min* (Honolulu: University of Hawai'i Press, 1989), Margaret K. Pai discusses her mother's ardent activism in Hawai'i, Korea, and later on the U.S. mainland during World War II. Presently, book-length autobiographies and biographies of Filipino and Asian Indian women during the late nineteenth and early twentieth centuries are lacking.

The challenges faced by American-born women to create hybrid lives and bridge two cultures and generations in the period of racial segregation prior to and during World War II are told in a number of works. Jade Snow Wong, *Fifth Chinese Daughter* (1945; reprint, Seattle: University of Washington Press, 1989), and Monica Sone, *Nisei Daughter* (1953; reprint, Seattle: University of Washington Press, 1987), are personal, and classic, accounts of their respective Chinese American and Japanese American childhood and adolescent lives during the 1930s and 1940s. In *Almost Americans: A Quest for Dignity* (Sante Fe, N.M.: Red Crane Books, 1997), Patricia Justiniani McReynolds shares her childhood and young adult memories of the 1930s and 1940s as she parented her Filipino-born father and Norwegian-born mother through the racism of that period, when interracial marriages and mixed-race children were less common. *Farewell to Manzanar* (New York: Bantam Books, 1973), by Jeanne Wakatsuki Houston and James D. Houston, reveals the hopes and tragedies of a Japanese American family before, during, and after internment through a young girl's eyes.

Other (auto)biographical works highlight contemporary women and reveal their active participation in the public sphere. In *Doing What Had to Be Done* (Philadelphia: Temple University Press, 1999), Soo-Young Chin gives voice to second-generation Korean American community leader, Dora Yum Kim, who in late adulthood maintains "a room of her own"—a separate dwelling—to ensure her sense of self. Grace Lee Boggs describes her long, intense life since the 1930s as an activist and political writer for African American social movement publications in *Living for Change* (Minneapolis: University of Minnesota Press, 1998). In *From a Native Daughter*, rev. ed. (Honolulu: University of Hawai'i Press, 1999), Haunani-Kay Trask integrates her personal struggles against institutional racism and gender discrimination in academe and her activism for Native Hawaiian rights with that of the efforts of Native Hawaiians for sovereignty.

In contrast to American-born experiences, many contemporary post-1965 memoirs convey the transnational character of new immigrant communities; the far-ranging impact of war, empire building, and colonialism; the reconciliation of different cultures; and the impact of family background and class on women's experiences. For example, in *Fault Lines* (New York: Feminist Press at the City University of New York, 1993), poet and author Meena Alexander, an "Indian, Other," explores her identity and emerging feminism through geographical locations—the Sudan, England, India, and New York City. Similarly, Shirley Geok-Lin Lim discusses her transculturation from a Malaysian girlhood and British colonial education to immigrant mother and Asian American academic in *Among the White Moon Faces* (New York: Feminist Press, 1996). In contrast, *Paper Daughter* (New York: HarperCollins, 1999), by M. Elaine Mar, recounts the author's journey from Hong Kong to Denver and then to Harvard and the painful cultural and class disparities of life around a working-class family restaurant.

War, dislocation, and survival are central to several works. In *Home Was the Land of Morning Calm* (Reading, Mass.: Addison-Wesley Publishing Company, 1995), Connie

Kang traces her Korean American family's struggle to survive as they relocated from North to South Korea, then to Japan, and finally to the United States between the 1950s and the 1990s. Duong Van Mai Elliott, *The Sacred Willow* (New York: Oxford University Press, 1999), describes four generations of her urban, educated Vietnamese family and the choices individuals made under French colonialism and during the U.S. war in Vietnam. In contrast, *When Heaven and Earth Changed Places* (New York: Doubleday, 1989), by Le Ly Hayslip, with Jay Wurts, traverses the traumatic life of a girl caught in the Vietnam War through adulthood and childrearing in America and a family reunion in Vietnam. Two powerful eyewitness accounts of life under the Khmer Rouge by Cambodian girls, now young adults, disclose their childhoods, family sufferings, and remarkable survival, as well as their life choices in the United States; see Chanrithy Him, *When Broken Glass Floats* (New York: W. W. Norton, 2001), and Loung Ung, *First They Killed My Father* (New York: HarperCollins, 2000).

Memoirs of transnational/transracial adoptees are also beginning to appear. In *A Single Square Picture* (New York: Berkley Books, 2002), Katy Robinson, who was Kim Ji-yun until the age of seven, narrates her personal odyssey as a Korean adoptee growing up in Salt Lake City, Utah, and her return to Korea twenty years after she left to learn about Korean culture and to locate her birth family.

Cambodian/Khmer American Women

The U.S. war in Southeast Asia, the refugee experience, and women's adaptive skills dominate the history of women from Cambodia, Laos, and Vietnam. Women's strategies to survive the Khmer Rouge and cultural, linguistic, and religious challenges in the United States are addressed through their voices in Usha Welaratna's *Beyond the Killing Fields* (Stanford, Calif.: Stanford University Press, 1993). In *Khmer American: Identity and Moral Education in a Diasporic Community* (Berkeley: University of California Press, 1999), Nancy J. Smith-Hefner examines gender ideology and socialization in Cambodia and the Cambodian American community, as well as women's efforts to reconstruct community in the Boston area in the late 1980s. Shiori Ui, "Unlikely Heroes," in Michael Burawoy, Alice Burton, Ann Arnett Ferguson, Kathryn J. Fox, Joshua Gamson, Nadine Gartrell, Leslie Hurt, Charles Kurzman, Leslie Salzinger, Joseph Schiffman, and Shiori Ui, eds., *Ethnography Unbound* (Berkeley: University of California Press, 1991), 161–77, considers how Cambodian American women's new economic and social roles in support of their families' survival contribute to their emergence as community leaders.

Two anthologies give voice to Cambodian, Hmong/Laotian, and Vietnamese American college students in the 1980s. They express their families' transformation by war and their refugee status, their struggles to live in "two worlds," and their hopes and aspirations for the future. See Katsuyo K. Howard, comp., *Passages: An Anthology of the Southeast Asian Refugee Experience* (Fresno, Calif.: Southeast Asian Student Services, California State University, 1990), and Lucy Nguyen-Hon-Nhiem and Joel Martin Halpern, eds., *The Far East Comes Near* (Amherst: University of Massachusetts Press, 1989).

Chinese American Women

Huping Ling, *Surviving on the Gold Mountain* (Albany: State University of New York Press, 1998), is an overview of Chinese immigrant women's lives from the 1840s to the 1990s, including the experiences of international students. Peggy Pascoe, "Gender Systems in Conflict: The Marriages of Mission-Educated Chinese American Women, 1847–1939," in Ruiz and DuBois, eds., *Unequal Sisters,* 2d ed. (1994), 139–56, uncovers the initiatives of Chinese American women who negotiated with the Presbyterian Mission Home to gain more autonomy for themselves and to establish marriages that gave them more power with their parents and spouses. Judy Yung, *Unbound Feet* (Berkeley: University of California Press, 1995), is a social history of Chinese women in San Francisco and their personal strivings between the 1840s and the 1940s. It includes descriptions of middle-class life prior to the 1960s and life histories of second-generation women and their community activities. Yung's *Unbound Voices* (Berkeley: University of California Press, 1999) is a documentary history of Chinese women in San Francisco that includes women's letters, essays, autobiographies, speeches, and oral histories, from the 1880s to the 1950s. For brief biographies and photos of pioneering women of the nineteenth and twentieth centuries, see Ruthanne Lum McCunn, *Chinese American Portraits: Personal Histories, 1828–1988* (San Francisco: Chronicle Books, 1988).

Lucie Cheng Hirata assesses women's work lives in "Chinese Immigrant Women in Nineteenth-Century California," in Carol Berkin and Mary Beth Norton, eds., *Women of America: A History* (Boston: Houghton Mifflin Company, 1979), 223–44, and in "Free, Indentured, Enslaved: Chinese Prostitutes in Nineteenth-Century America," *Signs* 5:1 (1979): 3–29. Hirata's path-breaking work views prostitution as a form of labor and part of the economic system, with a few Chinese American women being free agents and others subject to multiple layers of exploitation. In "Family, Economy, and the State: A Legacy of Struggle for Chinese American Women" in *Origins and Destinies,* ed. Silvia Pedraza and Rubén G. Rumbaut (Belmont, Calif.: Wadsworth, 1996), Esther Chow argues that Chinese American women and families developed different economic strategies to combine work and households as they negotiated changing economic forces in the United States from the 1840s to the 1990s.

Contemporary women's lives as garment workers, their multiple roles, and the limits of their socioeconomic mobility are discussed in Chalsa Loo's "Slaying Demons with a Sewing Needle: Gender Differences and Women's Status," in her *Chinatown: Most Time, Hard Time* (New York: Praeger Publishers, 1991), 189–210, and by Min Zhou and Regina Nordquist, "Work and Its Place in the Lives of Immigrant Women: Garment Workers in New York City's Chinatown," in Zhou and Gatewood, eds., *Contemporary Asian America* (2000), 254–77. In Margaret M. Chin's comparative study of Latina and Chinese garment workers, "When Coethnic Assets Become Liabilities," in *Migration, Transnationalization and Race in a Changing New York,* ed. Héctor R. Codero-Guzmán, Robert C. Smith, and Ramón Grosfoguel (Philadelphia: Temple University Press, 2001), 279–99, Chinese women workers express their heavy reliance on co-ethnic relations for obtaining work, as do Chinese employers for finding new workers. Xiaolan Bao, *Holding Up More than Half the Sky* (Urbana and Chicago: University of Illinois Press, 2001), examines the important role played by Chinese women immigrants from 1948 to 1992 in revitalizing both the garment industry and New York City's Chinatown, focusing on both their political activism and their changing notions of motherhood.

Two works on the American born give attention to their struggles to achieve a distinct Chinese American identity, especially in the pre–World War II era of racial segregation, and address gender differences in their households. Sucheng Chan considers identity construction through the turn of the twentieth century in "Race, Ethnic Culture, and Gender in the Construction of Identities among Second-Generation Chinese Americans, 1880s–1930s," in *Claiming America*, ed. K. Scott Wong and Sucheng Chan (Philadelphia: Temple University Press, 1998), 127–64. In *Of Orphans and Warriors* (New Brunswick: Rutgers University Press, 2000), Gloria Heyung Chun explores Chinese American culture and identity from the 1930s to the 1990s through various cultural formations.

On women's organizing efforts in contemporary history, see Miriam Ching Yoon Louie, who discusses Chinese American women's involvement in union work in *Sweatshop Warriors* (Cambridge, Mass.: South End Press, 2001), chap. 1. Women's leadership roles and strategies as community workers are examined in Lydia Lowe, "Paving the Way: Chinese Immigrant Workers and Community-Based Organizing in Boston," *Amerasia Journal* 18:1 (1992): 39–48, and in Stacey G. H. Yap, *Gather Your Strength, Sisters* (New York: AMS Press, 1989).

Filipino American Women

Filipino Americans are an understudied community, and Filipina experiences in particular during the pre-1965 period have yet to be adequately documented. Delia Aguilar San Juan poses questions for the study of Filipinas in "The Philippine Centenary: Urgent Feminist Questions," *Amerasia Journal* 24:3 (1998): 27–35. Aspects of women's history in the early migration period are explored in Fred Cordova, *Filipinos: Forgotten Asian Americans* (Dubuque, Iowa: Kendall/Hunt Publishing Company, 1983); Dorothy Cordova, "Voices from the Past: Why They Came," in *Making Waves* (1989), 42–49; and Marina E. Espina, *Filipinos in Louisiana* (New Orleans: A. F. Laborde and Sons, 1988). For contemporary life histories, see Yen Le Espiritu's *Filipino American Lives* (Philadelphia: Temple University Press, 1995).

Barbara Posadas discusses the formation of interracial Filipino families in "Crossed Boundaries in Interracial Chicago: Filipino American Families since 1925," *Amerasia Journal* 8:2 (1981): 31–52, and considers the daughters' lives in "Mestiza Girlhood: Interracial Families in Chicago's Filipino American Community since 1925," in *Making Waves* (1989), 273–82.

On the role of gender in recent Filipino immigration, see James A. Tyner, "The Social Construction of Gendered Migration from the Philippines," in Zhou and Gatewood, eds., *Contemporary Asian America* (2000), 207–28. Maruja Milagros B. Asis examines similarities and differences shared by Filipino and Korean American women with their male counterparts and with each other in "To the United States and into the Labor Force: Occupational Expectations of Filipino and Korean Immigrant Women,"

Papers of the East-West Population Institute, no. 118 (Honolulu: East–West Center, February 1991). On contemporary Filipinas who come to the United States as mail-order brides, see Raquel Z. Ordoñez, "Mail-Order Brides: An Emerging Community," in *Filipino Americans*, ed. Maria P. P. Root (Thousand Oaks, Calif.: Sage Publications, 1997), 121–42.

On professional Filipinas and their agency to emigrate for work and to maintain transnational families under contemporary global capitalism, see Rhacel Salazar Parreñas, "New Household Forms, Old Family Values: The Formation and Reproduction of the Filipino Transnational Family in Los Angeles," in Zhou and Gatewood, eds., *Contemporary Asian America* (2000), 336–53. See also Marujua M. B. Asis, "From the Life Stories of Filipino Women: Personal and Family Agendas in Migration," *Asian and Pacific Migration Journal* 11:2 (2002): 67–93.

The recruitment of Filipina workers to the United States as part of globalization is examined in a number of studies. Paul Ong and Tania Azores identify the opportunities and difficulties Filipinas face in the health professions in "The Migration and Incorporation of Filipino Nurses," in *The New Asian Immigration in Los Angeles and Global Restructuring*, ed. Paul Ong, Edna Bonacich, and Lucie Cheng (Philadelphia: Temple University Press, 1994), 164–95. In *Servants of Globalization* (Stanford: Stanford University Press, 2001), Rhacel Salazar Parreñas examines the individual lives of Filipina domestic workers in Rome and Los Angeles, including the emotional costs paid by women in their economic dislocation globally. Charlene Tung considers the work lives of Filipinas in California who provide home care to the elderly in "The Cost of Caring: The Social Reproductive Labor of Filipina Live-in Home Health Caregivers," *Frontiers* 21:1/2 (2000): 61–82. For the exploitation of Filipinas in the electronics industry, see Rebecca Villones, "Women in the Silicon Valley," in *Making Waves* (1989), 172–76.

On diversity among lesbian and bisexual Filipinas and changes in their personal lives and political activism over the past twenty years, see Christine T. Lipat, Trinity A. Ordona, Cianna Pamintuan Stewart, and Mary Ann Vbaldo, "Tomboy, Dyke, Lezzie, and Bi," in Root, ed., *Filipino Americans* (1997), 230–46.

Hmong/Laotian American Women

War, dislocation, and adaptation are at the center of most studies of Hmong and Laotian immigrants. Through multi-generational family studies, Hmong American women describe their lives in Laos before and during the U.S. war in Southeast Asia and their struggles as refugees to rebuild lives in America; see Sucheng Chan, ed., *Hmong Means Free* (Philadelphia: Temple University Press, 1994). In *The Changing Lives of Refugee Hmong Women* (Seattle: University of Washington Press, 1994), Nancy D. Donnelly details changes in marriage and courtship patterns, outlines the development of Hmong textile "cooperatives" in Seattle in the 1980s, and finds that women sought to maintain traditional gender relations even as they increased their economic power in the family. Lillian Faderman, with Ghia Xiong, in *I Begin My Life All Over* (Boston: Beacon Press, 1998), also discusses differences in the socialization of girls and boys and young women and men in Hmong society and in their generational adaptation in America.

Janet E. Benson uncovers the lives of Laotian and Vietnamese women who work in meatpacking plants in the Midwest and analyzes the impact of their employment on family survival and gender relations in "The Effects of Packinghouse Work on Southeast Asian Refugee Families," in *Newcomers in the Workplace*, ed. Louise Lamphere, Alex Stepick, and Guillermo Grenier (Philadelphia: Temple University Press, 1994), 99–126. In "Work, Politics, and Coalition Building," in *Community Activism and Feminist Politics*, ed. Nancy A. Naples (New York: Routledge, 1998), 310–25, Sharon Bays documents the rise of a women's multiethnic coalition in a central California town. Here Hmong women are developing new political styles and networks distinct from those of Hmong men, including a Laotian alliance across ethnicities that de-emphasizes clans.

In "Exploring and Transforming the Landscape of Gender and Sexuality: Hmong American Teenaged Girls," *Race, Gender and Class* 8:1 (2001): 35–46, Stacey J. Lee incorporates voices of Hmong American girls in examining the impact of intergenerational tensions and Hmong-versus-American cultural conflict over gender and sexuality on the schooling of high school–age daughters. Lee also uses Hmong American women's stories to document their struggles to gain a college education in the context of traditional expectations of early marriage and motherhood, racism, and welfare policies, in "The Road to College: Hmong American Women's Pursuit of Higher Education," *Harvard Educational Review* 67:4 (Winter 1997): 803–27. For moving accounts of the family experiences of Hmong and Laotian college students during the 1980s, see *Passages* and *The Far East Comes Near*, cited in the Cambodian/Khmer American women section, above.

Japanese American Women

For a general history, see Mei Nakano, *Japanese American Women: Three Generations, 1890–1990* (Berkeley: Mina Press Publishing, 1990). Studies on Japanese immigrant women as pioneers in Hawai'i and the American West during the first half of the twentieth century include Emma Gee, "Issei Women," in *Counterpoint*, ed. Emma Gee (Los Angeles: Asian American Studies Center, 1976), 359–64; Yuji Ichioka, "*Ameyuki-san*: Japanese Prostitutes in Nineteenth-Century America," *Amerasia Journal* 4:1 (1977): 1–22; Gail Nomura, "Issei Working Women in Hawaii," in *Making Waves* (1989), 135–48; Gail Nomura, "*Tsugiki*, a Grafting: A History of a Japanese Pioneer Woman in Washington State," in *Women in Pacific Northwest History*, ed. Karen J. Blair, rev. ed. (Seattle: University of Washington Press, 2001), 284–307; Patsy Sumie Saiki, *Early Japanese Immigrants in Hawaii* (Honolulu: Japanese Cultural Center of Hawaii, 1993); and Eileen Sunada Sarasohn, *Issei Women* (Palo Alto, Calif.: Pacific Books, 1998), which features eleven Japanese immigrant women's stories on family, community, work, racial discrimination, and internment. One of the few studies of the legacy of immigrant women's material culture considers the ways in which Japanese women modified traditional clothing for their lives in Hawai'i; see Barbara Kawakami's *Japanese Immigrant Clothing in Hawaii, 1885–1941* (Honolulu: University of Hawai'i Press, 1993).

The perception of Issei women as passive and accepting of their role as picture brides is challenged in Yuji Ichioka, "*Amerika Nadeshiko*: Japanese Immigrant Women in the United States, 1900–1924," *Pacific Historical Review* 49:2 (May 1980): 339–57, and in Laurie M. Mengel, "Issei Women and Divorce in Hawai'i, 1885–1908," *Social Process in Hawai'i* 38 (1997): 18–39. Evelyn Nakano Glenn's *Issei, Nisei, War Bride* (Philadelphia: Temple University Press, 1986) explores women's initiatives in paid domestic work across three generations and from different backgrounds, and how Japanese American women find meaning in it.

Studies of second-generation aspirations, family, work, identity, and cultural formation include Eileen Tamura, *Americanization, Acculturation, and Ethnic Identity: The Nisei Generation in Hawaii* (Urbana and Chicago: University of Illinois Press, 1994), and the works of Valerie Matsumoto, such as "Desperately Seeking 'Deidre': Gender Roles, Multicultural Relations, and Nisei Women Writers of the 1930s," *Frontiers* 12:1 (1991): 19–32 and "Japanese American Women and the Creation of Urban Nisei Culture in the 1930s," in *Over the Edge*, ed. Valerie J. Matsumoto and Blake Allmendinger (Berkeley: University of California Press, 1999), 291–306. On the life history of a Nisei woman educator and activist, see Gail M. Nomura, "'Peace Empowers': The Testimony of Aki Kurose, a Women of Color in the Pacific Northwest," *Frontiers* 22:3 (2001): 75–92. On the transnational experiences of three Nisei women who spent part of their adult years in Japan, see Eriko Yamamoto, "Miya Sannomiya Kikuchi: A Pioneer Nisei Woman's Life and Identity"; Mary Tomita, "Coming of Age in Japan"; and Nobuyo Yamane, "A Nisei Woman in Rural Japan," all in *Amerasia Journal* 23:3 (1997): 73–101, 165–80, and 183–96, respectively.

Community and family studies shed light on women's activities; gender roles; connections among family, work, and community survival; and the negotiations of Japanese Americans with mainstream society to maintain community. Examples include Lauren Kessler, *Stubborn Twig* (New York: Plume, 1994); Valerie J. Matsumoto, *Farming the Home Place* (Ithaca, N.Y.: Cornell University Press, 1993); and Linda Tamura, *The Hood River Issei* (Urbana: University of Illinois Press, 1993). Sylvia Junko Yanagisako identifies the importance of women-centered social networks in the making and maintenance of community across generations in *Transforming the Past* (Stanford: Stanford University Press, 1985).

There are many accounts of internment and camp experiences. Those with women's perspectives and experiences include Miné Okubo's *Citizen 13660* (Seattle: University of Washington Press, 1946, 1973, 1983, 1989), and Yoshiko Uchida's *Desert Exile* (Seattle: University of Washington Press, 1982), which also chronicles prewar life in Berkeley, California. See Gary Y. Okihiro, *Storied Lives* (Seattle: University of Washington Press, 1999), on the aspirations and initiatives of students who left the camps to pursue their college education during World War II and on the gender discrimination encountered by women in their community and in the larger society. For a glimpse of the experiences of a Japanese American woman stranded in Japan during World War II, see *Dear Miya: Letters Home from Japan, 1939–1946* (Stanford: Stanford University Press, 1995), by Mary Kimoto Tomita. For Nisei and Sansei women's experiences and voices in the struggle for redress, see Yasuko I. Takezawa, *Breaking Silence* (Ithaca, N.Y.: Cornell University Press, 1995).

Korean American Women

Studies on Korean immigrant women in early twentieth-century America include Alice Yun Chai's "Freed from the Elders but Locked in Labor: Korean Immigrant Women in Hawaii," *Women's Studies* 13 (1987): 223–34, and "Korean Women in Hawaii: 1903–1904," in *Women in New Worlds*, ed. Hilah F. Thomas and Rosemary Skinner Keller (Nashville: Abingdon Press, 1981), 328–44; Alice Yang Murray, "Ilse Women and the Early Korean American Community: Redefining the Origins of Feminist Empowerment," in Ruiz and DuBois, eds., *Unequal Sisters*, 3d ed. (2000), 205–13; Sonia S. Sunoo, "Korean Women Pioneers of the Pacific Northwest," *Oregon Historical Quarterly* 79:1 (Spring 1978): 51–63; Eun Sik Yang, "Korean Women of America: From Subordination to Partnership, 1903–1930," *Amerasia Journal* 11:2 (1984): 1–28; and Sun Bin Yim, "Korean Immigrant Women in Early Twentieth-Century America," in *Making Waves* (1989), 50–60.

On Korean wives of U.S. military servicemen whose experiences of intermarriage, raising mixed-race children, and marginalization by both U.S. society and the Korean American community differ from those of most Korean immigrant women, see Haeyun Juliana Kim, "Voices from the Shadows: The Lives of Korean War Brides," *Amerasia Journal* 17:1 (1991): 15–30; and Ji-Yeon Yuh, *Beyond the Shadow of Camptown* (New York: New York University Press, 2002), which also uses oral histories to explore the agency of Korean military brides and their coping strategies in the United States, including the role of food and the creation of support groups.

For Korean immigrant women's expectations and experiences in the contemporary labor force, see Maruja Milagros B. Asis, "To the United States and into the Labor Force" (1991), cited in the Filipino American women section, above. Studies on women's roles in post-1965 family businesses and the implications for the household include Kwang Chung Kim and Won Moo Hurh, "The Burden of Double Roles: Korean Wives in the USA," *Ethnic and Racial Studies* 11:2 (April 1988): 151–67. For ways in which recent immigrants cope with work and family and bridge the public and private spheres, see Alice Yun Chai, "Adaptive Strategies of Korean Immigrant Women in Hawaii," in *Beyond the Public/Domestic Dichotomy*, ed. Janet Sharistanian (New York: Greenwood Press, 1987), 65–99. The agency of contemporary immigrant women working as manicurists is discussed in Miliann Kang, "Manicuring Race, Gender and Class: Service Interactions in New York City Korean-Owned Nail Salons," *Race, Gender and Class* 4:3 (1996): 143–64.

Among Pyong Gap Min's works on Korean immigrant families and social change, see *Changes and Conflicts: Korean Immigrant Families in New York* (Boston: Allyn & Bacon, 1998). Immigrant women's changing ideology about gender roles in the household, family relations, work, and the family business are examined in In-Sook Lim, "Korean Immigrant Women's Challenge to Gender Inequality at Home," *Gender and Society* 11:1 (February 1997): 31–51, and Kyeyoung Park, *The Korean American Dream* (Ithaca, N.Y.: Cornell University Press, 1997). For chapters on feminist theory, work and family roles, ethnic identity, and other issues, see *Korean American Women: From Tradition to Feminism*, ed. Young I. Song and Ailee Moon (Westport, Conn.: Praeger, 1998).

Contemporary Korean immigrant women workers' activism—for example, against the sex industry and for health and safety in the workplace—is documented in Louie, *Sweatshop Warriors* (2001), chap. 3, cited in the Chinese American women section, above. Jung Ha Kim finds the church a site of contradictions, but with liberating opportunities for women, in "The Labor of Compassion: Voices of Churched Korean American Women," in *New Spiritual Homes*, ed. David K. Yoo (Honolulu: University of Hawai'i Press, 1999), 202–17. For contemporary life histories, see Elaine H. Kim and Eui-Young Yu, eds., *East to America: Korean American Life Stories* (New York: New Press, 1996).

Pacific Islander American Women

Pacific Islander Americans also constitute an understudied community. Native Hawaiians, the largest subgroup, predominate in the literature. First published in 1898 as an appeal to the American public to restore the Hawaiian monarchy and prevent the annexation of Hawai'i, the classic *Hawai'i's Story by Hawai'i's Queen*, by Queen Lili'uokalani (reprint, Tokyo: Charles E. Tuttle Company, 1977), continues to inspire generations of Native Hawaiians in their quest for sovereignty. Nathaniel B. Emerson's *Pele and Hiiaka: A Myth from Hawaii*, rev. ed. (Honolulu: 'Ai Pohaku Press, 1997), first published in 1915, has gained new prominence as the Native Hawaiian cultural renaissance focuses on the significance of these Hawaiian fire goddesses in shaping the identity of Native Hawaiian women. In *Native Land and Foreign Desires* (Honolulu: Bishop Museum Press, 1992), Lilikala Kame'eleihiwa describes the role of Native Hawaiian chiefesses in traditional cosmology and society, as well as the political and social changes that occurred with European and American contact. Jocelyn Linnekin's *Sacred Queens and Women of Consequence* (Ann Arbor: University of Michigan, 1990) is an exploration of the cultural values and social positions of Native Hawaiian women through the nineteenth century.

Several contemporary works focus on Native Hawaiian women's struggle for sovereignty and against colonialism. Noenoe K. Silva, "Kū'ē! Hawaiian Women's Resistance to the Annexation," *Social Process in Hawai'i* 38 (1997): 4–15, examines events at the turn of the twentieth century, whereas Haunani-Kay Trask, *From a Native Daughter*, rev. ed. (Honolulu: University of Hawai'i Press, 1999), considers the contemporary role and actions of Native Hawaiian women. In "Off-Island Hawaiians 'Making' Ourselves at 'Home': A (Gendered) Contradiction in Terms?" *Women's Studies International Forum* 21:6 (1998): 681–93, J. Kehaulani Kauanui analyzes the role of Native Hawaiians in the diaspora in the sovereignty movement and argues for the infusion of a feminist sensibility. In "Feminism and Indigenous Hawaiian Nationalism" *Signs* 21:4 (1996): 906–16, Haunani-Kay Trask calls attention to the significant role that indigenous women play in the sovereignty movement. In contrast, Karen Ito, *Lady Friends: Hawaiian Ways and the Ties That Define* (Ithaca, N.Y.: Cornell University Press, 1999), explores the ordinary and everyday social lives of Hawaiian women not involved in politics.

A feminist study of Guam, Laura Marie Torres Souder-Jaffery's *Daughters of the Island: Contemporary Chamorro Women Organizers on Guam* (Lanham, Md.: University

Press of America, 1992) documents the historical and influential role that women have held in Guam even under conditions of colonization and Catholicism. Using oral histories, Souder-Jaffrey assesses the leadership of specific Chamorro women who have sought to strengthen their communities through the strategy of social networks.

Studies of Pacific Islanders in the context of the U.S. continent and their lives as Pacific Islander Americans are beginning to appear. In *Pacific Voices Talk Story*, ed. Margo King-Lenson (Vacaville, Calif.: Tui Communications, 2002), fourteen narrators from a number of Pacific Islands who have settled largely in California share stories about their journey and adjustment to mainland life. In *Voyages: From Tongan Villages to American Suburbs* (Ithaca, N.Y.: Cornell University Press, 1997), Cathy A. Small utilizes an extended family history to chronicle the experiences of a generation of Tongan people who settled in California from the 1960s to the 1990s and the impact of their migration on village life and kin relationships.

South Asian American Women

Writings on women from South Asia tend to focus on the post-1965 period, and studies of Asian Indian women predominate. The recovery of the experiences of South Asian American women during the first half of the twentieth century is in great need. Kartar Dhillon, "The Parrot's Beak," in *Making Waves*, (1989), 214–22, provides a brief view of the childrearing, gender, and political perspectives of one of the first Sikh families in the United States at the turn of the twentieth century.

Three readers are concerned with the condition of contemporary South Asian American women. Chapters in Shamita Das Dasgupta, ed., *A Patchwork Shawl: Chronicles of South Asian Women in America* (New Brunswick, N.J.: Rutgers University Press, 1998), deal with patriarchy in South Asian American households, community tensions, ethnic and sexual identity, mother-daughter intergenerational dynamics, and domestic violence. *Emerging Voices*, ed. Sangeeta R. Gupta (Walnut Creek, Calif.: Altamira Press, 1999), includes chapters on how South Asian American women are redefining their lives, from notions of self and identity, including as bicultural women, to family, marriage, sexuality, and community issues. *Our Feet Walk the Sky: Women of the South Asian Diaspora* (San Francisco: Aunt Lute Books, 1993), edited by the Women of South Asian Descent Collective, is an anthology of personal histories, critical essays, and creative writings.

On work, the double burden, and survival strategies of recent immigrant women, see, among others, Amarpal K. Dhaliwal, "Gender at Work: The Renegotiation of Middle-Class Womanhood in a South Asian–Owned Business," in *ReViewing Asian America: Locating Diversity*, ed. Wendy L. Ng, Soo-Young Chin, James S. Moy, and Gary Y. Okihiro (Pullman: Washington State University Press, 1995), 75–85; Suvarna Thaker, "The Quality of Life of Asian Indian Women in the Motel Industry," *South Asia Bulletin* 2:1 (Spring 1982): 68–73; and Marcelle Williams, "Ladies on the Line: Punjabi Cannery Workers in Central California," in *Making Waves* (1989), 148–59.

Cultural, generational, and gender conflicts are the topics of a number of studies. For example, on aspects of Asian Indian immigrant women's changing roles and aspirations and second-generation women's formation of an ethnic identity and adaptation to two cultures, see Jean Bacon, *Life Lines: Community, Family, and Assimilation among Asian Indian Immigrants* (New York: Oxford University Press, 1996). The many publications of Shamita Das Dasgupta and Sayantani Dasgupta include "Public Face, Private Space: Asian Indian Women and Sexuality," in *Bad Girls, Good Girls*, ed. Nan Bauer Malgir and Donna Perry (New Brunswick, N.J.: Rutgers University Press, 1994), which discusses the impact of racial discrimination in the United States on young women's choices and the use of gender discrimination by the ethnic male leadership to present a "model" Indian community to American society. Rashmi Luthra explores the persistence of arranged marriages in "Matchmaking in the Classifieds of the Immigrant Indian Press," in *Making Waves* (1989), 337–44. In *Speaking the Unspeakable* (New Brunswick, N.J.: Rutgers University Press, 2000), Margaret Abraham analyzes "marital violence" in South Asian immigrant households in the United States and through women's voices documents the strategies abused women adopt to resist brutality and to organize with others and educate their communities against women's oppression.

Sources on women's role in community building include "Defining Community and Feminism: Indian Women in New York City," *Race, Gender and Class* 3:3 (1997): 95–111, by Madhulika S. Khandelwal, which focuses on women's leadership of community organizations in the 1980s. An analysis of South Asian women's groups in the United States appears in Jyotsna Vaid, "Beyond a Space of Our Own," *Amerasia Journal* 25:3 (1999/2000): 111–26. Chapters in Shah, ed., *Dragon Ladies* (1997), also address South Asian women's activism and their community-based organizations to combat domestic violence and promote feminism and empowerment.

Vietnamese American Women

As previously noted, war and the refugee experience are an integral part of the history of Southeast Asian women. The influence of America's gendered policies on Vietnamese American refugee women's adaptation in America is discussed in Gail Paradise Kelly, "To Become an American Woman: Education and Sex Role Socialization of the Vietnamese Immigrant Woman," in Ruiz and DuBois, eds., *Unequal Sisters*, 3d ed. (2000), 554–64. Van Luu, "The Hardships of Escape for Vietnamese Women," in *Making Waves* (1989), 60–72, considers Vietnamese women's difficult transition in their resettlement in the United States. In "What Is Winning Anyway? Redefining Veteran: A Vietnamese American Woman's Experiences in War and Peace," *Frontiers* 18:1 (1997): 145–67, Suzan Ruth Travis-Robyns describes the life of Nguyen Ngoc Xuan as one of many Vietnamese women whose sufferings in Vietnam and the United States also make them veterans of the Vietnam war. For life histories and other aspects of Vietnamese American women's history, see James A. Freeman, *Hearts of Sorrow: Vietnamese-American Lives* (Stanford: Stanford University Press, 1989) and *Changing Identities: Vietnamese Americans, 1975–1995* (Boston: Allyn and Bacon, 1995).

On the changing Vietnamese American household and women's strategies to negotiate gender and generational relations, see the works of Nazli Kibria, including *Family*

Tightrope: The Changing Lives of Vietnamese Americans (Princeton: Princeton University Press, 1993) and "Power, Patriarchy, and Gender Conflict in the Vietnamese Immigrant Community," in Zhou and Gatewood, eds., *Contemporary Asian America* (2000), 431–43. Nhi T. Lieu, "Remembering 'the Nation' through Pageantry: Femininity and the Politics of Vietnamese Womanhood in the *Hao Hau Ao Dai* Contest," *Frontiers* 21:1/2 (2000): 127–51, examines the cultural and gender politics of Vietnamese American communities as exemplified through beauty pageants.

Examining work, women's strategies, and changing gender roles, Craig Trinh-Phat Huynh explains why women operate nail salons in "Vietnamese-Owned Manicure Businesses in Los Angeles," in *Reframing the Immigration Debate*, ed. Bill Ong Hing and Ronald Lee (Los Angeles: LEAP Asian Pacific American Public Policy Institute and UCLA Asian American Studies Center, 1996), 195–203. On Vietnamese women workers in meatpacking plants and their family and gender relations, see Janet E. Benson, "Effects of Packinghouse Work" (1994), cited in the Hmong/Laotian American women section, above.

Vietnamese American college students of the 1980s give voice to their families' traumatic experiences and their hopes for the future through education in *Passages* and *The Far East Comes Near*, cited in the Cambodian/Khmer American women section, above. In *Growing Up American* (New York: Russell Sage Foundation, 1998), based on a study of a Vietnamese community in New Orleans, Min Zhou and Carl L. Bankston III find that cultural expectations placed on daughters by their refugee parents and economic realities in the United States have contributed to positive support for them to be educated, in order to enhance the family's income and to advance women's marriage opportunities.

This partial listing is meant to be suggestive of the rich literature that exists on Asian American and Pacific Islander American women as historical subjects with agency. In calling attention to such works in this essay and in this anthology, I hope that a more balanced and complete history can be achieved in the future. As noted by the absence of studies on women in many Asian American and Pacific Islander American groups, as well as by the gaps in topics and time periods, much more historical research remains to be done.

NOTE

This is a revised and updated version of an essay that first appeared in *Teaching Asian American Women's History* (Washington, D.C.: American Historical Association, 1997), chap. 4. I have included new scholarship and a section on Pacific Islander American women, replaced some works with others, and reorganized some subsections. Because of space limitations, not all works discussed in the earlier essay are included here. I thank Davianna McGregor, Gail Nomura, and Amy Stillman for their assistance with bibliographic sources on Native Hawaiian women.

"In Her Eyes"

An Annotated Bibliography of Video Documentaries on Asian/Pacific Islander American Women

Nancy In Kyung Kim

Faculty who teach Asian/Pacific Islander American women's history have used video documentaries as a pedagogical tool. Video documentaries can effectively provide visual images and illuminate perspectives that may not otherwise be covered in course readings or lectures. The purpose of this annotated bibliography is to offer a practical list of videos for instructors who teach Asian/Pacific Islander American women's history.

In selecting documentaries, I considered two major criteria. First, I chose to limit videos to those that placed Asian American and Pacific Islander American women central to the documentary. Made directly from their perspective or peering into their experiences at a particular historical moment, each documentary must be "in her eyes." Accessibility was the second criterion for the list. Instructors should be able to rent or purchase videos through distribution companies, with some exceptions. Therefore, many recently released independent films currently in the film festival circuit and those yet to be picked up by distributors are regretfully omitted.

With the many interdisciplinary approaches to documentary making, a few experimental videos are mixed in with the traditional documentary genre. Despite the variety, a common form emerged from the group: the personal narrative. Many documentaries focused on the film- or video-maker, who used her individual journey to uncover family history or to confront issues. The documentary thus contextualized an individual's experience with larger historical events.

In selecting videos, I also attempted to restrict documentaries to those with subjects in the United States and Pacific Islands. A few, however, concentrated on subjects located in Asia. I allowed this exception for those that address specific issues covered in Asian/Pacific Islander American women's course syllabi. Also included are documentaries considered dated and perhaps obsolete by some. Instructors showed these videos in early Asian/Pacific Islander American women's classes, and they may be useful to compare with contemporary documentaries addressing similar issues. Absent from the list are feature-length dramas such as *Picture Bride* and *When Heaven and Earth*

Changed Places. They convey key experiences of Asian/Pacific Islander American women's history and would likely be more accessible to pre-college-age viewers. However, those particular experiences would duplicate existing documentaries.

The bibliography is organized in alphabetical order by title, with a brief description of the video's content and suggestions for use in the classroom. In an early phase of the Asian/Pacific Islander American women's course development, faculty preferred to use an ethnic-specific framework to teach a historical immigration-based curriculum.[1] I chose not to distinguish videos by ethnic or cultural representation, with the exception of "Hawaiian" due to that group's significant underrepresentation in course curriculum. I categorized the videos by general, related topics typically covered in more recent courses, such as "family," "activism," and "labor." Ultimately, I hope this list will serve to show the glaringly absent issues, experiences, and perspectives in order to guide current and future film- and video-makers so that they may further contribute to an Asian/Pacific Islander American Women's Studies curriculum.

Most videos listed below are available through the following distribution companies:

National Asian American Telecommunications Association (NAATA)
Film Library
22-D Hollywood Avenue
Hohokus, NJ 07423
Tel: 800-343-5540
Fax: 201-652-1973
www.naatanet.org

Pacific Islanders in Communications
1221 Kapiolani Blvd. #6A-4
Honolulu, Hawai'i 96814
Tel: 808-591-0059
Fax: 808-591-1114
www.piccom.org

Third World Newsreel
545 Eighth Avenue, 10th Floor
New York, NY 10018
Tel: 212-947-9277
Fax: 212-594-6417
www.twn.org

Viewing Race Project
73 Spring Street, Suite 606
New York, NY 10012
Tel: 212-274-8080
Fax: 212-274-8081
www.viewingrace.org

Women Make Movies, Inc.
462 Broadway, Suite 500WS
New York, New York 10013
Tel: 212-925-0606
Fax: 212-925-2052
www.wmm.com

Annotated Bibliography

5 Girls, Maria Finitzo, Women Make Movies, 2001, 113 minutes.

5 Girls follows the high school adolescent lives of five girls from diverse backgrounds, living in or around Chicago. The same production company that made *Hoop Dreams* made this documentary. These girls struggle through family expectations, self-awareness, and relationships. Through this video, students can see commonalities and differences among girls of different ethnic and cultural backgrounds and at the same time compare the girls' experiences with their own.

Behind the Labels, Tia Lessin, Witness and Oxygen, 2001, 45 minutes.

Despite the perception that indentured servitude is long gone, garment workers arrive in Saipan with a large debt to repay. Mostly female workers from China, the Philippines, Thailand, Vietnam, and Cambodia are recruited to work for U.S.-owned manufacturing companies seeking cheap labor in the Commonwealth of the Northern Mariana Islands, a self-governing territory politically integrated with the United States. Because Saipan is among the U.S. territories, garment manufacturers profit from using the "Made in the USA" label, while they slide through regulation loopholes. *Behind the Labels* exposes the horrible working conditions and difficult experiences of Saipan's garment workers. Comparing Asian women seamstresses in Saipan with Asian women in the United States provides a global perspective on labor and the garment industry.

Between the Lines: Asian American Women's Poetry, Yunah Hong, Women Make Movies, 2001, 60 minutes.

Through interviews with fifteen Asian American female poets, Yunah Hong offers a look at how one's ethnic and gender identity and family history speak through creative expressions. This documentary would be effective in the "arts" section often included in Asian/Pacific Islander American women's courses and may inspire students to reflect on their creative voice.

Between Worlds, Shawn Hainsworth, University of California Extension Center for Media and Independent Learning, 1998, 75 minutes.

Between Worlds follows several Amerasians from Vietnam for six years. (Amerasians is the term typically used to describe children of U.S. military servicemen and Vietnamese women.) The documentary reveals their experiences, and those of their families, in refugee camps and for five years through adjustment to American culture in various parts of the United States. This documentary would be useful in discussing how war affects a generation of children, as well as in discussion of refugee experiences.

Beyond Black and White, Nisma Zaman, Women Make Movies, 1994, 28 minutes.

Through interviews and group discussions, the filmmaker, Nisma Zaman, compares her experiences and biracial identity formation with those of five other women of biracial backgrounds. Zaman is Bengali and Caucasian. This video is useful in exploring how media images and family form one's identity in the historical context of anti-miscegenation legislation and racial categorizations.

Blood, Sweat and Lace, Asian Immigrant Women's Advocates, 1994, 18 minutes.

When Lucky Sewing Company went bankrupt, its seamstresses were left without their pay, despite their production of dresses for Jessica McClintock. About a dozen of the workers sought support from the Asian Immigrant Women's Advocates (AIWA), an Oakland-based organization. The national Garment Workers Justice Campaign demanded back wages and worker protection from Jessica McClintock, action that led to a historic agreement and resolution in 1996. *Blood, Sweat and Lace* reveals the injustices in the garment-manufacturing industry and the archaic working conditions faced by these San Francisco workers. As the campaign continues to hold corporate retailers accountable, this documentary can be used to discuss women's labor and challenge the "model minority" image. This video is not available through the distribution groups listed. However, it may be found in university research libraries or possibly through AIWA.

Camp Arirang, Diana S. Lee and Grace Yoon Kyung Lee, NAATA, 1995, 28 minutes.

In the context of American military presence altering a country's economic system, this documentary shows the cooperation between the U.S. military and South Korean government to create a prostitution industry for American soldiers. Through interviews and archival footage, the lives of sex workers and their Amerasian children are examined. Although this documentary is set in Asia, it is relevant in discussing Asian war brides who immigrate to the United States in pursuit of the American Dream.

The Children We Sacrifice, Grace Poore, Women Make Movies, 2000, 61 minutes.

This documentary shares the stories of South Asian incest survivors and examines the social/cultural and psychological impact of such abuse. It includes statistics, poetry, art, and interviews with mental health professionals. The documentary was filmed in the United States, India, Sri Lanka, and Canada. Addressing an issue rarely discussed, *The Children We Sacrifice* gives voice to South Asian survivors of sexual abuse.

Daughter from Danang, Gail Dolgin and Vicente Franco, Independent Television Service, 2002, 80 minutes.

After twenty-two years, a Vietnamese mother is brought together with her Amerasian daughter. The reunion is not without challenges, however. They struggle with the effects of more than two decades of separation and the inevitable cultural differences.

Eating Welfare, Committee Against Anti-Asian Violence, 2001, 58 minutes.

More than 70 percent of the Southeast Asian community in the Bronx, New York, receive public assistance. *Eating Welfare* documents the community's organizing against welfare reform, which discriminatorily denies services to Southeast Asian refugees. Produced by the Committee Against Anti-Asian Violence, this video offers a view into youth direct-action organizing and advocacy for welfare rights. It is also useful for addressing issues of class and activism in Asian American women's courses.

First Person Plural, Deann Borshay Liem, NAATA, 2000, 56 minutes.

Nearly forty years ago, Deann was one of thousands of Korean children adopted by white American families. As an adult, Deann investigated her history and found that she was switched with another girl intended for adoption. The film chronicles her struggle to resolve the demands of two families, two cultures, and two nations; questions cultural assimilation as a concept; and considers alternative ways to address culture, race, family, and identity. With the growing community of transnational adoptees, this documentary delves into the complexities of identity, history and memory.

Four Women, Loni Ding, NAATA, 1982, 30 minutes.

This video explores the lives of four Asian American women—a social worker, a professor, a health clinic director, and a union business agent. Made twenty years ago, some may consider *Four Women* to be dated. However, it may be useful in discussions comparing occupations and career choices with those of young Asian American women today.

Frankly Speaking, Loni Ding, NAATA, 1982, 30 minutes.

Young Asian American women face many challenges as they become adults. High school students, teachers, employers, and counselors discuss their challenges. This documentary may be considered dated but may offer a basis for comparison to experiences of today's generation, two decades later.

From Hollywood to Hanoi, Tiana Thi Thanh Nga, 1993, 80 minutes.

Born in Saigon, Vietnam, Tiana and her family moved to the United States in 1966. This documentary follows her as she returns to Vietnam after twenty years. In her journey, she negotiates her violent memories with the roles she is asked to play as an actress in Hollywood. Distributed by Indochina Film Arts Foundation, 665 Chestnut Street (2nd Floor), San Francisco, CA 94133; Fax: 415-441-1783; E-mail: tianatiana@aol.com.

Gabriela, Trix Betlam, Women Make Movies, 1988, 67 minutes. Subtitled.

This documentary examines the history and contemporary struggles of women in the Philippines. Founded in 1984 in the Philippines, Gabriela is a mass women's organization representing diverse groups, with chapters in the United States. The documentary can be useful in discussing the power of a transnational social movement and global feminism.

Girls Like Us, Jane C. Wagner and Tina DiFeliciantonio, Women Make Movies, 1997, 57 minutes.

Girls Like Us follows four girls, ages fourteen to eighteen, in South Philadelphia. Through honest interviews and revealing footage, this documentary shows the working-class girls' struggles in growing up. The girls come from diverse racial backgrounds. Anna, who is Vietnamese American, deals with generational conflicts with her family.

The Global Assembly Line, Lorraine W. Gray, New Day Films, 1984, 58 minutes.

From clothing to electronics, *The Global Assembly Line* examines the global economy's impact on workers in Tennessee, Mexico, Silicon Valley, and the Philippines. This documentary could offer a basis for comparison to current industries in the United States and abroad, and covers the topic of labor in Asian/Pacific Islander American women's courses.

Hapa, Midori Sperandeo, NAATA, 2001, 26 minutes.

Hapa, also a term used to describe multiracial Asian Americans, raises many issues. The documentary focuses on hapa identity issues faced by Midori Sperandeo, with interviews with other individuals. The issues addressed include historical anti-miscegenation laws, struggles with identity, and the pull between ethnic communities. This documentary would complement a course section covering mixed-race Asian/Pacific Islander American women, as a growing number of students seek to explore that topic.

Happy Birthday Tutu Ruth, Ann Marie Kirk, Pacific Islanders in Communication, 1966, 28 minutes.

Struggling against assimilation and cultural genocide, ninety-year-old Ruth Kaholoa maintained Native Hawaiian cultural practices. This documentary reflects the Native Hawaiian experience in keeping their history and culture alive, despite historical pressures to disappear or to conform to the commodified tourist Hawaiian culture.

Hawai'i's Last Queen, Vivian Ducat, PBS: The American Experiences Documentary Series, 1997, 53 minutes.

Hawai'i's Last Queen documents the life of Queen Lili'uokalani, the last reigning constitutional monarch of the Kingdom of Hawai'i. Highly educated and a talented composer, Queen Lili'uokalani was overthrown in 1893 by American business interests with the help of U.S. naval forces when she sought to restore the power of the monarch and of Native Hawaiians through the promulgation of a new constitution. After several failed attempts, Hawai'i was annexed by the United States in 1898. Queen Lili'uokalani's leadership, actions, and writings resisting annexation, American rule, and assimilation continue to inspire the Native Hawaiian sovereignty movement. This documentary portrays an important part of Asian/Pacific Islander American women's history and would inspire discussion on women in leadership and women's role in the Native Hawaiian sovereignty movement.

Her Uprooting Plants Her, Celine Salazar Parreñas, Third World Newsreel, 1994, 17 minutes.

Based on interviews with Filipino families, *Her Uprooting Plants Her* is an experimental video that shares the stories of three sisters. The video raises issues of generational tensions and a sense of home. This video would be useful for students to reflect on and relate to their personal family stories.

Hollywood Harems, Tania Kamal-Eldin, Women Making Movies, 1999, 24 minutes.

Using Hollywood film clips from 1920 to the 1980s, Kamal-Eldin explores the construction of race, gender, and sexuality images to form fantasies of the exotic East. These images include the homogenization of East Asian representations with Arab, Persian, and Indian. This video is particularly useful in discussing sexualized racial formations and categorizations in light of post–September 11 racial profiling of "perceived" Middle Eastern Americans. *Hollywood Harems* may also be valuable as a followup to *Slaying the Dragon,* another documentary about images in Hollywood.

I Will Always Tell This Story, Lily Ng, NAATA, 1995, 7 minutes.

This documentary explores the struggle of a woman having to choose between staying in an abusive arranged marriage or losing her family and community connections. A short video, this may spark discussion on women's cultural expectation to make sacrifices for their family and community.

Issei Wahine, Ann Moriyasu, NAATA, 1991, 22 minutes.

Through "talk stories" told to her granddaughter, Koma Kokubun uncovers her family history on Hawaiian sugar plantations. The documentary integrates work songs and photographs. *Issei wahine* means first-generation immigrant woman. This video is useful in discussing the experiences of Asian Americans in Hawai'i in the early 1900s.

Jazz Is My Native Language: A Portrait of Toshiko Akiyoshi, Renee Cho, NAATA, 1983, 58 minutes.

A biography of Toshiko Akiyoshi, creator of Akiyoshi/Tabackin Big Band, this documentary shares her journey into prominence in American jazz. She has played with such renowned musicians as John Coltrane, Miles Davis, and Duke Ellington. Spotlighting this accomplished artist, *Jazz Is My Native Language* offers a role model to young Asian American women pursuing alternative careers in the arts and may be effective in conjunction with *Maya Lin: A Strong Clear Vision.*

Kelly Loves Tony, Spencer Nakasako, NAATA, 1998, 57 minutes.

Kelly Saeteurn is a pregnant seventeen-year-old high school graduate from a family of Lu Mien refugees from Laos. Her boyfriend Tony dropped out of junior high and has a criminal record. Addressing an often-neglected topic, *Kelly Loves Tony* reveals the tough realities and challenges of teenage pregnancy and cultural pressures.

Knowing Her Place, Indu Krishnan, Women Make Movies, 1990, 40 minutes.

Through experimental techniques, Krishnan explores the "cultural schizophrenia" many Asian American women experience. The video focuses on Vasu, an Indian American woman raised in the United States and India, and the cultural conflicts she feels in determining her gendered roles in family and society. *Knowing Her Place* is useful in discussing immigration, gender roles, and the tension between a cultural identity and a gender/feminist identity.

Mai's America, Marlo Poras, Women Make Movies, 2002, 72 minutes.

Mai, a "spunky Vietnamese teenager," visits the United States to study. She anticipated a Hollywood-like environment and instead encounters a mish-mash of characters in rural Mississippi. This documentary may not easily fit a typical Asian American women's course curriculum. However, it may offer a relatable perspective of recent immigrants' encounter with America.

Maya Lin: A Strong Clear Vision, Freida Lee Mock and Terry Sanders, NAATA, 1994, 98 minutes.

Maya Lin is a Chinese American artist, architect, and sculptor. This documentary explores Lin's creative processes in designing such works as the Civil Rights Memorial and the Yale Women's Table. Most significantly, it exposes the controversy of Lin, a young Asian American woman, designing the Vietnam Veterans Memorial, as is covered in the first half of the film. In addition to providing a role model of a young Asian American female artist, the documentary raises the issue of how an artist's race and gender politicize the art.

Miss India Georgia, Daniel Friedman and Sharon Grimberg, Viewing Race, 1998, 56 minutes.

This documentary follows four teenage contestants who prepare and participate in the annual Miss India Georgia competition. They share their thoughts and experiences of growing up in Atlanta and their relationships with family members in their teenage years. *Miss India Georgia* is a look at beauty pageants and what they represent to an immigrant South Asian community. In the classroom, this documentary can spark discussion about ethnic identity formation and what "beauty" means for young Asian/Pacific Islander American women.

Mitsuye and Nellie: Asian American Poets, Allie Light and Irving Saraf, Women Make Movies, 1981, 58 minutes.

The lives of Asian American poets Mitsuye Yamada and Nellie Wong are explored in this documentary. They share common experiences as women writers, yet varying histories as Japanese and Chinese Americans. Made more than twenty years ago, this documentary may be considered out of date. However, it may be useful in comparing experiences between generations.

Moving Mountains: The Story of the Yiu Mien, Elaine Velazquez, Filmmakers Library, 1991, 58 minutes.

Yiu Mien are people from Laos. During the Vietnam War they aided the CIA, which resulted in their loss of their land. This small group of refugees came from a society devoid of modern technology and was thrust into urban and suburban America. *Moving Mountains* captures the Yiu Mien's journey and adjustment to American culture. This documentary would shed light on a group's postwar displacement and acculturation to the United States.

Not Just Passing Through, Jean Carlomusto, Dolores Perez, Catherine Gund, Polly Thistlethwaite, Women Make Movies, 1994, 54 minutes.

This video presents four segments exploring the lives of lesbians in U.S. history and present. Shown primarily through June Chan's slide show, the third part focuses on Asian Lesbians on the East Coast and how the organization supported its members. With so little research on Asian American lesbian organizations, this documentary may offer a glimpse into how and why they created their own space.

Picturing Oriental Girls: A (Re)Educational Videotape, Valerie Soe, NAATA, 1992, 15 minutes.

This experimental video uses Hollywood film and television clips to reveal the exoticization of Asian American women. *Picturing Oriental Girls* can effectively spark discussion on how media images affect Asian American women's identity and experiences. However, *Slaying the Dragon* provides the historical context needed.

Precious Cargo, Janet Gardner, Independent Television Service, 2001, 56 minutes.

As the United States withdrew from Vietnam in 1975, Operation Babylift took twenty-eight hundred Vietnamese and Amerasian children with them. *Precious Cargo* follows several of these children in their journey back to Vietnam. These children, now adults, were adopted and raised in the United States. In their visit back, they confront their personal histories and compare the poor living conditions in Vietnam with their comparatively wealthy upbringing. This documentary deals with issues of war, mixed race, and transnational adoptions.

Quiet Passages: The Japanese American War Bride Experience, Chico Herbison and Jerry Schultz, NAATA, 1991, 26 minutes.

Thousands of Japanese women married U.S. servicemen during and after the 1950s. This documentary examines the lives of several "war brides" (also termed *military brides*) in the Midwest, using archival photographs and interviews with their children. War brides are an important part of Asian American women's immigration history.

Rabbit in the Moon, Chizu Omori, New Day Films, 1999, 85 minutes.

Two sisters, Emiko Omori and Chizuko Omori, seek to gather memories of their mother, who died soon after the family's release from the U.S. internment camps. Unexpectedly, they discover the history of 120,000 Japanese Americans unjustly interned by the U.S. government and the tumultuous experiences in and return from camp. This documentary can be used in a course syllabus that adopts a chronological or an ethnic framework. *Rabbit in the Moon* also can be juxtaposed with materials on comfort women, military prostitution, and war brides, under the general topic of "war/military impacts" on Asian and Asian/Pacific Islander American women.

Sa-I-Gu: From Korean Women's Perspectives, Dai Sil Kim-Gibson, Elaine Kim, Christine Choy, NAATA, 1993, 36 minutes.

Sa-I-Gu in Korean means April 29, referring to the 1992 Los Angeles Riots. This documentary gives a glimpse of the lives of Korean women store owners and their perspective on the riots. Despite only two weeks of filming, this documentary is useful in revealing women's role in merchant families and the Los Angeles Riots' impact on their lives. However, additional readings may be required to cover the historical and economic relationship between African American and Korean American communities.

Sambal Belacan in San Francisco, Madeleine Lim, Women Making Movies, 1997, 25 minutes.

This video discusses issues of home and homophobia through interviews with three Singaporean lesbians who immigrated to the United States to live openly with their sexual identities. A metaphor for these women's lives, *sambal belacan* is fragrant chili and shrimp paste, a mix of several cultural and ethnic groups. *Sambal Belacan in San Francisco* raises the question of Asian lesbians seeking sexual "freedom" in the United States as a push-pull factor for Asian American immigration.

Searching for Go-Hyang, Tammy Tolle, Women Making Movies, 1998, 32 minutes.

After over a decade with abusive adoptive parents, twin Korean American adoptee sisters go back to Korea and reunite with their biological parents. *Go-hyang* means "homeland" in Korean. With the growing population of Asian adoptees, now adults, this documentary is timely in presenting a personal journey of reconnecting to one's culture and history.

Separate Lives, Broken Dreams, Jennie Lew, NAATA, 1993, 47 minutes.

The Exclusion Act of 1882 prevented most Chinese from immigrating to the United States. *Separate Lives, Broken Dreams* shares how this discriminatory policy created a bachelor society in the United States, trans-Pacific split households, "paper sons," and "secrets" for generations to follow. The documentary reveals the conditions of the Angel Island immigration station, including the poignant stories of interrogations of Chinese immigrant woman, some separated from their children during interrogation. Starting roughly at the second half, the video shares the perspectives of "living widows," wives left behind in China and separated from their husbands for several decades, as well as the fate of wives who rejoined their husbands after decades of separation. This documentary would encourage discussion on how immigration policies significantly affect families and the psyche of an entire ethnic group. Also, it provides an opportunity to compare women's early participation in Asian immigration with the female-initiated immigration waves of post-1965.

Sewing Woman, Arthur Dong, NAATA, 1982, 14 minutes.

This documentary focuses on the life of Zem Ping, mother of the filmmaker, who emigrated from China and worked as a garment-factory seamstress for over thirty years. Made twenty years ago, this video would be useful to provide a link with current struggles for garment workers rights, perhaps in conjunction with the documentary *Blood, Sweat and Lace.*

Silence Broken: Korean Comfort Women, Dai Sil Kim-Gibson, NAATA, 1999, 57 minutes.

Comfort women is a euphemism for thousands of Korean women forced into sexual slavery by the Japanese army during World War II. This documentary includes testimonials from survivors who demand an apology and compensation from the Japanese government. The Japanese military also used comfort women from the Philippines, Thailand, and Burma. Former Korean comfort women speaking out have spurred an international movement for justice, including in the United States. This video is relevant in discussing Asian women in war times and contemporary transnational social movements.

Sin City Diary, Rachel Rivera, Women Make Movies, 1992, 29 minutes.

This video looks at prostitution in the Philippines around the U.S. Navy Base at Subic Bay. Rachel Rivera's personal experience as a Filipina American sets the video in a diary format. The film raises issues of U.S. military's impact on women and the economy.

Slaying the Dragon, Deborah Gee, NAATA, 1988, 60 minutes.

Used in many courses on Asian American women, *Slaying the Dragon* exposes how historical/political conditions, U.S.-Asia relations, and war affect media images of Asian women. The documentary also explores how these images and stereotypes of Asian women impact on Asian American women. The second half of the documentary discusses how Asian American filmmakers challenged stereotypes in the 1980s. Although the documentary was produced fifteen years ago, it continues to present a valuable overview of early Hollywood representations of Asians and Asian Americans. A followup discussion on contemporary representations is necessary for current students to find the relevancy to their experience in the twenty-first century.

Talking History, Spencer Nakasako, NAATA, 1984, 30 minutes.

Through oral histories, this documentary examines the immigration experiences of women from China, Japan, Korea, Laos, and the Philippines. This video would be useful to compare issues associated with immigration by ethnic group, including push-pull factors, cultural adjustment, and gender roles.

Then There Were None, Elizabeth Kapuʻuwailani Lindsey, Pacific Islanders in Communication, 1995, 26 minutes.

Made by a great-granddaughter of Hawaiian high chiefs and English seafarers who is also a former Miss Hawaiʻi, *Then There Were None* is Elizabeth Kapuʻuwailani Lindsey's personal documentary on Hawaiian history. Lindsey uses archival photographs, tourism promotional films, and music. She brings to light the struggle of Native Hawaiian people against outside forces and the sudden depopulation brought on by Westerners' diseases.

Unbidden Voices, Prajna Paramita Parasher and Deb Ellis, Women Making Movies, 1989, 32 minutes.

Unbidden Voices explores the life of Manjula Joshi, an Indian woman who works in a Chicago restaurant. This experimental video addresses immigration experiences, gender roles, and labor.

Voices of Challenge: Hmong Women in Transition, Candace Lee Egan, NAATA, 1996, 39 minutes.

Hmong women refugees from Laos faced significant changes in their lives when they arrived in the United States. In *Voices of Challenge*, Hmong women share their experiences negotiating traditional family expectations and their children's educational and career paths. Refugee experiences are frequently absent in immigration-based Asian American history courses. This documentary gives voice to that underrepresented community.

Who's Going to Pay for These Donuts, Anyway? Janice Tanaka, Women Making Movies, 1992, 58 minutes.

After forty years of separation, Janice Tanaka finds her father in a halfway house for the mentally ill. This video follows her journey of discovering family, history, and culture. It also shows the link between racism and mental illness.

Why Is Preparing Fish a Political Act? Russell Leong, NAATA, 1991, 20 minutes.

This video is about poet-activist Janice Mirikitani, who uses her grandmother's life of struggle as a point of departure to her own self-determination. This video would be useful in encouraging viewers to reflect on their personal family histories to inspire their social activism.

Xích-lô, M. Trinh Nguyen, NAATA, 1995, 20 minutes.

A Vietnamese American woman reflects on her personal life, her family, and war. Her reflections occur while riding on a pedicab (xích-lô) through Ho Chi Minh City. This video would be effective in addressing the impact of war on family and on the formation of one's identity.

Yuri Kochiyama: Passion for Justice, Rea Tajiri and Pat Saunders, NAATA, 1993, 57 minutes.

Yuri Kochiyama is a lifetime activist in various social justice movements. This video documentary presents her involvement in struggles for redress and reparations for Japanese Americans who were interned during World War II, political prisoners' rights, and the Black Liberation movement. It profiles a well-respected activist and leader among people of color.

Grouped by Topic

Activism

Blood, Sweat and Lace
Eating Welfare
Gabriela
Silence Broken: Korean Comfort Women
Why Is Preparing Fish a Political Act?
Yuri Kochiyama: Passion for Justice

Arts

Between the Lines: Asian American Women's Poetry
Jazz Is My Native Language: A Portrait of Toshiko Akiyoshi
Maya Lin: A Strong Clear Vision
Mitsuye and Nellie: Asian American Poets

Family

5 Girls
The Children We Sacrifice
Daughter from Danang
First Person Plural
Issei Wahine
I Will Always Tell This Story
Kelly Loves Tony
Knowing Her Place
Searching for Go-Hyang
Voices of Challenge: Hmong Women in Transition
Who's Going to Pay for These Donuts, Anyway?
Xích-lô

First-Person Narrative and Biography

First Person Plural
From Hollywood to Hanoi
Hapa
Happy Birthday Tutu Ruth
Hawai'i's Last Queen
Issei Wahine
Rabbit in the Moon
Searching for Go-Hyang

Then There Were None
Who's Going to Pay for These Donuts, Anyway?
Why Is Preparing Fish a Political Act?
Xích-lô
Yuri Kochiyama: Passion for Justice

Hawai'i

Happy Birthday Tutu Ruth
Hawai'i's Last Queen
Then There Were None

Immigrant and Refugee Experiences

Between Worlds
Issei Wahine
Her Uprooting Plants Her
Knowing Her Place
Moving Mountains: The Story of the Yiu Mien
Quiet Passages: The Japanese American War Bride Experience
Sambal Belacan in San Francisco
Separate Lives, Broken Dreams
Talking History
Unbidden Voices
Voices of Challenge: Hmong Women in Transition

Labor, Class

Behind the Labels
Blood, Sweat and Lace
Eating Welfare
Four Women
The Global Assembly Line
Sa-I-Gu: From Korean Women's Perspectives
Sewing Woman
Unbidden Voices

Lesbian/Bisexual

Not Just Passing Through
Sambal Belacan in San Francisco

Media Representations

From Hollywood to Hanoi

Hollywood Harems
Picturing Oriental Girls: A (Re)Educational Videotape
Slaying the Dragon

Mental Health

The Children We Sacrifice
Who's Going to Pay for These Donuts, Anyway?

Mixed Heritage

Between Worlds
Beyond Black and White
Hapa
Precious Cargo

Transnational Adoptees

First Person Plural
Precious Cargo
Searching for Go-Hyang

War and Military Presence in Asia

Between Worlds
Camp Arirang
From Hollywood to Hanoi
Moving Mountains: The Story of the Yiu Mien
Precious Cargo
Quiet Passages: The Japanese American War Bride Experience
Rabbit in the Moon
Silence Broken: Korean Comfort Women
Sin City Diary
Xích-lô

Youth

5 Girls
The Children We Sacrifice
Frankly Speaking
Girls Like Us
Kelly Loves Tony
Mai's America
Miss India Georgia

NOTE

I thank the following individuals for their valuable suggestions and feedback in helping me develop this bibliography: Shirley Hune, Davianna McGregor, Gail Nomura, Rhacel Parreñas, Amy Stillman, Linda Võ, and Judy Yung.

1. Nancy I. Kim, "The General Survey Course on Asian American Women: Transformative Education and Asian American Feminist Pedagogy," *Journal of Asian American Studies* 3:1 (February 2000): 37–65. See also Shirley Hune's Introduction in this book.

About the Contributors

XIAOLAN BAO is Professor of History at California State University, Long Beach. The author of "Feminist Collaborations between Diaspora and China," with Xu Wu, in *Chinese Women Organizing*; "Sweatshops in Sunset Park," in *International Labor and Working-Class History*; and *Holding Up More than Half the Sky: Chinese Women Garment Workers in New York City, 1948–1992*, her research has focused on Chinese American women workers, diasporic feminism, and women's movements in China.

SUCHENG CHAN is Professor Emerita of Asian American Studies and Global Studies at the University of California, Santa Barbara. The author of a dozen books, four of which have won prizes, she is the recipient of two Distinguished Teaching Awards from the University of California, Berkeley and the University of California, Santa Barbara.

CATHERINE CENIZA CHOY is Assistant Professor of American Studies at the University of Minnesota and the author of *Empire of Care: Nursing and Migration in Filipino American History*. A 2002–2003 AAUW (American Association of University Women) postdoctoral fellow, she is working on a new project that focuses on the history of the adoption of Asian children in the United States.

VIVIAN LOYOLA DAMES, MSW, Ph.D., is Associate Professor of Social Work/Women and Gender Studies at the University of Guam. Her doctoral dissertation (University of Michigan) analyzes American citizenship from the perspective of the Chamorros of Guam. An activist and scholar, she is also a leader in the formation of local advocacy organizations concerned with prison reform, land use and environmental issues, and social and economic justice for the poor.

JENNIFER GEE is an independent researcher who resides in the San Francisco Bay Area and currently serves on the Board of Directors of the Asian Women's Shelter. She has taught Asian American History at DeAnza College, and her doctoral dissertation (Stanford University, 1999) analyzes the screening of Japanese, Chinese, Korean, and South Asian women and men at the Angel Island immigration station from 1910 to 1940.

SHIRLEY HUNE is the Associate Dean for Graduate Programs in the Graduate Division at the University of California, Los Angeles, where she is also Professor of Urban Planning and Asian American Studies. She is currently working on projects related to minorities and women in higher education.

MADHULIKA S. KHANDELWAL is the Director of the Asian/American Center at Queens College, City University of New York. Author of *Becoming American, Being Indian: An Immigrant Community in New York City*, her interests are in the studies of immigrants, women, and the South Asian diaspora.

LILI M. KIM teaches U.S. history, feminist studies, and Asian American studies at Hampshire College in Amherst, Massachusetts. She is the author of "The Limits of Americanism and Democracy: Korean Americans, Transnational Allegiance, and the Question of Loyalty on the Homefront during World War II" (*Amerasia Journal*, Spring 2003) and is completing a book manuscript on the Korean American experience during World War II.

NANCY IN KYUNG KIM supports student empowerment as the Director of the Asian American/Pacific Islander Resource Center at the University of California, Santa Cruz. Her interests include Asian American feminist pedagogy, social movements, coalition building, and student leadership development.

ERIKA LEE is Assistant Professor of History at the University of Minnesota, where she teaches courses in American, immigration, and Asian American history. She is the author of *At America's Gates: Chinese Immigration during the Exclusion Era, 1882–1943*, and she is currently beginning a new book project on Asian immigration and exclusion in the Americas.

SHIRLEY JENNIFER LIM is Assistant Professor of History at SUNY Stony Brook and a writer, artist, and activist. She has completed a book manuscript, "Girls Just Wanna Have Fun: The Politics of Asian American Women's Public Culture, 1930–1960," and a second book project, "Subversive Sirens: Anna May Wong and Josephine Baker," currently captivates her investigatory prowess.

VALERIE J. MATSUMOTO is Associate Professor of History and Asian American Studies at UCLA. She is currently writing a book on Nisei women and the creation of urban youth culture in Los Angeles during the Jazz Age and the Great Depression; she is also researching Asian American women artists in California.

SUCHETA MAZUMDAR is Associate Professor of History at Duke University, where she teaches Chinese and Asian American history. She has recently co-edited, with Vasant Kaiwar, *Antinomies of Modernity: Essays on Race, Orient and Nation*.

DAVIANNA PŌMAIKAʻI MCGREGOR is a historian of Hawaiʻi and the Pacific and teaches as an Associate Professor of Ethnic Studies at the University of Hawaiʻi, Manoa. She is Native Hawaiian from the islands of Oʻahu and Hawaiʻi, who, as a member of the

Protect Kahoʻolawe ʻOhana, has been active in Hawaiian movements to reclaim sacred Hawaiian land.

GAIL M. NOMURA is Assistant Professor of American Ethnic Studies at the University of Washington. Co-editor of two anthologies on Asian American Studies and author of numerous chapters and articles on the history of Asian Americans, she is completing a book manuscript about the pre–World War II development of a Japanese American community on the Yakama Indian Reservation in Washington State and co-editing with Louis Fiset an anthology on the history of Japanese Americans and Japanese Canadians in the Pacific Northwest.

TRINITY A. ORDONA, Ph.D., is Associate Director of the UC San Francisco Lesbian Health Research Center and instructor in the Gay, Lesbian, Bisexual and Transgender Studies Department at the City College of San Francisco. She has a thirty-five-year history of civil rights activism and has received several awards for her grassroots organizing strategies, uniting Asian and Pacific Islander lesbian, bisexual, and transgendered people with their families and ethnic communities.

RHACEL SALAZAR PARREÑAS is Assistant Professor of Women's Studies and Asian American Studies at the University of Wisconsin, Madision. She is the author of *Servants of Globalization: Women, Migration, and Domestic Work.*

AMY KUʻULEIALOHA STILLMAN is Associate Professor of Music and American Culture and Director of Asian/Pacific Islander American Studies at the University of Michigan and a committed advocate on behalf of Hawaiian and Pacific Islander communities in Southern California. The author of *Sacred Hula: The Historical Hula ʻAlaʻapapa* and other publications, her research focuses on the history of Hawaiian and Tahitian music and dance performance.

CHARLENE TUNG is Assistant Professor of Women's and Gender Studies at Sonoma State University and is currently preparing a manuscript on Filipina migrant care workers in California. Her current research focuses on "border transgressions," including an oral history project on Taiwanese women's migration through the Americas, and analyses of gender, race, and sexuality in popular culture.

KATHLEEN UNO is an Associate Professor at Temple University, where she teaches Asian and Asian American history. The author of *Passages to Modernity*, she researches the history of Asian and Asian Pacific Island women and Asian social history, especially of family, children, women, and gender.

LINDA TRINH VÕ is an Assistant Professor in the Department of Asian American Studies at the University of California, Irvine. Her publications include *Contemporary Asian American Communities: Intersection and Divergences*, co-edited with Rick Bonus, and *Asian American Women: The "Frontiers" Reader* (forthcoming), co-edited with Marian Sciachitano.

JUDY TZU-CHUN WU, Assistant Professor of History at Ohio State University, has published articles on the Miss Chinatown USA Beauty Pageant and the gender and sexual identities of Dr. Margaret Chung (1889–1959). She is completing a biography of Chung, tentatively titled "Mom Chung of the Fair-Haired Bastards: Maternalism, Nationalism, and Sexuality."

JI-YEON YUH is Assistant Professor of History at Northwestern University and the author of *Beyond the Shadow of Camptown: Korean Military Brides in America*. She is currently working on a comparative study of ethnic Koreans in China, Japan, and the United States.

JUDY YUNG is Professor of American Studies at the University of California, Santa Cruz. She is the co-author of *Island: Poetry and History of Chinese Immigrants on Angel Island, 1910-1940* and the author of *Unbound Feet: A Social History of Chinese Women in San Francisco* and, most recently, *Unbound Voices: A Documentary History of Chinese Women in San Francisco*.

Index

CPSIA information can be obtained at www.ICGtesting.com
Printed in the USA
BVOW08s0325090116

432065BV00001B/1/P